PROGRESS IN UNDERSTANDING READING

PROGRESS IN UNDERSTANDING READING

SCIENTIFIC FOUNDATIONS AND NEW FRONTIERS

Keith E. Stanovich

FOREWORD BY ISABEL L. BECK

THE GUILFORD PRESS
New York   London

© 2000 The Guilford Press
A Division of Guilford Publications, Inc.
72 Spring Street, New York, NY 10012
http://www.guilford.com

Printed in the United States of America

This book is printed on acid-free paper.

Last digit is print number: 9 8 7 6 5 4 3

Library of Congress Cataloging-in-Publication Data

Stanovich, Keith E., 1950–
    Progress in understanding reading : scientific foundations and new frontiers /
  Keith E. Stanovich ; foreword by Isabel L. Beck.
      p.   cm.
    Includes bibliographical references and index.
    ISBN 1-57230-564-9 (cloth) — ISBN 1-57230-565-7 (pbk.)
    1. Reading.   2. Reading, Psychology of.   I. Title.

LB 1050 .S723 2000
428.4—dc21

                                                                00-022786

To Rich and Anne,
who have been with me from the very beginning
of this scientific journey

About the Author

Keith E. Stanovich is currently Professor of Human Development and Applied Psychology at the Ontario Institute for Studies in Education of the University of Toronto. He is the only two-time winner of the Albert J. Harris Award from the International Reading Association for influential articles on reading. In 1995 he was elected to the Reading Hall of Fame as the youngest member of that honorary society. In 1996 he was given the Oscar Causey Award from the National Reading Conference for contributions to research, and in 1997 he was given the Sylvia Scribner Award from the American Educational Research Association. Stanovich is a Fellow of the American Psychological Association (Divisions 3 and 15), the American Psychological Society, the International Academy for Research in Learning Disabilities, and is a Charter Member of the Society for the Scientific Study of Reading. He was a member of the Committee on the Prevention of Reading Difficulties in Young Children of the National Research Council/National Academy of Sciences. Stanovich is the editor of the volume *Children's Reading and the Development of Phonological Awareness* (Wayne State University Press) and the author of *How to Think Straight About Psychology* (6th edition, Allyn & Bacon) and *Who Is Rational? Studies of Individual Differences in Reasoning* (Erlbaum).

Foreword

When Keith Stanovich asked me to write the foreword to his new book, I felt honored, as I have long admired his work. He described the volume as a collection of selected papers divided into seven sections, each representing a strand of his work, and each introduced by a new context-setting chapter. When the manuscript arrived, the "warm, fuzzy" feeling I had initially experienced gave way to anxiety—when would I have time to read all of it? I was not very far into the manuscript when my anxiety was replaced with a twinge of excitement. In the Preface, Stanovich describes how and why he chose to include the papers and how he organized groups of papers to constitute sections. I enjoyed this brief description of his own work, and I suspected that the context-setting chapters were going to be enlightening. What an understatement! The truth is that I loved the context-setting chapters. (When editing this piece, one internal voice told me to be more sophisticated and reduce the hyperbole, but another said, "Be honest.")

Each of the context-setting pieces offered me something. Several introduced me to an issue that I had not been aware of, others pointed out some interpretations that I had missed when I read an original paper, and some colored in the backdrop of the times with primary hues. I was surprised to learn from the first context-setting chapter that the original theoretical underpinnings of Rich West and Stanovich's study of context effects on word identification were biased toward a top-down model. Specifically, the two young investigators had been enthusiastic about the notions presented in Frank Smith's *Understanding Reading* (1971), which included the position that poor readers were not adept at exploiting context for word recognition. But that is not what West and Stanovich's own research showed. Rather, they found that poor readers, in contrast to good readers, are more reliant on context to facilitate word recognition.

Stanovich uses this experience with research evidence that contradicted his starting notions to make three very important points that run throughout his work and the discussion of his work. First, real progress requires programmatic research; a study here and there is largely useless. Second, real progress requires converging evidence. In this regard, Stanovich highlights the point that one of the strands of his work is the development of "a theoretical synthesis of ideas by amalgamating the empirical results contributed by dozens of other investigators." And third, thoughtful people change their opinions on the basis of evidence.

Some of what Stanovich accomplishes with the context-setting chapters is very powerful. For example, rereading the Matthew effects paper (Chapter 10), with 15 years of additional experience and the addition of Stanovich's discussion and evaluation of the notions in it, was quite a stunning experience. Throughout the paper I had the feeling of "returning to the place where I started and seeing it clearly for the first time." Perhaps the majority who read the present volume have read the Matthew effects paper, but I recommend strongly that they do so again in light of the introductory chapter that precedes it.

One of the devices Stanovich employs in some of the context-setting chapters is to ask: "Well, did we get it right [at the time]?" His answers to that question are sometimes so interesting that I found myself reading the material as if it were a novel. To demonstrate, consider the following extracts: "Not bad as a first pass at a complicated concept." "Ten years later—right on the mark." "At a gross level the results have stood the test of time." "Although we were correct to emphasize the relative strength of the correlations . . . the linkages between . . . may be stronger than we implied." "Two of our conclusions now seem to be markedly understated."

Of course, everything does not turn out to be right, and when that is the case Stanovich announces it. When discussing his original characterizations of differences between dyslexic and garden-variety poor readers within the word recognition module, he talks about making two mistakes and he uses the mistakes to make a point about how "science proceeds by a Popperian falsification of earlier incorrect theoretical views." Before I read the next sentence I immediately thought, "What a great example for graduate students." I was most amused to find that Stanovich's next sentence was, "The graduate student might well learn from these examples."

Similarly, he doesn't hesitate to acknowledge instances when other scientists have an edge. He points out that he had "emphasized subword processing differences between high- and low-IQ poor readers that have not borne out under further empirical scrutiny . . . [Linda Siegel] had been right in her 1988 article . . . and I had been wrong in my article of the same year." That straightforward statement is followed by an enormously important concept: "We have here a lesson that protagonists in the Reading Wars might take to heart. In real science, disputes are answered empirically, and disputants can in fact cooperate in the empirical quest for an interpretation upon which both can agree."

In this regard Stanovich discusses "spirited" disgreements he has had with Foorman, Francis, Fletcher, and Lynn (1996) and Shaywitz, Holford, Holahan, Fletcher, Stuebing, Francis, and Shaywitz (1995). Presently, Stanovich says that he does not know whose interpretations will prevail. What he does know, however, is that one day Foorman et al. and Shaywitz et al. and Stanovich will be in agreement. Moreover, they "will have arrived at these agreements without the use of ad hominem attacks and personal vilification that has become common in the Reading Wars. . . . [T]hese disputes will end amicably because their end will be dictated by the data."

This statement brings me to Stanovich's last section, which begins with an introduction entitled "Putting Children First by Putting Science First: The Politics of Early Reading Instruction" and is followed by "Romance and Reality," a 1993 paper that was published in *The Reading Teacher,* and the address Stanovich gave when he received the Oscar Causey award from the National Reading Conference. I knew this section was coming, but when I got to it, I didn't want to read it because I had just come through an intellectual journey that was exhilarating both for what I did know about the issues concerned and for what I had learned. As such, I did not look forward to confronting how little of what is known is present in mainstream instruction.

But of course I read the chapter and, typical of a Stanovich piece, I learned from it. In the last introductory chapter, Stanovich attempts an explanation for why the best scientific evidence about the usefulness of systematic code instruction has not been incorporated into mainstream instruction. As Stanovich notes, I have attempted my own answers to this question. Nonetheless, I find Stanovich's explanation quite interesting. Given the "perverse logic" within the domain of reading education "where the bad seems to drive out the good," he suggests that in order to understand the neglect of systematic code instruction there is a need to turn to new theory. He offers memetic theory as defined in Chapter 19, a complicated notion that he explains well, and is certainly worth thinking about.

The last section also points to a hopeful notion for influencing mainstream instruction. Stanovich identifies that "the best scientists and the best teachers alike" are "ever the opportunistic practitioner," both have "'what works' epistemologies." This brought to mind learning that Stanovich had started his early context effects work biased toward a top-down model. My response was, "You too, Keith!" I began my own career as a teacher very biased toward a top-down model, although at the time I certainly didn't know that that was what it was. What I did know was what I had been taught in an undergraduate reading methods course: that when children had difficulty identifying a word, I should prompt them to use context. Well, Stanovich changed his opinion on the basis of research evidence, and I changed my opinion because it simply did not work. It has been my experience that when teachers who are frustrated are provided with some procedures for systematically teaching the code, they become convinced of its usefulness because it does work.

On another note, throughout the book a thought that kept coming to mind is that Stanovich is indeed "a scholar and a gentleman." The former characteristic need not be discussed, but the latter might be brought to the fore. He starts the book by talking about the volume as a representation of the progress *the field* has made over 25 years, he mentions every collaborator (more than 40) and every student who has worked on his projects (about 30), and he dedicates the book to Rich West, his fellow student in graduate school, and Anne Cunningham, a former graduate student. Similarly, he describes how profoundly he has been influenced by interactions with master teachers, such as his wife Paula, Anne Cunningham, and Ruth Nathan.

Finally, some words about the uses of this volume. One that kept coming to my mind was its use with graduate classes. I cannot wait to offer students the opportunity to read these papers against a backdrop in which an outstanding scientist tells what was going on at the time when he was engaged in a given research program—what was going on in the field and what was going on his mind. I even thought about how interesting it would be to attempt a study in which one class would be given papers from a section without the context-setting chapters while another class would have that benefit. However, I think this would constitute an ethical problem; I cannot deny students the best experience. In addition to its obvious use with students, this impressive array of fundamental research, synthetic chapters, and thoughtful essays—let alone the reference list—will be a boon to many of us as we write papers, recommend papers, or need specific data.

This book is a gift to the field. I look forward to talking about it with colleagues and using it with students. Thank you, Keith!

ISABEL L. BECK, PhD
University of Pittsburgh

Preface

This collection of work from over two decades of research is very much a tribute to the field. When my editor, Chris Jennison, and I first began talking about this project subsequent to my address at the meeting of the International Reading Association in 1998, we both thought that a book of this type would be a way of making good on my claim in that speech (Chapter 21 reprints a related address given to the National Reading Conference) that we have been through a remarkable 25-year period of scientific progress. This volume celebrates that progress. It represents a step back from the minutiae of individual studies in order to provide a broad view of what has been accomplished at a more general level—the level most often useful to teachers and other practitioners.

In the past 25 years we have made good on the promissory notes written by early pioneers such as Huey (1908/1968). We have made the study of psychological processes in reading a cumulative science, one with applications to problems of immense importance such as the prevention of reading failure. We have revealed many of the basic cognitive processes that underlie efficient reading performance. The links between these cognitive processes and the speed of early reading acquisition have been revealed—as have the links between these processes and the risk of reading difficulty. Home and school conditions that foster the rapid acquisition of reading and the prevention of reading difficulties are beginning to be understood (Adams, 1990; Burns, Griffin, & Snow, 1999; Byrne, 1998; Catts & Kamhi, 1999; Chard & Osborn, 1999; Hall & Moats, 1999; Morrow, Tracey, Woo, & Pressley, 1999; Pressley, 1998; Santa & Hoien, 1999; Scanlon & Vellutino, 1997; Snow, Burns, & Griffin, 1998; Stahl, Duffy-Hester, & Stahl, 1998; Thompson & Nicholson, 1999; Whitehurst & Lonigan, 1998; Whitehurst et al., 1999). Knowledge of the genetic and neurophysiological underpinnings of certain cases of reading difficulty and of reading processes in general has been gleaned

(Cardon et al., 1994; Grigorenko, 1999; Hohnen & Stevenson, 1999; Olson, 1999; Pugh et al., 1997; Shaywitz et al., 1998). It is truly an auspicious time in the history of reading research—seemingly a good time to sit back and take stock. Hence this volume.

The existence of this fundamental research base is itself reason for celebration. But it serves another function as well. As I try to argue in Part VII, equally important as the research itself is the example it provides of a model that is in opposition to the personal attacks and rhetorical posturing that seem to dominate discourse in educational debates about literacy. The field of reading education needs this model badly if it is ever to attain the level of professionalism that will make it immune from ill-informed political attacks by opponents of public education. My belief in the importance of substituting science for rhetoric has led me to devote an entire section of this book to my writings on the links between research and practice and the importance of the scientific values embodied in the former.

A certain degree of immodesty is a necessary prerequisite in putting together a collection of one's papers. There are several ways in which I hope that my hubris is mitigated. First, many of my most widely known contributions to the field (e.g., Stanovich, 1980, 1986b, 1991a) are research reviews and theoretical syntheses. Their very structure honors the remarkable scientific convergence mentioned above and discussed in Chapter 21. Second, my earlier contributions to various areas of the cognitive psychology of reading have been built upon and superseded by the subsequent work of others (as should be the case in any truly cumulative science). In the seven chapters that make up the part introductions I will make this abundantly clear. Finally, many of the original articles reprinted here have extensive reference lists—in some cases notoriously long—which in their combined form offer a comprehensive overview of research in the field of reading. Extensive references have been characteristic of my synthetic pieces because, from the earliest days in research, I have sought to emphasize the importance of *converging* evidence. Psychology in general is full of "one-shot" studies—interesting things that a single investigator came up with in a single study but that have gone nowhere theoretically (and the psychology of reading is certainly no exception here). I have tried to warn the field against this syndrome and to warn against drawing strong conclusions unless a clear scientific convergence was evident.

The process of evidence amalgamation in science is like a projector slowly bringing an unknown slide into focus. At first, the blur on the screen could represent just about anything. Then, as the slide is focused a bit more, many alternative hypotheses may be ruled out even though the image cannot be unambiguously identified. Finally, an identification can be made with great confidence. The early stages of the evidence amalgamation process are like the beginning of the focusing process. The ambiguous blur of the slide corresponds to contradictory data or to data that can be used to support many alternative hypotheses. In the articles reprinted here I have tried to focus our field's slides a little more clearly.

An emphasis on converging evidence is analogous to waiting for the slide to come into focus. Interestingly, on several occasions—in particular when writing for more practitioner-oriented outlets—I have been asked by editors or editorial assistants to "cut down quite a bit on the references" so that "we can focus the message for teachers." My reply to such requests has been that the references *are* the message—and that an emphasis on converging evidence is the only way that teachers will be freed of the "authority syndrome" that still pervades education.

These, then, are some of the points with which I would like to contextualize the scientific papers reprinted herein. Philosopher Michael Ruse (1999) has provided an additional perspective for contextualizing my contribution. Ruse notes how the growth, professionalization, and specialization of modern science diminishes the relative contribution of any one individual. Hence, in his historical survey of evolutionary theory, he prefaces his discussion of the modern period by noting that "the people chosen for discussion in the chapters that follow are primarily icons representing countless unmentioned others, rather than paragons who are necessarily overwhelmingly significant in their own right" (p. 124). This is very much how I view the present volume. This survey of my work serves as a prototype of how the field has advanced over this past 25-year period, and it rests on the contributions of countless named and unnamed others. In the ways mentioned above, I have tried to indicate clearly that these selected papers are exemplars of the progress the field has made in the past 25 years. They trace the field's progress through the writings of one active participant and his collaborators.

This volume is comprised of seven parts representing different strands of my research on the psychology of reading over the last 25 years. The parts are arranged in a rough chronological order, although many of the themes were pursued in parallel, as is common in any scientific program. I should say a brief word about the criteria for the selection of articles. At the time the selection was made, I was trying to choose the best exemplars of each of the themes from over 100 reading-related publications. In many cases, the selection was obvious purely on the basis of the attention the paper had received. That is, a perusal of the Social Sciences Citation Index clearly marked the paper as more influential than other related candidates. In other cases, the choice was more difficult, and I was forced to adopt several tie-breaking criteria. For example, in deciding between candidate articles, I chose to opt for the one with more contemporary relevance for ongoing debates in the field. I also opted for articles that would be of greater interest to practitioners. This is well illustrated in the section on context effects, where I chose three articles (Stanovich, 1980, 1984; West & Stanovich, 1978) on developmental trends and individual differences because they have relevance for current instructional debates. I did not include a host of articles with Richard West that I am most proud of and that represent some of our best science (Stanovich & West, 1981, 1983a; West & Stanovich, 1982, 1986) because they have less current practical relevance for practitioners. These articles contain studies of adult priming effects, syntactic effects, and sentence context effects that contributed greatly to theoretical advances in their day but that have been superseded by more recent work in these areas (e.g., Chwilla, Hagoort, & Brown, 1998; Masson, 1995; Stolz & Neely, 1995).

Similarly, work that David Bauer and I did on the spelling–sound regularity effect (Bauer & Stanovich, 1980; Stanovich & Bauer, 1978) is not reprinted here even though it followed closely on the seminal contributions of Baron and Strawson (1976) and Coltheart (1978). As discussed in Chapter 11, work on regularity/consistency has become quite refined in recent years (see Brown, 1997; Brown & Deavers, 1999; Plaut, McClelland, Seidenberg, & Patterson, 1996; Seidenberg & McClelland, 1989b; Share, 1995; Treiman et al., 1995), and theoretical developments have superseded these early papers.

An additional criterion that I applied to the selection of the part topics themselves was that they were chosen to represent those areas in which I have done programmatic research (on the order of at least a decade) rather than "one-shot" studies or research programs of limited duration. Thus, my two papers on measuring automaticity with the Stroop test (Stanovich, Cunningham, & West, 1981; West & Stanovich, 1979) did not warrant a separate section even though one (West & Stanovich, 1979) was listed among the 35 publications chosen as "classics" in 40 years of National Reading Conference publications (see *Journal of Reading Behavior*, 1992, 24, 505–532) and the other (Stanovich, Cunningham, & West, 1981) was listed as 13th-most-cited article in the history of the *Journal of Reading Behavior/Journal of Literacy Research* (McKenna & Robinson, 1999).

Each of the seven parts contains an introductory chapter that contextualizes the work historically and autobiographically. The introductory chapters then review the current status of the debate on the issues in question. I begin with my oldest contribution: the work on sentence context effects in word recognition. Next comes a part comprised of work on phonological awareness and the phonological core deficit model of reading disability—work from the 1980s that I have characterized as part of the "third wave" of research on phonological factors in reading acquisition and reading disability (see Chapter 5). Part III is devoted to my single most-cited paper, the so-called Matthew effects paper (Stanovich, 1986b). This paper interweaves all of the themes contained in the other six parts. For example, a central message of the Matthew effects paper was that context effects on word recognition are not the place to look for the source of reading difficulties (see Part I). The developmental model of reading difficulty proposed in the Matthew effects paper singled out phonological processes as a unique source of difficulty (Part II). Of course, the Matthew effects paper takes as a background assumption the importance of the development of automatic word recognition processes (see Part IV). Even more central to the Matthew effects paper was the notion that differences in reading acquisition speed themselves—through differential self-exposure to literacy activities—spawn increases in achievement disparities with age. Trying to find empirical evidence for this conjecture led to the productive program of research on the consequences of literacy described in Part V. Also present in the 1986 paper were my worries about the implications of Matthew effects for discrepancy definitions of reading disability. These worries were expressed in full-blown form in Stanovich (1991a; see Chapter 18 of the present volume) and led to my 1990s empirical and theoretical work on the discrepancy issue (see Part VI).

Finally, the Matthew effects paper really began to focus me more on the issue of how these findings about the reading process related to educational practice. As the autobiographical notes in the part introductions will make clear, my intellectual grounding throughout the 1970s was in cognitive psychology and cognitive developmental psychology. During the 1980s I was profoundly influenced by master teacher/researchers such as Anne Cunningham and Ruth Nathan. By the 1990s I was lecturing to learning disabilities groups, to the International Reading Association, to teachers' groups, and to groups of school psychologists. The basic research had had practical impact. It had also entered the messy world of the politics of educational practice. Although I have never been a front-line worker in the field of literacy education, as a researcher I have taken my responsibilities as a public communicator seriously. Thus this volume closes with two of my contributions to the debates on educational practice in the literacy field (see Part VII). The last part's introductory chapter (Chapter 19) also ties together my work on reasoning and rationality (Stanovich, 1998a, 1999b) with my work on the psychology of reading. Thus, Part III, centering around the Matthew effects paper, ties together themes from all of the other parts and from all aspects of my research. I will expand briefly on the contents of the remaining parts.

Part IV, on the importance of the word recognition process, reflects an insight that began to dawn on the field of reading in the 1970s and that has been heavily reinforced by research in the last two decades. That insight was that if we were ever going to understand the nature of reading difficulties, understanding the psychological subprocesses that mediated word recognition was a critical prerequisite. This is because so much of the variance in overall reading ability (comprehension) is accounted for by word recognition and because the proximal cause of most severe reading problems is difficulty with word recognition.

Part V describes the empirical work that I launched subsequent to the Matthew effects paper (Stanovich, 1986b) in order to test some of the conjectures about the effects of literacy contained in that paper. As is argued in that part, the positive effects of literacy experience must be empirically proven rather than merely assumed. This part describes the efforts of my research team to provide that empirical proof.

The final two parts contain my writings that are most relevant to policy issues. Part VI—on the role of discrepancy definitions in classifying individuals as reading disabled—is the more circumscribed of the two. Nevertheless, how this controversy is adjudicated has direct implications for how people are treated in our educational system.

In the final part (VII), I collect two papers in which I have directly commented upon the so-called Reading Wars, the dispute about which instructional approach is best in the early stages of reading instruction. Opinion in the reading community is quite severely bifurcated. I have published work that one critic has called "asinine"—in a professional journal, no less (see Chapter 21)—and other work that has earned me high praise: "[This is] one of the most impressive reviews of reading process research ever. [Stanovich] seems to have thought of every issue and dealt with it using the major studies relevant. . . . This is one of the truly great chapters in this or any other book on reading research findings" (Cunningham & Cunningham, 1991, pp. 367–368).

In both papers reprinted in Part VII and in Chapter 19 I have tried to argue that the scientific attitude—with all that it implies in terms of rigorousness, objectivity, tolerance for conflict, and response to evidence—is the only answer to the strife, public distrust, and unprofessional behavior that characterizes the field of reading education. In the papers reprinted in this part, issues of social justice play a prominent role, and I try to reorient how we think about the connection between these and certain instructional methods.

A Bibliography including all of my reading-related publications as well as my writings on topics outside of literacy—mainly reasoning, information processing, and the psychology and philosophy of rational thought—appears at the end of this volume. The other writings, while not directly related to literacy, do reflect the metaphilosophy with which I approach scientific problems.

By publishing this collection of papers and commentaries I hope to aid the field in its current task of synthesizing roughly 25 years of research on the scientific study of reading during which empirical and theoretical work has literally exploded in size and scope. Many of my most noted papers have been attempts to synthesize research on particular topics in the psychology of reading, and I hope that this volume can serve as another contribution in this vein. I feel that we are entering a period of intense specialization in the field in which attempts at synthesis will become ever more important just as they will become difficult. Specialization is good in science—it is a sure sign of scientific progress. Nevertheless, it presents problems for the outsider (and for the practitioner) who must make an extra effort to access information at the proper level and to make sure the information accessed represents a consensus in the field. In a sense, I am trying to aid the practitioner in this process by presenting a synthesis and recent history of the field in the form of my own intellectual and scientific autobiography—much as Linnea Ehri did in the compelling autobiography of her scientific career (Ehri, 1996; see also Ehri, 1998).

As anyone who knows my career realizes—and as those who don't can guess by reading the dedication page—I have been immensely fortunate in my collaborators. And the least of this good fortune has played itself out in science. The *most* important aspect of this good fortune has played itself out in friendships—friendships of in one case over 20 years and of another of over 25 years. The stories of my friendships and collaborations with Rich West and Anne Cunningham are told in Chapters 1, 5, and 13.

As I mentioned above, choosing papers for the volume was difficult. In some cases, after having made the selection decisions, it was a shock to look at the Table of Contents and see that some collaborators who had worked with me for a substantial period were not represented in the final papers selected. For example, Ruth Nathan worked with me throughout the 1980s and coauthored three substantial papers that did not quite make the final cut. One, our 1985 paper in *Child Development* (Stanovich, Nathan, West, & Vala-Rossi, 1985), is discussed in Chapter 1. Two others used the reading-level match design in the 1980s (Stanovich, Nathan, & Vala-Rossi, 1986; Stanovich, Nathan, & Zolman, 1988), when the field was still absorbing the lessons of that design from Bryant and Goswami (1986). Those studies are discussed in Chapter 5. Ruth's zest for life and her dedication to discovering what is best for children is a model for all practitioner/researchers.

Jim Cipielewski provided tremendous enthusiasm during the early days of work on the consequences of literacy project. My work with him and Linda Allen (Allen, Cipielewski, & Stanovich, 1992; Cipielewski, & Stanovich, 1992) is discussed in Chapters 15 and 16. Linda Siegel's role in bringing me to the Ontario Institute for Studies in Education of the University of Toronto (OISE/UT) is described in Chapter 17. The environment for scientific work on literacy, reading acquisition, and reading difficulties is abetted by a wealth of experienced colleagues here at OISE/UT such as Andy Biemiller, Esther Geva, Tom Humphreys, David Olson, Uri Shafrir, Judy Wiener, and Dale Willows. The same was true at Oakland University throughout the late 1970s and 1980s with the presence of my colleagues Ron Cramer, Larry Lilliston, Dean Purcell, and Bob Schwartz.

Scholars who have published with me and to whom I am grateful for their support include Linda Allen, David Bauer, Inger-Kristin Bjaalid, J. Kathryn Bock, Gordon Brown, Penny Chiappe, Jim Cipielewski, Barbara Cramer, Laura Echols, Alexandra Gottardo, John Hagen, Michele Harrison, Torliev Hoien, David Irwin, Dorothy Jeffreys, Perry Klein, Ingvar Lundberg, Jamie Metsala, Harold Mitchell, Ruth Nathan, David Olson, Robert Pachella, Denise Pollak, Dean Purcell, Walter Sá, Diane Salter, Bob Schwartz, David Share, Shahid Siddiqui, Robin Sidhu, Linda Siegel, Marty Singer, J. E. Keith Smith, Robert Solman, Paula Stanovich, Alan Stewart, Ron Stringer, Marilyn Vala-Rossi, Rick Wagner, Alex Wilkinson, Mark Wilson, Kathy Zehr, and Judy Zolman.

Students who have worked on my research projects throughout the years and who deserve my appreciation include: Linda Allen, Cheryl Anderson, Linda Ayres, David Bauer, Andrea Bubka, Penny Chiappe, Jim Cipielewski, Barbara Cramer, Laura Echols, Alexandra Gottardo, Jenny Gross, Michele Harrison, Caroline Ho, David Irwin, Dorothy Jeffreys, Carol Kelley, Jamie Metsala, Ruth Nathan, Jason Riis, Walter Sá, Diane Salter, Mike Seiler, Shahid Siddiqui, Robin Sidhu, Brenda Stringer, Ron Stringer, Maggie Toplak, Marilyn Vala-Rossi, Lesly Wade-Woolley, Joan Wolforth, and Judy Zolman.

Thanks also goes to those who have supported me in preparing this volume and in supporting the research that is reported in the many papers. The empirical research on the consequences of literacy has been made possible by consistent support received from the Social Sciences and Humanities Research Council of Canada. The work on reading difficulties and discrepancy definitions has been made possible by consistent support received from the Natural Sciences and Engineering Research Council of Canada. The work on context effects and phonological processing was supported by the National Science Foundation of the United States.

Denese Coulbeck and Walter Sá provided expert assistance in the preparation of this volume. Maggie Toplak did incredible work on the References. For 10 years Mary Macri has been essential to the smooth running of my research projects, and she continues to be a lifesaver. My editor at The Guilford Press, Chris Jennison, has become a friend more than a professional contact. No publisher could have a finer representative. Erudite, informed, enthusiastic, and knowledgeable—he proves that the generalist intellectual is not dead. Chris also proves that, in this age of corporatism and market imperatives, at least some publishers have a heart and a soul.

Longtime friend Marilyn Kertoy deserves my thanks for showing her support in so many ways. Her caring and concern has spanned this entire 25-year period and it could not have been more steadfast.

And of course, Paula, who has been my friend longest of all—my friend and love.

Acknowledgments

Appreciation is expressed for permission to reprint, in whole or in part and with revisions, the following works:

Chapter 2—West, R. F., & Stanovich, K. E. Automatic Contextual Facilitation in Readers of Three Ages (1978). *Child Development, 49,* 717–727. Copyright 1978 by the Society for Research in Child Development.

Chapter 3—Toward an Interactive–Compensatory Model of Individual Differences in the Development of Reading Fluency (1980). *Reading Research Quarterly, 16,* 32–71. Copyright 1980 by the International Reading Association.

Chapter 4—The Interactive–Compensatory Model of Reading: A Confluence of Developmental, Experimental, and Educational Psychology (1984). *Remedial and Special Education, 5,* 11–19. Copyright 1984 by PRO-ED, Inc.

Chapter 6—Stanovich, K. E., Cunningham, A., & Cramer, B. Assessing Phonological Awareness in Kindergarten Children: Issues of Task Comparability (1984). *Journal of Experimental Child Psychology, 38,* 175–190. Copyright 1984 by Academic Press, Inc.

Chapter 7—Explaining the Differences between the Dyslexic and the Garden-Variety Poor Reader: The Phonological-Core Variable-Difference Model (1988). *Journal of Learning Disabilities, 21,* 590–612. Copyright 1988 by PRO-ED, Inc.

Chapter 8—Stanovich, K. E., & Siegel, L. S. The Phenotypic Performance Profile of Reading-Disabled Children: A Regression-Based Test of the

Phonological-Core Variable-Difference Model (1994). *Journal of Educational Psychology, 86,* 24–53. Copyright 1994 by the American Psychological Association.

Chapter 10—Matthew Effects in Reading: Some Consequences of Individual Differences in the Acquisition of Literacy (1986). *Reading Research Quarterly, 21,* 360–407. Copyright 1986 by the International Reading Association.

Chapter 12—Concepts in Developmental Theories of Reading Skill: Cognitive Resources, Automaticity, and Modularity (1990). *Developmental Review, 10,* 72–100. Copyright 1990 by Academic Press, Inc.

Chapter 14—Stanovich, K. E., & West, R. F. Exposure to Print and Orthographic Processing (1989). *Reading Research Quarterly, 24,* 402–433. Copyright 1989 by the International Reading Associaton.

Chapter 15—Does Reading Make You Smarter?: Literacy and the Development of Verbal Intelligence (1993). In H. Reese (Ed.), *Advances in Child Development and Behavior* (Vol. 24, pp. 133–180). San Diego, CA: Academic Press. Copyright 1993 by Academic Press, Inc.

Chapter 16—Stanovich, K. E., Cunningham, A. E., & West, R. F. Literacy Experiences and the Shaping of Cognition (1998). In S. Paris & H. Wellman (Eds.), *Global Prospects for Education: Development, Culture, and Schooling* (pp. 253–288). Washington, DC: American Psychological Association. Copyright 1998 by the American Psychological Association.

Chapter 18—Discrepancy Definitions of Reading Disability: Has Intelligence Led Us Astray? (1991). *Reading Research Quarterly, 26,* 7–29. Copyright 1991 by the International Reading Association.

Chapter 20—Romance and Reality (1993/1994). *The Reading Teacher, 47*(4), 280–291. Copyright 1993 by the International Reading Associaton.

Chapter 21—Twenty-Five Years of Research on the Reading Process: The Grand Synthesis and What It Means for Our Field (1998). In T. Shanahan & F. Rodriguez-Brown (Eds.), *Forty-Seventh Yearbook of the National Reading Conference* (pp. 44–58). Chicago: NRC. Copyright 1998 by National Reading Conference.

Contents

PART I

THE ROLE OF CONTEXT EFFECTS IN MODELS OF READING

CHAPTER 1

Early Applications of Information Processing Concepts to the Study of Reading

The Role of Sentence Context

My first sustained contribution to the psychology of reading was the work on the role of sentence context in word recognition that is exemplified by the three papers reprinted in this section. Although I did a smattering of work on word and letter perception during this period (Purcell, Stanovich, & Spector, 1978; Stanovich, 1979), it was the work on context effects that had lasting influence. The lesson here for graduate students is that programmatic research has the most impact.

The lesson for the field more generally is that psychology is a "gradual synthesis" science, not a "sudden breakthrough" science. I devoted a chapter of my critical thinking text (Stanovich, 1998a) to just this point. In psychology and the psychology of reading we make progress by accumulating evidence from a host of interlocking studies, each of which may be of fairly low diagnosticity but which taken together present a coherent picture and warrant firm conclusions. We are a science that is custom-made for meta-analysis.

The genesis of the work on context effects occurred during my graduate student days at the University of Michigan in the early 1970s. After undergraduate study at Ohio State University with Harvey Shulman in information processing psychology and Jim Wise in decision theory, I arrived at the University of Michigan's experimental psychology program to study information processing. The effects of the "cognitive revolution" in psychology were still being felt.

A particular moment that looms large in retrospect (over 25 years later) occurred as I was sitting in my office in West Quad at Michigan working on an experiment for a laboratory course in developmental psychology. I had recently "crossed over" to do work in the developmental psychology area paralleling my research in experimental psychology. John Hagen had recommended me to Lorraine Nadelman as a graduate student teaching assistant (TA) for her developmental psychology lab course. The TAs were responsible for supervising undergraduates as they collected data from the children at Burns Park School to use in various experiments. Each of the TAs was responsible for devising one of the experiments, and I was in the office working on mine. I had decided to have the undergraduates do an experiment on the *Stroop effect*, the fact that people are much slower at naming the color in which a word is printed when the word itself is the name of an interfering color (e.g., the word *red* written in blue ink, to which the subject must respond "blue").

I was sitting in the lab making up the stimuli with an old Dymotape Labeller. I was surprised when another graduate student ambled past my open door, looked in, and said "Oh, the Stroop test." My surprise derived from the fact that I was using the test as a measure of the automaticity of word recognition, and that topic was not one that was close to the research interests of any of the faculty members in developmental psychology at the time. In the developmental area, aspects of social development, moral development, and traditional studies of memory were the dominant research interests. Having come to developmental psychology from experimental psychology, my interest in developmental problems was heavily colored by my immersion in the information processing framework of the (then) still relatively new cognitive revolution in psychology. I had not expected anyone in the developmental area to exactly share my interests and thus my surprise when someone recognized—from just a few bits of Dymotape—my Stroop test.

That graduate student was Richard West, and the rest is history. Well, I exaggerate. But some degree of hyperbole is warranted when discussing a 25-year-long collaboration. Surely we must represent one of the longest continuous collaborations in the psychology of reading—indeed, in psychology as a whole!

Soon after our "Stroop encounter," Rich and I were having regular meetings (joined sometimes by Joe Torgesen and Alex Wilkinson, fellow graduate students at Michigan) to discuss research on the reading process and to plan potential studies. We immediately became each other's main colleague and for the next 3 years used our collaboration to compensate for the absence of faculty who had as their primary interest reading-related topics. I was well versed in the latest information processing techniques for assessing the real-time operation of cognitive processes, and much of this knowledge was transferable to the problem of studying the word recognition process. I was also interested in individual differences in cognition and learning, in part due to the influence of my wife, Paula, who had just begun what was to become, at the time of this writing, a 25-year career in special education. I had sketched out a project on individual differences in basic information processing operations in individuals of varying cognitive ability and eventually did my third-year paper on that topic (published as Stanovich, 1978). I had also immersed myself in the literature on letter and word perception—again, though, from the perspective of cognitive psychology. Rich, however, was more conversant with the educational literature on reading, especially since he had recently attended a summer workshop on reading for graduate students and junior scholars sponsored by the Society for Research in Child Development (a workshop whose attendees—e.g., Rod Barron, Roger Bruning, Joe Danks, Linnea Ehri, Uta Frith, Peter Reitsma, Ellen Ryan, Gary Waller, Dale Willows—would later become the backbone of the psychology of reading field).

We both thought that the reading field seemed ripe for an infusion of knowledge and experimental techniques from allied fields such as cognitive psychology, developmental psychology, and psycholinguistics. We were convinced that many issues about the reading process that were debated in the educational literature could be clarified by the use of the information processing methods of cognitive psychology. One book that particularly piqued our interest at the time was the first edition of Frank Smith's *Understanding Reading* (1971). This book was terribly exciting to two young cognitive psychologists still feeling the excitement of the cognitive revolution in psychology. Smith's book was a very creative synthesis of many of the trends and concepts from the early days of the cognitive revolution, including Shannon's information theory, feature extraction models, redundancy, analysis-by-synthesis models of speech perception, and the "New Look" in perceptual research.

Beyond our generic enthusiasm for Smith's use of cognitive psychology to help understand the reading process, we also thought that Smith's *specific* theory had a great deal of plausibility given our intuitions as cognitive psychologists. In particular, we thought that his (what was later called) "top-down model" of word perception had a great deal of plausibility, and we thought that the individual difference hypotheses that Smith had derived were also probably true. Interestingly, this type of model became part of the theoretical foundation of the whole language movement that was to have such a great influence on reading education in the late 1980s and 1990s (I discuss this movement extensively in Part VII).

As I outline in the articles reprinted here as Chapters 2, 3, and 4, Smith's top-down view strongly emphasized the contribution of expectancies and contextual information. The word recognition process was thought to be heavily penetrated by background knowledge and higher level cognitive expectancies. One prediction derived from the top-down reading models that turned out to be very important concerned individual differences. Theorists who developed top-down models of reading consistently derived the prediction that skilled readers would rely less on graphic cues and more on contextual information than less-skilled readers. Smith's (1971) well-known hypothesis was that good readers were especially sensitive to the redundancy afforded by sentences, were particularly good at developing hypotheses about upcoming words, and were then able to confirm the identity of a word by sampling only a few features in the visual array. According to this hypothesis, good readers processed words faster not because their processes of lexical access were more efficient, but because their use of redundancy lightened the load on their stimulus–analysis mechanisms. In short, the skilled reader is less reliant on graphic cues and more reliant on contextual information than is the less-skilled reader:

> As the child develops reading skill and speed, he uses increasingly fewer graphic cues. (Goodman, 1976, p. 504)

> The more difficulty a reader has with reading, the more he relies on visual information; this statement applies to both the fluent reader and the beginner. (Smith, 1971, p. 221)

> One difference between the good beginning reader and the one heading for trouble lies in the overreliance on visual information that inefficient—or improperly taught—beginning readers tend to show, at the expense of sense. (Smith, 1973, p. 190)

These were the predictions that Rich West and I went on to test with reaction-time techniques derived from cognitive psychology. To our surprise, all of our research results pointed in the opposite direction: it was the poorer readers, not the more skilled readers, who were more reliant on context to facilitate word recognition (see Chapters 2 and 4). I write "to our surprise" because we embarked on these studies fully expecting to confirm Smith's (1971) views. It was his extrapolation of ideas from cognitive psychology into the reading field that had so excited us—two budding cognitive psychologists ourselves. The history of our work in this area is thus deeply ironic. We *did* start out with a theoretical bias, one consistent with the top-down view. But in real science one is *eventually* influenced by the evidence, regardless of one's initial bias, and the consistency of our findings finally led us away from the top-down view (see Adams, 1991, 1998, for the impact of this view on practice). I articulated an alternative view of the way that context worked at the word recognition level in my paper on interactive–compensatory models (Stanovich, 1980; reprinted in this volume as Chapter 3). Perfetti and Roth (1981) articulated a similar model at about the same time, one that also reflected the convergence of evidence that was beginning to become apparent.

I can still remember one of the first times I felt the true thrill of a scientific convergence in which I had participated. In the social sciences, where progress is fitful (two steps forward and one step back) and the inferences from any one experiment extremely ambiguous, the thrill of sharp convergence is rare. We read about it in autobiographies of scientists in other disciplines but rarely experience it ourselves. Thus I still remember the meeting of the Psychonomic Society in Washington, DC, in November 1977 where Rich and I came together, now as relatively new faculty members rather than as graduate students, and continued our collaboration (before the days of email, cheap phone rates, and routine Fed Exing). We had already written up and submitted the paper that was to become West and Stanovich (1978; reprinted here as Chapter 2) and were still puzzling over our failure to confirm the top-down predictions derived from Smith's (1971) model. At the Psychonomic Society meeting we attended a presentation by Chuck Perfetti (whom at the time I had yet to meet—indeed as a junior faculty member I was still starstruck when first meeting the people whose work I had read). There, we saw him present a slightly different context paradigm and report exactly the same trend that had so startled us: context effects were larger for the less-skilled readers. His work—later published as Perfetti, Goldman, and Hogaboam (1979)—became a critical part of the convergence that was synthesized in my interactive–compensatory model (see Chapter 3). The convergence from another laboratory working with its own paradigm played an important role in giving me the confidence to put forth the interactive–compensatory hypothesis. Our result was not a fluke. It was not dependent on the idiosyncrasies of our particular paradigm. It was not dependent upon our choice of words, or sentence contexts, or subjects, but instead appeared to be a replicable phenomenon.

The interactive–compensatory paper (Stanovich, 1980; reprinted as Chapter 3) remains one of my most cited papers (it has received over 350 citations and continues to be cited today, nearly 20 years after its publication). The 1984 paper in *Remedial and Special Education* (reprinted as Chapter 4) is less cited but remains a nice summary of our work during this period. Writing this paper was aided greatly by the additional convergence provided by our adult work (Stanovich & West, 1983a). Specifically, we had shown that the contextual effects displayed by adults could be made to mimic those displayed by children by degrading the visual stimuli—another effect consistent with the interactive–compensatory model.

In a paper from the same era not reprinted here (Stanovich, Nathan, West, & Vala-Rossi, 1985), but which I was tempted to include, we demonstrated a neat experimental effect and imported a new theoretical concept into reading theory. The neat experimental effect was that adults named a word (e.g., "tractor") just as fast when it was preceded by a related but incongruous incomplete sentence context (e.g., "the farmer planted the") as they did when it was preceded by a neutral sentence context. To a lesser extent this also held true for children. Theoretically, we took this finding to emphasize two things. First, the results were consistent with the two-process model we first outlined in the West and Stanovich (1978; reprinted as Chapter 2) paper and developed further in the papers reprinted as Chapters 3 and 4. If, as argued by Briggs, Austin, and Underwood (1984), only the attentional mechanism had been operative, the related incongruous condition should have displayed *inhibition* relative to the neutral condition. Alternatively, if only spreading activation had been operating, *facilitation* would have obtained for the related incongruous condition. That neither result was obtained seemed to be evidence of the operation of both mechanisms.

A more important theoretical landmark in the Stanovich et al. (1985) paper was our linking the findings to the issues raised in Fodor's (1983) then recently published *Modularity of Mind*. He conceptualizes modular input systems as those that are fast, automatic (obligatory and not capacity demanding), and informationally encapsulated. The latter is the most important aspect of modularity and means that a module operates autonomously—specifically, it is not under the direction of higher level cognitive structures and is not supplemented by real-world knowledge. Using this framework, we emphasized that the emerging consensus in the adult literature on context effects (e.g., Perfetti, 1985; Stanovich & West, 1983a) was that word recognition was modular, roughly in Fodor's sense. Context effects appeared to arise largely from the operation of an intramodule spreading-activation mechanism and not from a conscious, strategic process of expectancy generation. We summarized the outcomes of several recent developmental studies of context effects (e.g., Perfetti & Roth, 1981; Stanovich, West, & Feeman, 1981) as indicating that the word recognition module becomes more encapsulated as reading fluency develops. We argued that a series of recent findings (e.g., Gough, 1983; Mitchell, 1982; Perfetti & Roth, 1981; also see Chapter 3 of this volume) had suggested that skilled and/or older readers were more sensitive to contextual variables when the task that is employed taps comprehension processes but were actually *less* likely to use context to facilitate word recognition. We further argued that these trends were more easily accommodated by modular models of reading than by hypothesis-testing models that do not as strongly demarcate the word level of processing (e.g., Smith, 1971). The implications of the concept of modularity for reading theory are explored in more detail in Chapter 12.

A RETROSPECTIVE EVALUATION OF THE RESEARCH ON CONTEXT EFFECTS

Well, did we get it right? How well have these findings and theories held up over the years? If one stays at a fairly gross level, these questions are not hard to answer. At a gross level, the results have stood the test of time—as have the general theoretical analyses. As a first pass at a theory of contextual effects, the notion of interactive–compensatory processing has proven useful to the field, as has our importation of the modularity concept into the psychology of reading (see Chapter 12 for a discussion of these developments). Much work during the 1980s was concerned with replicating and extending the empirical trends we had originally highlighted in the work reprinted in Chapters 2 and 3. Many different priming paradigms were introduced into the literature, and they generally produced evidence convergent with our earlier insights (e.g., Becker, 1985; Ben-Dror, Pollatsek, & Scarpati, 1991; Briggs et al., 1984; Bruck, 1988, 1990; Perfetti, 1985; Pring & Snowling, 1986; Schwantes, 1985, 1991; Simpson & Foster, 1986; Simpson, Lorsbach, & Whitehouse, 1983). Work with other paradigms during that period confirmed the finding that when skilled and less-skilled readers are reading materials of comparable difficulty (an important control; see Stanovich, 1986b reprinted in the present volume as Chapter 10), the reliance on contextual information relative to graphic information is just as great—in many cases greater—for the less-skilled readers (Biemiller, 1979; Harding, 1984; Juel, 1980; Lesgold, Resnick, & Hammond, 1985; Leu, DeGroff, & Simons, 1986; Lovett, 1986; Nicholson, 1991b; Nicholson, Lillas, & Rzoska, 1988; Richardson, DiBenedetto, & Adler, 1982; Schwartz & Stanovich, 1981; Simons & Leu, 1987; Whaley & Kibby, 1981). The notion of compensatory processing was confirmed (Durgunoglu, 1988; Perfetti, 1985).

Of course, these data patterns and their associated theoretical explanations were not welcomed by whole language advocates. Their reaction to this empirical evidence is more extensively discussed in Part VII. Typical are instances chronicled in Mike Pressley's (1998) book, *Reading Instruction That Works: The Case for Balanced Teaching*. He quotes Frank Smith, who recommends guessing over decoding, and then notes that "what is so striking in reading Smith's writing, however, is the certainty of his claims. If you reread the quotes I provided, you see no hesitancy, no tentativeness" (p. 15). Likewise, Pressley (1998) feels that "Goodman is no less assertive than Smith in his writing . . . despite quite a bit of evidence to the contrary at the time of his writing" (p. 15). In Chapter 19 I discuss how the response to contradictory evidence is one of the key characteristics that teachers can use when evaluating the expertise of scholars in the reading field.

Several aspects of the interactive–compensatory paper (Chapter 3) stand out for me when rereading the paper now, more than 20 years after it was written. First, I was right to emphasize the insight that the compensatory assumption was *not* embodied in most top-down models of reading at the time. These models, for all their emphasis on interactiveness, posited a unidirectional individual difference prediction: higher level processes were posited to be always *less* implicated in the performance of poorer readers. In a sense these models were rigid: they did not accommodate the notion of a bidirectional flow of information that was dependent on the system's online needs—online needs that were a function of the extraction of stimulus information and of the ongoing contextual support combined with the ability to *use* that contextual support (Nation & Snowling, 1998; Tunmer & Chapman, 1998).

Another insight contained in the interactive–compensatory paper that I think was posited before its time was my stress on the necessity of distinguishing the presence of a knowledge base from the tendency to *use* that knowledge in the online reading situation (a distinction that will arise again in other sections of this volume—particularly in discussions of the use of phonological information). It was the failure to make this distinction that in part accounted for the confused nature of the context effects literature for such a long time (indeed, the distinction is still often ignored in educational discussions of the reading process). As I said in the interactive–compensatory paper,

The issue at hand is whether good readers have a greater tendency to use contextual redundancy to facilitate *ongoing* word recognition, *not* whether given virtually unlimited time, good readers can make better predictions. The question is not whether the good readers actually have better predictive abilities, but whether they are actually more prone to *rely* on such abilities to speed word recognition. (p. 45)

Prior to Perfetti's work and my own work with Rich West, much of the previous research had tapped the *ability* to predict words when that was the set task—not the *tendency* to do so during ongoing reading. Interestingly, the distinction here is not unlike the distinction between "abilities" and "dispositions" in the area of critical thinking—my other area of research interest (see Stanovich, 1999b; Stanovich & West, 1997). Finally, the discussion of the decoding epiphenomena explanation of reduced context effects in Stanovich (1984; reprinted as Chapter 4 in the present text) led me to write in the Matthew effects paper (see Chapter 10) what I still think is one of the better analyses of the confused notion of "word calling."

However, truly cumulative science changes. It moves forward. Unlike the rhetorical posturing of the Reading Wars, where the debate and the positions of the disputants are frozen (see Part VII), in *cumulative* science the debate progresses. People even change their opinions—sometimes radically (the evolution of the West–Stanovich view of context effects is a case in point; see Chapters 5 and 17 for further examples of marked changes in my theoretical views). After a period of consolidation in the 1980s, work on context effects in the 1990s began to become more transformative. Elaborations of interactive–compensatory ideas were proposed. For example, Nation and Snowling (1998) examined contextual facilitation in three groups of children who were matched on word recognition: a reading-disabled group, a younger non-disabled control group (a reading-level matched control), and a group of poor comprehenders (equal in age to the controls) who had subpar listening comprehension scores despite word recognition and pseudoword reading scores equal to those of the nondisabled control group. Consistent with the trends described in Chapters 2, 3, and 4, Nation and Snowling (1998) found that the reading-disabled individuals displayed larger context effects than the controls. However, poor comprehenders displayed less contextual facilitation than the nondisabled control group, a result that led Nation and Snowling (1998) to posit that the compensatory interactions might be limited in this group and presumably in any group of individuals who had cognitive deficiencies that impaired language prediction skills. Further, they speculated that their poor comprehenders might be subject to a Matthew effect (see Chapter 10) different from that described in Stanovich (1986b): poor comprehenders were posited to be at risk for poor development of word recognition skills because they lack the language prediction skills that are needed to add contextual constraints to partial phonological information. Thus they were posited to have a less efficient self-teaching mechanism (see Share, 1995, 1999; Share &

Stanovich, 1995). In elaborating the interactive–compensatory view and in positing a new subclass of Matthew effects, Nation and Snowling (1998) broadened the context of the original interactive–compensatory model.

Likewise, Tunmer and Chapman (1998) provide an elaborated notion of compensatory processing that bears similarities to that of Nation and Snowling (1998). They also view contextual cues as a supplement in situations where partial decoding has taken place, rather than as total substitutes for decoding. They build a complex model for the assumption that "good decoders do not need to rely on context as often because of their superior ability to recognize words in isolation; when they do rely on context they are much more likely to identify unfamiliar words than are less skilled readers" (Tunmer & Chapman, 1998, p. 60; see Share, 1995, for similar ideas). This notion contains the classic interactive–compensatory idea but elaborates and builds on it in an attempt to explain more of the variance in reading ability.

The Nation and Snowling (1998) and Tunmer and Chapman (1998; see also Share, 1995) contributions represent advances in our knowledge of context effects. My "first pass" at the theoretical issues, reprinted in Chapter 3, was certainly not meant to be the last word. Indeed, 6 years later I drew attention to the fact that "the relationship between the difficulty of the target word, the difficulty of the contextual material, the ability of the reader, and the amount of contextual facilitation is a complex one" (Stanovich, 1986b, p. 371). Tunmer and Chapman (1998) have since attempted to unravel some of these complexities.

My only reservation about the Nation and Snowling (1998) and Tunmer and Chapman (1998) work is that the important conclusions from both studies rely heavily on a particular metric of contextual facilitation with some peculiar properties. The metric used was one of proportion of potential improvement: the number correct in context minus the number correct in isolation divided by the number of errors in isolation. I have sympathy with how these investigators have struggled with the metric issue. The issue of different metrics in individual difference studies is a notoriously difficult one (see Chapman, Chapman, Curran, & Miller, 1994), and West and I wrestled with it ourselves in our earlier work. Our studies compared reaction times, and we settled on absolute differences once we assured ourselves that that metric tended to converge with alternative measures such as the relative difference or the residual of the context condition regressed on the neutral condition (see Chapman et al., 1994). Additionally, in the reaction-time situation, we felt that there was some merit in the argument that ceiling effects here are *real* ceilings—not artifacts. If lexical access beats process X, thus wiping out process X's effect, then that is not an artifact—it is the way the brain is structured with respect to the speed of the relevant processes.

However, comparing percent correct across two conditions, as did Nation and Snowling (1998) and Tunmer and Chapman (1998), may well introduce different complexities than does the simple comparison of reaction times. And the index chosen by these investigators does appear to have some problems.

Consider reader A who reads 90% correct in lists and 95% correct in context, and reader B who reads 20% correct in lists and 60% correct in context. According to the "proportion of potential improvement metric," both show the same contextual facilitation effect (.50). But surely reader B's reading has been virtually *enabled* by context, whereas reader A's reading has been simply *improved*. Or take a more extreme example: child Y reads 45 of 48 words correct in isolation and 47 of 48 correct in a passage. Child Z reads 24 in isolation and 40 in context. Child Z's reading has been qualitatively changed whereas child Y's improvement is psychologically barely discernible—yet they have the same score (.66) on the proportion of potential improvement metric.

Allerup and Elbro (1998) demonstrate in a more technical fashion what is wrong here. First, they point out that the proportion of potential improvement metric, by using a baseline of "relative gain from the isolation condition," controls for ceiling effects but not floor effects. They point out that one could equally relativize the contextual change to the "proportion of degradation in performance from the context condition." This transform completely changes the relationship between decoding skill and contextual facilitation. Note that in the examples above reader B's contextual sensitivity score calculated from this alternative (and equally justifiable) baseline is .66 ([60 − 20]/60), now considerably higher than that of reader A's score of .053 ([95 − 90]/95); and child Z's contextual sensitivity score (16/40) is now considerably higher than that of child Y (2/47). Allerup and Elbro (1998) demonstrate that the "proportion of potential contextual loss" has the reverse problem of the "proportion of contextual gain" statistic—the former controls floor effects but not ceiling effects and the latter controls for ceiling effects but not for floor effects. Allerup and Elbro (1998) demonstrate a metric—the logarithm of the quotient of the odds—that controls for both as well as having other desirable statistical properties. They demonstrate that when this metric is applied to the Tunmer and Chapman (1998) results they produce precisely the interactive–compensatory pattern: better readers display smaller contextual facilitation effects.

Despite these reservations about the metric used in the Nation and Snowling (1998) and Tunmer and Chapman (1998) studies, I believe that the work of these investigators (see also Walczyk & Taylor, 1996) represents the type of research needed to advance our knowledge of context effects beyond that of the interactive–compensatory model—an early attempt at a model that has stood the test of time as a first approximation pointing the way to the more specific and detailed model on which the field will no doubt converge.

C H A P T E R   2

Automatic Contextual Facilitation in Readers of Three Ages

RICHARD F. WEST and KEITH E. STANOVICH

There are undoubtedly numerous factors involved in the acquisition of proficiency in reading. The factors most frequently mentioned by reading researchers are the increasing ability to use contextual information, or redundancy, to facilitate the processing of written material (e.g., Gibson & Levin, 1975), and the gradual development of automatic-processing skills (e.g., LaBerge & Samuels, 1974). With respect to the use of contextual information, redundancy exists both within and between words. The role of within-word redundancy in letter and word recognition has been intensively investigated. In contrast to within-word redundancy, between-word redundancy has received relatively little experimental scrutiny. The relative dearth of research on between-word redundancy exists despite the fact that between-word redundancy is assigned a central role in contemporary reading theories (e.g., Gibson & Levin, 1975; Goodman, 1970; Smith, 1971).

Schuberth and Eimas (1977) investigated the use of context by presenting subjects with sentences that had their terminal word deleted. When a target appeared, the subject's task was to classify the target as either a word or a nonword as rapidly as possible. Sentence contexts were found to facilitate the classification of words that were predictable from the context. The lexical-decision task used by Schuberth and Eimas (1977) yielded findings that were consistent with those of tachistoscopic-recognition experiments (e.g., Tulving & Gold, 1963). Recent work (e.g., Fischler, 1977; Tweedy, Lapinski, &

Schvaneveldt, 1977) has focused on whether contextual facilitation results from conscious expectations or from involuntary priming of appropriate words—an issue addressed in this paper.

Schvaneveldt, Ackerman, and Semlear (1977) employed a lexical-decision task in a developmental investigation of the use of semantic context in word recognition. Second- and fourth-grade children were asked to make word–nonword decisions about targets in semantically related or unrelated contexts. A context consisted of the prior display of a single word that was either a high associate or a nonassociate of the target word. Decision times were faster for target words in the semantically related as opposed to the unrelated contexts. There was a marginal ($p < .10$) interaction between age and context condition. Interestingly, this interaction was due to the fact that the younger children showed a somewhat larger context effect. There was also evidence that, within each grade, the poorer readers made relatively greater use of context. The magnitude of the context effect for children of both grades was correlated with the vocabulary, spelling, and reading tests of the Iowa Basic Skills Achievement Test. All six of these correlations were in the negative direction (lower test scores tended to go with larger context effects), although only two reached statistical significance.

Since the ability to use contextual information is usually assumed to increase with age and reading ability, the findings of Schvaneveldt et al. (1977) are unexpected. However, recall that both the ability to use contextual information and the ability to process information automatically are assumed to be involved in the acquisition of proficiency in reading. Perhaps the developmental findings of this study are due to word recognition taking place more automatically for the more skillful readers. A process is considered to be automatic when it can take place without attention being directed to it (LaBerge & Samuels, 1974). Presumably a reader develops fluency by automating certain low-level processes such as letter and word identification so that attention can be allocated to higher-level functions such as comprehension.

[material omitted]

The present study investigates developmental changes in the influence of sentence context. In addition, the question of the relative influence of automatic word recognition and automatic contextual facilitation is explored. Fourth- and sixth-grade children and college students each performed three separate tasks. In task 1, the word-reading task, subjects were asked to read target words as rapidly as possible under the following three conditions: (a) with the prior display of a sentence context that was congruous with the target (e.g., "the dog ran after the" for the target "cat"), (b) with the prior display of a sentence context that was incongruous with the target (e.g., "the girl sat on the" for the target "cat"), and (c) without the prior display of a sentence context (e.g., only the word "the" preceding the target "cat"). This task will provide an indication of how the use of context, in a situation approximating actual reading, changes with age.

[*material omitted*]

METHOD

Subjects

The subjects were 48 fourth graders (24 males and 24 females), 48 sixth graders (24 males and 24 females), and 48 college students (22 males and 26 females). The children were recruited from three predominantly middle-class elementary schools. The fourth graders had a mean age of 9-9 (range 8-8 to 10-6), and their mean reading ability was at the 5-5 grade level as tested by the reading subtest level 1 of the Wide Range Achievement Test (WRAT) (Jastak, Bijou, & Jastak, 1965). The sixth graders had a mean age of 11-6 (range 10-4 to 12-3), and their mean reading ability was at the 7-5 grade level as tested by the WRAT. The college students were enrolled in an introductory psychology course and received credit toward course requirements for participating in this study. The mean age of the college students was 20-5 (range 18-0 to 32-0). Not surprisingly, their reading performance on the level 1 portion of the WRAT was generally at or near ceiling level (their mean score was 98 out of a possible 100 points).

Stimuli and Apparatus

Sixty-eight sentences were constructed so that their last two words were the words "the" and a noun that was highly predictable from the words that preceded it in the sentence (e.g., "The dog ran after the cat"). Second- and third-grade primers, Dolch words, and simple, high-frequency words (Kucera & Francis, 1967) were used in formulating the sentences. After the 68 sentences were constructed, they were organized into 34 sentence pairs (e.g., "the dog ran after the cat" was paired with "the girl sat on the chair"). The terminal word of each sentence was then deleted, and the resulting pairs of incomplete sentences were used as sentence contexts. The deleted nouns were used as word targets; from four to six letter X's were used as nonword targets. A sentence context and a target word were considered to be congruous when they had been derived from the same original sentence (e.g., "the dog ran after the" was congruous with the target "cat"). A sentence context and a target word were considered to be incongruous when they had been derived from opposite members of the original sentence pairs (e.g., "the girl sat on the" was incongruous with the target "cat"). Three of the original sentence pairs were used in deriving the stimuli for the practice trials, 27 for the experimental trials of tasks 1 and 2, and four for the trials of task 3.

The slides were back projected onto a translucent screen by two Kodak Carousel 760H slide projectors. Target onset was controlled by a Vincent Associates Uniblitz shutter that was positioned over the lens of the projector that contained the target slides. When the experimenter pushed a control button, the shutter was electronically opened, and the projected image of the target item appeared. Simultaneously, a National Electronic Systems Cristal stopwatch was started by the same push of the control button. When the subject verbally responded to the target, a voice-activated relay stopped the stopwatch and closed the shutter. The microphone that led to the voice-activated relay was held by the subject.

Procedure

Subjects were individually tested in a session that lasted between 20 and 30 min. First, the reading subtest level 1 of the WRAT (Jastak et al., 1965) was given to the subjects. Next, the subjects were handed a microphone and told to hold it approximately 10 cm from their mouth. For every subject, task 1 was performed prior to task 2, and task 3 was performed last.

Task 1 (Word-Reading Task)

In the word-reading task, subjects were asked to read aloud contexts that appeared on the screen in front of them. Approximately 0.5 sec after the subjects pronounced the last word of the context, which was always "the," a target word appeared. Subjects were instructed to read a target word as rapidly as possible when it appeared. In addition, the subjects were told that only the reading of the target word was timed, so they were free to read the contexts at a comfortable pace. Targets were read under the following three conditions: (a) with the prior display of a congruous-sentence context, (b) with the prior display of an incongruous-sentence context, and (c) without the prior display of a sentence context (only the word "the").

Two practice trials were given under each of the three context conditions. The practice trials were followed by nine experimental trials given under each of the three context conditions. The ordering of the three context conditions within the 27 experimental trials was random, with the constraint that each context condition occurred three times in every block of nine trials. A total of six different random orderings of the conditions were used across subjects. For the experimental trials of both tasks 1 and 2, all subjects saw the same set of 54 target words, but the assignment of these words to the two tasks and to the three context conditions was counterbalanced across subjects. In addition, each of the 54 sentence contexts was equally often congruous and incongruous with the target words across subjects. No subject saw the same target word or sentence context more than once in the course of the experiment.

[*material omitted*]

RESULTS

Of the 62 experimental trials presented to each subject, 2.3% were dropped from the data analysis because the voice-activated relay either failed to trigger (e.g., the relay was improperly adjusted, the vocal response was too quiet) or was triggered by irrelevant factors (the subject handled the microphone, coughing, etc.). The following types of responses were scored as errors: a response that took longer than 2,000 msec, an incorrect reading of a word in task 1, and a reading of a word instead of naming of a color in task 2. Across all trials the mean error rate was 4.1% for the fourth graders, 3.0% for the sixth graders, and 0.04% for the college students. Trials on which errors were made were dropped from the reaction-time analyses.

Task 1 (Word-Reading Task)

The mean reading times for the target words for each of the age groups and context conditions are displayed in Figure 2.1. The mean percentage of errors is indicated in parentheses. A two-way analysis of variance was performed on the reaction-time data with age as a between-subject factor and context condition as a within-subject factor. The analysis indicated a highly significant effect of age, $F(2, 141) = 54.56$, $p < .001$; context condition, $F(2, 282) = 49.90$, $p < .001$; and age × context condition interaction, $F(4, 282) = 4.62$, $p < .001$. Virtually identical results were obtained when an analysis of covariance was carried out on the reaction times with the percentage of errors as a covariate. As can be seen in Figure 2.1, the speed of reading target words increased steadily from fourth grade to college. Scheffé post hoc comparisons indicated that within each context condition, the mean length of reading time was significantly larger in the younger of every pairwise comparison of a younger and older group. In addition, large negative correlations were found between the WRAT scores and reading times within each condition (all subjects pooled: $r = -.73$ to $-.80$, $p < .001$; all children pooled: $r = -.63$ to $-.76$, $p < .001$).

From Figure 2.1 it is apparent that the context condition had an influence on word-reading times. The mean length of time required to read target words was significantly shorter in the congruous-context condition than in the no-context condition for the fourth graders ($p < .001$), sixth graders ($p < .005$), and college students ($p < .05$). The measure of the extent to which word reading was facilitated by a congruous context was the magnitude of the difference between the congruous context and no-context conditions. The size of the facilitation score (no-context condition reaction time [RT] minus congruous-context RT) did not significantly differ between any groups of subjects. However, a significant negative correlation was found between the WRAT score and the facilitation score (all subjects pooled: $r = -.35$, $p < .001$; all children pooled: $r = -.23$, $p < .025$). This negative correlation is analogous to that reported by Schvaneveldt et al. (1977). Better readers (as indicated by a standardized test) make less use of context.

As predicted, word reading was facilitated by congruous-sentence contexts. However, contrary to expectations, there was no evidence that the use of sentence context increased with age and reading ability. Indeed, the correlational data suggests that word-reading latencies were less influenced by the congruous context for the skillful, as compared to less skillful, readers.

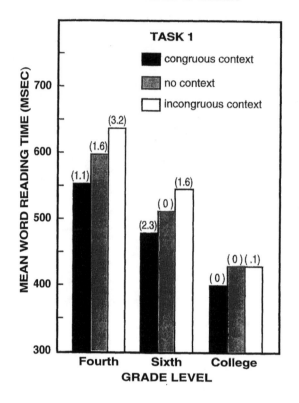

FIGURE 2.1. Mean word-reading times as a function of grade level and context condition for task 1. Mean percentage of errors indicated in parentheses.

The mean length of time required to read the target words was significantly longer in the incongruous-context condition than in the no-context condition for the fourth graders ($p < .001$) and sixth graders ($p < .05$), but not for the college students. The magnitude of the difference between the incongruous-context and no-context conditions was used in this study as the measure of the extent to which incongruous contexts interfered with word reading. None of the pairwise comparisons of interference scores (incongruous-context minus no-context condition RT) was significant. However, the comparison between fourth graders and college students did approach significance ($p < .06$). A significant negative correlation was found between the WRAT score and the interference score (all subjects pooled: $r = -.19$, $p < .05$; all children pooled: $r = -.29$, $p < .005$).

The prediction that the incongruous-sentence contexts would interfere with word reading was met for the two groups of children, but not for the adults. The expectation that the extent of this interference would increase with age and reading ability was not met. In fact, the post hoc analyses and the correlational data suggest that the less skilled readers were somewhat more influenced by the incongruous contexts than the more skilled readers.

In general, the results displayed in Figure 2.1 indicated that the ease with which target words were read increased with their predictability from the context. No developmental trend toward increased use of context was evident in the data. Fourth and sixth graders did not differ significantly in their use of context. In fact, when the data from the adults were taken into account, age × condition interactions indicated less use of context by the older subjects. The correlational results were also indicative of this pattern. The correlation between the WRAT scores and the facilitation and interference scores suggested that the less skilled readers relied more on context than the more skilled readers. These and other similar results (Schvaneveldt et al., 1977) can be explained by recourse to the concept of automatic processing. It is possible that the word-recognition processes of poorer readers are not so automated and are slow enough so that there is time for context to have a facilitating effect.

[*material omitted*]

DISCUSSION

The comparison of the congruous-context and no-context conditions of task 1 indicated that subjects of all three ages utilized sentence context to speed processing of the target word. However, there was no increase in contextual facilitation with age. In fact, the correlations involving WRAT scores suggested that the poorer readers made greater use of context. This conjecture was supported by the comparison of the no-context and incongruous-context conditions. Incongruous context slowed processing of the target word for children but had no effect on the reaction times of adults. It should be noted that when the results from the adult sample are interpreted within the context of the distinction between automatic pathway activation and conscious attention drawn by Posner and Snyder (1975a, 1975b), strong support is given for the notion that contextual facilitation in these subjects is due to automatic activation. Specifically, the benefit of a congruous context occurred without a corresponding cost in the incongruous-context condition.

[*material omitted*]

The results from tasks 2 and 3 support the contention that the greater use of context by younger and poorer readers in task 1 was due to the relative speed of automatic visual-recognition processes as opposed to the automatic processes that mediate syntactic and semantic redundancy. With increasing reading fluency, automatic word-recognition processes dominate performance, and recognition is so fast that the effect of contextual factors is mitigated. This notion contrasts with the conventional wisdom that reliance on context increases with age and reading ability. However, it is consistent with some other empirical results and at least one popular model of word recognition. The Schvaneveldt et al. (1977) study, mentioned earlier, found the semantic-context effect in a lexical-decision task to be greater for second graders than for fourth graders. Furthermore, correlations between the context effect and three subtests of the Iowa Basic Skills Test were all negative for both grades (although all were not significant). Samuels, Begy, and Chen (1975–1976), using a tachistoscopic-recognition task, reported data suggesting that single-word context had a greater effect on the performance of fourth graders who were poor readers than on the performance of good readers of the same age. In a tachistoscopic-recognition study of adults, Jackson and McClelland (1975) found that even with nonredundant materials good readers identified more words and letters. If use of redundancy were the only thing differentiating good from poor readers, no differences in performance would be observed on such tasks.

Seymour (1976) has discussed how Morton's (1969, 1970) logogen model of word recognition predicts that when sensory processes are relatively slow, nonsensory factors will have a greater effect on recognition time. Studies using adult subjects have tended to support this prediction. Meyer, Schvaneveldt, and Ruddy (1975) found that the semantic-context effect in the lexical-decision task is greater when the stimuli are degraded by visual noise. Degradation slows the feature-extraction process, allowing nonsensory processes to have a relatively greater influence. Similar results obtain when feature extraction is slowed by intensity reduction (Becker & Killion, 1977). Sanford, Garrod, and Boyle (1977) found that the association frequency of a previously displayed semantic category had a greater effect on naming words when the words were degraded. Finally, presentation probability has been shown to have a larger effect on naming numerals when the stimuli are degraded (Stanovich & Pachella, 1977). These results all support the logogen model's prediction that nonsensory factors will have a greater influence on performance when feature extraction (i.e., sensory processing) is slowed. It would not seem unreasonable to consider the developmental implications of this particular model. If the rate of sensory processing is slower in children, then the logogen model would predict that nonsensory factors would have a greater effect at younger age levels.

In summary, the present study has led to some important conclusions regarding the operation of automatic recognition processes and interword redundancy in reading. First of all, it appears that sentence context can automatically facilitate reading performance. However, the performance of more fluent readers seems to be dominated by rapid, probably automatic (in the sense of LaBerge & Samuels, 1974), word recognition. These recognition processes occur so fast that effects due to slower acting contextual factors are reduced. In less fluent readers these two sources of information are mediated by processes of a similar speed and both contribute to performance. It should be noted, however, that the relatively simple words used in the study would serve to exaggerate the influence of automatic word-recognition processes. Adults' use of context is probably greater when they read more difficult material.

CHAPTER 3

Toward an Interactive–Compensatory Model of Individual Differences in the Development of Reading Fluency

During the last two decades experimental psychologists have developed a renewed interest in phenomena that have a heavy cognitive component (e.g., mental imagery, psycholinguistics). Nowhere is this more apparent than in the literature on the reading process (see Venezky, 1977). Cognitive psychologists have recently applied their information processing perspective to many components of reading performance (cf. Massaro, 1975, 1978).

There was a strong tendency in early cognitive theorizing to depict information processing as a series of discrete stages, each performing a specific transformation on its input and passing on the new recoded representation as an input to a subsequent stage (Sperling, 1967; Sternberg, 1969; Theios, 1973). Since the sequence of processing operations proceeds from the incoming data to higher-level encodings, such conceptualizations have been termed "bottom-up" models. It is not surprising that, since these models were so influential in the early development of information processing theorizing, they were the first to be applied to reading. Thus, several bottom-up serial-stage models of reading and word recognition have been introduced into the literature (Geyer, 1970; Gough, 1972; LaBerge & Samuels, 1974; Smith & Spoehr, 1974). However, it is now reasonably well-established that such models are inadequate because they fail to account for many important empirical results in the reading literature. Rumelhart (1977) and Danks (1978) discuss many experimental phenomena (e.g., word, syntactic, and semantic context effects) that provide problems for bottom-up models. Serial-stage models of reading run into difficulty because they usually contain no mechanism whereby higher-level processes can affect lower levels. Samuels (1977) revised the LaBerge and Samuels (1974) model for just this reason.

TOP-DOWN MODELS

There exists, however, a class of models that conceptualize reading in a manner diametrically opposed to that embodied in serial-stage models. These have been termed "top-down" models because higher-level processes interact with, and direct the flow of information through, lower-level processes. Although several different top-down conceptualizations of reading exist (Goodman, 1976; Hochberg, 1970; Kolers, 1972; Levin & Kaplan, 1970; Neisser, 1967; Neville & Pugh, 1976–1977; Smith, 1971, 1973), they all have in common a view of the fluent reader as being actively engaged in hypothesis-testing as he proceeds through text. Since the reader is only sampling textual information in order to test hypotheses, the reading process is viewed as being driven by higher-level conceptual processes rather than by low-level stimulus analysis.[1, 2] In short, top-down analyses start with hypotheses and then attempt to verify them by processing the stimulus, whereas bottom-up analyses start by processing the stimulus (see Eisenstadt & Kareeve, 1975).

While the top-down hypothesis-testing models have often been attacked for excessive vagueness in their conceptualization, there are even more serious criticisms of the entire class of models. First, several authors (McConkie & Rayner, 1976; Samuels, Dahl, & Archwamety, 1974; Wildman & Kling, 1978–1979) have questioned the hypothesis-testing models because they require implausible assumptions about the relative speeds of the processes involved. Specifically, the generation of hypotheses about a subsequent word, or words, must take less time than is necessary to recognize the words on the basis of purely visual information; otherwise, the hypothesis generation is unnecessary. However, it seems unlikely that a hypothesis based on complex syntactic and semantic analyses can be formed in less than the few hundred milliseconds that is required for a fluent reader to recognize most words. This argument against hypothesis-testing models is reinforced by recent research indicating that fluent readers do not use conscious expectancies to facilitate word recognition (Mitchell & Green, 1978; Stanovich & West, 1979b). In summary, it appears that most top-down models have serious deficiencies as explanations of fluent reading. It will be argued later in this paper that their account of individual differences in reading skill is also inadequate.

INTERACTIVE MODELS AND THE COMPENSATORY HYPOTHESIS

A third class of theories is formed by those models that posit neither a strictly bottom-up nor strictly top-down processing, but instead assume that a pattern is synthesized based on information provided *simultaneously* from several knowledge sources (e.g., feature extraction, orthographic knowledge, lexical knowledge, syntactic knowledge, semantic knowledge). Rumelhart (1977) provides the best example of such a model, although Morton's (1969, 1970) logogen model embodies many of the assumptions of the interactive-processes conception at the level of word recognition.

As has been previously discussed by Mosenthal, Walmsley, and Allington (1978), interactive models differ from top-down models primarily in terms of the relative independence of processes at different levels. In top-down models, semantic processes direct lower-level processes, whereas in interactive models semantic processes constrain the alternatives of lower levels but are themselves constrained by lower-level analyses. Thus, each level of processing is not merely a data source for higher levels, but instead seeks to synthesize the stimulus based on its own analysis and the constraints imposed by both higher- and lower-level processes. Rumelhart (1977) argues convincingly that many experimental findings in the reading literature seem to require an interactive model for their explanation.

Although several authors have recently alluded to the potential of an interactive-processes model of reading and recognition (Lesgold & Perfetti, 1978; Levy, 1978; Marslen-Wilson, 1975; Pearson & Kamil, 1977–1978; Schwartz, 1980; Wildman & Kling, 1978–1979; Wisher, 1976), few have discussed the relation of the interactive model to current theorizing on the nature of individual differences in reading fluency. It will be argued here that an interactive model, when coupled with the assumption that the various component subskills of reading can operate in a compensatory manner, leads to a reconceptualization of the nature of individual differences in reading. Furthermore, this new model of individual differences can explain a series of results that, until now, had seemed paradoxical.

In order to make the compensatory assumption, we must first agree on the invalidity of bottom-up models of reading. That is, we must assume that it is not necessarily the case that the initiation of a higher-level process must await the completion of all lower ones. Once we have dispensed with bottom-up models, we are free to assume that a process at *any* level can compensate for deficiencies at any other level. This is the essence of the compensatory hypothesis. Notice that we are now free to consider a possibility that has been inadequately explored in the reading literature, namely, that higher-level processes can actually compensate for deficiencies in lower-level processes. Thus, a reader with poor word recognition skills may actually be prone to a greater reliance on contextual factors because these provide additional sources of information. It is precisely this possibility that is suggested by the interactive model developed by Rumelhart (1977).

Notice also that a compensatory assumption is not embodied in most top-down models of reading (e.g., Levin & Kaplan, 1970; Smith, 1971). In these models, higher-level processes (i.e., hypothesis-testing based on contextual expectancies) are usually *less* implicated in the performance of poorer readers. These models seldom consider the possibility that the poorer reader may compensate for a deficit in a lower-level process, such as letter or word recognition, by relying more on a higher-level knowledge source. In contrast, working from the interactive-processes conception, one might assume that, given a deficit in a particular process, the reader would rely more on other knowledge sources, *regardless* of their level. (In fact, Seymour, 1976, has previously discussed how Morton's logogen model predicts that, when stimulus analysis is relatively slow, nonsensory factors will have a greater effect on recognition time.) Thus, it is possible that, given a deficit in a lower-level process, poor readers might actually rely *more* on higher-level contextual factors. Evidence to be reviewed below indicates that this is sometimes the case.

It should be noted in addition that bottom-up models also contain no compensatory mechanism. In fact, they make the same prediction as the top-down models regarding the relatively greater reliance of the better reader on higher-level processes. This is because it is assumed that the efficiency of the good reader's lower-level stimulus–analysis processes free capacity for higher-level processes. Thus, the findings that, under certain circumstances, poorer readers show a greater reliance on higher-level processes also invalidates the bottom-up conception of individual differences in reading skill.

Masson and Sala (1978) have perhaps come closest to combining a compensatory hypothesis with an interactive model of reading (although see Frederiksen, 1978, and Perfetti & Roth, 1981). In order to explain results indicating that sentences originally read in transformed typography were recognized better than sentences read in normal typography, they argued that, due to the unfamiliarity of inverted typography, the data-driven stimulus–analysis mechanisms (Bobrow & Norman, 1975; Norman, 1976) were slowed, and decoding was more dependent on conceptually driven processing. This explanation suggests the possibility that a similar trade-off might occur when the data-driven operations are slower because of developmental immaturity and/ or unfamiliarity with written language, rather than the presence of an inverted typography. However, Masson and Sala (1978) did not extend their argument to deal with individual differences in reading ability or the development of reading fluency. In the present study, it will be shown that an interactive–compensatory model of reading is consistent with much research on individual differences in the use of orthographic structure and sentence context, and that many studies in this same literature present problems for bottom-up and top-down models. In the following review, studies that compared readers at different developmental levels and studies that compared skilled and less skilled readers at the same age will both be considered. The interactive–compensatory model is equally applicable to developmental and individual difference studies.

ORTHOGRAPHIC STRUCTURE EFFECTS

[*material omitted*]

SENTENCE CONTEXT EFFECTS AND TOP-DOWN MODELS

The way in which good and poor readers process contextual information has been frequently discussed in the reading literature. However, it is useful to distinguish two types of contextual processes. First, there are those that are involved in constructing a knowledge structure from the text, processes such as semantic integration (Bransford & Franks, 1971), the relation of new information to given information (Haviland & Clark, 1974), and all other strategic operations that facilitate comprehension of text. There exists some evidence indicating that these comprehension control processes are superior in the good reader, even when differential word-recognition abilities are controlled (Cromer, 1970; Guthrie, 1973; Jackson & McClelland, 1979; Oakan, Wiener, & Cromer, 1971; Smiley, Oakley, Worthen, Campione, & Brown, 1977; but see Perfetti & Lesgold, 1977, for a dissenting opinion). However, there is a second type of contextual processing that operates much differently than the comprehension strategies just described. This is the contextual hypothesis-testing that is posited by most theorists oriented toward top-down processing (Goodman, 1976; Hochberg, 1970; Levin & Kaplan, 1970; Neisser, 1967; Smith, 1971). According to these theorists, superior readers not only comprehend text better, but also use previously understood material to facilitate *ongoing* word recognition. Thus, Smith (1971) hypothesizes that, due to sensitivity to semantic and syntactic redundancy afforded by sentences, the good reader develops hypotheses about upcoming words and is then able to confirm the identity of a word by sampling only a few features in the visual display of a new word. Good readers should then process words faster since their use of redundancy lightens the load on their stimulus–analysis mechanisms. Poor readers, on the other hand, are less facile in their use of contextual redundancy, make incorrect or few hypotheses, are forced to process more visual information in order to recognize a word, and thus read slowly. Smith's (1971) view of reading difficulty is that "the more difficulty a reader has with reading, the more he relies on the visual information; this statement applies to both the fluent reader and the beginner. In each case, the cause of the difficulty is inability to make full use of syntactic and semantic redundancy, of nonvisual sources of information" (p. 221). It will later be argued that this conception of individual differences in reading ability is not supported by the empirical evidence. Before turning to this evidence, a recent study that questions the applicability of the hypothesis-testing models even to fluent reading will be discussed.

Levin and Kaplan (1970) have most forcefully stated the top-down hypothesis-testing view of reading. They characterize the fluent reader as one who

> continually assigns tentative interpretations to a text or message and checks these interpretations. As the material is grammatically or semantically constrained he is able to formulate correct hypotheses about what will come next. When the pre-

diction is confirmed, the material covered by that prediction can be more easily processed and understood. (p. 132)

However, as was previously mentioned, several authors (McConkie & Rayner, 1976; Samuels, Dahl, & Archwamety, 1974; Wildman & Kling, 1978–1979) have questioned whether hypotheses could be generated and tested with a speed that could facilitate ongoing word recognition. Mitchell and Green (1978) recently reported an important series of experiments that appear to answer this question in the negative. They employed a paradigm in which the subject presented a passage to himself on an on-line visual display by pressing a button that presented three words of the passage to be read. Successive presses of the button advanced the subject through the text three words at a time. The inter-response time served as an index of processing difficulty. Mitchell and Green (1978) failed to confirm an important prediction of the hypothesis-testing view that processing should be faster in more predictable parts of the text. Since the predictability of most sentences increases from beginning to end, processing difficulty, and hence inter-response time, should decrease as the reader progresses through the sentence. In fact, the data revealed a tendency to slow slightly as ordinal position in the sentence increased.

In further, more sensitive tests, Mitchell and Green (1978) found no tendency for a verb that permitted few structural continuations to speed the processing of the following three-word frame. The presence of a relative pronoun also had no effect on processing time. The results concerning semantically selective words were ambiguous. A post-hoc reanalysis of the data did indicate a tendency for semantically predictive words to speed subsequent processing, but the authors argued for an explanation of this effect that did not involve the facilitation of ongoing processing by prior predictions. However, this result is consistent with an explanation of sentence context effects presented by Stanovich and West (1979b; to be discussed below).

Although Mitchell and Green (1978) did not find sentence predictability to affect inter-response time, they did find that many other variables affected immediate processing. For instance, word frequency, display size, position in passage, and rated difficulty of the sentence all had significant effects on response time. Thus, it cannot be argued that their experimental technique was insensitive. Based on their failure to find predictability effects and their repeated observations of reliable display size and word frequency effects, Mitchell and Green (1978) concluded that reading rate is more dependent on the speed with which a reader can recognize words and construct a representation than on the ability to use predictions to facilitate word recognition. Note that these investigators do not deny that preceding context can affect comprehension processes, for there is ample evidence for such effects (e.g., Bransford & Johnson, 1973; Haviland & Clark, 1974). They are specifically arguing against the view that prior context can act to facilitate *ongoing* word recognition. Thus, they distinguish between the two types of contextual processing (for comprehension and for facilitation of word recognition) discussed at the beginning of this section. In a similar manner, it will now be argued that distinguishing the two types of contextual processes is useful in understanding the literature on individual differences in the development of fluency.

Smith (1971) has argued that the poor reader is deficient in both types of contextual processing. The hypothesis that the general comprehension strategies of better readers are superior will not be challenged here since there is some support for this position (Forrest & Barron, 1977; Guthrie, 1973; Oakan et al., 1971; Schwartz, 1977; Smiley et al., 1977). However, the idea that a greater ability to use contextual redundancy to facilitate word recognition also differentiates the good from the poor reader appears to be mistaken. This idea follows from a strong tendency of top-down theorists to assume that *every* higher-level "conceptual" process must be more implicated in the performance of more fluent readers. When empirical evidence contradicts this assumption, as was found in the literature on orthographic structure effects, top-down models run into problems. It will be argued that this assumption also fails to find support in the literature on contextual effects on lexical access in readers of differing abilities and that an interactive–compensatory model more easily accounts for the results.

THE EMPIRICAL LITERATURE ON SENTENCE CONTEXT EFFECTS

There is a body of research that is commonly cited as being supportive of the top-down notion that fluent readers are more reliant on contextual redundancy. Many of the studies (and/or the interpretations of them) fail to distinguish between the two types of contextual processing. Thus, while there are some studies that show that the comprehension strategies of good readers are superior, they are often incorrectly cited as showing support for the position that contextual redundancy actually facilitates word recognition (e.g., Klein's [1976] citation of Oakan, Wiener, & Cromer, 1971).

Another line of research has attempted to show that good readers are better at predicting words that are missing from an incomplete passage than are poor readers. The criticism of this research runs along the lines of the argument already presented in the section on orthographic structure effects. Specifically, the issue at hand is whether good readers have a greater tendency to use contextual redundancy to facilitate *ongoing* word recognition, *not* whether given virtually unlimited time good readers can make better predictions. The question is not whether the good readers actually have better predictive abilities, but whether they are actually more prone to *rely* on such abilities to speed word recognition. Thus, much of the previous research has tapped the presence of contextual knowledge, not its use, and once again many of the tasks resemble problem-solving rather than speeded recognition. For example, the cloze task, where the subject is asked to produce words that are missing from a passage, is obviously measuring the ability to consciously generate predictions under no time constraints. (Thus, the task does not tap potentially important automatic contextual effects; see below.) Consequently, the reported positive correlations between cloze performance and reading proficiency (Bickley, Ellington, & Bickley, 1970; Ruddell, 1965) should not be interpreted as indicating that good readers rely more on context to facilitate word recognition. It is more likely that comprehension processes are being tapped. For example, Perfetti, Goldman, and Hogaboam (1979) have shown that, although the predictive abilities of skilled fifth-grade readers were superior to those of less-skilled fifth-graders, the skilled readers' word recognition times were *less* affected by a prior sentence context, a finding corroborated by many studies to be discussed below (e.g., Schvaneveldt, Ackerman, & Semlear, 1977; West & Stanovich, 1978). Perfetti and Roth (1981) present a detailed explanation of how a good reader can be at once more *sensitive* to context but less *dependent* on it (due to the availability of information from other knowledge sources).

A study reported by Klein, Klein, and Bertino (1974) could be interpreted as indicating that the tendency to use prior context to speed word recognition increases with age. They employed materials consisting of word sequences that were printed with a space after every letter but no additional spaces between word boundaries. The subject's task was to go through the sequence and indicate with a slash the boundaries between words, the dependent variable being the number of words determined in a fixed period. The word sequence was either a random string of words or a coherent passage of sentences. Word demarcation was faster when coherent passages were used, and the difference in performance between the coherent and random conditions was an indication of the extent of context usage. Klein et al. found that both fourth- and sixth-grade readers identified more words in the coherent passage than in the random passage during a 90-sec search interval. The magnitude of the coherent/random difference was greater for the sixth-graders than for the fourth-graders, indicating a developmental increase in the use of context to speed word identification. There are, however, problems with this interpretation as well as with the word-boundary task itself. The boundary decisions take approximately 2½-3 sec per word, much slower than the less than 1 sec it takes fourth-graders to recognize most words. The unfamiliar orthographic configuration and the instructions to the subject make the task seem closer to an index of problem-solving skills than a measure of word identification in reading. Schwartz (1977) has stated that the Klein et al. (1974) result probably reflects the general strategic advantage of older children. If this interpretation is correct, then the study is not an adequate test of the hypothesis-testing view of the use of prior context by readers of different abilities. (See Goldsmith and Nicolich [1977] for indications of some additional problems in employing the word-boundary task as a measure of contextual facilitation in young children.) The research employing the word-boundary task shares with work on cloze task performance (Ruddell, 1965), whole-report tachistoscopic perception (Marcel, 1974), and memory tasks (Weinstein & Rabinovitch, 1971) the property that while it may be tapping important psychological processes, it is not a measure of the extent to which readers employ context to facilitate immediate word recognition.

Research that has more closely tapped the ability to use context to speed ongoing word recognition has shown support for the top-down notion that this process occurs during reading performance. However, the view of individual differences in reading ability proposed by the top-down theorists, that contextual facilitation is more implicated in the performance of better readers (e.g., Smith's [1971, 1973, 1975] oft-repeated statement that the good reader relies less on graphic cues), does not receive unanimous support. Instead, the research shows that even the very youngest readers use context to facilitate word recognition. In addition, many studies have failed to show the expected increase in contextual facilitation as reading fluency develops. Just as many, if not more, studies have shown contextual facilitation to *decrease* as reading fluency develops. Finally, recent research (e.g., Alford 1979; Fischler & Bloom, 1979; McConkie & Zola, 1981; Mitchell & Green, 1978; Stanovich, 1981a; West & Stanovich, 1978, 1979) has failed to uncover evidence favorable toward the hypothesis that the rapid word recognition of fluent readers is primarily due to an extensive use of contextual information. For example, McConkie and Zola (1981) examined eye fixation patterns as subjects read passages that contained critical words that were either highly constrained (i.e., were chosen 85% of the time when subjects were attempting to guess them in a cloze task) or relatively unconstrained (chosen less than 15% of the time in a cloze task). Highly constrained target words were just as likely to be fixated, and the fixation durations on highly constrained targets averaged only 14 msec shorter than the durations on the unconstrained targets.

The finding that in some situations poor readers rely more on context than do good readers presents problems for top-down models, which hypothesize that reading becomes more conceptually driven as fluency develops. However, such a finding presents no difficulty for the interactive–compensatory model, where knowledge sources at all levels contribute simultaneously to pattern synthesis and where a lower-level deficit may result in a greater contribution from higher-level knowledge sources. Thus, the interactive–compensatory conception allows for the reader with poor letter or word recognition skills to draw heavily on higher-level knowledge sources.

Studies of oral reading errors have been diagnostic in examining the relative contribution of graphic and contextual information to word recognition during reading. Biemiller (1970) studied the oral reading errors of a group of first-grade students from October to May and argued for the existence of three stages of reading acquisition during this period. In the first stage reading is dominated by the use of contextual information and few of the children's errors are graphically constrained. The second stage is one in which the proportion of nonresponse and graphically constrained errors increases markedly. Biemiller (1970) interpreted this stage as a transition period in which the children were moving from a context-using phase in which they were attempting to avoid using graphic information to a stage where their attention is more clearly focused on graphic information. The third stage is one where the children's oral reading errors are both contextually and graphically constrained. Across these three first-grade reading stages the increase in the percentage of graphically constrained errors was more marked than the increase in contextually constrained errors. The percentage of errors that were contextually appropriate rose from 74% in stage 1 to 83% in stage 3. However, the graphically similar responses rose from 19% in stage 1 to 44% in stage 3. Particularly striking is the fact that a large proportion of the errors of even the least fluent readers were contextually appropriate.

The results of Weber's (1970b) study of oral reading errors are largely consistent with those of Biemiller (1970). She found that approximately 90% of the oral reading errors of first-graders were grammatically acceptable with the preceding text and that good and poor readers were not distinguishable on the basis of the percentage of grammatically acceptable errors that they produced. Weber further analyzed the substitution errors in terms of their graphic similarity to the correct word. The graphic similarity scores of the better readers were higher than the scores of the poorer readers, indicating a greater attention to graphic information on the part of the better readers. This finding contradicts Smith's (1971) hypothesis that better readers are less reliant on graphic information and that the poor reader is a "slave to print." Instead, Weber (1970b) argues that

> these findings do not support the characterization of the relatively low achiever as a word-by-word reader. Rather, they suggest that children—no matter what their potential for acquiring literacy skills—bring to the task a fundamental linguistic ability, which in its rigidity shapes their reading responses into familiar language structure. (pp. 153–154)

In an additional study, Weber (1970b) observed that, once again, there was no significant difference between good and poor readers in the proportion of errors that were grammatically consistent with the preceding sentence context; however, good readers were more likely to correct errors that did not fit into the subsequent context of the sentence as it was written. These results suggest the distinction between the two types of contextual processing discussed above. Specifically, it appears that the ability to use previous context to speed lexical access does not differentiate good from poor readers (see also Rode, 1974). However, the general comprehension strategies needed to construct a coherent representation of the text appear to be superior in the better reader.

Perfetti and Roth (1981) report results from a study of oral reading errors that converge nicely with those of Weber (1970b) and Biemiller (1970). Perfetti and Roth found that both skilled and less skilled readers could trade off visual for contextual information, and that skilled readers were not more reliant on contextual information. Kolers (1972) has analyzed the oral reading errors of subjects who were reading geometrically transformed text. He found that, in terms of the linguistic pattern of substitution errors, dyslexic adolescents were not differentiated from normal readers. Kolers (1975) employed a similar technique with seventh-grade good and poor readers. He again found the pattern of substitution errors of poor readers to approximate that of good readers. On the basis of other evidence, Kolers (1975) argued that the good reader was, in fact, more sensitive to features of the typography.

Juel (1980) studied the oral reading errors made by second- and third-grade subjects. In her study, she analyzed the number of errors made on a set of target words that varied in decodability, frequency, number of syllables, and contextual constraint. The error analyses indicated that the good readers were predominately text-driven, whereas the poorer readers were more con-text-driven. Juel (1980) concluded, consistent with the position taken in this review, that

> researchers may be mistaken in interpreting those studies which show good read-ers can make use of contextual cues better than poorer readers as evidence that they actually do so in normal reading. It may be more efficient for good readers, with well developed decoding skills, to directly identify words in a text-driven manner than to "predict" words based on context. (p. 375)

[material omitted]

Studies that have measured oral reading latency have generally found re-sults consistent with the research on oral reading errors. Doehring (1976) found that even first-grade students read connected text faster than passages of random words. The mean contextual gain in seconds per syllable was actu-ally greater in the younger subjects, and the relative gain was invariant after second grade. Biemiller (1977–1978) observed similar results. His second-grade subjects also read connected text faster than random words. The abso-lute magnitude of the contextual facilitation (in seconds per word) was greater for the younger children; however, there was a slight tendency for older chil-dren and adults to show a larger relative gain.

Allington (1978a) tested the ability of good and poor fourth-grade read-ers to read connected text and random words. Both groups read the connected text faster, and an analysis of variance on the reading times indicated no inter-action between group and condition of presentation. However, since the read-ing latency of the good readers was lower, their relative contextual gain was greater. Statistical analyses of the accuracy of word identification indicated that the good readers were unaffected by experimental condition, but that the poor readers were more accurate reading connected words rather than ran-dom words. Allington (1978a) concluded that good readers were more reliant on context for fluency and poor readers were more reliant on context for ac-curacy. The findings of studies measuring reading latency dovetail with find-ings from studies of oral reading errors. The common pattern is that all read-ers appear to use context to facilitate word recognition. However, there seems to be no strong tendency for more fluent readers to show a greater reliance on context. In fact, just as often the opposite is true. It should be noted that there is nothing paradoxical about the conclusion that a process may be an important general determinant of reading speed yet not be a source of individual differences (see Perfetti & Roth, 1981). Graesser, Hoffman, and Clark (1980) found that macrostructure processes that integrate information from different sentences accounted for more variance in reading time than did microstructure processes (those operating on the words and syntax within a sentence). However, fast and slow readers differed mainly in microstructure processes.

Studies using somewhat different methodologies also support the above conclusion. Samuels, Begy, and Chen (1975–1976) investigated how the tachistoscopic exposure duration necessary to identify a word was affected by the prior presentation of an associate of the word. The exposure durations of fourth-grade students who were poor readers were affected just as much as the exposure duration of the good readers. The magnitude of the facilitation effect was actually greater in the poor readers. Schvaneveldt, Ackerman, and Semlear (1977) examined the effect of a single-word semantic context on lexical-decision times. They found that the previous presentation of a highly associated word facilitated the lexical-decision times of both second- and fourth-graders. The effect of semantic context was greater for the second-grade readers and, within each grade, the correlations between standardized reading measures and the magnitude of the context effect were all negative, indicating greater use of context by the poorer readers. Using full sentence contexts, Perfetti, Goldman, and Hogaboam (1979) and West and Stanovich (1978) found context to have a greater effect on the naming times of poorer readers. In a recent paper, Allington and Strange (1978) stated that

> the role of semantic and syntactic cues in fluent reading has been the basis for much recent controversy. While some have suggested that effective use of the contextual information provided by these cues is the determining factor in differentiating good and poor readers (Goodman & Goodman, 1977; Smith, 1976), others have argued that virtually all readers, regardless of achievement, employ semantic and syntactic cues and that other factors must account for achievement differences (Weber, 1970; Kolers, 1975; Allington & Strange, 1977; Allington, 1978a). (p. 56)

The bulk of the relevant research now appears to support the latter position.

The occasional tendency for the poorer readers to use context to a greater extent is not paradoxical if we keep in mind the distinction between the two types of contextual processing discussed above. Using hypotheses to facilitate word recognition may itself take cognitive capacity, thus leaving fewer resources for higher-level comprehension processes such as drawing implications or integrating new information with old. If the contextual facilitation observed in poorer readers is of a type that takes attentional capacity, then these readers may have less capacity left over for comprehension processes. The increased contextual facilitation that poorer readers sometimes display is probably an indication that their slow and nonautomatic word recognition skills make it necessary for them to draw on another knowledge source. However, if this source (prior contextual constraints) also requires attentional resources, then the comprehension of the poorer reader may suffer even though the additional knowledge source has aided in the recognition of individual words. This argument will be developed below.

AUTOMATIC AND ATTENTIONAL CONTEXT EFFECTS

West and Stanovich (1978) studied the effect of context on word recognition by having subjects of three ages name a target word that had been preceded by either an incomplete sentence that was congruent with the word, an incomplete sentence that was incongruent with the word, or simply by the word "the" (i.e., a no-context condition). Naming time was faster in the congruent condition than in the no-context condition. This contextual facilitation effect did not differ statistically across the three age groups in the study (fourth-graders, sixth-graders, and adults) and was actually somewhat larger in the times of the children. Within each age range, correlations involving a standardized reading measure indicated a slight tendency for poorer readers to show a greater contextual facilitation effect, a result consistent with previous research using a somewhat different paradigm (Schvaneveldt et al., 1977). A significant contextual inhibition effect (longer naming times in the incongruous-context condition than in the no-context condition) was found for both fourth-grade and sixth-grade subjects, but not for adults. In the adult group, mean naming times were virtually identical in the no-context and incongruous condition. (If the unpredictable condition of an experiment reported by Perfetti and Roth [1981] is comparable to the no-context condition of West and Stanovich, then the results of these two experiments are highly convergent.)

The pattern of results in the West and Stanovich (1978) study fits rather nicely within the framework of the two-process theory of expectancy developed by Posner and Snyder (1975a, 1975b). The Posner–Snyder theory has been applied to the semantic context effect in lexical decision tasks (Fischler, 1977; Neely, 1976, 1977) and can easily be generalized to sentence context effects of the type studied by West and Stanovich (1978). Briefly, Posner and Snyder (1975a, 1975b) proposed that semantic context affects recognition via two processes that act independently and that have different properties. (The two simultaneously acting processes in the Posner–Snyder theory are very similar to the two expectancy mechanisms originally proposed by Meyer and Schvaneveldt [1971].) The automatic-activation process occurs because, when stimulus information activates a memory location, some of the activation automatically spreads to semantically related memory locations that are nearby in the network. The automatic spreading-activation process is fast acting, does not use attentional capacity, and does not affect the retrieval of information from memory locations unrelated to those activated by the context. (For a fuller discussion, see Neely, 1977.) Thus, the automatic-activation process quickly results in a contextual facilitation effect, but does not cause an inhibitory effect when a word is incongruous with its preceding context. In contrast, the conscious-attention mechanism responds to a preceding context by directing the limited-capacity processor to the memory location of the expected stimulus. The conscious-attention mechanism is slow acting, utilizes attentional capacity, and inhibits the retrieval of information from unexpected locations because the limited-capacity processor must be "shifted" to a location some distance away in the memory network so that information can be read out.

Several recent studies of semantic context effects have provided some support for the two-process theory of Posner and Snyder (Fischler, 1977; Neely, 1977; Tweedy, Lapinski, & Schvaneveldt, 1977; Yates, 1978). In particular, the idea of contextual facilitation due to an automatic spreading-activation mechanism has received support (Fischler, 1977; Fischler & Goodman, 1978; Swinney, Onifer, Prather, & Hirshkowitz, 1978; Tversky, Havousha, & Poller, 1979; Underwood, 1977).

The results obtained by West and Stanovich (1978) can be interpreted as indicating that word recognition in adults is so fast that the target word can be named before the slow-acting conscious-attention mechanism can have an inhibitory effect (i.e., can direct the limited-capacity processor to a memory location far from the target word when it is preceded by an incongruous context). Instead, only the automatic spreading-activation component of contextual processing has time to operate before the word is recognized, thus resulting in contextual facilitation, but no corresponding inhibition in the reaction times of the adults. The word recognition processes of children, however, may be slow enough to allow the conscious-attention mechanism to have an effect. This results in both contextual facilitation and inhibition in the reaction times of the children. Thus, the Posner–Snyder theory explains the age differences without hypothesizing qualitative changes in syntactic and semantic processing across this particular age range. Rather, the seemingly discontinuous disappearance of the contextual inhibition effect between grade six and adulthood appears to be due, instead, to the gradual increase in word-recognition speed during this age range. Thus, for adults, word recognition is accomplished before the conscious-attention expectancy mechanism can have an effect. The two-process expectancy theory of Posner and Snyder can also account for the results of several recent studies indicating that poorer readers show greater contextual facilitation effects (e.g., Biemiller, 1977–1978; Perfetti, Goldman, & Hogaboam, 1979; Roth, Perfetti, & Lesgold, 1979; Schvaneveldt, Ackerman, & Semlear, 1977). This occurs because poorer readers have slower word-recognition times (Doehring, 1976; Perfetti & Hogaboam, 1975), and as word recognition is slower, there is a greater tendency for contextual facilitation to result from the conscious-attention, as well as the automatic-activation, mechanism.

In further experiments, Stanovich and West (1979b) found additional support for the Posner–Snyder theory. They obtained the same finding of contextual facilitation without inhibition in the response times of adult readers. More importantly, when target word recognition was slowed (via contrast reduction) to a speed comparable to that of the fourth-grade children, adults displayed a significant contextual-inhibition effect. (Roth, Perfetti, and Lesgold [1979] have also shown that, as regards the effect of context, visual degradation can cause the performance of skilled readers to mimic that of less-skilled readers.) Inhibition was also evident in the reaction times of the adults when the interval between the reading of the context and the onset of the target word was increased. Degrading the target word and increasing the response–stimulus interval both have the effect of delaying word recognition and thus providing the necessary time for the conscious-attention mechanism to become implicated in performance. These results support an interpretation of the developmental results of West and Stanovich (1978) in terms of the Posner–Snyder theory and also support the hypothesis that in the fluent reader it is through automatic activation rather than conscious prediction that context acts to speed word recognition. (See Stanovich [1981a] and Stanovich and West [1981] for a report of further tests of the Posner–Snyder theory.) The rapid word recognition of fluent readers simply short-circuits the conscious-attention mechanism. The Posner–Snyder theory thus posits a mechanism whereby the compensatory processing discussed above might work. Higher-level processes of conscious contextual prediction become implicated in performance when the bottom-up word-recognition processes are slowed. Whether the slowness of bottom-up processing is due to developmental immaturity or inadequate stimulus information appears to make no difference, since several studies have found that when fluent readers must identify visually degraded words their performance is more affected by prior context (Becker & Killion, 1977; Forster, 1976; Massaro, Jones, Lipscomb, & Scholz, 1978; Meyer, Schvaneveldt, & Ruddy, 1975; Sanford, Garrod, & Boyle, 1977; Sperber, McCauley, Ragain, & Weil, 1979).

A consideration of the way in which the two expectancy mechanisms of the Posner–Snyder theory act to compensate for slow word-recognition speed suggests an interesting distinction between types of compensatory processing. This is the distinction between an optional and an obligatory compensatory trade-off. An obligatory trade-off is one that is necessitated by the structure of the processing system. For example, according to Morton's (1969, 1970) logogen model, when the processing rate is slowed, factors affecting the evidence requirements of logogens (word detection devices) have a greater effect on performance (see Seymour, 1976). This trade-off is inherent in the structure of the system. In a similar manner, the increased facilitation produced by spreading activation when word recognition is slowed also represents an obligatory trade-off since spreading activation is automatic (not under subject control) and is a function of the structure of the semantic memory system. In contrast, the greater facilitation due to the formation of conscious expectancies that results when word recognition is slowed is an optional compensation. Conscious expectancy formation is under the control of the subject and need not necessarily be invoked when word recognition is slow (see Posner & Rogers, 1978).

[material omitted]

If one distinguishes two types of contextual processing that a subject might engage in, then the implications of the Posner–Snyder conception for theories of individual differences in reading ability become apparent. That is, a reader might use cognitive capacity in order to construct a new knowledge structure or to integrate new material into an old knowledge structure. On the other hand, a reader may also use the knowledge structures built up from previous context to aid in the processing of words that are currently undergoing recognition. Notice that the less cognitive capacity that is used to engage in the latter process, the more that is left over for the more important former processes. It is argued here that this is precisely what the fluent reader is doing. He recognizes words rapidly and mostly on the basis of physical cues, so that expectancy processes that draw cognitive capacity are not necessary. Thus his capacity is being used for comprehension, rather than for conscious prediction processes that aid individual word recognition. Based on the results of their studies of sentence context effects using a lexical-decision task, Fischler and Bloom (1979) argued similarly that "skilled readers, then, may not typically generate particular expectancies, even though it may result in slight facilitation of word recognition at no cost, because there is effort involved which may slow reading, and they simply will not be correct often enough for such a strategy to be worthwhile" (p. 12).

Note that the argument stated above does not imply that the word recognition of better readers is not facilitated by prior context. Quite the contrary, such facilitation is a reasonably well-established empirical fact. However, the facilitation displayed in the performance of the fluent reader is probably due to automatic-activation processes that use no cognitive capacity. One implication of this view is that prior context should facilitate the word recognition of poorer readers to a *greater* extent (since both automatic-activation and conscious-attention expectancy mechanisms are operative in these readers). However, the net result of using context in this way is that the poorer reader has less capacity left for integrative comprehension processes. The literature reviewed above is largely consistent with these predictions. Many studies have shown the poorer reader to be just as prone as the better reader to use context to facilitate word recognition and some studies have found poor readers to be more reliant on prior context. The prediction of the pure top-down models, that the word-recognition speed of poor readers is slow because they fail to use contextual information, finds little support in the literature.

It is interesting that the findings of a good deal of contextual processing on the part of poor readers have generally been ignored by reading theorists.

This has probably been because neither purely top-down models nor purely bottom-up models can easily handle these results. The compensatory hypothesis generally, and the Posner–Snyder theory in particular, render these findings understandable. It is the processing of the *good* readers that is primarily data-driven, in that it is the speed of their context-free word recognition that allows capacity to be freed for comprehension processes. This view is similar to the automaticity model of reading developed by LaBerge and Samuels (1974), in that both theories assume that efficient low-level recognition processes can free up capacity for higher-level processes. However, there are differences between the two models, and these differences center around the issues of what type of processing occurs at the word-recognition level and what happens when word recognition is slow and inefficient. The view presented above assumes that interactive–compensatory processing occurs at the word level, and that when word identification is slow, the reader can draw on higher-level knowledge sources (e.g., prior contextual constraints) to aid recognition. No such compensation involving contextual knowledge can occur in the LaBerge and Samuels (1974) model (although such a possibility may be present in the revised model; see Samuels, 1977). However, when the higher-level compensatory processes require capacity, they also serve to deplete the cognitive resources available to comprehension processes. Thus, the interactive–compensatory model and the LaBerge and Samuels (1974) model are in agreement on one important point, that fast and automatic word recognition is an important determinant of fluent reading.

The model presented above is also closely related to the limited-capacity model discussed by Lesgold and Perfetti (1978). The major difference, again, is that their model contains no mechanism for interactive–compensatory processing at the level of word recognition. Thus, the present model might best be conceptualized as a limited-capacity model with interactive–compensatory processing at the word level. It should be noted, however, that some recent studies have not found evidence for the performance linkages that are predicted by limited-capacity models of the type described above. Using somewhat different methodologies, Patberg and Yonas (1978) and Wilkinson, Guminski, Stanovich, and West (1981) found that disrupting the visual characteristics of the text so that reading was markedly slowed did not affect the memory or comprehension of the text. In a study of first- and second-grade children, Lovett (1979) found that the higher-order processing of sentential information was not related to decoding ability. It is possible that interactive processing is even more pervasive than that allowed for in the limited-capacity model with interactive–compensatory processing at the word level. Perhaps, as Wilkinson et al. (1981) have suggested, recognition and comprehension processes are so completely interactive that they maintain an equilibrium, whereby comprehension processes are meshed with recognition processes in such a way that the former can accommodate to changes in the latter. The issues are sufficiently complex, and the current empirical data sufficiently sparse, that the only reasonable conclusion at this point is that it remains for future research to elucidate whether a fully interactive model is to be preferred over a limited-capacity model with interactive processing at the word level.

WHERE ARE THE DIFFERENCES?

We are now in a position to consider the relative importance of three general loci of individual differences in reading skill, namely, context-free word recognition, the use of context to facilitate word recognition, and comprehension strategies.

The imprint of the hypothesis-testing models is evident in much of the theorizing on individual differences in reading skill. The dominance of the top-down perspective has been such that it is widely assumed that the ability to use context to facilitate word recognition is a major determinant of individual differences in reading ability. Evidence reviewed above suggests, to the contrary, that poor readers make use of prior context just as much, if not more, than good readers. Thus, it may be that good readers use context more effectively to monitor comprehension, whereas poor readers use it to aid word recognition.

There is evidence that the comprehension strategies of good readers are superior to those of the poor reader (Cromer, 1970; DiVesta, Hayward, & Orlando, 1979; Forrest & Barron, 1977; Guthrie, 1973; Jackson & McClelland, 1979; Oakan et al., 1971; Schwartz, 1977; Smiley et al., 1977). However, Perfetti and Lesgold (1977) argue convincingly that this is not the case. A review of this literature is beyond the scope of this paper. Suffice it to say that individual differences in reading performance could well be related to the ability to use sophisticated comprehension strategies. Instead, a more clear-cut case will be argued, namely, that context-free processes at the word and subword level are major determinants of individual differences in reading fluency. The three specific abilities that will be discussed are the ability to recognize words automatically (i.e., without using attentional capacity), the ability to rapidly recognize word and subword units, and the ability to recode print items into phonological form. The ability to recognize words automatically is important because it frees capacity for higher-level integrative and semantic processing. The speed of recognition, independent of the issue of automaticity, is another important factor in reading because rapid coding of information into short-term memory facilitates the integrative comprehension processes that operate on the information that is stored there (Lesgold & Perfetti, 1978; Perfetti & Lesgold, 1977). Finally, phonological coding abilities facilitate reading in two ways, by providing a redundant pathway for lexical access and by providing a more stable code for information that must be held in short-term memory.

There is some evidence from developmental studies indicating that better readers show a greater tendency to recognize words automatically (Guttentag & Haith, 1978; Pace & Golinkoff, 1978; West & Stanovich, 1979). However, the results from several studies (Ehri & Wilce, 1979; Golinkoff & Rosinski, 1976; Guttentag & Haith, 1978, 1979; Rosinski, Golinkoff, & Kukish, 1975; Stanovich, Cunningham, & West, 1979; West & Stanovich, 1979) have indicated that the recognition of words becomes automatized much earlier in reading practice than previously thought. In particular, the above studies suggest that most high-frequency words are automatized to adult levels by the third grade. Thus, the developing ability to recognize words automatically does not seem to be the main factor accounting for reading ability increases beyond the second grade. However, during the time that automaticity is developing, and even after a word is fully automatized, recognition time continues to decrease. The latter point is often lost in discussions that center on the automaticity concept itself, even though there is ample evidence in the literature documenting the fact that recognition time continues to decrease after words have become fully automatized. Several studies have failed to find an increase in automatic processing after the second- or third-grade reading level has been reached (Golinkoff & Rosinski, 1976; Guttentag & Haith, 1978, 1979; Rosinski, Golinkoff, & Kukish, 1975; West & Stanovich, 1979), but marked increases in word-recognition speed occur as children progress beyond the second-grade level of reading ability (Biemiller, 1977–1978; Perfetti, Finger, & Hogaboam, 1978; Perfetti & Hogaboam, 1975). Thus, it is possible that beyond the initial levels of reading fluency it is word-recognition *speed* rather than automaticity that is the major factor in skill development. Indeed, it is now reasonably well established that context-free recognition speed is a major determinant of individual differences in reading fluency.

Shankweiler and Liberman (1972) observed correlations in the range of .5 to .8 when word-naming speed and accuracy were correlated with paragraph-reading fluency. These high correlations were observed for second-, third-, and fourth-grade readers. Employing second-grade subjects, McCormick and Samuels (1979) found correlations of approximately −.55 between word-recognition speed and comprehension ability, and approximately .60 between word-recognition accuracy and comprehension ability. In a study where vocalization latency was carefully measured, Perfetti and Hogaboam (1975) found that third- and fifth-grade poor readers named even high-frequency words approximately 200 msec slower than good readers. Low-frequency words were named approximately 1 sec slower by the poorer readers. In further experiments, Perfetti, Finger, and Hogaboam (1978) found that third-grade poor readers named colors, digits, and pictures just as fast as good readers of the same age. However, the speed of naming words clearly differentiated the two groups (see also Staller & Sekuler, 1975). Biemiller (1977–1978) also found a strong relationship between reading ability and word-naming time in children. His argument, consistent with the previous review, is that

the high degree of association between the two non-contextual tasks and text reading times strongly suggests that the ability to use context to increase speed, while facilitating times for all readers, may not represent a major source of *indi-*

vidual differences in reading speed for text since a very large proportion of text time variance is associated with non-contextual measures. (p. 240)

The relationship between word-naming speed and reading ability also holds for adults. Using adult subjects, Mason (1978) found that good readers named words 57 msec faster than poor readers. Stanovich and Bauer (1979) also found a relation between reading ability and word-naming time, as did Butler and Hains (1979) and Frederiksen (1976). Jackson and McClelland (1975, 1979) found that, even when only fluent adult readers were considered, the ability to rapidly access over-learned memory codes distinguished skilled from less skilled readers. Mason (1980) has presented evidence to support a somewhat different hypothesis, that individual differences in reading fluency are in part due to differences in the speed of processing letter location information. Her research provides additional evidence favoring the more general hypothesis argued above, that differences between skilled and unskilled adult readers can be revealed using tasks that tap the speed of perceptual processing at the word level and below.

The ability to rapidly recode print items into a phonological form also appears to be related to reading ability (Barron, 1978a, 1978b, 1979, 1980; Perfetti & Lesgold, 1977; Spring & Capps, 1974; Spring & Farmer, 1975), even among relatively fluent adult readers (Goldberg, Schwartz, & Stewart, 1977). Perhaps it is this relationship that accounts for the finding that, for adults as well as children, the speed of naming pronounceable nonwords is one of the tasks that most clearly differentiates good from poor readers (Barron, 1978a; Firth, 197; Frederiksen, 1976; Hogaboam & Perfetti, 1978; Perfetti & Hogaboam, 1975; Seymour & Porpodas, 1980). Mason (1978) has argued that this relationship is due to the superior decoding skills of the better readers, but that decoding skill is an epiphenomenon of skilled reading in the adult. She suggested the intriguing hypothesis that nonword decoding tasks provide measures of linguistic awareness, which determined the ease with which reading *was* acquired in adult readers.

It is interesting to consider Mason's (1978) hypothesis in conjunction with other research on phonological processing, automaticity, and speed of word recognition. Certainly there exists much evidence indicating that phonological awareness, phonetic segmentation ability, and phonological recoding skills are important determinants of early reading success (Bradley & Bryant, 1978; Fox & Routh, 1975, 1976; Golinkoff, 1978; Jorm, 1979; Liberman, Shankweiler, Liberman, Fowler, & Fischer, 1977; Steinheiser & Guthrie, 1978; Torgeson & Murphey, 1979; Vellutino, 1977; Williams, 1980). This relationship may obtain either because phonological processing facilitates lexical access (see Barron, 1978a) or because it facilitates the formation of a stable code for the maintenance of information in short-term memory (e.g., Byrne & Shea, 1979; Shankweiler, Liberman, Mark, Fowler, & Fischer, 1979). Perhaps, as Mason (1978) suggests, an alphabetic writing system serves as a powerful reinforcer during the initial stages of reading only if the child has the phonological skills to make use of the alphabetic principle. However, children that do grasp the alphabetic principle are likely to read more and this additional practice leads to the development of the rapid, automatic, context-free word-recognition ability that is one key to fluent reading. Thus, adult good and poor readers are differentiated on word-naming tasks (which tap rapid context-free recognition) *and* nonword pronunciation tasks (which reflect the phonological skills that determined the ease with which they traversed the early stages of reading acquisition). Rozin and Gleitman (1977) summarize the research literature in a similar manner, stating:

> There seems to be strong evidence that good and poor readers, as well as younger and older individuals, will respond similarly to meaning distinctions and meaningful contexts. At the other extreme, the ability to read word lists aloud distinguishes very reliably between good and poor readers (Firth, 1972; Shankweiler & Liberman, 1972); the ability to make explicit phonological distinctions distinguishes between younger and older individuals and between good and poor readers. Apparently, an inability to notice and cope with phonological aspects of the language poses a stumbling block to reading acquisition. (pp. 97–98)

The work of Perfetti, Finger, and Hogaboam (1978) also leads to this conclusion. They summarized their results by stating: "The ability of the less skilled reader to use constraining knowledge as well as the skilled reader is established. The persistent differences between skilled and less skilled readers in reaction times to words and pseudowords seem to be due to processes of verbal coding, including processes operating on subword units" (p. 739).

CONCLUSION

Both top-down and bottom-up models of reading predict that higher-level conceptual processes will be more implicated in the performance of better readers. A review of the literature on the use of orthographic structure and the effect of contextual information on word recognition indicated that this prediction has not been borne out. It has been argued that an interactive–compensatory model of individual differences in reading ability best accounts for the pattern of results in the literature. Interactive models, best exemplified in the work of Rumelhart (1977), assume that a pattern is synthesized based on information provided simultaneously from several knowledge sources. The compensatory assumption states that a deficit in any knowledge source results in a heavier reliance on other knowledge sources, *regardless* of their level in the processing hierarchy. Thus, according to the interactive–compensatory model, the poor reader who has deficient word analysis skills might possibly show a *greater* reliance on contextual factors. In fact, several studies have shown this to be the case.

Word recognition during ongoing reading can be facilitated by expectancies based on the prior sentence context. Interactive–compensatory processing appears to be operating during this process, since poorer readers often show larger contextual facilitation effects than do good readers. The Posner–Snyder theory of expectancy provides an explanation of how this compensatory processing operates. When context-free word recognition is rapid, only the fast-acting spreading-activation process is responsible for contextual-facilitation effects. When word recognition is slow, the conscious-attention expectancy process has time to operate and provides another source of contextual facilitation. Thus, the reader with poor context-free word-recognition skills has an additional contextual expectancy process acting to aid his identification of a word. However, this additional contextual facilitation is purchased at a cost. The conscious-expectancy process uses attentional capacity and thus leaves fewer cognitive resources left over for comprehension operations that work on integrating larger text units. This trade-off among processes sharing a limited pool of cognitive resources is common to many information processing models (e.g., LaBerge & Samuels, 1974; Lesgold & Perfetti, 1978).

Given that the ability to use prior context to facilitate word recognition is not a skill that differentiates good from poor readers, there appear to be two general types of processes that good readers perform more efficiently than poor readers. Good readers appear to have superior strategies for comprehending and remembering large units of text. In addition, good readers are superior at context-free word recognition. There is some evidence indicating that good readers have automatized the recognition of word and subword units to a greater extent than poor readers. However, good readers recognize even fully automated words faster than poor readers. In addition, good readers appear to have superior phonetic segmentation and recoding abilities so that they can rapidly decode a word even when visual recognition fails. In short, the good reader identifies words automatically and rapidly, whether by direct visual recognition or phonological recoding. The existence of this rapid context-free word recognition ability means that the word recognition of good readers is less reliant on conscious expectancies generated from the prior sentence context. The result is that more attentional capacity is left over for integrative comprehension processes.

NOTES

1. The proliferation of nomenclature to describe these models may be confusing to the reader. When dealing with other treatments that use a different vocabulary, the reader would be advised to note that the following terms have been used in the literature to describe top-down and bottom-up processing. Top-down: conceptually driven, inside-out, reader-based, prediction-based, schema-driven, hypothesis-testing. Bottom-up: data-driven, outside-in, text-based, text-driven, decoding.

2. Of course, top-down models do allow that the reader may occasionally operate in a bottom-up mode (primarily when he is faced with a contextually meagre situation).

Similarly, Samuels (1977) has revised the LaBerge and Samuels (1974) model so that top-down processing can occur in some situations. Nonetheless, it is fair to say that there is a *strong preference* for conceptually driven processing in top-down models and for data-driven processing in bottom-up models. Thus, the notion of a processing mode preference, as opposed to a clear-cut dichotomous classification based upon processing directionality, may be preferable. The two classes of models are still distinguishable given this alternative conceptualization.

CHAPTER 4

The Interactive–Compensatory Model of Reading

A Confluence of Developmental, Experimental, and Educational Psychology

During the last ten years research developments in the psychology of reading have been nothing short of explosive. Both in terms of the quantity of empirical research and the quality of our theoretical explanations, progress has been steady and exciting. Because such work in the psychology of reading necessarily takes place at the interface between developmental, experimental, and educational psychology, a definable group of reading researchers has emerged who move with ease among these subareas of psychology.

An operational definition of a member of this group might be someone who in a two-year period publishes in *Child Development, Journal of Educational Psychology*, and *Memory and Cognition*; or perhaps in another two-year period publishes in the *Journal of Experimental Child Psychology, Reading Research Quarterly*, and the *Journal of Experimental Psychology*. This journal issue contains many fine exemplars of the category of researchers that I have in mind. In short, while research progress on many problems in psychology is hampered due to inadequate communication between specialty subareas, such communication is now taken for granted in the psychology of reading, to the mutual benefit of all subareas concerned.

CONTEXTUAL INFORMATION

I wish to review some of the highlights of my own research program, which will serve as a case study in the interaction of ideas from developmental, educational, and experimental psychology. Since its inception, this research program has involved the active collaboration of Richard F. West and, more recently, of Dorothy Feeman, Anne Cunningham, and Ruth Nathan. Our research interest for some years has focused on the interaction between stimulus information and contextual information in ongoing reading, and, more specifically, on how this interaction changes as reading fluency develops.

During the early stages of conceptualizing this research problem, Frank Smith's (1971) book *Understanding Reading* was particularly influential. He imaginatively synthesized some basic research in cognitive psychology and some educational observations into one of the most important "top-down" models of the reading process. Not surprisingly, given this top-down perspective, Smith emphasized the importance of contextual redundancy at all stages of the reading process. One clear developmental prediction deriving from his work is that the performance of the more fluent reader should be more dependent on contextual information.

Levels of Processing

Approaching this topic from an information processing perspective, we wondered whether Smith's developmental hypothesis was equally tenable at all levels of processing in reading, as Smith had argued. A review of the literature at the time (the mid-1970s) increased our curiosity. There was indeed considerable evidence that skilled readers were more facile at using contextual information at the level of text integration and comprehension. However, there was a general lack of evidence relevant to the accuracy of the prediction at the level of word recognition. Also, there was considerable looseness and confusion revolving around the use of the term "context effect." Miscitation was rampant.

Our background in cognitive psychology may have helped in our reading and organization of the educational literature. One major lesson of modern cognitive psychology (cf. Lachman, Lachman, & Butterfield, 1979) is that human performance can be analyzed, predicted, and explained by specific instantiations of models deriving from the general idea that human information processing results from the exchange of information between processing subroutines that operate at different levels in a partially hierarchical system. Thus, when discussing a particular variable, it is important to distinguish the level, or levels, in the processing system that are affected by the variable.

Generally, reading researchers have not been careful in specifying what level in the processing system was being tapped by the particular contextual manipulation employed in a given experiment. The point is that there can be many different *types* of context effects. For example, context can act to speed ongoing word recognition during reading. This is the effect that we were interested in studying. Alternatively, context can be used to facilitate the memory and comprehension of text (e.g., Bransford & Johnson, 1973), a very different type of context effect.

Ongoing Word Recognition

With this simple distinction in mind, we noticed that little, if any, of the research literature cited by Smith was relevant to what we might call "ongoing word recognition." Instead, memory tasks, cloze tasks, tachistoscopic tasks with unlimited guessing time, and other tasks that either reflected higher levels of processing or were only tangentially related to the real-time processing constraints of ongoing word recognition were inappropriately cited as if they confirmed Smith's developmental hypothesis at the level of word recognition (see Stanovich, 1980, 1982a, 1982b, 1982c).

Thus we were prompted to develop a sentence priming paradigm that we thought would more closely tap contextual effects at the level of word recognition. Subjects read aloud a sentence the final word (i.e., the target word) of which was missing. When the subject finished reading the incomplete sentence, the target word appeared, and the subject attempted to name it as fast as possible. Various contextual conditions can be created by manipulating the sentence context that precedes the target word. Three such conditions can be seen in Table 4.1.

In the congruous condition, the target word offers a meaningful completion of the sentence, it is moderately predictable and in many cases is semantically related to words in the context. In the neutral condition, the target word is not predictable from the context, nor is it related to words in the context. The incongruous condition is created by randomly rearranging targets and contexts.

If context is indeed used to speed word recognition, then recognition times in the congruous condition should be faster than the times in the neutral condition (a contextual facilitation effect). If contextual processes are operative in this situation, then one might imagine that such processes would slow the recognition of a word preceded by an incongruous context relative to the neutral condition (thus causing a contextual inhibition effect). Finally, the time difference between the incongruous and congruous conditions (the overall context effect) will serve as a general index of contextual sensitivity.

A Developmental Study

Our initial investigation was a developmental study in which we examined the performance patterns of fourth-grade, sixth-grade, and adult subjects (West & Stanovich, 1978). The results are presented in Figure 2.1 in the paper re-

TABLE 4.1. Examples of Contextual Conditions

Condition	Context	Target
Congruous	The soldiers flew in the	plane
Neutral	They said it was the	plane
Incongruous	The cowboy fired the	plane

printed as Chapter 2 in this volume. The data display two outstanding features. First, the *trend* in the contextual effects is actually in the opposite direction from what would be expected from Smith's hypothesis. The overall contextual effect diminishes as developmental level increases. Second, the *pattern* of the contextual effects changes with age. The children show mixed patterns of relatively equal facilitation and inhibition, whereas the adults display facilitation without inhibition.

Before proceeding further, let me note two points relevant to the interpretation of the data. All of the trends in our experiments are still apparent when contextual effects are expressed as proportions of the time in the neutral condition rather than as absolute time differences. Further, the effects are apparently stable enough to replicate across minor methodological variations. For example, Chuck Perfetti has worked extensively with paradigms similar to ours and has produced data that is highly convergent (see Perfetti, Goldman, & Hogaboam, 1979; Perfetti & Roth, 1981). Fred Schwantes has also replicated many of our results (Schwantes, 1981; Schwantes, Boesl, & Ritz, 1980).

A Longitudinal Study

Table 4.2 displays the data from a longitudinal study of second-grade children (Stanovich, West, & Feeman, 1981). The children were tested in the fall and spring of the school year. The study contains two manipulated variables that are orthogonal to the three basic context conditions. By manipulating the length and frequency of the target words, we created easy and difficult target word sets, sets whose neutral recognition time differed considerably. In addition, the subjects were given isolated word recognition practice on one half of the target words. This factor was varied orthogonally with context condition and word difficulty.

Focusing for the moment on the overall context effect, we see a trend sim-

TABLE 4.2. Mean Reaction Time as a Function of Context Condition, Word Difficulty, Practice, and Testing Period (Mean Percentage of Errors Is Indicated in Parentheses)

Testing period	Context condition					Overall context effect
	Congruous	No context	Incon	Facil	Inhib	
First testing period						
Practiced easy	669 (0.8)	765 (0.0)	749 (1.6)	96	−16	80
Practiced difficult	800 (0.0)	881 (0.8)	948 (3.3)	81	67	148
Unpracticed easy	685 (0.0)	816 (3.3)	840 (0.8)	131	24	155
Unpracticed difficult	825 (9.0)	1065 (13.3)	1186 (20.0)	240	121	361
Second testing period						
Practiced easy	658 (0.8)	711 (0.0)	718 (0.0)	53	7	60
Practiced difficult	744 (0.8)	869 (3.3)	906 (2.5)	125	37	162
Unpracticed easy	675 (0.0)	758 (0.8)	756 (0.8)	83	−2	81
Unpracticed difficult	760 (2.5)	849 (4.1)	949 (5.0)	89	100	189

ilar to that observed in our first study. Contextual effects diminish with development. We also see that the manipulated variables mimicked the effect of development. That is, contextual effects were smaller for easy words and practiced words. Looking at the pattern of effects, we also see a trend similar to the previous study. As word recognition becomes more rapid, the *pattern* of effects changes in the direction of facilitation dominance (larger facilitation effects than inhibition effects). In several conditions, the easy words show the pattern of facilitation without inhibition.

Finally, it should be mentioned that we have done extensive analyses of individual differences in our data. Basically, the results regarding skilled and less-skilled readers within an age level mimic the developmental trends. The better readers display smaller context effects and show more of a facilitation dominant pattern.

Two Variations

Table 4.3 displays the data from an experiment that involved two new features (see West, Stanovich, Feeman, & Cunningham, 1983). First, the stimulus materials, rather than being constructed by the experimenters, were randomly sampled from children's primers. Second, the length of the context preceding the target word was either one sentence (as in the previous experiments) or three sentences. The experiment employed second-grade and sixth-grade subjects. Context condition interacted with age.

As in previous experiments, younger readers displayed larger context effects. Thus, the basic phenomenon generalized to sentences that were more representative of actual school reading materials. Amount of context did not interact with context condition in either age group, and there was no three-way interaction. There was no statistically reliable tendency for context effects to be greater in the three-sentence condition, indicating that the contextual effects observed in this paradigm are arising primarily from the sentence containing the target word.

TABLE 4.3. Mean Reaction Times in Milliseconds (Mean Percentage of Errors Indicated in Parentheses)

Grade Context length	Context condition					Overall context effect
	Congruous	Neutral	Incon	Facil	Inhib	
Second grade						
One sentence	627 (7.0)	726 (6.3)	819 (9.4)	99	93	192
Three sentences	613 (7.0)	697 (3.1)	756 (9.4)	84	59	143
Sixth grade						
One sentence	511 (2.9)	554 (2.1)	601 (1.6)	43	47	90
Three sentences	487 (4.7)	540 (2.6)	599 (6.3)	53	59	112

Implications

What are the theoretical implications of these results? One of the most important is that Smith's developmental hypothesis regarding context use at the word level is falsified. The poorer reader does not seem less likely to use context to facilitate word recognition (*when* the context is adequately understood, a point to which I will return below). Evidence from a variety of paradigms is now converging with this conclusion. For example, studies of oral reading errors (Allington & Fleming, 1978; Batey & Sonnenschein, 1981; Biemiller, 1970, 1979; Cohen, 1974–1975; Coomber, 1972; Juel, 1980; Lesgold & Resnick, 1982; Perfetti & Roth, 1981; Richardson, DiBenedetto, & Adler, 1982; Weber, 1970a; Whaley & Kibby, 1981), timed text reading (Allington, 1978b; Biemiller, 1977–1978; Doehring, 1976), text disruption manipulations (Allington & Strange, 1977; Ehrlich, 1981; Schwartz & Stanovich, 1981; Siler, 1974; Strange, 1979), single-word priming (Schvaneveldt, Ackerman, & Semlear, 1977; Simpson & Lorsbach, 1983; Simpson, Lorsbach, & Whitehouse, 1983), and paragraph priming (Perfetti, Goldman, & Hogaboam, 1979; Schwantes, 1981, 1982). Smith's very valid hypothesis regarding developmental changes in context use at the level of text integration has apparently been inappropriately generalized to the level of word recognition.

THE INTERACTIVE-COMPENSATORY MODEL

In an attempt to develop theoretical alternatives to the "pure" top-down models such as Smith's, I have borrowed freely from ideas in the experimental psychology literature. Rumelhart's (1977) conceptualization of an interactive model of reading seemed particularly attractive, but we needed to supplement it before using it as a framework for the developmental results on context effects on word recognition.

To the basic interactive idea that recognition takes place via the simultaneous amalgamation of information from many different knowledge sources, I added what was termed the "compensatory assumption" (see Stanovich, 1980). This is simply the assumption that deficiencies at any level in the processing hierarchy can be compensated for by a greater use of information from other levels, and that this compensation takes place irrespective of the level of the deficient process.

While this seemed a fairly obvious addendum to the interactive idea, I have been surprised repeatedly at the extent to which educational researchers have responded to it as being "new," "surprising," or "interesting." I now think that the reason for this unexpectedly strong response is that thinking in reading education has been so dominated by the top-down models that inadequate consideration has been given to the alternative possibility that under some circumstances the poor decoding skills of less-skilled readers could lead them to rely more on contextual information (if it is available; see below). It is just this alternative that the interactive–compensatory model allows us to consider.

Two-Process Theory

Of course, the idea of interactive–compensatory processing still leaves us at a fairly global level of theorizing. However, some progress has been made at specifying in greater detail the actual mechanisms by which compensatory processing takes place and elucidating developmental changes in these mechanisms. Here again, the interchange of data and theory between developmental, experimental, and educational psychology has been apparent.

In previous papers, my research group has made use of the two-process theory of contextual expectancy developed by Posner and Snyder (1975a, 1975b) and Neely (1977). The idea is that contextual effects are mediated by two contextual mechanisms that may operate simultaneously, but that have different properties. One is an automatic spreading activation process operating in semantic memory. This mechanism is fast acting, uses little cognitive capacity, and causes facilitatory but not inhibitory context effects. The other mechanism is a process of specific contextual prediction that operates more slowly, utilizes attentional capacity, and causes facilitation and inhibition (see Stanovich & West, 1983a, for a fuller discussion).

There do exist other specific models of compensatory processing, for example, Becker's (1982) work on the verification model. However, we consider the Posner–Snyder theory the most useful in explicating developmental changes in contextual patterns for several reasons. For example, the recurring pattern of facilitation dominance in the reaction times of the adults suggests that the contextual effects of these subjects are mediated only through the automatic spreading activation mechanism. The greater trend toward inhibition in the times of children and poorer readers suggests that these readers make use of the mechanism of conscious contextual prediction. However, the reader's use of this mechanism is a distinctly mixed blessing. This compensatory mechanism will indeed speed the processing of congruous words, but will do so at the expense of cognitive capacity. Thus, less capacity remains for the comprehension processes that tend to be very capacity demanding.

In short, there is no substitute for automatic, efficient data-driven processing at the word level. Capacity must be freed for the all-important comprehension and text integration processes. The only contextual mechanisms that are ultimately advantageous are those that can facilitate word recognition automatically, without depleting the amount of cognitive resources that can be allocated to text-level processing (Stanovich, 1980; Stanovich & West, 1983a). Again, it should be stressed that the interactive–compensatory model makes heavy use of the idea of cognitive resource allocation that LaBerge and Samuels (1974) and Perfetti and Lesgold (1977, 1979) imported from cognitive psychology into the psychology of reading.

Finally, we think that the interactive–compensatory model—regardless of the ultimate scientific judgment of its merits—contributes to a healthy trend in reading research. Work in this area has accelerated the breakdown of the monolithic "top-down" versus "bottom-up" debate, offering a more complex scientific discussion. Essentially, the interactive–compensatory model fosters a perspective whose chief advantage is the recognition that the relative reliance on context shown by skilled and less-skilled readers may well change at different levels of the processing hierarchy.

The Decoding Epiphenomenon Explanation

Recently, my research group has, in a sense, tried to "recycle" our ideas back through the educational literature to see whether our theoretical terms in any way mapped into problems that have emerged independently in that literature. For example, what about the poor reader in relatively difficult materials who appears not to be making use of context? For years many educational theorists (e.g., Goodman, 1965, 1976) have assumed that such readers have learned certain inefficient strategies and have failed to learn contextual strategies. Goodman, for example, postulated overreliance on "phonic" strategies.

Our findings suggest a different interpretation. The less-skilled readers in our studies did not seem reticent to use context to facilitate word recognition. They reliably displayed context effects *when the context was adequately understood,* and here is perhaps the key to the seeming paradox. In many texts the slow and inaccurate word decoding processes of the poor reader may in fact degrade the contextual information that they receive, rendering it unusable. Under such conditions, the finding that poor readers rely less on context is not necessarily an indication that they *cannot* use context to speed word recognition. Rather, the finding may be an epiphenomenon of poor decoding skills. Indeed, since this is precisely what our results suggested (using materials that were within the ability of the poorer readers), we conducted a further study of first-grade children (Stanovich, Cunningham, & Feeman, 1984b).

A First-Grade Longitudinal Study

In the fall and spring of the school year we assessed the speed and accuracy with which the children read coherent story paragraphs and paragraphs of random words. A recognition efficiency score was constructed that reflected the mean number of words read correctly per second. In the fall and the spring both skilled and less-skilled readers recognized words more efficiently in the coherent than in the random paragraphs. Of course, the skilled readers were better in both types of paragraphs. The question we will ask is whether the poor readers are getting as much contextual facilitation as the good readers, *when at a comparable level of context-free decoding ability.*

Our data is relevant to this question because the mean random recognition efficiency of the less-skilled readers in the spring was similar to that displayed by the skilled readers in the fall. Thus, it is possible to ask if these two groups of readers were getting an equal contextual "boost" from the coherent paragraph when they were at similar levels of decoding skill.

Figure 4.1 displays a scatterplot in which the coherent paragraph efficiency score is plotted against the random efficiency score. The filled circles represent the data of the less-skilled subjects in the spring and the open circles represent the data of the skilled subjects in the fall. There is considerable overlap in the scores of the two groups, and it is clear that at a given level of random decoding efficiency the less-skilled readers get just as much recognition facilitation from the coherent paragraph. In fact, if anything, they seem to receive more facilitation. Thus, when at a similar level of decoding ability, poorer readers appear to receive as much contextual facilitation as the skilled readers. Our previous work (and that of Perfetti, Schwantes, and others) indicates that when the materials are well within the capability of the less-skilled readers, these children do show large context effects.

These findings appear to support the epiphenomenon rather than the strategy explanation of the contextual failures shown by poor readers. In short, our results converge with much other recent evidence (see Carr, 1981; Lesgold & Resnick, 1982; Mitchell, 1982; Perfetti & Roth, 1981; Richardson, DiBenedetto, & Adler, 1982; Stanovich, 1982b), indicating that it is not failure at the Goodman "guessing game" that characterizes the poor reader, but difficulty with the graphophonemic analysis of words.

FIGURE 4.1. Scatterplot displaying the relationship between coherent paragraph efficiency score and the random paragraph efficiency score. Open circles represent the scores of the skilled readers in the fall and the closed circles represent the scores of the less-skilled readers in the spring.

CONCLUSION

I will conclude by noting that while my work has focused on context effects on word recognition, other reading researchers are converging on several other conclusions regarding individual differences in reading ability. For example, it is becoming increasingly clear that the poorer reader often has subtle language problems that are independent of decoding ability (Andolina, 1980; Menyuk & Flood, 1981; Semel & Wiig, 1975; Vellutino, 1979; Vogel, 1974). Less-skilled readers have less efficient text comprehension strategies, are less adept at comprehension monitoring, and approach text more passively (Bransford, Stein, & Vye, 1982; Brown, 1981; Paris & Myers, 1981). These readers display less efficient text scanning strategies (DiVesta, Hayward, & Orlando, 1979; Garner & Reis, 1981), less sensitivity to text structure (Meyer, Brandt, & Bluth, 1980; Pearson & Camperell, 1981; Smiley, Oakley, Worthen, Campione, & Brown, 1977), and are less likely to elaborate the encoding of text (Levin, 1973; Merrill, Sperber, & McCauley, 1981; Pearson & Camperell, 1981). These strategic differences in the comprehension of text could result from a general lack of linguistic awareness on the part of the poor reader (Downing, 1980; Menyuk & Flood, 1981).

Regarding processes at the word decoding level, increasingly it is being recognized that early reading acquisition is critically dependent on some degree of phonological awareness (e.g., Calfee, Lindamood, & Lindamood, 1973; Fox & Routh, 1980; Lewkowicz, 1980; Liberman & Shankweiler, 1979). Recently, some imaginative longitudinal developmental studies have helped to untangle the correlation/causation problems in making inferences of this type. A particularly impressive longitudinal training study of four-year-old children who were followed up four years later was recently published by Bradley and Bryant (1983). This study provides strong evidence for a causal connection between phonological awareness and reading acquisition. On the negative side, it appears that eye movement patterning and processes of visual feature extraction are not critical loci of individual differences in reading ability (Carr, 1981; Rayner, 1978; Stanovich, 1982a; Vellutino, 1979). These processes appear to account for very little of the variance in reading skill.

In summary, the interactions of researchers in experimental, developmental, and educational psychology have led to significant progress in understanding reading, and there is every reason to expect this progress to continue. Further, we can expect that some of our general conclusions about individual differences in reading ability will gain in specificity as future research is guided by the trends already apparent. For example, an increasing number of multivariate studies (e.g., Singer & Crouse, 1981) will eventually begin to converge on estimates of the proportion of variance in reading ability accounted for by the processes that we already know are linked to reading skill. Such multivariate studies will undoubtedly need to incorporate a developmental component because it is likely that the relative importance of the various component processes of reading change as the general reading level of the sample under study increases. Finally, future research will provide stronger evidence of the existence of causal links between various subprocesses and reading ability, as well as evidence of the influence of developmental changes on such links.

PART II

PHONOLOGICAL SENSITIVITY AND THE PHONOLOGICAL CORE DEFICIT MODEL

CHAPTER 5

Early Reading Acquisition and the Causes of Reading Difficulty

Contributions to Research on Phonological Processing

After presenting some of our early context work at a meeting of the Society for Research in Child Development in the late 1970s, I was asked (I think somewhat skeptically) the following question: "If poor readers do not have problems with the 'psycholinguistic guessing game' [use of context], then what is the cognitive problem preventing them from reading fluently?" I thought this was a fair question and I set out to see whether I could contribute to answering it. The section at the end of the interactive–compensatory paper (Chapter 3) titled "Where Are the Differences?" was an attempt to summarize briefly what was known in the late 1970s. It is clear from rereading that section that I was already placing my bets on automatic context-free word recognition as the critical process. It is also clear that researchers such as Shankweiler and Liberman (1972), Bradley and Bryant (1978), Williams (1980), and Calfee, Lindamood, and Lindamood (1973) were already digging deeper and beginning to isolate the critical psychological processes at the subword level that determined individual differences in the acquisition of reading skill.

I was drawn to the smattering of results that had already appeared in the research literature that indicated that phonological awareness seemed to be of critical importance (e.g., Bradley & Bryant, 1978; Chall, Roswell, & Blumenthal, 1963; Liberman, Shankweiler, Fischer, & Carter, 1974). What might be termed the "first wave" of research on phonological awareness was represented by the work of Bruce (1964) and of Chall, Roswell, and Blumenthal (1963). They had alerted researchers to the importance of this process, but, unfortunately for these investigators and for the field, their work was really before its time. It was not until 10 years later with the seminal papers of Liberman et al. (1974) and Calfee et al. (1973) that there was a critical mass of researchers who could put these findings to good use and build upon them. This "second wave" of research, although still somewhat before its time (see Shankweiler, 1999, for more on the historical context of the second wave), did find enough kindling in the field to ignite some real interest.

My own contributions to establishing the importance of phonological processes in reading acquisition (see Chapter 6 and Stanovich, Cunningham, & Feeman, 1984a) were squarely in the "third wave" of research on phonological awareness—occurring at a time when research on these processes was beginning to explode. The over 200 citations received by the paper reprinted in Chapter 6 are probably due to the joint effects of this paper "catching the wave" (to use a surfing analogy) and simultaneously helping to create the wave. My participation in this part of the modern research synthesis in the psychology of reading (see Chapter 21) was profoundly affected by meeting my second career-long colleague: Anne Cunningham.

At the time that Anne and I first met, I was teaching an undergraduate statistics course at Oakland University. Because it was only the second time that I had taught the course, I was still a little nervous, so I only vaguely registered the student who engaged me after that first class meeting. She politely apologized for coming late and then tentatively advanced the proposition that she would need to come 15 minutes late for the rest of the term because she was a full-time teacher and would be driving to this late afternoon class from an outlying suburb of Detroit. I told her that was fine and gave the incident little thought at the time. I do remember becoming more aware of her as the term went by and getting used to her as she regularly, oh-so-quietly and unobtrusively slipped down the wall to a back-row seat (so as not to disturb me during lecture—she was clearly a "front-row" type of student!). Little did I know that this stealthy but polite latecomer would come to play such a large role in my life. As when looking back at so many things in history (Fischhoff's [1977] hindsight bias effect—which I've studied in another context—strikes again), it all seems so inevitable now: she took my experimental psychology lab course, she became involved in my research, we began to collaborate, we did research together at Clarkston Elementary School, she completed her master's degree with me at Oakland University. And it continued to play out from there: on to a doctoral degree in developmental psychology jointly supervised by Scott Paris and me, the Dissertation of the Year Award from the International Reading Association, and a productive research career leading up to her current positions as coordinator of the Joint Doctoral Program in Special Education and associate professor at the University of California, Berkeley. And, of course, a 25-year-long friendship.

In those productive late 1970s and early 1980s years we completed work on a variety of issues. For example, we did some work on the automaticity of word recognition using a Stroop paradigm. One article from this line of research (Stanovich, Cunningham, & West, 1981) was listed as the 13th-most-cited article in the history of the *Journal of Reading Behavior/Journal of Literacy Research* (see McKenna & Robinson, 1999). We also did some work on rapid naming (Stanovich, 1981b; Stanovich, Feeman, & Cunningham, 1983). Interestingly, given the current interest in rapid naming and the double deficit hypothesis (Bowers & Wolf, 1993; Levy, Bourassa, & Horn, 1999; Manis, Seidenberg, & Doi, 1999; Wolf, 1991a, 1997; Wolf & Bowers, 1999), we were among the first to suggest that the continuous list procedure was a more potent predictor of reading ability than the discrete trial procedure—a trend now widely accepted in the field (Bowers & Swanson, 1991; Share, 1995; Wagner, Torgesen, Laughon, Simmons, & Rashotte, 1993; Wolf & Bowers, 1999). But our most influential work from this period was our work on phonological awareness.

CONTRIBUTIONS TO RESEARCH ON PHONOLOGICAL AWARENESS

The paper reprinted as Chapter 6 of this volume no doubt served a consolidating function in what might be termed the third wave of interest on phonological awareness. At the time, such correlational predictive evidence was needed (more than it is today) to clearly establish the importance of the process of phonological awareness in early reading. Anne went on to publish her training study (Cunningham, 1990), which contributed to the consensus that developed in the 1990s that phonological awareness plays a causal role in early reading development (Adams, 1990; Brady & Shankweiler, 1991; Catts & Kamhi, 1999; Pressley, 1998; Shankweiler, 1999; Share & Stanovich, 1995; Torgesen & Wagner, 1998; Vellutino et al., 1996; Wagner et al., 1997). In the paper published as Stanovich, Cunningham, and Feeman (1984a), we elaborated a path model of the relationships among phonological awareness, decoding speed, listening comprehension, and general intelligence in early reading acquisition.

We can again ask the question that I posed in the introductory chapter of Part I: From the perspective of over 15 years, did we get things right? Again I feel that, grossly, we were on the mark. The high degree of commonality that we observed among the phonological awareness tasks has largely held up. Outside of tasks emphasizing the rime unit, the amount of commonality is high (Hatcher & Hulme, 1999; Hoien, Lundberg, Stanovich, & Bjaalid, 1995; Muter, Hulme, Snowling, & Taylor, 1998). Although occasionally a second factor appears (see Yopp, 1988), as long as the tasks are all reasonably focused at the phoneme level, there is considerable evidence that the "phonological g-factor" accounts for substantial variance (Hatcher & Hulme, 1999; Hoien et al., 1995; McBride-Chang, 1995; McBride-Chang, Wagner, & Chang, 1997; Wagner et al., 1997). Schatschneider, Francis, Foorman, Fletcher, and Mehta (1999) recently applied item-response theory to a battery of phonological awareness tasks and concluded that "these results showed that

TABLE 5.1. Examples of Correlations between Phonological Awareness (PA), Intelligence Test Performance (IQ), and Early Reading Ability (R)

Study	PA & R	IQ & R	PA & IQ
Bradley & Bryant (1985)	.52	.52	
		.45	
	.57	.51	
		.40	
Bryant et al. (1989)	.67	.66	.58
	.64	.42	.58
	.66		.61
			.28
			.46
			.34
Helfgott (1976)	.72	.41	
	.49		
Juel, Griffith, & Gough (1986)	.56	.34	.40
	.69		.36
	.67		.43
Lundberg, Olofsson, & Wall (1980)	.37	.19	.29
	.34	.15	.29
Share, Jorm, Maclean, & Mathews (1984)	.66	.47	
	.62	.50	
Stanovich, Cunningham, & Cramer (1984)	.47	.25	.55
Stanovich, Cunningham, & Feeman (1984a)	.43	.33	.29
	.44	.34	.07
Torneus (1984)	.33	.24	.30
	.41		.31
	.41		.42
	.52		.50
Tunmer & Nesdale (1985)	.48	.28	.11
Tunmer, Herriman, & Nesdale (1988)	.41	.10	.13
	.44	.34	.42
	.27	.11	
	.32	.43	
	.54		
Vellutino & Scanlon (1987)	.46	.34	
	.48	.39	
	.55	.39	
	.53	.32	
Yopp (1988)	.63		
	.66		
	.67		
	.55		
	.47		
	.71		
	.67		
	.72		
	.53		
Zifcak (1981)	.64	.27	
	.66	.33	

Note. Some PA correlations are averages of correlations from several different tasks employed in the study; in some cases multiple values are reported when different intelligence and reading tests were used in the same study, or children of different ages, or different subgroups; the time of PA assessment in these studies varied from prekindergarten, to kindergarten, to first grade.

phonological awareness, as measured by these tasks, appears to be well represented as a unidimensional construct, but the tasks best suited to measure phonological awareness vary across development" (p. 439).

On another issue—our emphasis on the relative independence of phonological awareness and general intelligence—we may have overstated the case for nonoverlap a bit in these papers. More recent and more comprehensive studies with larger sample sizes and more sophisticated statistical techniques have shown a tighter connection than we suggested in these papers (Wagner et al., 1993). We certainly were correct in pointing to the importance of the finding that phonological awareness accounted for variance in reading ability after variance due to general intelligence was partialled out. That finding has stood the test of time. Additionally, we were right to point to the startling nature of the finding that a 7-min (15-item) phonological awareness test correlates with reading ability more strongly than a comprehensive hour-long intelligence test. A nonexhaustive sampling of first-grade correlations revealing this startling pattern is provided in Table 5.1 (see Stanovich, 1992b). The mean correlation between the phonological measures and reading ability is .54 (median = .535), whereas the mean correlation between intelligence test performance and reading ability is .35 (median = .34).

Although we were correct to emphasize the relative strength of the correlations involving phonological awareness in the context of those involving general intelligence, the linkages between phonological processing and intelligence themselves may be stronger than we implied with our emphasis on the modularity of phonological processing. Using latent variable methods that provide a better estimate of the relationship, Wagner et al. (1993) found stronger relationships (see also Hohnen & Stevenson, 1999). Nevertheless, they emphasize that

> We do not believe that substantial correlations between phonological processing abilities and general cognitive ability are in conflict with the view that dyslexia is caused by a deficit in some aspect of phonological processing. . . . The only requirement is that the correlation be less than 1.0. If one examines a scatterplot of two variables that are correlated even at the level of .90, which is higher than any of our correlations between phonological processing abilities and reading, a small proportion of outlying points is the rule rather than the exception. (p. 100)

The causal model presented in Stanovich, Cunningham, and Feeman (1984a)—phonological awareness facilitating decoding skill, which in turn determines word recognition ability, which in conjunction with listening comprehension determines reading comprehension—while not particularly fine-grained, has largely stood the test of time. Phonological awareness contributes indirectly to reading comprehension ability through its direct effects on word recognition. Several similar path models echoed through the literature in subsequent years (e.g., Catts, Fey, Zhang, & Tomblin, 1999; Conners & Olson,

1990; Tunmer & Nesdale, 1985). Likewise, our emphasis on the uniqueness of decoding speed (i.e., its independent predictive variance from listening comprehension) was on the mark (even for adults; see Cunningham, Stanovich, & Wilson, 1990). That reading comprehension was uniquely predicted by decoding speed and listening comprehension in the Stanovich, Cunningham, and Feeman (1984a) paper could be interpreted within the context of Gough and Tunmer's (1986) influential paper on the "simple view" of reading that appeared soon after our article—and this did not go unnoticed in their seminal paper.

The bottom line on Chapter 6 is that two of our conclusions now seem to be markedly understated: (1) "The results of this investigation bode well for the future use of phonological awareness measures in both research and educational settings"; and (2) "The results bolster the construct validity of phonological awareness, indicate considerable comparability and interchangeability among the tasks used to measure the construct, and are encouraging as regards the possible use of such tasks in predictive test batteries." Subsequent work has moved well beyond these very general conclusions. Just as it was an advance to ask what was the primary individual difference variable underlying reading comprehension and to find the answer in "word recognition"; just as it was an advance to ask what was the primary individual difference variable underlying word recognition and to find the answer in "spelling–sound decoding skill"; just as it was an advance to ask what was the primary individual difference variable underlying spelling–sound decoding skill and to find the answer in "phonological awareness"; current researchers are moving on to ask the question of what is the primary individual difference variable underlying phonological awareness. A plethora of recent papers on variation in underlying phonological representations (Adlard & Hazan, 1998; Brady, 1997; Ceponiene, Service, Kurjenluoma, Cheour, & Naatanen, 1999; Cornelissen, Hansen, Bradley, & Stein, 1996; Edwards & Lahey, 1998; Elbro, 1996; Elbro, Borstrom, & Peterson, 1998; Fowler, 1991; Hulme & Snowling, 1992; McBride-Chang, 1996; McDougall, Hulme, Ellis, & Monk, 1994; Metsala, 1997a, 1997b, 1999; Metsala & Stanovich, 1995; Metsala & Walley, 1998; Mody, Studdert-Kennedy, & Brady, 1997; Snowling & Hulme, 1989; Swan & Goswami, 1997; Walley, 1993) promises to take us one step further toward a complete model of reading acquisition in terms of the psychological processes involved—as does work on neurophysiological and genetic underpinnings (Hynd, Clinton, & Hiemenz, 1999; Olson, 1999; Shaywitz, 1996). Additionally, much more information is now also available on adult reading-disabled individuals than was true at the time that Chapters 6–7 were first published. We now know with considerable confidence that adults with reading disabilities share the deficits in phonological awareness that have been identified in children (Bruck, 1992; Gottardo, Siegel, & Stanovich, 1997; Greenberg, Ehri, & Perin, 1997; Read & Ruyter, 1985; Scarborough, Ehri, Olson, & Fowler, 1998).

Finally, much work in the 1990s has served to contextualize the role of phonological awareness in a larger theory of the reading process—including the relationship of deficiencies in phonological awareness to deficiencies in other language processes. Catts et al. (1999) provide an outline of the role of oral language abilities outside the phonological domain in a full model of the determinants of reading comprehension.

THE TERMINOLOGY WARS

In a 1987 paper (Stanovich, 1987) I complained generally about the chaotic terminology in this area, and specifically about the ambiguity surrounding the term phonological awareness at that time. I suggested that "I almost feel that we should require dictionary appendices for all papers in this area so we would have some hope of untangling ourselves" (p. 515). Things are not quite so bad now. The main problem in the mid-1980s was that some investigators reserved the use of the term phonological awareness to refer to conscious access to the phonemic level of language and the ability to cognitively manipulate representations at this level, whereas others used it as an umbrella term to refer to any task that involved sensitivity to speech sounds.

Things are somewhat better now as investigators are much more careful to refer to phonemic awareness when they are referring to access to the phonemic level of language. In the 1987 paper I suggested that the term phonological sensitivity be used as an umbrella term to refer to any task that involves sensitivity to speech sounds. This suggestion is sometimes followed in the literature, but the term phonological awareness does seem to have become entrenched (see Gombert's [1992] distinction between metalinguistic and epilinguistic abilities).

I would still, however, reiterate the argument made at the end of Chapter 12 that linking any concept to the notion of awareness is a bad idea. Awareness will be seen as synonymous with consciousness by many, and consciousness is still a vexing concept within philosophy and cognitive science (Churchland & Churchland, 1998; Dennett, 1991). It can only cause confusion if it is used to do any conceptual work in our field. A more operationally straightforward conceptual term is needed than phonological awareness. But, just as the superiority of the Macintosh computer was not enough to displace the PC, the "meme" (Dawkins, 1976/1989 and Chapter 19, this volume) represented by the term phonological awareness is entrenched, and theories of thought contagion (see Blackmore, 1999; Lynch, 1996) would predict that it will be hard to dislodge. Just as I give in and use a PC occasionally even though I am addicted to the superior Macintosh computer, I also cannot resist the tidal wave of the term phonological awareness, and thus I use the term myself now, even though I still think phonological sensitivity is better. The latter does not have the connotations of metalinguistic awareness that may lead us theoretically astray.

This danger is well illustrated in Shankweiler's (1999) discussion of the history of the term within the Haskins group. He points out that "in the early years, we assumed that the critical insight leading to awareness was specifically metalinguistic" (p. 116) and notes that the speech-based representations that are later associated with print are part of the natural endowment for language: "We did not think of the underlying representations themselves as plastic. . . . If this view is right, then the emergence of phonological awareness is largely constrained by the development of the underlying representations" (p. 116). Shankweiler's (1999) theoretical chronology is shared by many of us in the field. And it is a fair bet that all of us emphasized the metalinguistic component of the construct phonological awareness too much because of the connotations of the term awareness—connotations not shared by the more operational term phonological sensitivity. In Chapter 19, I discuss why it is a bad idea to use terms to describe phenomena that carry too much theory with them. For example, in that chapter, I discuss how the term "emergent literacy" carries with it a theory of literacy acquisition—making the point that it is not a neutral operational term.

THE IMPORTANCE OF PHONOLOGICAL PROCESSING AS A FOUNDATIONAL ASSUMPTION

Soon after accepting the position as associate editor of the *Merrill-Palmer Quarterly* in 1986, I collected some of the third wave work on phonemic awareness and phonological sensitivity in a special issue. In the introduction to that issue (July 1987), I characterized this work (see Ehri, Wilce, & Taylor, 1987; Maclean, Bryant, & Bradley, 1987; Mann, Tobin, & Wilson, 1987; Perfetti, Beck, Bell, & Hughes, 1987; Vellutino & Scanlon, 1987) as representing a scientific success story that was all too rare in the social sciences, and I still think that this is true. In the middle of our intense scientific disputes, it is important not to forget the background assumptions that we all share. I made this point, I think, most forcefully at a symposium held in honor of Isabelle Liberman at the 1988 meeting of the Orton Society (Stanovich, West, & Cunningham, 1991). I pointed out that I thought that she helped to build the foundational assumptions about the importance of phonological processes that we now take for granted. Many researchers now share certain assumptions about reading that were far from established when Isabelle began making her seminal contributions to our understanding of reading acquisition (e.g., Shankweiler & Liberman, 1972; Liberman et al., 1974). Indeed, an outsider is in some sense in the best position to see the magnitude of the consensus. To the layperson, our refined disputes about precisely how to fractionate phonological abilities and how to trace the causal paths of each component will seem arcane; whereas the background assumptions that researchers in this area share will stand out in bold relief. We must remember this point when communicating current research on phonological processes to educators and parents (see Part VII). They should not mistake our disputes about highly spe-cific issues (e.g., Ehri, 1998; Goswami, 1998; Stahl & Murray, 1998) for dis-agreements about foundational assumptions.

For example, these disputes could (and have) been exploited by those hostile to explicit analytic instruction—just as disputes among evolutionary theorists have been exploited by creationists who misleadingly argue that these disagreements imply that the basic fact of human evolution itself is in question (rather than the importance of various evolutionary mechanisms). Such misuse of our theoretical disputes is already occurring. For example, Goswami's (1993, 1998) elegant work demonstrating the importance of the rime unit is sometimes used by whole language advocates to support their po-sition that segmenting at the phoneme level is never necessary. Likewise, the fact that most theorists view reading and phonological awareness as recipro-cally related ("Regarding phonological awareness to be a prerequisite for liter-acy, as we did, is not to deny that awareness and literacy are reciprocally re-lated"; Shankweiler, 1999, p. 116) does not allow the theoretical inference that phonological awareness is not causally potent in early reading acquisi-tion—again, an inference sometimes made in the whole language literature.

Thus, in the fractious but progressive manner of actual science, research-ers continue to refine their knowledge of phonological processes in reading de-velopment (Berent & Perfetti, 1995; Catts & Kamhi, 1999; Frost, 1998; Frost & Katz, 1992; Harm & Seidenberg, 1999; Jared, Levy, & Rayner, 1999; Liberman, 1999; Perfetti, 1994; Shankweiler, 1999; Tan & Perfetti, 1998; Vellutino et al., 1996). For example, the role of the rime unit in early reading development continues to be the subject of empirical and theoretical conten-tion (Bowey, 1999; Brown & Deavers, 1999; Goswami, 1998, 1999; Nation & Hulme, 1997). Which specific component of phonological awareness is the critical causal agent is the focus of increasing research attention (e.g., Byrne, 1998; Stahl & Murray, 1998). Methodological advances in measuring phono-logical awareness continue to be made (a paper on this issue by Byrne and Fielding-Barnsley [1993] remains undercited). Additionally, as noted previ-ously, interest in a processing level more basic than phonological sensitivity has heightened, as evidenced by the interest in exploring developmental change in the differentiation of phonological representations (e.g., Elbro, 1996; Fowler, 1991; Hulme & Snowling, 1992; Metsala & Walley, 1998) and in more basic timing mechanisms (e.g., Farmer & Klein, 1995; Mody et al., 1997; Tallal, Sainburg, & Jernigan, 1991). While encouraging work on the latter (Chiappe, Stringer, Siegel, & Stanovich, in press; Stringer, 1997), I con-tinue to believe that the former represents a more fruitful direction for the reading field. In a sense, I have thrown in my lot with the conclusion that Al Liberman (1999) articulated in his Outstanding Scientific Contribution Ad-dress to the Society for the Scientific Study of Reading: "The moral for the reading researcher and teacher is that the phonological underpinning of lan-guage holds the key to the reading process, as it does to speech" (p. 101).

LINKING DEVELOPMENTAL MODELS OF READING TO MODELS
OF INDIVIDUAL DIFFERENCES AND READING DISABILITY

One important trend that characterized work throughout the 1980s and 1990s was the attempt to link the emerging developmental model of reading acquisition (which, as outlined in Chapters 6 and 10, had a heavy phonological component) with work on reading disability. Prior to this period, work on reading disability and on normal reading acquisition had displayed a curious tendency to dissociate. Hypotheses about the cause of reading disability would spring up willynilly—without reference to anything that was known about reading development per se. Because models of normal reading development were not used to constrain models of reading disability in any way, it is perhaps not surprising that the latter simply proliferated with no pruning and cumulative progress in understanding.

In an article written together while he was on sabbatical in Toronto, David Share and I (Share & Stanovich, 1995) made the argument that models of development must be used to constrain models of disability, but that there was sometimes reluctance to use these constraints in the reading field. This has allowed speculations about the causes of individual differences in reading acquisition to be unconstrained by a specified model of the reading acquisition process itself. Confusion has reigned because studies of individual differences have uncovered a plethora of information processing tasks on which the performance of skilled and less-skilled readers differ. For example, Byrne (1992) has stated:

> One thing that could be said about this rather long list of possible causes of reading problems is that it is needed, because reading is multifaceted and because there are many kinds of problems. This is a standard line of reasoning . . . [but] given the uncertainty about a typology of reading difficulties and given that fewer explanatory constructs than reading problems may be needed, there may well be too much explanatory power for the job at hand. A way is needed to constrain the power. Economy of explanation characterizes the scientific endeavor and should be invoked in this branch of science. It is possible that the explanatory power available could be constrained if it were required that each of the many hypothetical causes of reading problems fits a well-worked-out account of the acquisition procedure. (p. 3)

However, few papers in the reading literature have attempted the type of integration that Byrne recommends: fitting the empirical research on individual differences with a model of the acquisition process (see Byrne, 1998; Shankweiler, 1999). Most investigators have either focused on developing generic developmental models of stages that all children traverse, or they have concentrated on looking for patterns of correlations in studies of individual differences. In some of the papers in this volume I have attempted the type of synthesis that Byrne is recommending (see also Share, 1995; Share &

Stanovich, 1995). In Chapter 7 I extrapolate the findings about individual differences in reading acquisition outlined in Chapters 3 and 6 (and in Chapter 10) into a model of reading disability: the phonological-core variable-difference model. Importantly, this chapter also introduces a research theme that was to continue for the subsequent decade: an examination of the notion of differing subtypes of poor readers. This theme was played out in terms of an examination of the validity of aptitude/achievement discrepancy definitions of reading disability (see Chapter 8 and Part VI), and then in terms of more process-based models of reading disability subtypes (see Stanovich, Siegel, & Gottardo, 1997).

THE PHONOLOGICAL-CORE VARIABLE-DIFFERENCE MODEL

The paper reprinted in Chapter 7 was written as a contribution for the 1988 Austin Research Symposium series held in Austin, Texas, and organized by Joe Torgesen (see Torgesen, 1990) and published in the *Journal of Learning Disabilities*. In this paper, I adopted the terminology from Gough and Tunmer's (1986) classic paper and speculated about the differences between the garden-variety poor reader (without IQ discrepancy) and the dyslexic poor reader (with IQ discrepancy). The paper is both a synthesis of previous research and a report of two studies from our research group (Stanovich, Nathan, & Vala-Rossi, 1986; Stanovich, Nathan, Zolman, 1988)—the latter study being one of the few longitudinal reading-level match investigations. This paper has also been heavily cited.

Taken retrospectively, the paper gets two very major issues right—the two concepts in the title. Explaining the phonological core deficit is at the heart of contemporary studies of reading difficulty (e.g., Blachman, 1997a; Catts & Kamhi, 1999; Elbro, 1996; Metsala & Walley, 1998; Morris et al., 1998). Chapter 8 describes the subsequent attempts of my research group to specify what I have termed the "phenotypic processing profile" of the disabled reader. Research has advanced to yield an understanding of the partial genetic basis of the phonological core deficit (Olson, 1999) and to provide some knowledge of that part of the deficit that might be experientially based (Castles, Datta, Gayan, & Olson, 1999; Olson, 1999; Stanovich, Siegel, & Gottardo, 1997). Important progress has been made in examining how this core deficit can be remediated and the difficulties involved in remediation attempts (Benson, Lovett, & Kroeber, 1997; Blachman, 1997a; Hatcher & Hulme, 1999; Lovett et al., 1994; Olson, Wise, Johnson, & Ring, 1997; Torgesen & Burgess, 1998; Torgesen, Wagner, & Rashotte, 1997; Vellutino et al., 1996; Wise, Ring, & Olson, 1999). We are just beginning to get a glimmer of the neurophysiological basis of the deficit (Hynd et al., 1999; Shaywitz, 1996).

The variable difference concept from the model described in Chapter 7 has also held up—it is the second major aspect of that paper to have been on the mark. The prediction here was in part a psychometric necessity. The differences between the garden-variety and dyslexic poor reader *outside* the word recognition module must play out in roughly the terms outlined in Chapter 7 if the field is using a coherent concept of general intelligence (however, Part VI will illustrate that, in the learning disabilities field, that very concept *is* often incoherent!). However, in characterizing the differences between these two groups *within* the word recognition module, I believe I made two interacting mistakes in this paper. These mistakes provide good examples of how science proceeds by a Popperian falsification of earlier incorrect theoretical views. The graduate student might well learn from these examples. Chapter 7 juxtaposed with Chapter 8 provides a beautiful exemplar from my own research career. Specifically, in Chapter 8 I became the coauthor of a theoretical view that is diametrically opposed to a theoretical conjecture that I made in the paper reprinted in Chapter 7—and I believe the field has benefited from the correction of this mistake. This is an example of the process Popper (1963) termed "conjectures and refutations." It is at the heart of the scientific process, yet is utterly absent from the debate about the evidence on the teaching of reading (a debate discussed in Part VII).

Many scientists have attested to the importance of understanding that making errors in the course of science is normal, that the real danger to scientific progress is the natural human tendency to avoid exposing our beliefs to situations where they might be shown to be wrong. Nobel Prize–winner Peter Medawar has said:

> Though faulty hypotheses are excusable on the grounds that they will be superseded in due course by acceptable ones, they can do grave harm to those who hold them because scientists who fall deeply in love with their hypotheses are proportionately unwilling to take no as an experimental answer. Sometimes instead of exposing a hypothesis to a cruelly critical test, they caper around it, testing only subsidiary implications, or follow up sidelines that have an indirect bearing on the hypothesis without exposing it to the risk of refutation. . . . I cannot give any scientist of any age better advice than this: *the intensity of the conviction that a hypothesis is true has no bearing on whether it is true or not.* (1979, p. 39)

In Chapter 8 we have an example of just what Medawar is talking about. I was able to continue making contributions to these issues because I was able to give up the hypothesis articulated in Chapter 7 that was leading me down the wrong path.

That wrong path involved two errors: one the interpretation of a data pattern and the other being an incorrect theoretical speculation. The error of data interpretation concerned the pseudoword performance displayed in Table 7.6. There is an indication in that table that seventh graders who were poor readers were performing worse than the two other reading-level matched groups on pseudowords—particularly on the accuracy measure. Nevertheless, it was not statistically significant and we accepted the null hypothesis at the time the paper was published. When Dick Olson reviewed the Stanovich, Nathan, and Zolman (1988) paper for *Child Development* he queried us on this point, but we were at the time more impressed by the commonality in performance across tasks. By the time the paper reprinted as Chapter 7 was published, though, I did feel it necessary to hedge with the statement that "in most instances the mean performance levels of the three groups were quite close (the possible exception being pseudoword naming)" (p. 597). Well, Dick is clearly justified in saying "I told you so" in this case. As his meta-analysis (Rack, Snowling, & Olson, 1992), subsequent work by others (e.g., Share, 1996) and our own subsequent work (Stanovich & Siegel, 1994; reprinted as Chapter 8) demonstrated, the group means of samples of all poor readers—including garden-variety poor readers—display a deficit in pseudoword reading in a reading-level match.

As will be noted by those who read Chapter 7 carefully, the theoretical error I made in the 1988 *JLD* paper was related to the error of data interpretation just mentioned. In that paper, I speculated that there would be a difference between the dyslexic and garden-variety poor reader in phonological processing—specifically, that the dyslexic readers would display a more severe phonological deficit. I believe that this speculation of mine has been falsified—in part by my own work, most notably the work with Linda Siegel (Stanovich & Siegel, 1994), a portion of which is excerpted as Chapter 8. In fact, the structure of processing within the word recognition module seems to be fairly similar for these two groups (see Chapters 8 and 17; Fletcher et al., 1994, 1998). The pseudoword performance deficit that was hinted at in my 1988 data is actually pointing me in the right direction because the children in our study were garden-variety poor readers. These nondiscrepant poor readers in our study *shared* the pseudoword naming deficit (compared to a reading-level control) with their higher IQ dyslexic counterparts.

In summary, the phonological-core variable-deficit model described in the *JLD* article reprinted as Chapter 7 had most of the basic trends right but it emphasized subword processing differences between high- and low-IQ poor readers that have not borne out under further empirical scrutiny. My work on this issue with Linda Siegel (reprinted as Chapter 8) demonstrated just how little the IQ-discrepancy variable can do as a predictor of subword processing characteristics. She had been right in her 1988 article (Siegel, 1988) and I had been wrong in my article of the same year (Stanovich, 1988a). We have here a lesson that protagonists in the Reading Wars (see Part VII) might take to heart. In real science, disputes are answered empirically, and disputants can in fact cooperate in the empirical quest for an interpretation upon which both can agree (see Chapter 17 for more of the historical context for my theoretical change on this issue).

As predicted by the variable-difference part of the model, however, once outside the word recognition module into wider domains of language and working memory, the differences between these groups do become significant. The chapters in Part VI describe in detail how I currently view the discrepancy issue—an issue of great practical as well as theoretical significance. The point here is to demonstrate by reference to Chapter 7 that my current view post-dates the publication of this paper and represents a theoretical change of no small magnitude.

Paralleling Popper's (1963) characterization of science as a series of con-jectures and refutations, I consider this particular conjecture from the 1988 paper to have been refuted. And in Chapter 8 the reader can see—quite specif-ically and empirically—why. In that paper Linda Siegel and I reported a large-sample comparison of poor readers both with and without reading–IQ dis-crepancy in the context of an analysis that was the statistical equivalent of a reading-level match design. To my knowledge, we were the first to report a continuous regression-based analysis that statistically simulated a reading-level design and that included contrasts capturing the discrepant nondis-crepant distinction.

PHONOLOGICAL PROCESSES: IS THAT ALL THERE IS? SUBTYPES OF READING DISABILITY

Given the strong emphasis on phonological processes in Part II, it is natural to ask whether I hold a "single factor" theory of reading difficulty (a view some-times attributed to me). The answer is "No." In fact, I do recognize additional sources of variance in reading ability and additional subtypes of reading *dis*-ability, but I will candidly admit that I do so reluctantly because of a bias that I am not reticent to reveal. The bias concerns a pretheoretical preference that cuts across most sciences. In every science—not only biology—there are "splitters" and "lumpers." The splitters tend to see idiosyncrasies, lack of fit, and discrepancies in new empirical findings—discrepancies which, for them, call for new concepts and/or theoretical change. The lumpers view the same discrepancies as random variation from an established pattern—variation which, for them, needs no additional explanation. For lumpers, the splitters' data pattern is a mere temporary perturbation, not a real anomaly. Lumpers hope that further experimentation will demonstrate that the discrepancy is simply random fluctuation. The splitters hope that with further experimenta-tion the perturbations will stand out as true anomalies and force theoretical adjustment.

The reason for my present preference for the lumper camp is that after spending my early career as a splitter—writing sentences like "Reading is a complex process determined by a multiplicity of factors"—around the mid-1980s I came to wonder whether our understanding of individual differences in reading had suffered from too much splitting. I certainly do think that edu-cational practice has suffered. Perhaps an overdose of arguments over fine dis-tinctions has made us underestimate how much progress we have made at a grosser level of analysis. Thus, in the mid-1980s I moved somewhat into the lumper camp. No doubt somewhere along the way I will have made the "lumper's error" by classifying together phenomena, tasks, and patterns that really call for theoretical differentiation. But studies of the sociology of science teach us that variability in pretheoretical views is advantageous for scientific evolution—just as it is for the gene pool (Kitcher, 1993). Because in our field there is plenty of incentive for splitting (it makes for "jazzier" journal articles), it has not hurt the field to have another lumper. As an exemplar of the latter, I have preferred to create broad subtypes—and thus to emphasize new predictors and new subtypes only after a fairly high criterion has been met.

Nevertheless, I feel that that criterion *has* been met. Despite the emphasis on phonological processing in my writings, studies in my own lab were some of the first to demonstrate that orthographic processing tasks can account for variance in reading ability over and above the variance explained by phonological processing tasks (see Cunningham & Stanovich, 1990, 1993, and Stanovich & West, 1989, reprinted here as Chapter 14). This finding has been replicated several times using a variety of different tasks (Barker, Torgesen, & Wagner, 1992; Braten, Lie, Andreassen, & Olaussen, 1999; Castles & Coltheart, 1993; Castles et al., 1999; McBride-Chang, Manis, Seidenberg, Custodio, & Doi, 1993; Olson, Forsberg, & Wise, 1994). This finding falsifies the so-called single-factor model of reading development across the reading ability continuum.

The analogous question in the domain of reading disability is whether there is another subtype of reading disability outside of the subtype defined by a phonological core deficit. Our research group has contributed to answering this question in the affirmative (see Stanovich, Siegel, & Gottardo, 1997), although with some crucial caveats. First, as long ago as the 1988 paper reprinted as Chapter 7, I felt that "there is growing evidence for the utility of distinguishing a group of dyslexics who have severe problems in accessing the lexicon on a visual/orthographic basis" (p. 601). But I also added the caveat that

> The problem encountered by these children is not similar to the "visual perception" problems popular in the early history of the study of dyslexia. . . . The older conceptualizations of visual deficits had the additional flaw that the purported problematic processes were too global and not modular enough. The actual problems in orthographic processing must be much more subtle and localized. . . . I am not prepared to say anything more specific about this issue, except that I would speculate that the problem involves something to do with the automatic and nonintentional induction of orthographic patterns. (p. 601)

More recent work on the orthographic processing deficit (e.g., Castles & Coltheart, 1996) would seem to support this conjecture.

My own work on reading disability subtypes has built upon the contribution of Castles and Coltheart (1993), who in turn had based their work on tow decades of seminal research by Max Coltheart. Briefly, in the early 1980s, researchers (e.g., Coltheart, Masterson, Byng, Prior, & Riddoch, 1983; Temple &

Marshall, 1983) began to present cases of developmental dyslexia where performance patterns mirrored those of certain classic acquired dyslexia cases (Beauvois & Derouesne, 1979; Coltheart, Patterson, & Marshall, 1980; Marshall & Newcombe, 1973; Patterson, Marshall, & Coltheart, 1985) and to interpret these cases of developmental dyslexia within the functional cognitive architecture assumed by dual-route theory (Carr & Pollatsek, 1985; Coltheart, 1978; Humphreys & Evett, 1985). The extrapolation from the acquired dyslexia literature to the interpretation of the performance patterns of developmental cases proved controversial, however (see Ellis, 1979, 1984; Frith, 1985; Snowling, 1983). For example, Bryant and Impey (1986) criticized the authors of the developmental case studies for not including control groups of nondisabled readers to form a context for their case descriptions.

Castles and Coltheart (1993) tried to answer these criticisms, first by demonstrating that their dual-route subtypes can be defined by reference to the performance of normal controls, and then by showing that the subtypes so defined are not at all rare in the dyslexic population. They analyzed the exception word and nonword reading performance of 53 dyslexic individuals and 56 nondyslexic chronological age (CA) controls. They were motivated by a desire to distill subgroups that were relatively skilled at sublexical processing (indexed by the reading of pseudowords) relative to lexical processing (indexed by the reading of exception words) and vice versa (or, to use the terms popularized in Olson's [e.g., Olson et al., 1989] influential studies, subgroups characterized by relatively unique deficits in phonological coding and orthographic coding).

Castles and Coltheart (1993) argued that subtypes of reading disability could be identified based on the *relative* imbalances on the two tasks. They defined their subtypes by running a regression line with 90% confidence intervals through the exception word by pseudoword plot for the control children. This regression line and confidence intervals are then superimposed upon the scatterplot of the performance of the dyslexic sample. Subjects falling below the lower confidence interval in this plot and not its converse (the pseudoword by exception word plot) qualify for the surface dyslexia subtype: they are unusually impaired on exception word reading relative to their performance on pseudowords when the relationship among these two subskills in the normal population is used as the benchmark. An analogous but opposite regression outlier criterion defines the phonological dyslexia subtype.

Using this procedure, Castles and Coltheart (1993) defined 16 surface dyslexics and 29 phonological dyslexics. They thus argued that the vast majority of children with reading disability in their sample (45 out of 53) displayed some type of dissociation. They concluded:

> The results reported here support the notion that a clear double dissociation exists between surface and phonological dyslexic reading patterns, with some children displaying a specific difficulty reading via the lexical procedure in the absence of any difficulty with the sublexical procedure and others showing precisely

the reverse pattern. . . . It would seem that these reading patterns are not rare phenomena, but are quite prevalent in the developmental dyslexic population. (p. 174)

However, conceptual and statistical interpretation of the Castles and Coltheart (1993) data was problematic for a reason argued by Bryant and Impey (1986) almost 10 years ago: the lack of reading-level (RL) controls. If the processing trade-offs involving the lexical and sublexical procedures are specifically bound up with the overall level that the reader has attained, then extrapolating from the reading patterns of children at a higher reading level is an inappropriate way of defining abnormal patterns of processing skills at a lower reading level. For example, Manis, Seidenberg, Doi, McBride-Chang, and Peterson (1996) found that 12 of the 17 phonological dyslexics defined by a CA comparison also qualified for that subtype based on regression lines derived from a reading-level control sample. However, when the performance of the 15 CA-defined surface dyslexics was examined, only *one* qualified for this subtype label when an RL control group was employed. In a reanalysis of the Castles and Coltheart (1993) data, Stanovich et al. (1997) demonstrated that this trend is present even in their original data. In a study using children three years younger than those investigated by Castles and Coltheart (1993) and Manis et al. (1996), Stanovich et al. (1997) also observed the same trend. The surface subtype disappeared when an RL control was employed. The phonological subtype was robust however—the majority of these reading-disabled children were also identified when an RL control group was used to determine the regression line.

Stanovich et al. (1997; see also Manis et al., 1996) argued that the surface subtype appeared to have the characteristics of a developmental delay. In contrast, phonological dyslexia seemed to reflect true developmental deviance. This conclusion was reinforced by examining performance comparisons between the surface dyslexics and RL controls on the other variables contained in the Stanovich et al. (1997) performance battery. Table 5.2 presents these comparisons. It is apparent that on only one variable, WRAT Spelling, were the two groups significantly different. The two groups of children performed similarly on several tasks not used to define the dyslexic subtypes (Rosner Auditory Analysis Test [AAT], wordlikeness choice task, two subtests of the Woodcock), as well as measures of syntactic processing and verbal working memory that were included in this study. The latter two measures add to the picture of developmental lag that seemed to characterize the surface subtype: these children had syntactic processing skills and verbal memory skills commensurate with their RL controls.

Comparisons of the phonological dyslexics to RL controls are in marked contrast to those involving the surface dyslexics. Table 5.3 indicates that here there were several significant differences between the groups. The phonological dyslexics were markedly inferior not only on the experimental pseudowords, which in part defined the groups, but also on the Woodcock Word At-

TABLE 5.2. Mean Differences between the Surface Dyslexics ($N = 15$) and the RL Controls ($N = 23$)

Variable	Dyslexics	Controls	t value
WRAT Reading (raw)	53.1	51.0	0.96
WRAT Spelling (raw)	33.7	31.4	2.09*
Woodcock Word Ident (raw)	46.4	42.6	1.09
Woodcock Word Attack (raw)	15.4	15.5	−0.04
Exception Words	4.8	6.4	−1.66
Regular Words	11.3	9.2	1.45
Pseudowords	19.2	16.8	1.96
Rosner AAT	21.5	21.1	0.17
Wordlikeness Choice	11.2	11.8	−0.69
Syntactic Proc (z score)	.256	.235	0.12
Working Mem (z score)	.090	.310	−1.03

*$p < .05$.

tack subtest (not used to define the groups). Their phonological problems were further indicated by a significant deficit in phonological sensitivity as indicated by their performance on the Rosner AAT. They were significantly *better* at reading exception words. One very interesting finding that serves to confirm the developmental deviancy of this group in the phonological/language domain was that phonological dyslexics performed significantly worse than these younger controls on the measures of syntactic processing skill and verbal working memory, perhaps indicating that these tasks are in part tapping their core phonological deficit.

TABLE 5.3. Mean Differences between the Phonological Dyslexics ($N = 17$) and the RL Controls ($N = 23$)

Variable	Dyslexics	Controls	t value
WRAT Reading (raw)	49.9	51.0	−0.58
WRAT Spelling (raw)	32.0	31.4	0.50
Woodcock Word Ident (raw)	46.8	42.6	1.28
Woodcock Word Attack (raw)	7.9	15.5	−5.07***
Exception Words	8.3	6.4	2.04*
Regular Words	7.2	9.2	−1.68
Pseudowords	9.9	16.8	−5.71***
Rosner AAT	13.9	21.1	−3.16**
Wordlikeness Choice	12.2	11.8	0.51
Syntactic Proc (z score)	−.473	.235	−3.15**
Working Mem (z score)	−.172	.310	−2.30*

*$p < .05$; **$p < .01$; ***$p < .001$; all two-tailed.

DIFFERING INTERPRETATIONS OF THE PHONOLOGICAL AND SURFACE SUBTYPES

Thus, although we agree that reliably identified subtypes can be identified using the Castles–Coltheart procedures, there is little in the Manis et al. (1996) and Stanovich et al. (1997) investigations that would refute the idea that the vast majority of reading-disabled individuals suffer from a phonological deficit. However, both those investigations (and Castles & Coltheart, 1993) serve to remind us that there is substantial variability within the reading-disabled sample and that the bivariate distribution of phonological and orthographic coding skill shows enough of a spread that investigations such as those of Castles and Coltheart (1993) and Stanovich et al. (1997) can partition a subject sample into two groups with quite different skill balances, including groups with quite mild phonological impairments (see Rack et al., 1992).

The notion in Stanovich et al. (1997) that virtually all reading-disabled children have some form of phonological deficit, but that this deficit varies in magnitude and in how it is conjoined with other processing strengths and weaknesses, is consistent with the recent large-scale multivariate study of reading disability subtypes conducted by Morris et al. (1998). These researchers concluded that their results were "consistent also with views of reading disability that postulate a core problem in the development of phonological awareness skills, with variable expressions in other domains that have been related to reading disabilities (e.g., verbal short-term memory and rapid serial naming; Stanovich, 1988a)" (p. 368).

Consider how the surface and phonological subtypes might arise through different combinations of relative phonological impairment and experience with print. Low print exposure might not have very dire consequences for a reader with high levels of phonological coding skill. When such a reader does open a book, phonological coding enables the reading process—irrespective of the inadequately developed orthographic lexicon. However, the situation is probably different for a reader with somewhat depressed phonological skills (and we must never forget that even the surface dyslexics have phonological processing problems to some degree). Without efficiently functioning phonological coding processes, a system designed for compensatory processing would actually draw more on orthographic knowledge—but in the case of the surface dyslexic, that orthographic knowledge may be lacking in part due to inadequate exposure to print. Thus, surface dyslexia may arise from a milder form of phonological deficit than that of the phonological dyslexic, but one conjoined with exceptionally inadequate reading experience. This is somewhat different interpretation of surface dyslexia (see also Manis et al., 1996; Snowling, Bryant, & Hulme, 1996) than the common one of differential impairment in a dual-route architecture (Castles & Coltheart, 1993).

In contrast, the phonological dyslexic pattern might become more apparent when a more severe pathology underlying the functional architecture of phonological coding (Castles & Coltheart, 1993; Coltheart, Curtis, Atkins, &

Haller, 1993; Coltheart et al., 1980; Coltheart et al., 1983; Patterson et al., 1985; Plaut & Shallice, 1994) is conjoined with relatively high levels of exposure to print. The latter would hasten the development of the orthographic lexicon (which is critical for the processing of exception words) but the former would be relatively refractory to direct remediation efforts (Lovett et al., 1994; Lovett, Warren-Chaplin, Ransby, & Borden, 1990; Vellutino et al., 1996) and result in relatively slow growth in the ability to read pseudowords (Manis, Custodio, & Szeszulski, 1993; Olson, 1994; Snowling, 1980). Phonological dyslexia should be more refractory to treatment than surface dyslexia (see Vellutino et al., 1996).

Based on this view of the two subtypes, Stanovich et al. (1997) posited that phonological dyslexia would show a higher heritability than surface dyslexia and that phonological dyslexics would be characterized by more exposure to print than surface dyslexics. Castles et al. (1999) recently reported data consistent with these two trends, although the data favoring the latter was weak. They found that the heritability of the reading deficit of a group of phonological dyslexics (.67) was higher than the heritability of the reading deficit of a group of surface dyslexics (.31). Conversely, the estimated shared environment influence on the reading deficit of the group of phonological dyslexics (.27) was lower than the estimated shared environment influence on the reading deficit of the group of surface dyslexics (.63). Castles et al. (1999) used the checklist-with-foils methodology that my research group has used to measure print exposure (see Part V) and found that, as predicted by Stanovich et al. (1997), the phonological dyslexics displayed significantly more exposure to print. This difference, however, was fairly small in magnitude. The reason that the absolute magnitude of the print exposure difference was small might have to do with the fact that the Castles et al. (1999) sample spanned a very large age range (from 8 to 18) and we have previously warned (Stanovich, West, & Harrison, 1995) that the use of differing populations of reading items across ages creates item-sampling problems for the checklist procedure and might compromise its validity (see the discussion of so-called quick probes in Chapter 13). I would conjecture that differences in print exposure would be larger in groups of phonological and surface dyslexics who were from a fairly narrow age span and thus more appropriate for the use of the checklist measures. Recently, Braten et al. (1999) supported this conjecture by finding that a group of children who were low in phonological coding skill, but high on orthographic coding skill, displayed unusually high levels of print exposure.

Although most researchers agree on a coherent theoretical interpretation of the phonological subtype, how to characterize the surface subtype theoretically is still somewhat puzzling (Castles & Coltheart, 1996). I remain skeptical, however, about linking the surface subtype to visual deficits (see Castles & Coltheart, 1996; Hayduk, Bruck, & Cavanagh, 1996; Hulme, 1988; Kruk, 1991; Stringer, 1997) or to temporal processing deficits (Chiappe et al., in press; Mody et al., 1997; Sidhu, Stringer, Chiappe, & Stanovich, 1999; Stringer & Stanovich, 2000; Studdert-Kennedy & Mody, 1995). Other viable possibilities remain, however. As argued above, one interpretation is stated primarily in terms of differences in print exposure. Another possibility is that the surface subtype relates in some way to the rate-disabled individuals identified by the double-deficit theorists and by other investigators (see Berninger, 1994; Bowers & Wolf, 1993; Levy et al., 1999; Lovett, Ransby, & Barron, 1988; Morris et al., 1998; Wolf & Bowers, 1999). I have previously speculated on individual differences in the ability to form orthographic representations (Stanovich, 1992; see also Ehri & Saltmarsh, 1995; Reitsma, 1983). A recent study by Samuelsson, Gustafson, and Ronnberg (1998) is suggestive regarding the latter idea.

The difficulties encountered in investigating the nature of orthographic processing deficits (Berninger, 1994, 1995) illustrate the problems that are encountered when trying to separate other processes from the phonological core. Phonological processing is so comprehensively intertwined with all aspects of reading (Berent & Perfetti, 1995; Frost, 1998; Perfetti, 1994) that it becomes very difficult to separate the "phonologically independent" processes that will be used in the identification of additional subtypes. This is why, although I remain confident that we will gain further knowledge of variance and subtypes beyond the phonological core, I believe that the emphasis on the phonological core in the papers in this section was essentially correct. These papers explore the basic pattern that the lumper looks to establish before introducing complications. I believe that the reading field has pretty much taken this evolutionary path. The phonological core has become the base to which theoretical complications can now be added. Additionally, investigators try to refine the knowledge of the core process by discovering its information processing and neurological underpinnings—for example, by explicating the notion of underspecified phonological representations (e.g., Elbro, 1996; Fowler, 1991; Metsala & Walley, 1998).

DIFFERENCES OUTSIDE THE CORE
AND THE PHONOLOGICAL/ORTHOGRAPHIC TRADE-OFF

There are two other important trends in the Stanovich and Siegel (1994) paper (see Chapter 8) that appear to be holding up. First, the characterization of the phonological-core variable-difference model outside of the phonological core appears to have been supported. In these more global processes (what Fodor [1983] calls "central processes"), there do seem to be differences between poor readers with high and low IQ. Siegel and I documented some of the memory and language differences in the 1994 paper. As I noted in the 1988 article (Chapter 7) and again in 1991 (see Chapter 18), these differences might well have implications for our expectancies about achievement outcomes (see Hatcher & Hulme, 1999).

Another trend highlighted in the Stanovich and Siegel (1994) paper was the indication that a different balance of phonological and orthographic skills characterizes reading-disabled children compared with younger nondisabled children reading at the same level—that reading-disabled children are relatively more impaired in phonological processing and relatively less impaired in orthographic processing. Subsequent to the the the publication of the Stanovich and Siegel (1994) article, Foorman, Francis, Fletcher, and Lynn (1996) published a paper using the continuous regression-based procedure we utilized in the 1994 paper but disputing our conclusion.

Although the amount of hindsight this time is small (scientific findings take longer than this to be digested and amalgamated; see Stanovich, 1998a), looking at the overall evidence in 1999, I think that we, rather than Foorman et al. (1996), got this one right. First, Foorman et al.'s (1996) pivotal analysis[1] was done on Woodcock Basic Reading w scores. From the regression parameters, Foorman et al. (1996) conclude that "nondisabled readers outperformed disabled readers on orthographic processing" (p. 650). A perusal of their Figure 4 indicates, however, that the regression lines are estimated from points that are about 80% nonoverlapping in the bivariate space. Nonlinear relations between orthographic processing and Woodcock Basic Reading w scores could account for the findings. Much more importantly, direct inspection of groups of subjects who actually do overlap in their w scores (i.e., who actually *are* matched on reading level) indicates that the conclusion of Foorman et al. (1996) reverses and instead the Stanovich and Siegel (1994) conclusion is supported. Between Woodcock w scores of 440 and 470 (where the groups overlap) reading-disabled children (both discrepant and nondiscrepant) score at least as high (perhaps higher) as nondisabled children. The scores of the reading-disabled children are definitely not lower, as implied in the conclusion drawn on page 650 of the Foorman et al. paper.

But independent of our interpretation of the Foorman et al. (1996) study, there probably is an even more compelling reason not to abandon the conclusion drawn by Stanovich and Siegel (1994) that reading-disabled individuals are somewhat less impaired in orthographic processing than they are in phonological processing. That reason is that the bulk of the available evidence converges with this conclusion (Castles et al., 1999; Frith & Snowling, 1983; Greenberg et al., 1997; Holligan & Johnston, 1988; Levinthal & Hornung, 1992; Olson, Kliegl, Davidson, & Foltz, 1985; Olson et al., 1989; Pennington et al., 1986; Rack, 1985; Snowling, 1980; Treiman, Goswami, & Bruck, 1990). In short, the principle of converging evidence (see Chapter 8 of Stanovich, 1998a) is operating again. It certainly is true that the evidence here is much, much less convergent than that for the phonological deficit. Nevertheless, evidence stronger than that provided by Foorman et al. (1996) will be needed to overturn it. However, new techniques for assessing individual differences in the sizes of the orthographic coding units being used during word decoding are coming online (e.g., Gottardo, Chiappe, Siegel, & Stanovich, 1999; Treiman, Mullennix, Bijeljac-Babic, & Richmond-Welty, 1995), and thus new tools may soon be applied to this controversy. Again, this theoretical and empirical disagreement will be resolved eventually by the data. As I shall discuss in Chapter 19, such a controversy provides a good model for the field of reading education which is stuck in the interminable Reading Wars. One of the lessons that can be learned from the scientific study of reading is how to settle disputes by empirical means—how investigators who begin with different theoretical views can converge on a common explanation of a phenomenon, as did Siegel and I on the discrepancy issue (see Chapter 17 for a further discussion of this example). Likewise, Foorman et al. (1996) and I will one day converge on a common view of orthographic differences—and we will do so without the rhetorical posturing or ad hominem attacks so common in the Reading Wars (see Chapter 19).

NOTE

1. Foorman et al. (1996) begin by presenting an odd set of analyses on *age*-adjusted scores when these scores are clearly inappropriate for regression analyses of the type introduced by Stanovich and Siegel (1994). I remain puzzled about why Foorman et al. (1996) imply in their Discussion section that we used such scores, when in fact we did not use age-adjusted scores as a principle covariate (as the covariate that was designed to mimic the reading-level match) in any of the analyses. A reading-level match (and its statistical equivalents such as our regression procedure) is just that—a match on reading *level*, not reading acquisition *rate* (which is what a statistical match on an age-adjusted score is).

CHAPTER 6

Assessing Phonological Awareness in Kindergarten Children

Issues of Task Comparability

with ANNE E. CUNNINGHAM and BARBARA CRAMER

$\mathbf{R}$esearchers interested in the cognitive determinants of early reading acquisition have increasingly focused on phonological awareness as a potentially important variable. There is now a substantial body of evidence indicating that tasks that in some way tap phonological awareness are moderate to strong predictors of the speed with which children acquire reading fluency in the early grades (Bradley & Bryant, 1978; Calfee, Lindamood, & Lindamood, 1973; Fox & Routh, 1976, 1980, 1983; Golinkoff, 1978; Helfgott, 1976; Jorm & Share, 1983; Liberman, 1973, 1982; Rozin & Gleitman, 1977; Treiman & Baron, 1981; Williams, 1980). The interest in this particular cognitive skill has been fueled by recent evidence indicating that the early development of phonological awareness is causally linked to rapid reading acquisition (Bradley & Bryant, 1983; Perfetti, Beck, & Hughes, 1981; Treiman & Baron, 1983; Williams, 1980).

A large number of different experimental paradigms have been used to assess phonological awareness, including rhyming tasks, phoneme segmentation tasks, matching tasks, phoneme substitution tasks, blending tasks, and phoneme counting tasks, to name just a few (see Lewkowicz, 1980, for a useful typology). The plethora of tasks, however, has made a consolidation of the knowledge gained from studies in this area very difficult. All of the tasks that have been used involve many cognitive processes (e.g., short-term memory, stimulus comparison, processing of task instructions) in addition to the phonological analysis ability that is the focus of interest. Without careful task analysis and comparison, it will remain unclear to what extent the predictive power of these tasks resides in the phonological ability or the other extraneous cognitive processes.

The present authors are not the first to recognize that a lack of direct task comparisons is the current Achilles' heel of the phonological awareness literature. After a thorough review of the existing research, Lewkowicz (1980) observed that

> there has been surprisingly little comparison, at least in print, of one phonemic awareness task with another. There has been little analysis of similarities and differences between tasks, of relative difficulty of tasks or of which tasks are most closely related to the reading process and are most likely to facilitate learning to read. In my opinion, this lack of in-depth analysis of phonemic awareness tasks and their relationship to reading has resulted in the obscuring of some important differences between the tasks, and, as a consequence, in the failure of researchers to focus on the most important tasks and questions that need to be asked about them. (pp. 686–687)

Three years later the situation remained much the same, and Backman (1983) concluded from her results that

> tasks which on the surface appear to be measuring the same phenomenon may in fact require different degrees of linguistic awareness, or may differ in their cognitive requirements. . . . We must not talk about phoneme segmentation per se in relation to reading, but segmentation within the context of a particular task. . . . Obviously, ease of understanding task requirements is intimately related to the phenomenon of "linguistic insight" we are interested in. (pp. 476–477)

Both Lewkowicz (1980) and Backman (1983) emphasized that differing cognitive requirements could lead to a divergence in the results obtained from different tasks. However, it is equally true that similar extraneous cognitive requirements could lead to a convergence of results from tasks that actually tap different aspects of phonological awareness (or that tap the same aspect to differing degrees). Actually, the literature on phonological awareness has shown considerable convergence despite the plethora of paradigms that have been used and the absence of extensive direct task comparisons. The fact that a wide variety of tasks has converged on similar conclusions in this area of research is encouraging. However, the general absence of direct comparisons between tasks in the published literature places arguments for convergence on shaky ground. Suspicion will always remain that the convergence is spurious, the result of the other cognitive and linguistic requirements of the phonological tasks. Thus, it is essential that some attempt be made to directly assess the relationships between phonological tasks and determine their degree of convergence. Otherwise, the impact of the strong results previously obtained in this research area may be muted due to lingering doubts about construct validity. Also, as Lewkowicz (1980) noted, multivariate studies of phonological awareness tasks would necessarily address another important question, that of potential task differences in predictive accuracy.

The present study attempted to address these issues. Ten different phonological tasks were administered to a group of kindergarten subjects. The tasks were of several different types, covering many of the categories (e.g., word-to-word matching, rhyme recognition, phoneme deletion, phoneme substitution, and identification of missing phoneme) included in the classification system developed by Lewkowicz (1980). Some tasks required abstraction of the initial phoneme, while others focused on the final phoneme. Finally, the critical linguistic construction that was used in the instructions to the child varied across tasks (e.g., "same," "different," "not same"). In short, the phonological task domain was widely sampled in terms of task type, location of phonological contrast, and task instructions. Whether the differing cognitive requirements of the tasks are reflected in the patterns of the performance relationships should be revealed by correlational analyses. Conversely, the same correlational analyses will give a rough indication of the degree to which these tasks tap a similar underlying construct of phonological awareness. It should be possible to detect performance convergences that are simply due to similarities in extraneous task requirements, because the latter varied between tasks to differing degrees.

The important issue of the relative predictive power of different phonological awareness tasks was addressed by obtaining a standardized measure of reading ability on the same subjects at the end of first grade. Thus, correlations between the performance on the phonological measures in kindergarten and reading achievement at the end of first grade could be assessed.

As more research attention focuses on the theoretical importance of measures of phonological awareness, practitioners will naturally question whether the relationships between these tasks and reading ability have any degree of practical utility. For example, the question of how these measures relate to other more global prereading assessment devices such as readiness tests and intelligence tests, and how all of these measures compare in predictive power, will be raised. These questions were also addressed in the present study by administering a standardized reading readiness test and a standardized general intelligence test to the sample of kindergarten subjects.

METHOD

Subjects

Fifty-eight subjects (29 males and 29 females) were recruited from three kindergarten classrooms in a predominantly middle-class elementary school. Nine subjects (4 males and 5 females) failed to follow the instructions on several tasks, leaving a total of 49 subjects for subsequent analysis. For example, several of these subjects scored zero on the substitute initial consonant and rhyme supply tasks because they gave random responses or semantic associates rather than rhymes. These subjects completed some of the other more difficult tasks, suggesting that their failure on the rhyme supply was due to a failure to understand the instructions. The status of these subjects as multivariate outliers was confirmed by using the objective methods described in Tabachnick and Fidell (1983). The mean age of the 49 subjects was 6 years and 2 months (SD = 4.4 months) at the time of testing. The children were administered a battery of 10 phonological tasks in May of the school year by the same experimenter. The prereading sections of the Metropolitan Readiness Tests (Form P, Level 2) were administered to all of the subjects. The mean prereading skills composite score was 47.9 (SD = 13.8; mean percentile rank = 47%). Forty-six of the 49 children were also administered the Otis–Lennon School Ability Test (Primary 1, Form R). The mean score on the Otis–Lennon was 37.8 (SD = 10.1), while the mean School Ability Index (IQ) was 103.8 (SD = 16.4). The two standardized measures were administered in late May and early June, following administration of the 10 phonological tasks. Thirty-one of the subjects (16 males and 15 females) were available for testing the following year. In May these children were administered the Reading Survey Test (Form JS, Primary Level 1) of the Metropolitan Achievement Tests. The mean raw score on this test was 42.3 (SD = 12.4) and the mean grade equivalent was 3.1 (SD = 1.6).

Tasks and Procedure

Ten phonological awareness tasks were individually administered to the subjects. Each task took approximately 10 min to complete and was administered on a separate day. The order of presentation was rhyme supply, rhyme choice, initial consonant same, final consonant same, strip initial consonant, substitute initial consonant, initial consonant not same, final consonant different, initial consonant different, and supply initial consonant. The subject's score on each task was the total number of correct responses, and the maximum score on each was 10. In tasks involving a multiple choice the position of the correct alternative was randomly determined and occurred with approximately equal frequency in all positions. The 10 experimental trials for each task were preceded by 3–5 practice trials during which the experimenter ensured that the child understood the task. On these trials the experimenter gave feedback on the correctness of the subject's response. In the case of an incorrect response the subjects were told the correct answer and why it was correct. Following the practice trials the subjects were told that the experimenter could no longer help them and that they were simply to try their best. Subjects were also always told that if they did not know the answer they were to guess.

Rhyme Supply

This task assessed children's ability to provide a word that rhymed with the target word. The 10 experimental words were *nose, pup, sky, toy, hill, wing, mouse, tip, note,* and *look.* The words were orally presented to the subjects. The subjects were told the experimenter would say a word aloud to them and that their task was to provide another word that rhymed or had the same ending sound as the target word. For practice, the experimenter instructed the subject to listen to the words *fish–dish.* The subjects were then told to say these words out loud. The subjects were told that both words ended with the *-ish* sound (that is, that they rhymed). Following the practice trials, the experimenter pronounced the 10 experimental words aloud to the subjects, and the subjects responded orally.

Rhyme Choice

In this task subjects were provided with the stimulus word and asked to choose 1 of 3 words that rhymed with it. The 10 experimental words were *star, mop, green, plane, clown, flash, cake, jump, box,* and *jeep.* The subjects were told to listen closely to the target word and the following 3 words. Their task was to choose a word that rhymed with the target word. The experimenter began with two explicit examples: "Listen to the word *pet.* Now say the word *pet.* Tell me which of these three words rhymes with *pet: barn, net, hand.*" The experimenter then explained to the child how he was correct or incorrect and the reasons why. Following the remaining practice trials, the 10 experimental trials were administered.

Substitute Initial Consonant

This task required subjects to isolate the initial sound of a word and then substitute a different sound to produce a new word. The 10 target words were *top, bell, lip, fed, gum, sick, pin, cat, sap,* and *cut.* The subjects were told that the experimenter was going to say a word, and that their task was to change the word by substituting the initial sound, thereby creating a different word. An example was provided by the experimenter: "If I say the word *go,* and then change the first sound by changing it to /n/ the new word will be *no.*" The experimenter then asked the subject to try to change the initial phoneme in the word *hang.* The subjects were told if they were correct or not and the reasons why. Following this example and the remaining practice trials the 10 experimental trials were administered.

Initial Consonant Same

This task consisted of 3 practice and 10 experimental multiple choice trials. The 10 experimental words were *milk, pear, fan, bone, soap, tent, leg, duck, nest*, and *key*. In the practice trials, subjects were instructed to listen closely to the beginning sound of the target word. The subjects were then instructed to say the target word aloud. The experimenter then pronounced the target word followed by 3 words. Their task was to decide which had the same initial sound as the target word.

Final Consonant Same

This task consisted of 3 practice and 10 experimental multiple choice trials. Each trial had a target word followed by 3 alternatives. The 10 experimental target words were *worm*, *cup*, *pan*, *beat*, *leaf*, *bud*, *house*, *hook*, *nail*, and *bug*. The subjects were instructed to listen closely to the target word and the 3 following words. Their task was to choose the word that shared the same ending sound as the target. A picture of the target word was provided for the subject. The picture remained in front of the subject during the trial. It was hypothesized that providing a picture of the target word would reduce memory load for the subject. This procedure, however, was followed only for this task. The experimenter provided the following example to the subject: "Say the word *meat* aloud and listen to the ending sound. If I say the word *meat* and then *fin*, *coat*, *glass*, which word would you say has the same ending sound as *meat*?" A picture of the target word was placed on the table in front of the subject when the experimenter said the word *"meat."* The experimenter then explained to the subject why the response was correct or incorrect and the remaining practice trials and the 10 experimental trials were completed.

Strip Initial Consonant

In this task subjects were required to delete the initial phoneme of a word and pronounce the embedded word that remained. This task was originally used by Bruce (1964) and Calfee, Chapman, and Venezky (1972) and adapted for this experiment. The 10 experimental words were *pink*, *told*, *man*, *nice*, *win*, *bus*, *pitch*, *car*, *hit*, and *pout*. The experimenter instructed the subjects to listen closely to the target word and then remove the first sound. The experimenter provided the example: "Listen to the word *task*. If you take away the /t/ sound, what word is left?" The subject was then told if he was correct or incorrect and why. After the remaining practice trials the 10 experimental trials were administered.

Initial Consonant Different

The subjects were told that the experimenter would read 4 words out loud to them. Their task was to listen closely to the beginning sound of each word and choose the word that had a beginning sound that was different from the other words. The experimenter instructed: "Say the words *bag*, *nine*, *beach*, and *bike*. Can you tell me which of these words had a different beginning sound—

bag, nine, beach, bike?" Following additional practice trials, the subjects were administered the 10 experimental trials. The 10 correct words were *ear, pop, hill, band, arm, give, van, cart, rice,* and *teeth.*

Initial Consonant Not Same

This task is structurally similar to the initial consonant different task except that the directions are phrased in a negative manner. The 10 experimental target words were *boy, doll, sun, kite, man, nest, fish, train, pie,* and *lamp.* The subjects were instructed to listen closely to the initial sound of the first word. The experimenter said: "I am going to say a word aloud followed by 3 more words. Your task is to tell me which word does not begin with the same sound as the first word. Say the word *mud.* Now say the words *mice, dig,* and *mouth.* Can you tell me which word did not have the same beginning sound as *mud?*" Each subject was told if their answer was correct or incorrect and the reasons why. Following the remaining practice trials the 10 experimental trials were administered.

Final Consonant Different

In this multiple choice task, subjects were asked to identify 1 of 4 words which had a final sound that was different from the others. Three practice and 10 experimental trials were administered. The 3 practice words were *rat, can,* and *log.* The 10 experimental target words were *ham, cup, leaf, flag, dress, wrist, ball, sand, rain,* and *desk.* The subjects were advised to listen closely to the 4 words the experimenter would read to them. Their task was to choose the word that had a different ending sound. For example, the experimenter said: "Listen to the following 4 words: *rat, dime, boat, mitt.* Say these words out loud. One of them has a different ending sound. Can you tell me which word has a different sound at the end of the word?" The experimenter then told the subjects when they were correct or incorrect and the reasons why. Following the 3 practice trials the subjects were informed that the experimenter could no longer help them and that if they could not choose the correct word that they should give their best guess.

Supply Initial Consonant

This task assessed the child's ability to isolate and produce the initial phoneme of a word. Subjects were orally presented a pair of words that were identical except that the initial phoneme had been deleted from the second word. The 10 experimental word pairs were *meal–eel, fill–ill, sit–it, land–and, near–ear, pair–air, bend–end, task–ask, date–ate,* and *can't–ant.* The subjects were told that they would be hearing words that were the same except for the beginning sound. For example, the experimenter said: "Say the word *cat.* Now say *at.* What sound do you hear in *cat,* that is missing from *at?*" The subjects were told the correct answer if they were unable to respond correctly. Following the remaining practice trials the 10 experimental trials were administered.

RESULTS

Descriptive statistics on each of the 10 phonological awareness measures are presented in Table 6.1. Hotelling's T, calculated with the 10 phonological tasks as the set of dependent measures, indicated no sex differences in the data ($T = 8.614$, F 1), so this variable will not be considered further. A perusal of the means reveals several patterns. The strip initial consonant task was the most difficult task. The mean score on this task was extremely low and the scores were positively skewed. The mode was zero (a score attained by 25 children), but 10 children attained a score of 8 or above. Thus, there is some indication of a bimodal distribution of responses, a pattern that has been observed before with the strip consonant task (see Calfee et al., 1972). Clearly this task exceeds the cognitive and phonological analysis capabilities of many kindergarten children. Nevertheless, the task was a moderately good predictor of first-grade reading and did correlate with other tasks that had more symmetrical distributions of responses (see below). The supply initial consonant task and both measures involving the final consonant were relatively difficult tasks (although note that the means are not directly comparable because the multiple choice nature of the latter two tasks probably restricts guessing responses).

TABLE 6.1. Phonological Awareness Measures: Descriptive Statistics

Task	Mean	SD	Skewness	Reliability	SMC	FL	Metro correlation
Strip initial consonant	2.53	3.67	1.16	.95	.59	.70	.42
Supply initial consonant	5.57	4.29	−.14	.95	.68	.79	.52
Initial consonant same	7.29	2.46	−.57	.83	.62	.76	.39
Initial consonant different	5.80	2.64	.18	.86	.71	.84	.60
Initial consonant not same	6.02	2.29	.08	.73	.74	.87	.51
Final consonant same	5.31	2.43	.46	.72	.64	.71	.40
Final consonant different	4.82	2.44	.57	.63	.68	.84	.45
Rhyme choice	7.71	1.91	−.66	.65	.35	.54	.30
Rhyme supply	8.57	1.26	−.71	.90	.20	.36	.11
Substitute initial consonant	8.63	1.33	−.77	.91	.13	.10	.09

Note. SMC = squared multiple correlation of each variable with all other variables. FL = factor loading.

Tasks where the critical sound contrast was at the beginning of the word were easier than those where the critical sound was at the end of the word. There was some statistical support for this trend. The mean in the initial consonant same task was higher than the mean in the final consonant same task, $t(48) = 5.88$, $p < .001$, and the mean in the initial consonant different task was significantly higher than the mean in the final consonant different task, $t(48) = 3.57$, $p < .01$. Marsh and Mineo (1977) also found that phoneme isolation performance was superior when the critical phonemic contrast was in the initial position, but this pattern interacted with phoneme class (continuants versus stops). A post hoc analysis of our data revealed no such interaction, error rates being very similar for continuants and stops in all tasks.

The three easiest tasks were substitute initial consonant, rhyme supply, and rhyme choice. Note that the substitute initial consonant task essentially requires the subject to produce a rhyme. It differs from the other two tasks only in the phrasing of the instructions, which do not explicitly mention rhyming. The superior performance on the three rhyming tasks confirms previous research and the reports of teachers that children often enter school with rhyming skills and that it is the easiest auditory analysis task to teach (see Jusczyk, 1977; Lewkowicz, 1980). Indeed, there is strong evidence that performance on these three tasks was at ceiling. The rhyming tasks had the three smallest standard deviations and the distributions of all three were characterized by negative skewness. The distribution of responses on the substitute initial consonant task illustrates the ceiling effect. The modal score was 10 (achieved by 16 of the subjects), and the next most frequent score was 9 (achieved by 14 subjects). The ceiling effects apparent in the three rhyming tasks probably account for the fact that these tasks were poor predictors of later reading achievement and were only weakly related to the other phonological awareness measures (see below). Essentially, they suffer from extremely restricted ranges, as indicated by the standard deviations in Table 6.1, and thus will necessarily fail to correlate with other variables.

The split-half reliability (Spearman–Brown corrected) of each task is also presented in Table 6.1. In general, the reliabilities of the 10 tasks ranged from low-moderate to high. The mean task reliability was .81. Of course, the magnitudes of the correlations displayed by a given task are limited by the reliability of the task, and this fact should be remembered when interpreting the obtained correlations. In general, however, a consideration of the reliabilities does not attenuate the conclusions drawn here, and in many cases consideration of the reliabilities serves to strengthen the apparent trends. For example, some tasks that were good predictors and that were strongly related to other tasks were only moderately reliable (initial consonant not same), while others that displayed weak relationships were highly reliable (rhyme supply and substitute initial consonant, although the high reliability may also be due to the ceiling effects in the performance on these tasks).

The interrelationships among the phonological awareness tasks are displayed in Table 6.2 which is a correlation matrix of the 10 measures. All cor-

TABLE 6.2. Intercorrelations of All Tasks

Task	2	3	4	5	6	7	8	9	10
1. Strip initial consonant	.49	.45	.57	.62	.66	.66	.30	.18	-.02
2. Supply initial consonant		.62	.68	.73	.41	.69	.47	.35	.01
3. Initial consonant same			.62	.74	.53	.60	.48	.20	.09
4. Initial consonant different				.70	.68	.72	.40	.28	.17
5. Initial consonant not same					.55	.71	.44	.34	.11
6. Final consonant same						.61	.39	.24	.06
7. Final consonant different							.40	.26	-.02
8. Rhyme choice								.32	.16
9. Rhyme supply									.13
10. Substitute initial consonant									

relations larger than .28 are significant at the .05 level. The major data pattern is apparent from a visual inspection of the matrix. The seven nonrhyming tasks show moderate to strong relationships with each other. The substitute initial consonant task does not correlate with anything. The rhyme choice and rhyme supply tasks show weak correlations with the other variables. This pattern is quantified in Table 6.1, which displays the squared multiple correlations (SMCs) of each variable as a dependent variable regressed on the other nine. The values for the seven nonrhyming tasks were very high, approaching their reliabilities in some cases. The seven nonrhyming tasks appear to have much common variance. In contrast, the SMCs of the rhyming tasks were very low (considering the number of predictor variables), ranging from a high of .35 for rhyme choice to a low of .13 for substitute initial consonant. Basically, the extremely restricted range of the scores on the rhyming tasks prevents them from correlating with anything.

The uniformly moderate to high correlations among the seven nonrhyming tasks was somewhat surprising given their different cognitive requirements and moderate reliabilities in some cases. The mean correlation between these seven variables was .62, which is quite high considering that their mean reliability is .81. Also surprising was the relative lack of clusters among the correlations of the seven nonrhyming tasks. The variables were relatively uniformly intercorrelated. These visual impressions from Table 6.2 were confirmed by a principle factor analysis carried out on the data of all 10 tasks. With squared multiple correlations serving as initial commonality estimates, only the first factor exceeded the eigenvalue > 1 criterion (the eigenvalue of the second factor was .398). This factor accounted for 47.8% of the total variance in the variables. A stable solution was reached after four iterations, and the factor loadings from this solution are displayed in Table 6.1. Predictably from the pattern of correlations in Table 6.2, the seven nonrhyming tasks had high loadings on the first principle factor, the rhyme choice task had a moderate loading, and the other two rhyming tasks had low loadings.

The last column of Table 6.1 displays the correlation between each of the phonological measures and the score on the Reading Survey Test of the Metropolitan Achievement Tests that was administered at the end of first grade. Correlations larger than .35 are significant at the .05 level. All seven of the nonrhyming tasks displayed significant correlations of moderate strength. Some idea of the relative magnitude of the difference in performance on the phonological tasks between readers of different abilities is provided by Table 6.3. There the 31 subjects who were assessed in the first grade have been split into a group of 16 less-skilled readers and a group of 15 skilled readers based on their score on the Reading Survey Test of the Metropolitan. The scores of the two groups were significantly different at the .001 level. The mean grade equivalent of the less-skilled group was 1.9 and the mean grade equivalent of the skilled group was 4.3. From Table 6.3 it is apparent that all of the measures except two of the rhyming tasks displayed significant differences between the two groups. It is interesting that the skilled group is near ceiling even on some of the nonrhyming tasks, whereas the performance of the less-skilled group is far from ceiling on any of these tasks. The median split thus gives some indication of the large performance disparity that is present on some of the nonrhyming tasks.

In attempting to assess how to best characterize the ability of the phonological tasks to predict first-grade reading levels, it is useful for comparative purposes to consider the results involving the Metropolitan Readiness Tests and Otis–Lennon IQ, two omnibus measures of cognitive skills that were also administered to these children in kindergarten. The prereading readiness test correlated .52 with first-grade reading ability and the correlation between the raw score on the Otis–Lennon and reading ability was .25. Thus, three of the

TABLE 6.3. Mean Scores on the Phonological Awareness Tasks as a Function of Reader Skill

Task	Skilled	Less Skilled	$t(29)$
Strip initial consonant	4.73	1.13	2.80*
Supply initial consonant	9.27	4.69	3.81*
Initial consonant same	9.20	7.00	3.43*
Initial consonant different	8.47	4.75	5.78*
Initial consonant not same	8.07	5.56	4.52*
Final consonant same	7.00	4.31	3.62*
Final consonant different	6.93	4.06	4.44*
Rhyme choice	9.07	7.44	2.82*
Rhyme supply	9.00	8.75	0.57
Substitute initial consonant	8.87	8.38	0.92

*$p < .01$.

seven nonrhyming phonological measures (each containing 10 items and taking less than 10 min to administer) predicted first-grade reading ability as well as a standardized readiness test containing six different subsections, and all of the nonrhyming phonological measures were superior to an omnibus IQ test. The mean correlation between performance on the seven nonrhyming phonological tasks and performance on the Metropolitan prereading readiness section was .68. The analogous mean correlation with the Otis–Lennon score was .55.

The trends already described were confirmed in a somewhat different way by regression analyses. A stepwise regression analysis with first-grade Metropolitan score as the dependent variable and the 10 phonological variables as predictors confirmed the essential redundancy and large variance overlap in the phonological measures. After initial consonant different and initial consonant not same were entered into the equation, no other variable made a significant contribution to explaining reading variance. Together, these two variables accounted for 66.2% of the variance in reading ability (adjusted R^2 = .638). Both regression coefficients were significant in the final analysis. The relatively high proportion of variance explained was not primarily due to the optimization criteria of the stepwise regression. The median proportion of variance explained by the 21 different pairs of nonrhyming phonological tasks was 57.6%. This figure is comparable to the 59.1% of the variance in first-grade reading ability that is accounted for when both the Otis–Lennon and Metropolitan readiness test were employed as predictors. An additional hierarchical regression analysis indicated that after the two phonological measures had been entered into the regression equation, the two standardized measures, when entered as a set, did not account for a significant additional proportion of variance.

DISCUSSION

Descriptively, the 10 phonological tasks broke down into three groups. Three tasks that required a rhyming response were very easy. Ceiling effects were apparent on these three tasks. The distribution of responses was negatively skewed and the variance was highly restricted. As a result of the restriction of range, these three tasks displayed low correlations with the other phonological tasks and with first-grade reading ability. One task (strip initial consonant) was extremely difficult. The distribution of responses on this variable was positively skewed and displayed a tendency toward bimodality. The other six measures were of intermediate difficulty and had distributions of responses that were more nearly symmetrical.

The seven nonrhyming tasks were highly interrelated. Despite the differing task requirements, there was every indication that these tasks were tapping a similar construct. The mean correlation between the seven tasks was quite high, considering the reliability of the measures. The squared multiple correlations for each of these variables were also quite high. The visual impression that the correlations in Table 6.2 are uniformly moderate and do not tend to cluster was confirmed by the factor analysis, which extracted only one factor upon which each of the seven variables loaded highly. Regression analyses predicting first-grade reading ability confirmed the essential redundancy of these seven variables. Stepwise regression stopped after only two variables had entered the equation. The proportion of variance accounted for did not change appreciably when pairs of variables not chosen by the stepwise procedure were used as predictors. Although caution in interpreting multivariate statistics is always advised when the subjects-to-variables ratio is in the range employed in our investigation, the convergence of all of the analyses suggests that the data patterns are probably robust.

Performance on each of the seven nonrhyming tasks was related to first-grade reading ability. The absolute magnitude of the performance difference between skilled and less-skilled readers is apparent in Table 6.3 and in many cases is quite large, considering that the partitioning represents not an extreme groups comparison but instead is a median split. At the end of kindergarten the skilled readers were near ceiling on several tasks, while the less-skilled readers were getting barely half of the items correct.

The correlational data also suggest that the seven nonrhyming tasks are quite impressive predictors of first-grade reading ability. All of the correlations with Metropolitan scores were significant and at least of moderate strength. The magnitude of the correlations must be considered in the context of the reliability of the tasks (each administered in a very short time span) and in the context of the type of correlations that are obtained when more comprehensive and carefully standardized measures of cognitive skills are employed. From this standpoint, the diagnosticity of the phonological measures was truly impressive. All seven nonrhyming measures correlated with first-grade reading more strongly than did a standardized IQ test (see Stanovich, Cunningham, and Feeman [1984a], where a similar result obtained when all the tests were administered at the end of first grade). Three of the phonological tasks displayed correlations with first-grade reading as large as those obtained from a standardized readiness test that was designed to tap a variety of reading-related cognitive skills. A stepwise regression of the Metropolitan scores on the phonological variables indicated that the latter explained 66.2% of the variance. When each possible pair of nonrhyming phonological measures served as predictors, the median proportion of variance explained was 57.6%. This compares to 59.1% explained by the Metropolitan readiness test and Otis–Lennon IQ in combination.

The results of this investigation bode well for the future use of phonological awareness measures in both research and educational settings. The wide variety of tasks that have been employed appear to be tapping a similar ability. Results from different investigations are probably not too contaminated by disparate task requirements. In fact, the degree of task convergence was quite a surprise to the present investigators who entered upon this investigation fully prepared to uncover the fact that the variance introduced by differing cognitive requirements would tend to obscure the underlying phonological abilities that were being tapped and would lead to vastly different patterns of task performance.

Finally, the uniformly moderate predictive accuracy of each task, coupled with the impressive predictive power when sets of these measures are used together, is an encouraging sign as regards future practical applications. While we must reiterate the caution that the relationship between reading ability and phonological awareness seems to be characterized by reciprocal causation (see Baron & Treiman, 1980; Ehri, 1979; Morais, Cary, Alegria, & Bertelson, 1979; Perfetti et al., 1981), the causal connection at the earliest stages of reading acquisition is probably most strong from phonological awareness to increased reading acquisition (Bradley & Bryant, 1983; Treiman & Baron, 1983).

CHAPTER 7

Explaining the Differences between the Dyslexic and the Garden-Variety Poor Reader

The Phonological-Core Variable-Difference Model

The field of learning disabilities (LD) is contentious and it has a checkered history. It is commonplace to bemoan the state of confusion and disagreement in the field. Here, however, I wish to focus on a positive trend that is discernible in current research. There has recently been an increasing recognition that the field in some sense "got ahead of itself," that educational practice simply "took off" before a thorough investigation of certain foundational assumptions had been carried out. Thus, much recent research has a "get back to basics" feel to it, as researchers double back to retrace crucial empirical and theoretical steps that were skipped during the mad rush to implement what we now know were nascent hypotheses rather than established empirical facts.

The signs that the field is making an attempt to establish itself on a firmer foundation are numerous. NICHD is supporting long overdue large-scale epidemiological and subtype investigations. The statistical and psychometric complexities of defining disabilities on the basis of behavioral and cognitive discrepancies are becoming more widely understood and are beginning to affect practice (McKinney, 1987; Reynolds, 1985).

The development I would like to focus on here is the recent flurry of work that goes back to the most critical foundational assumption underlying the learning disability concept: the concept of qualitative differences in cognitive/behavioral characteristics. I will confine the remaining discussion to reading disability—the most prevalent type of learning disability and also my particular area of expertise.

From the beginning, what has fueled both theoretical interest in dyslexia (and/or reading disability, specific reading retardation, etc.; the terms are used interchangeably here) and has justified differential educational treatment has been the assumption that the reading difficulties of the dyslexic stem from problems different from those characterizing the "garden variety" poor reader (to use Gough & Tunmer's [1986] term); or, alternatively, if they stem from the same factors, that the degree of severity is so extreme for the dyslexic that it constitutes, in effect, a qualitative difference.

I should mention as an aside that I view the interminable semantic debates in developmental psychology over what constitutes a qualitative as opposed to a quantitative difference as utterly futile and scientifically useless. Alternative terms would do equally well and probably would not trigger what are essentially linguistic debates. Nevertheless, I use the terms for convenience, ease of communication, and to make clear the connections with previous research.

What *is* important is the experimental contrasts that have operationalized the idea of qualitative difference and/or differential causation in the literature. This operationalization has been dominated by two different designs. One is the reading-level (RL) match design, where an older group of dyslexic children is matched on reading level with a younger group of nondyslexic children. The cognitive characteristics and reading subskills of the two groups are then compared. The logic here is fairly straightforward. If the reading subskills and cognitive characteristics of the two groups do not match, then it would seem that they are arriving at their similar reading levels via different routes, and this would support the idea of differential causation. In contrast, if the reading subskill profiles of the two groups are identical, this would seem to undermine the rationale for the differential educational treatment of dyslexic children and for their theoretical differentiation. If dyslexic children are reading just like any other child who happens to be at their reading level, and are using the same cognitive skills to do so, why should we consider their reading behavior to be so special?

The second major design—one pertinent not only to theoretical issues but also to the educational politics of LD—is to compare dyslexic children with children of the same age who are reading at the same level, but who are not labeled dyslexic. (Adapting the terminology of Gough and Tunmer [1986], this design will be termed the "garden-variety control" design.) Again, the inferences drawn are relatively straightforward: if the reading subskills and cognitive characteristics of the two groups do not match, then it would seem that the two groups are arriving at their similar reading levels via different routes. In contrast, if the reading subskill profiles of the two groups are identical, this would certainly undermine the rationale for the differential educational treatment of dyslexic children and would make dyslexic children considerably less interesting theoretically. As Fredman and Stevenson (1988) state, if "there is no clear distinction between the groups in terms of how they read, then the practice of identifying a special group of poor readers for special attention may no longer be necessary" (p. 105).

Unfortunately, the results of research employing both of these designs have been inconsistent. Empirically, there are reading-level match studies that have revealed similar processing profiles (Beech & Harding, 1984; Treiman & Hirsh-Pasek, 1985) and those that have identified differences (Baddeley, Ellis, Miles, Lewis, 1982; Bradley & Bryant, 1978; Kochnower, Richardson, & DiBenedetto, 1983; Olson, Kliegl, Davidson, & Foltz, 1985; Snowling, 1980; Snowling, Stackhouse, & Rack, 1986). Similarly, garden-variety comparisons have supported qualitative similarity (Fredman & Stevenson, 1988; Taylor, Satz, & Friel, 1979) and difference (Jorm, Share, Maclean, & Matthews, 1986; Rutter & Yule, 1975; Silva, McGee, & Williams, 1985).

The mixed results have troubled many in the field because they relate to some of the foundational assumptions of the concept of dyslexia as it is used in both research investigations and in educational practice. Indeed, these unresolved issues have provoked Andrew Ellis (1985) to ask, in an emperor-has-no-clothes fashion, "Is it worth studying dyslexia?" (p. 199)—and to further press the point:

> Does applying all the exclusionary tests discussed earlier to a group of poor readers in order to obtain a sample of high-grade, refined dyslexics actually yield a sample whose reading problems are qualitatively different from those of non-dyslexic rejects? Surprisingly this question seems to have received hardly any attention at all. . . . No one, it seems, has ever shown that the initial laborious screening is necessary in the sense that it produces a population of individuals whose reading characteristics are different from the great mass of poor readers. (pp. 199–200)

Ellis' use of the word "surprisingly" alludes to the point mentioned earlier—that the field of learning disabilities expanded and grew in virtual absence of the critical data needed to test its foundational assumptions. This situation has only recently begun to be remedied by researchers employing the two designs that I described above.

Unfortunately, as was mentioned, the results have been somewhat equivocal. It has not always been possible to differentiate the performance of dyslexic children from garden-variety poor readers or from younger reading-level controls. Thus, the field still invites skeptical questioning like that of Ellis, and challenges such as "it may be timely to formulate a concept of reading disability which is independent of any consideration of IQ. Unless it can be shown to have some predictive value for the nature of treatment or treatment outcome, considerations of IQ should be discarded in discussions of reading difficulties" (Share, McGee, & Silva, 1989, p. 12) or:

> If the dyslexic readers differ from poor readers along the same dimensions that differentiate poor readers from good, it cannot be concluded that the dyslexic

readers' performance is due to decoding processes specific to this group. Hence the results fail to provide evidence for the kind of qualitative differences between groups entailed by the standard view. ... If a term is to be reserved for those children who perform at the lowest end of the continuum, we suggest that it be something other than "dyslexic" or "reading disabled," which carry other connotations. Perhaps simply "very poor readers" would do. (Seidenberg, Bruck, Fornarolo, & Backman, 1986, pp. 79–80)

THE DEVELOPMENTAL LAG MODEL

One notable theoretical attempt to salvage the dyslexia concept has been the characterization of reading-disabled children as not qualitatively different, but as suffering from a developmental lag in reading-related cognitive processes. The developmental lag notion has a venerable history in the psychology of mental retardation (see Zigler, 1969). Its theoretical importance in the LD literature resides in the fact that, unlike the deficit models that emphasize qualitative difference, lag models predict that when older disabled and younger nondisabled children are matched on reading level, their performance should not differ on any cognitive tasks causally related to reading (see Fletcher, 1981). Thus, at least some of the results that are problematic for those wishing to distinguish dyslexic children (e.g., the similarities in some RL-control studies) are accommodated by the developmental lag theory.

However, there are several problems involved in conceptualizing and testing the lag notion. For example, predictions derived from the lag hypothesis depend critically on how the matching on reading level is done. It is somewhat surprising to find that researchers have been quite inconsistent in specifying exactly what "reading level" refers to in this literature or, for that matter, in the research employing garden-variety controls. Specifically, some investigations have matched children with reading comprehension tests (e.g., Bruck, 1988; Seidenberg, Bruck, Fornarolo, & Backman, 1985), while others have matched the children on word recognition skills (e.g., Olson et al., 1985; Treiman & Hirsh-Pasek, 1985). And finally, some have matched children using a composite of both word recognition and reading comprehension (Bloom, Wagner, Reskin, & Bergman, 1980; Jorm et al., 1986). Unfortunately, all of these investigations have been referred to as reading-level match studies, thus substantially increasing the difficulty of integrating the research findings in this area. It has been insufficiently recognized that the results and interpretation of an RL-match design may vary depending upon whether the matching is done with a comprehension test or with a word recognition test. We have suggested (Stanovich, Nathan, & Zolman, 1988) that future investigators refer to their designs as either decoding-level matches or comprehension-level matches.

The necessity of differentiating decoding-level (DL) matches from comprehension-level (CL) matches illustrates that researchers have really been asking two different questions. A study matching on comprehension is investigating whether the relative contributions of the subskills determining comprehension ability is the same in skilled and less-skilled readers. Studies that match subjects purely on the basis of decoding ability are asking the same question within the more restricted domain of the word recognition module; that is, they are asking whether the two groups perform equally on word recognition tests for the same or different reasons.

Consider, for example, the implications for the predictions derived from the developmental lag hypothesis if the matching in an RL study is done with a comprehension test and dyslexics—identified by strict discrepancy criteria— are the poor reader group. The two groups will presumably be close in intelligence. Of course, similar intelligence test scores at different ages mean different things in terms of the raw score or absolute level of performance on a given test or index of ability. Thus, when older dyslexics are matched with younger children progressing normally in reading, the former will have higher raw scores on the intelligence measure. It should then also be the case that the dyslexics will score higher on any cognitive task that is correlated with the raw score on the intelligence test, and of course there are a host of such tasks. This has implications for the expected outcome in a CL design.

The argument goes as follows. The best candidates for the critical loci of reading disability (see Stanovich, 1986b, 1988a) are tasks tapping a "vertical" faculty (i.e., processes operating in a specific domain; see Fodor, 1983) that is closely associated with reading but relatively dissociated from intelligence. According to the lag model, dyslexics lag in the development of certain vertical faculties and, as a result, their reading progress also lags. But consider that on any "horizontal faculty" cognitive processes (those operating across a variety of domains), like metacognitive awareness, problem solving, and higher-level language skills, the dyslexic should outperform the younger children (due to a higher mental age). However, when the reading test is a comprehension test, rather than a word recognition measure, the comprehension requirements of the test will implicate many of these higher-level processes. Thus, the psychometric constraints imposed by the matching in a CL investigation should result in a pattern that I have previously characterized as "compensatory processing" (Stanovich, Nathan, & Vala-Rossi, 1986).

The compensatory processing hypothesis begins by assuming the importance of phonological processing skills in early reading development (Bradley & Bryant, 1985; Liberman, 1982; Mann, 1986; Stanovich, 1986b, 1988a; Williams, 1984). From this assumption, and the psychometric constraints mentioned above, it follows that a rigorously defined sample of reading-disabled children should display performance inferior to the younger CL-matched children on phonological analysis and phonological recoding skills, but should simultaneously display superior vocabulary, real-world knowledge, and/or strategic abilities (i.e., superior performance on other variables that should be correlated with the raw score on the IQ test). The similar overall level of comprehension ability in the two groups presumably obtains because the dyslexic children use these other skills and knowledge sources to compensate for seriously deficient phonological processing skills. The key method-ological point is that in a CL match—even if a qualitatively similar develop-mental lag in a specific process is accounting for the reading difficulty of the dyslexic—we should not expect their performance to match CL controls on the critical causal processes. Such a prediction, commonly derived from the lag hypothesis, does not follow when the design is a CL match.

THE DEVELOPMENTAL LAG HYPOTHESIS
AND THE GARDEN-VARIETY POOR READER

The situation is different when the lag hypothesis is applied to CL compari-sons involving less-skilled readers defined simply on the basis of reading abil-ity relative to age. Such children are not statistically precluded from matching the complete cognitive performance profile of younger children who read at the same level. It is thus possible that population differences are the source of some of the empirical discrepancies in RL designs. These studies, like many in the dyslexia/LD literature, often fail to obtain a close IQ match between the dyslexic and nondisabled groups (Stanovich, 1986a; Torgesen & Dice, 1980). According to the hypotheses outlined here, any mismatch on IQ in a CL study will tend to change the pattern of results.

   With respect to the specifically disabled reader, I have argued that the in-terrelations of the processes that determine comprehension are different for the two groups in a CL match. However, it is important to note that even if compensatory processing does explain the similar levels of comprehension, this does not necessarily guarantee the applicability of an analogous explana-tion of similar levels of decoding in a DL match. That is, it is perfectly possible that the comprehension ability of disabled readers is determined by compensa-tory processing (relative to younger CL controls), but that the operation of their word recognition modules is similar (in terms of regularity effects, ortho-graphic processing, context effects, etc.) when compared to younger DL con-trols. (Note that from the compensatory hypothesis it follows that the DL-match controls for an older disabled group of readers will not completely overlap with the disabled group's CL controls.)

   Thus, in the case of the CL match, the finding of similar profiles across a wide variety of reading-related tasks is most likely to be observed with gar-den-variety poor readers. Such a finding would have implications for our un-derstanding of specific reading disability, because it follows that when one of these groups (garden-variety vs. dyslexic poor readers) displays a profile match in a broad-based CL study, the other is logically precluded from doing so. In short, if we could nail down one of the possible data patterns in one of the populations of interest, the decreasing degrees of freedom would go a long way toward constraining further theoretical speculation. This, then, is the the-oretical background that motivates the question we have asked in the research to be reported: Do garden-variety poor readers show matching profiles in a multivariate CL match that probes a variety of reading-related cognitive skills? I will report on two separate CL comparisons that are defined by a longitudinal research design.

A GARDEN-VARIETY CL MATCH

Our investigation (Stanovich, Nathan, & Vala-Rossi, 1986; Stanovich, Nathan, & Zolman, 1988) began as a multivariate study of the reading-related cognitive subskills of third- and fifth-grade children. The far left column of Table 7.1 displays the variables in this investigation. The main criterion variable was the score on the Reading Survey Test of the Metropolitan Achievement Tests, which is a test of reading comprehension. The Peabody Picture Vocabulary Test was employed as a measure of receptive vocabulary. Two measures of phonological sensitivity were employed: a rhyme production task and the odd-sound-out task popularized by Bradley and Bryant (1978, 1985). Response time, as well as errors, was assessed on these two tasks in an attempt to determine whether, for children of this age, speed might have a diagnosticity that accuracy lacks due to ceiling effects. In addition, it was thought that the speed instructions might serve to create more errors in the tasks and thus preclude ceiling effects that would ordinarily occur with children this old.

Discrete-trial letter- and picture-naming tasks were included because previous investigators (e.g., Denckla & Rudel, 1976; Wolf, 1984) have linked deficiencies in naming speed and accuracy to reading problems. Pseudoword naming, an indicator of phonological recoding ability and potent predictor of reading ability at all levels, is associated with three variables in Table 7.1. Since both accuracy and speed have tended to be diagnostic, both were assessed. In addition, overall pseudoword naming skill was assessed by combining z-score indices for both time and accuracy into a composite z-score variable. Word naming was assessed under two conditions: with and without a related prior context (here termed the neutral and related conditions). These two conditions were administered using the contextual priming methodology that Richard West and I have utilized extensively (see Stanovich & West, 1983a; West & Stanovich, 1978, 1982, 1986). A derived contextual facilitation variable was constructed by simply subtracting the mean time for word naming with related contexts from the mean time for word naming with neutral contexts.

Table 7.1 displays the intercorrelations among all of the variables for the third-grade children above the diagonal and for the fifth-grade children below the diagonal. Although there are many interesting relationships here, I will draw attention only to the top row, where the correlations with the Metropolitan scores are displayed. The strongest predictors of reading comprehension are scores on the Peabody and word naming times (particularly in related contexts). The phonological sensitivity tasks and pseudoword naming errors are

TABLE 7.1. Intercorrelations of All Variables

Variable	1	2	3	4	5	6	7	8	9	10	11	12	13	14
1. Metropolitan		.76*	-.50*	-.17	-.44*	-.02	-.07	-.18	-.16	-.45*	-.33*	-.72*	-.53*	.47*
2. PPVT[a]	.64*		-.48*	-.10	-.25	-.02	-.08	.00	.03	-.37*	-.15	-.51*	-.22	.59*
3. Rhyme production errors	-.43*	-.37*		.29*	.43*	.29*	.00	.12	-.25	.42*	.00	.50*	.35*	-.37*
4. Rhyme production time	-.29*	-.26	.24		.21	.06	-.20	-.14	.01	.28	.14	.20	.29*	.10
5. Oddity errors	-.38*	-.36*	.42*	.33*		.36*	-.02	.25	-.04	.42*	.16	.50*	.45*	-.19
6. Oddity time	-.29*	-.14	.30*	-.06	.13		.16	.15	.01	.22	.11	.26	.23	.11
7. Letter-naming time	-.30*	-.42*	.41*	.16	-.04	.16		.25	-.09	.02	-.06	.13	.00	-.25
8. Picture-naming time	-.38*	-.40*	.30*	.07	.18	.33*	.49*		-.15	-.16	-.20	.10	.00	-.20
9. Pseudoword-naming time	-.76*	-.54*	.67*	.30*	.30*	.31*	.43*	.48*		.23	.89*	.27	.33*	.06
10. Pseudoword-naming errors	-.52*	-.46*	.74*	.26	.42*	.18	.36*	.38*	.72*		.65*	.64*	.67*	-.08
11. Pseudoword z-score	-.73*	-.55*	.73*	.31*	.36*	.29*	.43*	.48*	.97*	.86*		.51*	.57*	.01
12. Word naming—related contexts	-.57*	-.36*	.34*	.15	.14	-.02	.27	.40*	.67*	.52*	.67*		.85*	-.45*
13. Word naming—neutral contexts	-.71*	-.53*	.61*	.23	.31*	.28*	.46*	.48*	.91*	.67*	.89*	.80*		.08
14. Contextual facilitation	-.36*	-.35*	.53*	.17	.30*	.48*	.37*	.22	.53*	.36*	.51*	-.11	.51*	

Note. Correlations for the third-grade children are above the diagonal, and correlations for the fifth-grade children are below the diagonal.
[a]PPVT = Peabody Picture Vocabulary Test.
* $p < .05$.

101

also moderate predictors. The far left column of correlations reveals similar, but not identical, relationships for the fifth-grade children. Here, every variable displayed a statistically significant relationship with reading ability, the strongest correlations involving pseudoword and word naming, in addition to the Peabody.

Table 7.2 presents the data of greatest interest. Here, the children in each grade are partitioned into skilled and less-skilled readers, and the mean on each variable is presented for each group. Importantly, the partitioning was done so that the skilled third-grade children and the less-skilled fifth-grade children formed a comprehension-level match, both obtaining similar grade equivalent scores on the Metropolitan (5.2 and 5.1, respectively). The critical comparisons are thus represented in the second and third columns from the left. A statistical test of the means for each variable for the CL-matched groups is presented in the far right column.

The results of the CL comparisons are easily summarized. The performance patterns of these two groups were remarkably convergent. They differed significantly on only one of the 13 variables listed in Table 7.2. The performance of the two groups was virtually identical on the Peabody, rhyme production errors, oddity errors, oddity response time, picture naming, pseudoword z-score, word naming speed in both related and neutral contexts, and contextual facilitation score. The fifth-grade children were 97 msec faster on the rhyme production task, but this difference was not significant. The fifth-grade students were also somewhat faster at pseudoword naming (again, not significantly so), but there are indications that this difference may be due to differential speed/accuracy trade-off criteria. Although the fifth-grade readers were somewhat faster at pseudoword naming, they made more errors than the third-grade readers. Consistent with the idea of a conservative criterion among the skilled third graders was the finding that skill differences within this grade were large in the error rates (3.43 vs. 1.44) but small in the naming times (984 msec vs. 956 msec). Given a possible difference in speed/accuracy criteria in the two age groups, the best comparison of performance on pseudowords is the z-score variable, where both performance indices are combined. On this variable the two CL-matched groups were very similar.

Thus, only one variable—letter naming time—differentiated the two groups. This variable is one that has been shown to track age much more strongly than reading ability in previous investigations (Jackson & Biemiller, 1985; Stanovich, Feeman, & Cunningham, 1983), and so its statistical significance in a CL match is predictable and empirically convergent. With this one exception, the reading-related cognitive performance profiles of these two groups of readers were highly similar. This pattern of performance similarities is consistent with a developmental lag model of the reading skill deficits displayed by the less-skilled fifth-grade children that extends over rather broad cognitive domains. Cognitively, they resemble younger children who are at the same stage of reading acquisition.

Two years later we conducted another similar investigation that had some

TABLE 7.2. Means for Each Task as a Function of Grade and Skill

Variable	Less-skilled third grade	Skilled third grade	Less-skilled fifth grade	Skilled fifth grade	Grade $F(1, 60)$	Skill $F(1, 60)$	Interaction $F(1, 60)$	Skilled third grade vs. less-skilled fifth grade $t(34)$
PPVT[a]	64.8	78.0	78.6	92.4	38.68*	35.40*	0.02	−0.26
Rhyme production errors	2.93	1.06	1.33	0.43	9.62*	15.03*	1.83	−0.60
Rhyme production time	1117	1050	953	937	5.92*	0.51	0.20	1.39
Oddity errors	6.71	4.61	4.89	3.71	4.49*	6.51*	0.52	−0.33
Oddity time	693	584	563	482	3.67	2.50	0.05	0.27
Letter-naming time	581	576	518	497	25.96*	0.81	0.32	3.16*
Picture-naming time	829	756	771	702	3.70	5.97*	0.01	−0.39
Pseudoword-naming time	984	956	870	696	13.81*	4.03*	2.13	1.12
Pseudoword-naming errors	3.43	1.44	2.11	0.64	3.67	9.75*	0.22	−0.88
Pseudoword z-score	0.64	0.12	−0.11	−1.14	13.42*	8.09*	0.87	0.55
Word naming—related contexts	672	508	494	463	30.54*	23.15*	10.63*	0.59
Word naming—neutral contexts	763	642	624	549	28.55*	20.08*	1.13	0.70
Contextual facilitation	92	134	130	86	0.11	0.01	8.14*	0.26

[a]PPVT = Peabody Picture Vocabulary Test.
* $p < .05$.

new design features (Stanovich et al., 1988). First, we tested children in three grades—third, fifth, and seventh—and formed a three-group CL match spanning all three grades. Virtually all such designs in the current literature involve only two-group comparisons. Embedded within this new multivariate investigation was a longitudinal follow-up of the third- and fifth-grade children in the previous investigation, now fifth and seventh graders, respectively. These children, plus additional children not tested before, formed part of the larger sample in the second investigation. This second testing enabled us to examine a situation virtually unreported in the literature and one with some interesting theoretical implications: namely, a longitudinal comparison of groups of children who, two years earlier, were CL-matched.

The Metropolitan Reading Survey Test was again the criterion reading measure. The tasks that were carried over into the follow-up study were the Peabody, letter naming, rhyming, pseudoword naming, word recognition, and contextual facilitation. The oddity task and picture naming were eliminated. Replacing them were several new tasks and variables dictated by developments in reading research and theory. Motivated by Cohen's work (e.g., Cohen, 1982; Cohen & Netley, 1981; Cohen, Netley, & Clarke, 1984) showing differential linkages between various types of memory tasks and reading ability, we adapted two memory tasks—one relatively nonstrategic and the other intended to be strategy loaded—for use in a multivariate battery like this one. The nonstrategic task was an adaptation of the running serial memory task investigated by Cohen and Netley (1981). The speed and unpredictability of the end of the stimulus sequence serve to preclude the use of memory strategies in the task. The strategic memory task was an adaptation of Brown's (1972) "keeping track" task, judged to be relatively strategy-loaded.

In this investigation the words named under neutral contextual conditions were subdivided in order to allow us to examine another variable. Half of the stimuli were regular words having common spelling-to-sound correspondences and half were exception words having uncommon spelling-to-sound correspondences (stimuli were chosen from those used in the investigation of Treiman & Hirsh-Pasek, 1985). Some recent studies (e.g., Backman, Bruck, Hebert, & Seidenberg, 1984; Manis, 1985; Morrison, 1984, 1987a; Waters, Seidenberg, & Bruck, 1984) have indicated that more skilled readers may display smaller spelling-to-sound regularity effects, presumably because of greater reliance on visual/orthographic mechanisms to mediate lexical access. Several theorists have viewed regularity effects as a window on the mechanisms operating in the word recognition module. Thus, regularity effects are the type of indicator one wants when comparing children of different ages who have arrived at similar levels of reading ability.

A final new measure was an articulation speed task adapted from the work of Hulme, Thomson, Muir, and Lawrence (1984). These investigators have linked articulation speed to memory span and Manis (1985) has observed a difference of 50 msec in production latency (the time to initiate the pronunciation of a known word) between disabled and nondisabled readers. Theoretically, the recent emphasis on the critical importance of the operation of the phonological module in the development of individual differences in reading (Liberman & Shankweiler, 1985; Mann, 1986; Stanovich, 1986b) also motivates an interest in articulation speed. While no theorist believes that the critical differences are actually located at the articulatory level, it could be that articulation speed taps into the module in a way that would make it act as a marker variable for phonological problems at deeper levels (see also Catts, 1986).

Table 7.3 contains a listing of all the variables that were analyzed along with the means for each of six groups defined by the factorial combination of grade and skill level based on a median split within each grade. Clearly, the comparisons of skill within each grade resulted in many significant differences. Perhaps a more comprehensible presentation of the results is contained in Tables 7.4 and 7.5, which display correlation matrices for a selected set of the variables. In order to reduce the size of these matrices, composite z-score variables were used for the rhyming task, pseudoword naming, regularity effect, and word naming in neutral context. Focusing again on the predictors of performance on the Metropolitan, we see that for the third-grade children (above the diagonal in Table 7.4) the strongest relationships were with pseudoword and word naming and to a lesser extent with the Peabody. For the fifth-grade children (below the diagonal, column 1) the best predictors were word naming and the Peabody. For the seventh-graders (Table 7.5), the Peabody was the best predictor, followed by pseudoword and word naming.

More important are the results displayed in Table 7.6, which are the means for the three CL-matched groups. It should be noted that because the fifth- and seventh-grade children took the same test, the match for these two groups was particularly good since they could be equated on actual raw scores. The third-grade children, who completed the Elementary rather than the Intermediate form of the test, were matched on grade equivalents and thus their match is psychometrically less secure. The resulting three groups represented a seventh-grade group considerably below average for their age, a fifth-grade group that is below average, and a third-grade group of above average ability.

Table 7.6 indicates that only two of the variables differed significantly across the three CL-matched groups. Letter naming was significantly faster for older children. This variable, however, was unrelated to reading ability (see Table 7.3). Thus, this study replicated the finding in our previous study and in the work of other investigators (e.g., Jackson & Biemiller, 1985) that letter-naming speed tracks chronological age more strongly than reading ability. The other variable to show a significant difference—articulation time—displayed a pattern similar to letter-naming time, although in even stronger form. As is clear from Tables 7.3–7.5, articulation time appears to be completely unre-

TABLE 7.3. Means of Variables for Skilled and Less-Skilled Readers in Each Grade

Variable	Third grade			Fifth grade			Seventh grade		
	Skilled	Less-skilled	$t(38)$	Skilled	Less-skilled	$t(40)$	Skilled	Less-skilled	$t(42)$
Metropolitan raw score	45.4	23.8	10.31**	48.2	28.1	11.55**	52.0	32.1	10.46**
Metropolitan grade equivalent	4.35	2.37	5.64**	8.00	4.02	9.07**	9.73	4.60	8.42**
PPVT[a]	73.4	69.8	1.45	83.4	73.9	3.25**	91.7	76.5	4.67**
Strategic memory task	14.1	12.5	1.86	15.0	14.1	1.21	16.0	14.8	1.71
Nonstrategic memory task (items)	27.3	23.4	2.23*	28.6	26.8	1.18	30.0	28.9	.78
Nonstrategic memory task (order)	21.3	15.2	2.66*	20.4	18.4	1.11	23.0	20.3	1.37
Letter-naming time	533	575	1.81	505	500	.26	461	474	1.04
Regular word-naming time	666	892	3.00**	633	648	.45	557	678	2.68*
Regular word-naming errors	1.30	2.60	3.19**	.76	1.81	3.53**	1.05	1.64	2.06*
Exception word-naming time	706	1006	4.27**	648	679	.99	588	743	3.12**
Exception word-naming errors	2.20	4.15	3.97**	1.05	2.00	3.13**	1.32	2.00	1.88
Mean neutral word-naming time	686	949	3.73**	641	663	.80	573	711	3.12**
Mean neutral word-naming errors	1.75	3.38	4.10**	.90	1.90	3.94**	1.18	1.82	2.40*
Neutral word z-score	-.061	1.260	4.42**	-.514	-.056	3.77**	-.577	.030	3.62**
Regularity effect (times)	40	114	2.04*	15	31	.58	32	65	.96
Regularity effect (errors)	.90	1.55	1.51	.29	.19	.30	.27	.36	.24
Regularity z-score	.084	.671	2.49*	-.269	-.232	.21	-.197	-.011	.86
Related word-naming time	518	675	2.89**	482	485	.16	422	495	3.77**
Related word-naming errors	.35	1.50	2.81**	.05	.48	3.07**	.14	.14	.00
Contextual facilitation	168	274	2.19*	159	178	.80	151	216	1.95
Pseudoword-naming time	828	1304	4.24**	807	854	.69	652	952	4.11**
Pseudoword-naming errors	2.75	7.25	5.55**	1.86	2.71	1.34	1.14	3.95	3.83**
Pseudoword z-score	-.181	1.267	5.84**	-.358	-.147	1.31	.707	.202	4.48**
Rhyming reaction time	1098	1127	.38	924	1058	1.74	1056	1081	.36
Rhyming errors	4.05	4.80	1.06	2.57	4.19	2.42*	2.68	4.14	2.42*
Rhyming z-scores	.157	.348	.82	-.527	.107	2.44*	-.232	.142	1.60
Articulation time	9290	9447	.37	8334	8577	.73	7604	7298	1.34

[a]PPVT = Peabody Picture Vocabulary Test.

* Difference between skilled and less-skilled readers significant at the .05 level (two-tailed test).

** Difference between skilled and less-skilled readers significant at the .01 level (two-tailed test).

TABLE 7.4. Intercorrelations of Variables for Third- and Fifth-Grade Children

Variable	1	2	3	4	5	6	7	8	9	10	11
1. Metropolitan		.50	.29	.29	-.13	-.34	-.21	-.69	-.38	-.37	-.72
2. PPVT[a]	.51		.22	.05	-.44	-.25	-.01	-.24	-.15	-.01	-.28
3. Strategic memory task	.15	.19		.28	-.13	-.30	-.15	-.12	-.20	-.15	-.15
4. Nonstrategic memory Task (correct order)	.25	.26	.05		-.05	-.23	-.25	-.03	-.08	.01	-.27
5. Articulation time	-.03	.04	.05	-.23		.46	-.08	.00	-.08	.24	.20
6. Letter-naming time	.02	.06	.08	.02	.54		.44	.36	.28	.30	.49
7. Rhyming z-score	-.32	-.03	-.17	-.16	.37	.17		.42	.21	.22	.41
8. Neutral word z-score	-.56	-.18	-.01	-.22	.19	.03	.39		.26	.56	.69
9. Regularity z-score	-.03	-.15	-.03	.03	-.17	-.06	-.02	-.06		-.01	.35
10. Contextual facilitation	-.19	-.08	.00	-.17	.07	.08	-.12	.42	-.09		.35
11. Pseudoword z-score	-.22	-.13	.00	-.13	.04	.07	.14	.36	-.10	.46	

Note. Correlations for the third-grade children are above the diagonal, and correlations for the fifth-grade children are below the diagonal. Correlations above .31 are significant at the .05 level (two-tailed).

[a] PPVT = Peabody Picture Vocabulary Test.

TABLE 7.5. Intercorrelations of Variables for Seventh-Grade Children

Variable	1	2	3	4	5	6	7	8	9	10
1. Metropolitan										
2. PPVT[a]	.70									
3. Strategic memory task	.31	.30								
4. Nonstrategic memory task (correct order)	.31	.18	.23							
5. Articulation time	.05	−.05	.04	.02						
6. Letter-naming time	−.36	−.18	−.10	−.19	.50					
7. Rhyming z-score	−.34	−.19	−.12	−.30	.06	.05				
8. Neutral word z-score	−.59	−.43	−.29	−.43	−.09	.43	.27			
9. Regularity z-score	−.20	−.06	−.17	−.10	−.04	.05	.08	.31		
10. Contextual facilitation	−.37	−.22	−.23	−.43	.13	.44	.25	.70	.08	
11. Pseudoword z-score	−.62	−.55	−.42	−.47	−.02	.36	.25	.77	.15	.76

Note. Correlations above .29 are significant at the .05 level (two-tailed).
[a]PPVT = Peabody Picture Vocabulary Test.

TABLE 7.6. Means for Groups Matched on Reading Ability

Variable	Third grade	Fifth grade	Seventh grade	$F(2, 61)$
Metropolitan grade equivalent	4.35	4.32	4.37	.01
PPVT[a]	73.4	74.4	76.7	.97
Strategic memory task	14.1	14.3	14.6	.24
Nonstrategic memory task (items)	27.3	26.8	28.5	.57
Nonstrategic memory task (order)	21.3	18.2	19.6	1.35
Letter-naming time	533	503	477	4.37*
Regular word-naming time	666	652	695	.50
Regular word-naming errors	1.30	1.64	1.58	.60
Exception word-naming time	706	678	752	1.23
Exception word-naming errors	2.20	1.88	2.05	.42
Mean neutral word-naming time	686	665	723	.98
Mean neutral word-naming errors	1.75	1.76	1.82	.03
Neutral word z-score	−.061	−.109	.061	.58
Regularity effect (times)	42	25	57	.45
Regularity effect (errors)	.90	.24	.47	1.93
Regularity z-score	.084	−.239	−.005	1.51
Related word-naming time	518	487	498	1.15
Related word-naming errors	.35	.40	.16	1.36
Contextual facilitation	168	178	226	1.56
Pseudoword-naming time	828	841	937	.89
Pseudoword-naming errors	2.75	2.48	4.05	2.07
Pseudoword z-score	−.181	−.205	.196	2.06
Rhyming reaction time	1098	999	1094	1.12
Rhyming errors	4.05	3.88	4.47	.47
Rhyming z-score	.157	−.082	.243	.91
Articulation time	9290	8471	7298	17.76**

[a]PPVT = Peabody Picture Vocabulary Test.
*$p < .05$; **$p < .001$.

lated to reading ability. However, it is strongly related to chronological age. Overall, then, with the exception of two variables that are relatively unrelated to reading ability, the performance profiles of these three groups of children displayed remarkable similarity. They had similar vocabularies, strategic and nonstrategic memory abilities, and rhyming ability. Their word recognition processes were very similar, as indicated by their context effects, regularity effects, and pseudoword naming ability.

There are several reasons why this uniformity of performance among the three CL-matched groups is striking. First, it is noteworthy in light of the varied set of tasks employed. Most previous RL-match investigations have used a much more restricted battery of tasks. In addition, when such a large number of statistical tests are run on a set of variables, some spurious significant differences could well appear. Also, one might worry if nonsignificant statistical results were observed in the presence of large absolute differences between the means, which might indicate that large variability and/or small sample sizes were rendering real differences nondetectable. However, this was clearly not the case, as in most instances the mean performance levels of the three groups were quite close (the possible exception being pseudoword naming). Finally, the analyses on the median splits (see Table 7.3) indicate that the design and measurement techniques were powerful enough to detect differences.

THE LONGITUDINAL COMPARISON

As mentioned previously, subgroups of the fifth- and seventh-grade children tested in 1986 had been tested two years earlier (in 1984), as third and fifth graders, respectively. Individual differences in reading achievement were quite stable. Correlations between Metropolitan raw scores in 1984 and 1986 were .93 and .78 for the fifth- and seventh-grade children, respectively. Table 7.7 presents the correlations between the 1986 Metropolitan scores and the variables assessed two years earlier. In general, the variables that predicted 1986 achievement were the same variables that had predicted concurrent achievement in 1984.

More interesting is the longitudinal comparison involving the previously CL-matched groups. What does the performance of these two groups—which two years earlier had been as displayed in Table 7.2—look like two years later? Are they still a CL-match? The performance of these two groups— matched on reading comprehension performance in 1984—is compared on the variables administered two years later in Table 7.8. Interestingly, the two groups are now no longer matched on reading comprehension ability. The raw scores on the Metropolitan Reading Survey are significantly different. In terms of grade equivalents, the skilled younger readers showed a gain of 2.8 years during the two-year period compared with 1.5 for the older less-skilled read-

TABLE 7.7. Correlations between Reading Ability and Tasks Administered Two Years Earlier

Variable	Fifth-grade children	Seventh-grade children
PPVT[a]	.74	.58
Rhyming errors	−.47	−.42
Rhyming time	−.15	−.26
Phonological oddity errors	−.53	−.49
Phonological oddity time	−.15	−.21
Letter-naming time	−.04	−.31
Picture-naming time	−.30	−.38
Pseudoword-naming time	−.12	−.61
Pseudoword-naming errors	−.23	−.59
Pseudoword z-score	−.24	−.65
Related word-naming time	−.53	−.34
Neutral word-naming time	−.38	−.51
Contextual facilitation	.44	−.37

Note. Correlations above .40 and .38 are significant at the .05 level (two-tailed) for the fifth- and seventh-grade children, respectively.

[a]PPVT = Peabody Picture Vocabulary Test.

ers. The results from the other variables do not indicate a large number of differences. However, there were significant tendencies for the younger readers to be superior in word naming accuracy in neutral contexts and in rhyme performance. The older children were significantly faster in the articulation task, a finding anticipated by the previous results indicating that this task is strongly linked to chronological age.

Most versions of the developmental lag hypothesis posit that there are acquisition rate differences between readers of differing skill: that skilled and less-skilled readers go through the same sequence of stages but at different rates. The hypothesis of rate differences clearly predicts that the younger skilled readers should show more growth in reading in a fixed amount of time than the older less-skilled readers. Most of the previous and conflicting research on this issue (e.g., Baker, Decker, & DeFries, 1984; Bruck, 1988; Trites & Fiedorowicz, 1976) has compared groups of similar chronological age but differing initial reading levels. Thus, the hypothesis must be assessed by evaluating a group by time interaction that is vulnerable to many artifacts. Perhaps a longitudinal CL-match design provides a less artifact-ridden method of assessing whether there are differential growth rates. Our results appear to reveal the predicted differential reading growth rates.

In summary, the results from the three-group CL-match longitudinal design converged with our earlier results. Both sets of results confirmed the hypothesis (Stanovich et al., 1986) that the performance of the unlabeled poor reader—those children who read poorly but do not necessarily fit the psychometric criteria for the label dyslexia—would show a broad-based developmental lag. It is hypothesized that this pattern will contrast with the results from studies where the reading-level match involves reading-disabled children defined by strict psychometric criteria.

TABLE 7.8. Performance of Groups Matched on Reading Ability in 1984 on the Tasks Administered in 1986

Variable	Skilled fifth-grade children	Less skilled seventh-grade children	t(26)
Metropolitan raw score	48.1	39.5	2.38*
Metropolitan grade equivalent	7.94	6.59	1.38
PPVT[a]	85.7	84.4	.36
Strategic memory task	15.1	15.6	.91
Nonstrategic memory task (items)	29.6	29.4	.13
Nonstrategic memory task (order)	21.9	20.3	.81
Letter-naming time	489	470	.99
Regular word-naming time	604	623	.41
Regular word-naming errors	.36	1.43	5.61**
Exception word-naming time	625	640	.34
Exception word-naming errors	.93	2.14	3.61**
Mean neutral word-naming time	614	632	.38**
Mean neutral word-naming errors	.64	1.79	5.43**
Neutral word z-score	−.687	−.184	3.74**
Regularity effect (times)	21	17	.20
Regularity effect (errors)	.57	.71	.41
Regularity z-score	−.133	−.096	.23
Related word-naming time	469	448	.73
Related word-naming errors	.07	.21	1.06
Contextual facilitation	145	184	.98
Pseudoword-naming time	789	746	.53
Pseudoword-naming errors	2.00	2.36	.33
Pseudoword z-score	−.362	−.367	.02
Rhyming reaction time	984	1140	1.93
Rhyming errors	2.36	3.50	1.76
Rhyming z-score	−.453	.121	2.18*
Articulation time	8131	7266	2.34*

[a]PPVT = Peabody Picture Vocabulary Test.
*p < .05; **p < .01.

A RESEARCH SYNTHESIS

In the following discussion I will try to amalgamate a number of findings and theoretical ideas into a coherent global model for understanding reading problems of both the garden-variety and dyslexic type. Although the "grain" of the model will be rather coarse, I would argue that we are better off with even a gross summary if it can help us to escape from the interminable definitional and semantic disputes that plague the LD field—and I think that my model does do this. My summary model builds on the basic result regarding garden-variety readers that I feel that my work has established. It supplements this empirical finding with some of the logical, statistical, and psychometric arguments that began my paper. Not the least important, however, is my reliance on the previous theoretical arguments and empirical results established by other investigators.

Here is what I think has been roughly established. First, Andrew Ellis (1985) is right that the proper analogy for dyslexia is not measles, but instead a condition like obesity. There is considerable evidence from a variety of different sources (Jorm, 1983; Olson et al., 1985; Scarborough, 1984; Seidenberg et al., 1985; Share, McGee, McKenzie, Williams, & Silva, 1987; Silva et al., 1985) that we are not dealing with a discrete entity but with a graded continuum. Several years ago, Rutter and Yule (1975) led researchers down a blind alley by reporting that there was a somewhat discontinuous "hump" near the bottom of the reading distribution, and this "hump" suggested a discrete pathology model to many investigators. However, there is now much converging evidence that indicates that the "hump" was a statistical artifact, perhaps involving ceiling effects on the tests (Rodgers, 1983; Share et al., 1987; Silva et al., 1985; van der Wissel & Zegers, 1985). There is in fact no "hump" in the distribution.

However, the fact that the distribution is a graded continuum does not render the concept of dyslexia scientifically useless, as many critics would like to argue. This is why obesity is such a good example—no one doubts that it is a very real health problem, despite the fact that it is operationally defined in a somewhat arbitrary way by choosing a criterion in a continuous distribution: "For people of any given age and height there will be an uninterrupted continuum from painfully thin to inordinately fat. It is entirely arbitrary where we draw the line between 'normal' and 'obese,' but that does not prevent obesity being a real and worrying condition, nor does it prevent research into the causes and cures of obesity being both valuable and necessary" (Ellis, 1985, p. 172). It follows that "to ask how prevalent dyslexia is in the general population will be as meaningful, and as meaningless, as asking how prevalent obesity is. The answer will depend entirely upon where the line is drawn" (p. 172).

Likewise, I think that it is also important to conceive of *all* of the relevant distributions of reading-related cognitive skills as being continuously arrayed in a multidimensional space and not distributed in clusters. In short, I accept the model of heterogeneity without clustering that has been discussed by Ellis (1985), Olson et al. (1985), Satz, Morris, and Fletcher (1985), and others. I further posit that the existence of heterogeneity without clustering is precisely the empirical fact that has obscured and stymied the search for discrete subtypes among dyslexic children. Ellis' (1985) discussion helps to shift our thinking into a quantitative mode which often helps to clarify precisely the things that the verbal debate obscures because of the inherent connotations of discreteness carried by many natural language terms.

Ellis notes that a categorical model is implicit in many discussions of dyslexic subtypes. This is the model that motivated the earlier, more naive attempts at finding a dyslexia typology. For example, the two dimensions that are often represented in such models (note that all of the same arguments would apply in a space of higher dimension) are the ability to access the lexicon on a visual/orthographic basis and phonological recoding ability. These dimensions are represented in the dysphonetic and dyseidetic dyslexic typology popularized by Bodor (1973) and recapitulated in the distinction between phonological and surface dyslexia in the literature on acquired dyslexia. These two groups are defined by severe deficits on one of the dimensions and normal ability on the other. The categorical model assumes that there are "galaxies" of dyslexics—and of nondyslexic readers as well. If this model were true, the subtyping literature would not have remained so confused for so long.

In contrast, in the dimensional model the poor readers are a heterogeneous lot, but they do not form clusters. I, like Ellis and several other investigators (e.g., Olson et al., 1985), believe that if we really want to have a useful concept of dyslexia, this is the model we must always keep in mind. Again, like in the obesity example, we may decide to arbitrarily partition the variability we observe and for various purposes treat the subgroups in a discrete fashion—but this again would be an arbitrarily imposed partitioning. Clearly, this state of affairs creates statistical problems for cluster analyses, but it is important to understand—via a logic similar to that in the obesity example—that such problems do not undermine the idea of forming abstract subtypes for certain theoretical or practical purposes:

> What the dimensional model predicts, however, is that there will be a complete and unbroken gradation of intermediate dyslexics linking such extreme cases. A dimensional model does not deny heterogeneity, only homogeneity of subtypes (cf. Olson, Kliegl, Davidson, & Foltz, 1985). It does not preclude the study of selected individuals to highlight dimensions of difference, nor does it prevent one from drawing conclusions about reading processes in general from the observed individual differences. It may, however, undermine an attempt to impose syndromes upon the dyslexic population. That is, the dimensional approach primarily creates problems for a syndrome-based version of preformism; other versions may be less affected by the denial of homogeneous subgroups. (Ellis, 1985, pp. 192–193)

[*Material omitted*]

THE PHONOLOGICAL-CORE VARIABLE-DIFFERENCE MODEL

The concepts inherent in the dimensional model outlined above can be generalized to account for contrasts between the dyslexic and the garden-variety poor reader. The bivariate distribution of reading and IQ is continuous, as is the univariate distribution of reading ability. What this means is that there is a continuous gradation between these two types of poor reader, defined by where they are on the bivariate relation of IQ and reading. That is, conditionalized at a given level of reading ability (low, in the case of the poor reader), the distribution of IQ is continuous, with an "unbroken gradation of intermediate cases" between the "pure" dyslexic (with relatively high IQ for that level of reading) and the "pure" garden variety (with a lower and more typical IQ). This means that to whatever extent the processing patterns of these two groups are dissimilar, that dissimilarity will be attenuated the closer to the "fuzzy" and arbitrary boundary between them we get. Or, to put it more concretely, studies employing dyslexics with somewhat depressed IQs and garden-variety poor readers with somewhat elevated IQs may be unable to detect whatever critical processing differences there are between the two groups.

And I do believe that such processing differences exist. They can be described within what I will term the phonological-core variable-difference model—actually, perhaps more of a framework than a model. The model rests on a clear understanding of the assumption of specificity in definitions of dyslexia (see Hall & Humphreys, 1982; Stanovich, 1986a, 1986b). This assumption underlies all discussions of the concept of dyslexia, even if it is not explicitly stated. It is the idea that a child with this type of learning disability has a brain/cognitive deficit that is reasonably specific to the reading task. That is, the concept of dyslexia requires that the deficits displayed by such children not extend too far into other domains of cognitive functioning. If they did, this would depress the constellation of abilities we call intelligence, reduce the reading–intelligence discrepancy, and the child would no longer be dyslexic. Indeed, he/she would have become a garden variety!

In short, the key deficit in dyslexia must be a vertical faculty rather than a horizontal faculty (see Fodor, 1983); that is, a domain-specific process (Cossu & Marshall, 1986) rather than a process which operates across a wide variety of domains. For this, and other reasons, many investigators have located the proximal locus of dyslexia at the word recognition level (e.g., Gough & Tunmer, 1986; Morrison, 1984, 1987a; Perfetti, 1985; Siegel, 1985; Vellutino, 1979) and have been searching for the locus of the flaw in the word recognition module. Research in the last ten years has focused intensively on phonological processing abilities. It is now well established that dyslexic children display deficits in various aspects of phonological processing. They have difficulty making explicit reports about sound segments at the phoneme level, they display naming difficulties, their utilization of phonological codes in short-term memory is inefficient, and their categorical perception of certain phonemes may be other than normal (see Liberman & Shankweiler, 1985; Mann, 1986; Pennington, 1986; Wagner & Torgesen, 1987; Williams, 1984). Importantly, there is increasing evidence that the linkage from phonological processing ability to reading skill is a causal one (Bradley & Bryant, 1985; Liberman & Shankweiler, 1985; Maclean, Bryant, & Bradley, 1987; Stanovich, 1986b, 1988a; Wagner & Torgesen, 1987). Presumably, their lack of phonological sensitivity makes the learning of grapheme-to-phoneme correspondences very difficult.

The model of individual differences I will present thus posits this core of phonological deficits as the basis of the dyslexic performance pattern. This is an oversimplification, since it ignores—at least temporarily—Bodor's (1973) dyseidetics, or surface dyslexics. I believe that there is growing evidence for the utility of distinguishing a group of dyslexics who have severe problems in accessing the lexicon on a visual/orthographic basis (see Stanovich, 1988a). But a crucial caveat is in order. I believe that the problem encountered by these children is not similar to the "visual perception" problems popular in the early history of the study of dyslexia, but now thoroughly debunked (Aman & Singh, 1983; Kavale & Mattson, 1983; Vellutino, 1979). In addition to the empirical evidence refuting this old view, I would add that the arguments presented here add to the negative convergence. The older conceptualizations of visual deficits had the additional flaw that the purported problematic processes were too global and not modular enough. The actual problems in orthographic processing must be much more subtle and localized. I am not prepared to say anything more specific about this issue, except that I would speculate that the problem involves something to do with the automatic and nonintentional induction of orthographic patterns (and thus would not be discernible under most intentional learning situations, e.g., most standard paired-associate learning paradigms). However, the smaller group of dyslexics with orthographic-core deficits would mirror the phonological-core group in all of the other processing characteristics of the model. What are those characteristics?

One important factor mentioned earlier was that of compensatory processing. CL-matched younger children should display superior word recognition skill and phonological abilities, whereas the older dyslexics should display superior vocabulary, memory, and real-world knowledge—the latter skills and knowledge presumably balancing the inferior word recognition skills to yield the equivalent reading comprehension performance (see Bruck, 1988). A similar trade-off should characterize comparisons of dyslexics and garden-variety poor readers matched on comprehension: poorer word recognition but superior "horizontal faculties" on the part of the dyslexics. There is some evidence supportive of this trend (Bloom et al., 1980; Fredman & Stevenson, 1988; Seidenberg et al., 1985).

A DL match should yield complementary results. The older dyslexics, matched at the word recognition level, should display superior reading comprehension. Similarly, dyslexics matched with garden-variety CA controls on decoding skill should display superior reading comprehension and horizontal faculties (see Bloom et al., 1980; Ellis & Large, 1987; Jorm et al., 1986; Silva et al., 1985).

For the majority of dyslexics with a phonological core deficit, a DL match with a younger group of nondyslexic controls should reveal another pattern of ability trade-offs: deficits in phonological sensitivity and in the phonological mechanisms that mediate lexical access—but superior visual/orthographic mechanisms and orthographic knowledge (an opposite but analogous pattern should obtain for those with an orthographic core deficit). Several investigations have shown this predicted pattern (Baddeley et al., 1982; Baron & Treiman, 1980; Bradley & Bryant, 1978; Kochnower et al., 1983; Olson et al., 1985; Snowling, 1980, 1981). A similar pattern should hold when dyslexics are compared to a CA garden-variety group. These, then, are the pattern of relationships that can be derived from the phonological core deficit of the dyslexic reader and the psychometric constraints inherent in the operational definition of dyslexia. (Note that Olson et al. [1985] have used similar ideas of compensatory processing to explain the variability *within* a dyslexic sample.)

In the phonological-core variable-difference model the term variable differences is used to contrast the performance of the garden-variety and the dyslexic reader. As outlined above, the cognitive status of garden-variety poor reader is well described by a developmental lag model. Cognitively, they are remarkably similar to younger children reading at the same level. A logical corollary of this pattern is that the garden-variety reader will have a wide variety of cognitive deficits when compared to CA controls who are reading at normal levels.

However, it is important to understand that the garden-variety poor reader does share the phonological problems of the dyslexic reader—though perhaps in less severe form—and the deficits appear also to be a causal factor in the poor reading of these children (Perfetti, 1985; Stanovich, 1986b). But for them the deficits—relative to CA controls—extend into a variety of domains (see Ellis & Large, 1987) and some of these (e.g., vocabulary, language comprehension) may also be causally linked to reading comprehension. Such a pattern does not characterize the dyslexic, who has a deficit localized in the phonological core. This core deficit is actually more severe (they show deficits in DL matches) than that of the garden-variety reader—whose performance matches younger DL controls—but it is not accompanied by other cognitive limitations.

One straightforward prediction that we then might derive is that the dyslexic's decoding problem will be more difficult to remediate. Interestingly, however, if the decoding problem can be remediated, then the contingent prognosis for the dyslexic child should be better—they have no additional cognitive problems that may inhibit reading comprehension growth. This prediction fits nicely with Gough and Tunmer's (1986) "simple view" of reading comprehension (R) as a multiplicative combination of decoding skill (D) and listening comprehension ability (C); in short, $R = D \times C$. If dyslexics and garden-variety poor readers are matched on reading comprehension (e.g., $.4 \times .9 = .6 \times .6$) and if (in some benign world) we were to totally remediate the decoding deficits of each, then the dyslexics would have superior reading comprehension ($1.0 \times .9 > 1.0 \times .6$).

The framework of the phonological-core variable-difference model fits nicely with Ellis' dimensional model described earlier. Consider the following characterization: As we move in the multidimensional space—through the "unbroken gradation of intermediate cases"—from the dyslexic to the garden-variety poor reader, we will move from a processing deficit localized in the phonological core to the global deficits of the developmentally lagging garden-variety poor reader. Thus, the actual cognitive differences that are displayed will be variable depending upon the type of poor reader who is the focus of the investigation. The differences on one end of the continuum will consist of deficits located only in the phonological core (the dyslexic) and will increase in number as we run through the intermediate cases that are less and less likely to pass strict psychometric criteria for dyslexia. Eventually we will reach the part of the multidimensional space containing relatively "pure" garden-variety poor readers who clearly will not qualify for the label dyslexic (by either regression or exclusionary criteria), will have a host of cognitive deficits, and will have the cognitively immature profile of a developmentally lagging individual. As we travel in this direction through the space the phonological core deficit will attenuate somewhat. That is, the phonological problem will attenuate in severity as the number of other deficits spreads. One would need an impressive multidimensional graphic to illustrate this more concretely, but I hope I have at least primed the imagination.

I believe that this phonological-core variable-deficit (PCVD) conceptualization provides a useful global framework within which to consider the plethora of controversial issues in the area of reading disabilities—issues of definition, subtypes, prevalence, etiology, process analysis, educational policy, remediation, and prognosis. For example, the framework provides an explanation for why almost all processing investigations of reading disability have uncovered phonological deficits, but also why some investigations have found deficits in *other* areas as well. This outcome is predictable from the fact that the PCVD model posits that *all* poor readers have a phonological deficit, but that other processing deficits emerge as one drifts in the multidimensional space from "pure" dyslexics toward garden-variety poor readers. Thus, the model's straightforward prediction is that those studies that revealed a more isolated deficit will be those that had more psychometrically select dyslexic readers. In short, the reading–IQ discrepancy of the subject populations should be significantly greater in those studies displaying more specific deficits. Presumably, studies finding deficits extending beyond the phonological domain are in the "fuzzy" area of the multidimensional space and are picking up the increasing number of processing differences that extend beyond the phonological domain as one moves toward the garden-variety area of the space.

This example of how the PCVD model clarifies and explains problematic findings in the LD literature is not a trivial one. I have previously discussed (see Stanovich, 1986a) how the research findings indicating multiple and somewhat global deficits threaten to make nonsense of the very concept of a learning disability. Escaping this paradox is a not inconsiderable problem for the LD field.

Nevertheless, I should not imply that the further necessary elaboration and quantification of the model will be an easy task. Numerous complications threaten to obscure its basically simple structure. I have already mentioned the likely existence of a smaller group of dyslexic readers whose core deficit is in the orthographic processing and lexical knowledge domain. Secondly, the model will need a stronger developmental component than it now has. The developmental lag characterization of the garden-variety poor reader is a step in the right direction but the appropriate developmental model for the dyslexic is largely unsketched. Some of the complications that elaboration of the developmental component entails have been discussed in my analysis (see Stanovich, 1986b, 1988a) of Matthew effects in reading: the fact that the early acquisition of reading skill results in reading/academic experiences that facilitate the development of other cognitive structures that lay the foundation for successful reading achievement at more advanced levels. In short, there are many rich-get-richer and poor-get-poorer phenomena resulting from the interaction of the cognitive characteristics of children and their academic and home environments. I have previously outlined (see Stanovich, 1986b) how such Matthew effects can lead to a pattern where poor readers display increasingly global cognitive deficits as they get older and how early modular deficits can grow into generalized cognitive, behavioral, and motivational problems. The existence of Matthew effects raises the startling possibility that a young dyslexic might actually develop into a garden-variety poor reader! Thus, these Matthew effects complicate the prediction of the developmental growth curves for reading ability and reading-related cognitive skills, but they simply must be accounted for.

CHAPTER 8

The Phenotypic Performance Profile of Reading-Disabled Children

A Regression-Based Test of the Phonological-Core Variable-Difference Model

with LINDA S. SIEGEL

Scientific reduction is the process whereby the laws and theoretical concepts at one level of analysis are mapped onto the laws and concepts of a more basic or fundamental level of scientific analysis (Churchland, 1979). The phenomenon of reading disability has been the subject of several such reductive efforts in the past decade. Investigators have attempted to characterize the functional neurophysiology of reading disability and to localize the information processing deficits of dyslexic readers in certain parts of the brain (e.g., Duane & Gray, 1991; Galaburda, 1991; Hynd, Marshall, & Gonzalez, 1991; Larsen, Hoien, Lundberg, & Odegaard, 1990; Steinmetz & Galaburda, 1991). Other researchers have attempted to analyze the genetics of dyslexia and to estimate the heritability of information processing operations that are particularly deficient in dyslexics (e.g., Olson, Wise, Conners, Rack, & Fulker, 1989; Pennington, Gilger, Olson, & DeFries, 1992; Plomin, 1991). More indirectly, reductive research programs are being carried out by investigators attempting to model dyslexic performance patterns with connectionist computer models (e.g., Hinton & Shallice, 1991; Seidenberg, 1992; Seidenberg & McClelland, 1989a; Van Orden, Pennington, & Stone, 1990). All of these reductive efforts are completely dependent upon an accurate characterization of the phenotypic performance pattern of reading-disabled children. In order for these research programs to succeed, we must first know who is reading disabled and, second, what is unique about the information processing characteristics of these individuals. Quite simply, investigators engaged in reductive research programs must know whose brain to scan, who to do a postmortem autopsy on, whose family to subject to linkage analysis, what tasks to subject to heritability analysis, and what performance patterns to try to mimic with computer models.

The behavioral phenomenon of dyslexia presents a problem for reductive research efforts because the classification criteria for the condition have long been in dispute (Ceci, 1986; Morrison, 1991; Rutter, 1978; Siegel, 1988, 1989; Siegel & Heaven, 1986; Stanovich, 1986a, 1991a; Vellutino, 1978). Equally contentious has been the ongoing debate about which processing deficiencies are uniquely characteristic of reading-disabled children (cf. Bruck, 1988, 1990; Lovegrove, 1992; Morrison, 1987a, 1991; Olson et al., 1985; Olson et al., 1989; Pennington, 1986; Siegel, 1992, 1993a; Siegel & Ryan, 1988; Stanovich, 1986a, 1988b; Tallal, Sainburg, & Jernigan, 1991; Vellutino, 1979; Willows, 1991; Wolf, 1991b). Reductive research efforts will continue to be hampered (indeed, such efforts may even be premature) until researchers succeed in coming to a consensual model of reading disability classification and until they can definitively establish what is unique about the cognitive processing profile of the reading-disabled child. For example, Pennington (1986) notes that "powerful genetic techniques are becoming increasingly available for the study of inherited, complex behavior disorders, including learning disabilities. Yet the utility of these techniques is directly affected by how we define the behavioral phenotype in question" (p. 69).

DEFINITIONAL PROBLEMS: THE ISSUE OF IQ DISCREPANCY

The question of who is reading disabled and that of what cognitive profile characterizes reading disability are seemingly separate. However, these issues have actually become conjoined because of the strange "cart-before-the-horse" history that has characterized the reading disabilities field (Stanovich, 1991a). One might have thought that researchers would have begun with the broadest and most theoretically neutral definition of reading disability—reading performance below some specified level on some well-known and psychometrically sound test—and then proceeded to investigate whether there were poor readers with differing cognitive profiles *within* this broader group. Unfortunately, the history of reading disabilities research does not resemble this logical sequence. Instead, early definitions of reading disability *assumed* knowledge of differential cognitive profile (and causation) within the larger sample of poor readers and defined the condition of reading disability in a way that actually served to preclude empirical investigation of the unproven theoretical assumptions that guided the formulation of these definitions!

This remarkable sleight-of-hand was achieved by tying the definition of reading disability to the notion of aptitude–achievement discrepancy (Ceci, 1986; Reynolds, 1985; Shepard, 1980; Siegel, 1989; Stanovich, 1991a). That is, it was assumed that poor readers of high aptitude—as indicated by IQ test performance—were cognitively and neurologically different from poor readers of low aptitude. The term dyslexia, or reading disability, was reserved for those children showing significant statistical discrepancies between reading ability and intelligence test performance. Such discrepancy definitions have become embedded in the legal statutes governing special education practice in many states of the United States (Frankenberger & Fronzaglio, 1991; Frankenberger & Harper, 1987), and they also determine the subject selection procedures in most research investigations (Stanovich, 1991a). The critical assumption that was reified in these definitions—in the almost total absence of empirical evidence—was that degree of discrepancy from IQ was meaningful: that the reading difficulties of the reading-disabled child with IQ discrepancy (reading-disabled, discrepant: RD-D) were different from those characterizing the reading-disabled child without IQ discrepancy (reading-disabled, nondiscrepant: RD-N).

One reason that the study of reading disability has remained so confused is that, until quite recently, we lacked empirical evidence that validated the foundational assumption that was driving classification of children for purposes of research and educational practice. In fact, the utility of aptitude–achievement discrepancy for understanding the cognitive basis of reading disability remains to be demonstrated. Ironically, the dominance of the discrepancy assumption has sometimes precluded the collection of the relevant data. Obviously, from the beginning, researchers should have made sure to include both RD-D and RD-N children in their samples so that the discrepancy assumption could be tested. What happened instead was that the discrepancy notion became so quickly reified in practice that researchers often culled RD-N children from their samples in order to attain "purer" groups, thus precluding the critical comparison of RD-D and RD-N children.

Thus, for many years, most investigations of reading disabilities lacked RD-N controls. They provided no indication of whether or not RD-N readers would have shown the same cognitive pattern as the RD-D children who were the focus of the investigation. Rutter and Yule's (1975) ground breaking investigation of differences between RD-D and RD-N children stood alone for nearly a decade. Only recently have a number of converging studies that included RD-N controls been reported (Fletcher et al., 1989, 1992, 1994; Jorm, Share, Maclean, & Matthews, 1986; Pennington et al., 1992; B. Shaywitz, Fletcher, Holahon, & Shaywitz, 1992; Siegel, 1988, 1989, 1992).

DIFFERENCES IN THE PROCESSING PROFILE
OF READING-DISABLED CHILDREN

The issue of whether there are cognitive differences between RD-D and RD-N children is related to the issue of whether the reading-related cognitive processes of reading-disabled individuals develop in ways different from those of nondisabled readers or whether they progress through the same sequence of stages at a slower rate (the latter situation is sometimes characterized as a developmental lag—see Stanovich, Nathan, & Vala-Rossi, 1986). This question of differential sequence or developmental lag can be investigated—and can potentially yield different answers—for groups of RD-N children as well as for samples of RD-D children. Traditional discrepancy-based definitions assume a differential outcome for the two groups (Stanovich, 1988a, 1991a)—one where the RD-N group displays a developmental lag and where the RD-D group displays a unique cognitive developmental sequence. However, little evidence exists regarding this critical assumption. Our investigation examines the developmental lag versus deficit issue.

One way to address the question of whether reading-disabled children are characterized by differences in developmental sequence is by examining cognitive profiles in a reading-level match design. The reading-level (RL) match design is one in which an older group of reading-disabled children is compared with a younger group of nondisabled children who are matched on reading level (Backman, Mamen, & Ferguson, 1984; Bisanz et al., 1984; Bradley & Bryant, 1978; Guthrie, 1973; Snowling, 1980). In the mid-1980s this design underwent a dramatic increase in popularity because it is more selective than the traditional chronological age (CA) match design in isolating processing differences between reading-disabled and nondisabled children. When reading-disabled children are compared with CA controls, it is well known that they display significant differences on a multiplicity of tasks (e.g., Stanovich, 1986a), thereby reducing the diagnosticity of any single difference (Bryant & Goswami, 1986; Goswami & Bryant, 1989). A particular difference in a CA design is thus open to an unusually large number of alternative explanations (Bryant & Goswami, 1986), including the very real possibility that the processing difference is the *result* of the different reading experiences of the two groups (Stanovich, 1986b, 1993a). In contrast, the number of tasks on which reading-disabled children display deficits relative to RL controls is much smaller. Additionally, any differences that are observed cannot be the *result* of differences in reading ability between the groups because the design eliminates such differences.

Nevertheless, viewed as a diagnostic tool to test whether a particular variable is causally linked to reading disability—in other words, when viewed as a sort of quasi-experiment—the RL design is fraught with methodological and statistical complications (Goswami & Bryant, 1989; Jackson & Butterfield, 1989). For example, regression artifacts are particularly prone to obscure inferences about single variables (see Jackson & Butterfield, 1989). The previous focus on the design as a kind of quasi-experimental method to test a causal hypothesis about a single variable (e.g., Backman, Mamen, & Ferguson, 1984; Bradley & Bryant, 1978; Bryant & Goswami, 1986) seems to have been misplaced (see Jackson & Butterfield, 1989). However, as a context for the comparison of cognitive profiles in a multivariate study, the design can still be of great utility (e.g., Bowey, Cain, & Ryan, 1992; Olson, Wise, Conners, & Rack, 1990; Siegel & Ryan, 1988; Stanovich, Nathan, & Zolman, 1988; Vellutino & Scanlon, 1987, 1989). For example, it provides one way to operationalize the question of whether readers progressing at different rates are going through the same developmental stages. If they are, then relationships among cognitive subskills should be the same for older disabled readers as they are for younger nondisabled readers at the same reading level. Any imbalance in cognitive subskills that appears when the two groups are compared is an indication that they must be reaching their similar levels of reading skills in different ways. Provided there is independent evidence from other types of designs indicating that the skills examined in the multivariate profile are indeed linked to reading ability, then mismatched cognitive profiles in an RL study are an empirical indication that the developmental paths by which the two groups came to their similar reading levels must be different. Note that this outcome is agnostic regarding the issue of what might be the cause of the different developmental paths—of which there may be many alternative explanations.

This use of the RL design—as an operationalization of developmental pattern differences in reading progress among children differing in rate of progress—is a more modest and less conceptually complex use of the design than its more customary use as a quasi-experimental test of a causal hypothesis concerning a single variable. It is the latter usage that has been the subject of the most intense methodological criticism. In contrast, Olson et al. (1990) have argued for the usefulness of the RL design in the former, more descriptive, manner:

> Our assumptions about the matching paradigm are modest. We do not assume that the groups are equivalent in reading experience, or that a deficit in a component skill would necessarily imply a causal role for reading disability, or that a deficit would imply its constitutional origin. . . . It is of interest to see whether the profiles of component skills are similar or different for the two groups. . . . Converging evidence would be required to determine the causal role and etiology of any significant deficits. (p. 272)

Similarly, Jackson and Butterfield (1989) note that "an RL match is more sensitive for determining whether fast- and slow-progressing readers are more different in some aspects of their performance than in others" (p. 397).

As Jackson and Butterfield (1989) have argued, the results of an RL study "need not imply any causal direction for the relationship between rate and skill pattern, but investigators often want to draw some directional, causal implications from their findings. Although one could think of rate of progress as determining skill patterns, directional hypotheses usually are concerned with the reverse possibility" (p. 388). In the present investigation—an attempt to characterize the phenotypic processing pattern of reading-disabled children with and without aptitude discrepancy—we are not primarily concerned with the reverse possibility. Instead, we will use the design for the former, more modest, purpose: to answer the straightforward operational question of whether disabled and nondisabled readers differ in pattern of cognitive skills.

A NEW ANALYTIC STRATEGY FOR THE READING-LEVEL DESIGN

However, there remain obstacles in using the RL design for even the purpose proposed here: identification of differences in cognitive pattern among children differing in rate of progress. Although some conceptual problems associated with the quasi-experimental use of the RL design are eliminated, other statistical problems such as the possibility of regression artifacts remain (Jackson & Butterfield, 1989). Additionally, such studies present investigators with many logistical problems. It is difficult for many investigators to procure enough matched subjects at any one age level to insure a powerful statistical test. This forces many investigators to collapse subjects across rather wide age ranges (e.g., Snowling, Stackhouse, & Rack, 1986), introducing possibly confounding variables. Problems with subject procurement have precluded most investigators from examining RL matches at more than one reading level (see Bisanz et al., 1984; Siegel & Ryan, 1988; and Szeszulski & Manis, 1987, for exceptions) and almost never have investigators included both RD-D and RD-N poor readers in RL studies. The latter is a particularly important missing dimension in investigations of reading disability—one that we attempt to remedy here by reporting an RL comparison of *both* RD-D and RD-N children.

We introduce in this report an analytic logic that removes many of the statistical artifacts of matched-groups RL designs and simultaneously allows investigators to use subjects over a wide range of reading levels in their study and still attain the empirical comparison that is the desired result of the traditional RL design. Our solution is to reconceptualize the entire logic of the RL design into the continuous framework of regression analysis. Other investigators have suggested reframing RL designs within a continuous framework (Bryant & Goswami, 1986; Jackson & Butterfield, 1989; Mamen, Ferguson, & Backman, 1986), but, to our knowledge, no investigation has utilized the procedure we describe here.

Our sample consisted of a large group of children whose reading level spanned a grade equivalent range of 1.0 to 5.8 on a standardized test of word recognition ability (the Reading subtest of the Wide Range Achievement Test [WRAT]). Within this sample, we defined three groups of readers[1]: (a) one consisting of children who were achieving normally for their age cohort (the nondisabled group: NRD); (b) a second group who was performing significantly below average for their age level and IQs (the RD-D group); and (c) a reading-disabled nondiscrepant group (RD-N) performing significantly below average for their age level, but commensurate with their IQs. The RD-D and RD-N groups are of course significantly older than the nondisabled group and, as a function of the selection criteria, the RD-D and NRD groups had IQs significantly higher than the RD-N group.

Employing a large set of theoretically relevant criterion variables (see below), we examined the performance of all three groups within this range of reading levels together in one regression analysis that has the following components. The criterion variable is regressed on WRAT reading grade level (and all significant power polynomials)—thus removing all of the variance in the criterion variable that is associated with overall reading level. Subsequent to WRAT reading level, two contrasts reflecting the group classifications are entered simultaneously into the equation: one contrast capturing the reading-disabled versus nondisabled comparison (RD-D and RD-N combined versus NRD) and the other the RD-D versus RD-N comparison. To whatever extent the criterion variable is associated with group classification independent of overall reading level, it will be reflected in significant beta weights (and explained variance) for these contrasts (see Cohen & Cohen, 1983; Darlington, 1990; Keppel & Zedeck, 1989). A significant beta weight for the first contrast becomes analogous to a processing deficit (or advantage, depending upon the sign) in a more traditional—and methodologically problematic—matched-groups RL design. A significant beta weight for the second contrast indicates that the performance of the RD-D children differs from that of RD-N children statistically equated on WRAT reading level. Alternatively, if performance on a variable tracks reading level, independent of the age at which children reach a given reading level or of the IQ of the reader, then subject classification (e.g., younger nondisabled reader, older discrepant disabled reader, older nondiscrepant disabled reader) should not be a significant predictor once reading level has been partialed out. In short, if a developmental lag model characterizes all poor readers, then once reading level is regressed out as a predictor of a reading-related cognitive subskill, subject categorization should not predict additional variance in the criterion variable.

Ours is a continuous, regression-based equivalent of the reading level design that has several advantages as an analytic strategy: (1) the logistical advantage of allowing subjects to be combined across several reading levels because there is no necessity to create a matched group at each reading level to be examined; (2) increased representativeness of the samples because case-by-case matching of subgroups on reading level is not required; (3) freedom from the regression confounds that plague the traditional matched extreme-groups RL design. As Jackson and Butterfield (1989) argue

> For purposes of maximizing external validity, statistical matching has at least two advantages over matching by sample selection. First, all samples will be representative of real populations whose identification can be replicated. Second, one can

analyze data using several different statistical procedures to see whether the pattern of results remains consistent with the same theoretical model. (p. 398)

Previous investigations utilizing the reading-level design have been precluded from employing the discrepancy/nondiscrepant criterion in part because the selection requirements of an additional category often prohibitively increase the number of matched subjects that the investigator must procure from a single grade level. Our analytic strategy allows the investigator to more easily embed a comparison between RD-D and RD-N children into their reading-level designs. The ability to combine subjects across several reading levels makes it easier to attain the requisite sample sizes within each of the psychometrically constrained RD groups. In our methodology, the comparison between RD-D and RD-N children is simply created by analyzing the independent contribution of an additional vector that is entered into the regression equation along with the basic contrast between reading-disabled and nondisabled children. When the two contrast vectors are entered simultaneously into the regression equation along with WRAT reading level (these two vectors are not orthogonal because the groups have unequal N's; see Keppel & Zedeck, 1989), the regression coefficient of the first vector reflects variance associated with the disabled/nondisabled classification independent of the discrepancy distinction and reading level, and the second vector reflects the variance in the criterion variable associated with the discrepant/nondiscrepant distinction independent of the disabled/nondisabled distinction and reading level. Thus, a test of the IQ-discrepancy assumption is captured elegantly in a design that is the logical equivalent of the traditional matched-groups reading level design.

THE THEORETICAL CONTEXT FOR THE NEW ANALYTIC STRATEGY

A theoretical context for our new analytic strategy is provided by the phonological-core variable-difference (PCVD) model of reading disability (Siegel, 1992; Stanovich, 1988a). The model provides a conceptualization within which to work out the implications of traditional definitions of dyslexia (Stanovich, 1991a). For example, traditional definitions rest on the assumption that groups of reading-disabled children defined by aptitude–achievement discrepancies have a brain/cognitive deficit that is reasonably specific to the reading task. The assumptions that are commonly made about the IQ tests used to create the RD-D category—and the psychometric logic involved—virtually requires that the deficits displayed by such children not extend too far into other domains of cognitive functioning. If they did extend into too many other domains, the probability that these domains would overlap with the constellation of abilities tapped by IQ tests would increase and the reading–intelligence discrepancy that defines this category of poor reader would disappear.

In short, standard psychometric assumptions would seem to require that the deficits displayed by RD-D children must display some degree of modularity and domain specificity, whereas this is not true for RD-N children. For this, and other reasons, many investigators have located the proximal problem of RD-D children at the word recognition level (e.g., Adams & Bruck, 1993; Bruck, 1988, 1990; Gough & Tunmer, 1986; Morrison, 1987a; Perfetti, 1985; Siegel, 1988; Siegel & Faux, 1989; Stanovich, 1986b) and have been searching for the locus of the flaw in the word recognition module.

Research in the last 10 years has focused intensively on phonological processing abilities and has indicated that dyslexic children display deficits in various aspects of phonological processing. They have difficulty making explicit reports about sound segments at the phoneme level, they display naming difficulties, their utilization of phonological codes in short-term memory is inefficient, their categorical perception of certain phonemes may be other than normal, and they may have speech production difficulties (e.g., Bentin, 1992; Bowey et al., 1992; Bradley & Bryant, 1978; Bruck, 1992; Bruck & Treiman, 1990; Goswami & Bryant, 1990; Kamhi & Catts, 1989; Lieberman, Meskill, Chatillon, & Schupack, 1985; Olson et al., 1989; Pennington, 1986; Perfetti, 1985; Snowling, 1991; Stanovich, 1986b, 1992a; Taylor, Lean, & Schwartz, 1989; Tunmer & Hoover, 1992; Williams, 1986; Wolf, 1991b). Importantly, there is increasing evidence that the linkage from phonological processing ability to reading skill is a causal one (e.g., Ball & Blachman, 1991; Bradley & Bryant, 1985; Byrne & Fielding-Barnsley, 1993; Cunningham, 1990; Hatcher, Hulme, & Ellis, 1994; Iverson & Tunmer, 1993; Lie, 1991; Lundberg, Frost, & Peterson, 1988; Mann, 1993; Torgesen, Morgan, & Davis, 1992). Whether all of these phonologically related deficits are reflective of a single underlying processing problem and whether all of them can be considered causal or are instead correlates is a matter for future research, but some important progress is being made on this issue (e.g., Fowler, 1991; Hansen & Bowey, 1994; Pennington, Van Orden, Kirson, & Haith, 1991; Pennington, Van Orden, Smith, Green, & Haith, 1990; Wagner, Torgesen, Laughon, Simmons, & Rashotte, 1993; Wagner, Torgesen, & Rashotte, 1994).

In the phonological-core variable-difference model (Stanovich, 1988a), the term variable difference refers to the key performance contrasts between the RD-N and the RD-D poor reader *outside* of the phonological domain. Although RD-D and RD-N children are assumed to share the phonological-core deficits which are the source of their word recognition problems, the RD-N child may have deficits in a wider variety of processes that are linked to reading ability and some of these (e.g., memory skills) are nonmodular processes. This framework provides an explanation for why almost all processing investigations of reading disability have uncovered phonological deficits, but also why some investigations have found deficits in many *other* areas as well (see Stanovich, 1988b). This outcome is predictable from the fact that the phonological-core variable-difference model posits that virtually all poor readers have a phonological deficit, but that other processing deficits emerge as one drifts in the multidimensional space from RD-D children toward RD-N children. Presumably, the studies finding deficits extending beyond the phonological domain are those containing a greater proportion of RD-N children. This follows from the model's more general prediction that differences between RD-D and RD-N children should increase as the processes tested become more central, less modular, and further removed from the phonological core. In contrast, both groups should look similar when tested on tasks that tap the phonological core deficit that they are assumed to share.

[*material omitted*]

Method

Subjects

[*material omitted*]

Table 8.1 displays the mean WRAT percentile score, estimated IQ, and age in months for each of the three groups at each of the five reading levels formed by combining all subjects at WRAT reading levels 1 through 5. From the table it is clear that the NRD group is performing at the WRAT level expected for their age (i.e., around the 50th %ile), whereas the RD-D and RD-N are both

TABLE 8.1. Mean WRAT Reading Percentile, IQ, and Age for the Samples of Nondisabled NRD) Children, Reading-Disabled Children with IQ Discrepancy (RD-D), and Reading-Disabled Children without IQ Discrepancy (RD-N) as a Function of Reading Grade Level on the WRAT

Variable	NRD	RD-D	RD-N
WRAT percentile			
Reading Grade Level 1	40.7 (3)	5.0 (85)	5.5 (28)
Reading Grade Level 2	47.0 (56)	10.2 (114)	6.8 (49)
Reading Grade Level 3	52.8 (89)	14.8 (66)	11.1 (49)
Reading Grade Level 4	55.9 (134)	14.1 (50)	9.6 (24)
Reading Grade Level 5	61.4 (117)	15.3 (26)	12.3 (17)
IQ score			
Reading Grade Level 1	106.7 (3)	106.5 (85)	73.3 (28)
Reading Grade Level 2	104.2 (56)	107.0 (114)	78.9 (49)
Reading Grade Level 3	102.8 (89)	102.6 (66)	79.2 (49)
Reading Grade Level 4	105.2 (134)	101.8 (50)	76.5 (24)
Reading Grade Level 5	104.7 (117)	104.3 (26)	81.4 (17)
Age in months			
Reading Grade Level 1	91.7 (3)	98.0 (85)	101.1 (28)
Reading Grade Level 2	91.0 (56)	112.5 (114)	121.1 (49)
Reading Grade Level 3	102.5 (89)	130.5 (66)	139.1 (49)
Reading Grade Level 4	112.3 (134)	147.1 (50)	157.5 (24)
Reading Grade Level 5	120.5 (117)	158.5 (26)	168.4 (17)

Note. The number of subjects in each group is indicated in parentheses.

performing substantially below expectation for their chronological age (approximately the 10th %ile). The NRD and RD-D groups have average IQ scores that are substantially higher than those of the RD-N group, which averages slightly below 80. The RD-D and RD-N are over two years older than the NRD groups matched to them on reading level.

Analysis

[material omitted]

PSEUDOWORD READING AND SPELLING

One of the most well replicated findings in reading disability research is that, compared to chronological-age controls, reading-disabled children have difficulty reading pseudowords (e.g., Bruck, 1990; Perfetti, 1985; Perfetti & Hogaboam, 1975; Siegel & Ryan, 1988; Snowling, 1981). It has been more difficult to determine whether reading-disabled children display deficits compared to reading-level controls, but a recent meta-analysis by Rack, Snowling, and Olson (1992) appears to indicate that this is the case. Whether this finding applies to RD-N poor readers as well as RD-D children is less well established, and we explore this issue here. Our battery of tasks contained five different measures of pseudoword reading and spelling.

[see original paper for methodological details omitted here]

Table 8.2 displays the mean performance on each of the pseudoword tests for each of the three groups at each of five WRAT reading levels. There was a consistent tendency for the two reading-disabled groups to perform less well than the NRD group at all reading levels and on all the tasks. In contrast, there were few systematic differences between the RD-D and RD-N groups. The results of the regression analyses conducted on the pseudoword reading and spelling tests are displayed in Table 8.3. The linear components of WRAT reading level and all significant higher order polynomials accounted for a substantial proportion of the variance in all cases. However, in all five of the analyses, the RD versus NRD contrast had a significant negative beta weight, indicating that the older reading-disabled children performed worse than the younger nondisabled children. Only two of the RD-N versus RD-D contrasts attained significance (Woodcock Word Attack and experimental pseudowords 1). The negative beta weight on this contrast indicated that the RD-D children outperformed the RD-N children. However, the beta weight was small in absolute magnitude (–.098 and –.091, respectively), and this contrast accounted for only 0.8% unique variance after the variance explained by WRAT reading level and the other contrast had been extracted. Overall, although there was a consistent tendency for reading-disabled children to underperform statistically matched RL-controls on pseudoword tasks, the pseudoword processing differ-

TABLE 8.2. Pseudoword Processing Performance (and *N*) as a Function of Subject Classification and Reading Grade Level on the WRAT

Variable	NRD	RD-D	RD-N
GFW pseudoword spelling			
Reading Grade Level 1	— (0)	1.0 (4)	1.2 (6)
Reading Grade Level 2	9.7 (18)	4.2 (12)	6.9 (15)
Reading Grade Level 3	15.9 (19)	9.4 (5)	11.0 (8)
Reading Grade Level 4	16.0 (17)	10.8 (10)	10.0 (6)
Reading Grade Level 5	23.1 (23)	17.6 (11)	23.3 (4)
GFW pseudoword reading			
Reading Grade Level 1	— (0)	1.6 (5)	1.0 (6)
Reading Grade Level 2	7.3 (18)	7.1 (12)	6.3 (16)
Reading Grade Level 3	23.6 (18)	19.1 (7)	12.7 (9)
Reading Grade Level 4	27.6 (17)	24.0 (10)	21.5 (6)
Reading Grade Level 5	41.3 (23)	31.9 (11)	36.0 (5)
Woodcock word attack			
Reading Grade Level 1	18.7 (3)	4.0 (78)	2.3 (18)
Reading Grade Level 2	16.9 (26)	14.2 (75)	6.2 (22)
Reading Grade Level 3	22.8 (41)	19.0 (37)	15.6 (30)
Reading Grade Level 4	28.2 (53)	26.4 (24)	22.8 (16)
Reading Grade Level 5	32.1 (50)	24.7 (12)	29.4 (12)
Experimental pseudowords 1			
Reading Grade Level 1	21.0 (2)	7.9 (37)	5.8 (6)
Reading Grade Level 2	24.2 (5)	18.9 (35)	15.8 (9)
Reading Grade Level 3	26.5 (15)	23.6 (19)	19.5 (12)
Reading Grade Level 4	28.4 (11)	25.1 (14)	25.0 (3)
Reading Grade Level 5	30.0 (13)	25.8 (5)	27.2 (5)
Experimental pseudowords 2			
Reading Grade Level 1	5.5 (2)	2.2 (36)	1.2 (6)
Reading Grade Level 2	12.6 (5)	6.6 (34)	5.0 (9)
Reading Grade Level 3	11.9 (15)	9.7 (19)	9.2 (12)
Reading Grade Level 4	13.9 (11)	10.6 (14)	9.0 (3)
Reading Grade Level 5	15.4 (13)	11.6 (5)	13.6 (5)

ences between reading-disabled children with average IQs and those with low IQs were either small or nonexistent.

FURTHER TESTS OF PHONOLOGICAL CODING SKILL

[*material omitted*]

TESTS OF ORTHOGRAPHIC CODING SKILL

Some previous research has suggested that reading-disabled children are relatively less impaired at orthographic coding than at phonological coding (Frith

TABLE 8.3. Regression Results for the Pseudoword Reading and Spelling Tasks

	Dependent variables				
	1.	2.	3.	4.	5.
	Multiple R				
WRAT grade level	.618**	.807**	.727**	.751**	.751**
Quadratic fit	NS	NS	.733**	.802**	.773**
	Beta weight in final equation				
RD vs. NRD contrast	−.226**	−.145**	−.175**	−.206**	−.252**
RD-N vs. RD-D contrast	.068	−.033	−.098**	−.091*	−.044
	Unique variance explained				
RD vs. NRD contrast	.048	.019	.023	.034	.050
RD-N vs. RD-D contrast	.005	.001	.008	.008	.002
	F ratio in final equation				
RD vs. NRD contrast	13.06	9.52	26.20	19.27	26.06
RD-N vs. RD-D contrast	1.21	0.50	9.87	4.24	0.89
	Sample size				
N	158	163	497	191	189

Note. Dependent variables:
1 = GFW Pseudoword Spelling
2 = GFW Pseudoword Reading
3 = Woodcock Word Attack
4 = Experimental Pseudowords 1
5 = Experimental Pseudowords 2
*$p < .05$; **$p < .01$; NS = not significant.

& Snowling, 1983; Holligan & Johnston, 1988; Olson, Kliegl, Davidson, & Foltz, 1985; Pennington et al., 1986; Rack, 1985; Siegel, 1993a; Snowling, 1980). However, it is still unclear whether disabled children display an actual superiority in orthographic processing compared with reading-level controls or whether their impairment in this domain is simply less severe compared to their phonological coding deficit. If the former is the case, then the word recognition performance pattern of reading-disabled children might be characterized as displaying compensatory processing: compared to RL controls, superiority in one type of coding (orthographic) is compensating for deficiencies in another type of coding (phonological). It would seem that the logic of the RL design and the previous finding of a phonological coding deficit (as measured by pseudoword reading) would almost require a compensatory superiority in *some* other skill involved in word recognition. If pseudoword reading is indicative of a processing subskill that contributes to the ability to recognize words, and if reading-disabled children perform more poorly than RL controls on this task, then they must have some other processing superiority that allows them to attain equivalent levels of word recognition. In order to test whether orthographic coding is indeed the compensatory mechanism, we examined performance on three different measures of orthographic coding skill. Another reason for focusing on orthographic coding skill is that connectionist theorists who have attempted to simulate aspects of reading performance (e.g., Seidenberg & McClelland, 1989a; Van Orden et al., 1990) have tended to concentrate on tasks with a heavy phonological component. Few studies have contained a thorough enough representation of orthographic tasks to draw the attention of theorists constructing connectionist models. Our task battery contained three measures of orthographic coding skill.

[see original paper for methodological details and table of means]

Table 8.4 displays the results of the regression analyses. Not surprisingly, WRAT reading grade level was the dominant predictor of performance on each of the three tasks. However, its association with performance on the PIAT Spelling Recognition ($R^2 = .60$) measure was much stronger than its association with performance on the wordlikeness choice task ($R^2 = .35$). Unlike the analyses of the pseudoword tasks, in two of the three analyses (PIAT spelling recognition and wordlikeness choice), the contrast between disabled and nondisabled children displayed a *positive* regression coefficient (although only the former was statistically significant)—indicating that disabled subjects perform better than the nondisabled subjects on these two tasks when WRAT reading grade level is controlled. This coefficient was significantly negative for the experimental spelling recognition task, although small in magnitude (unique variance explained = 1.3%). The word alternatives in this task were all short, high-frequency words. It is possible that, compared to the other two tasks, the two-alternative spelling recognition task might not require orthographic representations to be as elaborated and accurate. Nevertheless, collectively, the data from these three tasks indicates that the reading-level deficits of reading-disabled children are reduced on orthographic processing tasks.

The contrast between discrepant and nondiscrepant disabled readers does not attain significance in any of the analyses. As was the case with virtually all of the phonological coding tasks, RD-N children performed in a remarkably similar manner to the RD-D children when overall word recognition level was controlled.

THE SPELLING–SOUND REGULARITY EFFECT

*[see Metsala, Stanovich, and Brown (1998) in
the Bibliography for a review]*

Stimuli

The subjects were asked to name 36 regular (e.g., *gave*, *few*) and 36 irregular words (e.g., *have*, *sew*) taken from Baron (1979). Since the publication of

TABLE 8.4. Regression Results for Orthographic Coding Tasks

	Dependent variables		
	1.	2.	3.
	Multiple R		
WRAT grade level	.775**	.670**	.524**
Quadratic fit	NS	.686**	.568**
Cubic fit	NS	NS	.591*
	Beta weight in final equation		
RD vs. NRD contrast	.222**	−.121*	.107
RD-N vs. RD-D contrast	.006	−.021	.061
	Unique variance explained		
RD vs. NRD contrast	.041	.013	.009
RD-N vs. RD-D contrast	.000	.000	.003
	F ratio in final equation		
RD vs. NRD contrast	8.95	5.32	2.20
RD-N vs. RD-D contrast	0.01	0.14	0.83
	Sample size		
N	81	212	164

Note. Dependent variables:
1 = Spelling Recognition (PIAT)
2 = Experimental Spelling Recognition
3 = Wordlikeness Choice
*$p < .05$; **$p < .01$; NS = not significant.

Baron's (1979) paper, theories of lexical access have markedly evolved. Most theories now emphasize the concept of spelling–sound consistency, which more accurately connotes a continuous dimension of spelling–sound predictability than does the use of such terms as "regularity" or "exception" (Barber & Millar, 1982; Glushko, 1979; Patterson & Coltheart, 1987; Patterson & Morton, 1985; Rosson, 1985; Venezky & Massaro, 1987). We will retain the term spelling–sound regularity, however, to maintain consistency with past usage in the literature on reading disability. The issue of spelling–sound regularity/consistency is a complex one that has spawned voluminous research (Brown, 1987; Henderson, 1982, 1985; Humphreys & Evett, 1985; Kay & Bishop, 1987; Patterson, Marshall, & Coltheart, 1985; Rayner & Pollatsek, 1989; Rosson, 1985; Seidenberg, Waters, Barnes, & Tanenhaus, 1984; Venezky & Massaro, 1987). We are fully aware of the various controversies in this field (e.g., Stanovich, 1991b), but we address none of them here. For the purpose of the descriptive individual differences analysis that is our focus, it is necessary only to establish that these sets of words vary in their spelling–sound predictability, regardless of how defined (e.g., whether by small-unit regularity or large-unit consistency; see Patterson & Coltheart, 1987) and that these words are comparable to those used in other investigations that have used the RL design (e.g., Treiman & Hirsh-Pasek, 1985).

[see original paper for table of means]

Table 8.5 displays the results of the regression analyses. The first two analyses were conducted using performance on the regular and exception words, respectively, as the criterion variable. Not surprisingly, because the criterion variables reflect the ability to recognize words, WRAT reading grade level accounted for most of the variance. Nevertheless, the RD versus NRD contrast did attain significance in the exception word analysis. Although the sign of the beta weight is in the expected direction (indicating superior performance by the RD children on exception words), it is very small in magnitude (accounting for only 0.5% unique variance). The essential similarity in the performance of the RD and NRD children is bolstered by the separate regression analysis conducted on the magnitude of the regularity effect. Here, neither of the subject group contrasts is statistically significant. Overall, there is no indication in these results that disabled readers are relatively more impaired at reading regular words than exception words. Although this finding is theoreti-

TABLE 8.5. Regression Results for Regular and Exception Words

	Dependent variables		
	1.	2.	3.
	Multiple R		
WRAT grade level	.849**	.854**	.157
Quadratic fit	.914**	.920**	.170
Cubic fit	NS	NS	.281**
	Beta weight in final equation		
RD vs. NRD contrast	.021	.070*	−.106
RD-N vs. RD-D contrast	.022	.024	−.023
	Unique variance explained		
RD vs. NRD contrast	.000	.005	.011
RD-N vs. RD-D contrast	.000	.001	.001
	F ratio in final equation		
RD vs. NRD contrast	0.35	4.25	1.56
RD-N vs. RD-D contrast	0.36	0.49	0.08
	Sample size		
N	141	141	141

Note. Dependent variables:
1 = Regular Words
2 = Exception Words
3 = Regularity Effect
*$p < .05$; **$p < .01$; NS = not significant.

cally problematic (see below), it is consistent with the results from some other studies that have used a discrete-groups RL-match design (e.g., Beech & Harding, 1984; Ben-Dror, Pollatsek, & Scarpati, 1991; Olsen et al., 1985; Treiman & Hirsh-Pasek, 1985). Finally, differences in performance between RD-D and RD-N children were negligible in all three analyses.

ANALYZING PERFORMANCE OUTSIDE OF THE PHONOLOGICAL CORE: WORKING AND SHORT-TERM MEMORY

The processes analyzed so far have all been subcomponents of the word recognition (and spelling) process. Differences between reading-disabled children of differing IQs on these component word recognition subskills have been extremely few in number. However, the phonological-core variable-difference model of reading disability (see Siegel, 1992; Stanovich, 1988a, 1988b) predicts that such differences should increase as the processes examined become more central, less modular, and further removed from the phonological core. Therefore, we examined several working and short-term memory tasks with the analytic method previously described.

[*see original paper for methodological details and table of means*]

Table 8.6 displays the results of the regression analyses. On the two versions of the STM task (Rhyming and Nonrhyming) there is a tendency for the RD-D group to outperform the other two groups matched on reading level. This pattern is reflected in the regression analyses, which indicate significant negative beta weights for the RD-N versus RD-D contrast. Analyses on the magnitude of the rhyming effect yielded somewhat different outcomes. First, all three groups displayed inverted-U-shaped functions relating the magnitude of the rhyming effect to reading level, as has been suggested in a study by Olson, Davidson, Kliegl, and Davies (1984) using a related task. Ceiling effects might also contribute to this trend. However, indications of ceiling effects were mild in our data. The distribution of scores on the nonrhyming letters was negatively skewed, but only slightly so (the index of skewness was –.196). Only seven of 640 subjects achieved the maximum score on the task.

Because the function relating reading level and the rhyming effect takes on an inverted-U shape, it is misleading to draw conclusions from comparisons between NRD, RD-D, and RD-N children conducted at a single reading level. The complexity of the inverted-U-shaped function—and the tendency to draw conclusions from a single comparison reflecting only one slice through this complex function—probably accounts for some of the controversy surrounding individual differences in the rhyming effect in the reading literature (Bisanz et al., 1984; Hall, Wilson, Humphreys, Tinzmann, & Bowyer, 1983; Johnston, Rugg, & Scott, 1987; Shankweiler, Liberman, Mark, Fowler, & Fischer, 1979). To understand group differences in the magnitude of the rhyming effect it is necessary to sample across several reading levels as in the pres-

TABLE 8.6. Regression Results for Memory Tasks

	Dependent variables				
	1.	2.	3.	4.	5.
	Multiple R				
WRAT grade level	.526**	.474**	.053	.335**	.432**
Quadratic fit	NS	.482*	.088*	NS	NS
	Beta weight in final equation				
RD vs. NRD contrast	.169**	.023	−.165**	.260**	.124
RD-N vs. RD-D contrast	−.129**	−.160**	−.069	−.263**	−.232**
	Unique variance explained				
RD vs. NRD contrast	.023	.011	.021	.050	.012
RD-N vs. RD-D contrast	.016	.025	.005	.065	.053
	F ratio in final equation				
RD vs. NRD contrast	21.11	0.35	13.89	23.08	2.07
RD-N vs. RD-D contrast	14.94	20.99	2.93	29.81	9.06
	Sample size				
N	640	640	640	354	132

Note. Dependent variables:
1 = STM—Rhyming
2 = STM—Nonrhyming
3 = STM—Rhyme Effect
4 = Working Memory—Words
5 = Working Memory—Numbers
$*p < .05$; $**p < .01$; NS = not significant.

ent experiment (see also Siegel & Linder, 1984). As Olson et al. (1984) argue, "This curvilinear relation complicates the use of rhyming errors in recognition tasks, or confusion from similar items in recall lists, as evidence for phonetic memory in older disabled and normal readers" (p. 202).

The regression analysis on the rhyming effect presented in Table 8.6 indicates a significant quadratic trend (because of the inverted-U-shaped relationshiop trend), a significant negative beta weight for the RD versus NRD contrast (indicating larger rhyming effects for the nondisabled subjects), and no significant contrast between RD-D and RD-N children. The performance pattern revealed in the analysis of the rhyming effect was thus similar to that obtained on the pseudoword processing tasks: reading-disabled children performed differently from nondisabled children, but no differences between RD-D and RD-N children reached statistical significance. This finding may indicate that the rhyme effect is tapping into the same phonological deficit that is the cause of the alphabetic coding problems that are associated with reading disability.

The results from the two working memory tasks were fairly similar to those obtained from the STM task. Both regression analyses indicated positive beta weights for the RD versus NRD comparison (although only that for the Working Memory–Words task was statistically significant) and significant negative beta weights for the RD-D and RD-N comparison (indicating that RD-D children performed better than the RD-N children statistically matched on WRAT reading level). Thus, in contrast to the situation with tasks reflecting word-level processing, in the domain of short-term and working memory, there are performance differences between reading-disabled children at different IQ levels.

ANALYZING PERFORMANCE OUTSIDE OF THE PHONOLOGICAL CORE: LANGUAGE TASKS

In addition to memory tasks, our battery allowed for the investigation of another domain of processing that extended outside of the phonological deficit known to be associated with reading disability. As a further test of one of the central predictions of the phonological-core variable-difference model—that processing differences associated with IQ discrepancy should increase as the task requirements extend beyond phonological processing—we examined performance on a variety of language processing tasks.

[see original paper for methodological details and table of means]

Table 8.7 displays the results of the regression analyses. Across all six tasks, there was no strong tendency for reading-disabled children to perform differently from reading-level controls. Two of the tasks (the more difficult versions of the sentence correction and oral cloze measures) displayed significant contrasts between RD-N and RD-D children. The negative sign of these two beta weights indicates that the RD-D performed better than the RD-N children. There were no differences between these two groups on the grammatical closure task, sentence repetition task, error correction 1, and oral cloze 1.

Replication Using Other Discrepancy Criteria

All of the analyses presented so far have been based on an absolute IQ-cutoff criterion to differentiate RD-D from RD-N children. Here, we demonstrate that the patterns we have described are robust across different types of discrepancy criteria. The first alternative discrepancy criterion that we will examine is the standard-score discrepancy cutoff. Although it has well-known psychometric deficiencies (e.g., Fletcher et al., 1992; McKinney, 1987; Pennington, 1986; Reynolds, 1985; Shepard, 1980; Wilson & Cone, 1984; Yule, 1984), the standard-score discrepancy method is widely used in research and is the most commonly employed method of classifying children as learning disabled in the United States (Frankenberger & Fronzaglio, 1991).

TABLE 8.7. Regression Results for Language Tasks

	Dependent variables					
	1.	2.	3.	4.	5.	6.
	Multiple R					
WRAT grade level	.615**	.529**	.553**	.518**	.596**	.376**
Quadratic fit	NS	NS	.584**	.584**	.628**	NS
	Beta weight in final equation					
RD vs. NRD contrast	.109	.031	.001	.062	−.034	.035
RD-N vs. RD-D contrast	−.096	−.096	−.190**	−.099	−.236**	−.100
	Unique variance explained					
RD vs. NRD contrast	.010	.001	.000	.004	.000	.001
RD-N vs. RD-D contrast	.008	.009	.036	.009	.050	.010
	F ratio in final equation					
RD vs. NRD contrast	3.84	0.18	0.01	0.76	0.56	0.19
RD-N vs. RD-D contrast	3.39	1.74	8.32	1.99	34.69	1.59
	Sample size					
N	234	147	149	148	388	148

Note. Dependent variables:
1 = Grammatical Closure
2 = Sentence Correction 1
3 = Sentence Correction 2
4 = Oral Cloze Task 1
5 = Oral Cloze Task 2
6 = Sentence Repetition
*$p < .05$; **$p < .01$; NS = not significant.

[*material omitted*]

As in the previous analyses, differences between these subject groups become more apparent as the processes examined become removed from the phonological core. RD-D children outperformed RD-N children on the WRAT Arithmetic subtest, both short-term memory conditions, and on both working memory tasks. The two groups did not differ significantly in the magnitude of the rhyme effect in short-term memory, probably because this measure reflected the phonological processing deficit that they share. The results of the analyses conducted on the language processing tasks mirrored the results obtained using the IQ-cutoff procedure. RD-D children significantly outperformed the RD-N children on the sentence correction 2 and oral cloze 2 tasks. Coefficients for the RD versus NRD contrast were similar across the two methods of discrepancy classification.

The final criterion for discrepancy classification that we examined was a regression discrepancy criterion that is generally preferred to the standard-score discrepancy method (e.g., Fletcher et al., 1992; Reynolds, 1985). Although this method itself requires some complex decisions regarding the derivation of the regression equation (see Fletcher et al., 1992; Reynolds, 1985), for our purposes, most of these complications are not critical. The results were robust across various methods that we tried (deriving the equation from the normal sample, from norms, etc.).

[*material omitted*]

GENERAL DISCUSSION

The research conclusion that is at the heart of the phonological-core variable-difference model of reading disability (Siegel, 1992; Stanovich, 1988a) is that the critical processing deficit impairing the word recognition process of disabled readers lies in the phonological domain, a conclusion for which there is considerable converging evidence (e.g., Brady & Shankweiler, 1991; Bruck, 1992; Catts, 1991; Goswami & Bryant, 1990; Olson, 1994; Olson et al., 1989; Pennington et al., 1990; Perfetti, 1985; Snowling, 1991; Vellutino & Scanlon, 1987). The results reported here add three important elaborations to this conclusion.

First, an earlier conjecture that this phonological core deficit would be more severe for reading-disabled children with aptitude–achievement discrepancy (Stanovich, 1988a) appears to be false. Across seven comparisons conducted on different phonological coding tasks and on the rhyme effect in short-term memory, in only two cases was the contrast between RD-N and RD-D children significant (on the Woodcock Word Attack and experimental pseudowords 1 measures) when the absolute IQ-cutoff criterion was used. However, the obtained coefficients were small in magnitude (–.098 and –.091) and explained very little unique variance (0.8% in both cases). Most important is that the sign of the coefficient is in the opposite direction of the prediction: RD-D children outperformed the RD-N children. Results from the analyses using a standard-score discrepancy criterion and from those using a regression discrepancy criterion were highly convergent.

Taken as whole, these results provide no support for the notion that there are critical differences between RD-D and RD-N children in the phonological coding processes that are the proximal cause (see Gough & Tunmer, 1986) of their reading difficulties. Results from some other studies converge with the present findings by indicating that RD-N children demonstrate the same size of pseudoword reading deficit as do RD-D children (Felton & Wood, 1992; Fredman & Stevenson, 1988; however, see Pennington et al., 1992). The failure of this key prediction of the phonological-core model probably comes about because word recognition displays characteristics of acquired modularity (Humphreys, 1985; Perfetti & McCutchen, 1987; Seidenberg, 1985a; Stanovich, 1990b). The superior nonmodular, central processes of RD-D children apparently do not compensate for their phonological coding deficits in any way, because their word recognition performance is exactly commensurate with the performance of RD-N children who have the same level of word recognition skill. The processing skills and knowledge of RD-D children apparently cannot penetrate the word recognition module in order to facilitate its efficiency. This may reflect a form of informational encapsulation related to that originally described by Fodor (1983).

[material omitted]

A different balance of phonological and orthographic skills characterizes reading-disabled children compared with younger nondisabled children reading at the same level. On two out of three orthographic processing tasks (PIAT Spelling Recognition and wordlikeness choice) the performance of reading-disabled children was *under*predicted by their WRAT reading levels and, again, this was equally true for RD-D and RD-N children. Whether low phonological coding ability is due to developmental lag, neurological insult, or whatever, one thing that RD-D and RD-N children have in common is the struggle with the reading task that school entry makes inevitable. It may be that the necessity of confronting the demands of the reading task while lacking phonological sensitivity triggers the reorganization of skills we see in RD-D and RD-N children when either is compared to younger RL-matched controls (see Snowling, 1987). Thus, the differential phonological and orthographic processing skills may be indicating a pattern of compensatory processing. This trade-off among relative strengths in the processing subskills of disabled readers is consistent with the suggestive theoretical and empirical evidence indicating that phonological and orthographic coding abilities are at least partially separable (Barker, Torgesen, & Wagner, 1992; Bowers & Wolf, 1993; Castles & Coltheart, 1993; Cunningham & Stanovich, 1990, 1993; McBride-Chang, Manis, Seidenberg, Custodio, & Doi, 1993; Stage & Wagner, 1992; Stanovich, 1992b; Stanovich & West, 1989).

For the majority of reading-disabled children with a phonological deficit, a word recognition match with a younger group of nondisabled children seems to reveal a pattern of ability trade-offs: deficits in phonological sensitivity and in the phonological mechanisms that mediate lexical access, but relatively less impaired orthographic processing and storage mechanisms. Descriptively, it is important to be able to say that part of the phenotypic processing profile of disabled readers is a differential pattern of phonological and orthographic coding skills. However, it is unclear how to interpret this differential pattern of subskills because this processing pattern is open to alternative interpretations. For example, it may be interpreted as an inherent processing ability that is less impaired in reading-disabled children. Alternatively, it might be interpreted as a strategic choice—the product of consciously relying on other subskills in an attempt to overcome a phonological deficit. Another candidate might be an attentional explanation. Perhaps because phonological coding is difficult, disabled readers become very aware of the visual sequential redundancy in words. Finally, it is possible that disabled readers maintain word recognition levels equal to their younger nondisabled controls—despite inferior phonological coding skill—because they have had more exposure to print (Cunningham & Stanovich, 1990; Stanovich, 1993a; Stanovich & Cunningham, 1992, 1993; Stanovich & West, 1989). In short, they may require more exposure to words to reach a given level of word recognition skill.

[*material omitted*]

It would be interesting to see how easily a connectionist model of word recognition (e.g., Seidenberg & McClelland, 1989a) could simulate this type of compensation by deleting hidden units or lesioning the model but compensating by providing more exposure to words (see Brown, Loosemore, & Watson, 1993, for a related demonstration). Such an investigation might help to differentiate whether it is mere differential experience that accounts for this pattern or whether it is some experience-independent superiority in accessing orthographic representations that characterizes dyslexic readers. Alternatively, a connectionist model with too many hidden units might be the appropriate neural model. Galaburda (1991) has suggested that the atypical symmetry in the planum temporale found in dyslexics may be due to too many neurons rather than to too few. Interestingly, Seidenberg and McClelland (1989a) note that "it is known that in some cases, networks with too many hidden units 'memorize' the training examples, but fail to extract important regularities, and thus lack the ability to respond to novel inputs" (p. 561), and Besner, Twilley, McCann, and Seergobin (1990, p. 435) suggest that too many hidden units may be the reason that the data simulations of certain connectionist models show lower nonword reading performance (just as dyslexics) than they should. If the phenotypic performance pattern of poor readers is indeed inferior phonological coding and superior orthographic coding compared to reading-level matched younger controls, it may be that neurophysiological and connectionist models are converging on a coherent theory of why this is the case.

THE PARADOXICAL REGULARITY EFFECT

[*see Metsala, Stanovich, and Brown (1998) in the Bibliography*]

VARIABLE DIFFERENCES
OUTSIDE OF THE WORD RECOGNITION MODULE

The analyses conducted on the memory and language tasks test a critical prediction of the phonological-core variable-difference model of reading disability. In this model, performance differences between RD-D and RD-N children are predicted to increase as the processes tested become more central, less modular, and further removed from the phonological core (Siegel, 1992; Stanovich, 1988a).

[material omitted]

The analyses presented in the current study provide moderate support for the predictions of the phonological-core variable-difference model. In an academic achievement domain other than reading, specifically, arithmetic skill, the RD-D children outperformed the RD-N children, although the absolute magnitude of the difference was not large (an unweighted average across reading levels of 0.5 grade equivalents). Much stronger evidence for differential performance on nonmodular tasks operating across cognitive domains comes from the results of the memory tasks. Here there were robust differences between the RD-D and RD-N subjects on the STM–letters task (for both rhyming and nonrhyming letters), the working memory–words, and the working memory–numbers task. Thus, there were differences between these two groups when the task involved primarily storage functions (STM–letters) and when it implicated storage and capacity-demanding processing operations (working memory tasks). The beta weights for the RD-N versus RD-D contrasts were somewhat larger for the working memory tasks—as was the unique variance explained (6.5% and 5.3% versus 1.6% and 2.5%). Finally, three of the four overall RD versus NRD contrasts were significant (all but working memory - numbers) and all had positive signs, indicating that WRAT reading level underpredicted the performance of the older RD children. This finding is probably reflective of the influence of maturational factors that are independent of reading development. Also, it should be emphasized that these comparisons are relative to reading-level controls. The performance of the RD-D children would not be commensurate with chronological-age controls on most memory and language tasks (Siegel & Linder, 1984; Siegel & Ryan, 1988).

The results on the language tasks were less consistent than the results from the memory tasks. *[material omitted]* Performance differences on the language tasks may be somewhat less robust because the phonological deficits that characterize both RD-D and RD-N children may in fact disrupt performance on language tasks that ostensibly involved higher level language processing (Fowler, 1988; Mann, Shankweiler, & Smith, 1984; Shankweiler, 1989; Shankweiler, Crain, Brady, & Macaruso, 1992).

[material omitted]

THE PHENOTYPIC PERFORMANCE PATTERN OF READING-DISABLED CHILDREN

We have provided here a characterization of the phenotypic performance pattern of reading-disabled children that we argue could serve as a benchmark for reductive research programs. No comparable study has included RD-D and RD-N comparisons across the range of reading levels and tasks that we have examined here. Although reading-level designs have become much more common in the last five years, few studies have contained RD-D versus RD-N performance comparisons and simultaneously had RL controls (see Felton & Wood, 1992, for an exception).

An important strength of the data pattern we have described and of the framework we use to conceptualize the results—the phonological-core variable-difference model—is that it converges with other data in the literature. It thus provides a firmer foundation for reductive research efforts on reading disability (e.g., Pennington, 1991) that are examining the genetics of dyslexia, the heritability of reading subcomponents, neuroanatomical correlates, or performance patterns that can be mimicked by connectionist computer models. Many more group differences have been observed at the behavioral level than can be investigated by expensive, and thus resource-limiting, neuroanatomical and genetic investigations. Investigators seeking relationships in a more fundamental scientific domain must have confidence that the data patterns that they are attempting to reduce are not spurious. The data patterns we have described were robust enough within our own investigation, and display enough consistency when compared to other studies in the literature, that they appear to have passed this initial threshold of confidence. Other indications of group differences in the reading disabilities literature, while deserving of further investigation, have not passed this threshold. Such is the case, for example, with some data suggesting visual processing deficits that have been reported in the literature (Lovegrove, 1992; Lovegrove, Martin, & Slaghuis, 1986; Willows, 1991). Although these findings do deserve experimental attention, their replicability has not been established (Hayduk, Bruck, & Cavanagh, 1992; Kruk, 1991) and they simply do not exist in the context of the converging evidence and theory that characterize our knowledge of phonological-core deficits (Hulme, 1988; Shankweiler et al., 1992; Vellutino, 1979; Vellutino & Scanlon, 1987). Whether or not these visual deficits are eventually verified by converging evidence from a variety of laboratories, they are currently not the best candidates on which to focus reductive research techniques.

To summarize the phenotypic performance pattern we have characterized: Cognitive differences between RD-D and RD-N children all seem to reside outside of the word recognition module. These differences are consistently revealed on memory tasks and in academic domains other than reading and are present but somewhat attenuated in language processing tasks. With regard to word recognition processes themselves, RD-D and RD-N children show performance patterns that are remarkably similar. Both show pseudoword reading performance below that expected on the basis of their WRAT Reading levels. Both show performance on phonological coding tasks not involving production of a spelling or pronunciation (phonological choice task and pseudoword recognition) that is commensurate with their reading levels but inferior to chronological age controls. Both show indications of relative strength in orthographic processing skill: performance on some orthographic tasks is underpredicted by their WRAT reading levels. Both demonstrate spelling–sound regularity effects that are commensurate with their reading levels.

Contrary to previous conjectures (Stanovich et al., 1986; Stanovich et al., 1988), a developmental lag model in its strongest form does not fit the present results very well. That model predicts that once reading level is regressed out as a predictor of a reading-related cognitive subskill, subject categorization should not predict additional variance in the criterion variable. Only for the phonological coding tasks and the regularity effect was this the case. For all of the other tasks that we examined, at least one of the two contrasts was statistically significant. An advocate of a weakened version of the developmental lag model might argue, however, that on word-level processes, the maximum amount of unique variance explained by any categorization was 5.0%.

Importantly, the performance pattern we have described is extremely problematic for traditional conceptions of reading disability. As has often been pointed out (e.g., Pennington et al., 1992; Taylor & Schatschneider, 1992), the idea of defining dyslexia by reference to aptitude–achievement discrepancy gained credence because of the intuition that RD-D children were more likely to have a distinct etiology. The idea that some poor readers were different from others in terms of the genetic and/or neuroanatomical underpinnings of their disability was what fueled the enthusiasm for IQ-discrepancy measurement. Measuring IQ–achievement discrepancy was seen as a shortcut to the genetically and neurologically distinct group of poor readers that was assumed to exist. The discrepancy assumption survived for decades because there was no good evidence on the neurological, genetic, or phenotypic information processing differences between RD-D and RD-N children. Our data undercut one component of the discrepancy assumption: RD-D and RD-N children do not differ in the information processing subskills (phonological and orthographic coding) that determine word recognition. IQ discrepancy is not uniquely linked to the information processing pattern in the word recognition module that is the primary indicator of reading disability. Likewise, recent genetic analyses have not indicated differential genetic causation for children with and without IQ-discrepancy (Olson, Rack, Conners, DeFries, & Fulker, 1991; Pennington et al., 1992; Stevenson, 1991, 1992; Stevenson, Graham, Fredman, & McLoughlin, 1987). In short, neither the phenotypic nor the genotypic indicators of poor reading are correlated in any reliable way with IQ discrepancy. If there is a special group of reading-disabled children who are behaviorally, cognitively, genetically, and/or neurologically "different," it is becoming increasingly unlikely that they can be easily identified by using IQ discrepancy as a proxy for the genetic and neurological differences themselves. Thus, the foundational assumption that underlies decades of classification in both research and educational practice in the reading disabilities field is becoming increasingly untenable.

NOTE

1. Using the method to be described, various selection criteria can be explored within the same sample. Different cutoff values for reading disability can be examined (e.g., different percentile ranks on the reading test employed) as well as several different methods of defining aptitude/achievement discrepancy (e.g., absolute IQ cutoff score, standard score discrepancy, regression discrepancy). Some of the results of employing these alternative criteria will be reported below.

PART III

MATTHEW EFFECTS IN READING

CHAPTER 9

Tying It All Together

*A Model of Reading Acquisition
and Reading Difficulty*

No paper has defined my scholarly career in reading more than the "Matthew effects" paper published in Reading Research Quarterly in 1986. Hence its segregation in its own section in this volume. For this paper I received the Albert J. Harris Award at the meeting of the International Reading Association in 1988 in Toronto (where Anne Cunningham won the Dissertation of the Year Award—a happy and exciting coincidence for us). The Matthew effects paper has received over 500 citations, and it continues to be cited today, more than 10 years after its publication (it received 50 citations in 1998 alone). This paper was the first of my publications to have considerable impact on the field of reading practitioners where it resonated with some force. It is routinely reprinted in practitioner-oriented materials and publications. In fact, I still receive enthusiastic letters from teachers who are discovering it for the first time. This is because many publications directed at teachers have emphasized Matthew effects—for example, the very useful booklet for teachers in New Zealand and Australia prepared by Tom Nicholson (1991a) called *Overcoming the Matthew Effect: Solving Reading Problems across the Curriculum.*

Like the interactive–compensatory paper (Stanovich, 1980; Chapter 3) the Matthew effects paper was a review and theoretical synthesis of a diverse body of literature. But the Matthew effects paper is different from the interactive–compensatory paper in one interesting psychological respect. When I was writing the interactive–compensatory paper, I had no idea that it would become a "citation classic" (see Citation Classics, *Current Contents: Social and Behavioral Sciences*, October 31, 1988). I saw it as a logical theoretical progression that synthesized our early results (see Chapter 2 and Stanovich, West, & Feeman, 1981) with other related experiments in the literature. I did not envision how much the field would fixate on the top-down versus bottom-up debate in the ensuing decade—thus thrusting this paper into the center of those debates.

The Matthew effects paper provides a stark contrast to my myopia regarding the eventual impact of the interactive–compensatory paper. In contrast to the latter, while writing the Matthew paper I had a strong premonition that it would be influential and much cited. Primarily, I believe this was because all of the ideas in it were "ripe"—just sitting there waiting for someone to synthesize them. The field had become much more well populated with cognitive developmentalists and cognitive psychologists between the writing of the interactive–compensatory paper and the Matthew paper. There were simply many more people out there who could see the ripeness of the ideas. So, even if you hadn't written the Matthew paper yourself, you could immediately recognize the convergence of evidence that it articulated. Once I got the convergence in my head, I immediately saw how recognizable it was, and realized that others would recognize this as well. It probably represents in the most distilled form a skill for which I have been amply rewarded in the field of reading: arriving at a theoretical synthesis of ideas by amalgamating the empirical results contributed by dozens of other investigators.

So how does "Matthew" look with the perspective of 15 years' hindsight? First, it is a complex paper with many interlocking parts. In addition to its overall interlocking structure, there are many micropredictions and microtheories within it. For example, in the paper, I predicted that the causal relation between phonological sensitivity and word recognition ability might be developmentally limited (i.e., confined to the earliest stages of reading acquisition), and now there is some evidence supporting this view (Ehri & Soffer, 1999; however, see Wagner et al., 1997). The summary of work on context effects is an expansion and update of the work discussed in Part I. All of the comments there about how this work has progressed since then also apply to Chapter 10. The Matthew effects paper contains, I feel, a pretty good discussion of the complexities of the use of the term context effects. I also still like the discussion of reasons for why the theoretical confusions arose. Likewise, I feel that the section on the maddeningly misused term "word calling" was pretty much on the mark (see also Shankweiler et al., 1999). The section in the Matthew paper on rapprochement between theoretical perspectives is ironic in light of the 15 years of the so-called Reading Wars (see Part VII) that have elapsed between original publication of that paper and its reprinting in this volume. Nevertheless, I think I was on the mark in acknowledging the contributions of the top-down theorists while at the same time showing that the Popperian falsification of their view was contributing to cumulative progress:

> Once these alterations are made, it is possible to see more congruence between some of the insights that were the source of the top-down models and those of

more bottom-up models like verbal efficiency theory. For example, both classes of model are in agreement on the necessity of expending processing capacity on higher-level comprehension processes rather than on word recognition. . . . Long before most cognitive psychologists became interested in reading, top-down theorists were investigating critical processing issues in the domain of context use. The latter were responsible for the crucial insight that readers need to allocate attentional capacity to comprehension rather than to word recognition in order to become fluent. However, recent work by cognitive and developmental psychologists—some of whom are of a more bottom-up persuasion—has helped to specify accurately the key mechanism that allows capacity to be allocated to comprehension. This mechanism turns out to be efficient decoding rather than context use. Both groups of researchers have thus made important contributions to our current knowledge of the interrelationships between decoding, context use for word recognition, and comprehension. (p. 369)

Finally, the emphasis on differentiating the presence of a knowledge base from its use turned out to be useful not only in understanding context effects, but in more contemporary controversies such as the relation between reading ability and spelling–sound regularity (Metsala, Stanovich, & Brown, 1998; Rack, Snowling, & Olson, 1992).

The developmental model of reading acquisition articulated in the Matthew paper places phonological processing at the center of reading acquisition. Likewise, the Matthew paper relies heavily on the phonological core deficit model when talking about reading disability. As I noted in Chapter 5, this emphasis was largely justified. The self-teaching notion of Jorm and Share (1983) was also incorporated into the developmental model in the Matthew paper, and this model has continued to be elaborated in subsequent years (see Share, 1995, 1999; Share & Stanovich, 1995).

In the early 1980s, as these information processing issues (about context effects and phonological processing) were becoming clarified, I became concerned about how these issues interfaced with the larger contexts of literacy acquisition. Having spent a lifetime on the political left ("liberal" is not a dirty word in my household), I found particularly disturbing the empirical indications that schooling did not succeed in eliminating the achievement gaps that were apparent between children even as they entered school. One important conjecture in the Matthew paper was that exposure to print *outside* of school was a key contributing element in causing achievement differences that were apparent *inside* the classroom.

In short, there was a sad irony behind the literature reviewed in the Matthew paper and in the conclusions drawn from that literature. Schools create opportunities for learning and for acquiring critical skills and knowledge. But children then proceed to *use* those skills and that learning outside of school. Inevitably, there are individual differences in that knowledge and those skills. The differential reading skills thus acquired enable differential bootstrapping of further vocabulary, knowledge, and cognitive structures outside of school (see Part V, on the consequences of literacy). These bootstrapped knowledge bases then create further individual differences that are made manifest in differential performance as children grapple with subsequent in-school content and skills. There is empirical evidence for this sequence. For example, in a study that was not known to me when I was writing the Matthew paper, Hayes and Grether (1983) reported on the growth in reading comprehension and vocabulary of several thousand students in the New York City schools during the school year and during the summer. They found that the summer period, when the children were not in school, accounted for more of the gap between the high-achieving and the low-achieving students than did the period when the children were actually in school. They concluded that "very little of the enormous difference in word knowledge performance . . . appears to be attributable to what goes on in school; most of it comes from what goes on *out* of school" (p. 64). But, ironically, this differential skill use outside of school that sets the stage for these rich-get-richer effects is set up by the very literacy skills that are taught *in* school.

It should be noted that research by Huttenlocher, Levine, and Vevea (1998) and Morrison (Frazier & Morrison, 1998; Morrison, Griffith, & Alberts, 1997) indicating unique effects of the school year (as opposed to the summer) on cognitive development is not inconsistent with that of Hayes and Grether (1983). The latter focused on *variability* in cognitive skills, whereas the former focused on changes in the *mean levels* of groups of children. It is perfectly possible for mean levels of skills to be more affected during the school year rather than the summer and for the summer to be the main cause of the variability in those skills (McCall, 1981; Rutter, 1983). One can easily imagine a Matthew-like model that could account for such an effect. If during the school year the cognitive growth of all children is occurring and during the summer months the growth for only a subset of children is occurring, then mean levels will be increasing to a greater extent during the school year. However, if the particular children who are displaying growth during the summer are precisely those children who are already reading voraciously (and hence continue to read during the summer) and whose achievement is already at the top of the distribution, then the further growth spawned by the summer reading these children do will increase overall performance variance.

At the time I wrote the Matthew paper there was only scattered and unsystematic evidence relevant to the developmental model of achievement differences presented in the paper. Much of what I said in the paper was, at the time, speculation. As mentioned above, many other studies in subsequent years have confirmed, clarified, and amended aspects of the model (Anderson, 1996; Chall, Jacobs, & Baldwin, 1990; Crijnen, Feehan, & Kellman, 1998; Guthrie, Wigfield, Metsala, & Cox, 1999; Hayes & Ahrens, 1988; Jimerson, Egeland, & Teo, 1999; Juel, 1988; McBride-Chang, Wagner, & Chang, 1997; Senechal, LeFevre, Thomas, & Daley, 1998; Share, McGee, & Silva, 1989; Snow, Barnes, Chandler, Goodman, & Hemphill, 1991; Sticht, Hofstetter, & Hofstetter, 1996; van den Bos, 1989). In the subsequent decade, my own research group concentrated on empirically verifying many of the hypotheses articulated in the 1986 paper—in particular the hypothesis that early reading achievement differences lead to differences in reading volume that affect other cognitive and psycholinguistic processes (Cunningham & Stanovich, 1997; Stanovich, 1993a; Stanovich, Cunningham, & West, 1998; Stanovich, West, Cunningham, Cipielewski, & Siddiqui, 1996). This research program is described in Part V.

THE MATTHEW EFFECT VERSUS A MATTHEW EFFECT MODEL

It is clear from the research described in Part V that my focus in the years subsequent to the 1986 paper has been on the feedback effects caused by differential reading proclivities on other literacy-related cognitive skills. The research program summarized in Part V has this more substantive goal as its focus rather than the issue of increasing variance in cognitive skills themselves. I am referring here to a very useful distinction drawn by Bast and Reitsma (1998) in their study of Matthew effects: the distinction between the *Matthew effect* and the *Matthew effect model*. The former refers to the fan-spread effect on variability with time—that over time the variability in reading and reading-related cognitive skills increases. In contrast, a Matthew effect model

> attempts to account for these fan-spread effects. . . . The fan spread is, however, simply one component of the Matthew effect phenomenon. The most important feature of the model as proposed by Stanovich (1986b) is the underlying developmental pattern that causes the outcome. The phenomenon of increasing achievement differences is hypothesized to be caused by a specific developmental pattern of interrelations between reading skills and other variables. (Bast & Reitsma, 1998, p. 1373)

I like the distinction made by Bast and Reitsma (1998) because I think it might reorient empirical and theoretical efforts in a more fruitful direction. Much of the attention subsequent to the Matthew paper has focused on the fan-spread effect itself, whereas I was always equally concerned with the issue of how the engagement in literacy activities affects individual differences in cognitive skills (see Part V), regardless of whether a fan spread exists for that skill or not. Here I am referring to the fact that it is possible for reading experience to be a causal factor in cognitive growth whether or not it is a cause of a fan spread—the variability in a skill is in principle independent of its mean level (McCall, 1981; Rutter, 1983). In short, the issue of reciprocal causation involving reading experience is not totally coextensive with the issue of the fan-spread effect.

The studies by Bast and Reitsma (1998) and by Shaywitz, Holford, Holahan, Fletcher, Stuebing, Francis, and Shaywitz (1995) represent two of the most extensive empirical studies of the issues raised in my Matthew paper in recent years. I view the Bast and Reitsma (1998) study as a substantial contribution in its attempt to quantitatively test aspects of the developmental model. In contrast, I find the Shaywitz et al. (1995) study somewhat problematic.

Using structural equation modeling techniques, Bast and Reitsma (1998) studied a group of children longitudinally through the first three grades of school and found that there was a fan-spread effect for word recognition but not reading comprehension. More importantly, they constructed a Matthew effect model to explain the interacting relationships revealed by the waves in their longitudinal study. They found support for several reciprocal models that bear similarities to those that I speculated on in my 1986 paper. For example, Bast and Reitsma (1998) concluded that "the results indicate that good readers tended to read more frequently during leisure time than poor readers. These leisure time reading activities were related to differences in the size of the vocabulary at the end of second grade. In turn, vocabulary affected subsequent comprehension in reading" (p. 1387).

Unlike the Bast and Reitsma (1998) study, which focused on the various Matthew effect models (and was only incidentally concerned with the fan-spread effect), the Shaywitz et al. (1995) longitudinal study focused on examining fan-spread effects for both IQ and reading ability. For each of these variables, the slope of each subject's score over time was computed. Then the investigators looked to see whether this growth curve parameter increased as a function of the initial score on the variable—which would be evidence of a fan-spread effect (growth being faster for those with higher initial scores and slower for those with lower initial scores). The results of this study are marred, however, because of the choice of the metric for analysis. In their first analyses, Shaywitz et al. (1995) analyzed standard scores. This is problematic because no fan spread could possibly be demonstrated with percentiles or any type of standard score. This is because someone in the lower range of the distribution could only get relatively worse by "passing up" someone who is even lower—who themselves would be subject to a Matthew effect (and so on—the infinite regress is obvious).

For example, even if Matthew effects were operating, one would not expect the slope of percentile rank by grade functions to be correlated with the overall percentile rank. The percentiles of the higher scoring children are not going to rise. Passing up children with even higher percentile ranks would be the only way for high percentile children to have positive slopes, but the children with the even higher ranks should also be subject to Matthew effects and they should also rise—in an infinite regress. Fan-spread effects simply cannot be detected with such a metric. They are most likely to be detected with absolute measures of achievement such as vocabulary size (Walberg, Strykowski, Rovai, & Hung, 1984; Walberg & Tsai, 1983). In short, the Matthew hypothesis does *not* make the prediction that the slope of the standard score (or percentile rank) should be correlated with initial skill level. By definition, the standardization wipes out the possibility of increasing variability with age. The effect is statistically adjusted away by using standardized scores.

In their second analysis Shaywitz et al. (1995) used Rasch scores for the reading measure (composite Woodcock reading) rather than standard scores for their analyses. This metric seems a better choice than standard scores, which are clearly inappropriate for investigating fan-spread effects. However, the Rasch score results indicated an inverse fan-spread effect, that is, growth was faster for those low in ability. This is an astounding result. I certainly could conceive of a zero fan spread (all ability levels progressing at the same rate), but a negative fan spread seemed not credible. When do the poor readers catch up? Those of us who wished that a developmental lag model were true have been asking that question for decades (the answer being, of course, never—at least not without substantial instruction efforts). In fact, no one (especially teachers) I have asked about this result finds it remotely plausible. I was quite puzzled about how it could have come about and was stuck until I stumbled upon Lohman's (1999) discussion of Rasch scores and item-response theory methods. I was startled to read that

> more troubling is the fact that such methods can transform a raw score scale that shows a systematic increase in score variance with age into one that shows marked decrease in score variance with age (Hoover, 1984). Although score variance can reasonably remain steady or even decrease over time for closed-ended skills, there is little empirical or conceptual support for such effects in the complex, open-ended skills measured on school achievement tests. By the end of the grade school years, some low-scoring children are still struggling with elementary addition and subtraction, whereas their high-scoring peers are solving algebra problems. It makes little sense to say that somehow the variability in mathematics achievement or vocabulary knowledge has declined over the grade school years. Yet, this is precisely what happened when IRT methods were used to scale the California Achievement Tests. (pp. 62–63)

So perhaps here we have the reason for the strange results obtained by Shaywitz et al. (1995; see Bast and Reitsma [1998] for a further statistical critique of the Shaywitz et al. study, and Crijnen et al. [1998] for a growth-curve study of an educational intervention that focuses on Matthew effects). Finally, McBride-Chang, Wagner, and Chang (1997) conducted a growth-curve analysis like that of Shaywitz et al. (1995) and did find evidence of a fan-spread effect for phonological awareness.

MATTHEW EFFECTS AND LEARNING DISABILITIES

Nascent recognition that something was wrong with the concept of learning disabilities (LD) because its interrelationships with the concept of IQ had not been fully worked out is discernible in the Matthew paper. These problems receive extended discussion in Part VI of this book. As discussed there, the field did not heed my warning in the Matthew paper that "some of these conceptual problems are so serious that they threaten to undermine the entire field if they are not soon resolved" (p. 384). Instead, the field suffers through travesties such as the Boston University lawsuit (see Stanovich, 1999a) and hostile publicity in many media outlets (see Shalit, 1997). The undermining of the concept of LD continues—and public support for it in the sociopolitical domain is wavering. As I detail in Stanovich (1999a) and in Chapter 17 of this book in my comments on the Boston University case, this all could have been avoided if the field had adopted the self-critical attitude toward its relation with the IQ construct that I called for in my 1986 article; that I called for again in a much-cited 1991 paper (Chapter 18); again in a notorious 1993 paper (Stanovich, 1993b); and that I was finally forced to call for yet again in an invited commentary on the Boston University case in 1999 (Stanovich, 1999a). The mere existence of this series of papers warning of the same conceptual confusions and urging a self-critical stance on the field of LD suggests a lack of professionalism. Sadly, the LD field seems more than ever dominated by advocacy rather than science. In Chapters 17 and Stanovich (1999a) I discuss in detail why the public is rightly losing patience with such evidence-free advocacy. Thus, the LD section in the Matthew paper had a sad prescience. Rereading it 15 years after it was written saddens me.

MATTHEW EFFECTS AND POLITICAL TRENDS

My concern for poor-get-poorer effects in education was certainly affected by my interactions with master teachers such as my wife, Paula; Anne Cunningham, of course; and also Ruth Nathan, who had joined my research team as a PhD student in the early 1980s. And it was also affected by my politics. This is pretty clear from a reading of the section titled "Matthew Effects and the Less Skilled Reader" where I discuss organism–environment correlations and ability composition effects in classrooms. There, I lamented the Matthew effects caused by passive organism–environment correlations (Grigorenko, 1999; Scarr & McCartney, 1983), where "biologically unlucky individuals are provided with inferior social and educational environments, and the winners of the biological lottery are provided better environments" (p. 383), and pointed to the fact that these unfortunate correlations were in part socially determined.

Political trends of the late 1980s and 1990s have done nothing to attenuate these unfortunate correlations. We are, if anything, even more of a "winner-take-all society" (see Frank, 1999; Frank & Cook, 1995), where gross economic disparities are tolerated and where the economically advantaged make strenuous efforts to pass on these advantages to their children—and not the least of these efforts involve making sure that they are provided disproportionate educational advantages (Kelman & Lester, 1997). Junior is provided more tutoring in the vulnerable years, in addition to expensive SAT preparation a few years later—and a hunk of Fidelity Magellan when he turns 25 (Why can't those other lazy people just work harder and keep up?). In contrast, children not destined to appreciate the attractiveness of capital gains tax cuts or the beauty of the Roth IRA meet the savage educational inequalities described by Kozol (1991) when they enter school in the crucial years of literacy development. There are viable political solutions to this travesty (Ackerman & Alstott, 1999; Berliner & Biddle, 1995; Frank, 1999; Gitlin, 1995; Korten, 1999; Kuttner, 1998; Mander & Goldsmith, 1996; Schmookler, 1993), but I defer further comment along these lines until Chapter 19.

SOCIOCONSTRUCTIVISM IN THE MATTHEW PAPER

Aspects of the Matthew effects paper clearly show that I have some sympathy with socioconstructivist approaches. As Part VII will demonstrate, I only part company with this approach when its advocates adopt views emphasizing a radically relativistic ontology and deny the validity of the traditional criteria of science (operational definitions, replication, convergence, control, etc.). For example, I have previously (e.g., Stanovich, 1990a) acknowledged that although brain differences may exist that cause functional processing variations of the type that are related to academic success, it is still critical to examine the context in which differential behavioral outcomes occur. This is because how these differences are interpreted by society can have enormous consequences for children. In the Matthew effects paper I outlined how certain social structures can set up particularly bad interactions between the processing abilities with which a child approaches the task of reading and the educational milieu in which those abilities will be evaluated. Two examples that I employed were: (1) ability grouping within classrooms and schools and (2) political and social structures that dictate poorer educational environments for the economically disadvantaged. Both social policies ensure that it is just those children who are at risk for school difficulty who are provided with suboptimal educational resources (Berliner & Biddle, 1995; Bronfenbrenner, McClelland, Wethington, Moen, & Ceci, 1996; Kozol, 1991).

As a further example, consider the work of Stevenson and his colleagues (Stevenson, Stigler, Lee, Lucker, Kitamura, & Hsu, 1985; Uttal, Lummis, & Stevenson, 1988) on cross-cultural differences in educational achievement. His samples of Japanese and Taiwanese children outperformed his American sample, particularly in the area of mathematics; yet basic information processing differences—at least of the type revealed by common psychometric instruments—were virtually nonexistent. One looks to differences in cultural and school contexts for an explanation of the differential performance.

As a final example, consider that it appears that when epidemiologically based sampling methods and regression-based statistical definitions are used, the ratio of boys to girls in a sample of dyslexic children is much lower than the ratio that characterizes school- and clinic-based samples (Shaywitz, Shaywitz, Fletcher, & Escobar, 1990). The research programs that have uncovered this fact reflect biological, neuropsychological, and information processing frameworks, and virtually ignore socioconstructivist approaches. Nevertheless, the evidence that they have produced regarding differential sex ratios depending upon the source of the classification should, I submit, be of intense interest to researchers using a socioconstructivist perspective to understand how disabilities are in part cultural constructs. The lesson taught by this example is that evidence deriving from one framework can be of utility to a different research perspective, even when workers within the two frameworks are not consciously attempting to interact.

In short, I am not totally hostile to socioconstructivist approaches—nor have I only recently become aware of them. For example, consider the following discussion of the socially constructed nature of mental retardation as a disability category:

> Once one conceptualizes retarded individuals as comprising a surplus population, the culturally relative nature of the concept of retardation becomes obvious. It is rare to find a discussion of the full political and social implications of treating mental retardation as a culturally relative concept. This paper develops the argument that one can predict the effect of technological and economic developments on the lives of retarded individuals (and, to some extent, other handicapped persons) once one accepts the full implications of a socially relative concept of retardation. The position will also be taken that it is important for developing nations to recognize the interrelation of technological developments and the labeling of people as mentally disabled. Knowledge of the relationship can determine how a nation deals with its mentally retarded population. Indeed, it can even determine whether a nation will *have* such a population.

This is standard socioconstructivist stuff. The only thing remotely notable about the statement is that it was written over 20 years ago—considerably prior to the postmodernist/socioconstructivist vogue that has swept through education in the last decade. The statement was written by me (see Stanovich, 1978, p. 236), and was part of an address that I gave in the summer of 1978 to the Council for Exceptional Children's World Congress at the University of Stirling in Scotland. So I am not hostile to socioconstructivism and, as the statement proves, I am no johnny-come-lately to constructivist ideas.

This context needs to be understood when in Chapter 19 I consider the charge of whole language advocates that researchers who focus on information processing at the word level are somehow denying the important effects of context on reading growth. As I wrote in a 1990 article for the *Journal of Reading Behavior*, for a full understanding of a phenomenon, we need evidence from many different levels of analysis. This is as true when trying to understand literacy as it is for any other complex behavior. It is in this sense that I am in sympathy with the socioconstructivist perspective (the sense in which I am out of sympathy with this perspective will also be made clear in Chapter 19). Conversely, those who are working from socioconstructivist perspectives must acknowledge the importance of information processing and neurophysiological analyses of the reading process rather than display a knee-jerk hostility. These perspectives too are part of the full scientific model that we all seek: a model of the reading process acting in context.

CHAPTER 10

Matthew Effects in Reading

Some Consequences of Individual Differences in the Acquisition of Literacy

To synthesize the ever-growing body of literature on individual differences in the cognitive skills related to reading is difficult because of the plethora of relationships that have been found. Good and poor readers have been compared on just about every cognitive task that has ever been devised, and group performance differences have been observed on a large number of these tasks (see, for example, Carr, 1981; DeSoto & DeSoto, 1983; Mitchell, 1982; Palmer, MacLeod, Hunt, & Davidson, 1985; Share, Jorm, Maclean, & Matthews, 1984; Singer & Crouse, 1981; Stanovich, 1982a, 1982b, 1986a). Mounds of correlations and significant differences have been found. There is, then, at least one sense in which it can be said that we do not lack empirical evidence. The problem is in deciding what it all means.

The aim of this paper is to attempt to clarify the literature by drawing attention to some alternative ways of interpreting relationships between cognitive processes and reading ability. These alternative interpretations have all been discussed before by numerous authors (e.g., Bryant & Bradley, 1985; Byrne, 1986; Chall, 1983b; Donaldson, 1978; Ehri, 1979; Morrison & Manis, 1982), but their implications have not been fully explored—nor have they been brought together within a coherent framework, nor with a model of the development of individual differences in reading achievement.

PROBLEMS WITH THE EXISTING EVIDENCE

For many years, research on individual differences was plagued by the failure to carry out thorough process analyses on the experimental tasks employed.

159

Thus, it was rarely possible to ascribe any cognitive specificity to an observed group difference. This problem has partially been alleviated due to the general influence of a paradigmatic assumption of cognitive psychology: that performance on any single task is the result of the simultaneous or successive operation of many different information-processing operations. However, it took a long time for reading disability researchers to accept an implication of this assumption: that one could not merely observe a difference on, for example, a perceptual task, and then announce that "visual processing" was the key to reading failure, based on one's introspection about what the task tapped. It was sometimes hard to understand that no matter how large the performance difference observed on a single task, such an outcome represented not the end, but instead the beginning of a careful task analysis that one hoped would reveal the cognitive locus of the difference. The rise and fall of many of the popular hypotheses in the dyslexia literature mirrors this belated realization (see Vellutino, 1979).

Beyond the issue of inferring the appropriate process difference from task performance lies an even more vexing problem: that of inferring causation. After observing a performance difference in a purely correlational study and carrying out the appropriate task analysis, we are still left with the question of whether the processing difference thus isolated causes variation in reading achievement, whether reading achievement itself affects the operation of the cognitive process, or whether the relationship is due to some third variable. Also, there is the possibility of *reciprocal causation*: that there are causal connections running in both directions.

Complicating the picture even further is the possibility that the causal connections between variation in reading achievement and the efficiency of various cognitive processes may change with development. This possibility has been strongly emphasized by some researchers (e.g., Chall, 1983b; Satz, Taylor, Friel, & Fletcher, 1978), but has been inadequately reflected in much research on individual differences in the cognitive skills of reading. For example, it is possible that some relationships are *developmentally limited*—that individual differences in a particular cognitive process may be a causal determinant of variation in reading achievement early in development, but at some point have no further effects on the level of reading efficiency. In this case, a correlation between reading achievement and the efficiency of a cognitive process may obtain in adults because the efficiency of the cognitive process determined the ease with which the individual traversed earlier stages of the reading process—stages that laid the foundation for the present level of reading ability—but further progress is dependent on the development of processes other than the one in question. A residual correlation between the efficiency of the process and reading level remains as a remnant of a causal connection present during an earlier developmental stage.

The vast literature on individual differences in the cognitive processes of reading will only be fully understood when we are able to determine which performance linkages reflect causal relationships, which are developmentally limited, which are the result of third variables, which enter into relationships of reciprocal causation, and which are consequences of the individual's reading level or reading history. Achieving such a classification will be easier if it is recognized that certain relationships may change status at different levels of reading development. In this review some tentative classifications for some of the cognitive processes that have received considerable attention in recent research will be hypothesized. In order to provide a context for these hypotheses, I will first present a brief outline of a preliminary (and incomplete) model of the development of individual differences in reading skill.

A MODEL OF THE DEVELOPMENT OF INDIVIDUAL DIFFERENCES IN READING

Evidence is mounting that the primary specific mechanism that enables early reading success is phonological awareness: conscious access to the phonemic level of the speech stream and some ability to cognitively manipulate representations at this level. Although general indicators of cognitive functioning such as nonverbal intelligence, vocabulary, and listening comprehension make significant independent contributions to predicting the ease of initial reading acquisition, phonological awareness stands out as the most potent predictor (Share et al., 1984; Stanovich, Cunningham, & Cramer, 1984; Stanovich, Cunningham, & Feeman, 1984a; Tunmer & Nesdale, 1985). Indeed, phonological awareness tasks often correlate more highly with early reading acquisition than do omnibus measures such as general intelligence tests or reading readiness tests (Mann, 1984; Share et al., 1984; Stanovich, Cunningham, & Cramer, 1984; Stanovich, Cunningham, & Feeman, 1984a; Zifcak, 1981).

Of course, although the strength of these correlations serves to draw attention to phonological awareness, it is not proof that variation in awareness is causally connected to differences in the ease of initial reading acquisition. Proving causation requires much stronger evidence, and this evidence is much less plentiful than the purely correlational data. However, a growing body of data does exist indicating that variation in phonological awareness is causally related to the early development of reading skill. This evidence is of several different types. First, there are several studies showing that measures of phonological awareness predict reading ability even when the former are assessed very early in development (Bradley & Bryant, 1983, 1985; Fox & Routh, 1975; Share et al., 1984; Williams, 1984). Secondly, Tunmer and Nesdale (1985) reported a contingency analysis of their first-grade data which indicated that phonemic segmentation skill was a necessary, but not sufficient, condition for reading acquisition (see also Perfetti, Beck, & Hughes, 1981). In addition, the results of some recent longitudinal studies where cross-lagged correlational methods and/or structural equation modeling have been employed have led to the conclusion that early skill at phonological awareness leads to superior reading achievement (Perfetti et al., 1981; Torneus, 1984). Evidence supporting this conclusion also comes from reading-level match designs. When 10-year-old disabled readers perform worse on phonological tasks than nondisabled 6-year-old children reading at the same level (e.g., Bradley & Bryant, 1978), it is somewhat more difficult to argue that the latter are superior because they have had more reading experience. Last, and of course most convincing, are the results of several studies where phonological awareness skills were manipulated via training, and the manipulation resulted in significant experimental group advantages in reading, word recognition, and spelling (Bradley & Bryant, 1983, 1985; Fox & Routh, 1984; Olofsson & Lundberg, 1985; Torneus, 1984; Treiman & Baron, 1983).

It should be noted that several of the studies cited above have also supported Ehri's (1979, 1984, 1985) position that reading acquisition itself facilitates phonological awareness (see also Perfetti, 1985; Perfetti et al., 1981; Wagner & Torgesen, 1987), so that the situation appears to be one of reciprocal causation. Such situations of reciprocal causation can have important "bootstrapping" effects, and some of these will be discussed in this review. However, the question in this section is not which direction of causality is dominant. The essential properties of the model being outlined here are dependent only on the fact that a causal link running from phonological awareness to reading acquisition has been established, independent of the status of the opposite causal link.

Many researchers have discussed the reasons phonological awareness is important in early reading acquisition (see Gough & Hillinger, 1980; Liberman, 1982; Perfetti, 1984; Williams, 1984). A beginning reader must at some point discover the alphabetic principle: that units of print map onto units of sound (see Perfetti, 1984). This principle may be induced; it may be acquired through direct instruction; it may be acquired along with or after the buildup of a visually based sight vocabulary—but it must be acquired if a child is to progress successfully in reading. Children must be able to decode independently the many unknown words that will be encountered in the early stages of reading. By acquiring some knowledge of spelling-to-sound mappings, the child will gain the reading independence that eventually leads to the levels of practice that are prerequisites to fluent reading. The research cited above appears to indicate that some minimal level of explicit phonemic awareness is required for the acquisition of the spelling-to-sound knowledge that supports independent decoding.

It is apparently important that the prerequisite phonological awareness and skill at spelling-to-sound mapping be in place *early* in the child's development, because their absence can initiate a causal chain of escalating negative side effects. Biemiller (1977–1978; see also Allington, 1980, 1983, 1984) has documented how extremely large differences in reading practice begin to emerge as early as the middle of the first-grade year. In October, the children in the three most able groups in his sample read a mean of 12.2 words per child per reading session, the children in three average ability groups read 11.9 words per child per reading session, and the children in the two least able groups were not reading. By January, the mean for the most able groups was 51.9; for the average ability groups, 25.8; and for the least able groups, 11.5. In April the respective means were 81.4, 72.3, and 31.6. This of course says nothing about differences in home reading, which would probably be at least as large. Thus, soon after experiencing greater difficulty in breaking the spelling-to-sound code, poorer readers begin to be exposed to less text than their peers.

Further exacerbating the situation is the fact that poorer readers often find themselves in materials that are too difficult for them (Allington, 1977, 1983, 1984; Bristow, 1985; Forell, 1985; Gambrell, Wilson, & Gantt, 1981; Jorgenson, 1977). The combination of lack of practice, deficient decoding skills, and difficult materials results in unrewarding early reading experiences that lead to less involvement in reading-related activities. Lack of exposure and practice on the part of the less skilled reader delays the development of automaticity and speed at the word-recognition level. Slow, capacity-draining word-recognition processes require cognitive resources that should be allocated to higher-level processes of text integration and comprehension (LaBerge & Samuels, 1974; Perfetti, 1985; Stanovich, 1980). Thus, reading for meaning is hindered, unrewarding reading experiences multiply, and practice is avoided or merely tolerated without real cognitive involvement. The downward spiral continues—and has further consequences.

The better reader more rapidly attains a stage of proficiency where decoding skill is no longer the primary determinant of reading level. As word recognition becomes less resource-demanding by taking place via relatively automatic processes of visual/orthographic access, more general language skills become the limiting factor on reading ability (Chall, 1983b; Sticht, 1979). But the greater reading experience of the better reader has provided an enormous advantage even here. Reading itself is an important contributor to the development of many language/cognitive skills. For example, much vocabulary growth probably takes place through the learning of word meanings from context during reading (Nagy & Anderson, 1984; Nagy, Herman, & Anderson, 1985; Sternberg, 1985a). Similarly, much general information and knowledge about more complex syntactic structures probably also takes place through reading itself (Donaldson & Reid, 1982; Mann, 1986; Perfetti, 1985, pp. 172–173, 195). In short, many things that facilitate further growth in reading comprehension ability—general knowledge, vocabulary, syntactic knowledge—are developed by reading itself. The increased reading experiences of children who crack the spelling-to-sound code early thus have important positive feedback effects. Such feedback effects appear to be potent sources of individual differences in academic achievement (Walberg, Strykowski, Rovai, & Hung, 1984).

PARING DOWN THE NUMBER OF CAUSAL RELATIONSHIPS

It will be argued here that these bootstrapping effects of reading experience and other secondary effects have been inadequately considered in the extensive literature on individual differences in the cognitive processes of reading. Although it might seem that a consideration of the effects of these reciprocal relationships would complicate our models, it actually has great potential to clarify reading theory. If only a few of these reciprocal effects control a large portion of the variance in reading ability, we will be able to exercise parsimony elsewhere. Such a consideration will suggest that much of the explanatory power available from all of the variables that have been linked to reading ability in individual difference studies is superfluous; and this should spur us to eliminate some as causal factors accounting for variance in reading achievement.

It is only by trying to pare down the number of potential causal relationships by classifying some as spurious, some as consequences of reading, and some as developmentally limited that any clarity will be brought to the reading literature. In the remainder of this review some specific examples of candidates for possible "paring" will be discussed. A number of hypotheses are also advanced for incorporating reciprocal relationships and feedback effects within a general model of developmental changes in the cognitive processes related to reading. The tentative causal model I have outlined will be elaborated in the course of the discussion. Many of the hypotheses to be advanced are quite tentative, as the empirical evidence relating to several of them is far from definitive. The following discussion was not intended to be exhaustive, and it certainly will not present the final and definitive classification of process linkages, but hopefully it will serve to focus future research efforts.

The easiest processing differences to eliminate as causes of individual differences in reading ability should be those where performance differences arise merely because the individuals are reading at different levels—in short, situations where the efficiency of reading is determining how efficiently the cognitive process operates, rather than the converse. We will turn first to some possible examples of this type of relationship.

EYE MOVEMENTS: A CONSEQUENCE OF READING LEVEL

[material omitted]

CONTEXT EFFECTS ON WORD RECOGNITION: A CONSEQUENCE OF READING LEVEL?

Few areas of reading research are so fraught with confusion as are investigations of context use. One reason for this is that reading researchers have often failed to distinguish between levels in the processing system when discussing contextual effects (Gough, 1983; Mitchell, 1982; Stanovich, 1980, 1982b, 1984). The failure to distinguish the specific processing subsystems that are being affected by a particular experimental manipulation is one of the main reasons why there is still considerable looseness and confusion surrounding the term "context effect" in the reading literature. The point is that there can be many different *types* of context effects.

It will be argued here that the literature on context effects is considerably clarified if care is taken to distinguish the different types of context effects that are discussed in reading research. For example, the claim that variation in the use of context in part determines reading efficiency, and that contextual effects are more implicated in the performance of better readers, has often been made in the reading literature:

> Skill in reading involves not greater precision, but more accurate first guesses based on better sampling techniques, greater control over language structure, broadened experiences and increased conceptual development. (Goodman, 1976, p. 504)

> Guessing in the way I have described it is not just a preferred strategy for beginners and fluent readers alike; it is the most efficient manner in which to read and learn to read. (Smith, 1979, p. 67)

> The more difficulty a reader has with reading, the more he relies on the visual information; this statement applies to both the fluent reader and the beginner. In each case, the cause of the difficulty is inability to make full use of syntactic and semantic redundancy, of nonvisual sources of information. (Smith, 1971, p. 221)

> Less often the possibility is considered that use of context makes better readers. (Smith, 1982, p. 230)

It will be argued here that the truth of this hypothesis—that more fluent readers rely more on context—is critically dependent on the distinction between the use of context as an aid to *word recognition* and its use to aid *comprehension processes*. The claim appears defensible when referring to the latter, but appears to be largely incorrect when applied to the word-recognition level of processing.

We must first ask the question: Do less skilled readers use contextual information to facilitate word recognition when it is available; and if they do, to what extent do they rely on it? Many discrete-trial reaction-time studies of context effects have been conducted to investigate this question. Note that many of these studies have ensured the condition "when it is available" by using materials that were well within the reading capability of the least skilled subjects in the study. (This will become an important consideration in a later discussion.) Most of these studies have used priming paradigms where a context (sometimes a word, sometimes a sentence, and sometimes several sentences or paragraphs) precedes a target word to which the subject must make a naming or lexical decision response. Although this paradigm does not completely isolate the word-recognition level of processing (see Forster, 1979; Seidenberg, Waters, Sanders, & Langer, 1984; Stanovich & West, 1983a; West & Stanovich, 1982), it does so more than the other methodologies that have been used in the developmental literature. The finding has consistently been that not only do the poorer readers in these studies use context, but they often show somewhat larger contextual effects than do the better readers (Becker, 1982; Briggs, Austin, & Underwood, 1984; Perfetti, Goldman, & Hogaboam, 1979; Perfetti & Roth, 1981; Schvaneveldt, Ackerman, & Semlear, 1977; Schwantes, 1981, 1982, 1985; Schwantes, Boesl, & Ritz, 1980; Simpson & Foster, 1985; Simpson & Lorsbach, 1983; Simpson, Lorsbach, & Whitehouse, 1983; Stanovich, Nathan, West, & Vala-Rossi, 1985; Stanovich, West, & Feeman, 1981; West & Stanovich, 1978; West, Stanovich, Feeman, & Cunningham, 1983).

Some investigators have employed oral reading error analyses in order to examine individual differences in the use of context to facilitate word recognition. However, the use of the technique for this purpose is problematic. An oral reading error occurs for a variety of complex and interacting reasons (see Kibby, 1979; Leu, 1982; Wixson, 1979). Most critical for the present discussion is the fact that such errors often implicate levels of processing beyond word recognition. For example, hesitations and omissions are probably some complex function of word-recognition and comprehension processes (e.g., Goodman & Gollasch, 1980). Self-corrections in part reflect comprehension monitoring. Nevertheless, analysis of initial substitution errors has been used to throw light on the use of context to aid word recognition, and it is likely that these errors do partially implicate processes operating at the word-recognition level. So it is probably useful to consider this evidence if it is clearly recognized that it does not isolate the word-recognition level of processing as cleanly as the reaction-time studies.

Fortunately, there turns out to be no dilemma because the results of oral reading error studies largely converge with those of the reaction-time studies. When skilled and less-skilled readers are in materials of comparable difficulty (i.e., materials producing similar error rates), the relative reliance on contextual information relative to graphic information is just as great—in many cases greater—for the less-skilled readers (Allington & Fleming, 1978; Batey & Sonnenschein, 1981; Biemiller, 1970, 1979; A. S. Cohen, 1974–1975; Coomber, 1972; Harding, 1984; Juel, 1980; Lesgold & Resnick, 1982; Perfetti & Roth, 1981; Richardson, DiBenedetto, & Adler, 1982; Weber, 1970a; Whaley & Kibby, 1981). The findings from other paradigms, such as text disruption manipulations (Allington & Strange, 1977; Ehrlich, 1981; Schwartz & Stanovich, 1981; Siler, 1974; Strange, 1979) and timed text reading (Biemiller, 1977–1978; Doehring, 1976; Stanovich, Cunningham, & Feeman, 1984b), also converge with this conclusion.

Reconciling Differing Views on Context Use

In light of this evidence, it might seem difficult to understand how the claim that poor readers are less reliant on context for word recognition arose and gained popularity. There are several possible explanations, and they are not mutually exclusive. First is the tendency to conflate different levels of processing, discussed earlier. Skilled readers *are* more prone to use context to facilitate comprehension processes (see Stanovich, 1982b), so it is perhaps not surprising that there was a tendency to overgeneralize this relationship to the case of word recognition. Secondly, the popularity of the hypothesis may also have arisen from understandable confusion surrounding information processing concepts. For example, theorists proposing top-down models of reading have often defended the position that skilled readers rely less on graphic cues:

> As the child develops reading skill and speed, he uses increasingly fewer graphic cues. (Goodman, 1976, p. 504)

> But if in fact you are not making errors when you read, you are probably not reading efficiently, you are processing more visual information than you need. (Smith, 1979, p. 33)

> The more difficulty a reader has with reading, the more he relies on visual information; this statement applies to both the fluent reader and the beginner. (Smith, 1971, p. 221)

> One difference between the good beginning reader and the one heading for trouble lies in the overreliance on visual information that inefficient—or improperly taught—beginning readers tend to show, at the expense of sense. (Smith, 1973, p. 190)

Smith's (1971) well-known hypothesis is that, because the good reader is sensitive to the redundancy afforded by sentences, he or she develops hypotheses about upcoming words and is then able to confirm the identity of a word by sampling only a few features in the visual display. Good readers should then process words faster because their use of redundancy lightens the load on their stimulus–analysis mechanisms. Despite its surface plausibility, this notion is contradicted by much recent data.

Advances in eye movement technology have quite recently made available a host of powerful techniques for collecting data relevant to this hypothesis. The results of studies employing these new methodologies have consistently indicated that fluent readers rather completely sample the visual array—even when reading fairly predictable words (Balota, Pollatsek, & Rayner, 1985; Ehrlich & Rayner, 1981; Just & Carpenter, 1980; McConkie & Zola, 1981; Rayner & Bertera, 1979; Rayner, Inhoff, Morrison, Slowiaczek, & Bertera, 1981; Zola, 1984). Fluent readers are not engaging in the wholesale skipping of words, nor are they markedly reducing their sampling of visual features from the words fixated. Although Smith's (1973) conclusion that "it is clear that the better reader barely looks at the individual words on the page"

(p. 190) could not be evaluated at the time it was made, current research using the latest eye movement technology has rendered it untenable.

It appears that in the top-down models of reading, use of the features in the visual array was conflated with the cognitive resources necessary to process those features. In fact, it is not that the good reader relies less on visual information, but that the visual analysis mechanisms of the good reader use less *capacity*. That is, good readers are efficient processors in every sense: they completely sample the visual array *and* use fewer resources to do so. The good reader is not less reliant on the visual information, but the good reader does allocate less capacity to process this information. In short, it is important to note that the attentional resources allocated to graphic processing and the amount of graphic information itself are two different things.

Perhaps a third reason for the popularity of the context-use hypothesis as an explanation of differences in reading ability is that there is considerable confusion about the distinction between the importance of a mechanism as a determinant of a general developmental sequence and as a determinant of individual differences in the developmental sequence (McCall, 1981). The reasoning error involved seems to have been one of taking an idea that was valid in one sphere and extending it into a domain where it was not applicable. The error was not in emphasizing that context use occurs in reading, but in generalizing it as a mechanism that could explain individual differences. For example, research cited earlier indicates considerable use of context by early readers. This context use is clear from the reaction-time studies and from the fact that oral reading error studies of first-grade children have found that 70% to 95% of the initial errors are contextually appropriate (Biemiller, 1970, 1979; Weber, 1970). Note, however, that if the variability in context use is low relative to the variability in other factors that determine reading ability (phonological awareness, for example), then context use will not be strongly related to individual differences in reading ability, despite its importance as an underlying factor in every child's reading performance.

This point is similar to cautions researchers have raised about interpreting the effects of heredity and environment on intelligence test performance. It is often pointed out that if the variability in one factor is restricted, then the other will necessarily be more strongly related to individual differences. For example, individual differences in the intelligence scores among identical twins must be entirely due to environmental differences because they share the same genetic background. This of course does not mean that the general developmental sequence of identical twins is not partially under genetic control. However, although heredity is contributing to the development of the organism, it cannot be linked to individual differences in this case.

We must raise the question of whether an analogous phenomenon is occurring in the case of contextual facilitation. All the empirical evidence indicates considerable use of context by first-grade children, and models of first-grade reading acquisition often include at least one stage defined in part by context use. For example, Biemiller's (1970) proposed early reading stages include an initial stage of contextual dependency, a stage of increasing attention to graphic processing, and a stage where the integration of both graphic and contextual cues occurs. Bissex's (1980) case study can be interpreted within this framework; she particularly emphasizes the importance of the third stage, in which both contextual and graphophonemic information is used in an integrated manner. But even if we accept the importance of a stage of graphic and contextual cue integration, the question arises whether passage into this stage is blocked by the inadequate development of context-use skills or by the failure to develop skills of graphophonemic processing. All children may indeed go through this stage, but is the speed of its attainment actually determined by variation in context-use skills? The research reviewed above suggests that the answer may be no: stages may indeed exist that are defined in part by context use, but that the existence of such stages may misleadingly suggest that context use is a source of individual differences. Instead, it appears that compared to other prerequisite skills—such as phonological awareness—the variability in the ability to use context to facilitate word recognition is so relatively low that it may not be a major determinant of individual differences in reading acquisition. The very ubiquity of contextual facilitation—the thing that has led some theorists to single it out as a mechanism for generating ability differences—is precisely the thing that prevents it from being a cause of individual differences.

The hypothesis about context use among readers of differing skill generated from the top-down models thus needs several modifications in order to bring it into congruence with current research evidence. First, it is not that good readers are less reliant on visual information, but that they expend less capacity to process visual information fully. Secondly, the reason that they expend less capacity is not because they rely on context, but because their stimulus–analysis mechanisms are so powerful. These modifications are all more completely explicated in Perfetti's (1985) verbal efficiency theory. Once these alterations are made, it is possible to see more congruence between some of the insights that were the source of the top-down models and those of more bottom-up models like verbal efficiency theory. For example, both classes of model are in agreement on the necessity of expending processing capacity on higher-level comprehension processes rather than on word recognition. In fact, there are considerable grounds here for a rapprochement between the proponents of various global models of the reading process. Long before most cognitive psychologists became interested in reading, top-down theorists were investigating critical processing issues in the domain of context use. The latter were responsible for the crucial insight that readers need to allocate attentional capacity to comprehension rather than to word recognition in order to become fluent. However, recent work by cognitive and developmental psychologists—some of whom are of a more bottom-up persuasion—has helped to specify accurately the key mechanism that allows capacity to be allocated to comprehension. This mechanism turns out to be efficient decoding rather than context use. Both groups of researchers have thus made important contributions to our current knowledge of the interrelationships between decoding, context use for word recognition, and comprehension.

Compensatory Processing and Decoding Skill

The common finding that the magnitude of contextual facilitation effects is inversely related to the word-recognition skill of the reader has been seen as an example of interactive–compensatory processing (Perfetti & Roth, 1981; Stanovich, 1980, 1984; Stanovich, West, & Feeman, 1981) because it presumably results from the fact that the information processing system is arranged in such a way that when the bottom-up decoding processes that result in word recognition are deficient, the system compensates by relying more heavily on other knowledge sources (e.g., contextual information). The extent to which the compensatory processing in children is obligatory and the extent to which it is strategic is an issue of much complexity and is currently being debated in the literature (see Briggs, Austin, & Underwood, 1984; Simpson & Lorsbach, 1983; Stanovich, Nathan, West, & Vala-Rossi, 1985; Stanovich & West, 1983a), but the current evidence appears to indicate that to a considerable extent it is obligatory and automatic. It appears that reading skill is not determined by skill at contextual prediction, but rather that the level of word-recognition skill determines the extent to which contextual information will be relied on to complete the process of lexical access. The slower the word-decoding process, the more the system draws on contextual information. In the interactive–compensatory model, the magnitude of context effects is thus conceived to be largely a consequence of the efficiency of reading—making it analogous to the case of eye movements.

Perfetti (1985, p. 149) has provided the data that most convincingly demonstrate that the magnitude of contextual facilitation effects (at the word-recognition level) are a function of decoding skill. He has shown that words and individuals are "interchangeable." When the target word in a discrete-trial experiment is visually degraded so that the recognition speed of a good reader is as slow as that of a poor reader, the good reader shows as large a contextual effect as the poor reader. Increased word difficulty appears to operate in the same way (Perfetti et al., 1979; Stanovich, 1984; Stanovich & West, 1981, 1983a; Stanovich, West, & Feeman, 1981). Perfetti (1985) has shown that in his data there is a linear relationship between the contextual facilitation effect and the isolated word-recognition time across a wide variety of conditions of word difficulty, visual degradation, and reading skill. He concluded: "In other words, it does not matter whether a word's isolated identification time is measured from a high-ability or low-ability reader or from a degraded or normal word. The context effect simply depends on the basic word-identification time" (p. 149).

Unfortunately, the function relating word-recognition difficulty and the magnitude of the context effect presented by Perfetti (1985) turns out to be a special case rather than a completely generalizable relationship. It applies only under conditions where both the skilled and the less skilled readers have adequately processed the context. It is restricted to such conditions because the compensatory processing can only occur when the contextual information is available to supplement bottom-up analyses. Availability of context was ensured in the case of the reaction-time studies because materials were used in those studies that were well within the capability of the poorest readers; and it can be crudely controlled in the case of the oral reading error studies by looking at performance in materials where the overall error rates have been equated. However, in classroom reading situations, poorer readers will more often be dealing with materials that are relatively more difficult (Allington, 1977, 1983, 1984; Bristow, 1985; Forell, 1985; Gambrell, Wilson, & Gantt, 1981; Jorgenson, 1977), and in which they may experience decoding problems. These decoding problems will reduce the context available to the poorer reader. Thus, even though both groups may be reading the same materials, the poorer reader will have, in effect, less contextual information to utilize. This could lead such readers to display less contextual facilitation. (There may also be reader-skill differences in general knowledge and semantic memory that could affect contextual processing, but so little is known about this possibility that it will not be considered here.) The point is that we must eventually refine our theories of context use in order to distinguish the nominal context (what is on the page) from the effective context (what is being used by the reader).

Thus, in order to fully trace out the function relating contextual facilitation to the recognition time for the target word in isolation, we must consider another dimension: the difficulty of the material preceding the target word. And this added dimension will interact with reading skill in determining the amount of contextual facilitation observed. For a given target word, in very easy materials (at or below the reading level of the less skilled readers), poorer readers will show more contextual facilitation (Perfetti, 1985; Stanovich, 1980, 1984). But as the material becomes more difficult, this difference will disappear, and eventually a level of difficulty will be reached where the better readers display larger facilitation effects because the prior text (which forms the context for the word currently being recognized) is simply too difficult for the poorer readers to decode. In short, the relationship between the difficulty of the target word, the difficulty of the contextual material, the ability of the reader, and the amount of contextual facilitation is a complex one. Note, however, that taking the difficulty of the contextual material into account does not change the source of individual differences in contextual facilitation: they are directly determined by the decoding ability of the subject (and the difficulty level of the contextual material and of the target word).

Consideration of the difficulty factor may throw light on a question that is often raised in response to the reaction-time and oral reading error studies cited above: If poor readers use context so much, how can we explain the frequently reported description of problem readers as plodding through text, not using context, and understanding little? How should we interpret the performance of such readers? One interpretation that flows from the top-down perspective is that these children have learned inefficient word-recognition strategies:

> Excessive stress, in reading instruction and materials, on phonics or word attack skills, will tend to make recoding an end in itself, and may actually distract the child from the real end: decoding written language for meaning. (Goodman, 1968, p. 21)

> Trying to sound out words without reference to meaning is a characteristic strategy of poor readers; it is not one that leads to fluency in reading. (Smith, 1982, p. 145)

> If you had read the backwards passage aloud, incidentally, you probably would have sounded very much like many of the older "problem readers" at school, who struggle to identify words one at a time in a dreary monotone as if each word had nothing to do with any other. Such children seem to believe—and may well have been taught—that meaning should be their last concern. (Smith, 1978, p. 154)

An alternative conceptualization would view the lack of contextual facilitation shown by such a reader as the result of extremely poor decoding skills. The research reviewed above strongly supports the view that the word recognition of poor readers *is* facilitated by contextual information *when they understand the context.* When poor readers are in difficult materials, their slow and inaccurate word decoding processes may in fact degrade the contextual information that they receive, rendering it unusable (Kibby, 1979). The observation that, under such conditions, poor readers do not rely on context should not—according to this interpretation—be viewed as indicating that they *never* use context to facilitate word recognition.

Using a longitudinal research design, some colleagues and I (Stanovich, Cunningham, & Feeman, 1984b) tested these alternative explanations.

[material omitted; see Chapter 4]

A final point that emerges from the research on contextual facilitation effects is the importance of differentiating the presence of a knowledge base from the use of that knowledge. For example, Perfetti, Goldman, and Hogaboam (1979) found that the same skilled readers who displayed smaller context effects than less skilled readers on a word-recognition task were superior on a cloze-like prediction task. Of course, the finding that skilled readers possess superior prediction abilities is nothing new; it merely reconfirms older findings of a relationship between reading ability and cloze performance (Bickley, Ellington, & Bickley, 1970; Ruddell, 1965). What is new—and the important lesson in the Perfetti et al. (1979) results—is that the presence of prediction abilities does not necessarily imply that these abilities are *used* to facilitate ongoing word recognition. In fact, the Perfetti et al. (1979) results suggest just the opposite. Though the better readers possessed superior prediction abilities, they *also* were superior decoders, and the data appear to indicate that the latter is the critical causal mechanism sustaining fluent reading.

The context-free decoding efficiency of the better readers is so high that they are less in need of contextual support. They have more knowledge of contextual dependencies, but are simultaneously less reliant on this knowledge, because they possess other processing advantages that are more important for word recognition—namely, context-free decoding skills.

The Phenomenon of "Word Calling"

This discussion of contextual facilitation effects on word recognition is obviously related to the phenomenon described as "word calling" in the reading literature. Despite the frequency with which this term occurs in reading publications, it is rare to find an author who spells out the clear, operational meaning of the term as it is being used. However, the implicit assumptions behind its use appear to be as follows: (1) Word calling occurs when the words in the text are efficiently decoded into their spoken forms without comprehension of the passage taking place. (2) This is a bad thing, because (3) it means that the child does not understand the true purpose of reading, which is extracting meaning from the text. (4) Children engaging in word calling do so because they have learned inappropriate reading strategies. (5) The strategic difficulty is one of overreliance on phonic strategies. These assumptions can be detected in the following representative quotations:

> Trying to sound out words without reference to meaning is a characteristic strategy of poor readers. (Smith, 1982, p. 145)

> Preoccupation with teaching children to recode may actually short circuit the reading process and divert children from comprehension. It is even possible that children will reach a high level of proficiency in recoding, actually taking graphic input and recasting it as very natural sounding speech, with little or no awareness of the need for decoding for meaning. (Goodman, 1968, p. 20)

> In fact, few children who become remedial readers lack the ability to attack words. (Smith, Goodman, & Meredith, 1976, p. 270)

> Remedial reading classes are filled with youngsters in late elementary and secondary schools who can sound out words but get little meaning from their reading. (Goodman, 1973, p. 491)

The idea of a "word-caller" phenomenon embodying the assumptions outlined above has gained popularity despite the lack of evidence that it applies to an appreciable number of poor readers. There is no research evidence indicating that decoding a word into a phonological form often takes place without meaning extraction, even in poor readers. To the contrary, a substantial body of evidence indicates that even for young children, word decoding automatically leads to semantic activation *when the meaning of the word is adequately established in memory* (Ehri, 1977; Goodman, Haith, Guttentag, & Rao, 1985; Guttentag, 1984a; Guttentag & Haith, 1978, 1980; Kraut &

Smothergill, 1980; Rosinski, 1977). Inadequate attention has been directed to the possibility that "word calling" may simply be a consequence of a low level of reading ability. This might occur in a number of different ways. First, reports of "word calling" rarely definitively establish whether the words that are "called" are even in the child's listening vocabulary. If the child would not understand the meaning of the word or passage when spoken, then overuse of decoding strategies can hardly be blamed if the child does not understand the written words. In short, a minimal requirement for establishing "word calling" as defined by the assumptions outlined above is the demonstration that the written material being "called" is within the listening comprehension abilities of the child (see Gough & Tunmer, 1986; Hood & Dubert, 1983).

Secondly, it is necessary to show that the "word calling" is not a simple consequence of poor decoding. Although reasonably efficient decoding would appear to be an integral part of any meaningful definition of "word calling," decoding skills are rarely carefully assessed before a child is labelled a "word caller." Instead, a rough index of decoding accuracy is usually employed, and any child near the normal range on this index is considered a candidate for the label. As other investigators have previously noted (e.g., LaBerge & Samuels, 1974; Perfetti, 1985, 1986), one does not obtain a clear picture of a child's decoding abilities unless speed and automaticity criteria are also employed. It is quite possible for accurate decoding to be so slow and capacity-demanding that it strains available cognitive resources and causes comprehension breakdowns. Such accurate but capacity-demanding decoding with little comprehension should not be considered "word calling" as defined above. To the contrary, it is a qualitatively different type of phenomenon. Comprehension fails not because of overreliance on decoding, but because decoding skill is not developed enough.

CONSEQUENCES OF READING HISTORY AND PRACTICE

The previous sections have outlined how individual differences in eye movements and context use for word recognition may be considered to be consequences of the reading level of the subject. Because these cognitive processes operate primarily during the act of reading itself, they are most accurately assessed by experimental methodologies that do not depart too far from the real-time processing requirements of reading. These types of processes may represent one class of the consequences of reading: processing differences that arise due to the differential efficiency of ongoing reading in individuals of varying skill.

However, individual differences in other types of cognitive processes may be linked to reading because the processes are affected by the differential behavioral histories of individuals who acquire reading at varying rates. For example, as discussed in the introduction, readers of differing skill soon diverge in the amount of practice they receive at reading and writing activities.

They also have different histories of success, failure, and reward in the context of academic tasks. The long-term effects of such differing histories could act to create other cognitive and behavioral differences between readers of varying skill. Consider some possible examples. Many of the motivational differences between good and poor readers that are receiving increasing attention (see Johnston & Winograd, 1985; Oka & Paris, 1986) may well be consequences of the histories of success and failure associated with groups of differing skill. There is already some evidence suggesting that differences in self-esteem, rather than being the cause of achievement variability, are actually consequences of ability and achievement (Bachman & O'Malley, 1977; Maruyama, Rubin, & Kingsbury, 1981).

Ehri's (1984, 1985) work has elegantly demonstrated the effect that experience with print has on knowledge of sound structure and metalinguistic functioning. Others have speculated that the development of the ability to comprehend more complex syntactic structures is in part the result of reading experience (Donaldson & Reid, 1982; Mann, 1986; Perfetti, 1985). The status of the relationship between naming speed and reading ability is currently being debated by researchers, some of whom think that variation in this skill is a cause of reading ability differences, whereas others think it is a consequence of the differential reading histories of the subjects (M. D. Jackson, 1980; N. E. Jackson & Biemiller, 1985; Perfetti, 1985; Stanovich, 1986a; Wolf, 1984).

Torgesen (1985) has raised the interesting possibility that some of the memory performance differences between readers of varying skill might be consequences of reading once-removed. He speculated that, because a good deal of knowledge acquisition takes place via reading, the knowledge base of less skilled readers may be less developed because of their lack of reading practice. It has also been demonstrated that performance on many memory tasks is affected by the nature of the subject's knowledge base. The poorer reader might therefore display relative inferiority on such tasks due to a lack of reading experience (see Bjorklund & Bernholtz, 1986).

On a broader level, much of the literature on the consequences of literacy (Donaldson, 1978; Goody, 1977; D. R. Olson, 1977; D. R. Olson, Torrance, & Hildyard, 1985; Scribner & Cole, 1981) may be viewed as demonstrating the importance of some of the more global consequences of reading. This research also illustrates that it is a mistake to dismiss cognitive differences that are consequences of the reading histories of the individuals as unimportant. Such an unfortunate inference explains why many investigators resist the conclusion that individual differences in the process they are studying are actually caused by variation in reading skill. Surely the literature on the consequences of literacy—speculative and empirically sparse though it is—has at least suggested that the cognitive consequences of the acquisition of literacy may be profound. A few reading theorists have warned that we should be giving increasing attention to these types of effects. For example, Chall (1983b) has stated: "The influence of the development of reading and writing—'literate intelligence'—on general cognitive development has unfortunately been underestimated. Indeed, when reading development is delayed by personal or environmental factors or both, the effects on the person, unless given special help, are too often disastrous" (pp. 2–3).

THE READING-LEVEL MATCH DESIGN

Because of concern that some of the processing differences that have been attributed as causes of variation in reading ability are instead simple consequences of the overall level of reading or of the reading histories of the subjects, the reading-level match design has grown in popularity (Backman, Mamen, & Ferguson, 1984; Bryant & Goswami, 1986). In this research design, the performance of a group of older disabled readers is compared with that of a younger nondisabled group reading at the same level. The reading-level match design is often employed in order to rule out differential practice explanations of correlations between cognitive skills and reading ability. When 10-year-old disabled readers are found to perform worse on a cognitive task than normally progressing 6-year-old children (as in Bradley & Bryant, 1978), it is difficult to invoke the differential practice explanation; or at least, the inferior performance of the 10-year-olds is much less likely to be due to relative lack of experience than a performance deficit displayed in comparison to a control group of equal chronological age.

The recent exciting research on individuals with acquired dyslexia and the resulting debate about what these cases tell us about the nature of developmental dyslexia (Coltheart, Masterson, Byng, Prior, & Riddich, 1983; Ellis, 1984; Snowling, 1983) also point to the need for a reading-level match design, which should help to alleviate some of the interpretive problems in this research area. For example, the claim that the acquired dyslexic cases reveal a qualitatively distinct syndrome reflecting the breakdown of a specific mechanism that is the cause of their reading problems will only be sustained when it is demonstrated that the performance patterns observed do not merely reflect a depressed overall level of reading skill—in short, that normal children reading at the same level do not show similar performance patterns (Bryant & Impey, 1986; Prior & McCorriston, 1985).

The results from reading-level match designs also have important implications for developmental lag theories of variation in reading achievement (Beech & Harding, 1984; Fletcher, 1981; Stanovich, Nathan, & Vala-Rossi, 1986; Treiman & Hirsh-Pasek, 1985). These theories posit that the less skilled reader is traversing the same stages of cognitive development as the skilled reader, but at a slower rate. Thus, reading will be commensurately delayed because the prerequisite cognitive subskills are inadequately developed. The strong form of the lag hypothesis posits that the performance profiles of less skilled readers should be similar to those of younger readers at a similar level of achievement; that is, when older less skilled children and younger skilled children are matched on reading level, their performance should not differ on any other reading-related cognitive task (see Fletcher, 1981). However, Bryant and Goswami (1986) have pointed to the ambiguity inherent in null findings obtained with a reading-level match. That is, all processes—like eye movements—that are basically epiphenomena of the efficiency of reading will display precisely the pattern predicted by the developmental lag model. However, unlike the lag model, in which it is assumed that reading level is determined by the lagging cognitive processes, an alternative explanation in terms of the consequences of reading posits that the operation of the process is determined by the reading level.

DEVELOPMENTALLY LIMITED RELATIONSHIPS: PHONOLOGICAL AWARENESS AND PHONOLOGICAL RECODING ABILITY?

In the tentative causal model previously outlined, it was posited that phonological awareness is an enabling subskill in early reading, and that individual differences in this subskill contribute to variance in reading ability. A growing body of evidence appears to indicate that some level of phonological awareness is necessary for the discovery and exploitation of the alphabetic principle (Perfetti, 1984, 1985). The major advantage conferred by the alphabetic principle is that it allows children to recognize words that are in their vocabulary but have not been taught or encountered before in print. It is necessary for the child to make this step toward independent reading, and recognizing unknown words via phonological recoding seems to be the key to it (Ehri & Wilce, 1985; Jorm & Share, 1983). The point of phonological mediation is to provide the child with what Jorm and Share (1983) have termed a "positive learning trial" for an unknown word. Phonological mediation enables the child to associate a visual/orthographic representation of the word with its sound and meaning (Barron, 1986; Ehri, 1984, 1985). Once this early hurdle is cleared, the child will begin to attain the amount of reading practice that leads to other positive cognitive consequences.

However, just because phonological awareness enables word recognition via phonological recoding in beginning reading, it does not follow that this mechanism determines reading ability at all developmental levels. To the contrary, there is mounting evidence indicating that there is a developmental trend away from phonologically mediated word recognition in early reading stages toward direct, nonmediated visual access at more advanced stages of reading (Backman, Bruck, Hebert, & Seidenberg, 1984; Ehri, 1985; Ehri & Wilce, 1985; Juel, 1983; Reitsma, 1984; Waters, Seidenberg, & Bruck, 1984). (The controversy concerning the existence of an initial paired-associate learning stage will not be entered into here; see Ehri and Wilce [1985] and Gough and Hillinger [1980].) Early development of decoding skill leads to many positive learning trials that provide opportunities for visual/orthographic codes to become established in memory as future access mechanisms for the recognition of words (Barron, 1986; Ehri, 1984, 1985; Henderson, 1982; Jorm & Share, 1983). Of course, the efficiency with which visual/orthographic codes are established may depend upon more than just phonological recoding skill. That is, equally proficient phonological decoders may still differ in their ability to form visual/orthographic codes. But this caveat does not change the essential features of the present discussion.

It appears that for fluent adults the vast majority of words that are encountered in print are recognized by direct visual access (Ellis, 1984; Henderson, 1982; Mason, 1978; McCusker, Hillinger, & Bias, 1981; Seidenberg, Waters, Barnes, & Tanenhaus, 1984; Waters et al., 1984). Phonological information appears to be activated prior to lexical access only for low-frequency or very difficult words (McCusker et al., 1981; R. K. Olson, Kliegl, Davidson, & Foltz, 1985; Perfetti, 1985, p. 59; Seidenberg, Waters, Barnes, & Tanenhaus, 1984; Waters & Seidenberg, 1985). Reader skill appears to mimic the frequency variable: the less skilled the reader, the more likely it is that phonological information is activated prior to word recognition (Waters et al., 1984). The existing evidence is consistent with a class of models in which phonological codes are automatically activated as a consequence of visual processing, are not under strategic control, and are determined solely by the time course of visual access (Perfetti, 1985; Seidenberg, 1985b; Seidenberg, Waters, Barnes, & Tanenhaus, 1984). Note that, according to these models, phonological information is less implicated in the *lexical access* processes of the fluent reader. They do not claim that phonological information is not implicated in reading at all. Instead, they posit that even in the fluent reader, such information is activated postlexically, where it serves to support comprehension processes operating on the contents of working memory.

The developmental trend toward word recognition via direct visual access suggests that individual differences in phonological awareness and phonological recoding skills observed at advanced stages of reading may be examples of *developmentally limited* relationships: those where individual differences in processes that cause variance in reading ability early in development at some point cease to be causal factors. Thus, just as when we gaze at the night sky we are actually observing the past history of stars, when we measure differences in phonological decoding skills in adults we may be tapping the mechanisms that earlier in their developmental histories led different individuals to diverge in the rates at which they acquired reading skill, but are not currently causing further variation in reading fluency.

Of course, some indicators of phonological skill may be tapping the speed with which phonological information is accessed *postlexically*, and these—unlike the use of phonological information for decoding purposes—may still be a determinant of current reading ability. That is, the availability of the phonological information that follows lexical access in the more advanced reader may be a critical factor in determining reading ability. Because of the integrated nature of orthographic and phonological codes in the fluent reader (Ehri, 1984; Jakimik, Cole, & Rudnicky, 1984; Perin, 1983; Seidenberg & Tanenhaus, 1979), fast visual access rapidly and automatically activates the phonological codes that serve a reference-securing function in working memory which facilitates comprehension (Perfetti, 1985). This is why it is important to note that in this section we are concerned with the use of phonological information at a prelexical stage.

In their study of developmental changes in the use of spelling–sound correspondences, Backman, Bruck, Hebert, and Seidenberg (1984) emphasized the importance of a distinction already discussed: the distinction between the availability of knowledge and the actual use of that knowledge in the word-recognition process. They highlighted two important trends in their data. Older and more skilled readers displayed a greater tendency to recognize words without phonological mediation. They made fewer errors on words with homographic spelling patterns. At the same time, however, the more skilled readers were more rapidly expanding their knowledge of spelling–sound correspondences. This knowledge was indicated by a greater proportion of rule-governed errors and fewer errors on nonwords. These differences between readers of varying skill mirror an earlier developmental hypothesis of Venezky's (1976): "The reliance on letter–sound generalizations in word recognition slowly decreases as word identification ability increases, and the mature reader probably makes little use of them in normal reading. Nevertheless, the ability to apply letter–sound generalizations continues to develop at least through Grade 8" (p. 22).

The conclusion of Backman, Bruck, Hebert, and Seidenberg (1984) that "children's knowledge of spelling–sound correspondences is increasing at the very time they are learning to recognize many words without using it" (p. 131) parallels that of Perfetti et al. (1979) in the domain of context effects on word recognition. The latter investigators found that although good readers were better at contextual prediction, they were less dependent on such prediction for word recognition, demonstrating that the existence of a knowledge base does not necessarily mean that the information from it is used to facilitate word recognition. The studies by Perfetti et al. (1979) and by Backman, Bruck, Hebert, and Seidenberg (1984) both indicate that the operation of rapid visual-access processes short-circuits the use of other information.

Backman, Bruck, Hebert, and Seidenberg (1984) elaborated their conclusions by distinguishing between the pre- and postlexical activation of phonological information. They noted that the finding that less skilled readers rely more on prelexical phonological information

> does not mean that less skilled readers rely more on phonological information than do good readers, only that they utilize this information more in the *initial decoding* of words. . . . The confusion in the literature as to whether it is good or poor readers who rely more heavily upon phonological information in reading may be due in part to failing to distinguish between its pre- and postlexical functions. Poor readers may rely more upon this information, derived from spelling–sound knowledge, in word decoding, to their detriment; good readers may be

more facile in using phonological information that is accessed postlexically, facilitating text comprehension. (p. 131)

What the findings both of Backman, Bruck, Hebert, and Seidenberg (1984) and of Perfetti et al. (1979) emphasize is that in word recognition there is a developmental trend away from supplementing bottom-up processes of direct visual access with additional knowledge (spelling–sound correspondences and contextual expectancies). It appears that as reading skill develops, the word-recognition process during reading becomes increasingly modular (Fodor, 1983; Forster, 1979; Gough, 1983; Seidenberg, 1985a, 1985b; Seidenberg, Waters, Sanders, & Langer, 1984; Stanovich, Nathan, West, & Vala-Rossi, 1985; Stanovich & West, 1983a). That is, word recognition via direct visual access occurs more autonomously, and other knowledge sources tend to interact only with the *outputs* of completed word recognition, not with the word-recognition process itself. When the task demands it, adults can utilize phonological mediation to name a stimulus (as in pseudoword naming), but ordinarily this mechanism is not used to support their ongoing processes of word recognition.

The hypothesis that adult differences in phonological coding are remnants of an earlier causal relationship suggests many questions that will require investigation. Even if the hypothesis is correct, the developmental change in the linkage between reading ability and individual differences in phonological coding skill will have to be fully traced. An intriguing possibility—already suggested by some research (Barron & Baron, 1977; Kimura & Bryant, 1983; Reitsma, 1983)—is that visual access for most words begins to develop very rapidly (e.g., after only a few exposures), rendering phonological coding differences noncausal relatively early in development. Finally, note that in the case of phonological recoding the term developmentally limited may be a slight misnomer. Individual differences in this process may be less implicated in determining reading ability among older readers simply because fewer unknown words are encountered, but it may in fact be fully operative on those few occasions when such words occur.

Of course, phonological coding may be only one example of what might turn out to be a host of developmentally limited relationships. One intriguing candidate is individual differences in word-recognition efficiency itself. Although there is some evidence indicating that word-recognition efficiency is a causal determinant of reading skill (e.g., Biemiller, 1970; Blanchard, 1980; Herman, 1985; Lesgold, Resnick, & Hammond, 1985; Lomax, 1983), it has sometimes been difficult to demonstrate a causal connection, particularly in research employing adults and older children as subjects. For example, it has been surprisingly difficult to show that disrupting word-recognition processes diminishes comprehension (Levy, 1981; Masson & Sala, 1978; Wilkinson, Guminski, Stanovich, & West, 1981; but see Bowey, 1982) or that making word recognition more efficient results in better comprehension (Fleisher,

Jenkins, & Pany, 1979; but see Blanchard, 1980; Blanchard & McNinch, 1980; Herman, 1985). Thus, the possibility that the causal link between individual differences in word-recognition efficiency and comprehension is developmentally limited deserves further investigation.

SOME VARIABLES DISPLAY
RECIPROCAL CAUSATION: VOCABULARY

As mentioned in the introduction, one of the problems in conceptualizing the literature is that there are too many differences between good and poor readers. These differences lead to a plethora of explanations for reading failure, and in many cases the explanations are incompatible. Each investigator— emotionally wedded to his or her particular task(s)—likes to believe that his or her variable (and associated theory) is the key to understanding reading disability. The possibility that the difference observed is a consequence of the reading level or reading history is often not considered or, at most, is given a footnote or parenthetical comment. [*material omitted*]

Classifying relationships as either causes or consequences of reading ability of course does not exhaust the possibilities. Reading ability may be correlated with the efficiency of a certain cognitive process because both are linked to some third variable. For example, it is possible that a maturational lag in the general development of language abilities is what leads to the linkage between reading and phonological skills (Mann, 1984, 1986). Tallal (1980) has speculated on how a basic problem in processing rapidly presented information might serve to link low reading ability, speech disorders, and lack of phonological awareness.

Researchers investigating individual differences in reading have also become increasingly sensitized to the possibility that processes may be interlocked with reading in relationships of *reciprocal causation*: that individual differences in a particular process may cause differential reading efficiency, but that reading itself may in turn cause further individual differences in the process in question. There is mounting evidence that in the early acquisition stages this is precisely the status of phonological awareness and reading (Ehri, 1979, 1984, 1985; Perfetti, 1985, pp. 220–227; Perfetti, Beck, & Hughes, 1981). Individual differences in certain aspects of phonological awareness appear to be causally linked to variation in the ease of early reading acquisition; but initial success at cracking the spelling-to-sound code further develops phonological awareness and provides the experiences necessary for the acquisition of increasingly differentiated phonological knowledge and the ability to access it consciously. Ehri (1979, 1984, 1985) has provided the most convincing evidence for the effects of orthographic representations on phonological awareness.

However, as hypothesized in the previous section, in the case of phonological awareness there is probably a developmental limit on the time course of the reciprocal relationship. If reading is progressing normally, children may move quickly into stages where direct visual access predominates (Barron & Baron, 1977; Kimura & Bryant, 1983; Reitsma, 1983) and variation in phonological awareness is no longer the primary causal determinant of differences in reading ability. This example illustrates that hypotheses involving the concept of reciprocal causation must be framed developmentally. For example, assume that individual differences in a certain process (call it A) both cause differences in reading acquisition and in turn are also affected by reading. However, suppose that at some point, variation in A no longer causes variation in reading ability. Then it is important to investigate whether the "kickback" from reading to A occurs early enough for the newly facilitated A to affect subsequent reading acquisition. The research question concerns whether the "bootstrapping" occurs early enough for a true reciprocal relationship to develop, or whether the facilitation of A occurs too late for its extra efficiency to cause further achievement differences in reading. In the case of phonological awareness, evidence from a longitudinal study by Perfetti et al. (1981) suggests that a true reciprocal relationship may be occurring.

Nevertheless, if the conclusion of the previous section is correct, then this bootstrapping involving phonological awareness has some inherent limits. There will be a point when the facilitation of phonological awareness by reading becomes much less important because the level of phonological awareness is no longer determining reading ability. A more powerful reciprocal relationship would be one that was operative throughout reading development. The motivational differences that are associated with variability in reading ability (e.g., Butkowsky & Willows, 1980; Oka & Paris, 1986) may be involved in relationships of this type. In this section we will explore what may be another example of such a potent reciprocal relationship: the association between vocabulary development and individual differences in reading ability.

The correlation between reading ability and vocabulary knowledge is sizable throughout development (Anderson & Freebody, 1979; Mezynski, 1983; Stanovich, Cunningham, & Feeman, 1984a). Although, as in most areas of reading research, correlational evidence is much more plentiful than experimental evidence (Anderson & Freebody, 1979; Mezynski, 1983), there is a growing body of data indicating that variation in vocabulary knowledge is a causal determinant of differences in reading comprehension ability (Beck, Perfetti, & McKeown, 1982; McKeown, Beck, Omanson, & Perfetti, 1983; Stahl, 1983). It seems probable that, like phonological awareness, vocabulary knowledge is involved in a reciprocal relationship with reading ability, but that—unlike the case of phonological awareness—the relationship is one that continues throughout reading development and remains in force for even the most fluent adult readers.

There is considerable agreement that much—probably most—vocabulary growth takes place through the inductive learning of the meanings of unknown words encountered in oral and written language. It appears that the bulk of vocabulary growth does not occur via direct instruction (Jenkins & Dixon, 1983; Jenkins, Stein, & Wysocki, 1984; Nagy & Anderson, 1984; Nagy, Herman, & Anderson, 1985; Sternberg, 1985a; Sternberg, Powell, & Kaye, 1982). Also, there is substantial agreement among researchers that reading is a significant contributor to the growth of vocabulary. However, positions on this issue run from the conservative conclusion of Jenkins et al. (1984)—"Because we do not know how many words individuals know, we are seriously limited in accounting for changes in these totals. Whatever the totals, incidental learning from reading could account for some portion of the growth in vocabulary knowledge" (p. 785)—to the stronger position of Nagy and Anderson (1984): "We judge that beginning in about the third grade, the major determinant of vocabulary growth is amount of free reading" (p. 327).

The role hypothesized for vocabulary in this review will reveal a bias toward the stronger position of Nagy and Anderson (1984). The association between variation in vocabulary knowledge and reading achievement seems a good candidate for a strong reciprocal relationship. Much more evidence on the nature of both causal connections clearly is needed, but recent studies that are methodologically superior to earlier work have provided support for causal mechanisms operating in both directions. Also, some recent theoretical extrapolations support the plausibility of a reciprocal bootstrapping interaction between vocabulary and reading.

Although some earlier studies had failed to verify the relation, recent research has demonstrated a causal connection between vocabulary knowledge and reading comprehension (Beck et al., 1982; McKeown et al., 1983; Stahl, 1983). Regarding the reverse connection, there has also been some research progress. The most recent estimates of children's vocabulary sizes serve to emphasize the futility of expecting major proportions of vocabulary growth to occur via direct instruction; they also serve to reinforce the importance of learning word meanings from encountering words in different contexts during free reading (Nagy & Anderson, 1984). However, until quite recently the evidence for the assumption that much vocabulary growth occurs through inducing the meanings of unknown words from context during reading was virtually nonexistent. This is because, as many investigators have pointed out (e.g., Jenkins et al., 1984; Nagy et al., 1985), most previous studies have focused on the ability to *derive* meanings from context when that was the explicit task set, rather than on the extent to which meanings are naturally learned during reading. However, recent studies by Jenkins et al. (1984) and Nagy et al. (1985) have indicated that learning from context during reading does occur (but see Schatz & Baldwin, 1986). Furthermore, an analysis of the extent of the vocabulary learning in both studies, taken in conjunction with some reasonable estimates of children's reading volume and vocabulary growth, led Nagy et al. (1985) to conclude: "Despite the uncertainties, our analysis suggests that words learned incidentally from context are likely to constitute a substantial portion of children's vocabulary growth" (p. 250).

MATTHEW EFFECTS IN READING: THE RICH GET RICHER

If the development of vocabulary knowledge substantially facilitates reading comprehension, and if reading itself is a major mechanism leading to vocabulary growth—which in turn will enable more efficient reading—then we truly have a reciprocal relationship that should continue to drive further growth in reading throughout a person's development. The critical mediating variable that turns this relationship into a strong bootstrapping mechanism that causes major individual differences in the development of reading skill is the volume of reading experience (Fielding, Wilson, & Anderson, 1986; Nagy et al., 1985).

As previously discussed, Biemiller (1977–1978) found large ability differences in exposure to print within the classroom as early as midway through the first-grade year. Convergent results were obtained by Allington (1984). In his first-grade sample, the total number of words read during a week of school reading-group sessions ranged from a low of 16 for one of the children in the less skilled group to a high of 1,933 for one of the children in the skilled reading group. The average skilled reader read approximately three times as many words in the group reading sessions as the average less skilled reader. Nagy and Anderson (1984) estimated that, as regards in-school reading, "The least motivated children in the middle grades might read 100,000 words a year while the average children at this level might read 1,000,000. The figure for the voracious middle grade reader might be 10,000,000 or even as high as 50,000,000. If these guesses are anywhere near the mark, there are staggering individual differences in the volume of language experience, and therefore, opportunity to learn new words" (p. 328). There are also differences in the volume of reading outside of the classroom that are linked to reading ability (Fielding et al., 1986), and these probably become increasingly large as schooling progresses.

The effect of reading volume on vocabulary growth, combined with the large skill differences in reading volume, could mean that a "rich-get-richer" or cumulative advantage phenomenon is almost inextricably embedded within the developmental course of reading progress. The very children who are reading well and who have good vocabularies will read more, learn more word meanings, and hence read even better. Children with inadequate vocabularies—who read slowly and without enjoyment—read less, and as a result have slower development of vocabulary knowledge, which inhibits further growth in reading ability. Walberg (Walberg et al., 1984; Walberg & Tsai, 1983), following Merton (1968), has dubbed those educational sequences where early achievement spawns faster rates of subsequent achievement "Matthew effects," after the Gospel According to Matthew: "For unto every one that hath shall be given, and he shall have abundance: but from him that hath not shall be taken away even that which he hath" (XXV: 29).

The concept of Matthew effects springs from findings that individuals who have advantageous early educational experiences are able to utilize new educational experiences more efficiently (Walberg & Tsai, 1983). Walberg et al. (1984) speculated that

> those who did well at the start may have been more often, or more intensively, rewarded for their early accomplishments; early intellectual and motivational capital may grow for longer periods and at greater rates; and large funds and continuing high growth rates of information and motivation may be more intensely rewarded. Thus, rather than the one-way causal directionality usually assumed in educational research, reverberating or reciprocal states may cause self-fulfilling or self-reinforcing causal processes that are highly influential in determining educational and personal productivity. (p. 92)

In short, Walberg et al. (1984) emphasized that reciprocally facilitating relationships, like the one between vocabulary and reading, can be major causes of large individual differences in educational achievement.

The facilitation of reading comprehension by vocabulary knowledge illustrates a principle that has been strongly emphasized in much recent research on cognitive development: the importance of the current knowledge base in acquiring new information (Bjorklund & Weiss, 1985; Chi, Glaser, & Rees, 1982; Keil, 1984; Larkin, McDermott, Simon, & Simon, 1980). Sternberg (1985a) has articulated the point in the context of vocabulary: "Thus, vocabulary is not only affected by operations of components, [but] it affects their operations as well. If one grows up in a household that encourages exposure to words, then one's vocabulary may well be greater, which in turn may lead to a superior learning and performance on other kinds of tasks that require vocabulary" (p. 123). Thus, one mechanism leading to Matthew effects in education is the facilitation of further learning by a previously existing knowledge base that is rich and elaborated. A person with more expertise has a larger knowledge base, and the large knowledge base allows that person to acquire even greater expertise at a faster rate. An analogous Matthew effect in reading arises from the fact that it is the better readers who have the more developed vocabularies.

There are several factors contributing to Matthew effects in reading development. For example, the research cited above has pointed to reading exposure differences between individuals of different skill levels. This is an example of the important principle of *organism–environment correlation*: different types of organisms are selectively exposed to different types of environments. Recently, theorists have emphasized the importance of understanding that there are important organism–environment correlations that result from the child's own behavior (Lerner & Busch-Rossnagel, 1981; Plomin, DeFries, & Loehlin, 1977; Scarr & McCartney, 1983; Sternberg, 1985a; Wachs & Mariotto, 1978). Organisms not only are acted on by their environments; they also select, shape, and evoke their own environments. Particularly later in development (see Scarr & McCartney, 1983), a person has partly selected and shaped his or her own environment (sometimes termed *active* organism–

environment correlation) and has been affected by the environment's response to the particular type of organism (sometimes termed *evocative* organism–environment correlation).

The difference in volume of reading between readers of differing skill are partly due to these active and evocative organism–environment correlations. Children who become better readers have selected (e.g., by choosing friends who read or choosing reading as a leisure activity rather than sports or video games), shaped (e.g., by asking for books as presents when young), and evoked (e.g., the child's parents noticed that looking at books was enjoyed or perhaps just that it kept the child quiet) an environment that will be conducive to further growth in reading. Children who lag in reading achievement do not construct such an environment. Anbar (1986) noted the importance of these active and evocative organism–environment correlations in her studies of children who acquired reading before school: "Once the parents began to interact with their children around the reading activities, the children reciprocated with eagerness. The parents then intuitively seemed to follow the child's learning interests and curiosity, sensitively responding to requests for aid. One could say, therefore, that the parents facilitated the child's natural course of development" (p. 77).

[*material omitted*]

MATTHEW EFFECTS AND THE LESS SKILLED READER

Because Matthew, or rich-get-richer, effects have been shown to be an important source of achievement variance in many areas of schooling, researchers need to explore more fully the operation of such effects in the domain of reading. Also, of course, the other side of the coin, poor-get-poorer effects, may help to explain certain aspects of reading failure. For example, Matthew effects may arise from conditions other than those described above. In addition to the achievement differences that will occur as a result of the information processing efficiency of the better reader (e.g., Sternberg, 1985a) and the exposure differences resulting from active and evocative organism–environment correlations (e.g., Nagy & Anderson, 1984), there are also *passive* organism–environment correlations that contribute to rich-get-richer and poor-get-poorer effects.

[*material omitted*]

An example of a passive organism–environment correlation that contributes to Matthew effects is provided by the literature on the influence of a school's ability composition on academic achievement. The evidence, as summarized by Rutter (1983), indicates that "quite apart from the individual benefits of above-average intellectual ability, a child of any level of ability is likely to make better progress if taught in a school with a relatively high concentration of pupils with good cognitive performance" (p. 19). But of course a child of above-average ability is much more likely to reside in a school with a "concentration of pupils with good cognitive performance" (Jencks, 1972). Such a child is an advantaged organism because of the superior environment and genotype provided by the child's parents. The parents, similarly environmentally and genetically advantaged, are more likely to reside in a community which provides the "concentration of pupils" that, via the independent effects of school composition, will bootstrap the child to further educational advantages. Conversely, disadvantaged children are most often exposed to inferior ability composition in the schools that they attend. Thus, these children are the victims of a particularly perverse "double whammy."

Recently, Share et al. (1984) uncovered some fascinating ability–composition effects that illustrate how passive organism–environment correlations contribute to Matthew effects in the area of reading achievement. They investigated the relationship of 39 cognitive and home environment variables measured at kindergarten entry to reading achievement at the end of kindergarten and of Grade 1. (In Australia, the country of these subjects, formal reading instruction begins in kindergarten.) Share et al. (1984) tested over 500 subjects in many different classrooms located in several different schools. Their ability–composition analysis focused on phoneme segmentation ability because it was the single best predictor of reading achievement. Each child was assigned three phoneme segmentation scores. One was the child's own score on the phoneme segmentation test. Next, the mean score of each classroom was calculated and assigned to each child in that room. Finally, the mean score for each school was calculated and assigned to each child in that school. The zero-order correlations confirmed for phonological awareness—a critical determinant of the ease of initial reading acquisition—what is observed for ability in general: higher ability students are surrounded by higher ability peers. The correlation between individual and classroom phoneme segmentation ability was .59, and the correlation between individual and school phoneme segmentation ability was .45.

But does being surrounded by better phoneme segmenters make a difference in early reading? Apparently it does. The child's own phoneme segmentation ability at kindergarten entry correlated .65 with that year's reading achievement (correlations were similar for grade 1 reading achievement); the correlations involving the classroom and school means were .64 and .68. After *all* 39 cognitive and home background variables had been entered into a regression equation predicting end-of-kindergarten reading ability (the results were similar when grade 1 ability was the criterion variable), the school ability mean accounted for a statistically significant additional 9% of the variance. After the individual variables were entered, classroom mean accounted for an additional 5% of the variance in individual kindergarten achievement (again, statistically significant). Note that the 39 variables entered first include the child's own phoneme segmentation ability!

Although Share et al. (1984) have speculated on the reasons for these ability–composition effects (teacher responsiveness to ability differences, language interactions among the children, etc.), the issue of the precise mechanism involved is beyond the scope of this review. For the present purpose, the importance of the Share et al. findings is in the demonstration of an ability–composition effect—a passive organism–environment correlation that contributes to poor-get-poorer effects in achievement—in the domain of phonological awareness and reading. Unlike some of the unavoidable organism–environment correlations discussed by Scarr and McCartney (1983), this one is partially a function of social policy. It is controllable, perhaps unlike many such correlations that contribute to Matthew effects in education. Rutter (1983) emphasized this point in his conclusion:

> Nevertheless, the implication is that there are considerable disadvantages in an educational system that allows such an uneven distribution of children that some schools have intakes with a heavy preponderance of the intellectually less able. There can be no dodging the need to ensure a reasonable balance of intakes among schools, but the best way to do this is not obvious. (p. 20)

This example illustrates the importance of research aimed at uncovering the existence and causes of Matthew effects in reading, because a thorough understanding of the causes is a necessary prerequisite to sound social policy in education.

RECONCEPTUALIZING THE READING DISABILITY LITERATURE IN TERMS OF RECIPROCAL CAUSATION AND MATTHEW EFFECTS

A thorough exploration of the possible influence of reciprocal relationships and Matthew effects on observed performance profiles might help to clarify some problematic issues in the area of individual differences in reading ability. For example, reading disabilities would be better understood if some of the observed individual differences could be differentiated as cases of consequences of reading level or history, or as cases of reciprocal causation. Indeed, I will argue in this section that a consideration of the relationships between reading and other cognitive skills in terms of the concepts outlined above can help to resolve some recurrent problems in the area of reading disabilities (or dyslexia; these terms are used interchangeably in the following discussion). Some of these conceptual problems are so serious that they threaten to undermine the entire field if they are not soon resolved. For example, one assumption that is essential to all definitions of reading disability is the "assumption of specificity" (Hall & Humphreys, 1982; Stanovich, 1986a). This assumption underlies all discussions of the concept, even if it is not stated explicitly. Simply put, it is the idea that a child with this type of learning disability has a brain/cognitive deficit that is reasonably specific to the reading task. That is, the concept of a specific reading disability requires that the deficits displayed by such children not extend too far into other domains of cognitive functioning. If they did, there would already exist research and educational designations for such children (low intelligence, "slow learner," etc.), and the concept of reading disability would be superfluous.

The assumption of specificity is contained within virtually all psychometric and legal definitions of reading disability, and it is also quite salient in media portrayals of dyslexia. The typical "media dyslexic" is a bright, capable individual with a specific problem in the area of reading (the quintessential example of the white-collar worker who, through dictation, secretaries, and various office maneuvers, covers up the fact that he cannot read). In terms of the concepts I have developed in this review, such individuals have remained immune to the negative cascade of interacting skill deficits and Matthew effects surrounding reading. For example, their vocabularies and other language abilities have continued to develop without the benefit of reading, and they have (to some degree) avoided the negative motivational consequences of reading failure. It will be argued here that the number of such individuals—those who truly escape the snowballing consequences of reading failure—is much smaller than is commonly presumed.

A major problem in the area of reading disabilities research is that the literature on individual differences in the cognitive processes related to reading has undermined the assumption of specificity. When researchers went looking for cognitive differences between reading-disabled and nondisabled children, they found them virtually everywhere. The plethora of cognitive differences that have been uncovered threatens to undermine the concept of a reading disability because the existence of such differences calls into question the assumption of specificity and instead suggests that dyslexic children exhibit rather generalized cognitive deficits.

Consider the concatenation of processes that have been found to differentiate disabled from nondisabled readers. Not surprisingly, phonemic awareness and associated spelling-to-sound decoding skills are markedly deficient in disabled readers (Bradley & Bryant, 1978; Gough & Tunmer, 1986; Snowling, 1980, 1981). However, more general aspects of speech perception have been implicated by the findings of Brady, Shankweiler, and Mann (1983) that poor readers make more perceptual errors when listening to speech in noise, and the findings of Godfrey, Syrdal-Lasky, Millay, and Knox (1981) that disabled and nondisabled readers differ in the categorical perception of certain speech contrasts. Briggs and Underwood (1982) have presented evidence of a deficit in the speech code that is closer to articulatory in level, and Tallal (1980) has even uncovered processing deficits with nonspeech auditory stimuli. Of course, naming deficits have also long been associated with reading failure (Denckla & Rudel, 1976; Spring & Capps, 1974; Wolf, 1984). Thus, indications are that the speech and auditory processing problems of the disabled reader are multiple and pervasive.

Moreover, language processing differences have turned up at other levels. Syntactic knowledge and awareness seem to be deficient in disabled readers

(Bowey, 1986; Byrne, 1981; Hallahan & Bryan, 1981; McClure, Kalk, & Keenan, 1980; Menyuk & Flood, 1981; Newcomer & Magee, 1977; Semel & Wiig, 1975; Siegel & Ryan, 1984; Stein, Cairns, & Zurif, 1984; Vellutino, 1979; Vogel, 1974). Their performance is relatively low on tests of general listening comprehension and general linguistic awareness (Berger, 1978; Downing, 1980; Kotsonis & Patterson, 1980; Menyuk & Flood, 1981; Newcomer & Magee, 1977; Siegel & Ryan, 1984; Smiley, Oakley, Worthen, Campione, & Brown, 1977). Comprehension strategies that are very general seem to be deficient. Concatenating these findings with those on phonological awareness and speech cited previously, we seem to be uncovering a deficiency in a "specific" area that can only be labeled "language—in all its conceivable aspects." This is not the type of "specific" psychological disability that the originators of the idea of dyslexia had in mind.

Work on short-term memory as a psychological locus of the processing difficulties of disabled readers was originally motivated by the desire to uncover a specific "site" that was the source of reading problems. Although some proportion of the performance difference between normal and disabled readers on short-term memory tasks is almost certainly due to the specific phonological coding problems experienced by the latter (R. L. Cohen, 1982; Jorm, 1983; Torgesen & Houck, 1980), research on individual differences in memory performance soon pushed the mediating cognitive mechanisms far beyond an explanation purely in terms of phonological coding. Cognitive and developmental psychologists have linked many processing strategies to memory performance, and research has shown reading-disabled children to be deficient in their ability and/or willingness to employ virtually every one of these strategies (Bauer, 1977, 1979, 1982; Foster & Gavelek, 1983; Newman & Hagen, 1981; Tarver, Hallahan, Kauffman, & Ball, 1976; Torgesen, 1977a, 1977b, 1978–1979; Torgesen & Goldman, 1977; Wong, Wong, & Foth, 1977). These findings have led to characterizations of the underlying cognitive deficit of learning-disabled children that are strikingly general. For example, Torgesen's (1977a, 1977b) early work on memory functioning led him to characterize the learning-disabled child as an inactive learner, one who fails to apply even cognitive strategies that are within his or her capabilities.

Torgesen's notion is of course similar to currently popular ideas regarding the importance of metacognitive or executive functioning. Indeed, recent work on the performance of reading-disabled children has reinforced Torgesen's earlier position and explicitly tied his ideas in with recent views on metacognitive functioning (Baker, 1982; Bos & Filip, 1982; Foster & Gavelek, 1983; Hagen, Barclay, & Newman, 1982; Hallahan & Bryan, 1981; Wong, 1984). However, the tendency to link deficiencies in metacognitive functioning with reading disability will undermine the assumption of specificity. Recent conceptualizations (e.g., Baron, 1978; Campione & Brown, 1978; Sternberg, 1980, 1982, 1985a) have stressed that metacognitive awareness of available strategies is a critical aspect of intelligence! Thus, further developments along these lines will surely evolve a paradoxical conclusion: that reading-disabled children are deficient in a generalized ability to deal with cognitive tasks of all types (i.e., that they lack metacognitive awareness: a critical aspect of intelligence). This, of course, would be the death knell for the assumption of specificity, and hence the entire rationale for the concept of dyslexia would be undermined.

Escaping the Paradox: Subject Selection

There are at least three ways to escape the dilemma posed by the fact that the literature on individual differences in the cognitive processes of reading threatens to erode the fundamental assumption upon which the concept of dyslexia rests. One is to question the nature of the subject samples employed in the research. It may be that the less skilled children were not sufficiently disabled: that many studies contained substantial numbers of children who were experiencing only a moderate degree of reading difficulty and whose cognitive performance profiles—unlike those of the truly disabled reader—were characterized by mild but pervasive deficits. To the extent that some investigators have employed primarily school labeling as the criterion for forming subject groups—rather than scores on their own self-administered tests and strictly applied psychometric criteria—this criticism is appropriate.

Since the advent of the concept of a reading disability, it has repeatedly been pointed out that schools do not identify reading-disabled children in accord with the actual definitions of dyslexia prevailing in the professional literature (Ames, 1968; Bryan, 1974; Kirk & Elkins, 1975; Miller & Davis, 1982; Norman & Zigmond, 1980). We have come to think of a reading-disabled child—in the view that is certainly the one promoted by parent groups and the media—as a child with normal intelligence. But surveys of school-labeled reading-disabled children have consistently shown that even on nonverbal and performance intelligence tests, the mean score of the children does not approximate 100, but is usually closer to 90 (Anderson, Kaufman, & Kaufman, 1976; Gajar, 1979; Hallahan & Kauffman, 1977; Kirk & Elkins, 1975; Klinge, Rennick, Lennox, & Hart, 1977; Leinhardt, Seewald, & Zigmond, 1982; McLeskey & Rieth, 1982; Norman & Zigmond, 1980; Satz & Friel, 1974; Shepard, Smith, & Vojir, 1983; Smith, Coleman, Dokecki, & Davis, 1977; Tarver, 1982; Valtin, 1978–1979).

Thus, to the extent that school-labeled samples have been used, researchers have been comparing less skilled readers with mild IQ deficits to the normal control groups, and it is perhaps not surprising that a large number of performance differences have appeared. This problem extends even to research where an attempt has been made to match (or restrict the range of) the reading-disabled and control groups on other environmental variables (Fletcher, Satz, & Scholes, 1981; Hallahan & Kauffman, 1977; Klinge et al., 1977). For example, from a group of 108 learning-disabled children, Klinge et al. (1977) selected 30 children to match 30 controls on sex, race, age, socioeconomic status, and geographic community. Despite the matching, the mean performance intelligence test score of the learning-disabled group (94) was 9 points lower than that of the control group (103).

The problem is pervasive even in research studies that have attempted to match subjects on intelligence test scores. Although these procedures often ensure that the intelligence test scores of the reading-disabled sample approximate 100 and are not significantly different from those of the control group, it is almost invariably the case that the IQs of the disabled group turn out to be lower (Hall & Humphreys, 1982; Stanovich, 1986a; Torgesen, 1985). In a formal survey of the research literature, Torgesen and Dice (1980) found that the mean intelligence test scores of the learning-disabled groups averaged 6 points lower than those of the control groups. Wolford and Fowler (1984), in their survey, came to similar conclusions.

A discussion of the IQ matching problem leads naturally to a consideration of some of the statistical problems surrounding the concept of reading disability—statistical complications often unknown to the teachers and practitioners who are using the concept. For example, it is well known that performance on intelligence tests correlates with reading achievement. This correlation is usually in the range of .3 to .5 in the early elementary grades, but rises to the range of .6 to .75 in adult samples (see Stanovich, Cunningham, & Feeman, 1984a). An individual with a reading disability is by definition a person for whom this performance linkage does not hold, or at least for whom it is severely attenuated. Such a person has severely depressed performance on one variable (reading) but virtually normal performance on the other (intelligence test score). These individuals are statistical outliers, defined by their deviation from the regression line in a scatterplot of reading achievement scores against intelligence test scores. It is important to realize that because part of the outlier status of this group *must* be the result of measurement error, on a retesting (due to statistical regression) they will score lower on the IQ test (or highly related cognitive measure) and somewhat higher on the reading test (Crowder, 1984; Hall & Humphreys, 1982). Defining reading-disabled children on the basis of a single testing will conceal this fact and thus artificially magnify their outlier status (Shepard, 1980). A reading-disabled classification that partially reflects measurement error will contribute to the plethora of deficits obtained, because whatever cognitive tasks are administered become the "second testing" on which these subjects will regress to performance levels below those of their IQ-matched, nondisabled controls.

When we combine the purely statistical artifact of regression with the empirical fact, reviewed above, that the reading-disabled children in the schools and in research reports have mild IQ deficits, we may have a large part of the explanation for the tendency of the research literature to undermine the assumption of specificity. To some extent, the children in these samples *should* have small but pervasive cognitive deficits, because on one omnibus index of cognitive functioning (an intelligence test) they show a small deficit. They are not the extreme statistical outliers that the definitions of reading disability imply. Secondly, the moderate outlier pattern that they do display is, in part, measurement artifact.

The solutions to these statistical problems have clear implications for research and practice. Both practitioners and researchers should adopt a much stricter psychometric criterion for defining a child as reading-disabled. A second testing to insure that the bulk of the performance discrepancy is not measurement artifact is essential for accurate classification (see Shepard, 1980). It is only by isolating the true outliers that researchers can hope to obtain the evidence for specificity that the dyslexia concept requires if it is to be of scientific and practical utility. The parent groups who have pushed for ever-more-inclusive definitions of dyslexia (estimates from such groups often claim that anywhere from 10% to 30% of the school population should be so labeled) are indirectly undermining the concept. The wider the net that is cast, the greater will be the difficulties in distinguishing dyslexia from other educational designations (e.g., borderline retardation, EMR). Lack of restraint in applying the label is in part responsible for the failure of researchers to demonstrate consistently that the performance profiles of disabled subjects differ reliably from those of other poor readers (Algozzine & Ysseldyke, 1983; Bloom, Wagner, Reskin, & Bergman, 1980; Coles, 1978; Gottesman, Croen, & Rotkin, 1982; Taylor, Satz, & Friel, 1979), and it is one of the main reasons why the diagnostic utility of the concept of dyslexia continues to be questioned (Arter & Jenkins, 1979; S. Cohen, 1976; Coles, 1978; Gross & Gottlieb, 1982; Miller & Davis, 1982; Ysseldyke & Algozzine, 1979).

The best existing evidence in favor of demarcating reading disability as a qualitatively distinguishable behavioral concept comes from the epidemiological Isle of Wight study reported by Rutter and Yule (1975; Rutter, 1978; Yule, 1973). Their study contrasts with many others that have failed to distinguish reading-disabled children from other poor readers (Bloom et al., 1980; Coles, 1978; Taylor et al., 1979), and two of its critical features deserve attention. One was the use of regression procedures to define outliers (Horn & O'Donnell, 1984; Shepard, 1980; Wilson & Cone, 1984). But probably most important was their use of a conservative criterion for classifying a case as an outlier; as a result, only 3.7% of the subjects in their sample were classified as "specifics." A conservative criterion like that employed by Rutter and Yule (1975) is probably essential in forming samples that stand a chance of providing evidence consistent with the assumption of specificity. It seems reasonable to speculate that only studies that classify less than 5% of the sampled population as reading-disabled will stand a chance of uncovering evidence for specificity. When the proportion gets much above 5%, one will probably observe more generalized deficits.

Escaping the Paradox: Subtypes

A second way of putting the assumption of specificity on a firmer footing—and one that by no means excludes the previous recommendation of a conservative criterion—is suggested by the "subtypes" argument. This is the argument that there may be many subtypes of reading disability, and that if a research sample comprises several subtypes (each with a distinct, but different, single-factor deficit), the overall results from the sample will mistakenly seem to indicate multiple deficits. Although this is a logical possibility, the subtyping literature itself remains confusing (Jorm, 1983; Lundberg, 1985; R. K. Olson, Kliegl, Davidson, & Foltz, 1985; Perfetti, 1985; Stanovich, 1986a; Vellutino, 1979), and has produced no strong evidence implicating subtypes in the wide variety of deficits that have been observed. In fact, most researchers would probably find themselves having to agree that no "tight" subgroupings have been identified (Stanovich, 1986a) and to accept Jorm's (1983) statement that "there is no agreed-upon taxonomy of subtypes" (p. 312). However, newer research methodologies for evaluating the subtype hypothesis are just beginning to be evaluated (Doehring, Trites, Patel, & Fiedorowicz, 1981; Lovett, 1984; Torgesen, 1982). Pursuing the subtype hypothesis, in conjunction with using a conservative definition of reading disability, might establish a firmer empirical foundation for the assumption of specificity.

Escaping the Paradox: A Developmental Version of the Specificity Hypothesis

There is, however, a third alternative—again, not exclusive of searching for subtypes and using a conservative criterion—which may be theoretically the most interesting. This alternative is to hypothesize developmental change in the cognitive specificity of the deficits displayed by reading-disabled children—change that is in part a consequence of individual differences in reading acquisition and the reciprocal relationships between reading, other cognitive skills, and motivational factors. This hypothesis follows from the tentative causal model presented earlier.

According to this hypothesis, the performance of reading-disabled children is characterized by a relatively high degree of specificity upon entering school (see Jorm, Share, Maclean, & Matthews, 1986). The obvious candidate for the critically deficient process is phonological awareness. Thus, it is hypothesized that due to several incompletely determined—but undoubtedly complex and interacting—genetic and environmental causes (Chall, 1983b; S. Cohen, Glass, & Singer, 1973; Duane, 1983; Feitelson & Goldstein, 1986; Guthrie, 1981; Rutter et al., 1974; Stevenson et al., 1985), children who will later be candidates for the label of reading-disabled enter school with markedly underdeveloped phonological awareness, but with either mild deficits in other cognitive skills or none at all. Deficient phonological awareness makes it difficult for the child to understand the alphabetic principle and delays the breaking of the spelling-to-sound code. The differences in in-school exposure to text chronicled by Allington (1980, 1983, 1984) and Biemiller (1977–1978) begin to build up by the middle of the first-grade year. These exposure differences compound any out-of-school differences already present and leave reading-disabled children farther behind their peers in the development of the rapid, automatic processes of direct visual recognition. These processes enable the type of reading for comprehension that is more enjoyable than that encumbered by the cognitively demanding conscious process of "sounding out." The resulting motivational differences lead to further increases in the exposure differences between good and poor readers that are then exacerbated by further developments such as the introduction of more difficult reading materials.

Of course, the exact timing of this developmental sequence and of its feedback effects remains to be worked out. What is critical for the present discussion is the hypothesis that at some point, slower progress at reading acquisition begins to have more *generalized* effects: effects on processes that underlie a broader range of tasks and skills than just reading. That is, the initial specific problem may evolve into a more generalized deficit due to the behavioral/cognitive/motivational spinoffs from failure at such a crucial educational task as reading. For example, at some point reading exposure differences begin to result in marked divergences in the vocabularies of skilled and less skilled readers, and those vocabulary differences have implications for other aspects of language use. The same is probably true of syntactic knowledge and world knowledge.

Perhaps just as important as the cognitive consequences of reading failure are the motivational side effects. These are receiving increasing attention from researchers. Butkowsky and Willows (1980) manipulated success and failure in a reading and a nonreading task. The poor readers in the fifth-grade sample were less likely to attribute success to ability, and more likely to attribute it to luck or to the easiness of the task, than were the better readers. Following failure, however, they were more likely to attribute their performance to ability and less likely to attribute it to luck or task difficulty. The poorer readers also displayed less task persistence than the better readers. Their behavioral and attributional patterns displayed characteristics consistent with the concept of academic learned helplessness, which has been studied in several areas of educational achievement (Diener & Dweck, 1978; Fowler & Peterson, 1981; Johnston & Winograd, 1985; Licht & Dweck, 1984; Torgesen & Licht, 1983). Interestingly, the same behavioral and attributional patterns were displayed on the nonreading task as on the reading task, indicating that by this age, achievement-thwarting motivational and behavioral tendencies were being exhibited on tasks other than reading, even though the disabled group was constituted solely on the basis of lagging reading achievement. Thus, the learned helplessness that may have been the result of reading failure was beginning to influence performance on other cognitive tasks, perhaps eventually leading to an increasingly generalized inability to deal with academic and cognitive tasks of all types. Thus, not only the negative cognitive effects but also the motivational spinoffs of reading failure can lead to increasingly global performance deficits.

Butkowsky and Willows (1980) point to the possibility of a negative

Matthew effect in their paper—"These data provide convincing evidence in support of the notion that children with reading difficulties may display an eroding motivation in achievement situations that increases the probability of future failure" (p. 419)—and they suggest one mechanism contributing to this effect. They note that the lower persistence that is part of the learned helplessness pattern is self-defeating: "Children who give up easily in the face of difficulty may never persist long enough at a task to discover that success may, in fact, be possible. Such children may never spontaneously discover that they do possess the capacity to achieve outcomes that exceed their expectations" (p. 419).

Perfetti (1985) has explicated these proliferating Matthew effects and the related motivational problems using the framework of his verbal efficiency theory:

> The low-achieving reader starts out behind in terms of some of the linguistic knowledge on which this verbal processing system gets built. He falls farther behind as his reading experiences fail to build the rich and redundant network that the high-achieving reader has. By the time a fifth-grade student is targeted for remediation, the inefficiency (and ineffectiveness) of his (or her) verbal coding system has had a significant history. To expect this to be remedied by a few lessons in decoding practice is like expecting a baseball player of mediocre talent to suddenly become a good hitter following a few days of batting practice. This problem, the need for extended practice, is unfortunately coupled with the problem of motivation. (p. 248)

EVALUATING A DEVELOPMENTAL VERSION OF THE SPECIFICITY HYPOTHESIS

The hypothesis entertained here is that there is a developmental trend in the specificity of the disability: a specific cognitive deficit prevents the early acquisition of reading skill. Slow reading acquisition has cognitive, behavioral, and motivational consequences that slow the development of other cognitive skills and inhibit performance on many academic tasks. In short, as reading develops, other cognitive processes linked to it track the level of reading skill. Knowledge bases that are in reciprocal relationships with reading are also inhibited from further development. The longer this developmental sequence is allowed to continue, the more generalized the deficits will become, seeping into more and more areas of cognition and behavior. Or, to put it more simply—and more sadly—in the words of a tearful nine-year-old, already falling frustratingly behind his peers in reading progress, "Reading affects everything you do" (Morris, 1984, p. 19).

The presence of a developmental trend in the specificity of the disability may in part account for why the literature has failed to uncover strong evidence for specificity and instead has augmented the number of possible cognitive deficits: the subjects in many of the studies may have been so developmentally advanced that generalized cognitive deficiencies had begun to appear. This account is certainly true of studies of cognitive differences among adult readers of varying skill.

At present, there is little direct evidence with which to evaluate this developmental variant of the specificity hypothesis. Clearly, we need longitudinal research designs to obtain the most diagnostic data. Also, such a developmental trend may be difficult to detect because the period during which specificity might be observed could be quite short. Perhaps it is only in the very earliest stages of reading acquisition—when the seriously disabled readers may be harder to identify—that considerable cognitive specificity occurs. Again, the need for longitudinal data is obvious.

There are many other methodological, conceptual, and statistical problems in evaluating some of the predictions that follow from the hypothesis. One such prediction is that reading and the cognitive skills related to it should become more interrelated with development. Unfortunately, this predicted trend will probably be confounded with the fact that more complex cognitive processes are engaged mainly at the more advanced levels of reading (Chall, 1983b). For example, the more complex types of inferencing skills are necessary only when the material being read attains a certain level of difficulty. Thus, the correlation between reading and these cognitive skills will increase not only because of the consequences of differential reading experience, but also because the *task* of reading is changing (Chall, 1983b). Separating the operation of these two mechanisms could be extremely difficult.

Additionally, researchers who attempt to evaluate the hypothesis during the developmental stages that are critical—the very earliest reading acquisition stages—will encounter some statistical complications. For example, the reliability of some tasks may increase during this period, necessarily leading to changes in correlations. It is not surprising, given these difficulties, that there is currently little evidence to permit a strong test of the developmental version of the specificity hypothesis. Nevertheless, there are some suggestive trends in the literature that should at least motivate more definitive tests. The hypothesis is worth pursuing because—like the subtypes hypothesis, for which there is arguably little more evidence—it may provide a way of preserving the assumption of specificity (and the concept of dyslexia) in the face of the mounting body of data indicating pervasive cognitive deficiencies.

Developmental studies of multivariate relationships between reading-related cognitive processes have yielded suggestive evidence that the intercorrelation of subskills increases with age. In one study, we (Stanovich, Cunningham, & Feeman, 1984a) found that at the end of first grade, measures of phonological awareness, decoding speed, vocabulary, listening comprehension, and abstract problem-solving were only weakly correlated; but by the fifth grade, performance on these tasks was highly correlated. In the first grade the mean correlation between tasks tapping different cognitive skills was .24, whereas this correlation rose to .59 in the fifth grade. A similar trend runs through the correlations reported by Curtis (1980). Comparisons of other multivariate studies of reading-related skills in the early grades (e.g., Stevenson, Parker, Wilkinson, Hegion, & Fish, 1976) with adult studies (e.g., M. D. Jackson & McClelland, 1975, 1979) suggest a similar pattern.

[material omitted]

Bishop and Butterworth (1980) have reported one of the few longitudinal studies within the relevant age range, and their data are quite suggestive. They found that performance and verbal IQs assessed at age 4 were equally good predictors ($r = .36$) of reading ability at age 8; however, when assessed concurrently with reading ability at age 8, verbal IQ displayed a stronger relationship. Furthermore, the children in their sample who had reading problems at age 8 appeared to have lower verbal than performance IQ scores at age 8, but did not at age 4. These trends are consistent with the idea that success or failure at the initial stages of reading acquisition has effects on more general aspects of verbal intelligence.

Studies of reading-related cognitive skills in the early grades have consistently indicated that the different cognitive processes are only weakly interrelated. Our (Stanovich, Cunningham, & Feeman, 1984a) mean correlation of .24 is similar to that reported by other researchers, as follows: Blachman (1984), .30; Curtis (1980), .32, .27; Evans and Carr (1985), .39, .18; Share et al. (1984), .38; and Stevenson et al. (1976), .14, .26, .09, and .32. Although low reliabilities may be attenuating some of these correlations, these results do suggest the interesting possibility of considerable dissociation between the cognitive subskills related to reading when a child enters school. Such a relatively loose linkage between cognitive skills in the early grades would allow greater cognitive specificity among younger poor readers.

A similar pattern of relative dissociation appears when one examines the correlations between reading ability and scores on various intelligence tests. Although these correlations cluster in the ranges of .45 to .65 in the middle grades and .60 to .75 among adults, they are more commonly between .30 and .50 in the early elementary grades (see Stanovich, Cunningham, & Feeman, 1984a). Of particular interest is the finding that performance on phonological awareness tasks in kindergarten and first grade often predicts subsequent reading achievement better than intelligence tests that tap a variety of cognitive processes (Bradley & Bryant, 1983, 1985; Goldstein, 1976; Mann, 1984; Share et al., 1984; Stanovich, Cunningham, & Cramer, 1984; Stanovich, Cunningham, & Feeman, 1984a; Torneus, 1984; Tunmer & Nesdale, 1985; Zifcak, 1981). (Of course, it has long been known that letter knowledge prior to entering school is a better predictor of initial reading acquisition than IQ; see Chall, 1967; Richek, 1977–1978; Stevenson et al., 1976.)

Additionally, several studies have demonstrated that phonological awareness accounts for a statistically significant and sizable portion of variance in reading ability after the variance associated with standardized intelligence measures has been partialed out (Bradley & Bryant, 1983, 1985; Goldstein,

1976; Stanovich, Cunningham, & Feeman, 1984a; Tunmer & Nesdale, 1985). In short, some suggestive evidence does exist to indicate that, at school entry, phonological awareness is dissociated from other cognitive skills to such an extent that it could be the source of a specific reading disability: one that—according to the hypothesis outlined above—develops into a more generalized cognitive deficit.

BREAKING THE CYCLE OF INTERACTING SKILL DEFICITS

The discussion in several previous sections, emphasizing as it did the cycle of negative Matthew effects set in motion by reading failure, invites speculation on how the cycle is to be broken. Although this discussion has highlighted the importance of breaking the cycle, it has also hinted at the difficulty of doing so. One of the reasons that the cycle will be difficult for educators to break is that some of the Matthew effects are linked to events in the child's out-of-school environment. Also, as a result, certain interpretive problems are often encountered when one is attempting to evaluate the effects of interventions to facilitate reading achievement. In order to better understand these issues we may find it instructive to consider the interpretive problems in an area with analogous problems: research on schooling effects.

Findings on the effects of schooling on achievement appeared confusing and inconsistent until researchers generally recognized the importance of differentiating those factors that explain the variance in academic performance from those that determine the absolute level of performance (see McCall, 1981; Rutter, 1983). Rutter (1983) illustrated this point by pointing to Tizard's (1975) discussion of the fact that in the last 50–60 years, the average height of London children aged 7–12 has increased by nine centimeters—probably due to better nutrition—yet there has been no change in the variation in height among the children. Current variation is probably just as strongly determined by genetic factors as it always was, even though nutritional changes have raised the overall height of the population.

Understanding the effects of schooling on achievement requires that we understand the distinction drawn in the Tizard example. Although school variables explain very little of the *variance* in achievement (family background being the dominant factor), the *absolute level* of academic achievement is linked to a number of school variables (Rutter, 1983). This distinction provides a context for understanding Matthew effects in education. Raising the population's mean level of performance will not eliminate individual differences. In fact, raising absolute levels of performance might well *increase* performance variance, because high achievers will make better use of the new learning opportunities.

One might think that if overall performance levels rise, the lowest readers will eventually reach an acceptable level of achievement, one where they would no longer be considered "disabled." Unfortunately, ever-escalating absolute levels of performance will not necessarily be a panacea for the low-achieving student. Rising absolute levels of performance more often result in increased societal expectations, marketplace adjustments, and higher criteria of acceptable performance on the part of the public and employers (Levine, 1982; Resnick & Resnick, 1977).

In this context, note that researchers and educators who are focusing on the problem of reading disability are in effect aspiring to reduce the variance in reading ability (i.e., to bring up the lowest readers to some reasonable standard). The existence of negative Matthew effects that go beyond the school, and the history of research on the attempts to decrease achievement variability, suggest that educational interventions that represent a "more-of-the-same" approach will probably not be successful. The cycle of escalating achievement deficits must be broken in a more specific way to short-circuit the cascade of negative spinoffs. This suggests that the remedy for the problem must be more of a "surgical strike" (to use a military analogy).

[material omitted]

The conclusions drawn in this review will suggest what optimal specific remediation might be. I have hypothesized that if there is a specific cause of reading disability at all, it resides in the area of phonological awareness. Slow development in this area delays early code-breaking progress and initiates the cascade of interacting achievement failures and motivational problems. Fortunately, developmental delays in this ability can be detected fairly early. Several of the tasks used to assess this ability have been employed with preschool and kindergarten children (Bradley & Bryant, 1983; Fox & Routh, 1975; Stanovich, Cunningham, & Cramer, 1984; Williams, 1984). Recently, several studies have reported attempts to facilitate the development of phonological awareness and thus affect the speed of early reading acquisition. The most influential has been the study of Bradley and Bryant (1983, 1985), in which a group of 5- to 6-year-old children who had scored two standard deviations below the mean on a phonological awareness task were given 40 sessions of training in sound categorization stretching over a two-year period. A group matched on IQ and phonological ability received equivalent training in conceptual classification. The results indicated that the sound categorization training group was 4 months advanced in reading ability when assessed at age 8 (a group taught sound categorization with the aid of letters displayed a striking 8-month gain). This study provides strong evidence that early identification and subsequent training in phonological awareness can partially overcome the reading deficits displayed by many children whose phonological skills develop slowly.

A critic of the Bradley and Bryant (1983, 1985) study might argue that the achievement difference between the experimental and control groups appeared to be fairly small in magnitude (e.g., Yaden, 1984). However, one inference that follows from the argument presented here is that small achievement differences that appear early can be the genesis of large differences later in development. When viewed in light of possible Matthew effects and reciprocal relationships involving reading, the achievement differences observed by Bradley and Bryant (1983, 1985) can hardly be deemed unimportant. A longitudinal study by Jorm, Share, Maclean, and Matthews (1984) illustrates how phonological skills may generate individual differences in reading acquisition that multiply with development. They formed two groups of kindergarten children who differed on phonological recoding skill but were matched on verbal intelligence and sight-word reading. By the first grade the group superior in phonological recoding skill was 4 months advanced in reading achievement. Importantly, the two groups tended to diverge with time: the performance difference increased to 9 months by the second grade.

The Bradley and Bryant (1983, 1985) study illustrates an ideal way to attack the problem of snowballing achievement deficits in reading: identify early, remediate early, and focus on phonological awareness. But what is to be done at later points in development, when negative reciprocal relationships have already begun to depress further achievement? One answer is to aim an attack at a major bootstrapping mechanism: reading practice. A computer-aided reading system developed by McConkie and Zola (1985) exemplifies this approach (a similar system has been developed by R. K. Olson, Foltz, and Wise [1986]). The child reads text on a monitor attached to a computer. When the reader encounters a word that cannot be decoded, he or she touches the word on the screen with a light pen or mouse. McConkie and Zola (1985) explicitly acknowledge that thwarting Matthew effects was one of the motivations for developing their system: "Since there are probably many aspects of reading skill that develop primarily through extended involvement in reading, these people (with reading difficulties) have been essentially blocked from this further development" (p. 9).

[material omitted]

The purpose of this section was not to survey techniques for remedying or preventing reading failure, but to illustrate two research programs with particular relevance to the model of the development of individual differences in reading ability that has been outlined here. The studies of Bradley and Bryant (1983, 1985) and of McConkie and Zola (1985) represent two ways of attacking the problem of early reading deficits that spiral the child into a pattern of ever-increasing scholastic achievement problems. The work of the former investigators represents the strategy of prevention; that of the latter represents the strategy of intervention to attenuate one of the most pervasive causes of Matthew effects on achievement: differential practice.

CONCLUSIONS, SPECULATIONS, AND CAVEATS

In the foregoing, I have sketched the type of conceptualization of individual differences in reading and related cognitive processes that results from a consideration of the cognitive consequences of reading, reciprocal causation, organism–environment correlation, and developmental change. The review is not so much a complete model of the development of individual differences as an outline to be filled in by future research. It is hoped that this framework might help to clarify aspects of the existing research literature and to focus future experimental efforts. For example, the statement that reading ability is multiply determined has become a cliche. But the number of causal mechanisms may not be as large as is commonly believed. Some of the differences in cognitive processes that are linked with reading ability may actually be the effects of reading efficiency itself. Similarly, some of the individual differences in cognitive processes that are associated with reading ability in the adult (M. D. Jackson & McClelland, 1979; Palmer et al., 1985) may be remnants of the reading histories of the subjects. This would be especially true if the processes responsible for reading ability variation change several times during development, leaving behind differences in cognitive processes that were causal at earlier stages.

The framework I have outlined may also help to clarify thinking about other issues in reading research. Consider two examples. A moderately popular genre of individual differences research has been the attempt to identify readers who have similar ability but different cognitive profiles. Often researchers have implicitly assumed that when such qualitatively different patterns have been observed among less skilled readers, they represent differing etiologies of reading failure. This conclusion is a consequence of the "many different types of reading failure" assumption that guides most research. But perhaps more attention should be directed to the possibility that the qualitatively different processing patterns represent alternative ways of *coping* with a reading deficit that had a common cause. This alternative explanation looms larger when older subjects are the focus of the investigation.

A second example is provided by the recent flurry of exciting research on comprehension strategies and cognitive monitoring during reading (e.g., August, Flavell, & Clift, 1984). It is often assumed that what is being investigated is a set of cognitive abilities separate from those linked with word-recognition skill. However, as Perfetti (1984, p. 56; 1985, p. 244; see also Lovett, 1984) has noted, few such studies have included a comprehensive evaluation of decoding skill. This leaves open the possibility that the reading skill differences in comprehension strategies that are observed may be consequences of differing overall reading levels. The better readers could be decoding words more efficiently and thus have more cognitive resources available to allocate to comprehension. As Underwood (1985) has noted, "It is partly as a consequence of having automatic processes available that reading can be flexible" (p. 173). No doubt this is not the whole story. It is more likely that the comprehension strategy differences observed represent a combination of cognitive monitoring differences and the differential resource availability due to decoding skill variation. The point is that it is important—both practically and theoretically—to separate out the part of the relationship that is a consequence of reading level.

An emphasis on the importance of Matthew effects and reciprocal relationships will also help to highlight the necessity of providing some explanation of the massive individual differences in levels of acquired reading skill. Recall that Allington (1984) observed some skilled first-grade groups to be reading three times as many words a week as some less skilled groups. The differences among an adult population can be even more startling. Perfetti (1985, p. 10) has emphasized this point by noting that even among a self-selected and range-restricted group of college students, threefold differences in reading speed occur with regularity. If these large differences are indeed the result of Matthew effects, then research must begin to move beyond the mere chronicling of the achievement differences, and begin to specify and evaluate the mechanisms that produce the Matthew effects. Some of the progress already made on this problem has been outlined above. However, one important possible mediator of Matthew effects has so far been omitted because it deserves extended discussion beyond the scope of this review: instruction.

Despite some disagreement, researchers are increasingly uncovering support for Gough and Hillinger's (1980) provocative characterization of reading as an "unnatural act" (Barron, 1986; Byrne, 1984, 1986; Calfee, 1982, 1983; Donaldson, 1984; Donaldson & Reid, 1982; Ehri & Wilce, 1985; Masonheimer, Drum, & Ehri, 1984). Although it is popular for authors to cite examples of children who have acquired reading on their own—or, more often, have been able to identify some boxtop labels via paired-associate learning or guessing from context (Masonheimer et al., 1984)—for the vast majority of children the initial stages of reading must be traversed with the aid of some type of guided instruction from a teacher (who in the case of early readers may well be a parent; see Anbar, 1986; Durkin, 1982). Thus, because instruction must mediate the initial stages of reading acquisition, it could well interact with the child's initial level of cognitive skill to cause Matthew effects. Some of these effects will result from passive organism–environment correlations: Biologically disadvantaged children must learn in instructional environments (composed of teachers, schools, parents, etc.) that are inferior to those experienced by advantaged children (Rutter & Madge, 1976). Again, some part of this correlation is the result of social structures and is potentially manipulable, and some part of it is not.

Other Matthew effects may arise from evocative organism–environment correlations involving instruction. If Allington (1983) is correct that the reading instruction provided to less skilled readers is suboptimal in many ways, then a Matthew effect is being created whereby a child who is—for whatever reason—poorly equipped to acquire reading skill may evoke an instructional environment that will further inhibit learning to read. Certainly this was true of many of the ineffective visual training programs, which had the effect of removing from conventional reading instruction the very children who needed practice at actual reading. Calfee (1983) has previously speculated on such a mechanism's operating to cause reading disabilities:

> It is true that dyslexia is associated with many correlates of the individual—being a boy, poor preparation for school, language deficiencies, among others. . . . A plausible hypothesis, which cannot be rejected from the available data is that these characteristics serve as markers about what to expect of the child in school and which thereby determine the instructional program in which he or she is placed. (pp. 77–78)

If Matthew effects of this type are an appreciable source of ability variance, it will indeed be fortunate, because they are controllable.

In short, a major problem for future research will be to determine whether instructional differences are a factor in generating Matthew effects. In addition, it will be interesting to investigate whether any of the important consequences of the ease of initial reading acquisition arise indirectly from instructional differences determined by reading ability. Some progress has been made on these problems, as there is an increasing amount of good research appearing on the effects of instructional variations on cognitive processes and achievement (Alegria, Pignot, & Morais, 1982; R. C. Anderson, Hiebert, Scott, & Wilkinson, 1985; R. C. Anderson, Mason, & Shirey, 1984; Barr, 1974–1975; Duffy, Roehler, & Mason, 1984; Evans & Carr, 1985; Hiebert, 1983; Hoffman & Rutherford, 1984). Several other fruitful research programs would probably arise from attempts to specify the mechanisms that mediate the cognitive consequences of individual differences in reading acquisition.

PART IV

THE IMPORTANCE OF WORD RECOGNITION IN MODELS OF READING

CHAPTER 11

The Word Recognition Module

In the first *Handbook of Reading Research* published in 1984 (Pearson, 1984), Phil Gough (1984) began his review of word recognition by noting that "word recognition is the foundation of the reading process" (p. 225). I reiterated this conclusion in my chapter on word recognition (Stanovich, 1991b) in Volume 2 of the *Handbook* published in 1991 (Barr, Kamil, Mosenthal, & Pearson, 1991). At the end of the decade of the 1980s I wrote two review papers (Stanovich, 1990b, 1991b) summarizing the work on this foundational process that had taken place during the decade and the refinement in our conceptual understanding that had resulted. These two papers complement each other, yet there is some redundancy between them, and as a result I have decided to reprint here the paper that appeared in *Developmental Review* because it contained more new ideas, and the concepts it discusses—cognitive resources, modularity, lexical representations—are still the subject of intense theoretical interest.

The companion review article published in the *Handbook of Reading Research* did, however, provide some important context for understanding research on word recognition. By the time that paper was published, we were quite far down the road in our understanding of the importance of word recognition in the reading process. Gough's (1972) seminal "One Second of Reading" had been published, as had the automaticity model of LaBerge and Samuels (1974) which receives extended discussion in the paper reprinted as Chapter 12. Perfetti and Hogaboam (1975) had published their demonstration of the incredible potency of pseudoword reading as a predictor of reading difficulty, and their result had undergone extensive replication (Stanovich, 1981b; Perfetti, Finger, & Hogaboam, 1978). Nevertheless, the context for the statement that word recognition is the foundational process of reading was widely misunderstood at the time Volume 1 of the *Handbook* appeared (1984). It was still misunderstood at the time Volume 2 appeared (1991). And as the Reading Wars rage on into a new millennium (see Part VII), it is still widely misunderstood. Thus, it remains necessary to state that context yet again. Specifically, to emphasize the centrality of word recognition is not to deny that the ultimate purpose of reading is comprehension (Pressley, 1998). Neither does an emphasis on the fundamental role of word recognition in models of reading necessarily translate into particular instructional practices (see Ehri, 1998). The interface between models of reading and instructional practices is so complex that instructional prescriptions cannot be assumed simply from a knowledge of which processes receive emphasis in a particular model of reading (see Chapter 21).

Nevertheless, skill at word recognition is so central to the total reading process that it can serve as a proxy diagnostic tool for instructional methods. That is, while it is possible for adequate word recognition skill to be accompanied by poor comprehension abilities, the converse virtually never occurs. It has never been empirically demonstrated, nor is it theoretically expected, that some instructional innovation could result in good reading comprehension without simultaneously leading to the development of at least adequate word recognition ability (Chen & Vellutino, 1997; Gough, Hoover, & Peterson, 1996; Shankweiler et al., 1999). Because word recognition skill will be a by-product of any successful approach to developing reading ability—whether or not the approach specifically targets word recognition—lack of skill at recognizing words is always a reasonable predictor of difficulties in developing reading comprehension ability. As Pressley (1998) reminds us, "Even keeping in mind the caveat that reading is more than word recognition, however, the active processing of sentences and paragraphs cannot occur unless the reader can recognize individual words reliably and efficiently. That is why learning to decode is so important" (p. 45).

Although it has been amply documented that skill at recognizing words is strongly related to the speed of initial reading acquisition, and that this relationship is causal, it is true that as the general level of reading ability increases, the proportion of variance in reading ability accounted for by word recognition decreases and the proportion of variance in reading linked to listening comprehension abilities increases (see Chen & Vellutino, 1997; Stanovich, Cunningham, & Feeman, 1984a). Despite the fact that at the more advanced levels of adult reading skill comprehension ability becomes strongly related to listening abilities, even among adults word recognition efficiency accounts for a sizable amount of variance in reading ability. Not only does word recognition skill correlate with reading comprehension ability in adults (e.g., Bell & Perfetti, 1994; Ben-Dror, Pollatsek, & Scarpati, 1991; Bruck, 1992; Elbro, Nielson, & Petersen, 1994; Gottardo, Siegel, & Stanovich, 1997a; Liberman, Rubin, Duques, & Carlisle, 1985; Perfetti, 1985; Scarborough, 1984), it is actually an independent predictor. That is, word recognition skill predicts reading comprehension ability in adults even after variance due to listening comprehension ability has been partialed out. For example, Cunningham,

Stanovich, and Wilson (1990) demonstrated that word decoding skill accounted for significant additional variance in the reading comprehension ability of adult college readers even after measures of general intelligence, listening comprehension, sentence memory, and vocabulary were entered into a regression equation. Thus, efficient word recognition seems to be a necessary but not sufficient condition for good comprehension in adults, just as it is in children. While it is quite possible for an adult to have poor reading comprehension ability despite adequate word decoding skills—probably due to deficient general listening comprehension skills—it is highly unlikely that excellent reading comprehension will be observed in the face of seriously deficient word recognition skills (see Gough et al., 1996).

MODULARITY AND COGNITIVE RESOURCES

Once we move beyond demonstrating the general importance of word recognition, the much more complex task of characterizing the word recognition process remains. Two strands of this theoretical conceptualization are the focus of the paper reprinted as Chapter 12 (several more are mentioned later in this chapter). The first strand concerns the implications of conceptualizing word recognition as a modular process. As mentioned in Chapter 1, Stanovich, Nathan, West, and Vala-Rossi (1985) used a Fodorian (1983) notion of modularity to conceptualize the literature on reader skill differences in sentence context effects. The paper reprinted in Chapter 12 more completely draws out the implications of conceptualizing word recognition development as an instance of acquired modularity. The second theoretical focus of Chapter 12 is on limited-capacity resource models of individual differences in reading ability.

In the paper reprinted in Chapter 12 I lean quite heavily in favor of emphasizing the concept of representational quality and deemphasizing the concept of limited resources. Certainly the current research on self-teaching models (Share, 1995, 1999; Share & Stanovich, 1995) and phonological representations (Brady, 1997; Elbro, 1996; Fowler, 1991; Metsala & Walley, 1998; Shankweiler, 1999) is in the spirit of the former emphasis. Nevertheless, perhaps my theoretical piece is a bit too hard on the limited resource concept (see Pashler, 1998, for up-to-date coverage of the attentional and resource issues discovered in my 1990 paper; also see Stolz & Besner, 1999, and Walczyk & Taylor, 1996). It may be premature to jettison it completely. It is probably best to emphasize the possibility of theoretical coexistence between the two concepts. That is, in Chapter 12 I highlight Perfetti's (1992) view that properties such as speed and resource conservation are secondary concomitants of representation quality. But to say this is not to minimize the latter—just as in a true intertheoretic reduction (as opposed to intertheoretic elimination) the laws and concepts of the reduced level do not disappear (Churchland, 1979;

Stanovich, 1998b). Additionally, and importantly, for communication purposes—for teachers, parents, and so on—the limited-resource terminology might still be a better communication vehicle. Even if the resource terminology captures only emergent properties with no first-order causal significance, it still embodies for teachers crucial insights into the interrelationships in the processing system that perhaps representational language captures more accurately for researchers.

Another caveat that should have been emphasized more in the 1990 paper is that there are varying interpretations of the modularity concept. Fodor's (1983) view—emphasized in my paper—is a rather "hard-core" view. As Pinker (1997, pp. 30–31) points out, there are somewhat looser views of what a mental module is (for discussions of the interplay between connectionist and modular models, see Norris, 1990; Page, in press; Pinker, 1997). As he notes, "Mental modules need not be tightly sealed off from one another, communicating only through a few narrow pipelines. . . . Modules are defined by the special things they do with the information available to them, not necessarily by the kinds of information they have available" (p. 31).

Nevertheless, in retrospect I view my take on the issue as not bad as a first pass at a complicated concept—particularly in the context of a field dominated by top-down models. The strong view of a mental module that I borrowed from Fodor was a useful antidote for a field dominated by an opposing view. Although the paper reprinted in Chapter 12 seems highly theoretical, several of the theoretical issues raised are directly related to the metaphilosophical views that fuel the so-called Reading Wars about instructional practice discussed in Part VII—specifically, the contrasting top-down and bottom-up views of reading that characterize the proponents of whole language and the proponents of the importance of decoding skills phonics, respectively (see also Part I).

The emphasis given in my *Developmental Review* paper to understanding the unique stimulus ecology of the reading environment strikes me—10 years later—as right on the mark (see Pylyshyn, 1999). Here, the benefit of the Fodorian interpretation was quite apparent. The fundamental insight that an advantage accrues to encapsulation (modularity) when the specificity and efficiency of stimulus analyzing mechanisms is great relative to the diagnosticity of the background information that might potentially be recruited to aid recognition answers many theoretical questions that have arisen in the Reading Wars. It immediately becomes apparent that the stimulus ecology for which top-down processing is most adaptive—an impoverished stimulus embedded in highly diagnostic contextual information—is precisely the *opposite* of the stimulus ecology of reading. A modular organization—one that fits the assumptions of bottom-up models of word recognition—is clearly a more adaptive structure for the word recognition mechanism, because in reading a clear stimulus is embedded within contextual information of low diagnosticity (see Liberman, 1999, and Chapter 12).

THE HOLES IN "HOLISM"

There is another theoretical emphasis in Chapter 12 that has implications for the top-down and bottom-up models that frame the reading instruction wars. It is the emphasis in the paper on the theoretical utility of demarcating the word recognition level of processing from the comprehension level (see Gough & Tunmer, 1986; Nation, 1999). The chapter acknowledges that background knowledge saturates central processes of text inferencing and comprehension monitoring while at the same time modularity characterizes word recognition in the fluent adult. This assumption violates the extreme holism that characterizes the top-down models—held by the whole language advocates who are the public voice of the movement (see Part VII). These theorists strongly resist any theoretical separation of word recognition and comprehension.

Grundin's (1994) position is typical of whole language advocates: "The brain does not have separate compartments as the reading models suggest. The brain is highly integrated. . . . We must assume that the brain processes language in a holistic manner" (p. 8). But, contrary to Grundin's assertion, much recent work in cognitive neuroscience *does* support the notion of the separability of the cognitive/brain processes concerned with lexical access from those concerned with postlexical comprehension (e.g., Carr, 1992; Posner & Carr, 1992). Not only do separate brain architectures subserve word recognition and comprehension, but even *within* the word recognition module subprocesses are subserved by separate and localizable brain areas (e.g., Peterson, Fox, Posner, & Raichle, 1988; Posner, 1992; Posner & Carr, 1992; Posner, Peterson, Fox, & Raichle, 1988; Pugh et al., 1997; Pulvermuller, 1999; Shaywitz et al., 1998). Posner et al. (1988) conclude that

> the elementary operations forming the basis of cognitive analyses of human tasks are strictly localized. Many such local operations are involved in any cognitive task. A set of distributed brain areas must be orchestrated in the performance of even simple cognitive tasks. The task itself is not performed by any single area of the brain, but the operations that underlie the performance are strictly localized. This idea fits generally with many network theories in neuroscience and cognition. . . . In this article we review results of studies on cognitive tasks that suggest several separate codes for processing individual words. (p. 1627)

Posner and Carr (1992; see also Pulvermuller, 1999) review considerable evidence indicating that "visual, orthographic, semantic, and phonological-articulatory mechanisms clearly dissociate in the PET studies, which localize these coding systems in discrete (and widely separated) cortical regions" (p. 8). They argued:

> There appears to be at least a one-to-one correspondence between basic linguistic properties in need of computation and anatomically separated computational systems. . . . These imaging and lesion results show that the human brain computes linguistically relevant properties of words in a complex set of isolable systems . . .

To the extent that a computational model fails to incorporate this separation of mechanisms, it will lose at least biological fidelity and probably computational adequacy as well. (pp. 11–12)

In fact, whole language theorists such as Grundin (1994) appear to be in a position analogous to that of the author of an authoritative biology textbook published in 1931 that Dawkins (1998) discusses in his *Unweaving the Rainbow*. While acknowledging that atoms were, indeed, separate entities, the author argues:

> Not so the gene. It exists only as part of the chromosome, and the chromosome only as part of a cell. If I ask for a living chromosome, that is, for the only effective kind of chromosome, no one can give it to me except in its living surroundings any more than he can give me a living arm or leg. The doctrine of the relativity of functions is as true for the gene as it is for any of the organs of the body. They exist and function only in relation to other organs. Thus the last of the biological theories leaves us where we started, in the presence of a power called life or psyche which is not only of its own kind but unique in each and all of its exhibitions. (p. 90)

Dawkins (1998) tells us bluntly that "this is dramatically, profoundly, hugely wrong. And it really matters. Following Watson and Crick and the revolution they sparked, a gene can be isolated. It can be purified, bottled, crystallized, read as digitally coded information, printed on a page, fed into a computer, read out again into a test tube and reinserted into an organism where it works exactly as it did before" (p. 90).

The analogy here is direct. The field of reading research marches ahead by analyzing and fractionating reading processes to a now almost exquisite degree (Berent & Perfetti, 1995; Booth, Perfetti, & MacWhinney, 1999; Frost, 1998; Pugh et al., 1997; Pulvermuller, 1999; Rauner, 1998; Shaywitz et al., 1998), while whole language advocates merely reiterate slogans about "holism" that are supposed to trump the actual empirical research (see Part VII). Such advocates have tried to ignore the fact that the dominant theoretical preference in the science of reading has shifted considerable in the last decade and a half. This shift in the theoretical preferences of reading researchers represents a reversal of an intellectual trend of some years standing. Until the mid- to late 1980s, reading theory had been evolving in a fairly unidirectional manner. Theorists had been slowly abandoning the positivist-inspired early information processing models and moving toward more constructivist conceptualizations. Earlier models put the key information in the text and were concerned with its veridical transformation through information processing stages into an understanding almost completely constrained by the text itself. Schema theory, strategy approaches, and other constructivist accounts gradually altered this conceptualization by emphasizing that comprehension is determined by the reader's expectations and knowledge. However, empirical work in the late 1980s and early 1990s indicated that the strong constructivist assumptions were not squaring with what was becoming known about how the autonomous, encapsulated input processes that act on the external stimulus actually work. It was the flavor of this work, which was altering our basic theoretical conceptions, that I was trying to capture in the article reprinted as Chapter 12. At the time, constructivist assumptions in reading theory were being tempered by a consideration of how the external stimulus constrains central processes (e.g., Fodor, 1983)—a trend that has continued since that paper was published.

PROCESSING WITHIN THE WORD RECOGNITION MODULE: PHONOLOGICAL CODING

The issue of modularity concerns how enclosed and isolated the word processing module is from other information that could possibly be used to aid recognition. This issue was a centerpiece of both the *Developmental Review* paper (Chapter 12) and the *Handbook* paper. However, an issue also central to the *Handbook* chapter, but not to Chapter 12, was whether phonological processing mediates lexical access. This issue concerns the internal structure of the word recognition module itself, and I have intermittently engaged with it throughout my reading research career. For example, following on the heels of the seminal contributions of Baron and Strawson (1976) and Coltheart (1978), David Bauer and I did some of the earliest work on the spelling-to-sound regularity effect (Bauer & Stanovich, 1980; Stanovich & Bauer, 1978).

Although the issue of phonological recoding in lexical access dates back to Huey's (1908/1968) time and before, it was revived in modern form in a seminal paper by Rubenstein, Lewis, and Rubenstein (1971) in which they introduced what was termed the "phonological recoding hypothesis." As phrased by Gough (1984), "The phonological recoding hypothesis holds that the recognition of a printed word is mediated by its phonological form" (p. 235). There is an enormous literature on this issue; indeed, several reviews containing references to hundreds of papers have been published (Barron, 1986; Berent & Perfetti, 1995; Henderson, 1982; Humphreys & Evett, 1985; Patterson & Coltheart, 1987; Share, 1995). Importantly, we must reiterate one of the same cautions given in the discussions of context effects (see Chapters 3 and 4). That is, in understanding the role of phonological processes in reading, it is important to differentiate levels of processing. Virtually all theorists agree that phonological codes in working memory play some role in supporting comprehension processes. The major dispute has centered around the role of phonological processes in *word recognition*—in short, whether phonological coding is implicated in lexical access, and if so, how early in lexical access (questions that may need reframing for different orthographies; see Tan & Perfetti, 1998). Finally, it is also important to realize that the more contentious disputes surround the role of phonological coding in the word recognition processes of the fluent adult reader. A vast array of evidence points to the importance of phonological processes in early reading acquisition.

In the decade subsequent to the reintroduction of the phonological coding issue into reading theory by Rubenstein, Lewis, and Rubenstein (1971; see Gough's [1984] discussion of their seminal work), it was not difficult to generate data that seemingly indicated the influence of phonological factors on the two tasks most often taken to be measures of lexical access: naming and lexical decision (e.g., Baron & Strawson, 1976; Bauer & Stanovich, 1980; Gough & Cosky, 1977; Stanovich & Bauer, 1978). Much attention was focused on developing versions of what came to be called dual-route models (Coltheart, 1978; Forster & Chambers, 1973; Meyer, Schvaneveldt, & Ruddy, 1974). This class of model posits two alternate recognition pathways to the lexicon: a direct visual access route that does not involve phonological mediation (i.e., the lexical, orthographic, or addressed route) and an indirect route through phonology that utilizes stored spelling-to-sound correspondences (the sublexical, phonological, or assembled route). The size of the spelling-to-sound correspondences that make up the phonological route differ from model to model. Versions of dual-route models also differ in assumptions about the various speeds of the two access mechanisms involved and how conflicting information is resolved.

In all such views, however, the phonological route becomes a processing option (although not one necessarily under conscious control) that may or may not become implicated in performance depending upon the status of the other route (Patterson, Marshall, & Coltheart, 1985) and upon the nature of the words being read. Two important factors in the latter class are the frequency and the spelling-to-sound regularity of the words used as stimuli. Indeed, studies of the spelling–sound regularity effect in word recognition have become a major source of data for addressing questions about the role of phonological coding in word recognition (Brown, 1997; Metsala, Stanovich, & Brown, 1998; Plaut, McClelland, Seidenberg, & Patterson, 1996; Seidenberg & McClelland, 1989b).

Spelling–sound regularity refers to the nature of the mapping between the letters in the word and the sounds in its pronunciation. Regular words are those whose pronunciations reflect common small-unit spelling–sound correspondences (e.g., *made*, *rope*); irregular words are those whose pronunciations reflect atypical small-unit correspondences (e.g., *sword*, *pint*, *have*, *aisle*). Two important caveats must always be emphasized, however. First, although terms like "regular" versus "irregular" or "regular" versus "exception" appear often in the literature, regularity is a continuous variable, not a discrete category (Berndt, D'Autrechy, & Reggia, 1994; Berndt, Reggia, & Mitchum, 1987; Gottardo, Chiappe, Siegel, & Stanovich, 1999; Seidenberg & McClelland, 1989b; Treiman, Mullennix, Bijeljac-Babic, & Richmond-Welty, 1995; Venezky & Massaro, 1987; Ziegler, Stone, & Jacobs, 1997). Second, the issue of how best to define regularity is maddeningly complex and contentious. Two investigators in the area have referred to the complexities surrounding the concept of spelling–sound regularity as a "psycholinguistic hornet's nest" (Prior & McCorriston, 1985, p. 70). The extensive discussions of these complexities in the literatures of psycholinguistics and cognitive psychology stand in stark contrast to the glib statements about the alleged "irregularity" or "regularity" of English that are often tossed about in educational debates about the teaching of reading.

Disagreement about how to classify words in terms of spelling–sound regularity is common because the degree of regularity assigned depends greatly on the size of the coding unit that is assumed for spelling–sound correspondences (Treiman et al., 1995). Simply put, many more words are regular when large-unit mappings are employed (Henderson, 1982; Treiman et al., 1995; Venezky, 1970, 1999). For example, the *gh* of *light* seems irregular when considered as an isolated unit, because it has several different correspondences (*ghost, tough, light*), but in the *i—t* context, it is regular. That is, "ight," considered as a unit, maps regularly to /ayt/ (e.g., *light, fight, right, might*).

The results from early studies of the regularity effect were hard to integrate because a variety of different data patterns were obtained (Andrews, 1982; Bauer & Stanovich, 1980; Coltheart, Besner, Jonasson, & Davelaar, 1979; Parkin, 1982; Parkin & Underwood, 1983). However, a series of experiments by Seidenberg and colleagues (Seidenberg & McClelland, 1989b; Seidenberg, Waters, Barnes, & Tanenhaus, 1984; Waters & Seidenberg, 1985) confirmed the existence of an interaction between spelling–sound regularity and word frequency. Regularity effects are minimal or nonexistent for high frequency words and increase in magnitude as word frequency decreases. The existence of this interaction accounts for some of the inconsistencies across experiments because, in many cases, frequency varied from study to study in an uncontrolled fashion.

However, disputes about the mechanism that mediated the spelling–sound regularity effect continued to fuel research. For example, an influential set of experiments was conducted by Glushko (1979, 1981; see also Bauer & Stanovich, 1980) in which he found that regular words such as *gave* that had irregular neighbors (in this case, *have*) took longer to pronounce than regular words without irregular neighbors (e.g., *coat*). Similarly, nonwords such as *bint* that have word neighbors that are inconsistent in pronunciation (*pint, mint*) took longer to pronounce than nonwords without inconsistent word neighbors (e.g., *tade*). These findings, which seemed to indicate that word naming was affected by nearby lexical entries, motivated several investigators to explore models of word processing that involved only lexical entries and that did not accomplish phonological coding by employing small-unit, grapheme–phoneme correspondence rules.

One such lexical-analogy model (see Carr & Pollatsek, 1985; Henderson, 1982) was Glushko's (1979, 1981) activation-synthesis model, which he used to explain the aforementioned findings. In this model, visual letter strings activate orthographic codes at the word level based on letter similarity between the stimulus and the abstract letter codes of the orthographic representations. The resulting activated orthographic entries in turn activate phonological representations. The set of activated orthographic and phonological representations are integrated and synthesized and then sent to processes capable of executing naming and lexical decision responses.

Glushko's model, in conjunction with the seminal work of McClelland and Rumelhart (1981; Rumelhart & McClelland, 1982; see also Paap, Newsome, McDonald, & Schvaneveldt, 1982), anticipated the popularity of the distributed processing models in the subsequent decade of work on word recognition (Brown, 1997; Harm & Seidenberg, 1999; Metsala & Brown, 1998; Plaut et al., 1996; Seidenberg & McClelland, 1989b; Van Orden, Pennington, & Stone, 1990). The development of the lexical-analogy models such as the activation-synthesis model and its derivatives began a period during which the phonological coding hypothesis was reformulated somewhat. The classic form of the hypothesis—stated in terms of whether phonological codes are activated prior to or subsequent to lexical access—has been altered as researchers moved toward modeling regularity and consistency effects with distributed, connectionist networks that blur the distinction between phonological coding prior to lexical access and postaccess phonological activation (Harm & Seidenberg, 1999; Plaut et al., 1996; Seidenberg & McClelland, 1989b). For example, Perfetti (1985) emphasizes that, in his model of automatic speech activation within a connectionist network, "the question of speech recoding becomes irrelevant. Phonetic activation is not a first step to lexical access; rather, it is part of the access, sometimes reaching a high level prior to the completion of access and sometimes not. The former would look like 'recoding' and the latter would not" (p. 59).

Thus, the old issue of whether phonological recoding takes place prior to lexical access or not became recast into a more continuous model in the mid-1980s and early 1990s. In these new models, activation of phonological codes by letter codes is thought to take place almost immediately after stimulus onset, and these phonological codes immediately begin activating word codes, thus contributing to the ongoing word recognition process (see Berent & Perfetti, 1995; Booth et al., 1999; Frost, 1998). Perfetti's (1985) automatic speech activation model and Seidenberg's (1985c) time course model helped to demonstrate how ideas about parallel distributed processing might alter the nature of our questions about the role of phonological recoding in word recognition. Subsequent to these theoretical efforts, several theorists have attempted to develop more explicit computational accounts of the operation of the word recognition module (Brown, 1997; Harm & Seidenberg, 1999; Plaut et al., 1996; Seidenberg & McClelland, 1989b; Van Orden et al., 1990).

These connectionist, distributed processing models have had a decided impact on theorizing in cognitive psychology during the last decade. Such models simulate behavioral patterns by adjusting connections among networks of simple processing units based on feedback about the adequacy of the output from response units. Although they are not preprogrammed with rules as in more traditional simulation models in cognitive science, the connectionist models have displayed the capability to emit "rulelike" behavior. For example, connectionist models—after training—take longer to recognize words that depart from spelling-to-sound correspondence "rules" even though no such rules were used to structure the networks a priori. Seidenberg (1999) discussed how connectionist models lead to a different view of English orthography than do dual-route models. The latter tend to imply that the orthography is a mess—there is an important and large class of words (the "exception" words) that need a different route because they are so irregular. Connectionist models emphasize the fact that, as Seidenberg (1999) put it, "have" is not pronounced "banana." Its pronunciation has similarities to other words with which it shares orthographic overlap (*hive*, *had*, etc.). Even the notorious "pint" (a word residing on everyone's list of "exceptions") has three of four phonemes pronounced regularly. Connectionist models capture these facts of the predictability and nonarbitrariness of words deemed "exceptions" in ways that dual-route models do not. Connectionist models also give us a different slant on how much of the orthography should be considered "decodable."

Such models also provide a framework within which to conceptualize work on reading-disabled individuals (see Plaut et al., 1996). Gottardo, Chiappe, Siegel, and Stanovich (1999) used such a connectionist framework to explain their examination of decoding unit sensitivity with the regression-based procedures pioneered by Treiman et al. (1995). A consistent pattern running through our results is that the less-skilled readers are less sensitive to all measures of spelling–sound correspondence, regardless of unit size. Gottardo et al. (1999) suggested that their results might be indicating a continuum of differentiation and specificity in the coding of spelling–sound relationships detected by less-skilled nine-year-olds, skilled readers two years younger, and skilled nine-year-olds. Interpreted within a distributed connectionist framework, the results indicated that the less-skilled readers appeared to be at one end of the continuum—most sensitive to large-unit friends, but with distributed networks that have inadequately captured small-unit grapheme–phoneme correspondences as well as the inhibitory relationships involving large-unit enemies. The younger, skilled children had induced structural relationships involving large-unit friends, but also had more adequately coded structural relationships at the grapheme–phoneme level. Nevertheless, like the less-skilled readers, the younger controls had as yet failed to capture patterns of inhibitory relationships involving large-unit enemies. Finally, the skilled nine-year-olds appeared to have the most fully differentiated and tuned orthographic/phonological networks. Their patterns of responses indicated that they have coded large-unit facilitative and inhibitory relationships and that they are sensitive to small-unit grapheme–phoneme regularity as well.

THE SPELLING–SOUND REGULARITY EFFECT
AND READING DISABILITY

Nevertheless, in parallel with the connectionist theorists, dual-route theorists have also continued to refine their models (Coltheart, Curtis, Atkins, & Haller, 1993; Coltheart & Rastle, 1994). The result of the contention between these two theoretical camps has been a plethora of empirical results and theoretical insights that have been exploited by reading researchers interested in reading development and reading disability. For example, Jamie Metsala, Gordon Brown, and I (Metsala, Stanovich, & Brown, 1998) used the spelling-to-sound regularity effect, the techniques of meta-analysis, and connectionist insights to try to further specify the phenotypic processing profile of reading-disabled individuals. We pointed out that although the typical finding of a pseudoword reading deficit in a reading-level match (e.g., Rack, Snowling, & Olson, 1992; Stanovich & Siegel, 1994) has most often been interpreted within the context of dual-route models of reading, integrating the research on spelling-to-sound regularity effects with these models has been difficult. Given the indications of relative differences between disabled and nondisabled readers on the phonological and orthographic processing tasks discussed in Chapters 5 and 8, it has seemed to many investigators that the spelling-to-sound regularity effect should provide a converging pattern. Many investigators have argued that this seems to follow from the classic interpretation of the dual-route model of lexical access:

> The regularity effect provides an index of subjects' use of spelling-to-sound correspondences to pronounce familiar words. If dyslexic children are less able to apply their knowledge of these correspondences, they should show smaller regularity effects than normal readers. (Manis, Szeszulski, Holt, & Graves, 1990, pp. 229–230)

> The regular words are presumed to be processed by both the phonological and orthographic paths, while the exception words are confined to the orthographic path. In this model, disabled readers should show a smaller regular word advantage because their phonological coding is uniquely deficient. (Olson, Kliegl, Davidson, & Foltz, 1985, p. 18)

> If the less skilled readers are slower in activating phonological information than the skilled readers, then phonological information would be less likely to influence word recognition. As a result, they should be less likely than skilled readers to be faster on regular than exception words. (Barron, 1981, p. 305)

In short, the presence or absence of the spelling-to-sound regularity effect has been used as a marker for the efficient functioning of the phonological route. The regularity effect in reading has been considered to arise because sublexical spelling–sound correspondences can be used to correctly pronounce regular words, but not irregular words. The simultaneous activation of both routes for regular words will lead to consistent output, whereas this is not the case for irregular items. Therefore, regular words will have an advantage. However, if the phonological route is less available due to impairment, all words will be read by the lexical route and therefore the expected advantage for regular words should be eliminated or reduced.

However, the empirical literature on the nature of the regularity effect in reading-disabled samples is puzzling. Although some studies have found the expected interaction between subject group and spelling-to-sound regularity (Barron, 1981; Beech & Awaida, 1992; Frith & Snowling, 1983; Snowling, Stackhouse, & Rack, 1986), an even larger number of studies employing reading-level controls have not (Baddeley, Logie, & Ellis, 1988; Beech & Harding, 1984; Ben-Dror et al., 1991; Bruck, 1990; Holligan & Johnston, 1988; Olson et al., 1985; Stanovich, Nathan, & Zolman, 1988; Treiman & Hirsh-Pasek, 1985).

Metsala et al. (1998) meta-analyzed the existing findings and found that both reading-disabled and normally achieving readers displayed clear effects of spelling-to-sound regularity, but that the regularity effect size was the same across these two groups. It thus is the case that the observed pattern of empirical findings, taken as a whole (pseudoword reading deficit for reading disabled individuals in a reading-level match but not an attenuated regularity effect) cannot easily be explained within the classical, dual-route framework.

Metsala et al. (1998) suggested that this seemingly paradoxical pattern of findings can be explained by assuming that pseudoword reading places greater demands on phonological abilities than does the reading of regular and irregular real words because pseudoword reading is particularly dependent upon intact phonological representations. Furthermore, Metsala et al. (1998; see also Metsala & Brown, 1998) argued that this pattern can be modeled well by a connectionist network with varying representational quality (see Harm, Altmann, & Seidenberg, 1994; Harm & Seidenberg, 1999; Hulme, Snowling & Quinlan, 1991; Plaut et al., 1996). On this account, pseudoword reading is a more appropriate task for detecting impaired phonological representations than is word reading. This is because different connectionist models of reading have made different assumptions concerning the nature of phonological representations, and because models that have used certain types of phonological representations can be viewed as "impaired' in their phonological representations. These models, unlike models with "unimpaired" phonological representations, behave just like children with reading disability in that they exhibit a selective impairment in pseudoword reading, but show normal effects of spelling-to-sound regularity. The lack of sufficiently fine-grained phonological representations prevents the easy acquisition of spelling–sound correspondence information at the level of graphemes and phonemes, and the result is a model that exhibits normal effects of spelling-to-sound regularity, but impaired pseudoword reading.

Brown (1997) examined the issue directly, by comparing the performance of two small "toy" connectionist models that differed in the quality of their orthographic and phonological representations. The impaired representation model was given triple-based representations and the normal representation model was given representations of individual graphemes and phonemes (similar to those used in the model of Plaut et al., 1996; see Brown, 1997, for more details of the implementation and results). Both models were given a small vocabulary of words (including both regular and irregular items) and were required to learn the pronunciations of the items. An analogy to a reading-level match was used in comparing the performance of the models: results were scaled so that the models performed equally well on regular words. The ability of each of the models to read irregular words and pseudowords was then examined.

The results confirmed the hypotheses above. Each model performed worse on irregular than regular items, and this performance reduction was of approximately equal magnitude in the impaired and unimpaired models. However, when pseudoword reading performance was examined, the reduction in performance was substantially greater for the model with impaired phonological representations. Thus the results of computational modeling work within a connectionist framework support the suggestion that degraded phonological representations will lead to impaired pseudoword reading, but will not lead to reduced effects of spelling-to-sound regularity. This pattern is exactly the pattern of results that characterizes the performance of reading-disabled children (see Harm & Seidenberg, 1999, for even more advanced work on this issue).

Metsala et al. (1998) argued that the results of their meta-analysis and the review of the pseudoword reading deficit by Rack et al. (1992; see also Ijzendoorm & Bus, 1994) are consistent with the proposal that difficulties in phoneme-based representations underlie reading difficulties in reading-disabled children (e.g., Elbro, 1996; Fowler, 1991; Metsala & Walley, 1998; Shankweiler, 1999). If connectionist models are provided with impaired phonological representations, they, like the reading-disabled population assessed in our meta-analysis, showed impaired pseudoword reading but normal spelling-to-sound regularity effects. This appears to be because the use of fine-grained units (e.g., graphemes and phonemes) is particularly important in the reading of unfamiliar items (pseudowords) and, by extension, particularly important in the early stages of reading development when most words are still unfamiliar. Thus, work in this area is beginning to specify the nature of the processing internal to the word recognition module and link its functioning to variation in reading ability.

CHAPTER 12

Concepts in Developmental Theories of Reading Skill

Cognitive Resources, Automaticity, and Modularity

Most major concepts that are used in current reading theory can be traced back to Huey's (1908/1968) classic work, and the concepts of cognitive capacity and automaticity are no exception:

> Perceiving being an act, it is, like all other things that we do, performed more easily with each repetition of the act. To perceive an entirely new word or other combination of strokes requires considerable time, close attention, and it is likely to be imperfectly done, just as when we attempt some new combination of movements, some new trick in the gymnasium or new "serve" at tennis. In either case, repetition progressively frees the mind from attention to details, makes facile the total act, shortens the time, and reduces the extent to which consciousness must concern itself with the process. (p. 104)

As many histories of the study of reading have noted (Venezky, 1977), after Huey there was darkness—the behaviorist era led to a decrease in the type of cognitive theorizing about the reading process evident throughout Huey's work. Vague notions about cognitive capacity occasionally sputtered through the educational literature, but theorizing about the reading process in the manner of Huey was rare. Like many other information processing concepts, limited-resource theories were resurrected shortly after the cognitive revolution.

Here, we will trace the post-behaviorist era history of the limited-resource concept in theories of reading acquisition. Its resurgence and subsequent popularity was largely due to the influence of the automaticity theory of reading developed by LaBerge and Samuels (1974). Eventually, however, conceptual and empirical weaknesses in the automaticity concept as an explanatory construct in developmental reading theory were revealed. These problems arose at a time when the concept of modularity was being elaborated within cognitive science. Aspects of the modularity concept, such as information encapsulation, have the potential to account for some of the same developmental trends in reading performance that resource theory had explained. As a result, current reading theories have emphasized questions of representation quality and the nature of information exchange among semi-autonomous processes. The future of the resource concept in reading theory remains uncertain.

AUTOMATICITY THEORY: LABERGE AND SAMUELS

It was not until the classic paper by LaBerge and Samuels (1974) that ideas about cognitive capacity and resource use in the modern information processing sense were thoroughly reintegrated with reading theory. At the very beginning of their paper, LaBerge and Samuels (1974) outlined the basic limited-capacity argument that was accepted, either explicitly or implicitly, by reading researchers throughout most of the subsequent decade:

> During the execution of a complex skill, it is necessary to coordinate many component processes within a very short period of time. If each component process requires attention, performance of the complex skill will be impossible, because the capacity of attention will be exceeded. But if enough of the components and their coordinations can be processed automatically, then the loads on attention will be within tolerable limits and the skill can be successfully performed. Therefore, one of the prime issues in the study of a complex skill such as reading is to determine how the processing of component subskills becomes automatic. (p. 293)

There were several assumptions in Laberge and Samuels' treatment that became canonical for many reading researchers. First, their theory assumed a strong demarcation between word recognition processes and all post-lexical processing, because it was assumed that most, if not all, post-lexical comprehension processes would be resource-demanding and probably would not be good candidates for the development of acquired automaticity (in general; see Perfetti, 1985, pp. 102–106; Perfetti & Curtis, 1986). Most demonstrations of acquired automaticity thus focused on pre-lexical processes such as feature extraction, orthographic segmentation, and phonological coding. The examples in the classic LaBerge and Samuels paper were all of this type. Few assumptions about how capacity was allocated post-lexically were made. Instead, it was merely assumed that whatever the distribution of post-lexical capacity allocation, the key to optimal processing at this level was the reallocation of unneeded capacity from lower levels via the acquired automaticity of lexical access. Much subsequent theorizing in reading—such as Perfetti's (1985; Perfetti & Lesgold, 1977, 1979) influential verbal efficiency theory—contained variants of these assumptions.

Resource and Automaticity Models of Reading Acquisition

It will be noted that in emphasizing the concept of automaticity LaBerge and Samuels (1974) focused the attention of reading researchers on the flip-side of the processing resource question: namely, on processes that executed without depleting cognitive resources. In short, "the process of automatization was viewed as a gradual withdrawal of attentional involvement in performance" (Logan, 1985, p. 375). As Kahneman and Treisman (1984) have emphasized, "The study of attention underwent a significant paradigm shift during the decade of the 1970s, almost a reversal of figure and ground: the null hypothesis for research was inverted as the focus of interest moved from the nature of attention limits to the exploration of automatic processing" (pp. 29–30). This bias toward a focus on the degree of automaticity rather than on the direct assessment of resource use was also characteristic of the history of these concepts in the reading domain.

Interestingly, however, when LaBerge and Samuels (1974) attempted to operationalize their concept of automatic processing, they chose not to tackle directly the measurement problems inherent in assessing resource-free processing. Instead, they chose a correlated characteristic of capacity-free processing: obligatory execution, the tendency for an automatized process to execute regardless of where the conscious attention of the subject is directed. Specifically, they argued: "Our criterion for deciding when a skill or subskill is automatic is that it can complete its processing while attention is directed elsewhere" (p. 295).

This particular choice was to have important consequences for the subsequent history of the automaticity concept in reading theory. LaBerge and Samuels had implicitly equated the obligatory nature of an automatic process—its unconscious triggering and ballistic execution—with capacity-free processing. In addition, the use of processing resources was conflated with the idea of conscious attention and, conversely, lack of conscious attention was viewed as synonymous with resource-free processing. Only later was the necessity of theoretically separating the issues of obligatory execution, resource use, and conscious attention fully recognized (Humphreys, 1985; Logan, 1985; Paap & Ogden, 1981).

The tendency to intertwine resource use with conscious attention in reading theory was reinforced by the popularity of Posner and Snyder's (1975b) two-process model of cognitive expectancies. Although this model was originally developed within the context of the tasks, methods, and conceptual apparatus of experimental psychology, it eventually had a strong influence on theories of reading acquisition when it became integrated with automaticity theory. Posner and Snyder (1975b) also popularized the subsequently much-used priming methodology, whereby the subject is presented with a cue that predicts (probabilistically) a target stimulus. When the cue correctly predicts the target, response time to the latter is faster than a neutral baseline (a facilitation effect). However, when the cue incorrectly predicts the target, whether response time to the target will be slower (display an inhibition effect) depends importantly on certain conditions of the experiment.

Theoretically extrapolating from the results of a variety of these priming experiments, Posner and Snyder (1975b) outlined the time course and facilitative/inhibitory patterns of two different expectancy mechanisms: one a capacity-draining conscious mechanism and the other a resource-free automatic priming mechanism. According to Posner and Snyder, the conscious attention mechanism caused an inhibition of unexpected signals as well as the facilitation of expected signals, the former because "the mechanisms of conscious attention are limited in capacity and the use of these mechanisms by one signal will have inhibitory consequences for other signals" (p. 670). The automatic spreading activation process, in contrast, was posited to facilitate expected signals but not to inhibit the processing of unexpected ones: "Activation of a pathway in the memory system facilitates the processing of signals related to it, but there is no widespread inhibitory consequence of such activation" (p. 670). Posner and Snyder's (1975b) two-process model of expectancy was generalized to word recognition and single-word priming by Neely (1977), and to sentence processing situations in the empirical work of Stanovich and West (1979b, 1981, 1983a; West & Stanovich, 1978).

In my interactive–compensatory model of individual differences in reading (Stanovich, 1980), I used the Posner–Snyder expectancy framework to explain a longstanding paradox in the reading literature. It had consistently been found that children who were poor comprehenders invariably had poor word recognition skills. Additionally, and unexpectedly, however, they tended to show large linguistic context effects in many tasks. It had traditionally been assumed in reading theory that poor readers would display markedly attenuated contextual sensitivity (e.g., Smith, 1971).

These seemingly paradoxical findings were resolved, first by showing, via a review of the literature (Stanovich, 1980), that the greater contextual facilitation shown by poorer readers was confined to word recognition tasks and did not extend to reading tasks involving comprehension. It was then proposed that the contextual facilitation of word recognition could result from either of the Posner–Snyder expectancy mechanisms. The automatic spreading activation mechanism would result in contextual facilitation with no costs to other aspects of performance. In contrast, if the attentional mechanism was employed, it would likewise facilitate word recognition performance, but at the cost of depleting the cognitive resources available to other simultaneously operating processes. The performance paradox was explained by positing that the severely deficient word recognition processes of the less-skilled readers caused them to rely on the conscious expectancy process because of the additional facilitation that it provided—but at the cost of further depleting the resources available to higher-level comprehension processes. Fluent readers, in contrast, had word recognition mechanisms that were so efficient that they did not necessitate the use of the attentional mechanism and thus did not incur the costs of its use. The net result was that the poorer reader devoted more resources to the local level of word recognition, relied more on contextual mechanisms, but simultaneously further stressed an already inefficient comprehension system.

Subsequent developments confirmed the broad outlines of the interactive–compensatory model, although specific disputes arose over whether the Posner–Snyder two-process theory was the best way to conceptualize expectancy mechanisms (see Becker, 1982, 1985; Briggs, Austin, & Underwood, 1984; Leu, DeGroff, & Simons, 1986; Pring & Snowling, 1986; Schwantes, 1985; Simons & Leu, 1987; Stanovich, 1986b, 1992b, 1993c; Stanovich, Nathan, West, & Vala-Rossi, 1985; Stanovich & West, 1983a). During the same time period, Perfetti's (1985; Perfetti & Curtis, 1986; Perfetti & Lesgold, 1977, 1979) verbal efficiency theory was further developed and elaborated. This model shared many of the canonical assumptions of the LaBerge and Samuels (1974) automaticity theory, and conceptualized individual differences in much the same way as the interactive–compensatory model (see Perfetti, Goldman, & Hogaboam, 1979; Perfetti & Roth, 1981).

A DEVELOPMENTAL PARADOX

Ironically, however, during the very period when these resource-based models were gaining in popularity, the cognitive capacity notion as it applied to reading-related processes began to run into trouble. LaBerge and Samuels' original paper relied heavily on the catch-trial technique to demonstrate the properties of an automatic process. Generically, this methodology involves surprising the subjects with a few "catch trials" interspersed randomly within a sequence of trials that have oriented the subject's attention to some other stimulus. When the catch-trial stimulus appears, the subject has to reorient attention to that stimulus and remember precisely what he/she had been instructed to do with it. This attentional reorientation presumably takes some finite amount of time. The key manipulation concerns the prior familiarity with the catch-trial stimuli. The assumption is that only if the catch-trial stimulus was automatized would processing take place during the attentional shift. Nonautomatized stimuli, in contrast, would have to wait for the attentional shift to be complete before processing of them could begin.

LaBerge and Samuels (1974) presented several examples of different sets of stimuli that were processed equivalently when given direct attention, but that resulted in differential performance (in favor of the familiar stimuli) when the attentional reorientation of the catch-trial procedure was required. Presumably, the performance difference between two such stimulus sets reflects the additional processing that takes place for the familiar (automatized) stimuli while attention is being switched. Additionally, LaBerge and Samuels demonstrated that the performance difference between such stimulus sets decreased as the nonautomatized set received more practice.

Our purpose here is not to attempt a full methodological review of the catch-trial procedure, but only to emphasize that it was designed specifically to operationalize one particular criterion for deciding when a skill or subskill is automatic: "that it can complete its processing while attention is directed elsewhere" (LaBerge & Samuels, 1974, p. 295). This particular operationalization—obligatory execution not demanding a conscious control process—was to have considerable influence on developmental work on the automaticity concept and on reading theory in general.

Probably because the procedure is not data-efficient and because it requires rather complex instructions, the catch-trial procedure has never been a popular method for assessing automatic stimulus recognition in studies of children. Instead, researchers turned quite naturally to the Stroop paradigm, which seems to straightforwardly operationalize the idea of stimulus processing while attention is directed elsewhere. In the generic Stroop paradigm (see Dyer, 1973; La Heij, 1988; Jensen & Rohwer, 1966) the subject must respond by naming a simple property of a stimulus (naming the color of a patch, the name of a line drawing, or the number of items in an array) while in close proximity is a verbal stimulus (e.g., written word) that conflicts with the required response (e.g., the word "blue" written on a red patch to which the subject must respond by saying "red"). Automatic word recognition is inferred by the lengthened response time in the conflict situation compared to the baseline situation where there is no conflicting verbal stimulus. (Stroop effects can be explained by an output-interference theory [see Brainerd & Reyna, 1989], but such accounts have not figured prominently in the developmental reading literature.)

The interference caused by the conflicting written word becomes an index of automaticity via the argument that the Stroop task reflects the obligatory (indeed, unwanted) processing of the word even though the subject's attention is directed elsewhere. Actually, the Stroop task seems to be an extreme case of the "processing while attention is directed elsewhere" logic, because after several trials, most subjects not only are directing their attention "elsewhere" but are to actively attempting (unsuccessfully) to *ignore* the written word.

By the early 1980s, however, experiments that had employed variants of the Stroop task with children and that had examined developmental and reading-skill trends had uncovered a puzzling theoretical problem. Numerous studies (e.g., Ehri & Wilce, 1979; Guttentag & Haith, 1978, 1980; Posnansky & Rayner, 1977; Schadler & Thissen, 1981; Stanovich, Cunningham, & West, 1981; West & Stanovich, 1978, 1979) had indicated that automatic word recognition developed remarkably early in a child's instructional history. At least for words of moderate to high frequency (most current accounts emphasize that it is stimuli, not processes, that become automatized; see Logan, 1988;

Perfetti, 1992), robust indications of automaticity were present by the middle of the first-grade year, and by second or third grade many Stroop indicators of automaticity were at asymptote. This finding was at odds with the general (although mainly untested) assumption that the development of prelexical automaticity was a mechanism that fueled comprehension increases for a long period of fluency acquisition.

DIFFERENTIATING COMPONENTS OF AUTOMATICITY

What the puzzling developmental findings actually indicated was that the idea of obligatory/intentionless processing and that of resource-free processing had been too easily conflated in discussions of the automaticity concept. Direct experimental evidence supporting such a criticism was contained in the work of Paap and Ogden (1981; Ogden, Martin, & Paap, 1980). These investigators employed the dual-task methodology that had been used by experimental psychologists to index the differential capacity used by various cognitive processes. Posner and Boies (1971) did some of the seminal work that demonstrated the utility of the technique. The methodology involves defining a primary task, the cognitive components of which are to be assessed for capacity usage. Subjects become practiced at completing the primary task while sometimes responding to a probe (or secondary task) that occurs on random trials during the execution of the primary task. The probe is usually something like a white-noise tone to which the subject makes a single predetermined response, usually a button press. The reaction time to the probe becomes an index of the relative capacity usage of the primary-task processes occurring at the time of probe onset. The slower the reaction time to the probe (compared to a baseline where only the secondary task is being performed), the more cognitive capacity the overlapping process in the primary task is assumed to draw.

Paap and Ogden (1981) superimposed a probe task on the Posner–Snyder priming paradigm using letters as stimuli. Consistent with the Posner–Snyder idea of automatic priming, they found that a nonpredictive prime that the subjects were instructed to ignore still affected the processing of some subsequent stimuli, thus indicating obligatory processing of the letter. However, the ignored letters slowed the secondary probe relative to a baseline, indicating that basic letter encoding processes were not entirely free from capacity utilization, even though they displayed the characteristic of obligatory processing. Paap and Ogden (1981) concluded that "with respect to letter encoding, an automatic process is usually defined as a process that occurs without intention and without interfering with a concurrent secondary task. . . . The most significant general conclusion that can be drawn from these experiments is that the criteria of obligatory processing and interference-free processing should be disassociated" (p. 518).

Results like those of Paap and Ogden (1981) made researchers reconsider the linkages assumed in the automaticity framework that had been outlined by

LaBerge and Samuels. Subsequent work has reinforced the conclusion that the standard criteria for automaticity do not completely converge (see Humphreys, 1985; Kahneman & Chajczyk, 1983; Kahneman & Treisman, 1984; Logan, 1985; Zbrodoff & Logan, 1986). In particular, processes that are obligatory—in that they execute in the presence of the appropriate stimulus regardless of the direction of attention or of conscious intent—may still utilize cognitive resources. Thus, it cannot be assumed that measures of obligatory processing—such as the Stroop task—are direct indicators of capacity usage.

The dissociation between automaticity criteria demonstrated in the Paap and Ogden (1981) work dissolves the seeming paradox in the developmental studies employing the Stroop task. It appears that obligatory execution of word recognition processes develops quite rapidly, but that the speed and efficiency of execution, in terms of decreasing resource use, continue to develop even after recognition has become obligatory. Early theorists had described automatic processes as being fast, unconscious, obligatory, and effortless, and had implied that these properties were almost totally redundant. More recent theorizing has favored the position that "there are no strong theoretical reasons to believe in the unity of automaticity. The idea that the various properties should co-occur has not been deduced from established theoretical principles, although a number of theorists . . . have asserted it as if it were fact" (Zbrodoff & Logan, 1986, p. 118).

Developmental work has confirmed the finding that speed, obligatory processing, and capacity usage are at least partially dissociable. For example, it is clear that children's word recognition speed continues to decrease even after Stroop indices of obligatory processing are at asymptote (Ehri & Wilce, 1979; Stanovich, Cunningham, & West, 1981). In addition, Manis and colleagues (Manis, Keating, & Morrison, 1980; Horn & Manis, 1987; see also Lipps Birch, 1976, 1978) have extended the use of the dual-task probe technique to children (see Bjorklund & Harnishfeger, 1987; Guttentag, 1984b; Halford, Maybery & Bain, 1986; and Kee & Davies, 1988, for demonstrations in other domains). They found that this index of capacity usage does not track either the development of speed or the development of obligatory processing. Horn and Manis (1987) extended the work of Paap and Ogden (1981) by employing words as stimuli and testing first-, second-, third-, and fifth-graders. They argued that word recognition was obligatory but also capacity-demanding, and they concluded that "there may be a developmental asynchrony between automaticity in the sense of obligatory processing (Stroop-type test) and automaticity in the sense of limited attentional allocation" (p. 106).

Most recent research has thus focused on individual components of the several dissociable properties once lumped together under the automaticity rubric. The issue of resource usage has separated from issues of speed and obligatory execution. The moral of the experimental work with adults (Herdman & Dobbs, 1989; Humphreys, 1985; Logan, 1985; Paap & Ogden, 1981; Zbrodoff & Logan, 1986) and with children (Ehri & Wilce, 1979; Horn &

Manis, 1987; Manis et al., 1980; Stanovich, Cunningham, & West, 1981) is that the allocation of processing resources must be measured directly (for example, by a dual-task procedure) rather than by measures like Stroop interference. The latter cannot safely be used as a proxy measure of resource use because it is tapping a partially dissociable aspect of automaticity. Similarly, speed of execution is not synonymous with either obligatory execution, capacity usage, or conscious intent. Although we would surely expect some intercorrelations among these properties, each must be theoretically differentiated and measured with separate techniques.

MODULARITY IS KING: INFORMATION ENCAPSULATION

The recognition that Stroop indicators did not directly tap resource use rendered the developmental findings using this methodology somewhat less paradoxical, but ultimately did little to bolster limited-capacity models of reading. The reason for this was that the developmental trends involving the dual-task technique did not quite coincide with resource models of reading either (Horn & Manis, 1987). Thus, after almost 10 years of popularity, resource-based theories of reading began to engender increasing skepticism. When, in the early 1980s, an alternative concept began to garner the attention of researchers, models of reading based on cognitive resource limitations had already begun to lose their preeminence.

The focus in reading theory during the mid- to later 1980s shifted away from cognitive resource issues and toward another property associated with the automaticity concept. This property goes under a number of different names and has been discussed by several different investigators. Humphreys (1985) has described the property and some of its alternative terminology:

> If word processing does proceed involuntarily on at least some occasions, there are some interesting implications concerning the control of such operations. For instance, one possibility is that control operates locally so that once a set of word-processing procedures is activated, it runs to completion and cannot be amended by other higher order processes (i. e., it is "cognitively impenetrable"; see Pylyshyn, 1981). Such processes may be termed "functionally autonomous" (Forster, 1979). An implication of this is that word processing cannot be benefited by other ongoing processes (e.g., see Fodor, 1983). This is a different prediction from that which holds that the effects of word processing cannot be prevented (cf. the argument that processing is involuntary), since it is feasible that subjects are unable to prevent a particular process but they may still supplement it when required. (pp. 292–293)

The property of "functional autonomy" or "cognitive impenetrability" has garnered enormous attention since it was made the centerpiece of Fodor's (1983, 1985) controversial concept of modularity. Modularity, like automaticity, is a complex construct that conjoins a number of separate concepts.

Indeed, modularity and automaticity are partially overlapping constructs. For example, modular processes are fast and obligatory, like automatized processes. However, Fodor emphasized the concept of domain specificity as a feature of modularity, an idea missing from most discussions of automaticity.

More importantly, low resource use is not a defining feature of a modular process, as it was in early theorizing about automaticity. Fodor (1985) is at pains to point out that his modern version of a "vertical faculty psychology" does not share Gall's definition of lack of competition for horizontal resources: "I take the essential fact about modularity to be *informational* (not resource) encapsulation" (p. 37). Instead, it is the property of information encapsulation that is the defining feature of a modular process, according to Fodor. Information encapsulation (or "functional autonomy," or "cognitive impenetrability") means that the operation of a module is not controlled by higher-level processes or supplemented by information from knowledge structures not contained in the module itself:

> The claim that input systems are informationally encapsulated is equivalent to the claim that the data that can bear on the confirmation of perceptual hypotheses includes . . . considerably less than the organism may know. That is, the confirmation function for input systems does not have access to all of the information that the organism internally represents; there are restrictions upon the allocation of internally represented information to input processes. (1983, p. 69)

Fodor (1983) views processes such as basic speech perception and face perception as candidates for modular input systems and in his book cites numerous instances of where, in these domains, "at least *some* of the background information at the subject's disposal is inaccessible to at least some of his perceptual mechanisms" (p. 66). The enormous attention garnered by Fodor's book *Modularity of Mind* contributed to a trend already discernible in theories about individual differences in reading skill: a shift from concentration on issues of cognitive resource use to an emphasis on the issue of knowledge representation.

Although Fodor rejects the idea of acquired modularity and equivocates in applying the modularity concept to reading, many other cognitive scientists have endorsed the idea of acquired modularity as theoretically coherent (Forster, 1979; Humphreys, 1985; Logan, 1985; McLeod, McLaughlin, & Nimmo-Smith, 1985; Perfetti & McCutchen, 1987; Seidenberg, 1985; Sternberg, 1985b). Others have applied the modularity concept to the process of word recognition and its development (Forster, 1979; Perfetti, 1992; Perfetti & McCutchen, 1987; Seidenberg, 1985; Stanovich, 1986b, 1992b, 1993c; Stanovich, Nathan, West, & Vala-Rossi, 1985; Stanovich & West, 1983a). Interestingly, perhaps more actual empirical work has been done in the acquired domain of visual word recognition than in some of the other hypothesized modular domains that Fodor (1983) originally championed. In addition, it should also be noted that the theoretical claims in the area of visual word recognition have been more restricted to questions of the nature of information encapsulation (Seidenberg, 1985b; Stanovich & West, 1983a) and have not generally included the more far-reaching and tenuous claims that Fodor makes in his conceptualization of modularity (e.g., innateness, hard-wiring, specific ontogenic sequencing).

The important idea that information encapsulation could be acquired meshed perfectly with trends in the literature on context effects in the development of word recognition skills. Work emanating from tests of verbal efficiency theory (Perfetti, 1985; Perfetti & Roth, 1981) and from the interactive-compensatory model (Stanovich, 1980) had indicated that the effects of background knowledge and contextual information attenuate as the efficiency of word recognition processes increases (Perfetti, Goldman, & Hogaboam, 1979; Perfetti & Roth, 1981; Stanovich, West, & Feeman, 1981; West & Stanovich, 1978).

Thus, one major theoretical trend in developmental reading theory is to view word recognition as becoming increasingly encapsulated (informationally) as processing efficiency develops. Indeed, this trend in the developmental literature on reading is far more empirically well established than are any conclusions about resource use or obligatory processing. Thus, even before the appearance of Fodor's monograph, reading theorists had featured the concept of information encapsulation more prominently in their theories. For example, a critical principle from Perfetti's verbal efficiency theory is that "verbal efficiency is the quality of a verbal processing outcome relative to its cost to processing resources" (1985, p. 102). Thus, Perfetti's concept encompasses both the quality of the representation that is the output of a processing operation and the resources expended on the operation.

THE AUTONOMOUS LEXICON IN READING THEORY: INCREASING THE FOCUS ON REPRESENTATION

In subsequent elaborations of his theory, Perfetti (1992; Perfetti & McCutchen, 1987) has increased the emphasis on issues of representation quality and encapsulation and has decreased the emphasis on the issue of resource use. In its latest incarnation (Perfetti, 1992; Perfetti & McCutchen, 1987), verbal efficiency theory highlights the development of a large autonomous lexicon—orthographic/phonological representations of words that are precise enough that they can be accessed without the aid of background knowledge or contextual expectations—as the key to fluent reading. This emphasis is, of course, consistent with the evidence discussed earlier indicating that it is the word recognition processes of less-skilled readers that are characterized by interactive activation from higher-level knowledge sources such as contextual expectations (Perfetti & Roth, 1981; Stanovich, 1980). However, the new conceptualization is different from earlier versions of verbal efficiency theory (Perfetti & Lesgold, 1977, 1979) in that it deemphasizes issues of capacity use and intensifies the emphasis on the property of information encapsulation.

Perfetti (1992) argues that while encapsulated processes probably share characteristics of automatic processes such as their speed, obligatory execution, and low resource use, these properties are not primary, but are instead secondary concomitants of encapsulation. The key causal property is the development of a high-quality representation in memory that allows autonomous access:

> The entailments of acquired impenetrability . . . leave open the question of whether resources are required by the impenetrable process. It does assume that the impenetrable process cannot be penetrated or inhibited. A young reader might well have impenetrable processes that nevertheless require resources. However, it is generally the case that the potential for resource savings is a function of the representation quality just as impenetrability is. (p. 29)

Likewise, processing speed is the result of high-quality lexical representations. Speed is an outcome of the primary property—well-specified lexical representations—and thus is an imperfect indicator of encapsulation. Speed, in itself, however, is not the most important characteristic.

WHY MODULARITY?

If informational encapsulation, rather than resource allocation, has become the nexus of current theories of individual differences in reading ability, we must still address the question of how encapsulation determines increases in reading ability. In short, we may ask the question of why information encapsulation is a benefit to a processing system engaged in a task like reading. After all, one advantage of the resource notion was the common-sense way in which that mechanism explained reading growth. Freed resources from lower-level decoding processes were allocated to higher-level comprehension processes, which then operated with greater efficiency. Is there an equally parsimonious way in which information encapsulation accounts for increased reading efficiency with increased experience and practice? There is—and here again reading theory has marched in step with developments in cognitive science.

Discussing the computer analogy to human information processing that is popular in some domains of cognitive science, Fodor (1983) argues that researchers have inappropriately deemphasized the importance of making contact with the environment and have overly focused on Turing machines that are closed computational systems: "The sole determinants of their computations are the current machine state, the tape configuration, and the program, the rest of the world being quite irrelevant to the character of their performance; whereas, of course, organisms are forever exchanging information with their environments" (p. 39). What follows, according to Fodor, is that "what perception must do is to so represent the world so as to make it available to thought" (p. 40). In short, higher-level processing operations and inference-making processes will work more efficiently when perceptual processes deliver to them accurate representations of the world. The types of perceptual processes that do this best are modular ones—input systems that fire without accessing all of the organism's background information and beliefs. Modular cognitive processes are like reflexes in that "they go off largely without regard to the beliefs and utilities of the behaving organism" (1985, p. 2)

Modular processes are thus isolated from background knowledge, belief, and set. This confers two great advantages. One is the veridicality that results from the organism's ability to code—at least at some level—the features of the environment without distortion. As Fodor, in his inimitable style, points out: "The ecological good sense of this arrangement is surely self-evident. Prejudiced and wishful seeing makes for dead animals" (1985, p. 2). The second advantage—that of speed—follows along these same lines: "Automatic processes are, in a certain sense, deeply unintelligent; of the whole range of computational . . . options available to the organism, only a stereotyped subset is brought into play. But what you save by this sort of stupidity is *not having to make up your mind*, and making your mind up takes time" (1983, p. 64).

Referring to Ogden Nash's "If you're called by a panther / don't anther," Fodor argues that what the organism needs is a panther identification mechanism that is fast and that errs only on the side of false positives. Thus, "We do not want to have to access panther-identification information from the (presumably very large) central storage . . . on the assumption that large memories are searched slowly" (p. 70). In fact, even if such access were fast, it would not be efficacious because

> the property of being 'about panthers' is not one that can be surefootedly relied upon. Given enough context, practically everything I know can be construed as panther related; and I do not want to have to consider everything I know in the course of perceptual panther identification. . . . The primary point is to so restrict the number of confirmation relations that need to be estimated as to make perceptual identifications fast. . . . Feedback is effective only to the extent that, *prior* to the analysis of the stimulus, the perceiver knows quite a lot about what the stimulus is going to be like. Whereas, the point of perception is surely, that it lets us find out how the world is even when the world is some way that we don't expect it to be. (pp. 67, 71)

In short, an advantage accrues to encapsulation *when the specificity and efficiency of stimulus analyzing mechanisms is great relative to the diagnosticity of the background information that might potentially be recruited to aid recognition.* This is a point that has fundamental importance for reading theory.

MODULARITY AND READING THEORY

The debate in the cognitive science literature regarding the benefits of encapsulation finds immediate correspondence with issues in the reading literature. One of Fodor's (1983, 1985) recurring themes was that "poverty of the stimulus" arguments inherited from the "New Look" period of perceptual research had led cognitive psychology astray. An analogous argument has influenced reading theory during the last decade. For example, Kintsch's (1988) construction–integration model specifically rejects "New Look" and early AI assumptions (e.g., Schank, 1978) of context-driven and knowledge-saturated perceptual processing. In the construction phase of his model, a network of text-based propositions is formed and linked to knowledge structures in a purely bottom-up manner. In the integration phase, activation spreads through the network and stabilizes in a connectionist manner to determine a coherent interpretation. In the construction–integration model, text information contacts and shares activation with knowledge structures, but comprehension is not "driven" by knowledge-based expectations in the traditional top-down fashion. Thus, "modal models" of reading have migrated away from expectancy and "strong" schema theories (see Kintsch, 1988) toward theories stressing autonomous processing and connectionist architectures (Rumelhart & McClelland, 1986; Schneider, 1987; Sejnowski & Rosenberg, 1986; Tanenhaus, Dell, & Carlson, 1987; Tanenhaus & Lucas, 1987).

Similarly, models of reading acquisition and individual differences in reading ability were dominated for a considerable time by "top-down" conceptualizations that borrowed heavily from the New Look in perception (e.g., Smith, 1971). These models strongly emphasized the contribution of expectancies and contextual information in the process of word recognition. Using the current terminology, top-down models posited that developmental changes in reading skill were characterized by word recognition processes that were more heavily penetrated by background knowledge and higher-level cognitive expectancies. As previously discussed, when the appropriate developmental and individual differences data were collected, they demonstrated exactly the opposite: reading skill increases as word recognition processes become increasingly encapsulated (Perfetti, 1985, 1992; Perfetti & Roth, 1981; Stanovich, 1980, 1986b, 1992b, 1993c).

It appears that reading theory—at least regarding word recognition—went wrong in exactly the same ways as did perceptual theory in cognitive psychology. First, "poverty of the stimulus" arguments were overgeneralized. Reading theorists were considerably influenced by analysis-by-synthesis models of speech perception, and interactive models of recognition that derived from artificial intelligence work in speech perception (Rumelhart, 1977). The problem here is that the analogy to written language is not apt. The ambiguity in decontextualized speech is well known. For example, excised words from normal conversation are often not recognized out of context. This does not hold for written language, obviously. A fluent reader can identify written words with near perfect accuracy out of context. In short, the physical stimulus alone completely specifies the lexical representation in writing, whereas this is not always true in speech. The greater diagnosticity of the external stimulus in reading, as opposed to listening, puts a greater premium on an input system that can deliver a full representation of the stimulus to higher-level cognitive systems.

Another problem concerns the assumptions that have been made about the properties of contextual information. Laboratory demonstrations of contextual priming effects have often led to an overestimation of the magnitude of facilitation to be expected from contextual information, because these studies—often for sound theoretical reasons—employed stimulus materials that had strong semantic associations and that were vastly more predictable on a word-by-word basis than is natural text (Gough, 1983; Stanovich & West, 1983b). Also, the writings of top-down theorists—ignoring evidence on text redundancy—often give the impression that predicting upcoming words in sentences is a relatively easy and highly accurate activity. Actually, many different empirical studies have indicated that naturalistic text is not all that predictable. Alford (1980) found that for a set of SAT-type passages, subjects needed an average of more than four guesses to correctly anticipate upcoming words in the passage (the method of scoring actually makes this a considerable underestimate). Across a variety of subject populations and texts, a reader's probability of predicting the next word in a passage is usually between .20 and .35 (Aborn, Rubenstein, & Sterling, 1959; Gough, 1983; Miller & Coleman, 1967; Perfetti et al., 1979; Rubenstein & Aborn, 1958). Indeed, as Gough (1983) has shown, this figure is highest for function words, and is often quite low for the very words in the passage that carry the most information content.

Thus, we have in reading precisely the situation where an enormous advantage accrues to encapsulation: the potential specificity of stimulus analyzing mechanisms is great relative to the diagnosticity of the background information that might be recruited to aid recognition. In short, a consideration of the stimulus ecology of the reading task has converged with the actual empirical data on the development of word recognition skill and has led an increasing number of investigators to endorse the idea of the acquired modularity of the word recognition module.

Current reading theory is thus quite interestingly bifurcated. The idea that background knowledge should saturate central processes of text inferencing, comprehension monitoring, and global interpretation is now widely accepted (Anderson, 1984; Anderson & Pearson, 1984; Fincher-Kiefer, Post, Greene, & Voss, 1988; Paris, 1987; Paris, Lipson, & Wixson, 1983; Spiro, Bruce, & Brewer, 1980; Wixson & Peters, 1987), while at the same time the advantage of modularly organized input processes is acknowledged. Indeed, the dangers of cognitive penetrability at too low a level have become apparent in discussions of nonaccommodating reading styles (Kimmel & MacGinitie, 1984; Maria & MacGinitie, 1982; Stanovich & Cunningham, 1991). As Evans and Carr (1985) point out: "If print-specific encoding mechanisms send incomplete or erroneous data to the language comprehension processes, what could result but an incomplete or erroneous understanding of the text? In addition, the more powerful the language skills that are applied to the erroneous data, the greater the chance that a seemingly acceptable interpretation can be constructed" (p. 342). Of course, there is an analogy here to Fodor's "panther detector." The organism is much better off with a correct rendition of the stimulus as opposed to a sloppy stimulus representation and a geometric explosion of "panther-related" general information. Similarly, the reader is better off having the proper lexical entry activated.

THE FUTURE OF THE RESOURCE CONCEPT IN READING THEORY

This rather extended discussion of the place of the modularity concept in modern reading theory was necessary in order to fully explain the context in which reading researchers have gradually drifted away from the resource concept toward questions of representation quality and encapsulation. This shift has also characterized generic resource theory even outside of the reading area. For example, Logan's (1988) recent instance theory of automatization "reflects a shift from reliance on a general algorithm to reliance on memory for past solutions. Thus automatization reflects the development of a domain-specific knowledge base; nonautomatic performance is limited by a lack of knowledge rather than by scarcity of resources" (p. 501). Instance theory "accounts for many of the facts addressed by the modal view without assuming any resource limitations, attentional or otherwise" (p. 519).

It should not be inferred, however, that the resource concept is without supporters among reading theorists. Many researchers do believe that the capacity notion is still viable. It is just that the issues of the quality of lexical representations and of information encapsulation seem to many investigators to present more tractable theoretical problems, given our currently available empirical techniques.

There are several other reasons why the future of the concept of cognitive resources in reading theory will probably be characterized by only sporadic enthusiasm among reading researchers. First, the checkered history of the dual-task technique in experimental psychology has contributed greatly to the skepticism of investigators in allied fields. The literature on the methodological pitfalls and artifacts involved in using the technique seems to grow faster than the literature demonstrating that the technique can solve theoretical problems having to do with cognitive resources (Allport, 1980; Fisk, Derrick, & Schneider, 1986–1987; Howe & Rabinowitz, 1989; Jonides, Naveh-Benjamin, & Palmer, 1985; Lane, 1977; Logan, 1985; Logan, Zbrodoff, & Fostey, 1983; McLeod, 1978; Navon & Gopher, 1980; Salthouse, 1988).

In addition, the whole concept of generic cognitive resources, as it is commonly used in cognitive psychology, continues to come under conceptual attack (Allport, 1980, 1987; Brainerd & Kingma, 1985, Brainerd & Reyna, 1988, 1989; Hirst & Kalmar, 1987; Logan, 1985; Navon, 1984, 1985, 1989; Neumann, 1987). Navon's (1984) well-known critique severely questioned the falsifiability of the resource notion and concluded: "The claim that provisions for processing may be likened to resources drawn out of a limited reservoir does not seem to be entailed by the results of any known test: Alternative models that do not assume any limit on resources were seen to accommodate empirical findings predicted from this claim" (p. 231). Allport (1980) has leveled similar criticisms of unfalsifiability.

Thus, reading researchers seem to have become uncomfortable with using a task and a concept that seem to be so tenuous in the originating cognitive psychology literature. Reactions to research employing the technique in the reading domain have been decidedly lukewarm. For example, Britton and associates (Britton, 1980; Britton, Holdredge, Curry, & Westbrook, 1979; Britton & Tesser, 1982; Britton, Westbrook, & Holdredge, 1978) have imaginatively applied the dual-task technique in the domain of ongoing reading comprehension. However, some of the findings have been paradoxical, such as easier texts using more capacity (Britton et al., 1978), and the number of alternative explanations for any particular finding appears to be inordinately high (Britton, Glynn, Meyer, & Penland, 1982; Britton & Tesser, 1982; Larochelle, McClelland, & Rodriguez, 1980). Nevertheless, one would have suspected just a few years ago that the intriguing findings of the Britton group would have spawned more experimentation with this technique. Instead, there has been surprisingly little work by other investigators. One can only surmise that confidence in the task is at a low ebb and that interest in the whole resource concept is on the wane in reading theory.

Other attempts to empirically elaborate the generic resource concept within reading models have resulted in theoretical developments that undermined the concept. For example, the reading span task developed by Daneman and Carpenter (1980) initially seemed an excellent indicator of individual differences in central executive capacity. In this task, the subject reads aloud (or listens to) a series of increasingly longer sets of sentences and attempts to remember the last word in each sentence. However, the complexity and lack of process specificity of the task was criticized by Baddeley, Logie, Nimmo-Smith, and Brereton (1985):

> Both a strength and a weakness of the working memory span measure is its complexity. It involves a number of subcomponents, including comprehension, the selection and operation of strategies, learning, and recall. Its richness and complexity mean that it has a very good chance of capturing those aspects of working memory that are important, but at the same time it makes its interpretation very difficult. (p. 120)

Actually, Danemen and Tardif (1987) were quite aware of this criticism and themselves argued that "a legitimate concern about the reading span test is that it is too much like reading comprehension itself. . . . The complexity of the reading span processes makes interpretation of the correlation difficult" (p. 493). Thus, they conducted more thorough individual difference analyses and demonstrated that the "central executive capacity" presumed to underlie the original measure fractionated along domain-specific lines. These investigators recently concluded that "the findings of the larger study showed a high degree of domain specificity. . . . Reading is limited by a system specialized for representing and processing verbal or symbolic information only. . . . The picture suggests the need for abandoning the notion of a general and central limitation on information processing, a central executive" (Daneman & Tardif, 1987, pp. 501–502).

One additional reason for the relative unpopularity of the cognitive resource concept in current research on individual differences in reading is that the concept seems to have a ready affinity with g models of individual differences (Rabbitt, 1988; Salthouse, 1988). As Rabbitt (1988) notes:

> Many cognitive psychologists find the g model uninteresting. Most cognitive models treat the cognitive system as a highly differentiated structure in which component modules have considerable autonomy, but the g model is not concerned with whether or what modular sub-systems exist and merely predicts that if they do, they must all be affected by the presence or absence of a ubiquitous "brain grease." (p. 172)

Similarly, global trait models of individual differences in reading ability are currently exceedingly unpopular (Carr, Brown, & Vavrus, 1985; Carr & Levy, 1990; Cunningham, Stanovich, & Wilson, 1990; Frederiksen, 1980; Lipson & Wixson, 1986; Singer, 1982; Stanovich, Cunningham, & Feeman, 1984a). To the extent that the resource concept remains intertwined with the g construct, it will engender little enthusiasm among reading researchers concerned with individual differences.

However, it is always important to distinguish the theoretical usefulness of a concept as an explanation for individual differences in a skill from its centrality as an underlying general determinant of performance for all subjects. It is perfectly possible for a mechanism to enable a particular function, but not to be a generator of individual differences in the function (see Daneman & Tardif, 1987, pp. 506–507). This point continually needs reiterating in reading theory, because it is quite common for theorists to argue that a particular process, strategy, or mechanism is ubiquitous in reading and then go on to argue for the process as an underlying cause of individual differences. It is rarely considered that the very ubiquity of the process may be precisely the thing that prevents it from being a potent source of individual differences (Stanovich, 1986b, pp. 368–369). An analogous error commonly occurs in many areas of developmental and educational psychology where determinants of variability in a trait are often confused with the determinants of its absolute level or general developmental course (McCall, 1981; Rutter, 1983; Stanovich, 1986b,

p. 392). Thus, it may well be true that it is primarily in the area of individual difference theorizing where the resource concept seems to be losing ground. As a concept in a "modal model" of the generic reading process it may be more viable.

DIVORCING THE NOTION OF COGNITIVE RESOURCES FROM "CONSCIOUSNESS"

We have previously outlined how, in the area of reading theory, the undisciplined use of terms has contributed to ensnaring the cognitive resources concept in considerable confusion and has created seeming empirical paradoxes. For example, it was illustrated how the conflation of the idea of capacity-free processing with the notion of obligatory processing in the elaboration of the automaticity concept led to such a seeming paradox. There is, unfortunately, even further potential for conceptual confusion than has been outlined, and perhaps a few warnings are in order.

In describing the experience of automatic processing during reading, LaBerge and Samuels, in their original article, tell us: "Apparently we have not given a bit of attention to any of the decoding processes that have been transforming marks on the page into the deeper systems of comprehension" (1974, p. 314). Similarly, Posner and Snyder (1975b) reiterate the theme: "The mechanisms of conscious attention are limited in capacity" (p. 670). Both sets of investigators conflate automatic, resource-free processing with the lack of conscious attention and both simultaneously link capacity-demanding processing with conscious attention. Both of these seminal papers thus sustained a strong tendency to link resource use with conscious awareness. Again, this is probably a theoretical mistake. It is very conceivable that even processes that do not draw our conscious attention might utilize cognitive resources (Humphreys, 1985).

Indeed, the stronger point could be advanced that, as in many areas of psychology, the indiscriminate, and undiscriminating, use of folk terms such as "conscious" and "awareness" has contributed to the conceptual confusion in theorizing about resource issues and that the theoretical landscape would be clearer if the terms were barred altogether. This is not a new recommendation, although previous cautions have largely gone unheeded. It is well-established that our use of the term "conscious" is considerably confused (Armstrong & Malcolm, 1984; Dennett, 1969; Lyons, 1986; Rorty, 1979; Ryle, 1949; Smith & Jones, 1986; Wilkes, 1984); and this is surely not surprising since, as Hooker (1975) argues, "Language will surely be seen as a surface abstraction of much richer, more generalized processes in the cortex, a convenient condensation fed to the tongue and hand for social purposes" (p. 217).

In addition, connectionist models, modular brain theories involving semiautonomous processors, dissociation phenomena increasingly uncovered in neuropsychology and experimental psychology (Allport, 1980; Boden, 1988;

P. M. Churchland, 1988; Dennett, 1978; Hofstadter, 1985; Kihlstrom, 1987; Minsky, 1987; Navon, 1989; Nisbett & Ross, 1980; Nisbett & Wilson, 1977; Rollman & Nachmias, 1972; Springer & Deutsch, 1985; Tranel & Damasio, 1985)—all are putting tremendous stress on the integrity of our concept of "consciousness" (P. S. Churchland, 1983, 1986; Dennett, 1987, 1988; Rorty, 1979; Stich, 1983). It would seem best for resource theory to avoid linkage with such an unstable term.

Allport (1980) previously warned us that, 90 years after William James' analysis of attention,

> The word is still used, by otherwise hard-nosed information-processing psychologists, as a code name for consciousness. Questions regarding the limitations of concurrent human *performance* easily get confused with another, hidden agenda concerning the limitations of *consciousness*. Worse, "attention" (or "consciousness"?) is sometimes discussed as though it were yet another—but always unspecified!—information process. (p. 113)

Allport (1980) provides examples from a literature that Claxton (1980, p. 17) claims is "peppered with bits of double-speak." Quoting a common and widely used definition of controlled processes from Shiffrin and Schneider (controlled processes are "activated under control of, and through attention by, the subject"; 1977, p. 156), Allport asks:

> What can these terms mean? Is "the subject" equivalent to the whole system, long-term memory and all? ... Or does "the subject" refer to some sub-part of the system, a ghost-in-the-machine? ... And how does "attention" affect the nature of the processes, associative or otherwise, that can occur? ... The mechanism of "control processes" and presumably therefore of "attention" (which control processes supposedly require) is quite simply "the subject"! I sometimes wonder whether all those psychological theories that propose, as their central mechanism, a general-purpose limited-capacity central processor are not similarly homunculus theories, though sometimes better disguised. (pp. 122–124)

Philosophers have pressed this point even more forcefully. P. M. Churchland (1988) asks: "How could one possibly be blind and not know it? See with no visual field? Write freely but not read a word? Or sincerely deny ownership of arms and legs attached to oneself?" (p. 144). Yet these are all demonstrated phenomena in neuropsychology. P. S. Churchland (1986) argues:

> It is possible that the folk theory that gives "awareness" its meaning might turn out to be displaced by a superior theory. Accordingly, just as it turned out that there was no such thing as impetus, there may be no such thing as awareness. This is not as bizarre as it first sounds. Presumably there is some monitoring mechanism or other chugging away in the mind-brain in virtue of which our current employment of the concept "awareness" can get a foothold—just as there is something or other going on in the world in virtue of which the employment of

the concept "impetus" got a foothold. But we may misapprehend it, folk psychology may be a thoroughly muddled theory of mental business, and a newer and better theory may yield a more satisfactory characterization of it. (p. 309)

Although many cognitive psychologists still seem reluctant to heed Allport's (1980) advice, there are increasing signs that investigators are recognizing both that something is amiss with our terminology and that, fortunately, theoretical developments in the cognitive sciences do promise better conceptualizations. Kahneman and Treisman (1984) make this point in a discussion of the automaticity concept:

> The evidence of dissociation phenomena suggest that it may at times be as difficult to assign epistemic states to individuals as it is to assign such states to organizations. It now appears at least conceivable that future discussions of attention will be conducted within the framework of an organizational metaphor for the mind. ... It is disconcerting, but perhaps also encouraging, that many of the questions with which we have been concerned for years—including the question of automaticity that is the focus of this chapter—will turn out, in such a framework, to be slightly out of focus. Some "attentional" limits may turn out to be failures in the dissemination of information rather than its processing. (p. 56)

Navon (1989) has argued just this in his theory that explains "attentional" phenomena as decouplings and propagations in a distributed modular system.

Hopefully, there will be a continued retreat from conceptualizations that conflate resource use with "conscious attention." The concept of cognitive resources is currently in enough trouble, without taking on the added burden of our tenuous understanding of "consciousness." If there is a way out of the present thicket in which the concept of cognitive resources finds itself, it will be through a more thoroughly operational conceptualization, rather than through an even fuzzier folk psychology.

PART V

THE COGNITIVE CONSEQUENCES OF LITERACY

CHAPTER 13

Measuring Print Exposure

Attempts to Empirically Track
"Rich Get Richer" Effects

There were two theoretical trends in the mid-1980s that led to the body of work that my colleagues and I produced on the consequences of literacy. The first was the theoretical promissory note in the Matthew effects paper reprinted as Chapter 10. The consequences of literacy project described in this section was in part an attempt to deliver on some of the theoretical promises in that paper. There, I had made the case that out-of-school reading experiences were the cause of certain rich-get-richer effects in a variety of cognitive skills. However, at the time, there were few direct tests of this idea. Most of the relevant studies that I reviewed in that paper provided very indirect tests and their outcomes were subject to many alternative explanations. I had tried to distill whatever convergent conclusions I could in the absence of direct empirical tests. The absence of a direct empirical test was due to the two problems discussed extensively in the three papers reprinted in this section: (1) lack of valid and reliable measures of individual differences in exposure to print, and (2) the difficulty of inferring a specific causal path from evidence that was essentially correlational. Chapter 15 contains a detailed discussion of both of these problems and our attempts to address them.

The second theoretical impetus for the consequences of literacy project I began in 1987 was more indirect. It is related to an issue discussed in Chapter 5: that there were indications that phonological processing could not account for all of the observed variance in reading acquisition. In 1986 and 1987 I felt that it was time for our own research group (heretofore focused on phonological processing and contextual priming effects) to look at the issue of orthographic processing as a potential independent source of variance in reading ability.

At a lunch in an Italian section of Baltimore while attending the 1987 meeting of the Society for Research in Child Development, Rich West and I discussed the possibility of getting closure on our context work and gearing up for some studies on orthographic processing. The timing seemed to be right. We had accomplished much in our project on context effects (see Part I). Many things had been brought to fruition and we had achieved much closure on the questions we had raised over a decade earlier as graduate students. In a 1985 paper we had tied all of our earlier findings about individual differences in context effects to the (then recent) modularity notion (Stanovich, Nathan, West, & Vala-Rossi, 1985). We had published an 11-experiment paper in the *Journal of Experimental Psychology: General* a couple of years earlier outlining a massive set of convergent findings relevant to current theories of priming effects (Stanovich & West, 1983). We had extended our paradigm to study syntactic effects in a 1986 paper (West & Stanovich, 1986). We had recently clarified several artifacts in a couple of minor papers just finished (West & Stanovich 1988a, 1988b). The interactive–compensatory concept of context use (see Chapter 3) was now well established. The time seemed ripe to move on.

Looking at the road ahead, Rich and I shared most insights and really parted company on only one. We agreed that orthographic processing skills were the next obvious place to look for variance in reading ability that was independent of phonological processing ability. We agreed that although difficult, it would be possible to measure orthographic processing skill and that several investigators were already making considerable progress in that domain (see the review of the literature in Chapter 14). We agreed that exposure to print might be a uniquely efficacious predictor of this independent variance.

Our one (brief) parting of the ways concerned the mechanism for measuring print exposure. Over the summer of 1987 I worked on this problem by surveying the literature on what had previously been done. I was very motivated to come up with something good because such a measure would be a "twofer" for us. That is, it would serve two purposes. We thought print exposure might have a unique link to orthographic processing and we wanted to pin that relationship down. Additionally, the many theoretical speculations in my Matthew effects paper (Chapter 10) about the effects of out-of-school reading experience on a broad array of cognitive processes required a measure of print exposure if they were to be empirically tested. Of course, I knew in advance that we would be using a brute-force approach of including every type of measure that we could find: questionnaires, diaries, activity checklists, and so on (see Chapters 14 and 15). But I also knew that each of these measures had reliability and/or validity problems and that many of their validity problems stemmed from the social desirability factors that were so entwined with reporting on one's literacy habits. Although I was convinced that these social desirability problems could be overcome, I was initially stumped as to how.

I do not remember the precise moment when I thought of the checklist-with-foils procedure described in Chapters 14–16, but I do know that as soon as I had thought of it and before I had actually constructed an actual mock-up (which turned out to be the adult author version—magazines, comics, and children's titles came later) I was utterly confident that it would work. By "work" here I mean that the task would be reliable and be more valid than existing measures—primarily because it would more effectively circumvent social desirability problems.

It was regarding this confidence factor that Rich and I had a parting of the ways. I was utterly confident in the instrument before it was even constructed, but Rich remained somewhat skeptical. He and others, I think, were thrown off by the incredible briefness of the instrument (the subject scans through the author names in a couple of minutes) and the seeming triviality of the instrument (just "check a name" without independent verification of whether the author's work had even been read). Surely such a brief and (seemingly) cursory task could not predict as well as complicated and extensive tasks such as questionnaires, diaries, and interviews? But as the reader will see by perusing the first of our papers on this instrument (reprinted here as Chapter 14), from our first study onward the checklist instruments outperformed more traditional measures.

What made me so confident was the "quick probe" logic of the checklist method. I will explain the concept of a quick probe here because I think it has the potential to clarify certain confusions about experimental tasks that are quite widespread. The term "quick probe" I borrow from a 1985 paper of Daniel Dennett's titled "Can Machines Think?" that is reprinted in his 1998 collection *Brainchildren: Essays on Designing Minds* (all page numbers here are from the 1998 volume). In this paper, which is centered on a discussion of Turing's test, Dennett proposes the following test for whether a city is a great city (i.e., the type of city he would love). Dennett's test is whether or not on any randomly chosen day a person can do the following: (1) hear a symphony orchestra; (2) see a Rembrandt and a professional athletic contest; and (3) eat quenelles de brochet à la Nantua for lunch.

This operational definition of a great city Dennett termed a "quick-probe test." The point about a quick probe is *not* that the items in it are particularly important—nor that they are in any way exhaustive. Indeed, Dennett (1998) notes that "obviously, the test items are not all I care about in a great city. In fact, some of them I don't care about at all. I just think they would be cheap and easy ways of assuring myself that the subtle things I do care about in cities are present" (p. 10). The key characteristic of a quick probe is that it is associated with a very large number of characteristics that actually *do* define the concept of interest. So although Dennett might not care for Rembrandt, the presence of a Rembrandt in a city probably predicts a host of other things that he really does care about—for example, the presence of independent bookstores, jazz clubs, public radio stations, science museums, and restaurants that serve dim sum.

The quick probe is just that, a quick but risky way of getting at the larger set of characteristics that define the overall concept (in this case, the concept "cities I would like"). I write "risky" because there is always an outside chance that associations between the quick-probe characteristics and the concept of interest might be present for spurious reasons or, conversely, that the association might have been disrupted for some odd reason. As a humorous example of the former, Dennett (1998) points out that "if the Chamber of Commerce of Great Falls, Montana, wanted—and I can't imagine why—to get their hometown on my list of great cities, they could accomplish this by the relatively inexpensive route of hiring full time about ten basketball players, forty musicians, a quick-order quenelle chef, and renting a cheap Rembrandt from some museum" (p. 10).

In formulating his operational definition, Dennett is counting on the fact that Great Falls hasn't taken such steps. It's a risk—but probably a relatively safe one:

> I devised the test, of course, with the realization that no one would be both stupid and rich enough to go to such preposterous lengths to foil the test. In the actual world, wherever you find symphony orchestras, quenelles, Rembrandts, and professional sports, you also find daily newspapers, parks, repertory theaters, libraries, fine architecture, and all the other things that go to make a city great. My test was simply devised to locate a telling sample that could not help but be representative of the rest of the city's treasures. I would cheerfully run the risk of having my bluff called. (p. 10)

It is likewise with the famous test that Turing posited as the operational definition of whether a computer could think: that the computer could carry on an intelligent conversation. It was not that Turing thought that holding a conversation encompassed all we could possibly mean by the term "thinking." He was obviously aware that thinking encompassed much more. Instead, the ability to hold a conversation was merely a quick probe. Turing was making the bet that "nothing could possibly pass the Turing test by winning the imitation game without being able to perform indefinitely many other intelligent actions" (p. 6). According to Dennett,

> Turing realized, as anyone would, that there are hundreds and thousands of telling signs of intelligent thinking to be observed in our fellow creatures, and one could, if one wanted, compile a vast battery of different tests to assay the capacity for intelligent thought. But success on his chosen test, he thought, would be highly predictive of success on many other intuitively acceptable tests of intelligence. (p. 6)

This quick-probe logic is used in most psychometric instruments. Such instruments do not claim to be exhaustive inventories of human abilities but instead provide quick probes into a much larger panoply of skills. The quick-probe logic is, in turn, often not understood by critics of psychometric testing. Faced with the item "pusillanimous" on a vocabulary test, critics are often unreflectively quick to ask questions like "Who said that you're not intelligent if you don't know the word *pusillanimous*?" or "I know plenty of people who do fine without the word *pusillanimous*" or "I know what it means but I've never used this word, so how can it be so important that it is included on this test?" The answer to these questions is, of course, that *pusillanimous* has no specific importance at all—in and of itself. It is merely a quick probe. Just as cities with Rembrandts in them tend to have many other good things in them, people who know the word *pusillanimous* tend to know many other similarly difficult words. The item "pusillanimous" is simply a stand-in for these hundreds of other words.

Of course, there is always the chance that someone with a large vocabulary somehow missed out on learning *pusillanimous* or that someone with a small vocabulary just happened to learn it. The psychometric logic here is simply to increase the sample of quick probes so that it becomes increasingly unlikely that chance or spurious circumstances produced the results. Just as Dennett conjoined three items in order to make sure that Great Falls (clearly somewhere he doesn't want included in his set of great cities) doesn't fortuitously have a Rembrandt and make the cut—vocabulary tests are composed not just of the word *pusillanimous* but of several dozen similar words. While you might just know *pusillanimous* through sheer luck, it is likely that if you know the meanings of the words *substratum, nuance, denouement, confluence, suffuse, ubiquitous, languor, unction*, and *eventuate* you really do have a large vocabulary.

The recognition checklists discussed in Chapters 14–16 have the same quick-probe logic—and the same psychometric sampling logic of a vocabulary test. Like the example of the latter, it probably means little if someone does not recognize the name Judith Krantz. We are not saying that there is anything uniquely important about Judith Krantz for understanding a person's literacy experiences (surely). But we *are* saying that someone who doesn't recognize any of the names Isaac Asimov, Bill Bryson, Judy Blume, Tom Clancy, John Grisham, Stephen King, Judith Krantz, Frank McCourt, James Michener, Bob Woodward, Tom Wolfe, and John Updike is probably not immersed in a culture of print. These names are quick probes into a person's literacy environment. Not knowing them is the equivalent of saying that a city doesn't have a Rembrandt, a quenelle chef, or a symphony orchestra. If a city doesn't, it is probably a poor candidate for a great city (by Dennett's standards).

Note that the quick-probe nature of the recognition checklist logic is emphasized in Chapter 15 where I deal with a common question that comes up about the checklists: "What if a subject knows the author name but has never read anything that the author has written?" The answer is that this is no problem whatsoever as long as a basic quick-probe assumption is preserved: that the name be known because of engagement in literacy-based activities. Under this assumption, some ways of obtaining knowledge of an author's name al- though not having read their work are problematic whereas others are not. For example, hearing about a magazine or an author on television without having been exposed to the actual written work is problematic. But as men- tioned in Chapter 15, postexperimental interviews reveal a number of in- stances where name knowledge is reflective of immersion in a literate environ- ment even though the author's specific works have not been read. People can see an author's books in a bookstore, see an author's book in the "new fic- tion" section at a library, read a review of the author's work in a magazine, see an advertisement in the newspaper, or the like. All of these ways of gaining knowledge of an author's name are proxies for reading activities, despite the fact that the particular author had not actually been read. Thus, in all of these situations the author names are acting like the efficient quick probes that they are.

GOALS ACCOMPLISHED BY THE PRINT EXPOSURE PROJECT

Two versions of the checklist-with-foils task (the Author and Magazine Rec- ognition Tests) were unveiled in a 1989 paper published in *Reading Research Quarterly* (reprinted here as Chapter 14). In this series of studies we accom- plished all of our initial goals. We verified that orthographic processing skill predicted variance in word recognition and spelling that was unaccounted for by phonological processing; we linked this unique orthographic processing variance to individual differences in print exposure measured in various ways; and we established the reliability and validity of the Author and Magazine Recognition Tests.

A little over a year later, Anne Cunningham and I (Cunningham & Stanovich, 1990) published our first work with children using the checklist- with-foils methodology. Aided by Ruth Nathan's immense knowledge of chil- dren's literature, we developed a Title Recognition Test for children. As in the 1989 study, we demonstrated that, for children too, orthographic processing skill predicted variance in word recognition and spelling that was unac- counted for by phonological processing and that this independent ortho- graphic variance could be linked to print exposure (see also Cunningham & Stanovich, 1993). The Title Recognition Test was further refined and a chil- dren's Author Recognition Test developed in further work with Jim Cipiel- ewski and Linda Allen (Allen, Cipielewski, & Stanovich, 1992; Cipielewski, & Stanovich, 1992)—then graduate students but now valued senior col- leagues and friends. More work on the validity of the checklist-with-foils pro- cedure for children was reported in Allen et al. (1992) and validity work with adults was reported in West, Stanovich, and Mitchell (1993). The work from the first 5–7 years on the consequences of literacy and the correlates of expo- sure to print was summarized in a chapter in *Advances in Child Development and Behavior* (reprinted here as Chapter 15). Five more years of work on the consequences of literacy is summarized in the paper reprinted here as Chapter 16 (Stanovich, Cunningham, & West, 1998), which was a chapter contributed to a Festschrift for Harold Stevenson. Harold, along with John Hagen, had helped Rich West and me organize a seminar on reading research when Rich and I were graduate students at the University of Michigan. This paper also formed the basis for my Sylvia Scribner Award Address to Division C of the American Educational Research Association in San Diego in 1998. I chose to highlight the print exposure research in the address because of its connection to Sylvia Scribner's work—a connection detailed most explicitly in Chapter 15.

As will be clear from Chapters 15 and 16, the main goals that I had for this project were largely accomplished. First, we empirically established the existence of phonologically independent orthographic processing variance and showed that print exposure had a unique link to that orthographic processing variance—a link that other investigators have since replicated (Barker, Torgesen, & Wagner, 1992; Braten, Lie, Andreassen, & Olaussen, 1999; Chateau & Jared, in press; McBride-Chang, Manis, Seidenberg, Custodio, & Doi, 1993; Olson, Forsberg, & Wise, 1994). Attacking this issue empirically required us to invent and refine our checklist-with-foils methodology for assessing individual differences in print exposure. With these measures, we have studied diverse samples of readers, including a sample of individuals with a mean age of 79 years (Stanovich, West, & Harrison, 1995), as well as the reading habits of first graders (Cunningham & Stanovich, 1993; Salter & Stanovich, 1996). We have examined relationships longitudinally (Cipielewski & Stanovich, 1992; Echols, West, Stanovich, & Zehr, 1996) as well as cross-sectionally.

I have been pleased to see that the methodology and tasks have been adapted by other investigators and used for disparate purposes—for example, in twin studies of genetic and environmental determinants of reading subprocesses (Castles, Datta, Gayan, & Olson, 1999; Olson et al., 1994). They have also been used to study parents' knowledge of children's literature (Senechal, LeFevre, Hudson, & Lawson, 1996). The basic data patterns that we have uncovered have been replicated using variants of our methodology in other parts of Canada (Chateau & Jared, in press; Senechal et al., 1996), the United States (Barker et al., 1992; Hall et al., 1996; Lewellen et al., 1993), Great Britain (Stainthorp, 1997), The Netherlands (de Groot & Bus, 1995), China (McBride-Chang & Chang, 1995), Norway (Braten et al., 1999), and Taiwan (Lee, 1996). Populations such as second language learners (Jackson, Lu, & Ju, 1994), Spanish speakers (Rodrigo, McQuillan, & Krashen, 1996), and learning-disabled individuals (McBride-Chang et al., 1993) have also been examined using variants of our methodology. Sticht, Hofstetter, and Hofstetter (1996) studied a sample by telephone that was representative of the demographics in the U.S. Census. It has even been tested on a prison population (Rice, Howes, & Connell, 1998).

The second major goal achieved by this research program was that many of the theoretical speculations in my Matthew effects paper (Chapter 10) were tested empirically. Variance in exposure to print was rather specifically linked to a variety of cognitive outcomes, including variation in vocabulary, knowledge structures, verbal fluency, and other aspects of psycholinguistic processing (see Chapters 15 and 16, and Siddiqui, West, & Stanovich, 1998). The inherently conservative nature of the regression logic (particularly in the longitudinal analyses; see Cipielewski & Stanovich, 1992; Echols, West, Stanovich, & Zehr, 1996) that we used to address the issue of specificity is being more generally recognized. Speaking of an analogous set of analyses, Manis, Seidenberg, and Doi (1999) argued that

> it is important to note that the autoregression technique factors out both prior reading skill and growth in reading that is predictable from prior reading skill (expected growth). Thus, only the relation of RAN and phoneme awareness to unexpected growth in reading is being evaluated in these studies. If the variables have stable individual differences, there may be very little unexpected growth and, hence, small contributions of the predictors. In other words, the autoregression studies leave open the possibility that the contribution of RAN and other factors to predictable growth in later reading may be substantial. (p. 133)

READING MAKES YOU SMARTER BUT NOT WISER

The range of outcomes in the verbal domain that have been specifically linked to print exposure has been so broad that it led me to (perhaps rather cheekily) title the *Advances* paper "Does Reading Make You Smarter?" If by "smarter" we in part mean verbal ability, then it is clear that I regard the answer to this question as "Yes." Having established some very basic linkages to verbal skills, we have more recently moved toward examining whether there are specific connections between exposure to print and more elaborate thinking skills—linkages that have been posited by various literacy theorists in the humanities and social sciences (see the discussion in Chapter 15). We have focused on the property of cognitive decontextualization that has been emphasized by many different literacy theorists (Akinnaso, 1981; Denny, 1991; Donaldson, 1993; Goody, 1977, 1987; Havelock, 1963, 1980; Luria, 1976; D. Olson, 1977, 1994; Ong, 1967, 1982; see Stanovich, 1999b, for an extensive discussion of decontextualized reasoning). An interest in decontextualized reasoning skills as a foundation of rational thought goes back at least to Piaget (1926), who considered the concept of decentration as pivotal in children's cognitive development.

One indicator of decontextualized thought that has been of interest at least since the work of Luria (1976) is syllogistic reasoning (see Sá, West, & Stanovich, 1999; Scribner & Cole, 1981; Stanovich, 1999b; Stanovich & West, 1998). Siddiqui, West, and Stanovich (1998) examined the associations between print exposure and performance on such a syllogistic reasoning task, as well as the association with a vocabulary measure of knowledge of mental-state verbs. The correlation of print exposure with mental-state verb knowledge (.46) was higher than that with syllogistic reasoning performance (.30). Additionally, print exposure predicted unique variance in mental-state vocabulary performance after controls for general ability were invoked, but it was not a unique predictor of syllogistic reasoning performance in similar analyses. Thus, exposure to print was not uniquely linked to decontextualized reasoning (as many literacy theorists maintain).

The pattern in the Siddiqui et al. (1998) study has replicated across many of our experiments in which we have examined several aspects of decontextualized reasoning (Sá et al., 1999; Stanovich, 1999b; Stanovich & West, 1997, 1998). Print exposure always displays a zero-order correlation with measures of decontextualized reasoning, but in a majority of cases when controls for general cognitive ability are invoked print exposure is not a unique predictor. In the minority of cases where it remains a significant unique predictor, the proportion of unique variance explained is quite low. Such a pattern is quite different from that involving vocabulary and variables related to verbal ability. In those domains print exposure always remains a unique predictor even after stringent controls for general ability are invoked (see Guthrie, Wigfield, Metsala, & Cox, 1999), and the proportion of unique variance explained is often quite substantial (see Chapters 15 and 16). Somewhat to our consternation (every member of my research group being a strong advocate of literacy), the effects of print exposure on decontextualized reasoning appear to be weak. Somewhat sadly, I have tentatively concluded that reading makes you smarter but not wiser. This conclusion, although again expressed in a somewhat provocative and cheeky way, is actually reinforced by my theoretical work on reasoning (Stanovich, 1999b) in which I have argued that cognitive ability is an individual difference variable at the algorithmic level of analysis in a cognitive model, whereas variation in decontextualized thought is in part due to individual differences at the intentional level of analysis. The two can thus easily dissociate—as appears to be the case when their relation to print exposure is examined.

FUTURE WORK ON EXPOSURE TO PRINT

Given the results discussed in the previous section, clearly it is within the verbal domain that future work on exposure to print will prove most fruitful. In the vocabulary domain, the time seems right for some more microanalyses of the effects of print on vocabulary development. New technologies for measuring vocabulary relationships in text are developing rapidly, and connectionist technologies show much promise. For example, Landauer's latent semantic analysis (Landauer, 1998; Landauer & Dumais, 1996, 1997) is incredibly promising and provides a refined way of measuring the density and complexity of semantic relationships in texts. The connectionist model that implements the analysis could be used to measure the semantic richness of texts that people are reading or the semantic complexity of their written products.

Landauer's (1998) work with latent semantic analysis also drives home the importance of print exposure, because this work has demonstrated how the paradox of vocabulary growth—how children's vocabularies grow at prodigious rates despite the seeming inefficacy of direct instruction in vocabulary—can be explained by the effects of mere exposure. Specifically, when a word is encountered in the context of other known words, it is not just the representation of the unknown word that is sharpened, but that of all related words in the lexicon (which in the abstract includes *all* words in the lexicon, although at some lexical distance the effect becomes vanishingly small). Landauer (1998) emphasizes that "we believe that central human cognitive abilities often depend on immense amounts of experience, and that theories that cannot be applied to comparable data may be fundamentally wrong, or at least unprovable" (p. 163).

Latent semantic analysis reflects a more fine-grained analysis of the texts that people are reading, and I hope that such more fine-grained methodologies will be applied in future work on the cognitive consequences of print exposure. Indeed, in several of the papers I published on the effects of print exposure I tried to draw attention to the work of Hayes (1988; Hayes & Ahrens, 1988) and his research with a computer system (LEX) for measuring lexical density. This work has not received as much attention in the reading research community as it deserves. Additionally, I have found that teachers are quite interested in it, and that it serves a motivational function for them in that it reinforces their belief in the power and efficacy of print.

During the last decade, many teachers have found themselves to be embattled advocates for print as they try to ward off the effects of an increasingly image-oriented culture; rampant commercialization of all the symbolic aspects of life (including the schools, which have made themselves into Pepsi billboards—often for trivial amounts of money); and the latest computer hype from corporations and administrators. Teachers who have invested a lifetime in the culture of books are made to feel inadequate because they are not familiar with the latest technological gizmo that has been placed (without their consent) in their classrooms as part of the latest "campaign" on which the school board spent thousands while the school library languishes (see Neuman, 1999).

So what I give such teachers is not a motivational speech but some of the raw statistics that Hayes and Ahrens (1988) have generated from their LEX system. Table 13.1 illustrates the three different categories of language that were analyzed by Hayes and Ahrens (1988): written language sampled from genres as difficult as scientific articles and as simple as preschool books; words spoken on television shows of various types; and adult speech in two contexts varying in formality. The words used in the different contexts were analyzed according to a standard frequency count of English (Carroll, Davies, & Richman, 1971). This frequency count ranks the 86,741 different words in

TABLE 13.1. Selected Statistics for Major Sources of Spoken and Written Language (Sample Means)

	Rank of median word	Rare words per 1,000
Printed texts		
Abstracts of scientific articles	4,389	128.0
Newspapers	1,690	68.3
Popular magazines	1,399	65.7
Adult books	1,058	52.7
Comic books	867	53.5
Children's books	627	30.9
Preschool books	578	16.3
Television texts		
Popular prime-time adult shows	490	22.7
Popular prime-time children's shows	543	20.2
Cartoon shows	598	30.8
Mr. Rogers and *Sesame Street*	413	2.0
Adult speech		
Expert witness testimony	1,008	28.4
College graduates to friends, spouses	496	17.3

Note. Adapted from Hayes & Ahrens, 1988. Copyright 1988 by Cambridge University Press. Adapted by permission.

English according to their frequency of occurrence in a large corpus of written English. So, for example, the word "the" is ranked number 1, the 10th most frequent word is "it," the word "know" is ranked 100, the word "pass" is ranked 1,000, the word "vibrate" is 5,000th in frequency, the word "shrimp" is 9,000th in frequency, and the word "amplifier" is 16,000th in frequency. The first column, labeled "Rank Median Word," is simply the frequency rank of the average word (after a small correction) in each of the categories. So, for example, the average word in children's books was ranked 627th most frequent in the Carroll et al. (1971) word count, the average word in popular magazines was ranked 1399th most frequent, and the average word in the abstracts of scientific articles had, not surprisingly, a very low rank (4389th).

What is immediately apparent is how lexically impoverished is most speech, as compared to written language. With the exception of the special situation of courtroom testimony, the average frequency of the words in all of the samples of oral speech is quite low, hovering in the 400–600 range of ranks. The relative rarity of the words in children's books is in fact greater than that in all of the adult conversation, except for the courtroom testimony. Indeed, the words used in children's books are considerably rarer than those in the speech on prime-time adult television (which of course has been *intentionally* stripped of low-frequency words so as not to scare off the audience). The categories of adult reading matter contain words that are considerably rarer than those heard on television.

These relative differences in word rarity have direct implications for vocabulary development. Opportunities to acquire new words occur when an individual is exposed to a word in written or oral language that is outside their current vocabulary. That this will happen vastly more often while reading than while talking or watching television is illustrated in the second column of Table 13.1. That column lists how many rare words per 1,000 are contained in each of the categories. A rare word is defined as one with a rank lower than 10,000—roughly, a word that is outside the vocabulary of a fourth to sixth grader. For vocabulary growth to occur after the middle grades, children must be exposed to words that are rare by this definition. Again, it is print that provides many more such word-learning opportunities. Children's books have 50% more rare words in them than does adult prime-time television and the conversation of college graduates. Popular magazines have roughly three times as many opportunities for new word learning than does prime-time television and adult conversation. Assurances that "what they read and write may make people smarter, but so will any activity that engages the mind, including interesting conversation" (Smith, 1989, p. 354) are overstated, at least when applied to the domain of vocabulary learning. The data in Table 13.1 indicate that conversation is not a substitute for reading. An oral culture plus visual images (increasingly the environment of children) is no substitute for print.

Baines (1996) has done an interesting analysis of the lexical consequences of the transition from the written to the oral. He analyzed the vocabulary differences between books and the movies that had been made from those books. For example, Table 13.2 contains an analysis of the words in *To Kill a Mock-*

TABLE 13.2. Analysis of Words in the Movie and Book Versions of *To Kill a Mockingbird*

Script	Book
ugly	up
under	us
until	use
up	used
upstairs	upon
us	until
used	upstairs
	unceiled
	unpainted
	uncontrollable
	uncrossed
	under
	undress
	unhitched
	unique
	unless
	unlighted

Note. From Baines (1996). Copyright 1996 by the International Reading Association, Inc. Reprinted by permission.

ingbird. On the left are all of the words beginning with the letter *u* that appear in the script of the movie. On the right side are all of the words beginning with the letter *u* that appear in the book. Table 13.3 displays a similar analysis of *Wuthering Heights*. On the left are all of the words beginning with the letter *i* that appear in the script of the movie. On the right side are all of the words beginning with the letter *i* that appear in the book. Immediately apparent is the severe "lexical pruning" that occurs when a story goes from book to screen.

It is sometimes argued or implied that the type of words present in print but not represented in speech are unnecessary words: jargon, academic doublespeak, elitist terms of social advantage, or words used to maintain the status of the users but that serve no real functional purpose. A consideration of the frequency distributions of written and spoken words reveals this argument to be patently false, as is readily apparent from a perusal of some words that do not occur at all in two large corpora of oral language (Berger, 1977; Brown, 1984), but that have appreciable frequencies in a written frequency count (Francis & Kucera, 1982), for example, the following words: *participation, luxury, maneuver, provoke, reluctantly, relinquish, portray, equate, hormone, exposure, display, invariably, dominance, literal, legitimate, and infinite*. The words are not unnecessary appendages, concocted by the ruling class

TABLE 13.3. Analysis of Words in the Movie and Book Versions of *Wuthering Heights*.

Script	Book	
I'd	I'd	I'll
I'll	I've	idea
I'm	ideas	ideal
I've	idleness	idiot
icy	if	ill
If	in	is
ill	into	it's
ills	illusions	imagined
imp	impressed	impulse
improved	incoherent	irks
in	indefinite	indoors
indeed	indignant	induced
injured	inexquisite	instant
inside	inquiring	instead
insolent	inscribed	instinct
into	inscription	invalid
introduce	interesting	interposed
irony	interrogatively	
is	introduction	
isn't		
It		
it's		

Note. From Baines (1996). Copyright 1996 by the International Reading Association, Inc.. Reprinted by permission.

to oppress those who are unfamiliar with them. They are words that are necessary to make critical distinctions in the physical and social world in which we live. Without such lexical tools, one will be severely disadvantaged in attaining one's goals in a technological society. D. Olson (1986) has argued that

> the distinctions on which such questions are based are extremely important to many forms of intellectual activity in a literate, society. It is easy to show that sensitivity to the subtleties of language are crucial to some undertakings. A person who does not clearly see the difference between an expression of intention and a promise or between a mistake and an accident, or between a falsehood and a lie, should avoid a legal career or, for that matter, a theological one. (p. 341)

Olson's statement reflects a stark fact about modern technological societies: they are providing lucrative employment only for those who acquire increasingly complex verbal skills and vocabulary (Bronfenbrenner, McClelland, Wethington, Moen, & Ceci, 1996; Frank & Cook, 1995; Gottfredson, 1997; Hunt, 1995, 1999). The large differences in lexical richness between speech and print are a major source of individual differences in those complex verbal skills.

NOTE

1. I should mention that it is not necessarily typical that our disagreements are resolved in my favor. In the course of a 25-year collaboration at least as often the opposite happens. For example, Rich has the unerring ability to predict the effects of research technology better than I can. There exist numerous examples of innovations that I have dubbed "fads" only to have them become an essential part of our research operation years later.

CHAPTER 14

Exposure to Print and Orthographic Processing

with RICHARD F. WEST

Much recent research has focused on phonological processing abilities—phonological awareness, use of phonological codes in short-term memory, rapid name retrieval—as determinants of individual differences in reading acquisition (Liberman & Shankweiler, 1985; Lundberg, Frost, & Peterson, 1988; Mann, 1986; Stanovich, 1982a, 1986b, 1988a; Wagner, 1988; Yopp, 1988). This focus is justified because a large body of recent research has linked differences in phonological processing skills to word recognition difficulties in both children and adults (Bradley & Bryant, 1985; Olson, Kliegl, Davidson, & Foltz, 1985; Pennington, 1986; Perfetti, 1985; Read & Ruyter, 1985; Vellutino & Scanlon, 1987). Nevertheless, despite the importance of phonological variables in explaining variance in the acquisition of word recognition skill, it is possible that another class of factors could explain additional variance. Although the correlations between phonological processing skill and word recognition ability are quite high, they still probably leave some reliable word recognition variance unaccounted for (Stanovich, Cunningham, & Cramer, 1984; Wagner, 1988; Wagner & Torgesen, 1987; Yopp, 1988). In addition, some investigators have argued that the development of a minimal level of phonological sensitivity is a necessary but not sufficient condition for the development of efficient word recognition processes (Gough, Juel, & Griffith, 1989; Juel, Griffith, & Gough, 1986; Tunmer & Nesdale, 1985). That is, while virtually no child with deficient phonological processing skills develops reading ability with ease, some children with adequate phonological sensitivity lag behind in the development of word recognition effi-

259

ciency. If phonological processing is a necessary but not sufficient condition for the development of adequate word recognition skill, this implies that there may be another cognitive "sticking point" for some children—a second critical locus of variance in word recognition skill.

Some recent empirical research and theoretical speculation has raised the possibility that variance in the ability to form, store, and access orthographic representations accounts for some of the residual variance in word recognition not accounted for by phonological factors. Reitsma (1983) gave children practice at recognizing a set of words with standard spellings and three days later tested their recognition of these words and a matched set of homophonic spellings of the words. Among a group of first-grade readers, only four trials of practice led to superior performance on the standard spellings three days later. However, a group of learning-disabled children two years older but approximately matched to the first graders on reading level did not perform better on the standard spellings even after six trials of practice. This result suggests that specific problems in forming visual–orthographic representations may characterize some less-skilled readers. Reitsma (1983) concluded that "facility in decoding does not automatically predict the capability of learning to recognize the unique letter sequence of words" (p. 335).

Case studies of adults with acquired surface dyslexia (Patterson, Marshall, & Coltheart, 1985) have suggested that there exist reading problems specifically associated with difficulties in accessing and/or forming representations in the orthographic lexicon. Clinical studies of dyslexic children have also repeatedly suggested the existence of a subtype of poor readers with unique difficulties in dealing with the visual representations of words (e.g., Bodor, 1973), although the interpretation of this clinical work is very equivocal (Hooper & Hynd, 1985; Olsen, Kliegl, Davidson, & Foltz, 1985; Perfetti, 1985). Nevertheless, some studies of individual differences across the normal continuum of ability have suggested that children show marked differences in their tendency to utilize print-specific information when recognizing words (Baron & Treiman, 1980; Bryant & Impey, 1986; Freebody & Byrne, 1988; Treiman, 1984).

Some current theoretical views are also consistent with the idea of orthographic processing skill as an independent source of word recognition variance. For example, the three stages in Frith's (1985) model of reading acquisition are characterized by the development of logographic, alphabetic, and orthographic skill, respectively. Developmental arrest prior to or early in the alphabetic stage would lead to the most common type of poor reader: those with deficient phonological and spelling-to-sound decoding skills. Developmental arrest at the next stage results in reading problems more closely associated with orthographic processing problems. Frith's (1985) model, then, is consistent with the idea of phonological skills as necessary but not sufficient for the full development of word recognition fluency.

However, despite some convergent evidence for the idea of individual differences in orthographic processing skill, there are also some reasons to question the hypothesis of orthographic processing as an independent source of variance. For example, it is clearly the case that a child with efficiently functioning phonological coding processes will develop a richer orthographic lexicon due to a greater number of "positive learning trials" (Jorm & Share, 1983) with words: instances where accurate decoding leads to the complete phonological representation of a word becoming associated with its visual form. Such positive learning trials lead to the amalgamation of orthographic and phonological representations in memory (Barron, 1986; Ehri, 1980, 1984, 1987), and the amalgamated orthographic representation is what eventually enables rapid and efficient processes of direct access to the lexicon.

Thus, there is little doubt that the development of orthographic processing skill must be somewhat dependent on phonological processing abilities. The critical question for research is whether the development of the orthographic lexicon is *entirely* parasitic on the operation of phonological processes. For example, Gough et al. (1989) argue that word-specific knowledge must be acquired in addition to spelling–sound decoding skill and that the development of the orthographic lexicon depends on factors in addition to phonological decoding skill. They point to the fact that children who are equally skilled at reading regular words vary considerably in their ability to read exception words. Gough et al. (1989) speculate that the ability to read exception words essentially depends on how much children practice their decoding skills.

This conjecture naturally raises the question of whether there are differences in exposure to print that are independent of phonological decoding skills. The problem is that even if differences in orthographic processing abilities had as their proximal cause differences in exposure to print, reading practice may simply be determined by how skilled the child is at phonological coding. If this is the case, then orthographic processing differences could not serve as a unique source of reading variance. Such differences would be indirectly parasitic on the phonological processing abilities that directly cause print exposure variance. This conjecture yields the prediction that print exposure differences should not account for variance in the quality of the orthographic lexicon, once phonological skill has been partialled out.

The two studies of adult readers that we will report represent an initial attempt to address these two interrelated questions: First, can orthographic processing ability account for variance in word recognition and spelling once all of the variance associated with phonological processing skill has been partialled out? Secondly, can orthographic processing variance be linked to print exposure differences that, again, are independent of phonological processing skill?

In Study 1 we assessed the relative volume of print exposure using two different classes of method. One of the methods involved a new instrument which may be of considerable use in future studies designed to investigate the effects of reading volume. The measures of print exposure were linked to indices of the quality of the orthographic lexicon derived from spelling performance. This experiment allowed a crude test of whether print exposure differences can be linked to orthographic processing differences after variance due to phonological ability has been partialled out. A much more refined test of this hypothesis is reported in Study 2, an investigation employing multiple indices of phonological and orthographic processing skill.

STUDY 1

In Study 1 we attempted to measure reading volume in two different ways. One of these resulted in the development of a new index of print exposure designed to eliminate one of the most serious problems with standard questionnaires about reading activity: their tendency to be confounded by social desirability factors (Paulhus, 1984). In short, most adults—especially college students—know that it is a "good thing" to read and thus may be prone to differentially exaggerate how much they engage in this activity. Our new index of exposure to print eliminates this confounding factor.

In our initial experiment we attempted to link the indices of print exposure with the ability to spell segments of words that had ambiguous or irregular sound-to-spelling correspondences. We examined spelling in our initial experiment because, as Perfetti (1992) has argued, "Reliable, confident, and facile spelling is an index of a high quality representation" (p. 28). We focused on ambiguous spelling segments and irregular words because such stimuli are excellent probes of the ability to form and access orthographic representations, independent of phonological skills.

Method

Subjects

The subjects were 61 undergraduate students (10 males and 51 females) recruited through an introductory psychology subject pool.

Spelling Tasks

> *Experimental Spelling Test.* [*material omitted*]
> *Wide Range Achievement Test—Spelling.* [*material omitted*]
> *Composite Spelling Performance.* [*material omitted*]

Print Exposure Measures

The Reading and Media Habits Questionnaire. The full reading and media habits questionnaire is presented in Appendix A of the original Stanovich and West (1989) paper. The reading questionnaire contained six questions that were answered by choosing one of several multiple-choice alternatives. The questions probed whether the student read for pleasure, read books in addition to those for college courses, owned a library card, subscribed to or bought magazines, visited bookstores, or read newspapers. The responses on these six questions were scored in the direction of higher scores reflecting more reading and then were summed to give a composite index of print exposure. Three open-ended items asked the subjects to name all of the magazines they subscribed to or bought regularly, name and locate the last bookstore they visited, and to name two favorite authors/writers. Four remaining questions probed television viewing habits. [*material omitted*]

The Author Recognition Test. The Author Recognition Test was explicitly designed to circumvent the problem of questionnaire contamination by tendencies toward socially desirable responses (Paulhus, 1984). This problem is particularly acute in cases like the present one where relatively educated people are being asked questions about a socially valued activity such as reading. Data to be presented below will indicate that the recognition questionnaire to be described here is a more sensitive index of exposure to print than are traditional questionnaires like the Reading Habits Questionnaire.

The logic by which the Author Recognition Test (ART) circumvents the social desirability problems inherent in most reading exposure measures is a simple, yet powerful one. In the ART subjects indicate whether or not they are familiar with the name of a particular popular author/writer by putting a check mark next to the name. There are 50 names of writers/authors on the ART. What prevents the subject from simply checking all of the names is the fact that they are mixed in with 50 foils—names of people who are not popular writers/authors. Thus, the tendency to have a low criterion for checking a name will result in the checking of foils as well as actual authors. In essence, the ART has a signal detection logic. It is a proxy measure of reading activity, obviously not intended to measure absolute levels of print exposure—as were the diary studies of children (e.g., Anderson, Wilson, & Fielding, 1988)—but instead designed as a measure reflecting relative individual differences in exposure to print. Although checklist procedures have been used before to assess print exposure (Chomsky, 1972), they have not been employed in the context of a detection-type method that uses foils to control for differential response criteria. It was hoped that this measure would prove more valid than some of the more traditional questionnaire measures; and, indeed, we will report correlations in this experiment and the next that are higher than those typically obtained with more standard questionnaire methods (Nell, 1988; Walberg & Tsai, 1984).

The 50 authors appearing on the ART are listed in Appendix B of the original Stanovich and West (1989) paper. The list is dominated by "popular" authors. That is, it is not composed of "highbrow" writers who would be known by only the most highly educated or academically inclined readers. Instead, many of the book authors regularly appear on best-seller lists and most have sold hundreds of thousands, if not millions, of volumes. Indeed, some were on the best-seller lists at the time this study was conducted. Similarly, the newspaper and magazine columnists are syndicated in hundreds of mainstream newspapers and in wide circulation magazines (e.g., *Newsweek*). Several authors have syndicated newspaper columns and have authored best-selling books (e.g., Andrew Greeley).

Circulation figures confirm that the authors on the ART are indeed popular writers. Fourteen of the 50 authors were on the *Publishers Weekly* (March 11, 1988) lists of top hardback sellers for 1987 and these 14 authors accounted for sales of over 7,172,000 hardback volumes in that year. Indeed, nine of the top 15 hardback fiction best-sellers on the 1987 list were by writers listed on the Author Recognition Test. The figures from mass-market paperback sales are even more impressive. Sixteen of the writers on the Author Recognition Test authored a mass-market paperback that sold over 1,000,000 copies in 1987. These 16 authors were responsible for 27 different books that sold over a total of over 67,000,000 copies on the paperback market. A total of 22 of the 50 writers on the ART appear on at least one of the *Publishers Weekly* (March 11, 1988) best-seller lists for 1987. These are figures for the year 1987 only. Cumulating lists from previous years would take in many more of the authors on the ART. Clearly, these circulation figures demonstrate that, for the most part, the authors on the ART produce popular works for the general public.

Although no statistical sampling of authors was carried out, an attempt was made to mix writers from a wide variety of genres. Thus, most major categories of nonfiction (e.g., sports, science, politics/current events, humor, religion, history, biography, business/finance) and fiction (e.g., mystery/detective, romance/gothic, spy/intrigue, occult/supernatural, historical novels, Westerns, short stories, science fiction) were represented. In constructing the list, authors were selected who were most likely to be encountered outside of the classroom, so that the ART would be a proxy measure of out-of-school print exposure. Thus, an attempt was made to avoid authors who are regularly studied in the school curriculum. None of the authors appears in Ravitch and Finn's (1987) survey of the high-school literature curriculum. Perhaps only James Baldwin comes close to being a "curriculum author." In short, the ART was intentionally biased toward out-of-school reading, because it was intended as an indirect measure of free-reading volume.

The 50 foils in the ART were names taken from the Editorial Board of Volume 22 (1987) of *Reading Research Quarterly*. It was thought a safe assumption that these names would be unfamiliar to any subjects in the study and, of course, few would argue that they represent "popular" authors. (Although P. E. Bryant—with 10 false alarms, the most alluring foil—would seem to have a good start on a career as a popular writer. He is already more "well-known" than his neighbor on the list, Anthony Burgess.) The 100 names were listed in alphabetical order, mixing targets and foils. Full names were used in all cases except where the individual habitually used initials (e.g., S. E. Hinton).

The instructions to the subject read as follows: "Below you will see a list of 100 names. Some of the people in the list are popular writers (of books, magazine articles, and/or newspaper columns) and some are not. You are to read the names and put a check mark next to the names of those individuals who you know to be writers. Do not guess, but only check those who you know to be writers. Remember, some of the names are people who are not popular writers, so guessing can easily be detected." These instructions resulted in only a few foils being checked. The mean number of foils checked per subject was .90. The most foils checked by any subject was 9 (one individual). But the mode was zero ($N = 35$), and 55 of the 61 subjects checked 2 foils or less. Only four foils caused three or more false alarms (Rebecca Barr, P. E. Bryant, James Flood, Robert Tierney).

For each subject, the number of correct targets identified was recorded as well as the number of foils checked. The reliability of the number of correct items checked was .84 (Cronbach's alpha). To take into account possible differential thresholds for guessing, a derived score was calculated for each subject whereby the number of foils checked was subtracted from the number of correct targets identified (Snodgrass & Corwin, 1988). This derived score was used in the analyses that follow, although it was highly correlated with the raw number of correct identifications ($r = .96$). Other corrections for guessing resulted in virtually identical correlational results.

The Magazine Recognition Test. The logic and structure of the Magazine Recognition Test (MRT) was analogous to that of the ART, but was designed to tap a possibly different type of out-of-school reading. Although, the ART contains writers whose work appears in magazines and newspapers, it is nevertheless heavily biased toward authors of books. The MRT was thus designed to balance the ART by sampling magazine reading exclusively.

[material omitted]

Results

Overall Spelling Performance and Print Exposure

The mean performance on the MRT (23.8, $SD = 6.3$) was higher than that on the ART (9.3, $SD = 5.7$), reflecting a greater recognizability for magazines.

The ability to predict overall spelling performance from print exposure depended critically on the measure of reading volume employed. The Author Recognition Test displayed a significant correlation with the composite spelling z-score ($r = -.46$, p .01; note that the negative sign occurs because the composite spelling z-score is an error measure), whereas the performance on the MRT did not ($r = -.05$). The Reading and Media Habits Questionnaire displayed little relation to spelling ability. None of the six multiple-choice questions on reading habits correlated significantly with the composite spelling z-score; nor did a composite variable that combined these six questions ($r = -.09$). However, one of the open-ended questions did display a relationship. This question asked subjects to name their two favorite authors/writers and was scored 2, 1, 0, according to whether the subject wrote down two names ($N = 37$), one name ($N = 10$) or left the question blank ($N = 14$). Interestingly, this rather crude index correlated $-.35$ ($p < .01$) with spelling ability. None of the questions involving television habits correlated with spelling ability; neither did the open-ended question that required the names of magazines regularly read or subscribed to ($r = .06$).

Table 14.1 presents a correlation matrix of variables reflecting performance on the ART, performance on the MRT, a composite of the multiple-choice questions from the Reading Habits Questionnaire, the favorite authors question, the number of magazine subscriptions, the composite spelling z-score, the number of critical errors on the WRAT, and the number of critical errors on the Experimental Spelling Test. Correlations greater than .25 are significant at the .05 level (two-tailed).

It can be seen that the five variables that are measures of print exposure generally display significant and moderate correlations with each other (median correlation = .34). However, only two of them—the ART and the favorite authors question—bear any relation to spelling performance.

The Experimental Spelling Test and Print Exposure

Table 14.2 presents the correlations among performance on the ART, performance on the favorite authors question, and the errors on the three different types of ambiguous segments on the Experimental Spelling Test. An interesting pattern emerges in this set of correlations. Both reading volume measures show higher correlations with errors on the Morphophonemic segments than with errors on the Orthographic segments and higher correlations with errors on the Exception segments than with errors on the Morphophonemic segments. The trend in the correlations is not due to differential variability. The standard deviations of the errors on the three different types of segments were

TABLE 14.1. Intercorrelations among Variables in Experiment 1

Variable	1.	2.	3.	4.	5.	6.	7.
1. Author Recognition Test							
2. Magazine Recognition Test	.36						
3. Reading Habits Composite	.38	.36					
4. Favorite Author	.33	.25	.35				
5. Magazine Subscriptions	.30	.33	.62	.17			
6. Composite Spelling z-score	−.46	−.05	−.09	−.35	.06		
7. WRAT—Critical Segment Errors	−.38	−.13	−.13	−.36	.06	.79	
8. EST—Critical Segment Errors	−.43	−.11	−.06	−.34	.02	.90	.63

TABLE 14.2. Intercorrelations among Variables

Variable	1.	2.	3.	4.
1. Author Recognition Test				
2. Favorite Author	.33			
3. Orthographic Segment Errors	−.19	−.05		
4. Morphophonemic Segment Errors	−.33	−.31	.39	
5. Exception Segment Errors	−.45	−.41	.40	.35

1.32, 1.43, and 1.39, respectively. Neither correlation involving Orthographic segments was statistically significant. A test for difference between dependent correlations (Cohen & Cohen, 1975, p. 53) indicated that the correlation involving Exception segments was significantly larger than that involving Orthographic segments for both the favorite authors question, $t(58) = 2.71$, $p < .01$, and performance on the ART, $t(58) = 2.07$, $p < .05$. Thus, the less predictable the spelling pattern from surface rules, the greater the association between performance on the pattern and print exposure.

Print Exposure Effects That Are Independent of Phonological Skill

In the Introduction we raised the issue of whether print exposure differences can be linked to variability in orthographic processing skill once phonological processing variance has been partialled. Study 2 will examine this question in considerable detail by utilizing multiple measures of each of the processing constructs. However, Study 1 does contain a crude measure of phonological coding skill in the number of nonphonetic spelling errors on the Experimental Spelling Test. This (inverse) measure of phonological coding skill was entered first into a regression equation predicting the composite spelling z-score and it explained 33.5% of the variance. When the best measure of print exposure (performance on the ART) was entered next into the regression equation, it accounted for a statistically significant 11.9% ($p < .01$) of additional variance in spelling ability.

Similar outcomes were observed when the critical errors on the WRAT and on the Experimental Spelling Test (EST) were used as criterion variables. Number of nonphonological errors accounted for 29.9% of the variance in the number of critical WRAT errors, and performance on the ART an additional 6.9% ($p < .05$). Number of nonphonological errors accounted for 21.2% of the variance on the EST critical errors, and ART performance an additional 11.2% ($p < .01$). Interestingly, ART performance did not account for significant variance in Orthographic segment errors after the number of nonphonological errors was entered, but did account for significant additional variance in Morphophonemic errors (7.3%, $p < .05$) and Exception errors (12.5%, $p < .01$), a finding consistent with the conjecture that the precision of the orthographic lexicon is at least partially determined by differences in print exposure.

All of these preliminary results do provide a tentative indication that it is possible to link variance in exposure to print not associated with phonological ability to the quality of orthographic representations. In short, orthographic processing differences might not be completely parasitic on the development of phonological processing abilities—a conjecture tested more thoroughly in our next experiment.

STUDY 2

Method

[see original paper for details of the Method]

Results

General Relationships

In order to present some of the basic descriptive statistics and to give some indication of the skill-related variability in the data, the sample was split into skilled (*N* = 84) and less-skilled (*N* = 96) readers based on performance on the Woodcock Word Identification subtest (unequal numbers of subjects resulted from tied scores). The means and standard deviations of the untransformed variables are presented in Table 14.3, along with a statistical test of the difference between the means of the two groups. From Table 14.3 it is apparent that there are differences favoring the skilled group on all of the experimental variables, and most of the differences are statistically significant.

A more complete display of all of the interrelationships among the variables in the study is displayed in Table 14.4, which presents a correlation matrix for the primary variables. Z-score composites of reaction times and errors were used to characterize performance on the orthographic choice task, phonological choice task, pseudoword naming, exception word naming, strange word naming, and combined word naming. Correlations greater than .15 are significant at the .05 level (two-tailed). Note that all measures composed of speed and/or time scores will have negative correlations with reading ability and the recognition tests.

[material omitted]

As a predictor of word recognition ability, the ART was roughly as good as most of the laboratory and spelling measures. The results of Experiment 2 replicated those of Study 1 in indicating that the ART is more strongly linked to spelling ability than the MRT—the difference between the dependent correlations of −.42 and −.11 was statistically significant ($t[177] = 4.35, p < .001$). However, Study 2 indicated that this result generalized to a wide variety of reading-related processing measures—the ART was more highly correlated with every single variable in the study.

The laboratory tasks of orthographic and phonological processing dis-

TABLE 14.3. Means and Standard Deviations (in Parentheses) for Skilled and Less-Skilled Readers

Variable	Skilled	Less-skilled	$t(178)$
Woodcock Word Identification (raw)	100.6 (1.7)	94.5 (3.6)	14.41**
Woodcock Word Identification (%)	73.9 (8.8)	45.6 (12.7)	17.08**
Woodcock Passage Comprehension (raw)	60.4 (3.8)	56.8 (4.8)	5.51**
Author Recognition Test	13.8 (6.0)	9.4 (5.6)	5.06**
Magazine Recognition Test	26.9 (6.2)	25.5 (6.6)	1.46
WRAT—Critical Errors	5.50 (2.7)	8.49 (3.6)	6.24**
EST—Critical Errors	8.25 (3.1)	10.57 (3.1)	5.04**
EST—Orthographic Errors	1.58 (1.1)	2.07 (1.5)	2.47*
EST—Morphophonemic Errors	2.42 (1.5)	3.16 (1.6)	3.20**
EST—Exception Errors	4.25 (1.5)	5.34 (1.1)	5.82**
Phonological Choice Task—RT	949 (177)	1086 (334)	3.37**
Phonological Choice Task—Errors	2.88 (2.0)	4.53 (3.1)	4.20**
Pseudoword Naming—RT	635 (126)	716 (198)	3.20**
Pseudoword Naming—Errors	0.67 (1.0)	1.78 (2.2)	4.19**
Orthographic Choice Task—RT	666 (99)	683 (103)	1.08
Orthographic Choice Task—Errors	3.74 (2.2)	4.27 (2.2)	1.62
Homophone Choice Task—RT	710 (102)	728 (114)	1.09
Homophone Choice Task—Errors	2.18 (1.7)	2.91 (2.2)	2.49*
Regular Words—RT	502 (56)	536 (80)	3.22**
Exception Words—RT	527 (68)	582 (107)	4.00**
Exception Words—Errors	0.64 (0.7)	1.04 (1.1)	2.84**
Strange Words—RT	606 (88)	672 (124)	4.02**
Strange Words—Errors	1.00 (0.92)	2.06 (1.4)	5.93**
All Words Combined—RT	537 (63)	583 (96)	3.73**
All Words Combined—Errors	1.68 (1.2)	3.27 (2.3)	5.67**

*$p < .05$; **$p < .01$.

played convergent validity. The orthographic and homophone choice z-scores displayed a correlation of .58, and the phonological choice and pseudoword z-scores displayed a correlation of .60. The four correlations among these tasks across categories were considerably lower (.29, .31, .35, .29).

Orthographic Processing as an Independent Predictor

Analyses that examined the two orthographic measures as a set (orthographic choice z-score and homophone choice z-score) indicate that they can account for significant unique variance in word processing after the phonological measures have been partialled out—but only when there are an appreciable number of irregular words in the task. For example, the orthographic measures as a set account for no unique variance in Woodcock Word Identification in a hierarchical regression by sets (see Cohen & Cohen, 1975) with phonological choice z-score and pseudoword naming z-score entered before the two orthographic measures. However, when the All Words Combined z-score was the criterion measure, the orthographic tasks accounted for significant additional variance after the two phonological tasks had been partialed out (6.7%, $p < .01$). The ability of the orthographic measures to account for variance in

TABLE 14.4. Intercorrelations among Variables in Experiment 2

Variable	1.	2.	3.	4.	5.	6.	7.	8.	9.	10.
1. Woodcock Word Identification										
2. Woodcock Passage Comp	.51									
3. Author Recognition Test	.50	.36								
4. Magazine Recognition Test	.25	.29	.45							
5. WRAT—Critical Errors	-.63	-.44	-.41	-.17						
6. EST—Critical Errors	-.50	-.26	-.31	-.04	.66					
7. Composite Spelling z-score	-.60	-.34	-.42	-.11	.82	.91				
8. Orthographic Choice z-score	-.24	-.29	-.32	-.03	.32	.33	.39			
9. Homophone Choice z-score	-.29	-.25	-.33	.00	.35	.42	.46	.58		
10. Phonological Choice z-score	-.47	-.27	-.27	-.07	.34	.32	.35	.29	.31	
11. Pseudoword Naming z-score	-.51	-.28	-.35	-.06	.50	.45	.52	.35	.29	.60
12. Regular Words—RT	-.34	-.20	-.31	-.06	.37	.28	.35	.47	.36	.42
13. Exception Words z-score	-.54	-.31	-.40	-.18	.51	.35	.45	.36	.30	.46
14. Strange Words z-score	-.60	-.43	-.45	-.26	.50	.41	.52	.42	.39	.45
15. All Words Combined z-score	-.61	-.40	-.45	-.21	.56	.43	.55	.47	.41	.50

Variable	11.	12.	13.	14.
12. Regular Words—RT	.57			
13. Exception Words z-score	.57	.69		
14. Strange Words z-score	.65	.66	.67	
15. All Words Combined z-score	.69	.77	.88	.90

the All Words Combined z-score but not Woodcock Word Identification is probably due to the fact that the former measure is based on a word set more heavily weighted with irregular words (two-thirds are irregular in some way). It is not due to the fact that it shares a speed component with the orthographic and homophone choice tasks and that Woodcock Word Identification does not. When the speed component is eliminated by using only the number of errors on regular, exception, and strange words combined as the dependent measure, the orthographic tasks still account for significant additional variance when entered as a set of predictors subsequent to the phonological measures (5.5%, $p < .01$).

Finally, after the variance associated with the two phonological tasks is partialled, the orthographic tasks account for a significant additional proportion of variance in spelling the irregular segments of the EST: Orthographic (4.1%, $p < .05$), Morphophonemic (5.0%, $p < .05$), Exception (6.9%, $p < .01$); and in spelling the critical segments on the WRAT (4.5% $p < .05$). Thus, at least when tasks are weighted with irregular words, it does seem possible to isolate orthographic processing variance independent of phonological processing abilities.

Print Exposure as an Independent Predictor

As in Study 1, performance was better on the MRT (26.2, $SD = 6.5$) than on the ART (11.5, $SD = 6.2$); although, overall, performance was somewhat better than in Study 1, probably due to the presence of more upper-level students in the second sample. Appendixes B and C of the original Stanovich and West (1989) paper list the percentage of correct recognition for each of the items on the ART and MRT.

[material omitted]

With the exception of Woodcock Passage Comprehension, for no variable was the MRT a significant predictor after performance on the ART had been entered into a regression equation, whereas the ART always accounted for significant unique variance after performance on the MRT was entered. Thus, we will focus on the ART as a measure of print exposure in the analyses that follow.

The ART is a remarkably unique predictor, consistently accounting for additional variance in word recognition skill after factors known to be strongly related to decoding skill have already been partialled out. For example, together, the phonological choice z-score and pseudoword naming z-score form a powerful set of measures of phonological coding skill. As a set, they have a multiple R with Woodcock Word Identification of .55. Nevertheless, the ART accounts for an additional 10.5% of the variance after these two phonological tasks have been entered into the regression equation ($p < .001$). Similarly, the ART accounts for significant additional variance in the All

272 THE COGNITIVE CONSEQUENCES OF LITERACY

Words Combined z-score (4.4%, $p < .001$) after the two phonological tasks have been partialled.

Tests of the uniqueness of the ART can be pushed quite far, with surprisingly positive outcomes. For example, we can add the number of non-phonological errors on the EST as an additional measure of phonological skill. When all three measures of phonological skill are in a regression equation predicting Woodcock Word Identification (multiple $R = .60$), the ART still accounts for significant additional variance (8.6%, $p < .001$).

Finally, the ART accounts for substantial unique variance even after tasks tapping both phonological and orthographic processing have been entered into a regression equation. After two phonological variables (phonological choice z-score and pseudoword naming z-score) and two orthographic variables (orthographic choice z-score and homophone choice z-score) had all been entered, the ART accounted for significant additional variance in Woodcock Word Identification performance (9.5%, $p < .001$), All Words Combined z-score (2.2%, $p < .01$), and composite spelling z-score (2.8%, $p < .01$).

Linking Variance in Print Exposure to Orthographic Processing

If orthographic processing differences are indirectly dependent upon phonological processing abilities that directly cause print exposure variance, then the ART should not account for variance in orthographic processing ability once phonological skill has been partialled. However, this prediction is repeatedly falsified in our data. Table 14.5 presents several relevant regression analyses.

[material omitted]

An interesting pattern emerges on the EST. The ART is not a unique predictor of spelling performance on the Orthographic or Morphophonemic segments, but is a unique predictor of the more irregular Exception segments. An analogous finding characterized the relationships involving the three different classes of stimuli in the word naming task. After the two phonological measures were entered as predictors of regular word naming time, performance on the ART could not significantly improve the regression. However, as a predictor of exception word z-score and strange word z-score, ART performance significantly increased the proportion of variance accounted for. Thus, the ART seems to account for more additional variance when the subject has to deal with tasks requiring a precise orthographic representation—that is, in tasks involving irregular words. Thus, there do appear to be differences in orthographic processing that are independent of phonological skill and that are in part linked to print exposure differences.

Principal Components Analysis

[material omitted]

TABLE 14.5. Unique Print Exposure Variance after Phonological Coding Variance Is Partialled Out

Dependent variable	Predictors	Multiple R	R^2 change
Orthographic Choice	Phonological Choice		
	Pseudoword Naming	.362	.131**
	Author Recognition Test	.416	.042**
Homophone Choice	Phonological Choice		
	Pseudoword Naming	.333	.111**
	Author Recognition Test	.406	.054**
Spelling: WRAT Critical Segments	Phonological Choice		
	Pseudoword Naming	.504	.254**
	Author Recognition Test	.560	.059**
Spelling: EST Orthographic Segments	Phonological Choice		
	Pseudoword Naming	.389	.151**
	Author Recognition Test	.409	.016
Spelling: EST Morphophonemic Segments	Phonological Choice		
	Pseudoword Naming	.362	.131**
	Author Recognition Test	.365	.002
Spelling: EST Exception Segments	Phonological Choice		
	Pseudoword Naming	.319	.102**
	Author Recognition Test	.379	.041**
Regular Word Naming	Phonological Choice		
	Pseudoword Naming	.577	.333**
	Author Recognition Test	.588	.013
Exception Word Naming	Phonological Choice		
	Pseudoword Naming	.587	.345**
	Author Recognition Test	.621	.040**
Strange Word Naming	Phonological Choice		
	Pseudoword Naming	.657	.431**
	Author Recognition Test	.697	.054**

$*p < .05; **p < .01.$

Do Phonological Processing and Print Exposure Jointly Account for All of the Variance in Orthographic Processing Skill?

[*material omitted*]

Do phonological processing ability and print exposure account for all of the variance in orthographic processing skill? The analyses in Table 14.6 address this question. Three tasks are employed to first extract the phonological processing variance, then both the ART and the Magazine Recognition Test are used to extract the variance associated with print exposure.

[*material omitted*]

The results consistently indicate that variability in phonological processing skill and differences in print exposure do not exhaust the reliable variance in orthographic processing.

We have made some initial attempts to analyze this independent orthographic variance, but have been largely unsuccessful. Rather than looking in

TABLE 14.6. Unique Orthographic Processing Variance after Phonological Coding and Print Exposure Variance Is Partialled Out

Dependent variable	Predictors	Multiple R	R^2 change
Woodcock Word Identification	Phonological Choice Pseudoword Naming Nonphonological Spelling Author Recognition Test	.604	.365**
	Magazine Recognition Test	.677	.094**
	WRAT Critical Segments	.735	.081**
All Words Combined Performance	Phonological Choice Pseudoword Naming Nonphonological Spelling Author Recognition Test	.714	.510**
	Magazine Recognition Test	.744	.044**
	WRAT Critical Segments	.769	.038**
All Words Combined Performance	Phonological Choice Pseudoword Naming Nonphonological Spelling Author Recognition Test	.714	.510**
	Magazine Recognition Test	.744	.044**
	Orthographic Choice Task	.759	.023**
Spelling: WRAT Critical Segments	Phonological Choice Pseudoword Naming Nonphonological Spelling Author Recognition Test	.625	.391**
	Magazine Recognition Test	.657	.041**
	EST Critical Segments	.751	.132**
Spelling: EST Critical Segments	Phonological Choice Pseudoword Naming Nonphonological Spelling Author Recognition Test	.548	.301**
	Magazine Recognition Test	.562	.015
	Homophone Choice Task	.594	.037**
Homophone Choice Task	Phonological Choice Pseudoword Naming Nonphonological Spelling Author Recognition Test	.434	.188**
	Magazine Recognition Test	.492	.054**
	Orthographic Choice	.645	.174**

*$p < .05$; **$p < .01$.

the visual domain for the underlying sources of orthographic processing ability differences, it may be more fruitful to pursue Frith's (1980, 1985) hypothesis that such problems may result from a habitual shallow and nonanalytic processing style when encountering words. For example, it might be informative to examine the performance of individuals with orthographic processing problems but without phonological coding difficulties or inadequate print exposure on refined measures of contextual facilitation of word recognition (Stanovich, Nathan, West, & Vala-Rossi, 1985; Stanovich & West, 1983a).

Discrepancies between Reading Comprehension Ability and Print Exposure

Since the ART was such a potent predictor of word processing ability, it is interesting to speculate about the cognitive implications of a mismatch between reading comprehension ability and amount of print exposure.

[*material omitted*]

The results in Table 14.7 are easy to summarize. The word processing performance of individuals high in print exposure but relative low in reading comprehension ability is superior to that of individuals high in reading comprehension ability but with little print exposure. This analysis again confirms the diagnosticity of the ART as a proxy measure of print exposure differences that in part determine word processing efficiency.

DISCUSSION

The experiments reported here seem to have accomplished two things: (1) We appear to have been successful in developing a measure of print exposure that can account for word processing variance not explained by phonological factors. (2) It is suggested that some of the nonphonological variance accounted for by print exposure is linked to individual differences in orthographic processing. We will take up each of these conclusions in turn.

TABLE 14.7. Differences between Subjects with Low Comprehension Ability but High Print Exposure ($N = 41$) and Subjects with High Comprehension Ability but Low in Print Exposure ($N = 34$)

Variable	Locom/Hiprint	Hicom/Loprint	$t(73)$
Woodcock Passage Comprehension	56.4	61.7	10.97†
Author Recognition Test	15.7	7.3	11.65*
Woodcock Word Identification	98.0	96.7	1.64
Magazine Recognition Test	28.4	24.8	3.06*
WRAT—Critical Errors	7.05	6.91	.18
EST—Critical Errors	9.22	9.82	.87
EST—Nonphonological Errors	.32	.88	2.08*
Composite Spelling z-score	−.117	.011	.68
Phonological Choice Task z-score	−.218	.163	2.14*
Pseudoword Naming z-score	−.255	.155	2.81*
Orthographic Choice Task z-score	−.179	−.022	1.15
Homophone Choice Task z-score	−.158	.083	1.96
Regular Words—RT	508	536	2.02*
Exception Words z-score	−.165	.148	2.02*
Strange Words z-score	−.167	.061	1.55
All Words Combined z-score	−.184	.145	2.09*

* Significant difference favoring Locom/Hiprint.
† Significant difference favoring Hicom/Loprint.

There is little doubt that scores on the ART are a relatively potent and unique predictor of reading and spelling ability. Study 1 and 2 both demonstrated the ability of ART performance to predict variance in spelling ability—particularly the ability to spell irregular words—after the substantial variance due to differences in phonological coding ability had been partialled out. Study 2 demonstrated that this conclusion also holds for word recognition performance.

It is important to emphasize, however, that although our analyses have focused on linking print exposure variance to orthographic processing, we are not arguing that the effect of print exposure is restricted to print-specific processing. To the contrary, the ART had significant correlations with all the phonological measures in the studies; in the principle components analysis the ART had moderate loadings on both the orthographic and the phonological factors; and phonological processing superiority was also indicated for the Locomop/Hiprint group in Table 14.7. It is quite likely that fully operative decoding processes depend on extensive experience with how the orthography maps phonology (Perfetti, 1992). Conversely, as mentioned in the introduction, it is likely that efficiently functioning decoding processes make reading more pleasurable and lead directly to more extensive reading. Thus, we have taken the bidirectional linkage between print exposure and phonological processing as a basic assumption and have focused our efforts on relating print exposure to orthographic processing variance not linked to phonological processing abilities.

While the ART was a potent predictor, the logically analogous MRT was a much weaker correlate. It is not presently clear what to make of this difference. Potential explanations for the differential predictiveness are not hard to generate. For example, it could be relevant that the ART contains a sizable number of book authors. Previous studies have found book reading to be a better predictor of various educational outcomes than magazine or comic book reading (Anderson, Wilson, & Fielding, 1988; Greaney, 1980; Kirsch & Jungeblut, 1986; Nell, 1988). The differences in the present studies could be the result of differences in depth of processing across types of reading material. Alternatively, encounters with magazines may be more haphazard, more likely to occur through the electronic media or in public places such as doctors' offices.

However, it may not be necessary to invoke such explanations. Since these were the first versions of both print exposure scales, it is possible that the selection of items on the ART was simply more judicious. This possibility is consistent with subsequent pilot work with revised versions of both instruments where psychometrically poor items were removed or replaced. Although no data is available on tasks comparable to those in this study, the revised version of the MRT appears to be able to predict vocabulary differences as well as the ART.

It is interesting that in Study 1 the multiple-choice measures of book reading on the Reading and Media Habits Questionnaire did not display the same link with spelling ability as did the ART. One indication that it is so-cial desirability that may be distinguishing the ART from traditional ques-tionnaires as a measure of print exposure comes from the only item on the Reading and Media Habits Questionnaire to show a relation to spelling ability—an open-ended question asking the respondent to write down the names of their two favorite authors. Like the ART, but unlike multiple-choice formats, this is somewhat of a performance measure—it cannot be faked. Either the subjects can think of two names of authors or they cannot. Similar to the ART—but unlike multiple-choice questions—guessing is not a useful strategy.

The convergence of the ART with this item, and the divergence of these two measures from the other indicators, supports the conjecture that they both are more valid indicators of print exposure because they are less contam-inated by social desirability factors. Indeed, there is little doubt that, for what-ever reasons, people overestimate their reading ability and exaggerate their tendencies to read (see Ennis, 1965; Sharon, 1973–1974).

[material omitted]

The diagnosticity of the ART was confirmed in our comparison of outlier subjects: those high in reading comprehension ability and low in print expo-sure versus those low in reading comprehension and high in print exposure. It was the high print exposure subjects who had the superior word-level process-ing skills, despite being less skilled in certain postlexical text processing opera-tions (inferred from their reading comprehension performance).

Analyses conducted with the ART indicated that some of the substantial variance in print exposure that is independent of phonological ability is partially linked to individual differences in orthographic processing. If all or-thographic processing differences are indirectly dependent on phonological processing abilities that directly cause print exposure variance, then print ex-posure differences should not account for orthographic variance once phono-logical skill has been partialled. This prediction appears to have been falsified. If print exposure differences simply tracked how skilled the readers were at phonological coding, then the ART should not serve as a unique predictor of variance in orthographic processing—but in fact it does.

It should be noted, however, that the residual print exposure variance is not linked *only* with orthographic processing, because the ART accounted for significant reading and spelling variance after *both* phonological and ortho-graphic measures were entered into regression equations. This is probably be-cause the ART taps vocabulary knowledge as well as phonological and ortho-graphic processing factors. Specifically, some of the words contained on the Woodcock, on the All Words Combined reaction time measure, and on the spelling tests are so infrequent that they are probably unknown to some of the subjects. One would commit errors on all these tasks, regardless of the effi-ciency of one's phonological skills, if some of the words were unfamiliar. The ART probably taps this overall word knowledge and thus predicts even more variance than can be accounted for by phonological and orthographic processing.

Our study demonstrated, in the orthographic domain, how reading might itself develop skills and knowledge bases that then serve to enable more efficient subsequent reading. Individual differences in print exposure are now being identified as a potent source of the developmental increase in the variance in certain knowledge bases such as vocabulary (Anderson et al., 1988; Hayes, 1988; Hayes & Ahrens, 1988; Nagy & Anderson, 1984; Stanovich, 1986b). We are just beginning to understand the cognitive mechanisms by which reading volume differences act to create rich-get-richer and poor-get-poorer effects in educational achievement.

CHAPTER 15

Does Reading Make You Smarter?

Literacy and the Development
of Verbal Intelligence

I. INTRODUCTION

What role do experiential differences play in determining variation in cognitive growth? This question has been at the heart of much theorizing in developmental psychology. Enthusiasm for experiential explanations of differences in cognitive growth has waxed and waned over the years, as has interest in explanations based on genetic inheritance. For example, interest in genetic determinants of differences in cognitive skills increased considerably in the 1980s (Plomin, DeFries, & McClearn, 1990; Thompson, Detterman, & Plomin, 1991), and some once-popular experiential hypotheses went out of favor altogether. Theories in which literacy is posited to be a determinate of individual differences in cognitive growth provide a case in point. Differential experience with print was once an important mechanism in many theories of cognitive change (Greenfield, 1972; Olson, 1977). In the 1980s, the idea that the acquisition of literacy has profound cognitive consequences went seriously out of favor (Erickson, 1984; Gee, 1988; Scribner & Cole, 1981; Street, 1984, 1988).

In this chapter, I argue that we should reconsider experience with print as an explanatory mechanism that can account for cognitive change. My argument begins with a review of selected literature on the consequences of literacy in which I claim that a role for reading experience in theories of cognitive change seems to have been prematurely dismissed. I then introduce a methodology for studying the cognitive consequences of literacy within a literate society that could help to revive research interest in this hypothesis.

II. THE RISE OF THE "GREAT DIVIDE" THEORIES

Theories in which literate and nonliterate individuals and societies are posited to exhibit important cognitive differences have been termed "Great Divide" theories (Erickson, 1984; Olson & Torrance, 1991; Scribner & Cole, 1981). As will be discussed below, in the 1980s the term was most often used pejoratively (e.g., Street, 1984). Great Divide theories can be partitioned according to whether they are primarily concerned with the indirect, mediated effects of literacy—habits of thought derived through cultural immersion in a literate society—or the direct, nonmediated effects of literacy on a particular individual's cognitive processes and knowledge structures (Goody, 1987; Scribner & Cole, 1978). For example, illiterates, or people who engage only marginally in literacy activities, may derive certain cognitive benefits from participation in a literate culture. These have been termed the mediated effects of literacy (Goody, 1987, pp. 217–252), and anthropologists and historians have done much work to assess these culturally mediated consequences of literacy. In contrast, psychologists have been more concerned with examining the individual effects of having personally engaged in reading/writing activities (Scribner & Cole, 1978, 1981).

Great Divide theorists are further differentiated according to whether they posit a continuous range of effects—that is, effects that are linked to variation in print-related activities that exist even within literate populations. Greenfield's seminal (1972) work provides a case in point. Based on her cross-cultural research in Africa, Greenfield (1972) posited that facility with written language developed a set of cognitive competencies that were more elaborate than those associated with purely oral language. Her argument was based on the differences in context dependency between written and oral language:

> If a speaker of an oral language depends upon the surrounding context to communicate his message, then effective communication presupposes a common context and common point of view for both listener and speaker. The speaker, moreover, must assume that this is the case. He is, therefore, egocentric. . . . Speech based on a written language, in contrast, must be relatively independent of context for a number of reasons. (p. 170)

The central thesis of Greenfield's argument was that "context-dependent speech is tied up with context-dependent thought, which in turn is the opposite of abstract thought" (p. 169). Greenfield outlined several examples of how context-independent language fosters abstract thought and problem solving. Although most of her discussion derived from her work done among the Wolof of Senegal, Greenfield (1972) extended her hypotheses to encompass cultural subgroups in the United States who were not illiterate but who had less exposure to written language. That is, she championed a continuous version of the Great Divide hypothesis by positing that differences in degrees of print exposure within even a generally literate society also have cognitive consequences.

Greenfield's hypotheses concerning the direct effects of literacy on an individual reader's cognition paralleled theories of the effects of literacy at the societal level that were popular among anthropologists and historians (Akinnaso, 1981; Goody, 1977, 1987; Havelock, 1963, 1980; Musgrove, 1982; Ong, 1967, 1982). Goody's influential writings (1977, 1980; Goody & Watt, 1968) contain hypotheses about the effects of literacy at the level of societies and cultures rather than individuals:

> The specific proposition is that writing, and more especially alphabetic literacy, made it possible to scrutinise discourse in a different kind of way by giving oral communication a semi-permanent form; this scrutiny favored the increase in scope of critical activity, and hence rationality, scepticism, and logic to resurrect memories of those questionable dichotomies. It increased the potentialities of criticism because writing laid out discourse before one's eyes in a different way; at the same time increased the potentiality for cumulative knowledge, especially knowledge of an abstract kind, because it changed the nature of communication beyond that of face-to-face contact as well as the system for the storage of information; in this way a wider range of "thought" was made available to the reading public. . . . [It] enabled man to stand back from his creation and examine it in a more abstract, generalised, and rational way. (1977, p. 37)

Elaborations of this argument have echoed throughout the anthropological and historical literature on the effects of literacy (Havelock, 1963, 1980; Musgrove, 1982; Ong, 1982). Ong (1982) made the case for the cognitive effects of literacy most strongly: "Without writing, the literate mind would not and could not think as it does, not only when engaged in writing but normally even when it is composing its thoughts in oral form. More than any other single invention, writing has transformed human consciousness" (p. 78). The causal mechanism emphasized by Ong (1982) was a variant on the Goody/ Greenfield theme: "Writing fosters abstractions that disengage knowledge from the arena where human beings struggle with one another. It separates the knower from the known" (pp. 43–44).

Olson (1977, 1986b, 1988) has presented a related causal theory of how literacy comes to influence thought. In his important 1977 essay Olson contrasted texts (written prose statements) with utterances (informal oral-language statements). His thesis—which he made clear was intended to apply to both the societal and individual consequences of literacy—was that: "There is a transition from utterance to text both culturally and developmentally and this transition can be described as one of increasing explicitness, with language increasingly able to stand as an unambiguous or autonomous representation of meaning" (p. 258). Olson emphasized the importance of the assumption that meaning resides autonomously within the text and "the consequences of that assumption, particularly of the attempts to make it true" (p. 258). The highest form of the autonomous text ideal is the essayist technique: "The more fundamental effects of this approach to text was on the writer, whose task now was to create autonomous text—to write in such a manner that the sentence was an adequate, explicit representation of the meaning, relying on no implicit premises or personal interpretations" (p. 268). He argued that

> logical development in a literate culture involves learning to apply logical operations to the sentence meaning rather than to the assimilated or interpreted or assumed speaker's meaning. Development consists of learning to confine interpretation to the meaning explicitly represented in the text and to draw inferences exclusively from that formal but restricted interpretation. . . . The developmental hypothesis offered here is that the ability to assign a meaning to the sentence per se, independent of its nonlinguistic interpretive context, is achieved only well into the school years. (pp. 274–275)

Hypotheses of the type put forth by Greenfield, Goody, and Olson came to be termed "Great Divide Theories" because of the number and importance of the cognitive consequences of literacy that were assumed. Among these were:

> Logical and analytic modes of thought; general and abstract uses of language; critical and rational thought; a skeptical and questioning attitude; a distinction between myth and history; the recognition of the importance of time and space; complex and modern governments (with separation of church and state); political democracy and greater social equity; economic development. . . . It leads to people who are innovative, achievement oriented, productive, cosmopolitan, politically aware, more globally (nationally and internationally) oriented. (Gee, 1988, p. 196)

III. GREAT DIVIDE THEORIES UNDER ATTACK

By the late 1970s and early 1980s the Great Divide position had garnered considerable support and momentum. However, by the late 1980s the situation had changed drastically. By then, many scholars had accepted Graff's (1979, 1986, 1987) characterization of the Great Divide theory as the "literacy myth" and Gee (1988) was claiming that "at least in academic circles, the literacy myth is on its last legs" (p. 196). What happened to cause such a rapid and extreme theoretical reversal?

Not surprisingly, a number of interacting factors acted in concert to cause the collapse of the "literacy myth." First, literacy's effects at the societal level were brought into question by historical studies indicating that literacy was intertwined with certain cultural effects in a much more intricate and interactive way than was implied by some of the simpler theories that emphasized unidirectional causation. For example, the link between economic development and national levels of literacy has turned out to be much more complex than originally thought. Literacy levels are as much a consequence of economic development as they are its cause (Fuller, Edwards, & Gorman, 1987; Graff, 1986, 1987; Kaestle, 1991; Wagner, 1987).

The plausibility of literacy having an effect on cognition at the level of individuals has also been questioned. Some researchers have questioned the distinctions between utterance and text that served as the guiding assumptions of Great Divide theorizing. Clearly, for example, oral speech in formalized settings can contain all the features associated with written text: detachment, certain types of subordination, integration, nominalization (Biber, 1986; Chafe & Danielewicz, 1987; Feldman, 1991; Nystrand, 1987; Redeker, 1984; Tannen, 1982). Similarly, written texts need not always contain these features. Thus, utterances can sometimes have the characteristics of text and vice versa. Acceptance of the idea that the features of utterance and text that were allegedly responsible for differential cognitive effects were different only probabilistically rather than in a discrete sense had the effect of making the "divide" seem less "great."

Adding to these second thoughts about the consequences of literacy was a radical social critique that conceived of literacy as just one more mechanism used by powerful groups to maintain social privilege. For example, Street (1984) claimed that "the actual examples of literacy in different societies that are available to us suggest that it is more often 'restrictive' and hegemonic, and concerned with instilling discipline and exercising social control" (p. 4), and that "schooling and techniques of teaching literacy are often forms of hegemony" (p. 11). Another author titled her book *The Violence of Literacy* and argued that American society "stakes much on the oppressive powers of literacy" (Stuckey, 1991, p. 30) and that "it is possible that a system of ownership built on the ownership of literacy is more violent than past systems, however. Though it seems difficult to surpass the violence of systems of indenture, slavery, industrialism, and the exploitation of immigrant or migrant labor, literacy provides a unique bottleneck" (p. 18). Gee (1988) echoed the argument that "literacy has been used, in age after age, to solidify the social hierarchy, empower elites, and ensure that people lower in the hierarchy accept the values, norms and beliefs of the elites, even when it is not in their self-interest" (p. 205).

In short, the social effects of literacy are no longer universally viewed as positive—at least by some educational theorists. Great Divide theories seemed, to these same scholars, to be a case par excellence of blaming the victims. Thus, the popular social critiques of the 1980s were used as weapons against any theory of the consequences of literacy that posited substantial cognitive effects following from differential engagement in literacy activities. Because people *do* differentially engage in literacy activities, any such effects were bound to create cognitive inequalities that most neo-Marxist and socioconstructivist theorists were committed to denying. Great Divide theories ran straight into the brick wall of cultural and epistemological relativism that was a foundational assumption of these social critiques (for discussions, see Gellner, 1985; Hollis & Lukes, 1982; Musgrove, 1982; Shweder, 1991; Siegel, 1988; Sperber, 1985). The critiques seemed to rest on the tenuous assumption that literacy creates enormous sociopolitical differences that are not associated with any concomitant cognitive differences.

IV. THE DEATH BLOW TO GREAT DIVIDE THEORIES: SCRIBNER AND COLE

Thus, a confluence of academic critiques in the 1980s undermined hypotheses about the effects of literacy. However, another factor was probably more influential than all the academic critiques combined. This factor was the investigation into literacy effects among the Vai in Africa by Scribner and Cole (1981).

The work of Scribner and Cole provides one of the firmest foundations for the assaults on the "literacy myth" and it is repeatedly cited in critiques of Great Divide theories:

> In the Scribner and Cole study, literacy in and of itself led to no grandiose cognitive abilities. (Gee, 1988, p. 203)

> The Vai findings caution us against such generalizations as are often made: that writing promotes general mental abilities. (Akinnaso, 1981, p. 175)

> Cole and Scribner point toward an interpretation that contradicts the usual view that literacy leads inevitably to higher forms of thought. . . . Such research may also control the assumptions and expectations that students carry to studies of literacy—such as presupposing literacy to be "liberating" or "revolutionary" in its consequences. There are, I suggest, better reasons to expect the opposite to be more often the case. (Graff, 1987, pp. 23–24)

> Scribner and Cole (1981) conclude that literacy per se contributes only marginally to cognitive development. (Nystrand, 1987, p. 236)

Scribner and Cole's investigation was groundbreaking because they sought to separate the effects of literacy from the effects of schooling. The confounding of these two factors in earlier research (e.g., Greenfield, 1972; Luria, 1976) rendered tenuous any conclusions about the effects of literacy per se. Scribner and Cole took advantage of the fact that three scripts are in use among the Vai and that each script is associated with a particular context. English is learned in school and is used in formal settings (e.g., dealings with the government); Arabic is used for reading, writing, and memorizing the Koran; and an indigenous Vai script is transmitted outside of institutional settings and is used in personal correspondence and for some business purposes. Although some of the Vai are fluent in multiple scripts and some are illiterate, the fact that some individuals are familiar with only one script allows the separation of schooling effects from literacy effects. The comparison of Vai monoliterates with illiterates and individuals schooled in English is particularly diagnostic.

Scribner and Cole found no specific effect of Vai literacy on a number of tasks tapping general cognitive processes, including geometric sorting tasks, taxonomic categorization tasks, memory tasks, and syllogistic reasoning problems. Scribner and Cole concluded that "effects of nonschooled literacies are spotty and appear on only a few performance measures. . . . These surely disappoint the grand expectations and lofty theories that inspired us to undertake this line of investigation" (pp. 130–132). The authors further argued that the findings "lay to rest some misconceptions about the psychology of literacy that went unchallenged in the past for lack of empirical data. First, it is clear from the evidence we reviewed that nonschooled literacy, as we found and tested it among the Vai, does not produce general cognitive effects as we have defined them. The small and selective nature of Vai script and Arabic influences on cognitive performance precludes any sweeping generalizations about literacy and cognitive change" (p. 132). Only when Scribner and Cole changed the focus of their research program to metalinguistic tasks more tightly and specifically linked to reading and writing (e.g., grammatical judgment, rebus reading, integrating syllables) did they find any specific effects of Vai literacy.

Despite the existence of some "spotty effects" (p. 244), Scribner and Cole's summary conclusion has been accepted by many investigators:

> Our results are in direct conflict with persistent claims that "deep psychological differences" divide literate and nonliterate populations. On no task—logic, abstraction, memory, communication—did we find all nonliterates performing at lower levels than all literates. Even on tasks closely related to script activities, such as reading or writing with pictures, some nonliterates did as well as those with school or literacy experiences. We can and do claim that literacy promotes skills among the Vai, but we cannot and do not claim that literacy is a necessary and sufficient condition for any of the skills assessed. (p. 251)

One indirect effect of the widespread acceptance of interpretations of the Scribner and Cole results was that in the 1980s very few cognitive and developmental psychologists conducted empirical studies on the individual consequences of literacy. The seeming conclusiveness of the Scribner and Cole investigation and the difficulty of conducting studies on these issues dampened enthusiasm for new empirical investigations of the effects of literacy. In the rest of this chapter, I reopen the issue, first by arguing that the consensus against the idea of profound cognitive consequences of literacy was arrived at too hastily and then by introducing a methodology for studying the cognitive consequences of literacy within a generally literate society.

V. PREMATURE CLOSURE ON THE CONSEQUENCES OF LITERACY?

Although acknowledging the groundbreaking nature of the Scribner and Cole project, I still would point out that their results are often overinterpreted in the literature on literacy. A major issue that is often glossed over—but that, interestingly, was raised by Scribner and Cole themselves—is whether the nature of Vai literacy was such that it provided a valid test of the claims of Great Divide theorists. Olson (1977), for example, was clear that the literacy on which he staked his claim is the high-level literacy characterized by the use of an essayist style. Goody (1987, p. 252), in his argument for the cultural effects of literacy, was also clear that he referred to the type of literacy that enables the reader to have access to a wide range of the world's accumulated knowledge. Vai literacy is simply not of this type. Individuals typically do not learn the Vai script until their late teens or twenties. It is used primarily for personal letter writing among people who know each other and for conducting business with those with whom one is familiar. Vai writing does not contain the autonomous essayist form that Olson (1977) argued is the causal mechanism that spurs cognitive change. Instead, the letter writing that looms so large in the society of Vai-script literates is highly personalized—assuming elaborate shared knowledge between the letter writer and the recipient (Scribner & Cole, 1981, pp. 71–75). Finally, the Vai have no libraries in this script that can be used by individuals to access the world's storehouse of knowledge.

Scribner and Cole themselves admitted that "literate practices among the Vai are far more restricted than in technologically sophisticated societies. . . . Cultural heritage is transmitted orally in a way that does not depend upon texts. . . . It does not open doors to vicarious experience, new bodies of knowledge, or new ways of thinking about major life problems" (p. 238). They flatly conceded that "Vai script literacy does not fulfill the expectations of those social scientists who consider literacy a prime mover in social change" (p. 239). This admission is most often omitted in the discussions by authors who use Scribner and Cole's work to attack the "literacy myth." Theorists who refer to Scribner and Cole's work often put forth their interpretations without the qualifications introduced by the original authors—another case of prophets' disciples being more fanatical than the prophets themselves. In short, Scribner and Cole's research—influential and provocative though it was—should not be considered the final word on the issue of the cognitive consequences of literacy, although surely it would be foolish not to build on their insights.

VI. STUDYING THE DIRECT CONSEQUENCES OF LITERACY WITHIN A LITERATE SOCIETY

A. Introduction

Unfortunately, Scribner and Cole's innovative and costly project is unlikely to be replicated, so that resolving the issues using a variant of their methodology is not going to be possible. However, the cognitive consequences of literacy can be studied without necessarily using a cross-cultural comparison. I will describe here a procedure for studying the cognitive consequences of literacy within a generally literate society. In developing the procedure, we exploited the fact that even within a generally literate culture, individuals vary tremendously in degree of exposure to print (Anderson, Wilson, & Fielding, 1988;

Guthrie & Greaney, 1991; Guthrie & Seifert, 1983). Even among a group of individuals who have the same level of assessed reading comprehension ability, remarkably large differences are found in their degree of engagement in print-related activities (Stanovich & West, 1989) and the correlates of this natural variation can be studied. Comparing literates and illiterates is the exclusive design of choice only if the effects of literacy are believed to be completely discontinuous—with no cognitive consequences of variation in amount of print exposure among literate individuals. We speculate that the discontinuity assumption is false and that there is measurable cognitive variation among people who differ only in the amount of reading that they do.

In choosing which variables to focus on in our initial investigations, my research group was again influenced by the outcomes of Scribner and Cole's investigation. In a sense, we started where Scribner and Cole finished. That is, in the first part of their investigation, they concentrated on looking for effects of literacy on tasks that tapped developmental change in general cognitive processes. The tasks in the second part of their investigation—rebus reading, integrating auditory information, word pronunciation, and communication games—were more closely tied to aspects of Vai literacy and specific effects of literacy on these tasks were easier to demonstrate. In our research program on the cognitive consequences of differences in print exposure, we have inverted the investigative chronology of Scribner and Cole by starting with tasks that are more closely linked to literacy skills. Contingent upon positive outcomes in these domains, we have examined more general cognitive processes. Thus, we established our methodology (see Stanovich & West, 1989) by examining criterion variables—orthographic knowledge and spelling—that should clearly be linked to individual differences in print exposure. We then expanded the set of criterion variables to encompass broader domains such as vocabulary, cultural knowledge, and verbal fluency.

B. The Research Strategy

In our methodology, we attempted to correlate differential engagement in reading activities with various cognitive outcomes that have been associated with the acquisition of literacy. However, such an experimental logic, if not supplemented with additional methodological controls, will yield data subject to an inordinately large number of alternative explanations. Levels of print exposure are correlated with too many other cognitive and behavioral characteristics. Avid readers tend to be different from nonreaders on a wide variety of cognitive skills, behavioral habits, and background variables (Guthrie, Schafer, & Hutchinson, 1991; Kaestle, 1991; Zill & Winglee, 1991). Attributing any particular outcome to print exposure uniquely is thus extremely difficult.

We have utilized a hierarchical regression logic first introduced by Anderson, Wilson, and Fielding (1988) to deal with this problem. The logic of the regression analysis allows any control variables entered first into the regression equation to explain any variance that they can in the criterion variable. Following these control variables, the measures of print exposure are entered. Thus, the procedure allows the the investigator to assess whether reliable variance remains to be explained after the control variables are entered and whether print exposure is associated with this remaining variance. In our analyses, we first regressed out ability measures most likely to lead to spurious relationships before examining the linkage between print exposure and criterion variables.

This procedure of reducing possible spurious relationships by first partialing relevant ability measures was used in our early investigations of subword processes in reading. For example, in previous work we had demonstrated that, independently of decoding ability, variation in print exposure among adults predicts variation in specific types of orthographic knowledge (Stanovich & West, 1989). Similarly, in a study of children's performance (Cunningham & Stanovich, 1990) we found that after partialing out IQ, memory ability, and phonological processing abilities, print exposure accounted for significant variance in orthographic knowledge and word recognition. The logic of our analytic strategy is quite conservative because in certain analyses we have actually partialed out variance in abilities that are likely to be developed by print exposure itself (Stanovich, 1986b). However, the explanatory ambiguities surrounding a variable such as print exposure have led us to continue to structure the analyses in a "worst case" manner, as far as print exposure is concerned.

C. Assessing Print Exposure: The Diary Technique

A variety of methods have been used to assess individual differences in exposure to print. For example, a variety of questionnaire and interview techniques have been used to assess relative differences in print exposure (e.g., Estes, 1971; Guthrie, 1981; Guthrie & Greaney, 1991; Guthrie & Seifert, 1983; Lewis & Teale, 1980; Sharon, 1973–1974; Walberg & Tsai, 1984), but many of these are encumbered with reliability and validity problems. A more valid method—but also a more logistically complicated one—is the use of daily activity diaries filled out by subjects (Anderson et al., 1988; Greaney, 1980; Greaney & Hegarty, 1987; Rice, 1986; Taylor, Frye, & Maruyama, 1990). Activity diaries yield estimates of the actual amount of time spent on literacy activities and are generally more valid than interview or questionnaire instruments (Carp & Carp, 1981).

Anderson et al. (1988) utilized the activity diary method to estimate the amount of time that fifth-graders (10–11 year-olds) spent reading in their nonschool hours. They found that time spent reading predicted fifth-grade reading comprehension after the variance in second-grade (7–8 year-olds) reading comprehension had been controlled. This result seems to indicate that exposure to print was a contributor to individual differences in growth in reading ability over the elementary school years. My research group has completed a series of investigations in which we attempted to determine whether the specific correlates of print exposure can be extended beyond the demonstration by Anderson et al. (1988). We have employed the activity diary method in some of our own studies.

Our method of collecting daily activity records was adapted from the nonschool time diary investigation of Anderson et al. (1988), but we also attempted to improve on their methods in several respects (see Allen, Cipielewski, & Stanovich, 1992). Our daily activity record-keeping procedure was designed to minimize the time students would need to spend on it; to minimize the necessity for adding and subtracting minutes or converting hours into minutes; and to maximize student judgment accuracy. We collected data over a 3-week period and thus obtained estimates of the average number of minutes per day that the children in our fifth-grade (10–11 year-old) sample spent in various activities when they were outside of school.

Table 15.1 shows the mean and median minutes per day spent during the nonschool hours in the various categories of activity that were listed on the activity records (with the exception of All Reading, which is a composite of the categories book reading, comic reading, and other reading). The figure for book reading in the table includes only those instances in which the child could give at least a fragment of the title or a character from the book (a procedure adapted from Anderson et al., 1988). In contrast, All Reading, the most liberal category, included all instances where book reading was indicated on the diary sheets.

The fact that the means were generally larger than the medians reflects the positive skew of most of the variables, particularly the reading variables. The positive skew of reading time has repeatedly been observed in activity di-

TABLE 15.1. Minutes Spent per Day in Various Activities by a Fifth-Grade Sample[a]

Activity	Mean	Median	SD
All reading	21.3	16.0	19.4
Reading books	10.2	5.0	15.0
Reading comics	2.1	0.0	4.0
Other reading	5.8	3.5	8.4
Television watching	83.2	68.0	65.5
Eating	52.9	54.6	19.1
Homework	49.0	45.0	26.9
Just playing around	35.7	26.0	32.7
Playing outdoor games	25.7	18.0	25.2
Talking	17.0	13.6	12.9
Family activities	18.0	13.9	18.2
Playing indoor games	14.5	8.6	19.1
Practices	14.3	8.0	18.4
Hobbies	7.9	0.0	17.5
Chores	6.6	5.0	6.4
Lessons	4.5	0.0	7.0
Other	62.6	60.0	35.0

[a]Allen, Cipielewski, and Stanovich (1992). Weekdays and weekends are proportionately represented.

ary studies (Anderson et al., 1988; Greaney, 1980). Although some of our categories were different from those of the Anderson et al. (1988) study, those that were common were ordered similarly in the two studies. For example, television watching was the most frequent activity and book reading was far down the list in both studies. Our fifth-graders watched less television (83.2 min versus 131.1 min) and did more homework (49.0 min versus 18.9 min) than the Anderson et al. fifth-graders. These differences might reflect the use of different populations—a private school in our study, public schools in the Anderson et al. (1988) study. Previous studies have shown private/public school differences in television and homework habits (Coleman, Hoffer, & Kilgore, 1982).

Despite differences in the estimates in other categories, our estimates of book reading time (mean and median of 10.2 and 5.0 min, respectively) are very close to those obtained in the Anderson et al. study (10.1 and 4.6 min). Certain rough generalizations thus hold across the two studies: fifth-graders (10–11 year-olds) spend around 5 minutes per night reading books for pleasure outside of school, roughly one-tenth the amount of time they spend watching television. These figures call to mind the many studies of school achievement in which American children scored poorly and in which their poor performance was linked to excessive television watching, low levels of homework, and little reading (Applebee, Langer, & Mullis, 1988; Chen & Stevenson, 1989; Stevenson, Stigler, Lee, Lucker, Kitamura, & Hsu, 1985).

Our specific concern, however, was whether children's reading volume related to their achievement and whether such a linkage could be shown to have any specificity. Book reading time (logarithmically transformed; see Allen et al., 1992; Anderson et al., 1988) correlated .39 with a standardized test of vocabulary knowledge. We attempted a further assessment of the specificity of the relation between book reading and vocabulary development by conducting a hierarchical regression analysis in which the standardized vocabulary test was the criterion measure and in which performance on a standardized mathematics test was forced into the equation first as a control for general school learning ability. When entered second, book reading time explained an additional 9.7% of the variance and this unique variance explained was statistically significant ($p < .01$). Thus, the linkage between vocabulary and book reading time remains even when variability in general academic performance is partialed out.

D. Assessing Print Exposure: The Recognition Checklist Technique

In the study described in section VI.C we employed a comprehensive activity recording methodology in which children accounted for all of their out-of-school time over a period of 3 weeks. This methodology provides not only estimates of relative differences in print exposure among children, but also estimates of the actual amount of time (in minutes per day) spent on literacy activities. However, the measurement of absolute amounts of reading activity and the methodologies used to achieve such measurement have a number of associated problems. First, the daily activity diary methodology requires extensive cooperation from teachers and students. Children must record, either at the end of the day or on the following morning, their activities from the day before and these recordings must be checked by a teacher or other adult to assure that the scale is being used properly. Such a level of participant involvement may discourage many investigators from using the technique.

An additional problem is that the retrospective estimation of periods of time is a notoriously difficult task, even for adults (Bradburn, Rips, & Shevell, 1987; Burt & Kemp, 1991). This difficulty places some limits on how valid such estimates can be, even for a group of conscientious and well-motivated children. Finally, social desirability is a potential confound: responses may be distorted because of tendencies to over-report socially desirable behaviors (Furnham, 1986; Paulhus, 1984)—in this case, to report more reading than actually takes place. Independent evidence indicates that social desirability does distort self-reports of book reading by adults (Ennis, 1965; Sharon, 1973–1974; Zill & Winglee, 1990). The extent to which it is a factor in children's self-reports of reading time is unknown.

However, the correlates of differential exposure to print can be studied without estimating absolute amounts of reading minutes per day. Only an index of relative differences in exposure to print is required. Thus, one can use measures of print exposure that do not have some of the drawbacks of the activity diary method. My research group (Cunningham & Stanovich, 1990, 1991; Stanovich & West, 1989) has attempted to develop and validate measures of individual differences in print exposure that were designed: (a) to yield estimates of relative differences in print exposure in a single 5–10 min session, (b) to have very simple cognitive requirements (i.e., not requiring retrospective time estimates), and (c) to be immune from contamination from the tendency to give socially desirable responses.

The first measures we developed were designed for use with adult subjects. The Author Recognition Test (ART) and the Magazine Recognition Test (MRT) both exploited a signal detection logic whereby actual target items (real authors and real magazines) were embedded among foils (names that were not authors or magazine titles, respectively). Subjects simply scan the list and check the names they know to be authors on the ART and the titles they know to be magazines on the MRT. The measures thus have a signal detection logic. The number of correct items checked can be corrected for differential response biases that are revealed by the checking of foils. Although checklist procedures have been used before to assess print exposure (Chomsky, 1972), our procedure is unique in using foils to control for differential response criteria (see Stanovich & Cunningham, 1992, for examples of the stimuli).

[material omitted; see description of ART and MRT in Chapter 14]

This checklist method has several advantages. First, it is immune to the social desirability effects that may contaminate responses to subjective self-estimates of socially valued activities such as reading. Guessing is not an advantageous strategy because it is easily detected and corrected for by an examination of the number of foils checked. Further, the cognitive demands of the task are quite low. The task does not necessitate frequency judgments, as do most questionnaire measures of print exposure, nor does it require retrospective time judgments, as does the use of daily activity diaries. Finally, the measures can be administered in a matter of a few minutes.

These checklist tasks are of course proxy indicators of a person's print exposure rather than measures of absolute amounts of reading in terms of minutes or estimated words (Anderson et al., 1988). The fact that the measures are very indirect proxy indicators is problematic in some contexts, but it is also sometimes a strength. Clearly, hearing about a magazine or author on television without having been exposed to the actual written work is problematic. The occurrence of this type of situation obviously reduces the validity of the tasks. However, a postexperimental comment sometimes made by adult subjects in our studies is worth noting: some subjects said they knew a certain name was that of an author, but had never read anything that the author had written. When questioned about how they knew that the name was a writer, the subjects often replied that they had seen one of the author's books in a bookstore, had seen an author's book in the "new fiction" section at the library, had read a review of the author's work in *Newsweek*, had seen an advertisement in the newspaper, etc. In short, knowledge of that author's name was a proxy for reading activities, despite the fact that the particular author had not actually been read. Thus, although some ways of gaining familiarity with author names would reduce validity (TV, radio), most behaviors leading to familiarity with the author names are probably reflections of immersion in a literate environment.

We have developed analogous checklist measures for assessing children's exposure to print. One task is the Title Recognition Test (TRT), a measure that has the same signal detection logic as the adult ART and MRT, but involves children's book titles rather than authors as items. This children's measure shares the same advantages of immunity from socially desirable responding, objective assessment of response bias, low cognitive load, and lack of necessity for retrospective time judgments. The TRT consists of an intermixed list of actual children's book titles and foils for book names (see Allen et al., 1992, and Cunningham & Stanovich, 1991, for examples of stimuli). The titles utilized were selected from a sample of book titles generated in pilot investigations by groups of children ranging in age from second grade (7—8 years-old) through high school, by examining various lists of children's titles, and by consulting teachers and reading education professionals knowledgeable about current trends in children's literature. In selecting the items to appear on the TRTs used in our investigations, we attempted to choose titles that were not prominent parts of classroom reading activities in the schools in which our studies were to be conducted. Because we wanted the TRT to reflect out-of-school rather than school-directed reading, we attempted to avoid books that were used in the school curriculum. Thus, if the test is used for this purpose, versions of it will necessarily differ somewhat in item content from classroom to classroom and from school to school. To complement the TRT, we have also developed children's versions of the ART (see Allen et al., 1992). The score on all of these checklists—both child and adult versions—was the proportion of correct items checked minus the proportion of foils checked.

[*material omitted*]

E. Validating Checklist Measures of Print Exposure

Because Anderson et al. (1988) have established the reliability and validity of the activity diary method of estimating print exposure, their methodology might well be considered the canonical method for assessing print exposure. Thus, we have used it as a baseline for assessing other methods. In an attempt to see whether questionnaire and recognition checklist measures of print exposure were measuring the same construct as the home reading-time estimates from children's daily activity diaries, we included all these methods in a study of 57 fifth-grade (10–11 year-olds) children (Allen et al., 1992).

Table 15.2 shows a correlation matrix of all the media exposure measures utilized in the study. The variables are (1) book reading minutes as estimated from the activity diary, (2) and (3) two versions of the TRT, (4) one version of the ART, (5) a comics recognition checklist instrument modeled on the TRT, (6) number of preferences for reading on a questionnaire structured around forced-choice between activities, (7) a reading disposition item from a typical reading habits questionnaire, (8) the recreational reading and (9) academic reading scales from the Elementary Reading Attitude Survey (ERAS, a public-domain questionnaire designed to give teachers an easy method of assessing attitudes toward reading; see McKenna & Kear, 1990), (10) the diary estimate of minutes of television watching each night, (11) number of choices of television on the activity preference scale, and (12) a composite of television items from a typical media habits questionnaire.

Generally, the print exposure measures had significant correlations with each other and the television exposure measures were significantly inter-correlated. The print and television measures did not correlate with each other. In fact, most of these correlations were negative, although many did not attain statistical significance. This pattern of correlations suggests that the measures have both convergent and discriminant validity.

In Table 15.2 we can examine more closely the question of whether the time estimates of reading activity derived from the diary method correlate with the recognition checklist measures that we have developed. These correlations are, in fact, substantial when we consider that these tasks had modest reliabilities (ranging from .68 to .86). Corrected for attenuation (Ghiselli, Campbell, & Zedeck, 1981, p. 241), the correlations of book reading minutes

TABLE 15.2. Intercorrelations of Differing Measures of Reading Habits

Variable	1.	2.	3.	4.	5.	6.	7.	8.	9.	10.	11.
1. Book Reading (diary)											
2. TRT—Form 1	.48*										
3. TRT—Form 2	.43*	.65*									
4. ART	.52*	.70*	.52*								
5. Comics Recognition	.11	.38*	.27	.35*							
6. Activity Preference—Reading	.25	.34*	.34*	.35*	.40*						
7. Reading Disposition Question	.41*	.56*	.54*	.49*	.31*	.47*					
8. ERAS—Recreational	.37*	.39*	.37*	.34*	.24	.55*	.54*				
9. ERAS—Academic	-.08	-.05	.12	-.05	.03	.30*	.10	.52*			
10. Television (diary)	-.32*	-.20	-.17	-.26	.14	.03	-.18	-.10	.06		
11. Activity Preference—TV	-.13	-.09	-.04	-.27*	-.11	-.40*	-.22	-.02	-.09	.33*	
12. Television Composite	-.22	-.22	-.19	-.18	-.01	-.07	-.32*	.06	.26	.63*	.44*

Note. Correlations involving Book Reading (diary), TRT (form 1), ART, Activity Preference—reading, Reading Disposition Question, and all television measures are based on an N of 57. Correlations involving Comics Recognition are based on an N of 53. Correlations involving TRT (Form 2) and the ERAS are based on an N of 43.
*Correlations significant at the .05 level (two-tailed).

from the activity diaries with the two forms of the TRT are .65 and .59, and with the ART, .70. Additionally, the correlation between the two forms of the TRT was acceptably high as a parallel-forms reliability coefficient, and the correlations of these forms with the ART were acceptably high as concurrent validity estimates. Collectively, these results indicate that the recognition checklist measures are tapping a common construct with book reading minutes as estimated from the daily activity records.

Book reading minutes from the activity diaries did not, however, correlate with the comics recognition measure, and the comics recognition measure correlated only modestly with the TRT and ART. This finding is consistent with previous results indicating that comic book reading is, functionally, somewhat different from book reading (Anderson et al., 1988; Greaney, 1980).

As a further method of exploring the relationships among the reading habits and attitudes measures, the variables were subjected to several methods of factor analysis (see Table 15.3 for a typical solution). [*material omitted*]

The checklist measures were also analyzed with the regression logic described earlier, to examine whether these print exposure measures can account for variance in vocabulary development after scores on a mathematics achievement test had been entered into the regression equation. The results for each of the four recognition checklist measures are present in Table 15.4. The outcome at the second step indicates whether each recognition checklist measure can predict vocabulary scores after controlling for general learning ability in a largely nonverbal domain. Three out of four checklists (TRT 2, ART, and comics recognition) could do so.

A further test of the convergent validity of the checklist measures is provided by examining step 3 of the regressions, where the diary book reading time estimates were forced into the equation as the third variable. Investigating whether the diary estimates can predict variance after the checklist

TABLE 15.3. Factor Loadings for All Measures after Varimax Rotation

	Factor		
Measure	1	2	3
1. Book Reading (diary)	.629	—	—
2. TRT—Form 1	.870	—	—
3. TRT—Form 2	.661	—	—
4. ART	.768	—	—
5. Comics Recognition	.419	—	—
6. Activity Preference—Reading	.442	—	.596
7. Reading Disposition Question	.674	—	.292
8. ERAS—Recreational	.437	—	.660
9. ERAS—Academic	—	—	.697
10. Television (diary)	—	.669	—
11. Activity Preference—Television	—	.423	—
12. Television Composite	—	.900	—

Note. Factor loadings lower than .250 have been eliminated.

TABLE 15.4. Hierarchical Regressions Predicting Vocabulary Scores

Step	Variable	Statistic			
		R	R^2	R^2 change	F to enter
1.	Mathematics Subtest	.407	.166	.166	10.93**
2.	TRT Form 1	.472	.223	.063	3.96
3.	Book Reading (diary)	.524	.275	.052	3.80
1.	Mathematics Subtest	.274	.075	.075	3.57
2.	TRT Form 2	.432	.187	.112	5.93*
3.	Book Reading (diary)	.462	.213	.026	1.41
1.	Mathematics Subtest	.407	.166	.166	10.93**
2.	ART	.583	.340	.174	14.24**
3.	Book Reading (diary)	.595	.354	.014	1.18
1.	Mathematics Subtest	.400	.160	.160	10.27**
2.	Comics Recognition	.565	.319	.159	12.39**
3.	Book Reading (diary)	.636	.405	.086	7.52**

Note. The first and third regressions are based on an N of 57, the second regression is based on an N of 46, and the fourth is based on an N of 56.
*$p < .05$; **$p < .01$.

measures have been entered addresses the question of whether the vocabulary variance explained by the checklist measures overlapped with that explained by the book reading measure from the diary. In three of the four regressions, once the checklist measure was entered, book minutes from the diary no longer independently predicted vocabulary scores. Thus, the variance in vocabulary scores explained by book reading minutes is variance that is largely shared with the checklist print exposure measures.

VII. THE SPECIFIC COGNITIVE CORRELATES OF PRINT EXPOSURE

A. Print Exposure as a Contributor to Growth in Comprehension Ability

The preceding section indicates that the recognition checklists have convergent and discriminant validity as measures of print exposure. They therefore facilitate investigation of the specific cognitive correlates of exposure to print because they provide an alternative to the logistically difficult activity diary technique. Thus, my research group has embarked upon a series of studies in which we employed recognition checklist measures and the regression logic outlined previously to see whether print exposure is a specific predictor (i.e., after various ability controls are employed) of a variety of verbal skills.

First, we asked whether the recognition checklist measures of print exposure predict growth in reading ability throughout the elementary school years, as did the diary estimate of book reading time employed by Anderson et al. (1988). The regression analyses presented in Table 15.5 were addressed to this issue. They display the results of a study (Cipielewski & Stanovich, 1992) in which growth in reading comprehension ability was tracked by administering the comprehension tests from the Stanford Diagnostic Reading Tests and Iowa Tests of Basic Skills (ITBS) to 82 fifth-graders who had been administered the comprehension subtest from the ITBS in the third grade (8–9 year-olds). The regressions are hierarchical forced-entry analyses for prediction of fifth-grade reading comprehension ability. Third-grade reading comprehension was entered first, followed by a recognition checklist measure of print exposure (either a version of the TRT or the ART). Thus, the analyses are essentially addressed to the question of whether the indicators of exposure to print can predict individual differences in growth in reading comprehension from third grade to fifth grade.

In three out of four cases, print exposure measures predicted variance in fifth-grade reading comprehension ability after third-grade reading comprehension scores had been partialed out. [*material omitted*]

B. Print Exposure as a Contributor to Growth in Other Verbal Skills

In several studies, we asked whether print exposure contributes to growth in other cognitive skills. There are a number of reasons for expecting that the answer to this question might be affirmative. The study described in the preceding subsection indicated a unique contribution of print exposure to the explanation of reading comprehension, and reading comprehension is an extremely

TABLE 15.5. Hierarchical Regressions Predicting Fifth-Grade Reading Ability

Step	Variable	R	R^2	R^2 change	F to enter
	Fifth Grade Stanford Reading Comprehension				
1.	Iowa Comprehension (Third)	.645	.416	.416	54.06**
2.	Title Recognition Test	.725	.526	.110	17.38**
	Fifth Grade Stanford Reading Comprehension				
1.	Iowa Comprehension (Third)	.591	.349	.349	34.89**
2.	Author Recognition Test	.655	.430	.081	9.02**
	Fifth Grade Iowa Reading Comprehension				
1.	Iowa Comprehension (Third)	.545	.297	.297	33.78**
2.	Title Recognition Test	.609	.371	.074	9.25**
	Fifth Grade Iowa Reading Comprehension				
1.	Iowa Comprehension (Third)	.485	.236	.236	20.95**
2.	Author Recognition Test	.503	.253	.017	1.56

Note. The spanner headings identify the dependent variables in the regression analyses.
**$p < .01$.

broad skill. A large body of research has demonstrated that reading skill is linked to a wide range of verbal abilities: vocabulary, syntactic knowledge, metalinguistic awareness, verbal short-term memory, phonological awareness, speech production, inferential comprehension, semantic memory, and verbal fluency form only a partial list (e.g., Oakhill & Garnham, 1988; Perfetti, 1985).

In certain domains, reading is especially likely to be a substantial contributor to cognitive growth. For example, as a mechanism for building content knowledge structures (Glaser, 1984), reading seems to be unparalleled (Goody, 1987). The world's storehouse of knowledge is readily available for those who read, and much of this information is not usually attained from other media (Comstock & Paik, 1991; Huston, Watkins, & Kunkel, 1989; Iyengar & Kinder, 1987; Postman, 1985; Zill & Winglee, 1990). Further, if we consider vocabulary to be one of the primary tools of verbal intelligence (Olson, 1986a), then we have another mechanism by which print exposure may influence cognition because reading appears to be is a uniquely efficacious way of acquiring vocabulary (Hayes, 1988; Hayes & Ahrens, 1988; Nagy & Anderson, 1984; Nagy & Herman, 1987).

In a study of fourth-, fifth-, and sixth-grade children (Cunningham & Stanovich, 1991), we examined whether print exposure accounts for differences in vocabulary development once controls for both general and specific (i.e., vocabulary relevant) abilities were invoked. The analyses displayed in Table 15.6 illustrate some of the outcomes of this study. Three different vocabulary measures were employed as dependent variables: a word checklist measure of the written vocabulary modeled on the work of Anderson and Freebody (1983; see also White, Slater, & Graves, 1989; Zimmerman, Broder, Shaughnessy, & Underwood, 1977), a verbal fluency measure where the children had to output as many words as they could that fit into a particular category (e.g., things that are red; see Sincoff & Sternberg, 1987), a group-administered version of the Peabody Picture Vocabulary Test (PPVT). Age was entered first into the regression equation, followed by scores on the Raven Progressive Matrices as a control for general intelligence. As a second ability control more closely linked to vocabulary acquisition mechanisms (see Gathercole & Baddeley, 1989), we entered phonological coding ability into the equation. [material omitted]

The results of the first three analyses displayed in Table 15.6 indicate that for each of the vocabulary measures, the TRT accounted for significant variance after the variance attributable to performance on the Raven and the phonological coding measure had been removed. The last two regressions indicate that this was also true for two additional criterion variables in the study: spelling ability and performance on the general information subtest of the WISC.

Similar relationships involving print exposure were found in a study of adult subjects (Stanovich & Cunningham, 1992). The first set of analyses partialed out general ability as measured by two nonverbal tasks before enter-

TABLE 15.6. Unique Print Exposure Variance after Age, Raven, and Phonological Coding Are Partialed Out

		Statistic			
Step	Variable	R	R^2	R^2 change	F to enter
		Word Checklist			
1.	Age	.103	.011	.011	1.41
2.	Raven	.457	.209	.198	32.57**
3.	Phonological Coding	.610	.372	.163	33.49**
4.	TRT	.683	.466	.094	22.52**
		Verbal Fluency			
1.	Age	.043	.002	.002	0.24
2.	Raven	.231	.053	.051	6.89**
3.	Phonological Coding	.477	.228	.175	28.47**
4.	TRT	.582	.339	.111	21.02**
		PPVT			
1.	Age	.230	.053	.053	7.29**
2.	Raven	.393	.154	.101	15.60**
3.	Phonological Coding	.403	.162	.008	1.21
4.	TRT	.516	.266	.104	18.19**
		Spelling			
1.	Age	.179	.032	.032	4.31*
2.	Raven	.414	.172	.140	21.95**
3.	Phonological Coding	.656	.430	.258	58.51**
4.	TRT	.713	.509	.079	20.42**
		General Information			
1.	Age	.224	.050	.050	6.84**
2.	Raven	.362	.131	.081	12.05**
3.	Phonological Coding	.410	.168	.037	5.68*
4.	TRT	.492	.242	.074	12.37**

Note. The spanner headings identify the dependent variables in the regression analyses.
*$p < .05$; ** $p < .01$.

ing the print exposure measures as predictors. The dependent variables were a variety of indicators of verbal intelligence, including two vocabulary measures (the Nelson–Denny vocabulary subtest and the PPVT), a reading comprehension measure (Nelson–Denny), a measure of history and literature knowledge taken from the National Assessment of Educational Progress, a cultural literacy test, a composite measure of spelling performance, and a verbal fluency measure.

A second set of analyses provided a much more stringent test of the ability of the print exposure indicators to account for unique variance. The analyses in Table 15.7 partial from the dependent variables reading comprehension ability in addition to the nonverbal ability measures. Structuring the analyses

TABLE 15.7. Unique Print Exposure Variance after Nonverbal Abilities and Reading Comprehension Ability Are Partialed Out

Step	Variable	Dependent variables					
		1.	2.	3.	4.	5.	6.
		Cumulative R					
1.	Figural Analogies	.316	.278	.280	.270	.238	.205
2.	Raven	.488	.405	.369	.363	.362	.243
3.	Nelson–Denny Comprehension	.684	.541	.599	.600	.582	.323
4.	ART	.738	.688	.677	.803	.625	.423
4.	MRT	.725	.636	.660	.770	.589	.356
		R^2 change					
1.	Figural Analogies	.100**	.077**	.079**	.073**	.057**	.042**
2.	Raven	.138**	.087**	.057**	.059**	.074**	.017*
3.	Nelson–Denny Comprehension	.230**	.129**	.222**	.227**	.208**	.045**
4.	ART	.076**	.180**	.100**	.286**	.052**	.075**
4.	MRT	.058**	.112**	.077**	.234**	.008	.023*

Note. Dependent variables: 1 = Nelson–Denny Vocabulary; 2 = PPVT; 3 = History and Literature (NAEP); 4 = Cultural Literacy Recognition; 5 = Spelling Composite; 6 = Verbal Fluency.
*$p < .05$; **$p < .001$.

in this way is not meant to imply that print exposure is not a determinant of reading comprehension ability. Indeed, there are strong grounds for believing that exposure to print does facilitate growth in comprehension ability (Anderson et al., 1988; Hayes, 1988; Juel, 1988; Stanovich, 1986b). Thus, these analyses have allowed the Nelson–Denny comprehension measure to steal some of the variance that rightly belongs to the print exposure measures. The reason for structuring the analyses in this conservative manner was to ensure a stringent test of whether the print exposure measures could predict performance on the criterion variables after possibly spurious relationships with general ability had been controlled.

The results illustrated in Table 15.7 indicate that the ART was able to account for additional variance in all of the variables even after reading comprehension ability had been partialed out along with nonverbal ability. The MRT accounted for unique variance in four out of five cases (the exception being spelling performance).

[material omitted]

These data, and those presented in our studies of children, refute the argument that experiential factors are not implicated—or are of secondary importance—in explaining performance on vocabulary measures.

[material omitted]

C. Print Exposure and Incidental versus Intentional Learning

In a further study of college students (West & Stanovich, 1991), we attempted to sample knowledge domains that varied on the dimension of whether they reflected conscious, intentional learning of material in formal educational settings or whether they in part implicate the acquisition of information incidentally and informally in nonschool settings. This study also included SAT test scores as a stringent control for spurious relationships involving general ability.

Our two key measures of formal, school learning were the students' college grade point average and a content test on material from the subjects' major field. Our other two knowledge measures—a vocabulary measure and a cultural literacy test—are amalgamations of information acquired from formal schooling and from incidental learning in nonschool settings. Because the ART and MRT were designed to measure free-reading habits and not in-school study diligence, they would be expected to explain more unique variance on measures of knowledge acquired outside a formal school setting. We partialed out general ability as measured by SAT total scores (see Table 15.8) before entering the print exposure measures as predictors of the student's GPA, the Area Concentration Achievement Test in Psychology (ACAT; Austin Peay State University, 1990), performance on a vocabulary checklist, and a cultural literacy test.

The results for the four dependent variables diverged considerably. Neither of the print exposure measures predicted GPA or ACAT performance when entered after SAT performance, whereas each of the exposure measures accounted for significant additional variance on the vocabulary measure and on the cultural literacy test. This result is predictable if GPA and ACAT performance are assumed to reflect the intentional learning of school material. In

TABLE 15.8. Hierarchical Regression Analyses

		Dependent variables			
Step	Variable	GPA	ACAT	Vocab	CLT
		Cumulative R			
1.	SAT	.343	.306	.510	.381
2.	ART	.345	.306	.564	.570
2.	MRT	.360	.348	.583	.558
		R^2 change			
1.	SAT	.118*	.093*	.260*	.145*
2.	ART	.001	.000	.058*	.180*
2.	MRT	.011	.028	.080*	.167*

Note. Dependent variables: GPA = grade point average; ACAT = Area Concentration Achievement Test in Psychology; Vocab = vocabulary checklist; CLT = cultural literacy test.
*$p < .01$.

contrast, the vocabulary and cultural literacy measures reflect the amalgamation of information acquired from formal schooling and from incidental learning in nonschool settings.

D. The Recognition Checklists and Reading in the Real World

In another study (West, Stanovich, & Mitchell, 1993) we attempted to validate the checklist print exposure measures by seeing whether they were associated with individual differences in reading observed in a nonlaboratory setting where reading occurs. The setting chosen for our study was an airport passenger waiting lounge. This is a setting where reading occurs via the free choice of the subject. If individual differences in free reading in a setting such as this can be related to performance on the recognition checklist tasks, this would strongly bolster the construct validity of the checklist measures as indicators of individual differences in print exposure.

The study involved unobtrusive observations of individuals in a waiting lounge at National Airport in Washington, DC. Individuals sitting by themselves were the potential subjects. Such individuals were selected and monitored unobtrusively for 10 consecutive minutes. If they were not reading at the beginning of the observation period and continued sitting by themselves without reading or having reading matter in sight for the entire 10-minute period, they were classified as nonreaders. If they were reading at the beginning of the observation period and continued reading for the entire 10-minute period they were classified as readers. Individuals whose behavior did not fall into one of these categories did not enter the sample. Subsequent to the observation, the individual was approached by the experimenter, was asked for consent to participate in the study and to fill out several experimental measures, and then was debriefed. Slightly less than 10% of the potential subjects refused to participate.

Table 15.9 displays the results of a comparison of the readers ($N = 111$) and nonreaders ($N = 106$) on a few of the measures. The groups were significantly different on the ART, the MRT, and a newspaper recognition test. However, they were not different on measures of exposure to television and film. This pattern of differences provides evidence of ecological validity for the recognition checklist measures. They were reliably linked to direct observations of the behavior of interest (free reading) in a situation where investigators do not intrude upon the process.

Importantly, the readers were also superior on measures of vocabulary and general knowledge (a cultural literacy recognition test). However, as the last two rows in Table 15.9 show, the readers were also older and had more education. Although the correlations of reading with age and education probably represent real relationships in the population and should not be interpreted as confounds, we nevertheless carried out analyses designed to examine whether airport reading was related to the print exposure measures after the effects of age and education had been statistically controlled and found that it was (see West et al., 1993).

TABLE 15.9. Differences between Readers and Nonreaders

Variable	Nonreaders	Readers	t value
Author Recognition Test	.401	.635	7.75*
Magazine Recognition Test	.598	.751	5.21*
Newspaper Recognition Test	.370	.529	6.12*
Television Recognition Test	.426	.468	1.87
Film Recognition Test	.292	.320	1.10
Vocabulary Checklist	.516	.731	7.57*
Cultural Literacy Recognition	.600	.770	7.00*
Age	35.3	41.4	3.28*
Education	15.2	16.5	4.25*

Note. df = 211 for the vocabulary checklist, 213 for the MRT, 214 for film recognition, and 215 for all other variables.
*p < .01.

[material omitted]

Not surprisingly, given our earlier results, the checklist measures of print exposure were also significant predictors of vocabulary after age and education were partialed out.

[material omitted]

This study successfully demonstrated the ability of the recognition checklist measures to predict reading behavior in a real life setting—one where the target behavior is not influenced by the presence of an experimenter. The construct validity of the tasks has now been bolstered by demonstrating linkages with other measures of print exposure (e.g., the diary method; see Allen et al., 1992) and by demonstrating their ability to predict behavior in a natural environment.

Print exposure, whether measured by the 10-minute airport probe or by the recognition checklist measures, was significantly linked to vocabulary and cultural knowledge in this study even after controls for age and education were invoked. This finding converges with the previously reported studies that have indicated that print exposure can predict a variety of behavioral outcomes even when some rather stringent controls for general cognitive ability and background characteristics are employed.

VIII. SUMMARY AND CONCLUSIONS

The studies reported here represent the first steps in the development of a new research paradigm for studying the unique cognitive correlates of literacy. Reading experience exhibits enough isolable variance within a generally literate society to be reliably linked with cognitive differences. Research on such links is therefore facilitated because the consequences of engaging in literacy activities can be studied without necessarily obtaining totally illiterate samples or setting up cross-cultural comparisons. Issues that are at least analogous issues to those raised in cross-cultural research can be studied within literate societies with a paradigm such as this, and therefore the speed with which we can answer questions about the cognitive consequences of literacy may be greatly increased because more studies can be carried out, larger samples can be studied, and the range of the cognitive domains tapped can be widened.

Research in this area appears to have been stifled because of the widespread acceptance of the most extreme interpretations of the outcome of Scribner and Cole's (1981) investigation—interpretations that have slowly diffused throughout the literature without being accompanied by any new data. These conclusions are fueled by a powerful social critique which advances the argument that the positive cultural and economic effects of literacy have been overstated—indeed, that literacy is, if anything, a repressive force (Auerbach, 1992; Street, 1984, 1988; Stuckey, 1991). Educational theorists such as Frank Smith accused the educational establishment of "overselling" literacy and have argued that "literacy doesn't generate finer feelings or higher values. It doesn't even make anyone smarter" (1989, p. 354).

The data reported herein appear to indicate that these theorists could well be wrong in this conclusion. If "smarter" means having a larger vocabulary and more world knowledge in addition to the abstract reasoning skills encompassed within the concept of intelligence, as it does in most layman's definitions of intelligence (Stanovich, 1989a; Sternberg, 1990), then reading may *well* make people smarter. Certainly our data demonstrate time and again that print exposure is associated with vocabulary, general knowledge, and verbal skills even after controlling for abstract reasoning abilities (as measured by such indicators as the Raven). Although nothing can turn our correlational data into true experimental findings, the converging patterns of relationships—most importantly, the indication that reading habits predict growth in verbal abilities in longitudinal investigations (see also Anderson et al., 1988; Juel, 1988)—certainly imply a role for reading experience in a comprehensive theory of cognitive growth (its role is at least as well supported as many other mechanisms that have attained popularity in developmental psychology).

Thus, investigators who attempt to supplement purely genetic accounts of differences in mental ability by speculating about variables in children's ecologies that could account for cognitive change (e.g., Ceci, 1990) might well find print exposure worth investigating, because the variables they choose must have the requisite potency to perform their theoretical roles. An important class of such variables would be those that have long-term effects because of their repetitive and/or cumulative action. Schooling is obviously one such variable (Cahan & Cohen, 1989; Ceci, 1990, 1991; Morrison, 1987b). However, print exposure is another variable that cumulates over time into enormous individual differences. For example, Anderson et al. (1988) have found hundredfold differences in word exposure among fifth-grade (10–11 year-old) children and order of magnitude differences in opportunities to learn vocabulary words (see also Hayes & Ahrens, 1988). From the time of at least the fifth grade, an avid reader is seeing literally millions of words a year (Anderson et al., 1988). Thus, whatever cognitive processes are engaged over word or word-group units (phonological coding, semantic activation, parsing, induction of new vocabulary items) are being exercised hundreds of times a day. This amount of cognitive muscle-flexing might be expected to have some specific effects. Reading volume is thus an explanatory variable that should be more routinely considered when attempting to predict individual cognitive outcomes and group trends. For example, print exposure might be a useful explanatory variable that can be called upon when trying to explain group trends such as declining verbal SAT scores (Wirtz, 1977), historical changes in intelligence test performance (Flynn, 1987), or differential changes in fluid versus crystallized intelligence with aging.

The results reported here do not, of course, reveal anything about the *causes* of differences in exposure to print. Certainly, environmental differences (cultural opportunities, parental modeling, quality of schooling) may be a contributing factor (Anderson et al., 1988). But personality dispositions toward literacy activities may also play a role, and the environmental and/or genetic determinants of such behavioral propensities are completely unknown (but see Plomin, Corley, DeFries, & Fulker, 1990). We must be careful to avoid the "sociologist's fallacy" of failing to recognize that a seemingly environmental variable like print exposure could—via the influence of the parent-constructed home literacy environment—carry genetic variance (Plomin & Bergeman, 1991). Nevertheless, Olson (1991) analyzed the heritability of the deficit in performance on the print exposure checklist measures shown by dyslexic twins in the Colorado Reading Project and found that the hypothesis of zero heritability could not be rejected.

What are the mechanisms by which print exposure comes to be an independent predictor of variance in the criterion variables studied in this investigation? Several mechanisms are possible. First, the distributions of language structures that people are exposed to in print are different from those encountered in speech. Evidence for this conjecture is most strong in the lexical domain. Work by Hayes (1988; Hayes & Ahrens, 1988; see also Akinnaso, 1982; Biber, 1986; Chafe & Danielewicz, 1987; Corson, 1985) has indicated that moderate to low frequency words—precisely those words that differentiate individuals with high and low vocabulary sizes—appear much more often in common reading matter than in common speech. These relative differences in the statistical distributions of words in print and in oral language have direct implications for vocabulary development.

Most theorists agree that a substantial proportion of vocabulary growth during childhood occurs indirectly through language exposure (Miller & Gildea, 1987; Nagy & Anderson, 1984; Nagy, Herman, & Anderson, 1985; Sternberg, 1985a, 1987). Furthermore, many researchers are convinced that exposure to print is a more potent source of vocabulary growth than is exposure to oral language (Hayes, 1988; Hayes & Ahrens, 1988; Krashen, 1989; Nagy & Anderson, 1984; Nagy & Herman, 1987; Stanovich, 1986b). If most of one's vocabulary is acquired outside formal teaching, then the only opportunities to acquire new words occur when an individual is exposed to a word in written or oral language that is outside the current vocabulary. That such exposure will happen vastly more often while reading than while talking or watching television is illustrated in research by Hayes and Ahrens (1988). They studied how many rare words per 1,000 are contained in various categories of language. A rare word was defined as one with a rank lower than 10,000 in the Carroll, Davies, and Richman (1971) count—roughly, a word that is outside the vocabulary of a fourth–sixth grader (9–12 year-old). For vocabulary growth to occur after the middle grades, children must be exposed to words that are rare by this definition. Hayes and Ahrens (1988) found that print provides many more such word-learning opportunities. Children's books contain 50% more rare words than does adult prime-time television and the conversation of college graduates. Popular magazines have roughly three times as many opportunities for new word learning as prime-time television and adult conversation. The data presented by Hayes and Ahrens (1988) indicate that conversation is not a substitute for reading.

To a lesser extent, a similar situation holds for other language systems, including syntax (Purcell-Gates, 1988). Although all syntactic constructions can be found in all types of language, more complex syntactic constructions are disproportionately found in text (Akinnaso, 1982; Biber, 1986; Redeker, 1984). Of course, complex syntactic constructions are also found disproportionately in types of speech that are text-like, such as judicial proceedings, planned speeches, and college lectures (Biber, 1986; Chafe & Danielewicz, 1987); nevertheless, the findings establish that the average person experiences these syntactic constructions disproportionately in print (Chafe & Danielewicz, 1987; Purcell-Gates, 1988; Redeker, 1984). In short, print exposure might be expected to contribute to skill in verbal domains because print is a source of exceptionally rich stimulation.

Another mechanism by which print exposure might lead to cognitive change is its role as a builder of the individual's knowledge base. In recent years, cognitive and developmental psychologists have strongly emphasized the importance of domain knowledge in determining information processing efficiency (Bjorklund, 1987; Ceci, 1990; Chi, Hutchinson, & Robin, 1989; Keil, 1984; Scribner, 1986). Yussen (1990) summarized the view as follows: "Much of what develops in children's memory is neither changes in basic capacity nor changes in strategies available to children but, instead, the richness of knowledge about a topic or about the concepts embedded in the material put to children to remember in various experimental tasks. This is called content" (p. 677). Print is a uniquely rich source of content. Personal experience provides only narrow knowledge of the world and is often misleading and unrepresentative (Baron, 1985, 1988; Dawes, 1988; Gilovich, 1991; Kahneman, Slovic, & Tversky, 1982; Nisbett & Ross, 1980). The most commonly used electronic sources of information (television, radio) lack depth (Comstock & Paik, 1991; Hayes & Ahrens, 1988; Huston, Watkins, & Kunkel, 1989;

Iyengar & Kinder, 1987; Zill & Winglee, 1990). Only print provides opportunities for acquiring broad and deep knowledge of the world. Research indicates that reading has higher correlations with world and cultural knowledge than does television viewing (Allen et al., 1992; West et al., 1993; West & Stanovich, 1991; Zill & Winglee, 1990).

Cognitive theories in which individual differences in basic processing capacities are viewed as at least partly determined by differences in knowledge bases (e.g., Ceci, 1990) indirectly provide a mechanism through which print exposure influences cognitive efficiency. Print is simply a more distal factor that determines individual differences in knowledge bases, which in turn influence performance on a variety of basic information processing tasks (see Ceci, 1990). This link explains why some of the relations found in our studies between print exposure and criterion variables such as general knowledge and vocabulary should not be criticized or dismissed as representing "narrow" effects. If the theories of cognitive development in which domain knowledge is emphasized have some truth to them, then demonstrating effects on such knowledge structures is an important finding because whatever causal power accrues to content knowledge in these theories also partially accrues to print exposure as a mechanism of cognitive change.

Finally, in any attempt to explain tendencies of early achievement disparities to increase with age (e.g., Jorm, Share, Maclean, & Matthews, 1984; Stanovich, 1986b), print exposure is, again, a variable that may have some explanatory power. For example, Hayes and Grether (1983) studied the growth in reading comprehension and vocabulary of several thousand students in the New York City schools during the school year and during the summer. They found that the summer period, when the children were not in school, accounted for more of the gap between the high achieving and low achieving students than did the period when the children were actually in school. They concluded that "it now appears that non-school periods may have contributed a majority of the differentials in reading and word knowledge noted among the six sets of schools" (pp. 65–66). "In short, very little of the enormous difference in word knowledge performance . . . appears to be attributable to what goes on *in* school; most of it comes from what goes on *out* of school" (p. 64). Demonstrating that the pattern uncovered by Hayes and Grether can be explained in terms of specific variables in children's ecologies would be important, and print exposure might play a role in such an explanation.

The Hayes and Grether result may represent an instance of what have been termed "Matthew effects" in literacy development: educational sequences in which early and efficient acquisition of reading skill yields faster rates of growth in reading achievement and other cognitive skills (see Stanovich, 1986b; Walberg & Tsai, 1983). The term "Matthew effects" derives from the Gospel According to Matthew—"For unto every one that hath shall be given, and he shall have abundance: but from him that hath not shall be taken away even that which he hath" (XXV: 29)—and refers to rich-get-richer and poor-get-poorer effects embedded in the sociodevelopmental context of schooling. For example, children who are already good comprehenders may tend to read more, thus spurring further increases in their reading comprehension abilities and increasing the achievement differences between them and their age-mates who are not good comprehenders and not avid readers (Chall, Jacobs, & Baldwin, 1990; Juel, 1988; Share & Silva, 1987; Share, McGee, & Silva, 1989; Stanovich, 1986b; van den Bos, 1989). Thus, free reading choices may explain part of the puzzle—and the pressing social problem—of widening achievement disparities between the educational haves and have-nots.

CHAPTER 16

Literacy Experiences
and the Shaping of Cognition

with ANNE E. CUNNINGHAM and RICHARD F. WEST

Reading is a popular topic in cognitive development and education. Within cognitive developmental psychology, for example, there is a considerable literature on the individual differences in the cognitive processes that support efficient reading performance (Carr & Levy, 1990; Gough, Ehri, & Treiman, 1992; Perfetti, 1985; Share & Stanovich, 1995). A popular research strategy has been the cognitive correlates approach (see Pellegrino & Glaser, 1979; Sternberg, 1990) in which investigators attempt to determine whether individual differences in particular cognitive processes or knowledge bases can serve as predictors of reading ability (e.g., Carr & Levy, 1990; Jackson & McClelland, 1979). The causal model that is implicit in such analyses locates individual differences in the cognitive subprocesses prior to reading ability. The focus of this chapter somewhat inverts the causal model implied in most of this research. That is, many researchers have attempted to specify individual differences in the cognitive processes that support efficient reading performance. In contrast, very little attention has been focused on the reciprocal possibility that exposure to print itself affects the development of cognitive processes and declarative knowledge bases.

In contrast to the relative inattention to the consequences of reading experience displayed by developmental psychologists, the literature on the cognitive consequences of literacy in the humanities and social sciences outside of psychology is large (Gee, 1988; Goody, 1977, 1987; Graff, 1986, 1987; Havelock, 1963, 1980; Kaestle, 1991; Ong, 1967, 1982; Stock, 1983). Over the past three decades, scholars such as Goody (1977, 1987), Olson (1977,

1994), and Ong (1982) have promulgated a view which has come to be called the Great Divide theory: that literacy fosters logical and analytic modes of thought; critical attitudes; propositional knowledge; and abstract uses of language. However, in the 1980s, the Great Divide theory received what seemed like a death blow from the much publicized study of Scribner and Cole (1981), who examined literacy effects among the Vai in Africa. The fact that some unschooled individuals in this society were familiar with an indigenous script allowed the separation of schooling effects from literacy effects. Scribner and Cole (1981) found no specific effect of literacy on a number of tasks tapping general cognitive processes, including taxonomic categorization tasks, memory tasks, and syllogistic reasoning problems. The extremely innovative separation of literacy and schooling in the Scribner and Cole investigation led to an almost instant acceptance of their main conclusions in the literature on the consequences of literacy.

The seeming conclusiveness of the Scribner and Cole (1981) investigation dampened enthusiasm for new empirical studies of the effects of literacy. Unfortunately, Scribner and Cole's (1981) innovative and costly project is unlikely to be replicated, so that resolving the issues using a variant of their methodology will not be possible. However, the cognitive consequences of literacy can be studied without necessarily using a cross-cultural comparison. Our methodology exploits the fact that even within a generally literate culture, individuals vary tremendously in degree of exposure to print. Furthermore, even among a group of individuals who have the same level of assessed reading comprehension ability, remarkably large differences are found in their degree of engagement in print-related activities (Stanovich & West, 1989), and the correlates of this natural variation can be studied. Comparing literates and illiterates is the exclusive design of choice only if the effects of literacy are believed to be completely discontinuous—with no cognitive consequences of variation in amount of print exposure among literate individuals. Our research program is predicated on the view that the discontinuity assumption is false and that there is important cognitive variation among people who differ only in the *amount* of reading that they do. We do not wish to dispute the fact that there may be important cognitive implications of the literacy/illiteracy divide, only that there is other, less discrete, variability in literacy practices that deserves exploration. Our research conclusions are thus restricted to the more continuous variation in reading experience.

INDIVIDUAL DIFFERENCES IN DECLARATIVE KNOWLEDGE: ALTERNATIVE VIEWS

An important theoretical motivation for this research program is provided by theories of cognitive development which have strongly emphasized the importance of declarative knowledge (Alexander, 1992; Bjorklund, 1987; Ceci, 1990, 1993; Chi, 1985; Chi, Hutchinson, & Robin, 1989; Hoyer, 1987; Keil,

1984; Scribner, 1986). Given that the knowledge-dependency of cognitive functioning is a central tenet of many contemporary developmental theories, it is surprising that there has not been more attention directed to a question that such theories seem to naturally prompt: Where does knowledge come from? This question seems to be addressed only implicitly by theories emphasizing knowledge-dependency—the most common implication being that individual differences in domain knowledge are, for the most part, a product of experiential differences. In contrast, some investigators have explicitly argued against the experiential assumption implicit in the declarative knowledge literature. These alternative hypotheses can be illustrated by using vocabulary knowledge as an example.

Vocabulary is a knowledge base that is important for many aspects of psycholinguistic processing; and it is certainly tempting to attribute variability in vocabulary size to experiential differences. For example, there is considerable evidence indicating that children's vocabulary sizes are correlated with parental education and indicators of environmental quality (Hall, Nagy, & Linn, 1984; Mercy & Steelman, 1982; Wells, 1986). Thus, it has been argued that vocabulary differences are primarily the result of differential opportunities for word learning. This conjecture might be termed the *environmental opportunity hypothesis*.

The environmental opportunity hypothesis is countered by theorists who emphasize that differences in vocabulary are caused by variation in the efficiency of the cognitive mechanisms responsible for inducing meaning from context. Proponents of what we might call the *cognitive efficiency hypothesis* argue that experiential factors are not implicated—or at least are of secondary importance—in explaining vocabulary differences. For example, Sternberg (1985a) has argued that "simply reading a lot does not guarantee a high vocabulary. What seems to be critical is not sheer amount of experience but rather what one has been able to learn from and do with that experience. According to this view, then, individual differences in knowledge acquisition have priority over individual differences in actual knowledge" (p. 307). Jensen (1980) has stated the cognitive efficiency hypothesis in even stronger form:

> Children of high intelligence acquire vocabulary at a faster rate than children of low intelligence, and as adults they have a much larger than average vocabulary, not primarily because they have spent more time in study or have been more exposed to words, but because they are capable of educing more meaning from single encounters with . . . . The vocabulary test does not discriminate simply between those persons who have and those who have not been exposed to the words in context. . . . The crucial variable in vocabulary size is not exposure per se, but conceptual need and inference of meaning from context. (pp. 146–147)

It is important to realize that cognitive efficiency explanations of this type are generic and are not necessarily restricted to the domain of vocabulary acquisition. They could, in theory, apply to knowledge acquisition in virtually any domain. Ceci (1990) has discussed how in an attempt to undermine developmental theories that emphasize the importance of knowledge structures in determining intelligent performance, advocates of the cognitive efficiency hypothesis argue that "intelligent individuals do better on IQ tests because their superior central-processing mechanisms make it easier for them to glean important information and relationships from their environment" (p. 72). The cognitive efficiency hypothesis thus undercuts all developmental theories that emphasize the importance of knowledge structures in determining intelligent performance by potentially trivializing them. According to the cognitive efficiency view, these differences in knowledge bases may affect certain cognitive operations all right, but the knowledge differences themselves arise merely as epiphenomena of differences in the efficiency of more basic psychological processes. Knowledge differences thus become much less interesting as explanatory mechanisms of developmental differences because they are too proximal a cause.

MEASURING THE SPECIFIC EFFECTS OF PRINT EXPOSURE

As part of a broad-based research program examining the impact of reading experience on cognitive development (Echols, West, Stanovich, & Zehr, 1996; Stanovich, 1993a; Stanovich & Cunningham, 1992, 1993), we have put to test the cognitive efficiency hypothesis by examining the experiential variable that presents perhaps the most serious challenge to it: exposure to print. Before embarking on these investigations, we were faced with two fundamental problems: (1) How do you measure individual differences in exposure to print? (2) How should you interpret any associations between cognitive outcomes and print exposure that are observed? We will turn first to the former question.

[material omitted; see Section VI.C of Chapter 15]

ALTERNATIVE METHODS FOR ASSESSING EXPOSURE TO PRINT

[material omitted; see Sections VI.D, VI.E, and VII.D of Chapter 15]

PRINT EXPOSURE AS A CONTRIBUTOR TO GROWTH IN VERBAL SKILLS

[material omitted; see Section VII.B of Chapter 15]

EXPOSURE TO PRINT AND DECLARATIVE KNOWLEDGE

In other studies, we have focused even more directly on content knowledge by addressing the question "Where Does Knowledge Come From?" Stanovich and Cunningham (1993) examined general ability, print exposure, and exposure to other media sources as determinants of individual differences in content knowledge. This study contained a particularly stringent test of the cognitive efficiency explanation of individual differences in knowledge acquisition. The subjects were 268 college students, and the strong test is displayed in Table 16.1. The criterion variable is a composite index of performance on five general knowledge measures. Four measures of general ability were entered prior to print exposure: high school grade point average, performance on the Raven matrices, on an SAT-type mathematics test, and the score on the Nelson–Denny Reading Comprehension Test. This set of tasks surely exhausts the variance attributable to any general ability construct; and general ability does account for a substantial proportion of variance in the general knowledge composite (multiple R of .63). When entered as the fifth step, a composite measure of exposure to television accounted for no additional variance. However, a composite index of exposure to print accounted for a substantial 37.1% of the variance when entered after the four ability measures and television exposure.

This pattern replicated in each of the five measures of general knowledge we employed, including a homemade instrument we called the Practical Knowledge Test. This task was designed to address the criticism that our other measures of general knowledge were too academic—that they tapped knowledge that was too esoteric or elitist, and that was not useful in daily life. We thought this a dubious criticism by the way—many items on these measures were mundane and concrete questions such as "In what part of the body does the infection called pneumonia occur?" Nevertheless, in the Practical Knowledge Test, we bent over backward to devise questions that were directly relevant to daily living in a technological society in the late twentieth century. For example, What does the carburetor in an automobile do? If a substance is carcinogenic it means that it is *blank*? After the Federal Reserve Board raises the prime lending rate, the interest that you will be asked to pay on a car loan will generally increase/decrease/stay the same? What vitamin is highly concentrated in citrus fruits? When a stock exchange is in a "bear market," what is happening? and so forth.

The results indicated that more avid readers in our study—independent

TABLE 16.1. Hierarchical Regression Analyses Predicting General Knowledge Composite

Step	Variable	R	R^2 change	F to enter	Final beta	Final F
1.	HS GPA	.372	.139	42.82**	.020	0.32
2.	Raven	.447	.061	20.30**	.016	0.20
3.	Mathematics Test	.542	.094	35.07**	.165	18.19**
4.	N–D Comprehension	.630	.103	45.11**	.112	9.87**
5.	Television Composite	.630	.000	0.06	−.039	1.68
6.	Print Composite	.876	.371	417.63**	.720	417.63**

*$p < .05$; **$p < .01$.

of their general abilities—knew more about how a carburetor worked, were more likely to know who their U.S. Senators were, more likely to know how many teaspoons are equivalent to one tablespoon (3), more likely to know what a stroke was, and what a closed-shop was in a factory, etc. One would be hard pressed to deny that at least some of this knowledge is relevant to living in the United States in the late 20th century.

In other questions asked of these same subjects, we attempted to probe areas that we thought might be characterized by *mis*information. We then attempted to trace, in our individual difference analyses, the "cognitive anatomy" of this misinformation. One such question concerned the sizes of the world's major religions, and was designed to assess awareness of the multicultural nature of the modern world. The question was phrased as follows: "The 1986 *Encyclopedia Britannica* estimates that there are approximately nine hundred million people in the *world* (not just the United States) who identify themselves as Christians. How many people in the world (not just the United States) do you think identify themselves as _____?" Space was then provided on the form for the subjects to make estimates of the number of Moslems, Jews, Buddhists, Hindus, etc.

We will focus here on the estimates of Moslem and Jewish people because of our a priori hypothesis that availability effects caused by televised coverage of Israel in the United States had skewed the perception of this ratio. While the median estimate in our sample of the number of Jewish people (20 million) was quite close to the actual figure of 18 million according to the 1990 *Universal Almanac*, the number of estimated Moslems—a mean of 10 million— was startlingly low (817 million is the estimate in the *Universal Almanac*). For each subject, we calculated the ratio of the Moslem to Jewish estimates to see how many subjects were aware of the fact that the number of Moslems is an order of magnitude larger (the actual estimated ratio is approximately 33:1 according to the *World Almanac*; 45:1 according to the *Universal Almanac*). The median ratio in our sample was 0.5. That is, 69.3% of our sample thought that there were more Jewish people in the world than Moslems.

This level of inaccuracy is startling given that approximately 40% of our sample of 268 students were attending one of the most selective public institutions of higher education in the United States (the University of California at Berkeley). We have explored the correlates of this particular misconception in a variety of ways. In the following analysis, we scored a subject's ratio "correct" if it was 1.0 or greater—admittedly a ridiculously liberal scoring criterion, but one necessitated by the fact that only 8.2% of the sample produced a ratio of 20:1 or greater. Table 16.2 presents a breakdown of the scores on this question based on a median split of the print composite and television composite variables. There is a clear effect of print exposure on the scores on the question and a significant effect of television viewing, but the effects were in opposite directions. Print exposure was associated with higher scores on the question but television exposure was associated with lower scores. Scores among the group high in print exposure and low in television exposure were

TABLE 16.2. Proportion "Correct" on the Moslem/Jewish Question as a Function of Print and Television Exposure

High print		Low print	
Low TV	High TV	Low TV	High TV
.614	.419	.298	.236

highest (61.4% of this group getting the item quote "correct") and the lowest scores were achieved by those high in television exposure and low in print exposure (only 23.6% of this group responding with a ratio of at least 1.0). Regression analyses confirmed that these relationships were not due to differences in general ability.

Similarly, we have analyzed a variety of other misconceptions in a number of other different domains—including knowledge of World War II, the world's languages, and the components of the federal budget—and all of them replicate the pattern shown for this question. The cognitive anatomy of misinformation appears to be one of too little exposure to print and over reliance on television for information about the world. Although television viewing can have positive associations with knowledge when the viewing is confined to public television, news, and/or documentary material (Hall, Chiarello, & Edmondson, 1996; West & Stanovich, 1991; West et al., 1993), familiarity with the prime-time television material that defines mass viewing in North America is most often negatively associated with knowledge acquisition.

We have conducted a study using a much older population in order to investigate the extent to which age-related growth in declarative knowledge can be accounted for by differential experience with print (Stanovich, West, & Harrison, 1995). Although much research effort has been expended on describing cumulative growth in crystallized intelligence, we know little about the experiential correlates of knowledge growth in older individuals. For example, educational experience is a predictor of intellectual functioning in older individuals (e.g., Schwartzman, Gold, Andres, Arbuckle, & Chaikelson, 1987). It is assumed that education (which is received early in life) in part determines the extent and quality of many intellectual activities later in life. It is presumably these later activities that are so crucial to the preservation of cognitive capacities. Thus, while considerable development of cognitive skills and abilities can result from formal educational experiences, it is the life-time use of these skills that is assumed to have the beneficial effect.

In this study, we investigated the extent to which age-related growth in declarative knowledge can be accounted for by differential experience with print. We compared the performance of 133 college students (mean age = 19.1 years) and 49 older individuals (mean age = 79.9 years) on two general knowledge tasks, a vocabulary task, a working memory task, a syllogistic reasoning task, and several measures of exposure to print.

The older individuals outperformed the college students on the measures of general knowledge and vocabulary, but did significantly less well than the college subjects on the working memory and syllogistic reasoning tasks—the standard dissociation between fluid and crystallized intelligence found in the literature (Baltes, 1987; Horn & Hofer, 1992; Salthouse, 1988). However, a series of hierarchical regression analyses indicated that when measures of exposure to print were used as control variables, the positive relationships between age and vocabulary, and age and declarative knowledge, were eliminated (in contrast, the negative relationships between age and fluid abilities were largely unattenuated). The results are consistent with the conjecture that—in the domain of verbal abilities—print exposure helps to compensate for the normally deleterious effects of aging (see also Smith, 1996).

DEVELOPING A LIFELONG READING HABIT

Given that lifelong reading habits are such strong predictors of verbal cognitive growth, what is it that predicts these habits? That is, so far, the analyses have treated exposure to print as a predictor variable of criterion abilities such as reading comprehension. However, it is generally agreed that comprehension ability and exposure to print are in a reciprocal relationship (Anderson et al., 1988; Stanovich, 1986b, 1993a). We have examined this reciprocal relationship in a longitudinal study. We had available extensive cognitive profiles of a group of children who had been tested as first graders in 1981 (see Stanovich, Cunningham, & Feeman, 1984a). About one half of this sample were available 10 years later for testing as eleventh graders. At that time, we administered a set of reading comprehension, cognitive ability, vocabulary, and general knowledge tasks, as well as several measures of exposure to print. We were thus able to examine what variables in the first grade predicted these cognitive outcomes in the eleventh grade.

Table 16.3 displays the results from an analysis in which we addressed the question of whether the speed of initial reading acquisition in the first grade could predict the tendency to engage in reading activities 10 years later, even after the current level of reading comprehension ability is taken into account. Entered first in the hierarchical regression is eleventh-grade reading comprehension ability (Nelson–Denny performance) in order to remove the direct association between print exposure and contemporaneous reading ability. Listed next in the table are alternative second steps in the regression equation. All three measures of first-grade reading ability (MAT, Gates, and WRAT) predicted significant variance (slightly over 10%) in eleventh-grade print exposure even after eleventh-grade reading comprehension ability had been partialed out!

The table indicates that the two measures of cognitive ability administered in first grade (Raven and PPVT) did not account for unique variance in print exposure once eleventh-grade reading comprehension ability had been partialed out. Finally, third- and fifth-grade measures of reading ability

TABLE 16.3. Hierarchical Regression Analysis Predicting Exposure to Print in the Eleventh Grade

Step	Variable	R	R^2 change	F to enter	Partial r
1.	Grade 11 N–D Comp	.604	.364	14.34**	—
2.	Grade 1 Metropolitan	.696	.121	5.61*	.435
2.	Grade 1 Gates	.681	.100	4.45*	.396
2.	Grade 1 WRAT	.686	.106	4.78*	.408
2.	Grade 1 Raven	.632	.035	1.39	.234
2.	Grade 1 PPVT	.641	.047	1.89	.270
2.	Grade 3 Metropolitan	.765	.221	11.09**	.588
2.	Grade 5 Metropolitan	.719	.153	6.72*	.484

Note. N–D Comp = Nelson–Denny Reading Comprehension Test.
*$p < .05$; **$p < .01$.

account for even more variance in print exposure than does the first-grade measures. Thus an early start in reading is important in predicting a lifetime of literacy experience—and this is true regardless of the level of reading comprehension ability that the individual eventually attains. This is a strong finding because it indicates that, regardless of the student's level of reading comprehension in the eleventh grade, if the student got off to a fast start in reading (as indicated by his/her first-grade reading ability score) then he/she is are more likely to engage in more reading activity as an adult. Early success at reading acquisition is thus one of the keys that unlocks a lifetime of reading habits. The subsequent exercise of this habit serves to further develop reading comprehension ability in an interlocking positive feedback logic (Juel, 1988; Juel, Griffith, & Gough, 1986; Snow, Barnes, Chandler, Goodman, & Hemphill, 1991; Stanovich, 1986b, 1993a).

CONCLUSION

Our work on the cognitive correlates of exposure to print has demonstrated that a strong version of the cognitive efficiency account of knowledge acquisition is clearly falsified by the data we have presented. Print exposure accounted for a sizable portion of variance in measures of vocabulary and general knowledge even after variance associated with general cognitive ability was partialed out. Thus, at least in certain domains, and at least as measured here, individual differences in declarative knowledge bases—differences emphasized by many contemporary theories of developmental growth—appear to some extent to be experientially based.

Researchers and practitioners in the reading education community are nearly unanimous in recommending that children be encouraged to spend more time engaged in literacy activities outside of school (e.g., Adams, 1990; Anderson, Hiebert, Scott, & Wilkinson, 1985). From a cultural standpoint, this recommendation is virtually unassailable. What has been less clear, however, is the empirical status of the tacit model of skill acquisition that often underlies the recommendation to increase children's free reading. The tacit model is basically one of accelerating skill development via practice. It is thought that more exposure to print via home reading will lead to further growth in reading comprehension and related cognitive skills. As plausible as this tacit model sounds, until quite recently, there was actually very little evidence to support it. Most of the available evidence was correlational—for example, research demonstrating that avid readers tend to be good comprehenders (see Guthrie & Greaney, 1991, for a review)—and did not contain any statistical controls of possible third variables. These zero-order correlations are ambiguous because they are open to the interpretation that better readers simply choose to read more—an interpretation at odds with the tacit model of skill development via practice that underlies efforts to increase children's free reading. The pattern of regression results in our studies suggests that print exposure does appear to be both a consequence of developed reading ability and a contributor to further growth in that ability and in other verbal skills—thus they bolster the emphasis on reading experience that currently prevails in the reading education community. The results also strengthen the case for advocating a more prominent role for reading activity in general theories of cognitive development (Booth & Hall, 1994; Guthrie, Schafer, & Hutchinson, 1991; Hayes, 1988; Olson, 1994; Stanovich, 1986b, 1993a; Stanovich & Cunningham, 1993).

Cognitive theories that view individual differences in basic processing capacities as at least partly determined by differences in knowledge bases (e.g., Ceci, 1990, 1993) elucidate a mechanism by which print exposure can be said to influence cognitive development. Print exposure is simply a more distal factor that determines individual differences in knowledge bases, which in turn influence performance on a variety of basic information processing tasks (see Ceci, 1990). If the theories of cognitive development in which declarative knowledge is emphasized have some truth to them, then demonstrating effects on such knowledge structures is an important finding because whatever causal power accrues to content knowledge in these theories also partially accrues to print exposure as a mechanism of cognitive change.

There are, in fact, several possible mechanisms by which print exposure could become a mechanism for the growth and preservation of crystallized knowledge. Reading is a very special type of interface with the environment, providing the organism with unique opportunities to acquire declarative knowledge. The world's storehouse of knowledge is readily available for those who read, and much of this information is not usually attained from other sources. Personal experience provides only narrow knowledge of the world and is often misleadingly unrepresentative (Baron, 1985, 1994; Dawes, 1988; Gilovich, 1991; Nisbett & Ross, 1980; Stanovich, 1994b, 1996a). The most commonly used electronic sources of information (television, radio) lack depth (Comstock & Paik, 1991; Hayes & Ahrens, 1988; Huston, Watkins, & Kunkel, 1989; Iyengar & Kinder, 1987; Zill & Winglee, 1990). For example, most theorists agree that a substantial proportion of vocabulary growth during childhood and adulthood occurs indirectly through language exposure (Miller & Gildea, 1987; Nagy & Anderson, 1984; Nagy, Herman, & Anderson, 1985; Sternberg, 1985a, 1987). Obviously, the only opportunities to acquire new words occur when an individual is exposed to a word in written or oral language that is outside the current vocabulary. Work by Hayes (1988; Hayes & Ahrens, 1988; see also Akinnaso, 1982; Biber, 1986; Chafe & Danielewicz, 1987; Corson, 1995) has indicated that moderate to low frequency words—precisely those words that differentiate individuals with high and low vocabulary sizes—appear much more often in common reading matter than in common speech. These relative differences in the statistical distributions of words in print and in oral language have direct implications for vocabulary development.

In summary, when speculating about variables in people's ecologies that could account for cognitive variability, print exposure is worth investigating, because such variables must have the requisite potency to perform their theoretical roles. A class of variable that might have such potency would be one that has long-term effects because of its repetitive and/or cumulative action. Schooling is obviously one such variable (Cahan & Cohen, 1989; Ceci, 1990, 1991; Ferreira & Morrison, 1994; Morrison, Smith, & Dow-Ehrensberger, 1995; Varnhagen, Morrison, & Everall, 1994). However, print exposure is another factor that varies enormously from individual to individual and that cumulates over time. We have shown here that these individual differences are associated to a strong degree with individual differences in general knowledge across the life span and with individual differences among individuals of roughly similar age.

PART VI

DISCREPANCY DEFINITIONS OF READING DISABILITY

CHAPTER 17

Reading Disability Classification

Are Reforms Based on Evidence Possible?

The paper reprinted in this section, and two companion essays (Stanovich, 1993b, 1999a), are all more conceptual in nature, and more concerned with policy issues, than most of the previous chapters. The paper does, however, derive from the empirical falsification that was discussed in Chapter 5. In the 1988 paper in the *Journal of Learning Disabilities* (*JLD*; see Chapter 7) I had speculated that the discrepancy-defined poor reader would have a more severe phonological deficit than the garden-variety poor reader without reading-IQ discrepancy. No sooner than had the ink dried on my paper when Linda Siegel published her classic paper in the *Canadian Journal of Psychology* (Siegel, 1988) indicating that this was not so. Shortly afterward, she published her target article in the *JLD* (Siegel, 1989), and I was one of the commentators on that article (along with scholars such as Scott Baldwin, Tanis Bryan, Steve Graham, Karen Harris, C. K. Leong, Reid Lyon, Ed Meyen, Lee Swanson, Joe Torgesen, Sharon Vaughn, and Bernice Wong). Almost immediately I began to backtrack on the theoretical speculation in my 1988 paper.

In fact, I was ripe for theoretical change because I had expressed reasonable skepticism in the 1988 paper. For example, I had noted that "the results have been somewhat equivocal. It has not always been possible to differentiate the performance of dyslexic children from garden-variety poor readers" (p. 591) and that the "results have troubled many in the field because they relate to some of the foundational assumptions of the concept of dyslexia as it is used in both research investigations and in educational practice" (p. 591). I proceeded to quote sections of articles by Ellis (1985) and by Seidenberg, Bruck, Fornarolo, and Backman (1986) that were skeptical of the discrepancy notion (see Chapter 7). In short, I had noted how surprisingly difficult it had been to that date to unequivocally demonstrate differences between discrepancy-defined and nondiscrepant poor readers on many of the critical processes of word recognition. It was surprising to me because I think I had pretty much uncritically absorbed—like so many in this field—the basic assumption that IQ discrepancy would pick out a neurological difference and a differential etiology. Although in retrospect I am embarrassed at how uncritically I had accepted assumptions that the field of learning disabilities had never adequately tested (see Chapters 8 and 18 of this volume), I am at least comfortable with the fact that I did respond rather quickly to the preponderance of evidence when it began to point in a direction opposite to my assumptions.

Spurred by Siegel's (1988, 1989) two papers—combined with my own doubts raised in the 1988 *JLD* paper—I began to reorient my theoretical position. I now felt that a better default hypothesis was precisely the one that Siegel (1988, 1989) had so boldly advocated: that there were no important differences between discrepancy-defined and nondiscrepant poor readers within the word recognition module. I held back on her even more provocative claim that there were no comprehension differences because this would have violated the variable difference concept within the phonological-core variable-difference model, and this was wise because there probably are comprehension differences outside the word recognition module (e.g., Hatcher & Hulme, 1999). In a keynote address to the 1989 meeting of the International Academy for Research in Learning Disabilities (IARLD) in Ann Arbor, I explored more thoroughly the implications of this restricted version of Siegel's claim. Future work on this issue was also ensured at the Ann Arbor meeting because, at a lunch at the Michigan League, Linda continued her adroit recruitment of me to come to the Ontario Institute for Studies in Education (a successful recruitment abetted the following year by Anne Jordan and Merl Wahlstrom).

In the Ann Arbor address, I also explored the broader social implications of discrepancy definitions (implications that broadened even further in two subsequent papers, (Stanovich, 1993b, 1999a), as well as how the concept of intelligence interacts with the discrepancy definitions that were foundational for the learning disabilities field. I began a process in this paper (to be carried even further in Stanovich, 1993b, 1999a) of trying to force the field to face up to the responsibilities entailed by making discrepancy—and hence the concept of intelligence—foundational for the learning disabilities field. My feeling was that the field had ducked the responsibility of defending the intelligence concept.

In any case, the IARLD address was rewritten and published in *Reading Research Quarterly* (*RRQ*) in 1991 (here reprinted as Chapter 18). It immediately had a substantial impact, as evidenced by numerous requests for me to speak on the topic of discrepancy definitions, queries from school psychologists and administrators, and requests to write for somewhat new audiences. For example, I was asked to critique the classification criteria for developmental reading disorder in DSM-III-R (see Hooper, Hynd, & Mattison, 1992). The *RRQ* paper also immediately began to rack up a substantial number of citations. It was listed in the February 7, 1994, issue of *Current Contents: Social and Behavioral Sciences* as the fifth most cited publication in education for the period 1991–1993. Additionally, the paper received the 1992 Albert J. Harris Award from the International Reading Association—giving me the honor of being the only person to have won that award twice.

The paper reprinted in Chapter 18 is an odd hybrid (as is the case with the other major papers on this topic, Stanovich, 1993b, 1999a). It reviews the literature, it advances theoretical speculations, and it explores social implications. On standing the test of time, I would score this paper about an 8.5 out of 10. I think the social implications of the discrepancy notion of learning disability that I discussed then are currently as relevant as they ever were, and this discussion is updated in my more recent piece (Stanovich, 1999a). The discussion of intelligence as an index of potential in the learning disabilities field was, I think, a useful addition to the literature critical of how IQ has become reified in learning disabilities definitions (see Kelman & Lester, 1997; Stanovich, 1999a). The discussion of the assumption of specificity in the 1991 paper reiterates and expands on my original discussion of this concept in an important volume by Torgesen and Wong (Stanovich, 1986a) where I first pointed out the problematic psychometric implications of the learning disability concept. The assumption of specificity and its psychometric corollaries have yet to be fully understood by learning disabilities practitioners—and researchers as well have not fully thought through its implications.

In the 1991 paper, I tried to draw attention to the fact that intelligence is a superordinate construct for the notion of learning disabilities (a theme even more salient in Stanovich, 1999a) and that simple intellectual honesty requires the field to deal with the psychometric and conceptual problems surrounding the notion of IQ. Additionally, in that paper I wished to flush out the hidden assumptions about life potential (and who has a moral claim on resources) that often hide behind the learning disabilities label. In the 1991 paper, I explored the implications of various types of IQ measures for defining severe discrepancy. The implicit concepts of potential lurking in various intelligence measures are examined as well as their psychometric implications. This examination leads inexorably to the consideration of an old warhorse—listening comprehension—as a baseline for discrepancy measurement. I outline the features that recommend this measure (although some of the reliability and validity problems I pointed to then still remain; see Badian, 1999; Fletcher et al., 1998), but then proceed to undermine it by noting how a consideration of Matthew effects in cognitive development blurs the sharp aptitude/achievement distinction that is necessary to sustain the discrepancy concept even when based on listening comprehension.

If I were to write this paper again, I would include a discussion of a point emphasized by Fletcher et al. (1998): that the excessive focus on discrepancy definitions thwarts early intervention efforts because such classification often takes place rather late in an academic career. Instead, a more inclusive approach, such as that advocated in Stanovich (1996b) would "enhance early identification and intervention for children with LD, which has been hindered by the IQ-discrepancy model" (Fletcher et al., 1998, p. 186).

The paper reprinted as Chapter 18 began what was to become a trend in my papers on the discrepancy issue. Specifically, the paper, and its two companions (Stanovich, 1993b, 1999a), was characterized by a heavy dose of "if–then logic." In these papers, my goal was less to push a certain view of reading, reading disability, or educational classification. Instead, I wanted to reveal the implications of the classification concepts that were used in the field. My strategy was to say "if *this* is your concept of reading disability, then such and such follows." For example, *if* your concept of learning disability rests on the assumption of specificity, then the learning disability *cannot* be due to deficiency in a cognitive mechanism that is likely to have broad-based effects.

DYSRATIONALIA: A SWIFTIAN EPISTEMOLOGICAL BENDER

This "if–then logic" became even more apparent in my 1993 article published in the *JLD*. This logic probably became more apparent because my impatience with the field had increased since my 1989 IARLD address. This was noticed by many commentators. For example, Ashton (1996) noted that, compared with the discussion in Stanovich (1991a), in my later papers "the argument against discrepancy measures is expressed in a more radical and striking way" (p. 131). This is quite true. The change in emphasis came about, however, for a very straightforward reason: in the interim, more evidence had accumulated. The evidence subsequent to the Stanovich (1991a) publication simply warranted a stronger conclusion.

Part of that evidence subsequent to the 1991 paper was the result of my collaboration with Linda Siegel. The most well-known paper from that collaboration (Stanovich & Siegel, 1994) is reprinted in the current volume as Chapter 8 in Part II. At the 1989 American Educational Research Association (AERA) meeting in San Francisco and at the IARLD meeting in Ann Arbor we had discussed the possibility of my joining her and the other literacy researchers at the Ontario Institute for Studies in Education. By late 1991 we were working together in Toronto. The data we were analyzing for our paper subsequently published in 1994 was in my mind as I was writing the so-called dysrationalia article published in 1993.

The dysrationalia article had been started a couple of years earlier while I was on sabbatical at the University of Cambridge as a guest of Usha Goswami. However, the vehemence with which the challenges to the field were expressed was increased by the knowledge of the data that was to appear as Stanovich and Siegel (1994)—hence Ashton's (1996) correct observation that in articles after the 1991 *RRQ* paper "the argument against discrepancy measures is expressed in a more radical and striking way" (p. 131). Indeed, in an article in the magazine *Lingua Franca* in March 1998, a reporter characterized my 1993 *JLD* article as a "Swiftian epistemological bender" (Metcalf,

1998). I took this as a profound compliment. My favorite author, George Orwell, was often dubbed "Swiftian," so I was more than comfortable with the comparison. As for "epistemological bender," if we take this to mean "disruptive of what the field thinks it knows," then this is precisely what I intended by coining a new disability category called dysrationalia. Of course, in structuring the article in the way that I did, I ran the risk that it's if–then logic would be missed by some readers, which is apparently what happened for one *New Republic* reporter (Shalit, 1997) and the president of Boston University (Stanovich, 1999a).

In the dysrationalia paper, I attempted to push the if–then logic used in the earlier 1991 article as far as it would go. The heart of the dysrationalia article is the if–then cascade triggered by the fact that "the logic of discrepancy-based classification based on IQ test performance has created a clear precedent whereby we are almost obligated to create a new disability category when an important skill domain is found to be somewhat dissociated from intelligence" (p. 502). This premise highlights the foundational role played by intelligence in the definition of learning disabilities. It also suggests that any alteration in our concept of intelligence will have concomitant effects on the concept of learning disability. For example, at the end of the article, I explore the markedly contrasting effects on the dysrationalia disability category for two alternative conceptions of intelligence. Under one view of intelligence dysrationalia disappears. Under the other, it has as much conceptual status as reading disability itself.

The situation is again an if–then. Do we want disability categories to appear and disappear as notions of intelligence evolve and change, as they continue to do (Sternberg, 1990; Sternberg & Detterman, 1986)? If such instability in disability categories is thought to be undesirable, then it must be recognized that it results directly from the reliance on discrepancy measurement and its concomitant IQ dependency. If we do not want to recognize dysrationalia and a host of other similar disability categories that might be concocted, then we must again recognize that these categories follow directly from the field's fixation on discrepancy measurement.

DESTROYING THE VERY CONCEPT OF DYSLEXIA?

The 1991 *RRQ* article (Chapter 18) and the 1993 *JLD* article were soon followed by our (Stanovich & Siegel, 1994) empirical analysis of processing inside and outside the word recognition module by discrepancy-defined and garden-variety poor readers (see Chapter 8). This article was published back to back in the *Journal of Educational Psychology* with a paper by Fletcher, Shaywitz, Shankweiler, Katz, Liberman, Stuebing, Francis, Fowler, and Shaywitz (1994) that came to essentially the same conclusion: that within the word recognition module—in terms of phonological and orthographic processing efficiency—the two groups performed in a remarkably similar manner (see also Fletcher et al., 1998; Francis et al., 1996; Share, 1996). Differences did begin to appear once the task tapped more extensively outside of the word recognition module—just as predicted by the phonological-core variable-difference model (see Chapter 7). I updated and summarized this evidence later in the *Journal of Child Psychology and Psychiatry* (Stanovich, 1994a) and in the journal *Dyslexia* (Stanovich, 1996b).

By the mid- to late-1990s there were signs that the message was beginning to get through. At least one researcher lamented that "the most incisive, and latterly most damaging, analyses have been presented by Stanovich (1988a, 1988b, 1991, 1994; Stanovich & Siegel, 1994), who has not only defined the theoretical agenda for dyslexia research, but has also come close to destroying the very concept of dyslexia" (Nicolson, 1996, p. 194). Again, I think that this statement was made in consternation, but I took it as a compliment—a compliment if by dyslexia we mean only children with reading difficulties who have reading/IQ discrepancies. As I tried to indicate in the title of my 1996 *Dyslexia* article—"Toward a More Inclusive Definition of Dyslexia"—I think the field would have been much better off to have started with a more inclusive definition of reading disability that made no discrepancy differentiation. The field could have then proceeded to more systematically explore whether different partitionings based on various psychometric and demographic characteristics did carve out groups with differing cognitive profiles and etiologies. Such a definition would have put us on the right foot with respect to what the proper null hypothesis should be: that we should assume similarity until empirical evidence established reliable differences between groups. As discussed in the Stanovich and Siegel (1994; see Chapter 8) article, failure to adopt the proper null hypothesis precluded a test of the discrepancy assumption. Instead of including a discrepancy versus garden-variety comparison in their studies, researchers often culled the garden-variety children from their samples!

How have the extent tests—those in Stanovich and Siegel (1994), Fletcher et al. (1994; Fletcher et al., 1998) and others (e.g., Felton & Wood, 1992)—stood the test of time? The skepticism toward discrepancy measurement apparent in Chapters 8 and in Stanovich (1993b, 1994a, 1996b) was based on lack of evidence or null findings on four basic issues: (1) no evidence that the pattern of information processing skills that underlie the word recognition deficits of poor readers are different for poor readers of low and high IQ; (2) no evidence that the neuroanatomical defects that underlie the cognitive deficits of these two groups are different; (3) no evidence that low and high IQ poor readers respond differently to treatment; and (4) no evidence for differential etiology in the two groups based on different heritability of the component deficits. The evidence on points #1 and #2 seems as it was when I wrote the article reprinted here, but the evidence on points #3 and #4 has evolved a bit since that article was written.

Regarding point #1, although there is some recent conflicting evidence, the preponderance of evidence still indicates that the primary indicators of reading difficulty at the word recognition level do not differentiate poor readers with discrepancy from those without. For example, several studies have compared the performance of poor readers with high and low IQs and have found that they display equivalent pseudoword reading deficits (Ellis, McDougall, & Monk, 1996; Felton & Wood, 1992; Fredman & Stevenson, 1988; Share, 1996; Siegel, 1988, 1989, 1992; Stanovich & Siegel, 1994). Similarly, the two groups display roughly equal deficits in phonological segmentation skills[1] (Fletcher et al., 1994, 1998; Foorman, Francis, Fletcher, & Lynn, 1996; Hurford, Schauf, Bunce, Blaich, & Moore, 1994). On measures of orthographic processing, where reading-disabled children are generally less impaired, the groups again display no differences (Foorman et al., 1996; Fredman & Stevenson, 1988; Siegel, 1992; Stanovich & Siegel, 1994). The evidence on naming deficits is inconclusive (Goswami, Schneider, & Scheurich, 1999; Swan & Goswami, 1997). The spelling–sound regularity effect, often interpreted as an indicator of the relative reliance on phonological and orthographic coding processes, appears to be of a similar magnitude in reading-disabled children and younger reading-level controls (Metsala, Stanovich, & Brown, 1998) and this appears to be true for both poor readers without aptitude/achievement discrepancies (Beech & Harding, 1984; Stanovich, Nathan, & Zolman, 1988; Treiman & Hirsh-Pasek, 1985) and for those with such discrepancies (Baddeley, Logie, & Ellis, 1988; Ben-Dror, Pollatsek, & Scarpati, 1991; Brown & Watson, 1991; Bruck, 1990; Holligan & Johnston, 1988; Siegel & Ryan, 1988; Watson & Brown, 1992). Finally, the two groups appear to have identical growth curves for reading development (see Francis, Shaywitz, Stuebing, Shaywitz, & Fletcher, 1996) and for component skills of word recognition (Foorman, Francis, & Fletcher, 1995). In summary, there is still no converging empirical evidence indicating that the processing mechanism accounting for the primary word recognition problems of high-IQ poor readers is different from the processing mechanism accounting for the primary word recognition problems of low-IQ poor readers.

On point #2, neuroanatomical differences have yet to be demonstrated—primarily because of the lack of empirical evidence. For example, neuroanatomical studies have indicated that atypical brain symmetries and other cortical anomalies are associated with reading disability (Galaburda, 1994; Hynd, Clinton, & Hiemenz, 1999). However, there is as yet no indication that these neuroanatomical correlates of reading disability show any association with degree of reading-IQ discrepancy. For example, in the Larsen, Hoien, Lundberg, and Odegaard (1990) study of planum temporale symmetry, reading-IQ discrepancy was defined using the Raven Matrices test. The use of a nonverbal test that displays very low correlations with reading and other verbal skills (Stanovich, Cunningham, & Feeman, 1984a) might well have resulted in a sample containing several subjects with depressed verbal IQs and/or below average full-scale IQs. Such subjects might well have been classified as garden-variety poor readers using another IQ measure (Stanovich, 1991a; Chapter 18). Thus, this particular study might well be providing indirect evidence against the hypothesis that these atypical symmetries are unique to discrepancy-defined poor readers.

On point #3—whether low- and high-IQ poor readers respond differently to treatment—there was little definitive evidence at the time Chapter 18 was written. However, since then, some suggestive evidence has come to light in the work of Hatcher and Hulme (1999) and Wise, Ring, and and Olson (1999). The former found that, in individual difference analyses of their training study (see Hatcher, Hulme, & Ellis, 1994), higher IQ children at risk for reading difficulties did not gain more in word recognition ability over the testing period but they did gain more in reading comprehension ability.

However, two caveats are required in the interpretation of the Hatcher and Hulme (1999) analyses. First, in an analysis of individual differences in response to their training intervention, Wise et al. (1999) did find that the higher IQ children gained more in word recognition skill. There are numerous differences between the studies that will need to be examined in order to reconcile this difference (e.g., the Wise et al. sample was 2 years older and of overall higher IQ). Second, in the Hatcher and Hulme (1999) study IQ was only a unique predictor of comprehension gains in one of the four conditions of their experiment (the reading practice only condition). In the other conditions (control, phonology-only training, reading-practice-plus-phonology condition), IQ was not a significant independent predictor of comprehension gains (although it was when the four groups were amalgamated; see also Olson et al., 1999).

Taking the overall trends of the Hatcher and Hulme (1999) study (greater comprehension gains for high IQ children, but not great word recognition gains) at face value, however, they fit in quite well with Gough and Tunmer's (1986) simple model of reading and with the prediction derived from it that I articulated in my 1988a paper (see Chapter 7). Specifically, I argued there that

> if the decoding problem can be remediated, then the contingent prognosis for the dyslexic child should be better—they have no additional cognitive problems that may inhibit reading comprehension growth. This prediction fits nicely with Gough and Tunmer's (1986) simple view of reading comprehension (R) as a multiplicative combination of decoding skill (D) and listening comprehension ability (C); in short, $R = D \times C$. If dyslexics and garden-variety poor readers are matched on reading comprehension (for example, $.4 \times .9 = .6 \times .6$) and if (in some benign world) we were to totally remediate the decoding deficits of each, then the dyslexics would have superior reading comprehension ($1.0 \times .9 > 1.0 \times .6$)." (Stanovich, 1988a, p. 602)

As I argue in Chapter 18, a listening comprehension measure provides an estimate of the reading level that a reading-disabled child might obtain if his or her word recognition deficit were totally remediated (see Chen & Vellutino,

1997; Gough & Tunmer, 1986). To the extent that an IQ measure is correlated with listening comprehension, it serves the same function.

Of course, the findings of Hatcher and Hulme (1999) could also be viewed as additional indications of the trend predicted by the phonological-core variable-difference model that was confirmed in Stanovich and Siegel (1994; see Chapter 8); that there *are* differences between high and low discrepancy groups outside of the word recognition module (see Olson et al., 1999). However, it is important to note that any such differences are not indicators of the core processing problem that caused the word recognition deficit that triggered the diagnosis of reading disability in the first place: phonological coding difficulties probably resulting from deficient phonological awareness due to segmental language problems (see Part II).

On point #4—differential etiology in the two groups based on different heritability of the component deficits—the evidence has also been evolving. An amalgamation of earlier studies (e.g., Fletcher, 1992; Olson, Rack, Conners, DeFries, & Fulker, 1991; Pennington, Gilger, Olson, & DeFries, 1992; Stevenson, 1991, 1992; Stevenson, Graham, Fredman, & McLoughlin, 1987) failed to provide strong evidence that indicators of genetic etiology were correlated with degree of aptitude–achievement discrepancy. However, recent studies by the Colorado group (Olson, 1999) have reported a trend in the expected direction (higher heritability for the group deficit of the higher IQ poor readers), so conclusions on this issue are clearly premature. What is much clearer is that research on the phenotypic performance profile of children with reading difficulty indicates similar proximal causes (see Coltheart & Jackson, 1998) for poor readers with and without aptitude–achievement discrepancy.

The findings of Hatcher and Hulme (1999) on differential response to treatment—as well as the differential genetic associations recently reported by Olson (1999) begin to put the the discrepancy-defined reading disability concept on slightly better footing than I argued for in the paper reprinted as Chapter 18. A few caveats are in order, however. First, such findings do not automatically justify the allocation of differential educational resources to different types of poor readers. Advocates of differential educational treatment still have a difficult job of justification to do—they must still defend a theory of social justice that warrants the differential treatment (see Stanovich, 1999a). It should be remembered that the genetic findings occur in the presence of no phenotypic differences in the cognitive processing profiles of the groups. The proximal cause of reading difficulty in the two groups remains the same. It simply appears that there is a quantitative difference in the matrix of etiological factors that lead to the common proximal deficit in both groups. This remains a thin reed upon which to justify the multimillion dollar learning disabilities classification industry (Kelman & Lester, 1997). And with a comment like that, I have clearly arrived at the social policy issues that are the focus of my most recent statement on this issue (Stanovich, 1999a).

SOCIAL POLICY AND LEARNING DISABILITIES

Social policy issues have loomed larger in my writings as time has progressed. Papers such as those reprinted as Chapter 2 (from 1978) and as Chapter 6 (from 1984) were focused virtually exclusively on basic research concerns and issues. Things change quite a bit with the Matthew effects paper (Chapter 10), which contains discussions of several social and educational policy issues. In the 1990s I was increasingly pressed to comment on policy issues. In a 1990 paper in the *Journal of Reading Behavior* (Stanovich, 1990a), I gave my view of the "paradigm wars" in educational research as they were playing out in studies of the reading process. In my 1994 Distinguished Educator article in the *Reading Teacher* (discussed in Chapter 19 and reprinted as Chapter 20) I stepped into the center of the Great Debate in reading instruction (Adams, 1990; Chall, 1967, 1983a), and I spoke most directly to the social context and politics of the so-called Reading Wars in my Oscar Causey Award address to the National Reading Conference in 1997 (see Chapter 21).

Likewise, the discrepancy issue was raised in the Matthew effects article, which contained a discussion of the assumption of specificity. I worried about the discrepancy issue in the 1988 *JLD* article (Chapter 7); dealt with it explicitly in the 1991 *RRQ* (Chapter 18) and 1993 *JLD* articles; and published an extensive series of statistical analyses on it in the 1994 *Journal of Educational Psychology* paper (Chapter 8). I entered the policy fray on this issue again in 1997 (Stanovich & Stanovich, 1997) when the British journal *Educational Psychology in Practice* asked my wife and me to comment on some papers they had published on the "discrepancy wars." Thus, it was hardly a shock when Richard Sparks emailed me in late 1997 to participate as a commentator for a special series in the *JLD* on the so-called Boston University (BU) case. A group of students had brought suit against BU, charging that eligibility criteria for qualifying as learning disabled were burdensome, procedures for granting accommodations were not reasonable, and that course substitutions in mathematics and foreign language were precluded. I had been following the BU case in the media, but I had not yet read the judge's decision until I took it and the six *JLD* series papers (authored by the lawyers and expert witnesses for both sides) on our post–silver wedding anniversary vacation in the summer of 1998. I also threw in Kelman and Lester's *Jumping the Queue* (1997) which I had just become aware of but had not read.

I took the materials on the BU case to our favorite place on earth—the North Coast of Cornwall—and there I wrote my commentary on the BU case and its implications (Stanovich, 1999a). And I will admit that I wrote it in some anger. My anger was not primarily directed at the judge's decision (although it did have its problems), and not primarily directed at the BU president, whose remarks and actions in part spawned the case (although he was, indeed, clueless). My anger was directed at the field. Here it all was—all of the problems I had been writing about for over a decade—indeed, all of the problems others before me had been writing about for a decade (at least) before I started. All of the conceptual confusion, all of the thoughtless advocacy, all of the pseudoscientific mumbo jumbo—it was all there in the BU case. A decade earlier I had written:

> The field of learning disabilities has a checkered history that is littered with contention, false starts, fads, dead ends, pseudoscience, and just a little bit of hard-won progress. It seems as though the field is constantly getting into scrapes, is always on probation, is never really secure. Why is this? Surely one of the reasons is that, when borrowing ideas from allied fields such as developmental psychology, neuropsychology, and cognitive psychology, the LD field has displayed a remarkable propensity to latch onto concepts that are tenuous and controversial. Examples of this tendency are legion, ranging from visual process training to the concept of minimal brain damage. The LD field seems addicted to living dangerously. However, even in the context of such a history, the decision to base the definition of a reading disability on a discrepancy with measured IQ is still nothing short of astounding. (Stanovich, 1989a, p. 487)

Everything I said in this quote (and more) came home to roost in the BU case a decade later. I remain frustrated that somehow we cannot seem to get the hard-won research knowledge in the field to infuse practice—and that frustration shows in my *JLD* piece. Nevertheless, I stand by virtually everything I said in my commentary—even though I know many in the LD community will not be happy with it. As contemporary rationality theorists have demonstrated (Damasio, 1994; deSousa, 1987; Oatley, 1992) passion does not *necessarily* imply error.

Nevertheless, I do fear that the *JLD* paper on the BU case will be misunderstood. The inability to carry on nuanced debate around the issue of learning disabilities has been characteristic of the educational literature since the concept was invented. History gives little reason for optimism here. No doubt certain commentators will say that I am advocating reduced services for individuals with disabilities when everywhere I argue just the opposite—and in fact I deal specifically with this misunderstanding. And this will sadden me because it will reflect a continuing dilemma in my academic career (one that I will discuss further in Chapter 19): how to reconcile my scientific values with my political values.

Politically I am a man of the Left. But like Orwell, I desire to be a *thinking* man of the left. All political creeds tempt people to check their brains at the door. This is certainly true of the political right in North America. The Right says it stands for stable social structures, traditional values, stable families, cohesive communities, and free-market capitalism. But the last of these does not cohere with the previous four. There is no more continuously disruptive force in the world than unrestricted capitalism. The business pages of our newspapers and our corporate-controlled electronic media constantly tell us that capitalism's "creative destruction" (leaving behind old ways of production in order to promote the more efficient and new) is what produces our impressive material wealth, and this may well be true (for the moment, we will not argue this point). But among the most notable things that are "creatively destroyed" by capitalism are traditional values, stable social structures, families, and cohesive communities. The temporary employment agency, Manpower, is the largest employer in the United States, having more people on its payroll than General Motors (Sennett, 1998). Amid the downsizing and outsourcing there exists no traditional loyalty. Amid the buyouts and globalism, cohesive communities count for nothing (more important is that they make it cheaper in Guadalajara). So in order to sign on to this particular version of right-wing politics, you have to check your brain at the door by ignoring this glaring inconsistency among the matrix of beliefs that you are supposed to hold.

But the Left has its own "check your brain at the door" views as well (this is what Orwell wrote so eloquently about in *Homage to Catalonia* [1952] and other works; see Orwell & Angus, 1968). This is what the controversies over "political correctness" (PC) are all about. When discussing social policy surrounding learning disabilities, surely we do not want a situation where one cannot call for a rational discussion of the allocation of educational resources without triggering the charge that one is denying disabled individuals their rights. However, the plaintiffs in the BU case certainly did try to co-opt all of the PC language of disability rights. But the purpose of my essay was to question the automatic associations that the mere mention of the word "rights" has in people's minds. The complications here are myriad and I tried to illustrate a few—for example, in the discussion of the continuous nature of reading disabilities. Where does the "right" to extra time on tests begin?—at 16 standard score points of reading achievement below IQ, or at 15, 14, 13, 12? *All* of these students could use the extra time to good effect—to say nothing of the poor readers without discrepancy whom I tried to draw attention to in the essay. The situation does not lend itself at all to the language of "rights" but instead to the language of a zero-sum trade-off of resources among many different groups—all of whom might benefit. I stand by my contention in the essay that the case for extra resources based on reading/IQ discrepancy has yet to be made. The unintended consequences of such a policy can be brought to the fore by considering cases where services are not offered to those lacking such discrepancies.

Consider the case of Cedric Jennings, movingly described in Ron Suskind's marvelous book *A Hope in the Unseen* (1998). Cedric survived a career of harassment at an inner-city high school in Washington, DC—harassment generated in part by his devotion to his studies. He often skipped achievement awards ceremonies for fear of verbal and physical intimidation. He went home to study diligently in his room in a bleak apartment block—a home that his valiant single mother tried to hold together. Mother and son had lived through several evictions and periods of hunger between welfare checks. His mother struggled to procure work and did succeed, but this barely helped. The family simply became part of a low-wage economy in the United States that is little better than welfare. Nevertheless, Cedric succeeded in being accepted by

Brown University. Despite an immense capacity for work, his high-school background did not prepare him for Brown—for its vocabulary, for its demands of nuanced and responsive argument rather than memorization. The cultural knowledge (see Hirsch, 1987, 1996) assumed in virtually all his courses and conversations was not available at his alma mater, Ballou High School.

After much struggle in his courses, Cedric was sent to an academic tutor who, Suskind (1998) tells us,

> fires off a long list of questions, her clipboard poised: any allergies? any family members prematurely grey? any relatives who stutter? She then asks Cedric to write a sentence so she can carefully examine the way he holds his pencil. These are some of the strange, medicine-man tests to identify learning disabilities. For most of her students, she quickly identifies some strain of learning disability (a broadly applicable label) that allows them special provisions for test-taking and general classwork. "Have you ever had any trouble in school?" she asks, because she hasn't hit any obvious LD markers. "Always a good student?" (pp. 238–239)

No, Cedric did not have a severe discrepancy—just years and years of hard work in an impoverished educational atmosphere that was bound to leave him behind the requirements of Brown no matter how hard he worked. Thus, we have the peculiar logic of present-day university services and accommodations: extra time on tests for a score on a neuropsychological test—but not for hearing gunfire in school, traveling to school through hazardous territory, being discouraged by peers, having no quiet place to study, having dated textbooks. No extra time, no accommodations for these things—no, sorry Cedric, you lack a severe discrepancy.

REFRAMING THE ISSUE

I think that one of the most useful sections of my essay on the BU case is the section on alternative framings of an issue where I borrowed from the decision theory literature on framing effects (e.g., Schick, 1997; Tversky & Kahneman, 1981). The theme of that section was that we should not hide zero-sum situations behind touchy-feely language—because, behind the touchy-feely language, someone is getting hurt. To use the example discussed there, the issue is not "Should a deduction be allowed for home mortgage interest?" The issue society should be debating is whether renters should pay *more* tax in order that home owners can pay *less*. As two economists describe the situation, "By requiring higher tax rates, subsidies cause everything else to be penalized. . . . The point is that these features are enormously popular because they have been enshrined as 'tax reductions,' but these exact same features probably wouldn't stand a chance as stand-alone policies" (Slemrod & Bakija, 1996, pp. 113, 141).

In short, some positions will withstand a revealing zero-sum scrutiny and others will not. For example, I would hazard a guess that "capital gains tax break" will not survive a reframing as "Should wage earners pay more taxes in order that stockholders can pay less?" Likewise, certain educational trade-offs will survive the scrutiny and others will not. For example, I would support the proposition that "most youngsters should get slightly fewer resources so that a blind child can be accommodated to benefit from school" and I would bet that most other people would as well. This proposition would survive the public policy debate. Likewise, changing "Should we help deaf kids?" into "Should most youngsters get slightly fewer resources so that a deaf child can be accommodated to benefit from school?" would make little difference. The altered proposition would survive the public policy debate.

In contrast, changing the proposition from "Should learning disabled children be helped?" to "Should most youngsters get slightly fewer resources so that some children are more able to perform commensurate with their IQs?" does alter the debate considerably. It is not that there are not some good arguments in favor of the altered proposition. I in fact think that there *are* some, though they are in no way as definitive as those applying to the blind child. The point is that these arguments have not been made at all in the LD literature, and in my paper on the BU case I speculated about why. I think a type of PC is coming into play here. While it is PC to "advocate for services," it is not PC to talk about trading off relative levels of resources among students and, more importantly, it is definitely not PC to advocate for individuals based on their relatively high IQ—nor is it PC to defend intelligence tests (or even the concept of intelligence) upon which the LD concept rests.

On the latter point, I think Kelman and Lester (1997) are right on the mark in pointing out the tendency of LD advocates to obscure their endorsement of the most traditional IQ notions (e.g., that an IQ is a measure of educational potential). Such an endorsement clearly follows from the advocates' position that "society is especially obligated to try to ensure that all students develop skills congruent with the expectations we derive from their IQ tests" (p. 175). I emphasized this in my BU piece by pointing out that there is little difference between the LD field's notions of intelligence and those of Jensen (1998) or Herrnstein and Murray (1994)—all of whom are bête noirs for leftist academics.

More than trying to defend a specific position in the dispute, I want all the sides to acknowledge the implications in their positions and to resolve the contradictions. This again is consistent with the if–then logic of Chapter 18 and with my interest in fostering critical thought (Stanovich, 1998a, 1999b). If there are contradictory implications in your beliefs, you really do have to *choose* in order to have a rational set of beliefs. In the right-wing example used above, the point is that you *can't* have traditional values, stable social structures, stable families, cohesive communities, *and* have feverish, unrestrained global capitalism as well. You have to decide which you value more. Similarly, you cannot advocate for extra resources for one group of children without acknowledging that another group will get less and defending this as a reasonable trade-off. And you cannot advocate for an LD concept based on discrepancy without defending the most traditional assumptions about psychometric IQ (e.g., that it is a measure of educational potential). My goal was summarized well in a quote from Jacques Barzun (1959) in which he said that "the intention of my words was not so much to persuade as to direct attention to incongruity and disease; this book is a pathology of the subject, of which the fundamental principle resides in just this conditional proposition: if–then. The argument was in fact a choice: if you want this you must have, or do, *that*" (p. 251).

NOTE

1. Recently, Olson et al. (1999) reported evidence contradicting this trend in that they found a significant difference between groups of high-IQ and low-IQ poor readers (equated for word recognition ability) on a phonological awareness task (Pig Latin). However, the outcome (better performance by the high-IQ children) was in the direction *opposite* to the prediction in my 1988 paper (Chapter 7; see also the discussion in Chapter 5) and to the finding that might be expected psychometrically. That the finding was in this direction presents a theoretical puzzle. It would seem that the high-IQ group has two important processing characteristics going in their favor, yet they cannot parlay either into word recognition performance better than that of garden-variety poor readers. Specifically, the discrepant group has superior central processing ability (as indicated by their IQs) *and* superior phonological awareness, yet cannot use *either* to facilitate word recognition. This is a puzzling finding, but I have a theoretical explanation for it. Perhaps the variance in the Pig Latin task that is associated with IQ is the *non*phonological variance that is implicated in any cognitive task. This would explain why the phonological awareness difference did not cash out in terms of differences in word recognition. Thus, the conjecture is that maybe these two groups are similar on the underlying phonological trait but that they differ on the extraneous processing requirements of the task. This of course leads to a prediction: the less of the latter in a task, the more similar the groups will be.

CHAPTER 18

Discrepancy Definitions of Reading Disability

Has Intelligence Led Us Astray?

The concept of dyslexia and/or reading disability[1] has been controversial in the reading community. In this essay, I will argue that a major source of contention and theoretical confusion surrounding the term dyslexia stems from an almost perverse insistence on utilizing the concept of intelligence in definitions of dyslexia. It is argued that more educationally relevant aptitude indicators, long suggested by reading educators, would be preferable to intelligence measures. However, we will end on a sobering note by arguing that all attempts at aptitude/achievement discrepancy measurement are plagued by the reciprocal relationship between reading and various cognitive skills—reciprocal effects that, with time, serve to undermine the distinction between aptitude and achievement.

INTELLIGENCE VIEWED AS "POTENTIAL"

The initial formulation of professional and legal definitions of reading disability all emphasized the existence of discrepancies between actual school achievement and assumed intellectual capacity. During the 1960s and 1970s, several proposed definitions of reading disability had considerable influence on both research and service delivery debates. The definition of the World Federation of Neurology had many features that became canonical for many researchers and practitioners. Specific developmental dyslexia was characterized as "a disorder manifested by difficulty in learning to read despite conventional instruction, adequate intelligence, and socio-cultural opportunity. It is dependent upon fundamental cognitive disabilities which are frequently of constitutional origin" (Critchley, 1970, p. 11).

This particular definition highlighted the well-known "exclusionary criteria" that subsequently caused much dispute in discussions of dyslexia (e.g., Applebee, 1971; Ceci, 1986; Doehring, 1978; Eisenberg, 1978; Rutter, 1978)—in particular, it requires "adequate" intelligence to qualify for the dyslexia label. The exclusionary criteria became the indirect way of operationalizing the assumption of neurological etiology in the absence of direct evidence of neurological dysfunction.

The use of exclusionary criteria were carried over into the definition of learning disability employed in the landmark Education for All Handicapped Children Act (PL 94-142) passed in 1975:

> Specific learning disability means a disorder in one or more of the basic psychological processes involved in understanding or in using language spoken or written, which may manifest itself in an imperfect ability to listen, think, speak, read, write, spell, or to do mathematical calculations. The term includes such conditions as perceptual handicaps, brain injury, minimal brain dysfunction, dyslexia, and developmental aphasia. The term does not include children who have learning problems which are primarily the result of visual, hearing, or motor handicaps, of mental retardation, of emotional disturbance, or of environmental, cultural, or economic disadvantage.

Again, the exclusion of poor reading achievement due to mental retardation highlights the requirement of a mismatch between aptitude and achievement.

The National Joint Committee for Learning Disabilities responded to criticisms of the exclusionary criteria by proposing that "these disorders are intrinsic to the individual and presumed to be due to central nervous dysfunction. Even though a learning disability may occur concomitantly with other handicapping conditions (e.g., sensory impairment, mental retardation, social and emotional disturbance) or environmental influences (e.g., cultural differences, or inappropriate instruction, psycholinguistic factors), it is not the direct result of those conditions or influences" (Hammill, Leigh, McNutt, & Larsen, 1981); thus emphasizing that the mere presence of other impairments or of environmental deprivation should not exclude children from the LD categorization (see also Kavanagh & Truss, 1988).

All of these professional and legal definitions highlight the same salient feature: the fact that a dyslexic child has an "unexpected" disability in the domain of reading, one not predicted by his/her general intellectual competence and socioeducational opportunities. Practically, this has meant a statistical assessment of the difference between objectively measured reading ability and general intelligence (Frankenberger & Harper, 1987; Kavale, 1987; Kavale & Nye, 1981; Reynolds, 1985; Shepard, 1980). Typically, very little effort is expended in ascertaining whether adequate instruction has been provided or whether the child suffers from sociocultural disadvantage—in short, in ascertaining whether the disability is "intrinsic to the individual." So much conceptual confusion has surrounded the more operational discrepancy criterion that researchers and theoreticians have been reluctant to take on the potential additional complications of the other criteria. In short, despite repeated admonitions that the diagnosis of reading disability should be multidimensional (Johnson, 1988; McKinney, 1987; Senf, 1986; Tindal & Marston, 1986), in actual educational practice it is the assessment of a discrepancy between aptitude as measured by an individually administered intelligence test and reading achievement that is the key defining feature (Frankenberger & Harper, 1987).

The popularity in educational practice of the use of the concept of intelligence as a benchmark in the definition of reading disability is puzzling, however. Surely one would be hard-pressed to find a concept more controversial than intelligence in all of psychology! It has been the subject of dispute for decades, and this shows no sign of abating. Current work on individual differences in intelligent functioning continues to produce exciting findings and interesting theories (Baron, 1985; Ceci, 1990; Ceci & Liker, 1986; Sternberg, 1985a, 1988), but no consensual view of the intelligence concept (Sternberg & Detterman, 1986). Even though much progress has been made in both empirical and theoretical domains, quite fundamental disputes remain. For example, some investigators have recently emphasized more contextualized approaches to the study of intelligence (Ceci, 1990; Ceci & Liker, 1986; Sternberg, 1985a, 1988; Sternberg & Wagner, 1986), whereas others have been advocating more decontextualized biological approaches (Vernon, 1987).

Yet despite the controversy surrounding intelligence in the cognitive, developmental, and psychometric literature, it was adopted as a foundational construct for the definition of dyslexia. Oblivious to the ongoing debates, the learning disabilities field seems to have avoided worrying about the issue by simply adopting a variant of E. G. Boring's dictum and acting as if "Intelligence is what The Psychological Corporation says it is!" The choice of IQ test performance as the baseline from which to measure achievement discrepancies was accepted by teachers, schools, professional organizations, and government agencies in the absence of much critical discussion or research evidence. Until quite recently, the field seems never to have grappled very seriously with the question of why the benchmark should have been IQ. It is thus not surprising that the concept of intelligence is the genesis of so many of the conceptual paradoxes that plague the concept of dyslexia (Stanovich, 1986a, 1986b, 1988b).

Why was professional assent to the use of IQ test scores in the discrepancy definition given so readily? Undoubtedly there were many reasons, but probably one factor was the belief that IQ scores were valid measures of intellectual potential. Certainly an extreme form of this belief can be seen in the promotional activities of many advocacy groups and in media portrayals. The typical "media dyslexic" is almost always a very bright child who is deeply troubled in school because of a "glitch" (assumed to be biologically based; see Coles, 1978, 1987; McGill-Franzen, 1987) that prevents him or her from reading. The subtext of the portrayal clearly implies that the tragedy of the situation is proportionally greater because the child's great "potential" remains unlocked. This media portrayal has now entered the realm of folk belief, for there exists a popular myth that dyslexia is the "affliction of geniuses" (Adelman & Adelman, 1987; Coles, 1987), if anything, *more* likely to occur in very bright people. This popular belief in the idea of "unlocked potential" undoubtedly helped to fuel the rapid expansion of the learning disabilities field.

One major problem, however, was that most psychometricians, developmental psychologists, and educational psychologists long ago gave up the belief that IQ test scores measured potential in any valid sense. Indeed, standard texts in educational measurement and assessment routinely warn against interpreting IQ scores as measures of intellectual potential (Anastasi, 1988; Cronbach, 1984; Thorndike, 1963). At their best, IQ test scores are gross measures of current cognitive functioning (Detterman, 1982; Humphreys, 1979). Indeed, many theorists would dispute even this characterization. Siegel (1988, 1989), for example, attacks the representativeness of several typical IQ tasks and outlines the objections of many theorists. Without entering into the details of all of these debates, the point is that an IQ test score is not properly interpreted as a measure of an individual's potential. Thus, to the extent that this misinterpretation contributed to the practice of measuring discrepancies from IQ scores, then this practice was misconceived from the beginning. In short, we have been basing systems of educational classification in the area of reading disabilities on special claims of unique potential that are neither conceptually nor psychometrically justifiable.

However, advocates of current practices might counter some of these criticisms by arguing that, despite conceptual difficulties, a strictly empirical orientation would support current procedures. That is, an advocate of the status quo might argue that all of the philosophical and conceptual criticisms are beside the point, because measuring discrepancy from IQ in the current manner distinguishes a group of children who, cognitively and behaviorally, are sufficiently distinct that the use of current procedures is justified on empirical grounds. Here we are getting to the heart of many recent research disputes.

THE CONSTRUCT VALIDITY OF THE CONCEPT OF DYSLEXIA

The vast majority of poor readers in the schools are, of course, not characterized by severe discrepancies between their reading ability and assessed intelligence (Eisenberg, 1979). Their below-average reading performance is predictable from their general cognitive abilities. They are what Gough and Tunmer (1986) term "garden-variety" poor readers, and they tend to be more numerous than discrepancy-defined poor readers. The critical assumption that has fueled theoretical interest in the dyslexia concept from the beginning—and that has justified differential educational classification and treatment—has been that the degree of discrepancy from IQ is meaningful: that the reading difficulties of the dyslexic stem from problems different from those character- izing the poor reader without IQ discrepancy; or, alternatively, if they stem from the same factors, that the degree of severity is so extreme for the dyslexic that it constitutes, in effect, a qualitative difference.

The operationalization of this assumption for purposes of empirical tests has been dominated by two different research designs. One is the reading-level match design, where an older group of dyslexic children is matched on read- ing level with a younger group of nondyslexic children. Without entering into the methodological thicket surrounding the use of this design to infer causa- tion (Goswami & Bryant, 1989; Jackson & Butterfield, 1989; Vellutino & Scanlon, 1989), the procedure of profile comparison in a reading-level design seems at least a minimally acceptable operational method for testing the cog- nitive differentiability of dyslexic poor readers. The logic here is fairly straightforward. If the reading subskills and cognitive characteristics of the two groups do not match, then it would seem that they are arriving at their similar reading levels via different routes. In contrast, if the reading subskill profiles of the two groups are identical, this would seem to undermine the ra- tionale for the differential educational treatment of dyslexic children and for their theoretical differentiation. If dyslexic children are reading just like any other child who happens to be at their reading level, and are using the same cognitive skills to do so, they become much less interesting from a theoretical point of view.

The second major design—one pertinent not only to theoretical issues but also to the educational politics of reading disability—is to compare dyslexic children with children of the same age who are reading at the same level, but who are not labeled dyslexic because they have lower IQs. Adapting the termi- nology of Gough and Tunmer (1986), I have termed this design the "garden- variety control" design (Stanovich, 1988a). Again, the inferences drawn are relatively straightforward. If the reading subskill profiles of the two groups do not match, then this is at least consistent with the assumption that they are ar- riving at their similar reading levels via different routes. In contrast, if the reading subskill profiles of the two groups are identical, this would certainly undermine the rationale for the differential educational treatment of dyslexic children and would again make dyslexic children considerably less interesting theoretically.

Unfortunately, well-controlled studies employing the garden-variety con- trol and reading-level match designs have begun to appear in sufficient num- bers only recently. For a considerable period, the dyslexia literature was domi- nated by studies employing only chronological-age controls, a design of low diagnosticity (Bryant & Goswami, 1986). It was not until the mid-1970s that we had the data from the groundbreaking epidemiological comparison of dys- lexic and garden-variety poor readers conducted by Rutter and Yule (1975), and only in the last five years or so has their data been supplemented by other garden-variety control investigations. Additionally, only recently have enough studies employing reading-level matches been accumulated so that patterns were discernible.

Part of the reason for the malaise and soul-searching that periodically overtakes learning disabilities researchers and practitioners (Coles, 1978, 1987; Lyon, 1987; Senf, 1986; Stanovich, 1989b; Swanson, 1988; Vaughn & Bos, 1987; Vellutino, 1979) is that the field plunged ahead into the domains of educational practice and diagnosis without setting itself on a firm foundation by first unequivocally demonstrating the empirical differentiability that would establish construct validity for the reading disability concept. We will review the evidence that does exist below.

The Phonological-Core Variable-Difference Model of Dyslexia

Before summarizing the current state of the evidence on the cognitive differentiability of dyslexic poor readers I will outline what patterns, *given* our current conceptions of dyslexia, our data *should* show, in the best of all possible worlds. I have summarized the idealized situation in a model that I have termed the phonological-core variable-difference framework (Stanovich, 1988a).

The model rests on a clear understanding of the assumption of specificity in definitions of dyslexia (see Hall & Humphreys, 1982; Stanovich, 1986a, 1986b). This assumption underlies *all* discussions of the concept of dyslexia, even if it is not explicitly stated. It is the idea that a child with this type of learning disability has a brain/cognitive deficit that is reasonably specific to the reading task. That is, the concept of dyslexia requires that the deficits displayed by such children not extend too far into other domains of cognitive functioning. If they did, this would depress the constellation of abilities we call intelligence and thus reduce the reading/intelligence discrepancy that is central to all current definitions.

In short, the key deficit in dyslexia must be a domain-specific process (see Fodor, 1983) rather than a central cognitive mechanism with widely distributed effects. For this, and other reasons, many investigators have located the proximal locus of dyslexia at the word recognition level (e.g., Bruck, 1988, 1990; Gough & Tunmer, 1986; Morrison, 1984, 1987a; Perfetti, 1985; Siegel, 1985, 1988; Siegel & Faux, 1989; Stanovich, 1986b, 1988b) and have been searching for the locus of the flaw in the word recognition module.

Research in the last ten years has focused intensively on phonological processing abilities. It is now well established that dyslexic children display deficits in various aspects of phonological processing. They have difficulty making explicit reports about sound segments at the phoneme level, they display naming difficulties, their utilization of phonological codes in short-term memory is inefficient, their categorical perception of certain phonemes may be other than normal, and they may have speech production difficulties (Ackerman, Dykman, & Gardner, 1990; Cossu, Shankweiler, Liberman, Katz, & Tola, 1988; Kamhi & Catts, 1989; Liberman & Shankweiler, 1985; Lieberman, Meskill, Chatillon, & Schupack, 1985; Mann, 1986; Pennington, 1986; Pratt & Brady, 1988; Reed, 1989; Snowling, 1987; Taylor, Lean, & Schwartz, 1989; Wagner & Torgesen, 1987; Werker & Tees, 1987; Williams, 1984, 1986; Wolf & Goodglass, 1986). Importantly, there is increasing evidence that the linkage from phonological processing ability to reading skill is a causal one (Adams, 1990; Bradley & Bryant, 1985; Bryant, Bradley, Maclean, & Crossland, 1989; Lundberg, Frost, & Peterson, 1988; Lundberg & Hoien, 1989; Maclean, Bryant, & Bradley, 1987; Perfetti, Beck, Bell, & Hughes, 1987; Stanovich, 1986b, 1988b; Treiman & Baron, 1983; Wagner, 1988; Wagner & Torgesen, 1987). Presumably, lack of phonological sensitivity makes the learning of grapheme-to-phoneme correspondences very difficult. There is evidence for reciprocal causation here as well (Ehri, 1987; Ehri, Wilce, & Taylor, 1987; Morais, Bertelson, Cary, & Alegria, 1986), but a full discussion of this issue is beyond the scope of this essay and not necessary to the following argument.

Thus, there is now voluminous evidence indicating that phonological deficits are the basis of the dyslexic performance pattern. This is an oversimplification, because it ignores the possibility of core deficits in the realm of orthographic processing. In fact, there is growing evidence for the utility of distinguishing a group of dyslexics who have severe problems in accessing the lexicon on a visual/orthographic basis (see Stanovich, 1992b; Stanovich & West, 1989). Suggestive evidence comes from the work on acquired reading disability that has revealed the existence of surface dyslexia (Patterson, Marshall, & Coltheart, 1985), a condition where the affected individual appears to have difficulty forming and/or accessing orthographic representations of words in memory. Indirect evidence also comes from multivariate investigations indicating that efficient phonological processing is a necessary but not sufficient condition for attaining advanced levels of word recognition skill (Juel, Griffith, & Gough, 1986; Tunmer & Nesdale, 1985).

But as regards visual/orthographic processing deficits, two crucial caveats are in order. First, there is a very large body of evidence indicating that this group of children must be numerically quite smaller than the group with phonological difficulties (Aaron, 1989a; Freebody & Byrne, 1988; Gough & Hillinger, 1980; Liberman, 1982; Liberman & Shankweiler, 1985; Pennington, 1986; Perfetti, 1985; Vellutino, 1979). One reason they must be very small in number is that they have not obscured the identification of phonological problems in samples that were not preselected for subtypes. Secondly, the problem encountered by these children seems to be not at all similar to the "visual perception" problems popular in the early history of the study of dyslexia, but now widely recognized to have been overstated (Aman & Singh, 1983; Morrison, Giordani, & Nagy, 1977; Stanovich, 1986a; Vellutino, 1979). The actual problems in visual/orthographic processing must be much more subtle and localized than these older views suggested. Some research has indicated the presence of such visual deficits (Lovegrove & Slaghuis, 1989; Martin & Lovegrove, 1988; Solman & May, 1990; Willows, 1991), but the issue remains controversial (Hulme, 1988). Irrespective of how this research dispute is eventually resolved, it is the case that any smaller group of dyslexics with visual/orthographic core-deficits would mirror the phonological-core group in all of the other processing characteristics of the model. What are those characteristics?

In the phonological-core variable-difference model (Stanovich, 1988a), the term variable difference refers to the key performance contrasts between the garden-variety and the dyslexic poor reader. The cognitive status of the garden-variety poor reader appears to be well described by a developmental lag model. Cognitively, they are remarkably similar to younger children reading at the same level (Stanovich, Nathan, & Vala-Rossi, 1986; Stanovich, Nathan, & Zolman, 1988). A logical corollary of this pattern is that the garden-variety reader will have a wide variety of cognitive deficits when compared to chronological-age controls who are reading at normal levels. However, it is important to understand that the garden-variety poor reader does share the phonological problems of the dyslexic reader, and these deficits appear also to be a causal factor in their poor reading (Juel, 1988; Juel, Griffith, & Gough, 1986; Perfetti, 1985; Stanovich, 1986b). But for the garden-variety reader the deficits—relative to CA controls—extend into a variety of domains (see Ellis & Large, 1987) and some of these (e.g., vocabulary, language comprehension) may also be causally linked to reading comprehension. Such a pattern should not characterize the dyslexic, who should have a deficit localized in the phonological core.

The phonological-core variable-difference model assumes multidimensional continuity for reading ability in general and for all its related cognitive subskills. That is, it conceives of all of the relevant distributions of reading-related cognitive skills as being continuously arrayed in a multidimensional space and not distributed in clusters. There is considerable evidence from a variety of different sources supporting such a continuity assumption (Ellis, 1985; Jorm, 1983; Olson, Kliegl, Davidson, & Foltz, 1985; Scarborough, 1984; Seidenberg et al., 1985; Share, McGee, McKenzie, Williams, & Silva, 1987; Silva, McGee, & Williams, 1985; Vogler, Baker, Decker, DeFries, & Huizinga, 1989). However, the fact that the distribution is a graded continuum does not necessarily render the concept of dyslexia scientifically useless, as some critics charge. Ellis (1985) has argued that the proper analogy for dyslexia is obesity. Everyone agrees that the latter condition is a very real health problem, despite the fact that it is operationally defined in a somewhat arbitrary way by choosing a criterion in a continuous distribution.

The framework of the phonological-core variable-difference model meshes nicely with the multidimensional continuum notion. The model conceives of the differences between the dyslexic and the garden-variety poor reader as a matter of degree, rather than kind. Consider the following characterization: As we move in the multidimensional space—from the dyslexic to the garden-variety poor reader—we will move from a processing deficit localized in the phonological core to the global deficits of the developmentally lagging garden-variety poor reader. Thus, the actual cognitive differences that are displayed will be variable depending upon the type of poor reader who is the focus of the investigation. The differences on one end of the continuum will consist of deficits located only in the phonological core (the dyslexic) and will increase in number as we run through the intermediate cases that are less and less likely to pass strict psychometric criteria for dyslexia. Eventually we will reach the part of the multidimensional space containing relatively "pure" garden-variety poor readers who will not qualify for the label dyslexic (by either regression or exclusionary criteria), will have a host of cognitive deficits, and will have the cognitively immature profile of a developmentally lagging individual.

This framework provides an explanation for why almost all processing investigations of reading disability have uncovered phonological deficits, but also why some investigations have found deficits in *other* areas as well (see Stanovich, 1988b). This outcome is predictable from the fact that the phonological-core variable-difference model posits that virtually all poor readers have a phonological deficit, but that other processing deficits emerge as one drifts in the multidimensional space from "pure" dyslexics toward garden-variety poor readers. Presumably, the studies finding deficits extending beyond the phonological domain are those using more lax psychometric criteria for sampling poor readers and are picking up more children from the garden-variety area of the space.

The phonological-core variable-difference model provides a parsimonious but realistic way of conceptualizing the idea of dyslexia. The model preserves at least some of the clinical insights of practitioners within the learning disabilities field who prefer traditional assumptions; yet its emphasis on continuity removes some of the more objectionable features of the term dyslexia—features which have actually stigmatized the term within some reading research subcommunities. Parsimony aside, however, what is the current state of the empirical evidence that bears on the model? Quite frankly—mixed.

Empirical Evidence for the Cognitive Differentiability of Dyslexic Children

The data from investigations employing reading-level match designs was once a confusing mass of contradictions (see Stanovich et al., 1986), but has recently become considerably clarified. Olson, Wise, Conners, and Rack (1990; Rack, Snowling, & Olson, 1992) have recently completed a meta-analysis of these studies that explains some of the discrepancies in the literature. It appears that the cognitive profiles of discrepancy-defined dyslexic readers will not match those of younger reading-level controls. The dyslexics are actually inferior in the phonological processing domain (Aaron, 1989b; Baddeley, Ellis, Miles, & Lewis, 1982; Bradley & Bryant, 1978; Bruck, 1990; Holligan & Johnston, 1988; Kochnower, Richardson, & DiBenedetto, 1983; Lundberg & Hoien, 1989; Olson et al., 1985; Olson, Wise, Conners, Rack, & Fulker,

1989; Siegel & Faux, 1989; Siegel & Ryan, 1988; Snowling, 1980, 1981; Snowling, Stackhouse, & Rack, 1986). Although there are some exceptions to this pattern in the literature (Baddeley, Logie, & Ellis, 1988; Beech & Harding, 1984; Bruck, 1988; Treiman & Hirsh-Pasek, 1985; Vellutino & Scanlon, 1987), most of these can be explained by a variety of factors that Olson et al. (1990; Rack et al., 1992) discuss in their meta-analysis. The data from reading-level designs thus provide at least some modest support for the construct validity of the concept of dyslexia.

It has been even more difficult to empirically differentiate dyslexic subjects in garden-variety designs. While some garden-variety comparisons have supported the idea of qualitative difference (Aaron, 1987, 1989b; Ellis & Large, 1987; Horn & O'Donnell, 1984; Jorm, Share, Maclean, & Matthews, 1986; Rutter & Yule, 1975; Silva et al., 1985), other investigations have demonstrated that it can often be surprisingly difficult to differentiate discrepancy-defined dyslexic readers from garden-variety poor readers (Fredman & Stevenson, 1988; Siegel, 1988, 1989; Taylor, Satz, & Friel, 1979). Even Olson et al. (1989) have failed to find a correlation between degree of discrepancy within their sample of dyslexic twins and the degree of phonological deficit, a statistical test not quite equivalent to a garden-variety control design but troublesome nonetheless.

Regardless of how one views the muddled research evidence from the garden-variety designs, there is one conclusion that is forced by the very fact that the literature is so full of contradictions: namely, that this research has demonstrated how surprisingly difficult it is to demonstrate cognitive differences among poor readers of differing IQs. I say surprising because it is *intelligence* that is supposed to be the more encompassing construct. Consider, for example, some data recently published by Siegel (1988). It is *reading skill* and *not* IQ that separates subject groups more strongly on such variables as visual processing, phonological processing, ITPA performance, cloze performance, sentence correction tasks, short-term memory tasks, working memory tasks, of course spelling, but also arithmetic performance, which tracks reading more closely than IQ. As a general cognitive probe, reading ability seems to be more a more sensitive indicator than IQ test performance.

ADDITIONAL PROBLEMS OF CONSTRUCT VALIDITY

Such findings are cause for some soul-searching. Indeed, the empirical picture is, if anything, even more incomplete than I have portrayed it here, for there is still inadequate data on several other foundational assumptions. For example, outside of the pioneering work of Lyon (1985), there is very little data on differential response to treatment. There are, for example, no good data indicating that discrepancy-defined dyslexics respond differently to various educational treatments than do garden-variety readers of the same age or than younger nondyslexic children reading at the same level (Pressley & Levin,

1987; van der Wissel, 1987). This is not a trivial gap in our knowledge. Differential treatment effects are, in large part, the raison d'être of special education.

We are equally unenlightened on several other crucial issues. The data on differential prognosis for reading are contradictory. Rutter and Yule (1975) found differential growth curves for specifically disabled and garden-variety poor readers. The garden-variety poor readers displayed greater growth in reading but less growth in arithmetic ability than the specifically disabled children. However, this finding of differential reading growth rates has failed to replicate in some other studies (Bruck, 1988; Labuda & DeFries, 1989; McKinney, 1987; Share et al., 1987; van der Wissel & Zegers, 1985).

Until convincing data on such issues as differential response to treatment are provided, the utility of the concept of dyslexia will continue to be challenged because the reading disabilities field will have no rebuttal to assertions that it is more educationally and clinically relevant to define reading disability without reference to IQ discrepancy (Seidenberg, Bruck, Fornarolo, & Backman, 1986; Siegel, 1988, 1989). For example, Share, McGee, and Silva (1989) still see fit to argue that "it may be timely to formulate a concept of reading disability which is independent of any consideration of IQ. Unless it can be shown to have some predictive value for the nature of treatment or treatment outcome, considerations of IQ should be discarded in discussions of reading difficulties" (p. 100). In short, the learning disabilities field is still in need of the large-scale experimental demonstrations that, compared to groups of garden-variety poor readers, discrepancy-defined poor readers show differential response to treatment and prognosis—and for further evidence that the reading-related cognitive profiles of these two groups are reliably different.

DEEPER CONCEPTUAL PROBLEMS: THE ISSUE OF INTELLIGENCE

We are thus right back to the issue of why IQ scores should have been the benchmark from which to measure discrepancy in the first place. Indeed, it is surprising that for so long the concept of intelligence received so little discussion in the learning disabilities literature. Researchers and practitioners in the field seem not to have realized that it is a foundational concept for the very idea of dyslexia. As currently defined, IQ is a superordinate construct for the classification of a child as reading disabled. Without a clear conception of the construct of intelligence, the notion of a reading disability, as currently defined, dissolves into incoherence.

But problems with the IQ concept are legion. Consider the fact that researchers, let alone practitioners, cannot agree on the type of IQ score that should be used in the measurement of discrepancy. For example, it has often been pointed out that changes in the characteristics of the IQ test being used will result in somewhat different subgroups of children being identified as discrepant and also alter the types of processing deficits that they will display in comparison studies (Bowers, Steffy, & Tate, 1988; Fletcher et al., 1989; Lindgren, De Renzi, & Richman, 1985; Reed, 1970; Shankweiler, Crain, Brady, & Macaruso, 1992; Siegel & Heaven, 1986; Stanley, Smith, & Powys, 1982; Torgesen, 1985; Vellutino, 1978). Yet it is not hard to look in the research literature and find recommendations that are all over the map.

For example, a very common recommendation that one finds in the literature is that performance and/or nonverbal IQ tests be used to assess discrepancy (e.g., Beech & Harding, 1984; Perfetti, 1985, p. 180, 1986; Siegel & Heaven, 1986; Stanovich, 1986a; Thomson, 1982), because verbally loaded measures are allegedly unfair to dyslexic children. In complete contrast, in a recent issue of *Learning Disabilities Research* devoted to the issue of measuring severe discrepancy, Hessler (1987) argues for the use of *verbally loaded* tests because "using a nonverbal test of intelligence because an individual has better nonverbal cognitive abilities than verbal cognitive abilities does not, of course, remove the importance of verbal processing and knowledge structures in academic achievement; it only obscures their importance and perhaps provides unrealistic expectations for an individual's academic achievement" (p. 46).

Of course, the use of full scale IQ scores results in some unprincipled amalgamation of the above two diametrically opposed philosophies but is still sometimes recommended precisely *because* the field is so confused and so far from consensus on this issue (Harris & Sipay, 1985, p. 145). Finally, there is a sort of "either" strategy that is invoked by investigators who require only that performance *or* verbal IQ exceed 90 in dyslexic samples (e.g., Olson et al., 1985). As Torgesen (1986) has pointed out, the naturally occurring multidimensional continuum of abilities guarantees that such a criterion ends up creating more discrepancies with performance IQ.

Are there any implications in all of these differing practices beyond just the confusion created? Indeed, there are. First, there are implied value judgments in the measure used as a proxy for aptitude. Secondly, there are implications in just the research domain that was the focus of our earlier review: the empirical differentiation of dyslexic children from poor readers without aptitude/achievement discrepancy. We shall take up each of these implications in turn.

VALUE JUDGMENTS INHERENT IN DIFFERENT INDICES OF "POTENTIAL"

It is rarely noted that the use of certain types of intelligence tests in the operationalization of dyslexia often conceals conceptions of "potential" that are questionable, if not downright illogical. Consider again some of the hidden assumptions behind the often-heard admonition that verbally loaded intelligence tests are unfair to dyslexic children, and that performance IQ measures provide "fairer" measures of the reading potential of such children.

Typical arguments are that "the instrument (WISC-R) is confounded and not a true measure of potential. The learning disability itself is reflected clearly in the IQ performance" (Birnbaum, 1990, p. 330) and that "computing an IQ from items shown to be specifically associated with dyslexic difficulties may be an underestimate" (Thomson, 1982, p. 94). But it is not at all clear—even if one accepts the problematic notion of educational "potential"—that the spatial abilities, fluid intelligence, and problem-solving abilities tapped by most performance tests provide the best measures of the potential to comprehend verbal material. To the contrary, it would appear that verbally loaded measures would provide the best estimates of how much a dyslexic reader could get from written text if their deficient decoding skills were to be remediated.

As Hessler (1987) notes:

> There are different types of intelligence, and they predict academic achievement differently. . . . In fact, the performance score accounts for so little academic achievement that there is reason to question its relevance for use as an ability measure to predict academic achievement. It is therefore a mistake to use any test of intelligence as an ability measure for predicting academic achievement in a severe discrepancy analysis simply because it is called a test of intelligence, without demonstrating some ability to predict academic achievement. (p. 45; see also Lyon, 1987, pp. 78–79)

Consistent with this interpretation, van der Wissel (1987) has demonstrated that the extent to which an IQ subtest separates dyslexic from garden-variety children is *inversely* related to how highly the subtest correlates with reading achievement. It is a paradoxical situation indeed when the indicators that best make this subgroup discrimination are those that do *not* relate to the criterion performance that drew professional attention in the first place: reading failure.

It goes largely unnoticed that when people make the "fairness" argument for the use of nonverbal tests they in fact jettison the notion of "potential," at least in its common meaning. They cannot mean the potential for verbal comprehension through print if the decoding deficit were remediated, since this is not what IQ tests—particularly the performance tests they are recommending—assess. What people who make the "verbal IQ scores are unfair to dyslexics" argument are asserting—implicitly—is that if we had a society that was not so organized around literacy, dyslexics would have the potential to do much better. True. But recognize that this is a *counterfactual* premise that contradicts more common usages, to the advantage of some and to the disadvantage of others. But it simply makes little sense to adopt linguistic usages of the term "potential" that require the assumption that literacy-based technological societies will be totally reconstructed.

We seem to find it difficult to use this crude cognitive probe—an IQ score—as a circumscribed behavioral index without loading social, and indeed metaphysical (Scheffler, 1985), baggage onto it. If these tests *are mere* predictors of school performance, then let's treat them as such. If we do, then performance IQ is manifestly not the predictor that we want to use, at least in the domain of reading prediction. An alternative conception of potential to apply in cases like dyslexia—where educational achievement in a particular domain is thwarted due to a circumscribed, modular dysfunction—was suggested previously: the degree of improvement in the particular educational domain that would result if the person's dysfunction were totally remediated.

THE IMPLICATIONS OF USING DIFFERENT IQ MEASURES FOR DIFFERENTIATING DYSLEXIC FROM GARDEN-VARIETY POOR READERS

The choice of different aptitude measures also relates strongly to the possibility of isolating a modular dysfunction, perhaps in the phonological domain (Liberman & Shankweiler, 1985; Stanovich,1988b), that might have some genetic specificity and neurological localizability. The point is this: Do we really want to look for a group of poor readers who are qualitatively differentiable in terms of etiology and neurophysiology? Officials at the National Institutes of Health (NIH) who are funding several program projects on the neurological, genetic, and behavioral underpinnings of dyslexia certainly want to look for such a group (Gray & Kavanagh, 1985). Many in the learning disabilities field share their enthusiasm for the quest to isolate—behaviorally, genetically, and physiologically—a select group of "different" poor readers.

Let us, for purposes of argument, accept this as a goal whether we believe in it or not. I want to argue that if we do, a somewhat startling conclusion results. The conclusion is that we must move away from measures of abstract intelligence as benchmarks for discrepancy analysis and toward more educationally relevant indices. In short, to get NIH's neurologically differentiable groups we need an aptitude benchmark of more educational relevance than IQ—than of nonverbal IQ in particular, contrary to some common recommendations.

However, it must be emphasized that the context for any such discussion must be the voluminous body of prior research on the cognitive correlates of individual differences in reading achievement. Our knowledge of the structure of human abilities in this domain puts severe constraints on the ability patterns that can be observed in studies of dyslexia. For example, an extremely large body of research has demonstrated that reading skill is linked to an incredibly wide range of verbal abilities. Vocabulary, syntactic knowledge, metalinguistic awareness, verbal short-term memory, phonological awareness, speech production, inferential comprehension, semantic memory, and verbal fluency form only a partial list (Baddeley, Logie, Nimmo-Smith, & Brereton, 1985; Byrne, 1981; Carr, 1981; Chall, 1983b; Cunningham, Stanovich, & Wilson, 1990; Curtis, 1980; Evans & Carr, 1985; Frederiksen, 1980; Harris

& Sipay, 1985; Jackson & McClelland, 1979; Just & Carpenter, 1987; Kamhi & Catts, 1989; Palmer et al., 1985; Perfetti, 1985; Rapala & Brady, 1990; Rayner & Pollatsek, 1989; Siegel & Ryan, 1988, 1989; Stanovich, 1985, 1986a; Stanovich, Cunningham, & Feeman, 1984a; Stanovich, Nathan, & Zolman, 1988; Vellutino, 1979; Vellutino & Scanlon, 1987).

In contrast, the nonverbal abilities linked to reading are much more circumscribed (Aman & Singh, 1983; Carr, 1981; Daneman & Tardiff, 1987; Hulme, 1988; Lovegrove & Slaghuis, 1989; Siegel & Ryan, 1989; Stanovich, 1986a; Vellutino, 1979; but see Carver, 1990, for an opposing view). Here, the abilities associated with reading are more likely to be distinct and domain-specific (e.g., orthographic storage, processing of certain spatial frequencies). In the verbal domain, however, there are many more abilities that are related to reading and that are more likely to have more global influences (e.g., inferential comprehension, verbal STM, vocabulary), thereby affecting general verbal IQ. Therefore matching dyslexics and nondyslexics on performance IQ will necessarily lead to broad-based deficits on the verbal side. But even if there are visual/orthographic deficits linked to reading disability, the converse is not true. Because there are not as many reading-related nonverbal processes and because those that do exist will certainly be more circumscribed than something like vocabulary or verbal memory, verbal IQ matching will not necessarily result in dyslexic subjects with severely depressed performance IQs.

We will now travel across the continuum of potential aptitude candidates for discrepancy measurement with this research context and the goal of differentiating dyslexic children in mind. It immediately becomes apparent that the use of reading achievement discrepancies from performance IQ will make it extremely difficult to cognitively differentiate dyslexic children from other poor readers. Such performance-discrepancy dyslexics—because they are allowed to have depressed verbal components—will have a host of verbal deficits, some at levels higher than phonology, and they will not display the cognitive specificity required of the dyslexia concept. Torgesen (1986) has discussed how definitional practices that require only that verbal *or* performance scales be over some criterion value will have the same effect. The verbal scale is allowed to be considerably under that of the nondisabled control group, and it is not surprising that, subsequently, a broad range of verbal deficits are observed (see Vellutino, 1979). A behaviorally and neurologically differentiable core deficit will be virtually impossible to find, given such classification. As Bowers et al. (1988) note, "Should the subtle language processing deficits differentiating dyslexics from normal readers have considerable overlap with verbal intelligence, then it will be impossible to distinguish the causes of dyslexia from the causes of poor reading associated with lower general verbal ability" (p. 307).

In contrast, discrepancies based on verbal aptitude measures would be likely to isolate a more circumscribed disability that may be more readily identifiable by neurophysiological and/or genetic methods. Such a procedure would preclude the possibility of deficits in broad-based verbal processes. It could potentially confine deficits exclusively to the phonological module. For example, Bowers, Steffy, and Tate (1988) demonstrated that if only performance IQ was controlled, dyslexic subjects were differentiated from non-dyslexics on the basis of rapid naming performance and on digit span and sentence memory. However, controlling for verbal IQ removed the association between reading disability and memory abilities. Importantly, an association with rapid naming remained. In short, verbal IQ control resulted in the isolation of a more circumscribed processing deficit.

Similarly, verbal IQ–based discrepancy measurement would be much more likely to demarcate a visual/orthographic deficit, if one exists (see Lovegrove & Slaghuis, 1989; Solman & May, 1990; Willows, 1991). Verbal-IQ matching in a comparison study would, of course, allow the performance IQ of the dyslexic group to fall below those of the control group. But since the number of nonverbal abilities linked to reading is much more circumscribed in the nonverbal than in the verbal domain, the groups would not become un-matched on a commensurately large number of abilities. Additionally, subtle, visually based deficits would not be "adjusted away" by a procedure of performance-IQ matching. Thus, verbal-IQ control provides a greater opportunity for these visual/orthographic deficits—much harder to track than those in the phonological domain—a better chance to emerge in comparison studies.

In summary, by adopting verbal IQ as an aptitude measure we would be closer to a principled definition of potential in the reading domain: as the academic level that would result from instruction if the person's dysfunction were totally remediated. We would also be more likely to isolate a circumscribed deficit that would at least be more amenable to cognitive and neurological differentiation than are the samples of children defined by other methods.

CAN WE DO WITHOUT IQ? AN ALTERNATIVE PROPOSAL

But, if we have come this far down the road of altering our treatment of IQ, why not go all the way? The learning disability field's seeming fixation on intelligence has driven a wedge between groups of investigators in the reading research community (McGill-Franzen, 1987). We have, for example, two organizations concerned with reading—the Orton Society and the International Reading Association (IRA)—who hold conventions with almost totally non-overlapping attendees, a strange state of affairs indeed and one directly attributable to how different subgroups within the reading community view the concept of dyslexia.

There is, however, a proposal for conceptualizing reading disability that could well result in a rapprochement between groups like the IRA and the Orton Society. It is in fact a proposal that has been around for quite some time, but has never gotten a proper hearing because studies and definitions of dyslexia have so strongly emphasized the measurement of intelligence. In fact, many educationally oriented reading researchers have long suggested that measuring the discrepancy between reading ability and *listening comprehension* would be more educationally relevant and would seem to have been a more logical choice in the first place (see Aaron, 1989a; Carroll, 1977; Carver, 1981; Durrell, 1969; Gillet & Temple, 1986; Gough & Tunmer, 1986; Hood & Dubert, 1983; Royer, Kulhavy, Lee, & Peterson, 1986; Spring & French, 1990; Sticht & James, 1984). Certainly a discrepancy calculated in this way seems to have more face validity and educational relevance than the traditional procedure (Aaron, 1989a; Durrell & Hayes, 1969; Hoover & Gough, 1990; Spache, 1981). Children who understand written material less well than they would understand the same material if it were read to them appear to be in need of educational intervention. Presumably, their listening comprehension exceeds their reading comprehension because word recognition processes are inefficient and are a "bottleneck" that impedes comprehension (Gough & Tunmer, 1986; Perfetti, 1985; Perfetti & Lesgold, 1977). Listening comprehension correlates with reading comprehension much more highly than full scale or even verbal IQ. Children simultaneously low in reading and listening do not have an "unexplained" reading problem (Carroll, 1977; Hoover & Gough, 1990), and we must always remember that the idea of "unexplained" reading failure is the puzzle that enticed us into the idea of dyslexia in the first place.

As with verbal IQ but only more so, listening comprehension isolates a modular deficit, because in a comparison study dyslexic subjects would not become unmatched from nondyslexics on a host of reading-related verbal abilities. Additionally, even though the idea of visual deficits as an explanation of dyslexia is out of favor at the moment, this "layman's conception of dyslexia" (not totally without support in the literature; see Lovegrove & Slaghuis, 1989; Solman & May, 1990; Willows, 1991) would receive a fairer test if discrepancies from listening comprehension were the criteria for subject selection in research. Any potential visual deficits would not be "adjusted away" by performance-IQ matching. Thus, not only would we get a better chance of demarcating the modular phonological deficits that are of great interest in current work on dyslexia (Liberman & Shankweiler, 1985; Stanovich, 1988b), but more tenuous hypotheses in the visual domain would get a fairer hearing.

In short, a large reading discrepancy from listening comprehension has probably isolated—as well as we are ever going to get it—a modular decoding problem that then may or may not be amenable to genetic and neurological analysis in the manner of the ongoing NIH program projects. It is indeed ironic that measuring discrepancies from listening comprehension—a procedure often suggested by those hostile to the dyslexia concept—may be just the procedure that allows those working from a neurological perspective to succeed in their quest.

There are, of course, several obstacles to implementing procedures of measuring reading disability with reference to discrepancies from listening comprehension. For example, while several individual measures of listening comprehension ability have been published (Carroll, 1972, 1977; CTB/

McGraw-Hill, 1985; Durrell & Hayes, 1969; Spache, 1981), it may be the case that none have been standardized across the range of ages, nor attained the psychometric properties, to serve as an adequate measure from which to assess discrepancy (Johnson, 1988). Other complications may also arise, such as hearing problems or unfamiliarity with standard English. However, many of these problems are no more severe for listening comprehension measures than they are for certain IQ tests. It is encouraging that work on listening comprehension as a diagnostic benchmark has recently been increasing in quantity, and some important progress is being made (see Aaron, 1989a; Carlisle, 1989; Hoover & Gough, 1990; Horowitz & Samuels, 1985; Royer, Sinatra, & Schumer, 1990; Spring & French, 1990).

Consider, though, how some of the other complications in this proposal illuminate the arguments previously outlined. From what type of material should we assess listening comprehension? One possibility is simply to employ oral presentations of text material (Hoover & Gough, 1990). This is often done in research investigations and is the method employed in most standardized measures of listening. Of course, such material will have the syntax, vocabulary, and language structures of text which, as is well known, differ somewhat from speech (Hayes, 1988; Hayes & Ahrens, 1988; Chafe & Danielewicz, 1987). An alternative procedure would be to orally present more naturalistic nontextual language. Which method is preferable obviously depends upon the question being asked. But if our goal is to qualitatively distinguish reading disability, then the choice is orally presented *text*. Performance on this material will correlate more highly with reading comprehension and, most importantly, discrepancies will result more specifically from decoding problems. In contrast, severe underachievement based on prediction from naturalistic language comprehension is more apt to implicate, in addition, more global difficulties with text structures that result from environmental causes such as lack of print exposure.

This comparison between the oral presentation of naturalistic speech and that of textual material is analogous in form to the choice between IQ measures that was discussed earlier. We want the measure that is more highly correlated with the criterion—reading—because such a measure will more cleanly isolate an unexpected, separable, modular failure in a more circumscribed cognitive domain—the critical intuition and assumption that has fueled interest in dyslexia from the time of Hinshelwood (1895, 1917) to the present.

In light of the arguments above, it is important to state that educational practitioners may well want to demarcate children high in nonverbal abilities and simultaneously low in both listening and reading ability and to give them special attention (this is a policy/political issue). But such children should not be considered dyslexic. They do not have a domain-specific difficulty in the area of reading if their general listening skills are also depressed. They may well present an important educational problem worth identifying and dealing with, but it is simply perverse to call them *reading* disabled. In a contentious field, one of the few areas of agreement is that "the current sine qua non of learning disabilities is unexpectedly low achievement" (McCleskey, 1989, p. 435). We surely do not expect a child who does not comprehend spoken language to *read* well. Their poor reading is not unexpected; therefore they are not reading disabled. If the child would not understand the material were it spoken to them, then it is highly unlikely that they will understand it when reading it (Carroll, 1977; Hoover & Gough, 1990). It cannot be emphasized enough that to say this is not to deny that the child has an educational problem. It is simply to call for more logical consistency in our application of educational terminology and hence in our classification.

AN ADDITIONAL COMPLICATION IN DISCREPANCY MEASUREMENT: MATTHEW EFFECTS

There remains, however, a further obstacle to measuring reading disability by reference to aptitude/achievement discrepancy—irrespective of the indicator used for the aptitude benchmark. Let us again consider the recommendation against the use of verbally loaded tests for discrepancy measurement. This admonition stems from the either tacit or explicit assumption that the reading difficulties themselves may lead to depressed performance on such measures. One reason that this may occur is because of so-called Matthew effects associated with reading: situations where reading itself develops other related cognitive abilities (see Stanovich, 1986b; Walberg & Tsai, 1983). But the recognition of such phenomena perniciously undermines the whole notion of discrepancy measurement by weakening the distinction between aptitude and achievement. It serves to remind us that the logic of the learning disabilities field has implicitly given all of the causal power to IQ. That is, it is reading that is considered discrepant from IQ rather than IQ that is discrepant from reading. However, this is a vast oversimplification, because there are potent effects running in both directions.

Much evidence has now accumulated to indicate that reading itself is a moderately powerful determinant of vocabulary growth, verbal intelligence, and general comprehension ability (Hayes, 1988; Hayes & Ahrens, 1988; Juel, 1988; Share, McGee, & Silva, 1989; Share & Silva, 1987; Stanovich, 1986b; Stanovich & West, 1989; van den Bos, 1989). These Matthew effects (reciprocal causation effects involving reading and other cognitive skills) highlight a further problematic aspect of discrepancy-based classification. Do we really want to withhold certain types of educational treatments from children whose poor reading is accompanied by equally subpar IQs (or listening comprehension) when we know that the poor reading may at least in part be a direct cause of the low IQs and listening comprehension ability? The possibility of Matthew effects precludes us from assuming that the poor listening comprehension or verbal intelligence could not be enhanced by better reading.

Thus, Matthew effects are interrelated in some very complicated ways with the conceptual logic of discrepancy-based disability definitions. It appears, then, that any discrepancy-based conceptualization is going to require considerable refinement based on how Matthew effects alter the course of development, bringing education-related cognitive skills more into congruence with age. Thus, conceptually justified discrepancy-based classification—even from listening comprehension—will be maddeningly tricky to carry out in a principled fashion.

CONCLUSION: IS DISCREPANCY MEASUREMENT WORTH THE EFFORT?

Much of the best recent research in the learning disabilities field has a "back to basics" feel to it (see Ceci, 1986; Torgesen & Wong, 1986; Vaughn & Bos, 1987), because it has increasingly been recognized that the field somehow got ahead of itself—that educational practice simply "took off" before a thorough investigation of certain foundational assumptions had been carried out. Thus, researchers have had to double back to retrace crucial empirical and theoretical steps that were skipped during the field's rapid expansion.

The history of the concept of dyslexia has followed a confused "cart before the horse" path in part because too many practitioners and researchers accepted at face value claims that IQ tests were measures of special "unlocked potential" in particular groups of children with low reading achievement. We have seen that in the area of reading disability the notion of unlocked potential was misconceived, because it was defined in a way that did not relate to the critical prediction in this domain: the prediction of how much growth in reading comprehension ability would be expected if the decoding deficit that was the proximal cause of the disability were to be totally remediated.

An alternative proposal for measuring aptitude/achievement discrepancies with reference to listening comprehension ability was explored and found to be superior to that of IQ assessment. Nevertheless, it was argued that complications stemming from the increasing difficulty of differentiating aptitude from achievement as a child gets older will plague all definitional efforts based on the discrepancy notion. Problems such as these have led to Siegel's (1988, 1989) suggestion that reading disability be defined solely on the basis of decoding deficits, without reference to discrepancies from aptitude measures. Whether or not her proposal is adopted, the learning disabilities field is simply going to have to face up to the implications of current research findings, namely that: (1) defining dyslexia by reference to discrepancies from IQ is an untenable procedure; (2) much more basic psychometric work needs to be done in order to develop a principled method of discrepancy measurement from listening comprehension or some other verbal aptitude indicator; (3) If the field is unwilling to do the spade work necessary to carry out #2, or deems the potential benefit not worth the effort, then the only logical alternative is to adopt Siegel's proposal to define reading disability solely in terms of decoding deficiencies, without reference to aptitude discrepancy.

The learning disabilities field has been so carried away with the face validity of the notion that achievement discrepancies from aptitude *should* be important (given our standard psychometric assumptions and theories) that it has completely forgotten where the burden of proof lies. Since there is considerable evidence that in the case of reading ability we are dealing with a continuum; that reading disability is not a discrete condition; and that the multivariate relations between reading ability and a variety of cognitive skills form a continuous space (Ellis, 1985; Jorm, 1983; Olson et al., 1985; Scarborough, 1984; Seidenberg, Bruck, Fornarolo, & Backman, 1985; Silva et al., 1985; Vogler et al., 1989), the correct null hypothesis is that there are no qualitative differences in reading-related cognitive subskills between dyslexic and garden-variety poor readers. The burden of proof is on those claiming that there are such differences, because these assumed differences have been used to justify a new diagnostic category and associated educational practices.

In short, we are still in need of data indicating that the cognitive processing of dyslexic and garden-variety poor readers reading at the same level is reliably different, the data indicating that these two groups of poor readers have a differential educational prognosis, and the data indicating that they respond differently to certain educational treatments. This is, of course, the data that should have be presented in the first place—that is, prior to the rapid expansion of discrepancy-based learning disabilities as a diagnostic and educational category. That we lack such basic data at this late date in the learning disability field's development speaks volumes about the current state of educational research and practice in this area.

NOTE

1. The terms "reading disability," "dyslexia," and "specific reading retardation" are used interchangeably in this essay. No connotations of differential etiology or cognitive pattern are to be implied by the use of the various terms. Indeed, exploring the evidence on differential cognitive patterns is one of my goals here. Additionally, it is to be emphasized that this essay is focused on school-based classification. These issues have a somewhat different histories in the literatures of neuropsychology and clinical practice (Doris, 1986; Hynd & Hynd, 1984; Monaghan, 1980), and the latter are beyond the scope of this essay.

PART VII

THE READING INSTRUCTION DEBATE: COMMENTS ON THE "READING WARS"

CHAPTER 19

Putting Children First by Putting Science First

The Politics of Early Reading Instruction

If it is true that the discrepancy debate (see Chapter 17) is a confusing mix of science and politics, the so-called Great Debate about reading instruction (more commonly called the Reading Wars in current popular publications)—the debate between whole language advocates and proponents of the importance of decoding skills—is an even stranger amalgamation of research and politics. Fortunately, the best teachers have often been wise enough to incorporate the most effective practices from the two different approaches into their instructional programs (see Chapter 21 and Pressley, 1998). However, many other practitioners are confused by the marked disparities between the opinions that are articulated within their professional literature.

A SAD POLITICAL IRONY

To my mind, one of the saddest aspects of the Reading Wars is that they have fostered internecine conflicts *within* the political left. If one didn't know better, one might think that there is tacit collusion going on between the whole language movement and the reactionary right in the United States. We have seen such seeming paradoxes before. Margaret Thatcher's dominance of British politics during the 1980s was assured by the emergence of the so-called "loony left" within the Labour Party, which caused it to lose credibility with the public and spend a decade in the wilderness trying to reconstruct itself after massive self-inflicted internal injuries. Political correctness (PC) in the United States serves the same function as did the "loony left" of the old Labour Party in Britain. As many commentators have pointed out (e.g., Gitlin, 1995), the victims of PC are more often moderate liberals than the hard-core supporters of the political right. The latter don't give a fig about the fine distinctions made among the terms in the gender and racial language wars. It delights them that they talk in ways that enrage the PC crowd. The speech codes promulgated on university campuses throughout the 1990s caused distress not to the right wing, but to those on the left who were strong free-speech advocates and to leftists more dedicated to issues of economic justice than identity politics (see Gitlin, 1995, for a detailed discussion). PC did not bother the right at all—instead, it provided a convenient foil. Like the loony left in Britain, it divided progressive forces and discredited them among the general public. Had it done so in the aid of a full-scale attack on the forces of global capitalism, one may well have concluded that at least the resulting disarray was in pursuit of a larger goal—but it did not. The PC advocates stormed the English and education departments of universities rather than Chase Manhattan. Hegemonic male pronouns in memos were deemed more important than the chemicals Monsanto pours into the ecosphere or than the fact that our television news comes to us courtesy of General Electric.

These analogies are quite relevant to the Reading Wars because this is just the role that the most extreme (and hence most vocal) segments of the whole language camp serve in the current debate. Here, for example, is the sequence that has been carried out with such depressing regularity in the 1990s:

1. Whole language proponents advocate a model of the reading process that is at variance with the scientific data (see Chapter 20).
2. Whole language proponents link that model with the aspects of whole language philosophy that are legitimately good and upon which virtually no researchers disagree (see Chapter 20).
3. Reactionary forces point to the evidence that the model of reading is incorrect (evidence that does exist—it is the evidence that the whole language theorists ignored) and use the lack of professionalism implied by their failure to respond to evidence to justify an agenda of educational cutbacks, privatization, union busting, and teacher bashing.

The unfortunate point here is that the lack of professionalism is *real*. A first-grade teacher who is unaware of the importance of phonological awareness in reading acquisition or of the importance of explicit code instruction for some children is either acting in an unprofessional manner or has been trained by faculty members in schools of education who are not basing practice on established scientific knowledge.

The sad irony—and the thing that makes the analogy with the loony left apt—is that the researchers who the extreme whole language advocates attack[1] are almost without exception fellow political progressives.[2] So the efforts of the whole language advocates to grab the political high ground are misplaced. Proponents of the importance of decoding skills are *also* fighting to rid society of the "savage inequalities" that Kozol (1991) so eloquently wrote about. If the politically active whole language advocates *really* wanted to win the battle against reactionary political forces, they would drop their misguided opposition to systematic instruction in the alphabet code and stop dividing the progressive forces into "camps."

Ironically, the primary casualties of the Reading Wars are disadvantaged children who are not immersed in a literate environment and who are not taught the alphabetic code—precisely the children that progressive forces most want to aid. As Adams's (1990) book makes clear, research has shown that a very efficient way to generate large social class differences in reading achievement is to implement an extreme whole language curriculum that short changes the explicit teaching of spelling–sound relationships (see Foorman, Francis, Fletcher, Schatschneider, & Mehta, 1998; Scanlon & Vellutino, 1997). The evidence on this issue reinforces Pressley's (1998) point that

> one part of any strategy to prevent disadvantaged children from being upwardly mobile would be to deny them effective literacy instruction, employing the most convincing scientific analyses available to determine effectiveness. I sincerely believe that those who would deny such instruction to children for whatever reason are, in fact, working on behalf of those who might prefer to prevent the disadvantaged from becoming more advantaged. (p. 37)

In short, when explicit teaching of the components of the alphabetic code is shortchanged in early reading instruction, the middle-class children end up reading fine because they induce the code through their print-rich home environments and/or explicit parental tuition.

Why do whole language advocates (just like the loony left in Britain) direct so much bile and hostility (see Footnote 1 and McKenna, Stahl, & Reinking, 1994) at researchers who share the very same goals of providing educational opportunities for all children—especially those who are socially disadvantaged? I think there are some specific factors that account for this hostility and also some general philosophical factors as well. I shall discuss these in turn, starting with some of the more specific issues that separate the camps in the Reading Wars and then move to the more general cultural trends of which whole language is a part.

SPECIFIC DISPUTE #1: HOW "NATURAL" IS THE PROCESS OF READING ACQUISITION?

The disagreement about the necessity of teaching decoding skills follows from the background assumptions of the two camps concerning whether reading acquisition should be characterized as an "unnatural" task (Gough & Hillinger, 1980) or as a "natural" task (Goodman, 1986) for young children. Typical of the latter view is the statement from Goodman's (1986) popular book for parents and teachers, *What's Whole in Whole Language?*:

Why do people create and learn written language? They need it! How do they learn it? The same way they learn oral language, by using it in authentic literacy events that meet their needs. Often children have trouble learning written language in school. It's not because it's harder than learning oral language, or learned differently. It's because we've made it hard by trying to make it easy. Frank Smith wrote an article called "12 Easy Ways to Make Learning to Read Hard." Every way was designed to make the task easy by breaking it up in small bits. But by isolating print from its functional use, by teaching skills out of context and focusing on written language as an end in itself, we made the task harder, impossible for some children. (p. 24)

The way that this passage equates written language learning with oral language learning illustrates a recurring theme in the whole language literature: that learning to read is just like learning to speak. However, as many cognitive psychologists have pointed out (see Adams, 1990; Adams & Bruck, 1993; Byrne, 1998; Byrne & Liberman, 1999; Liberman, 1999; Liberman & Liberman, 1990; Perfetti, 1991, 1994; Shankweiler, 1999; Share & Stanovich, 1995), the use of the "reading is like speech" analogy ignores the obvious facts that all communities of human beings have developed spoken languages but only a minority of these exist in written form; that speech is almost as old as the human species, but that written language is a recent cultural invention of only the last three or four thousand years; and that virtually all children in normal environments develop speech easily by themselves, whereas most children require explicit tuition to learn to read and substantial numbers of children have difficulty even after intensive efforts on the part of teachers and parents. The argument of Liberman and Liberman (1990) is typical of scientific thinking on the oral/written language distinction:

Reflecting biological roots that run deep, speech employs a single, universal strategy for constructing utterances. All languages form all words by combining and permuting a few dozen consonants and vowels, meaningless segments that we will sometimes refer to, loosely, as phonemes. On the other hand, scripts, being artifacts, choose variably from a menu of strategies. Some, like the one we use, represent the phonemes. Others represent the more numerous syllables. Still others, like the Chinese, take the considerably more numerous morphemes as their irreducible units. . . . Surely it is plain that speech is biologically primary in a way that reading and writing are not. Accordingly, we suppose that learning to speak is, by the very nature of the underlying process, much like learning to walk or to perceive visual depth and distance, while learning to read and write is more like learning to do arithmetic or to play checkers. (p. 55)

For an exposition of this argument every researcher and practitioner in reading should read Al Liberman's (1999) elegant and erudite address to the Society for the Scientific Study of Reading when he (along with Isabelle Liberman and Don Shankweiler) received the Outstanding Contribution Award of that organization. There, he lays out, with exquisite precision, the role of phonology in reading, why speech is easy and reading is hard, and why the model of language held by the extreme whole language advocates does not square with linguistic science (see also Byrne, 1998; Perfetti, 1994; Shankweiler, 1999). Contrary to the "reading is natural" view, research has consistently supported the view that reading is *not* acquired naturally, in the same way as speech (Adams, 1990; Byrne, 1998; Gough, 1993; Gough & Hillinger, 1980; Gough & Juel, 1991; Gough, Juel, & Griffith, 1992; Jorm & Share, 1983; Masonheimer, Drum, & Ehri, 1984; Seymour & Elder, 1986; Share, 1995, 1999).

The emphasis on analytic language skills in recent research highlights another specific point of contention between different camps in the reading wars: Do children best acquire reading skill in a holistic manner or through direct instruction that emphasizes analytic attention to language components (e.g., phonemes, words, etc.)?

SPECIFIC DISPUTE #2: ANALYTIC VERSUS HOLISTIC APPROACHES TO READING ACQUISITION

Research indicates that successful reading acquisition seems to require the development of an analytic processing stance toward words that is probably not the natural processing set adopted by most children (Byrne, 1998) and that some children have extreme difficulty in adopting such an analytic processing set. The latter group of children will, as a result, have considerable difficulty building up knowledge of subword spelling–sound correspondences—and such knowledge appears to be almost a necessary prerequisite of fluent reading (Adams, 1990; Adams & Bruck, 1993; Foorman et al., 1998; Gough et al., 1992; Jorm & Share, 1983; Shankweiler, 1999; Shankweiler et al., 1999; Share, 1995; Snowling, 1980).

What makes the analytic processing set difficult for some children? As argued elsewhere in this volume, to induce subword spelling–sound correspondences, children must become sensitive to the subword units in both the written word and in the representation of the spoken word. As outlined in Part II, research indicates that some children have problems dealing with subword units of speech representations. Becoming aware of the segmental structure of language appears to be a prerequisite for rapid reading acquisition in an alphabetic orthography.

Thus, it is not surprising that researchers have moved to earlier developmental levels to demonstrate the efficacy of training in phonological processing skills. They have demonstrated that training kindergarten and preschool children in phonological sensitivity skills and alphabetic coding can lead to faster rates of reading and spelling acquisition (Adams, 1990; Ball, 1993; Ball & Blachman, 1991; Blachman, Ball, Black, & Tangel, 1994; Blachman, Tangel, Ball, Black, & McGraw, 1999; Bradley & Bryant, 1983, 1985; Byrne, 1998; Byrne & Fielding-Barnsley, 1993; Cunningham, 1990; Evans & Carr,

1985; Foorman et al., 1998; Hatcher & Hulme, 1999; Hatcher, Hulme, & Ellis, 1994; Iversen & Tunmer, 1993; Lie, 1991; Lundberg, Frost, & Peterson, 1988; Scanlon & Vellutino, 1997; Torgesen, Morgan, & Davis, 1992; Tunmer & Nesdale, 1985; Vellutino et al., 1996). Some beneficial effects have been observed as well for older reading disabled children despite great variability in how well the training transfers for this group (Blachman, 1997; Lovett et al., 1994; Olson, Wise, Johnson, & Ring, 1997; Torgesen & Burgess, 1998; Torgesen, Wagner, & Rashotte, 1997; Wise, Ring, & Olson, 1999). Because these training programs invariably involve the segmentation of words, this research evidence flies in the face of the frequent admonitions from whole language advocates not to fractionate language:

> Careful observation is helping us to understand better what makes language easy or hard to learn. Many school traditions seem to have actually hindered language development. In our zeal to make it easy, we've made it hard. How? Primarily by breaking whole (natural) language up into bite-size, but abstract little pieces. It seemed so logical to think that little children could best learn simple little things. We took apart the language and turned it into words, syllables, and isolated sounds. Unfortunately, we also postponed its natural purpose—the communication of meaning—and turned it into a set of abstractions, unrelated to the needs and experiences of the children we sought to help. (Goodman, 1986, p. 7)

A large database now contradicts this position. Liberman and Liberman (1990; see also Liberman, 1999; Perfetti, 1991, 1994, 1995) argue that, from a linguistic perspective, this is not surprising:

> Communication among nonhuman animals is different in a critically important way, for, so far as anyone has been able to determine, the natural animal systems have no phonology (nor do they have syntax, for that matter), and, as a consequence, their message-carrying potential is severely limited. Lacking the phonological structures that make lexical generativity possible, nonhuman animals can convey in their natural communication only as many word-meanings as there are distinctively different signals they can make and perceive, and that is, at most, a few dozen. . . . Thus, in contrast to language, which is lexically open because word meanings are conveyed by arranging and rearranging meaningless signal elements, the nonhuman systems attach meaning directly to each element and are, as a consequence, tightly and irremediably closed. We see, then, that language would pay a terrible price if it were not phonologically based. Perhaps it would be of some comfort to the Whole Language people that in such a nonphonological world there would be no "bite-size abstract little pieces" for teachers to break a word into. . . . Each word would be conveyed by an unanalyzable signal, so meaning would be conveyed directly, just as Whole Language seems to think it should be. Unfortunately, there would not be many words. (pp. 56–57)

The admonition not to "break up" language is not very helpful to teachers faced with children who are struggling in reading. In contrast, the growing knowledge of the role of phonological processing in reading holds out great hope for educational applications. First, phonological sensitivity can be assessed very early in development, prior to school entrance (Blachman, 1989; Catts & Kamhi, 1999; Lonigan, Burgess, Anthony, & Barker, 1998; Maclean, Bryant, & Bradley, 1987; Whitehurst & Lonigan, 1998). Second, the research cited above indicates that phonological sensitivity can be increased through appropriate preschool experiences, and that such training results in a significant increase in of word recognition and spelling skills. This training is even more effective when combined with practice in recognizing letter–sound correspondences (Adams, 1990; Bradley & Bryant, 1985; Byrne, 1998; Hatcher et al., 1994; Share, 1995). All of this research converges with the findings from instructional-comparison studies of slightly older children indicating that a code emphasis is more efficacious in early reading instruction than holistic programs that deemphasize phonological analysis and letter–sound training— particularly for poor readers (Adams, 1990; Adams & Bruck, 1993; Brown & Felton, 1990; Chall, 1983a, 1989; Evans & Carr, 1985; Felton, 1993; Foorman, Francis, Novy, & Liberman, 1991; Foorman et al., 1998; Iversen & Tunmer, 1993; Scanlon & Vellutino, 1997; Tunmer & Nesdale, 1985).

Of course these conclusions have been disputed by those in the whole language camp who are fervidly antianalytic in their assumptions and who wish to deny evidence of the effectiveness of any analytic approach to instruction. Over the years (from roughly the early 1980s when the research began reaching critical mass to now, 20 years later) the claims of the extremists have become even more bizarre. For example, Grundin (1994) states that researchers finding evidence for the effectiveness of teaching explicit decoding skills assume that "word recognition—or rather word pronunciation—amounts to reading" (p. 9) and that such researchers argue that "all we have to do is decide how to teach word reading" (p. 9).

Contrary to these assertions, the investigators who have conducted the studies on the importance of phonological sensitivity and decoding have not assumed that "reading amounts to word recognition" and do not assert that we do not need to worry about reading development once decoding skills are established (Adams, 1990; Anderson, Hiebert, Scott, & Wilkinson, 1985; Chard & Osborn, 1999; Pressley, 1998). It is, in fact, impossible to track down any such assertions in the writings of the investigators who are being criticized. Such criticisms are often hurled—without any specific attribution— at researchers whose findings support the importance of decoding skills. In contrast, there is substantial evidence in the published literature that investigators who have demonstrated the importance of phonological sensitivity and decoding such as Marilyn Adams (1990, 1999; Adams, Foorman, Lundberg, & Beeler, 1998) have stressed that the goal of reading is comprehension and that instruction must emphasize understanding, even when such instruction takes place at the letter–sound level (see Cunningham, 1990, for an example).

Typically, the passages from Grundin's (1994) article given above were accompanied by no citations—no quotes from actual researchers who had stated such things. These mysterious straw men are part of the process of demonizing decoding that takes place with regularity in our field. As I write, the April 1999 issue of *The Reading Teacher* has appeared in my mailbox. In an article there, the reader is told that criticisms of whole language have come from "researchers who seemed mired in a single-dimensional world, where attention to the quest for meaning was placed in juxtaposition to sequential curricula organized primarily in terms of phonetic [*sic*] elements. The development of vocabulary, wide reading, and contextual analysis were portrayed as enemies of literacy" (Joyce, 1999, p. 667). I really would like to know which of my research colleagues believes that vocabulary and wide reading are the "enemies of literacy." I will never find out, however, because again no citations are provided—no quotes from researchers who have ever said such things.

In the absence of any evidence that a researcher actually has made such a statement, such charges should be taken for what they appear to be: strawmen assertions designed to trigger negative associations in the mind of the reader. This is increasingly the type of rhetoric that passes for debate in our literature, however (see the section on the "Meme Wars" below). Rather than presenting an argument or alternative evidence, polemicists instead try to trigger negative associations designed to turn teachers away from phonics and trigger positive associations that will bind them to whole language (see Stahl, 1998, for an excellent discussion of the use of these techniques; also see McKenna et al., 1994).

THE BROADER PHILOSOPHICAL DISPUTE

In Chapter 20, I characterize the position of the whole language advocates as standing Canute-like against the evidence. Why the Canute-like stance, when Chapter 20 (and Adams, 1991) lays out how easy the rapprochement might be? Of course there are psychological factors such as belief bias, motivated reasoning, and belief perseverance operating.[3] But the increasingly vitriolic attacks on researchers in the whole language literature (see Footnote 1; Ehri, 1998; McKenna et al., 1994) have an air of desperation about them—the air of people losing their grip as the evidence turns against them. As more and more teachers—through publications such as California Reading Initiative (1999), Hall and Moats (1999), McGuinness (1997), McPike (1998), Pressley (1998), Reading Coherence Initiative (1999), Snow, Burns, and Griffin (1998), and Stahl, Osborn, and Lehr (1990)—become aware of the evidence, the extreme whole language advocates will begin to lose their influence. Their recognition of this impending loss of influence has no doubt contributed to their escalating rhetoric and the increasingly vitriolic attacks that characterize their writings.

The implications of evidence can be painful for those whose positions on instructional debates in education are philosophically driven rather than data-driven. Note that shifting meta-philosophical trends are no problem at all for the true scientist. Scientists, like teachers (see Chapter 21), are dedicated pragmatists. They follow the data and the productive hypothesis—theories and metaphilosophy be damned. A falsified hypothesis can often lead to an advance, so why get angry when the data surprises us? Of course, a falsified theory can be inconvenient for a scientist. For example, one might have geared up one's lab to test a certain theory, and it might take years to get back up and running to test a different hypothesis. But this is rarely true in reading research. Had I been wrong about phonological processes around 1984, let's say, and had faulty visual processing been shown then to be the key to reading difficulty, it would have taken me no more than a few months to gear up to study these types of processes. I could have cadged together the right equipment from various places in my university and quickly been ready to contribute to the emerging trends in visual processing. There is no reason why a scientific career studying those processes would not have been as fulfilling and fruitful as the course I did take if that's where the data had led me. What purpose would it have served to pour vitriol on the researchers who discovered the visual link? A personal attack would not have made the data go away.

Disputes about general educational philosophy are not the same, however. It has been common for those in such debates to quote studies and use research as weapons. But the key indicator that the evidence is not being used in a truly scientific sense is observing what happens when the data trend turns. Changing trends in evidence cause changes in *actual* scientific theory. To a philosophical stance they are an annoyance to be dispensed with.

Note the difference between the resolution of disputes in science and those in education. In Chapter 5 I took issue with the interpretation of the data in a paper by Foorman, Francis, Fletcher, and Lynn (1996). I gave there a spirited refutation of their data interpretations (as they had done with the interpretations in Stanovich & Siegel, 1994). Likewise, in Chapter 9 I took strong exception to the data interpretations of Shaywitz et al. (1995)—as they had done with some previous interpretations of Matthew effects. I do not know how either of these two disputes will eventually be resolved by future data—that is, I do not know which of us will eventually prevail in either of these disputes. But I do know two things. First, one day Foorman et al. (1996) and I will be in agreement on the nature of orthographic processing differences and one day Shaywitz et al. (1995) and I will be in agreement on the nature of the fan-spread effect. Second, I know that we will have arrived at these agreements without the use of the ad hominem attacks and personal vilification that has become common in the Reading Wars. In short, these disputes will end (unlike the interminable Reading Wars). And they will end amicably because their end will be dictated by the data. Three groups of scientists, all striving for the truth (a truth that none assumes they know in advance), will continue onward and find some new scientific issue to dispute and then resolve using converging data upon which we can all agree. Several things characterize this sequence in science in a way that distinguishes it from the Reading Wars: issues are resolved (they do not drag on interminably) and scientists move on to other things; they are resolved because the convergence of the data leads to a scientific consensus.[4]

What we have seen in the reading literature over the past couple of decades is in some sense a natural experiment. We have seen what different people do when the data change—when the evidence moves against them. This natural experiment is the perfect test of whether the original position was in fact scientifically based or instead a philosophical stance not based in evidence.

As discussed in Chapter 11, in the 1990s a backlash against the more extreme elements of the constructivist conceptualization in reading theory began to set in (exemplified in Chapter 12; see also Gough, 1995). It was increasingly recognized that strong constructivist assumptions were not squaring with what is now known about the importance of autonomous, encapsulated input processes in reading. Reading theory is being tempered by a consideration of how the external stimulus constrains comprehension (see Perfetti & McCutchen, 1987; Chapter 12). In contrast to these developments in cognitive science, writing and polemic in reading education is more extremely constructivist than ever (see Goodman, 1996; Taylor, 1989; Weaver, 1989; for a commentary on the flavor of these writings, see McKenna et al., 1994).

Instead of following the scientific evidence and altering their educational prescriptions, whole language theorists have simply thrown in their lot with the antiscientific relativism that has swept the humanities, social sciences, and departments of education throughout the 1990s (Gough, 1995; Gross & Levitt, 1994; Gross, Levitt, & Lewis, 1997; Haack, 1998; Sokal & Bricmont, 1998). This is a sad development, leaving education again stranded on the shoals of irrationalism—arrayed against science when science is in fact the wellspring of modern society and a source of humane values (Bronowski, 1973, 1977; Dawkins, 1998; Medawar, 1990; Stanovich, 1998a; Wilson, 1998). As discussed in Chapter 21, the situation becomes even worse when whole language proponents try to separate progressive social values from the scientific values of objectivity, data-driven interpretations, and the embrace of theoretical change in the face of contradictory evidence. The only remedy for this sad state of affairs is to build into teacher preparation much-needed instruction in scientific thinking and values.

THE "PARADIGM" SMOKESCREEN

In the paper reprinted as Chapter 20 I tried to expose the misleading use of Thomas Kuhn's notion of paradigm in the Reading Wars. In my Research Awards Address to the 1994 meeting of the International Reading Association in Toronto, I was able to elaborate on this theme a little more. I wish to draw attention to those remarks here because such a discussion highlights the use of the "paradigm smokescreen" to obscure inconvenient data.

The extreme constructivism exemplified in many whole language writings derives in part from adherence to a coherence theory of truth. This theory is contrasted with the correspondence theory that is held by most researchers in the psychology of reading (indeed, by most researchers in any domain of science). *Correspondence* theories of truth are easy to understand because, at a superficial level, they represent the view of the person in the street: put simply, there is a real world out there that exists independently of our beliefs about it, researchers form theories about this world, and the theories that track the world best are closer to the truth and thus provide a better basis for action. This is why planes don't fall out of the sky, why bridges rarely collapse, and why my headache medication works more often than not. In short, correspondence theories endorse *realist* assumptions about the world: that an independent reality exists separately from my thoughts and perceptions. We know about that reality when different investigators agree that they have made convergent observations. Duplication of findings by other critical investigators is deemed crucial under this view because only when such intersubjective agreement is reached are we confident that we are tracking an investigator-independent reality.

In contrast, most *coherence* theories reject realism and instead argue that knowledge is internally constructed—that our evolving knowledge is *not* tracking an independently existing world, but that *internally* constructed knowledge literally *is* the world. Variants of this view are apparent in some of the extreme forms of constructivism that are currently being promulgated in the educational community. Philosopher Michael Devitt (1991) explains how modern constructivism is the amalgamation of Kantian ideas with 20th-century epistemological relativism (see also Hacking, 1999). The criterion of truth for such a view is the coherence of the belief system: Do the beliefs fit together in a reasonably logical way? Do they make sense to the person constructing the beliefs? For example, presenting such a view to the audience of the *Harvard Educational Review,* Mishler (1990) stated that when interpreting interviews, for him, it is irrelevant whether the responses correspond to or mirror objective reality, because "a concern with distortion places the burden of validity claims on the wrong shoulders. Instead of assuming reality as a criterion, a potential warrant concerns *only* whether the responses make sense to the respondent" (p. 427).

Pure correspondence and pure coherentist views are both incomplete (see Ruse, 1999, for a nuanced discussion). In actual scientific practice, there is always a tension and interplay between the two. However, while coherence criteria (and their associated philosophical stance of constructivism) are currently quite popular, I want to explain why I still feel that teachers—when evaluating knowledge claims—should not lose sight of correspondence criteria.

First, I would make sure—in the midst of a lot of confusing rhetoric—that teachers really understand what proponents of epistemic relativism are actually saying. Philosopher Larry Laudan (1990) chooses to highlight the break with realism that constructivism entails, telling us that the doctrine "can be defined, to a first order of approximation, as the thesis that the natural world and such evidence as we have about that world do *little* or *nothing* to constrain our beliefs" (p. viii). Pulling no punches about the relativism of a coherence view, Mishler (1990), in the same essay quoted above, calls the concepts of reliability and objectivity "shibboleths— rhetorical strategies that serve a deviance-sanctioning function" (p. 420). Here we have laid bare the epistemic relativism that is underlying most of the extreme coherentist and constructivist views now popular in the educational literature. This is the thoroughgoing relativism that Kuhn's paradigm notion is (often mistakenly) used to promote.

Why do I think that such a thoroughgoing relativism is not a useful tool for a teacher? First, there is a vast philosophical literature on the self-refuting nature of an epistemic relativism (e.g., Haack, 1998; Nagel, 1997; Siegel, 1980, 1987, 1997)—that is, on just the type of debased Kuhnian notion that is so popular in the educational literature—yes, the one we all have heard a thousand times: "You are locked in your paradigm and I in mine. You cannot impose criteria developed within your paradigm to evaluate mine because the conceptual meaning of those criteria are inexplicable within my paradigm which has generated its own internally coherent criteria." Note the link to our earlier discussion here. The one universal criterion that *might* be imposed— tracking an investigator-independent real world—is finessed by an epistemic relativism rooted in a rejection of realism. In short, "We construct our own worlds, so there is no independent reality to adjudicate"—this is the stratagem that is used to dismiss the data that provides the scientific consensus on reading that I have outlined throughout this volume.

But as has been pointed out dozens of times in the philosophical literature—though never to the audiences of undergraduates or teachers who are subjected to this initially beguiling notion—the stratagem is deeply flawed. For example, in philosopher Donald Davidson's (1984) famous essay "On the Very Idea of a Conceptual Scheme," he notes that

> currently, there is much talk of conceptual schemes. Conceptual schemes, we are told, are ways of organizing experience; they are points of view from which individuals, cultures, or periods survey the passing scene. There may be no translating from one scheme to another, in which case the beliefs, desires, hopes, and bits of knowledge that characterize one person have no true counterparts for the subscriber to another scheme. Reality itself is relative to a scheme: what counts as real in one system may not in another. Now this conceptual relativism is a heady and exotic doctrine, or would be if we could make good sense of it. The trouble is, as so often in philosophy, it is hard to improve intelligibility while retaining the excitement. (p. 183)

The dominant metaphor of conceptual relativism—that of incommensurable points of view—seems to betray an underlying paradox, says Davidson: "The idea of incomparable points of view make sense, but only if there is a common coordinate system on which to plot them; yet the existence of a common system belies the claim of dramatic incomparability" (p. 184). This claim of whole language theorists, that they *know* that paradigms are incommensurable, is a transcendental claim of absolute knowledge. Totally contrary to what they seem on the surface to imply, the whole language theorists are actually making the strong claim that only *they* have unique access to multiple schemes. Only *they* have access to the meta-level where the compatibility of the coordinate systems of differing perspectives can be assessed. They are actually claiming that only *they* have access to a "God's-eye view."

The paradigm smokescreen is often reinforced by another strategy: that of setting up and then knocking down a straw-man version of a more traditional view that no scientist or philosopher of science would recognize. This common tactic involves stating an extremely authoritarian view of traditional science, acting like constructivists were the first to notice problems with this view, and then implying that once the straw man is demolished, epistemological relativism is the only alternative.

To be specific, traditional empirical science does *not* claim to yield certain knowledge; does *not* reject the idea of a plurality of methods; does *not* claim that the scientific method involves the use of a "formal algorithm," a fixed logic, or unchanging rules (Mishler, 1990, p. 418); does *not* recognize *only* laboratory studies as valid; and does *not* yield laws that ignore the context of the phenomenon. These are all caricatures regularly seen in the literature excoriating research that has demonstrated the importance of word recognition in the reading process.

The lesson here is simple. Teachers should not fall prey to facile, inaccurate, straw men designed to make the traditional correspondence view of science seem unpalatable—seemingly leaving the teacher with the "new paradigm" embodied in extreme whole language views as the only alternative. If teachers want a conceptualization that recognizes that observation is theory-laden and takes this into account, that is tentative in its knowledge claims, that recognizes its inherent fallibility, that recognizes that phenomena are conditioned by contexts and tries to take that concept into account, that uses a plethora of methods and logics, and whose methods can be employed outside the laboratory as well as in, then modern science fits the bill exactly.

Richard Shweder (1991), an anthropologist supportive of ethnographic methods in the social sciences, and one quite sympathetic to the "new paradigm" view, has warned that the latter, in its embrace of relativism, has

> ironically, however, despite its egalitarian intentions . . . [lent] support to a world based on intellectual domination and power assertion. The relativist views the understandings of others as self-contained, incommensurate, ideational universes (i.e., "paradigms"): across these universes there is no comparability, no common standard for rational criticism. Consequently, people's changes of ideational worlds (which do happen) can be explained by the relativist only in terms of domination, force, or non-rational conversion. And for disagreements, the only means

of adjudication is force—there is nothing to discuss [because of incommensurability]. When consensus [not the world] is the final arbiter of what is real, numbers count, and the powerful and/or the masses have their way. (p. 121)

Shweder is discussing a well-known conundrum for constructivist positions—but again one rarely discerned in the reading literature—namely, the issue of how to adjudicate *disputes* about knowledge claims. And one cannot avoid the issue of adjudication. As I outline in Chapter 21, a basic assumption of the paradigm smokescreen has been obscured from teachers, and this basic assumption has tremendous costs for our field. The assumption is that we (different sides in the Reading Wars) cannot really talk to each other—that insurmountable barriers exist between conceptual universes that are so fundamental that conversation is literally impossible. I am arguing here that in order to avoid this distressing conclusion—that continuing conversation among people in the reading field is futile and might as well cease—adherence to the correspondence notion of truth is essential.

In fact, the correspondence view is actually saying very *little*, and certainly less than people think. It says merely that there is a real world out there to talk about. It says that that world may be approached with a variety of different methods, techniques, and inquiry devices, but nevertheless we can *talk* about it with each other, and perhaps reach agreement, because we are indeed triangulating the same world with our different methods. This is in fact how teachers already adjudicate their differing opinions about different children, for example.

In reading, as in many fields, Liam Hudson's (1989) admonition is especially appropriate: "Many more of our prime movers than we realize may be in the grip of luminous metaphors, quasi-poetic or quasi-philosophical visions, hobbyhorses, obsessions, and ideés fixes. While providing the necessary driving force, such visions are bound to be at odds with the fabric of everyday science—not just with the patience of its methods, but with the answers it can ultimately be expected to give" (p. 1201). What teachers most definitely need is some grounding in the the "fabric of everyday science." Additionally, the reading field has been blessed with many "prime movers" whose poetic visions provided a motivating force for researchers and practitioners. But the field has been likewise cursed with the side effects of these luminous metaphors. Unfortunately, many whole language writings directed at teachers are authored by "prime movers" whose ideas are at odds with the patience of scientific methods.

MEME WARS: HOW AND WHY THE WHOLE LANGUAGE DISINFORMATION CAMPAIGN CONTINUES

Who is damaged by the whole language disinformation campaign? Interestingly, it is not the research scientists who are the focus of the attacks. Nor are the scientific research programs attacked in the whole language polemics in any way threatened. Who is hurt the most are the teachers who do not have access to the actual scientific information about the reading process, and the children (usually children from economically deprived backgrounds) who are utterly dependent on teachers to reveal the alphabetic code for them so that they can acquire the tool that will unlock all of their subsequent education: reading.

The scientific issues that relate most directly to the educational questions that are at the center of the Reading Wars are no longer in doubt. Many complicated theoretical issues remain the subject of intense dispute, of course, but regarding the basic practical issue of whether we would expect systematic instruction in alphabetic coding to facilitate the reading of the students at risk for reading difficulties there is little dispute in the scientific community. On this restricted conclusion the evidence was already pretty clear by the time Chapter 10 was published in 1986. It was even clearer when Chapter 20 was published in 1994. It it is even more clear now. Again, this is not meant to deny a host of more detailed scientific issues that *are* in dispute. It is merely to establish that on the most general and basic issue that divides the camps in the Reading Wars there is no scientific dispute (as discussed in Chapter 20, on most other issues, such as teacher empowerment the camps are not in disagreement).

We are thus faced with a puzzle. If the evidence is so clear, why can't science prevail? Why isn't the best scientific information being transmitted to teachers? It is not that the people spreading misinformation about the efficacy of code training have ulterior motives. It is not that teachers don't want to do what is best for their students. We need a new way to explain why the misinformation wins and the scientific information loses in this domain. I am convinced that we need to introduce some new concepts into our discussion of why this is happening. I intend to do just this in the present section by suggesting that we need to import concepts from the study of the evolution and the spread of ideas. When one turns to this literature (e.g., Blackmore, 1999; Lynch, 1996) one finds many discussions of conditions where the truth value of an idea is not the primary determinant of its spread. I will begin with an anecdote and then move on to a more formal discussion.

The anecdote highlights the dilemma we are in. At the 1999 meeting of the Society for the Scientific Study of Reading (SSSR) in Montreal I was standing at the back of the room during one of the concurrent sessions when Marilyn Adams gestured for me to join her out in the hall. She proceeded to show me an article in a recent National Council for Teachers of English (NCTE) publication containing gross distortions of the work of several researchers, including Adams herself, Barbara Foorman, and me. Throughout the remainder of the conference I queried many colleagues as to whether they thought anything should be written in response to these distortions (interestingly, no offer of reply to this vitriolic attack had come to any of us from the NCTE editor). I was relieved to see the response of my colleagues. The response of the majority—after seeing the unscholarly and ad hominem nature of the attack—was basically "Forget it, it's not worth your time." This was a relief, because I had no desire to spend precious time responding to myriad errors and misrepresentations in a very long paper (which turned out to be an excerpt from a book!). The time spent could in no way advance science—the distortions in the article were utterly obvious to anyone who had been following the actual scientific literature. Any time spent in replying would come at the cost of delaying my own current writing and ongoing studies.

Indeed, it is easy to rationalize nonresponse in a situation such as the one I've just described. One would spend one's whole life correcting such errors. There are whole books of misinformed critiques of the research literature published by Heinemann on a regular basis—and the NCTE as an organization seems dedicated to presenting distorted representations of the research literature to teachers. This situation is not unlike that of physical and social scientists and their response to the ESP reports presented in the media (see Stanovich, 1998a, for a discussion of this case). What scientist wants to stop his research, put it on hold, and begin replying to each bogus report of the existence of paranormal powers reported to the general public? That would be the end of one's research career because the task would never end. The very ubiquitousness of the misinformation demoralizes those who might otherwise be prone to correct it. Correspondingly, what researchers want to drop their research and respond to each distortion of science that some postmodern theorist communicates to the public?

As Gross and Levitt (1994) note about this related example, postmodernist critiques that distort science are

> unlikely to affect scientific practice and content; nor will they penetrate the attitudes of those who study the philosophical implications of science from a position of genuine familiarity. The danger, for the moment at least, is not to science itself. What is threatened is the capability of the larger culture, which embraces the mass media as well as the more serious processes of education, to interact fully with the sciences, to draw insights from scientific advances, and, above all, to evaluate science intelligently. (p. 4)

The same is true for the whole language disinformation campaign. The actual science of the psychology of reading has not been harmed. The Society for the Scientific Study of Reading and the *Journal of Educational Psychology* are as healthy as ever—new data and new theories are brought forth at conferences and in journals in greater profusion than ever, and we understand more and more about the reading process every day. The damage has been done once again to teachers who could know more about the reading process but don't; to teachers who could learn better teaching techniques than they utilize presently; and to children at risk for reading difficulty who need those teachers most.

The anecdote related above does, however, reveal the underlying logic of

the evolution and spread of beliefs and ideas in the domain of reading education. To be more specific, it reveals the peculiarly perverse logic where the bad
seems to drive out the good. That logic is so perverse that indeed we need to
turn to a new language and theory to understand it. The language is the language of belief propagation deriving from memetic theory (Blackmore, 1999;
Lynch, 1996). Blackmore (1999) provides the broadest and most readable introduction to memetic theory, although Richard Dawkins introduced the term
"meme" in his famous 1976 book *The Selfish Gene.* The term "meme" refers
to a unit of cultural information and is meant to be understood in rough
(rather than one-to-one) analogy to a gene. Blackmore (1999) defines the
meme as the instructions for behaviors and communications that can be
learned by imitation broadly defined (in the sense of copying by the use of language, memory, or any other mechanism) and that can be stored in brains (or
other storage devices). Collectively, genes contain the instructions for building
the bodies that carry them. Collectively, memes build the culture that trans-
mits them. Like the gene, the meme is a true replicator in the sense of the distinction made in theoretical biology between replicators and interactors
(Dawkins, 1976/1989; Hull, 1988). Replicators are entities that pass on their
structure relatively intact after copying and interactors are "those entities that
interact as cohesive wholes with their environments in such a way as to make
replication differential" (Hull, 1988, p. 27). In the context of the present discussion, the interactor is the human being in whose brain a particular meme is
residing.

The key idea in memetic theory is that the meme is a true selfish
replicator in the same sense that a gene is. By "selfish" we do not mean a gene
or a meme that makes people selfish. Instead, we mean that they are true
replicators that act only in their own "interests." The anthropomorphic language about genes and memes having interests is shorthand for the complicated description of what is actually the case: that genes/memes that perform
function X make more copies of themselves, copy with greater fidelity, or have
greater longevity—and hence will leave more copies in future generations. Or,
as Blackmore (1999) states it, "The shorthand 'genes want X' can always be
spelled out as 'genes that do X are more likely to be passed on.' This is the
only power they have—replicator power. And it is in this sense that they are
selfish" (p. 5).

Once we have understood the meme—the basic unit of culture—as a true
replicator, we are in a position to understand how memetic theory helps to
clarify certain phenomena of belief propagation. The fundamental insight triggered by memetic theory is that a meme may display fecundity and longevity
*without necessarily being true or helping the interactor (the human being
holding the belief) in any way.* Memetic theorists often use the example of a
chain letter. Here is a meme: "If you do not pass on this message to five people
you will experience misfortune." This is a true meme, an idea unit, in the form
of an instruction for a behavior that can be copied and stored in brains. It has
been a reasonably successful meme. A relatively large number of copies of this

meme have been around for most of the 20th century. Yet there are two remarkable things about this meme. First, it is not true; the reader who does not pass on the message will *not* experience misfortune. Second, the interactor who stores the meme and passes it on will receive no benefit; the interactor (human being in this case) will be no richer or healthier or wiser for having passed it on. Yet the meme survives. It survives because of its *own* self-replicating properties. Memes are independent replicators. They do not necessarily exist in order to help the interactor (those who hold the belief) they exist because through memetic evolution they have displayed the best fecundity, longevity, and copying fidelity—the defining characteristics of successful replicators.

Memetic theory has profound effects on our reasoning about ideas because it inverts the way we think about beliefs. Personality and social psychologists are traditionally apt to ask what it is about particular individuals that leads them to have certain beliefs. The causal model is one where the interactor determines what beliefs to have. Memetic theory asks instead what is it about certain memes that leads them to collect many "hosts" for themselves. The question is not how people acquire beliefs (the tradition in social and cognitive psychology) but how do beliefs acquire people. Indeed, this type of language was suggested by Dawkins (1976/1989) himself who, paraphrasing Nick Humphreys, said that "when you plant a fertile meme in my mind you literally parasitize my brain, turning it into a vehicle for the meme's propagation in just the way that a virus may parasitize the genetic mechanism of a host cell" (p. 192). Dawkins (1976/1989) argues that "what we have not previously considered is that a cultural trait may have evolved in the way it has, simply because it is *advantageous to itself*" (p. 27).

With Dawkins's point in mind we are now in a position to extract from the writings of the memetic theorists (e.g., Blackmore, 1999; Lynch, 1996) a taxonomy of reasons for meme survival. The first two classes of reason are the ones that are traditional in our folk psychology. The last reflects the new perspective of memetic theory:

1. Memes survive and spread because they are helpful to the interactors that store them (most memes that reflect true information in the world would be in this category).
2. Memes spread because they facilitate the spread of the genes that make good hosts for these particular memes (religious beliefs that urge people to have more children would be in this category; see Lynch, 1996).
3. Memes survive and spread because of the self-perpetuating properties of the memes themselves.

Categories #1 and #2 are uncontroversial and are standard fare in the disciplines of cultural anthropology and evolutionary psychology, respectively. Category #3 introduces new ways of thinking about beliefs as symbolic instructions that are more or less good at colonizing brains. Lynch (1996) and Blackmore (1999) discuss many subcategories of meme survival strategies under the general category #3, including proselytizing strategies, preservation strategies, persuasive strategies, adversative strategies, freeloading strategies, and mimicking strategies. For example, Lynch (1996) discusses proselytizing meme transmission and uses as an example the belief that "my country is dangerously low on weapons" which he argues illustrates proselytic advantage:

> The idea strikes fear in its hosts. . . . That fear drives them to persuade others of military weakness to build pressure for doing something about it. So the belief, through the side effect of fear, triggers proselytizing. Meanwhile, alternative opinions such as "my country has enough weaponry" promote a sense of security and less urgency about changing others' minds. Thus, belief in a weapons shortage can self-propagate to majority proportions—even in a country of unmatched strength. (pp. 5–6)

Another potential subclass of self-preservative properties of memes are their adversative properties, their ability to "change the selective environment to the detriment of competing memes" (Blackmore, 1999, p. 27) or to influence their hosts to attack the hosts of competing memes (see Lynch, 1996), or to neutralize the ability of competing memes to spread. Additionally, in category #3 are symbionts (memes that are more potent replicators when they appear together) and memes that *appear* to be advantageous to the interactor but are not—the freeloaders and parasites that mimic the structure of helpful memes and deceive the host into thinking that the host will derive benefit from them. Advertisers are of course expert at constructing meme parasites—memes that ride on the backs of other memes. In fact, advertisers are creators of so-called memeplexes (coadapted meme complexes), sets of memes that tend to replicate together (see Blackmore, 1999; Speel, 1995).

And now we have a sufficient conceptual structure for what is the obvious inference to which we are building: advocates of whole language have created a better memeplex than the advocates of a role for explicit phonics. Again, from the previous discussion it should be clear what "better" means in this content: a more successful replicator. These more efficient replicative qualities of the whole language memeplex occur despite the fact that some of the component memes in the memeplex do not serve the interests of the interactors (teachers) and despite the fact that many of them are false (they do not reflect the way that the reading process actually works).

THE READING NURTURANCE MEMEPLEX

Consider Adams's (1991) characterization of the whole language memeplex as the interconnection of five issues (see Chapter 20 for a discussion): (1) teacher empowerment, (2) child-centered instruction, (3) integration of reading and writing, (4) a disavowal of the value of systematic phonics instruction, and (5) subscription to the view that children are naturally predisposed toward written language acquisition. We might term this the Extreme Whole Language Memeplex (I use the adjective "extreme" because of propositions #4 and #5). Propositions #4 and #5 happen to be false but they have been conjoined here with three other very appealing memes. Interestingly, #4 and #5 are the only propositions that separate many advocates of phonics from whole language philosophy. That is, we could easily imagine a memeplex that conjoined #1 through #3 with #6: many children need systematic phonics instruction and #7: because children are not naturally predisposed toward the analytic processing requirements of written language acquisition (see Byrne, 1998). Call this the Reading Nurturance Memeplex. It is what Hall and Moats (1999) are referring to when they note that

> while some educators are resisting change in their entrenched belief systems, the research community is developing an even better understanding of how people learn to read. Reading experts are recommending comprehensive, balanced, informed instruction in which all parts of reading are taught well. This new approach is much more than an unsatisfactory compromise between two schools of thought. The more sophisticated approach emphasizes the importance of specific skills for specific children at specific times, in the context of a literature-rich program. No pieces are left out. (pp. 26–27)

Propositions #4 and #5 ride along in the Extreme Whole Language Memeplex despite their falsity because the other propositions with which they are conjoined are immensely appealing. Proposition #1 is bound to be popular with teachers, and proponents of the importance of decoding skills would also support the proposition. The meaning of #2 is very indeterminant but there is no question that it is a "warm fuzzy"—that it makes us feel good regardless of whether we can or cannot determine how it cashes out in terms of the treatment of children. Research from both camps supports proposition #3 (Treiman, 1998), so it has the advantage of strong empirical support. Thus, propositions #4 and #5 of the Extreme Whole Language Memeplex are riding parasitically on #1–#3. They are not symbionts, however. The package of five is not fitter as a replicating unit than is the Reading Nurturance Memeplex. The Extreme Whole Language Memeplex does in fact lose some fitness because of the empirical falsity of #4 and #5—as witnessed by the backlash against the failures of whole language in California, Texas, and other localities throughout the late 1990s (see Chapter 21).

Unfortunately for the field of reading—and for many disadvantaged children—we haven't really tried to advance the Reading Nurturance Memeplex because we haven't conjoined #6 and #7 with #1–#3 or with some similarly warm and fuzzy memes that would be popular and easily accepted. Instead, we have let the adversative strategies of extreme whole language advocates disrupt the formation and spread of the Reading Nurturance Memeplex. For example, we have allowed proposition #6 of that memeplex (many children need systematic phonics instruction) to be associated with noxious memes such as "skill and drill," "rote learning," "teacher-proof materials," and "tracking." As Hall and Moats (1999) point out, teachers "have been prejudiced against teaching skills because they mistakenly assume that the instruction must be rote, boring or meaningless for children" (p. 20; see Stahl, 1998, for a useful discussion).

There is no question that the whole language advocates have won the terminology war. They have repeatedly been successful in getting the field to accept seemingly neutral terms that actually carry with them parts of the Extreme Whole Language Memeplex. For example, the terms "emergent literacy" and "invented spelling" are not neutral terms. They are not descriptions of certain operationally defined performance patterns in early literacy. These terms convey a theory of early literacy acquisition (i.e., that it is natural and will normally progress without much formal tuition)—namely, proposition #5 of the Extreme Whole Language Memeplex (precisely one of the two propositions that is without empirical support; see Byrne, 1998; Liberman, 1999; Liberman & Liberman, 1992; Perfetti, 1991).

Whole language proponents are prone to use the term "authentic tasks" when characterizing their position—leaving, of course, the "inauthentic" ones to the advocates of systematic decoding instruction. Indeed, the term whole language is itself a deceptive meme that carries with it positive connotations of completeness that are utterly at variance with the facts. As many cognitive scientists have noted (e.g., Byrne, 1998; Byrne & Liberman, 1999; Hall & Moats, 1999; Liberman, 1999; Perfetti, 1991, 1994, 1995; Shankweiler, 1999), whole language has a hole in it. It is missing the very critical aspect of language that unlocks earlier reading acquisition for *all* children—not just those from privileged literacy-rich homes. That factor is instruction in the analytic nature of the language and of the orthography (see Byrne, 1998). That instructional process might well be termed an inclusionary reading practice because it ensures that all children will be provided with the tools of literacy. Proposition #4 of the Extreme Whole Language Memeplex is in fact an *exclusionary* practice because it ensures that some children (disproportionately the disadvantaged) will lack the full set of literacy tools. As Pressley notes, "Whole language theorists, such as Goodman (1993), had it about half right with respect to the development of reading skills. Yes, authentic reading and writing are important in the development of literacy, but systematic instruction in skills is also very important" (1998, p. 21).

Pointing out that it is the Reading Nurturance Memeplex that actually contains more inclusionary practices helps put an end to the hijacking of the terms of social justice by the Extreme Whole Language Memeplex. It is time to stop the adversarial strategy of the latter memeplex and take the language of social justice back. Nothing "empowers" readers more than learning the alphabetic principle. Many teachers are already proponents of the Reading Nurturance Memeplex—we just have to bring this reality to the surface for them by hooking a name to the beliefs and thus ending the stranglehold of the few figures promulgating the Extreme Whole Language Memeplex. Blackmore (1999) discusses the idea of "meme fountains" (individuals who spread ideas profusely) and "meme sinks" (individuals who copy memes but don't spread them). The Extreme Whole Language Memeplex has been spread by some prolific meme fountains, but as far as talking with teachers is concerned, most scientists are meme sinks.

So now with the new perspective of memetic science established, we can revisit my anecdote about the Montreal SSSR meeting. Unless we learn to package scientific information about the reading process in a more palatable fashion (as something like the Reading Nurturance Memeplex), we are going to lose the meme wars. We are meme fountains in the community of our scientific peers but we are meme sinks in the world of teachers. Scientists (like myself) are busy designing studies and analyzing data. Occasionally we get asked to write for publications such as *The Reading Teacher* (TRT), which are read by significant numbers of practitioners, and occasionally we do accept the invitation (see Chapter 20). Nevertheless, we need many more scientists who are willing to become meme fountains for teachers on a regular basis (for such heroic examples, see Adams, 1990; Burns, Griffin, & Snow, 1999; Consortium on Reading Excellence, 1999; Cunningham, Moore, Cunningham, & Moore, 1995; Hall & Moats, 1999; Pressley, 1998; Snow, Burns, & Griffin, 1998; Sternberg & Spear-Swerling, 1996; Thompson & Nicholson, 1999). But we are always going to be outnumbered here. The stark fact is that if you think you know the truth without having to collect any data, that saves a lot of time!

Ehri (1996) describes aspects of the scientific mode of communication that contribute to the "bad driving out the good" logic operating in reading. She notes that:

> the history of reading instruction has followed the course of a pendulum, with fashion swinging between phonics-oriented approaches and meaning-based approaches. Those who determine fashion control practice. The personality characteristics most effective in this enterprise are not likely those of the scientist. . . . Scientists never feel fully certain of their beliefs. They do not tend to view results of a study as definitive. . . . As a result of the tentative nature of their ideas, scientists are reluctant to make pronouncements. This may keep them from moving into the world of practice and strongly espousing a particular approach to instruction. Without a strong advocate to preach the implications of research findings for practice, the findings get ignored or suppressed in the impatient, profit-oriented, fashion conscious practical world (pp. 198–199)

And there is another factor operating here. Some memes are reliant for their survival on other coadapted memes. Any memes that appeal to evidence are reliant on another complex set of coadapted beliefs: the scientific memeplex. And the problem is that this is a minority memeplex. If it is a minority memeplex but also a prerequisite for understanding the evidence on the reading process, we have a problem. The only answer to the problem (as I argue in Chapter 21) is to give teachers the skills to understand the scientific literature for themselves. Teachers must be freed from the "gurus" that plague them or else the field of education will continue to be characterized by pendulum swings and fads.

Science does not swing from idea to idea like a pendulum—it builds cumulatively (see chapter 8 of Stanovich, 1998a). The cumulativeness of science—and the reasons *why* it is cumulative—is one of the critical principles that we must communicate to teachers in their teacher preparation. As mentioned in Chapter 21, the most basic principles of science are not difficult or arcane. They could easily be incorporated into teacher preparation, as they are into the methods training received by psychology majors when they are undergraduate sophomores (see Stanovich, 1998a).

Interestingly, in these times when many are concerned about teacher autonomy, there is nothing that has greater potential for making teachers autonomous scholars than a knowledge of the scientific process and the ability to evaluate scientific evidence—that is, to be independent evaluators of knowledge claims. Such skills not only provide the best protection against gurus and fads, but they provide other benefits as well. They provide teachers with tools to win intellectual battles with (often misinformed) principals, school boards, parents, school psychologists, and other ancillary supervisors and personnel that attempt to dictate teacher practice. For example, in my own experience, many teachers completing my reading research course have used the scientific principles taught there to fight off bogus "remedies" for reading disabilities in their schools. They have confronted the principals, learning disabilities specialists, and inservice gurus with the appropriate questions: "Has the evidence for this treatment been published in peer-reviewed scientific journals?" "If so, in what journals? I would like to provide the involved teachers with reprints of the studies." "Have the studies that have been done on this treatment been more than case studies?" "Have they involved some type of control group?" "Is the proposed mechanism by which this treatment works consistent with the 30-year consensus in the voluminous literature on the determinants of reading disability?" "Have the results been replicated by independent researchers?" These are basic questions, and in my experience they can be used by teachers to great effect.

THE TWO PAPERS REPRINTED HERE

Chapter 20 was published in the December 1993–January 1994 issue of *The Reading Teacher* as part of its Distinguished Educator Series. Although the Matthew effects paper (Chapter 10) had "broken through" beyond the research community and had been read by many practitioner audiences, "Romance and Reality" exposed many teachers to the research evidence on the issues covered in this volume for the first time. I know this because this article spawned a torrent of letters from teachers to me. Most of them had not been reading the research literature (nor had the faculty who had taught them in teacher training), but they did read TRT. I had served as a meme fountain for a new group!

The "Romance and Reality" article reprinted here as Chapter 20 also brought down a torrent of abuse from whole language extremists. Many of these individuals had seen no need to address my research evidence directly in the scientific literature with studies of their own. They were unconcerned about the actual evidence. And they were unconcerned about the theoretical debates about reading difficulty and reading acquisition that were going on in the literature as long as the scientists were just talking among themselves. But they became incensed when a scientist threatened to block the stranglehold they have on the flow of ideas within the domains that really determine practitioners' beliefs (publications such as TRT, inservice providers, schools of education in universities). I mentioned above that, as a researcher, information dissemination is not my primary activity, but I was happy to have contributed a bit with the TRT article and also happy that in the 1990s we have seen the proliferation of research-based publications directed at teacher audiences (Adams, Foorman, Lundberg, & Beeler, 1998; Ayres, 1998; Burns, Griffin, & Snow, 1999; Byrne & Fielding-Barnsley, 1991; California Reading Initiative, 1999; Catts & Kamhi, 1999; Catts & Vartianen, 1993; Chard & Osborn, 1999; Cunningham et al., 1995; Gaskins, Ehri, Cress, O'Hara, & Donnelly, 1997; Goswami, 1996; McGuinness, 1997; McPike, 1998; Pressley, 1998; Reading Coherence Initiative, 1999; Stahl, Osborn, & Lehr, 1990; Stein, Johnson, & Gutlohn, 1999; Sternberg & Spear-Swerling, 1996; Torgesen & Bryant, 1993).

The paper reprinted as Chapter 21 was based on my Oscar Causey Award Address to the meeting of the National Reading Conference in Scottsdale, Arizona, in December 1997. I had been honored with the Causey Award for outstanding contribution to research the year before in Charleston, South Carolina. This paper is a rich mix of musings on science, reading practice, and politics. The latter two loom so large because late 1997 was a very politicized time in the history of reading education. The situation in California was the subject of much discussion, the so-called Houston study (see Foorman et al., 1998) was generating heated discussion, and state legislatures were stepping in to regulate practice in literacy education. The beginning of the backlash against the failures of the extreme forms of whole language had begun in earnest. Many were worried that the pendulum would again swing too far back in the other direction, and there were also worries that teacher autonomy was threatened. To the extent that the latter two outcomes have indeed been fostered by hasty legislative action, I still stand by the points made in my Causey Address and the warning I gave there. That warning was that if the extremists in the whole language movement persist in cutting the reading education field off from the scientific evidence on reading acquisition and reading difficulty, then the resulting lack of professionalism will be seized upon by right-wing politicians hostile to teachers (and also by well-meaning but intrusive reformers), and legislatures will be tempted to prescribe teacher preparation and practices.

I suggested in the Causey Address that in contrast to the grim future that is guaranteed if we persist in ignoring evidence,

> the field could choose another course—a course that would assure our professional autonomy. That course is to present a united front to the public—united around our basic research findings—a front that would not stifle debate, that would still contain spirited debate about the practical implications of the basic facts about the reading process—but that would establish not only our knowledge but our shared entry into the community of science where issues are ultimately decided by empirical means. (Stanovich, 1998a, p. 54)

Were the field to do so we could present more of a united front to those threatening teacher practice with restrictive legislation. We could also form a more united front against the reactionary and corporate forces that are arrayed against teachers and public education. Instead, as mentioned in the TRT article, groups who share socially progressive goals for children and society have become divided over whether we should say to a child "s makes the /s/ sound"! This of course is doubly ironic because saying "s makes the /s/ sound" is an inclusionary educational practice: it helps precisely those children who will otherwise be left behind.

In his review of the work of the Committee on the Prevention of Reading Difficulties for the National Research Council of the National Academy of Sciences[5] (Snow, Burns, & Griffin, 1998)—a committee on which I served in the years 1996–1998—Pearson (1999) echoed my warnings about threats to teacher autonomy. While making it absolutely clear that he opposes legislative mandates, Pearson (1999) cautions:

> We have a professional responsibility to forge best practice out of the raw materials provided by our most current and most valid readings of research. . . . If professional groups wish to retain the privileges of teacher perogative and choice that we value so dearly, then the price we must pay is constant attention to new knowledge as a vehicle for fine-tuning our individual and collective views of best practice. This is the path that other professions, such as medicine, have taken in order to maintain their professional perogative, and we must take it, too. My fear is that if the professional groups in education fail to assume this responsibility squarely and openly, then we will find ourselves victims of the most onerous of legislative mandates. (p. 245)

Pearson (1999) then points to the contrary view in education—spawned by the excessive relativism and constructivism that has infused literacy theory in the last 2 decades—that teaching is too "situated" and research too "indeterminate" to mesh with any notion of best practices. Pearson (1999) argues that this position comes, however, with great political and professional burdens. First, it sells short the genuine accumulation and convergence of results we have achieved. . . . While we all respect the need for teachers to be able to adapt to individual needs and situations, we cannot, as a matter of policy, assert that all instruction is dependent and contingent. Third, it obscures the grave political reality I just outlined. Politics and politicians set policies, and they will set them with whatever intellectual resources are made available to them. We have an obligation, I believe, to make sure that policies are informed by the best, most current, and most convergent knowledge we can provide. (p. 245)

Progressive educators armed with an incorrect process model of reading and reading acquisition are sitting ducks for the potshots of right-wing teacher bashers. A much more formidable foe for the latter would be progressive educators armed with evidence and a research consensus—educators and researchers acting in solidarity, with utmost professionalism, to advocate for increased educational resources for all our children. Instead, we (advocates of progressive social policies) are trumped when our own Reading Wars are used to advance a right-wing agenda.[6]

In his still-relevant study of poverty in the North of England, *The Road to Wigan Pier*, George Orwell (1937/1989) explored the reasons why the Left could not seem to form a united front against the forces of the capitalist right. In the controversial second half of the book (his left-wing publisher inserted a Foreword disavowing the second half of the book) Orwell lamented the Left's tendency to slice and dice itself into small subgroups—none large enough to face up to corporate power (a phenomenon repeated 50 years after Orwell wrote with the "identity politics" of the 1980s and 1990s; see Gitlin, 1995):

> Obviously the Socialist movement has got to capture the exploited middle class before it is too late. . . . Socialists have a big job ahead of them here. They have got to demonstrate, beyond possibility of doubt, just where the line of cleavage between exploiter and exploited comes. Once again it is a question of sticking to essentials; and the essential point here is that all people with small, insecure incomes are in the same boat and ought to be fighting on the same side. Probably we could do with less talk about "capitalist" and "proletarian" and a little more about the robbers and the robbed. . . . It has got to be brought home to the clerk, the engineer, the commercial traveller . . . that they *are* the the proletariat, and that Socialism means a fair deal for them as well as for the navvy and the factory-hand. They must not be allowed to think that the battle is between those who pronounce their aitches and those who don't; for if they think that, they will join in on the side of the aitches (pp. 210–211)

We might paraphrase Orwell's admonition to socialists and turn it into an admonition to the different sides in the Reading Wars. We might say something like:

> Obviously those who support public education have got to get the voting public and taxpayers on their side before it is too late. Politically progressive educators have a big job ahead of them here. They have got to demonstrate, beyond possi-

bility of doubt, just where the line of cleavage is between those truly concerned with educating children and those with a corporate agenda of privatization and tax-cutting. Once again it is a question of sticking to essentials; and the essential point here is that researchers and teachers on different sides of the Reading Wars ought to be fighting on the same side against those determined to gut public education and to attack the professional integrity of teachers. Probably we could do with less talk about certain research and instructional activities being "authentic" and others "inauthentic" and a little more about who wants to rob children of classroom resources to give the already wealthy tax cuts. It has got to be brought home to the whole language advocate that researchers showing the effectiveness of alphabetic coding for children at risk are not their enemy. These advocates must stop trying to write their natural allies out of the political fight for educational resources just because these allies come to somewhat different scientific conclusions. We must not create a cleavage between our progressive politics and scientific truth. It undercuts progressive political positions with the public if the price of joining the progressive coalition is that our belief in objective truth and scientific evidence must be jettisoned. It of course brings the political views into question if this steep price is the cost of holding them.

We must stop creating a progressive politics where to be of the left you must oppose science (see Gross & Levitt, 1994; Gross, Levitt, & Lewis, 1997; Haack, 1998). We must stop expelling people from the progressive coalition unless they check their brains at the door. We must stop putting social justice at war with truth. This was Jacob Bronowski's great plea in a lifetime of writings on science and human values: "It is this opposition between what we think of as the kindly values of family . . . on the one hand, and the stern values of science on the other, which threatens to demoralize society in the age of plenty. . . . Somehow we think it remote from reality to face the facts; somehow we think it possible to be good without being wise" (Bronowski, 1977, pp. 202–203).

The cleavage between progressive social policies and scientific research that the extreme whole language advocates have caused in the field has many negative effects, not the least of which is that it gives right-wing forces a club with which to attack teacher autonomy and progressive educational reforms. It certainly gives them a powerful argument to make against alloting increased resources to education. Why spend extra money on things like lower class sizes, say the right-wing ideologues, when university schools of education are inculcating teachers with a model of reading development that does not square with the scientific evidence? I think that they are wrong—that the question is somewhat of a non sequitur—but nonetheless, the question has powerful resonance with parents and voters. Faculties in schools of education *do* have a lot to answer for. I myself would like to know why they teach an outmoded, 30-year-old notion of a "psycholinguistic guessing game" that has been superseded by modern research (indeed, that was superseded some time ago—see Part I).

In her seminal book, Adams (1990) notes without understatement that "reading may be the most politicized topic in the field of education" (p. 13).

And sadly, her book demonstrates what has been lost through the excessive politicization of the subject. Much is known about early reading. The information we have could be used to improve practice. This is all amply demonstrated in Adams's book. Most importantly, her volume and others like it (e.g., Snow et al., 1998) highlight the key differences between the polemics that often pass for scholarship in the field of education and true scientific research.

An actual research synthesis is often a kludge (in computer science, an inelegant but successful solution to a problem). It unashamedly uses methods, theories, and findings from a variety of areas with no concern for philosophical consistency. It is highly opportunistic and pragmatic. Philosophically based educational polemic is just the opposite. Here, everything must be consistent. Everything must be perfectly in line with the basic philosophical principles that serve as the foundation of the view. The foundational assumptions here are not subject to alteration by empirical evidence. They are chiseled in stone. When given the choice between data and the philosophical assumptions, the assumptions are preserved every time. Stahl (1998) pointed to an example of this syndrome when he quoted Goodman's (1992) statement that "whole language teachers are beyond eclecticism" (p. 361) and Deegan's (1995) attack on teachers who hold what I call in Chapter 21 a "what works" epistemology: "Essentially, a 'what works' argument represents a position hostile to theory. On the contrary, the challenge of whole language is to constantly assess practice by referring to theory; anything less is simply not whole language. 'What works' can never be justification for practice" (p. 692).

To the contrary, as I argue at the end of Chapter 21, the best scientists and the best teachers alike are less concerned about being philosophically consistent. Both are ever the opportunistic practitioner. This is why I characterized both as having "what works" epistemologies. This commonality between researchers and teachers has been another casualty of the dreadful Reading Wars. Teachers are grounded in empiricism (systematic observation), as are scientists. They share a critical fallibilism (changing theories on the basis of evidence) with scientists. They share realist assumptions (that there is an actual fact of the matter that we converge on while using our differing perspectives) with scientists. These commonalities have become obscured amid the efforts to demonize scientific work that does not lead to whole language conclusions (specifically propositions #4 and #5 discussed above).

Whole language advocates like to imply that the insights of teachers and those of researchers are at variance with one another. Nothing could be farther from the truth. Teachers often do observe exactly what the research shows: that most of their children who are struggling with reading have trouble decoding words. In an address full of wisdom and reason, presented to the Reading Hall of Fame at the 1996 meeting of the International Reading Association, Isabel Beck (1996) illustrated this point by reviewing her own intellectual history (see Beck, 1998, for an archival version). She relates her surprise upon coming as an experienced teacher to the Learning Research and Development Center at the University of Pittsburgh and finding "that there were some people there (psychologists) who had not taught anyone to read, yet they were able to describe phenomena that I had observed in the course of teaching reading" (Beck, 1996, p. 5). In fact, what Beck was observing was the triangulation of two empirical approaches to the same issue—two perspectives on the same underlying reality. And she also came to appreciate how these two perspectives fit together: "What I knew were a number of whats—that is, what some kids, and indeed adults, do in the early course of learning to read. And what the psychologists knew were some whys—that is, why some novice readers might do what they do" (pp. 5–6).

Near the end of her essay, Beck speculates on why the Reading Wars have dragged on so long without resolution and posits that it is due to the power of a particular kind of evidence: evidence from personal observation. The vehemence of whole language advocates is no doubt sustained because "people keep noticing the fact that some children or perhaps many children—in any event a subset of children—especially those who grow up in print-rich environments, don't seem to need much more of a boost in learning to read than to have their questions answered and to point things out to them in the course of dealing with books and various other authentic literacy acts" (Beck, 1996, p. 8). But Beck points out that it is equally true that proponents of the importance of decoding skills are also fueled by personal observation: "People keep noticing the fact that some children or perhaps many children—in any event a subset of children—don't seem to figure out the alphabetic principle, let alone some of the intricacies involved without having the system directly and systematically presented" (p. 8).

I think Beck is basically correct that personal observation is trumping all other evidence here. But clearly we have lost sight of the basic fact that the two observations are not mutually exclusive: one doesn't negate the other. Additionally, of course, this is just the type of situation that the scientific method was invented to address (see Stanovich, 1998a)—when we need a consensual view that triangulates differing observations across observers. We proceed to develop operational definitions that all investigators can replicate and therefore check the data trends themselves. And in this domain, as discussed in Chapters 20 and 21, the data has converged nicely. Nothing in the scientific consensus negates the fact that some children "don't seem to need much more of a boost," but the same research base does strongly support Beck's conclusion that

> from the multiple lenses of having taught first graders . . . from being familiar with large bodies of research . . . from engaging in my own lines of related research; from watching my own two children . . . from visits to current primary grade classrooms, the most significant understanding that I have about beginning reading is that it is crucial that children gain control of the print to speech mapping system early. And it won't happen for a substantial number of children if we don't do it systematically. But doing it systematically does not need to diminish the development of a language-rich environment. (p. 12)

Beck's conclusions reinforce an admonition of Frank Smith's from some years back. He expressed the sentiment that teachers should not be turning to researchers for advice as to what specifically they should do in the classroom, but should instead ask for basic information on the nature of the reading process, which they can then use to arrive at their own decisions:

> Instead of inquiring what they should do, which can never be answered with the generality they expect, they should ask what they need to know in order to decide for themselves. (1983, p. 3)
>   Teacher training institutions seem often to expect teachers of reading to do their jobs without a basic understanding of the topic they are concerned with. . . . Most teachers are often left with a patchwork of conflicting practical suggestions and a belief that the nature of reading is either too obvious to require analysis or too mysterious to be discussed. Yet the nature of reading cannot be ignored. . . . There is no alternative to acquiring understanding of reading itself. (1979, pp. ix–x)

Precisely. And a 25-year research consensus has converged on an understanding of reading itself—an understanding summarized in several seminal research syntheses that have been published throughout this period (Adams, 1990; Anderson, Hiebert, Scott, & Wilkinson, 1985; Byrne, 1998; Catts & Kamhi, 1999; Chall, 1983a; Ehri, 1987, 1995, 1997; Frost, 1998; Metsala & Ehri, 1999; Perfetti, 1985, 1994; Rayner, 1998; Shankweiler, 1999; Share, 1995; Snow et al., 1998; Sternberg & Spear-Swerling, 1999; Thompson & Nicholson, 1999).

I hope that the collection of my work published here will help to add to that synthesis and also to the efficiency with which it is communicated to teachers. It has been a fascinating ride this career of mine in reading: from meeting Rich West as a graduate student at Michigan in the early 1970s—and then Anne Cunningham when I was a newly minted assistant professor—to the honor of being inducted into the Reading Hall of Fame in 1995 and then serving on the Committee on the Prevention of Reading Difficulties for the National Academy of Sciences from 1996 to 1998. This has been an extraordinarily productive period in which we have begun to really crack the mysteries of the reading process by arriving at a scientific synthesis—a synthesis put together through the work of literally hundreds of investigators. I am proud to have played my part in this scientific achievement.

NOTES

1. The invective since the 1994 and 1998 papers reprinted here has gotten even worse—both on the listservs and in print. Mindful of memetic theory (Blackmore, 1999), I do not wish to make the situation worse by citing sources for the invective (the examples with sources in Chapter 21 are enough to give the flavor). I will just note that a scientist who has contributed decades of work to research on how struggling children can be helped to read has been called the "lyin' king" on listservs re-

peatedly. Others (myself included) were called "spin doctors" in a book published by the National Council of Teachers of English (NCTE) and advertised in publications of the International Reading Association. I was among another group of researchers who were accused of the "rhetoric of insincerity" in an NCTE journal. The magazine *American Educator*, an organ of the American Federation of Teachers (AFT), a teachers' union, publishes an absolutely wonderful issue on "The Unique Power of Reading" (McPike, 1998) and, because some of the articles mention the importance of decoding, the magazine's editors are excoriated with blustering comments on the National Reading Conference listserv such as "as a lifelong supporter of unions I am sickened by AFT joining the campaign of those who would destroy teacher unions to mandate a paradigm of reading instruction which treats teachers as technicians to be controlled" (Goodman, July 31, 1998). In her intellectual autobiography Linnea Ehri (1996, 1998) describes a session at an American Educational Research Association meeting in which traditional researchers—those not carrying out action research, ethnographic research, or using collaborative methods—were described as "academic rapists." The list of such unscholarly encounters in our professional community lengthens daily—primarily due to a few individuals who unfortunately have disproportionate influence.

2. This is certainly true in the present case. The Stanovich family has more labor union experience and progressive politics in it than that of most postmodernist theorists with whom I am familiar. Many researchers, like me, are rooted in values of economic justice that were spawned by our working-class backgrounds. I have never really needed a situated cognition theorist to find out for me through his or her research that working-class people think in complex ways. My father did superbly well with the complex mass of data in the *Daily Racing Form* despite continuing exposure to the toxic fumes present in the spray-paint booth at the General American Transportation Corporation.

3. See the many citations of research on these psychological processes in Stanovich (1999b) where their basic characteristics are explained: interpreting evidence in terms of ones own theories, letting one's desires that a conclusion be true interfere with evidence evaluation, and maintaining beliefs in the face of contradicting evidence.

4. In her intellectual autobiography Linnea Ehri (1998) describes scientific disagreements with Phil Gough, Connie Juel, and Usha Goswami that have this same characteristic.

5. In arriving at a consensus view on the prevention of reading difficulties, this panel drew heavily on the 25-year research convergence on the nature of the reading process that is described in this volume.

6. Right-wing political forces continually attack public education and use as a club the claim that reading is not being taught as well as in the "good old days" despite the fact that this claim is false. Longitudinal indicators consistently show that children are reading at least as well as they ever did (Berliner & Biddle, 1995; Campbell, Voelkl, & Donahue, 1997; Stedman, 1996). The "crisis" of low literacy levels results because of rising *demands* for literacy—not because absolute levels of literacy are falling.

CHAPTER 20

Romance and Reality

When, in preparation for this essay, I began thinking about the various components of my research program over the past twenty years, I realized that they could be divided into two categories: research I have done that almost everyone likes and research I have done that not everybody likes. I thought that this distinction might be worth exploring in this essay because it may well say more about the current state of the field of reading than it does about my research itself.

RESEARCH I HAVE DONE THAT ALMOST EVERYONE LIKES

In this category would go some of my research which has demonstrated that certain ways of classifying children having reading difficulties may be untenable. For example, one idea that has a long history in the learning disabilities field is that less-skilled readers who display a discrepancy with a measure of "aptitude" (typically defined as performance on an intelligence test) are different from poor readers who do not display such a discrepancy. It was thought that the reading-related cognitive characteristics of these groups were different and that they needed different types of treatment. Nevertheless, recent research and theory has brought these assumptions into question (Siegel, 1989; Stanovich, 1988a, 1991b). It appears that children having difficulties in reading who have aptitude/achievement discrepancies have cognitive profiles that are surprisingly similar to children who do not. Also, to a large extent, these groups respond similarly to various educational interventions. Although some in the learning disabilities community have not found this research to be palatable, IRA audiences and the vast majority of teachers have not only felt very comfortable with these research conclusions, but also vindicated by them.

Even more popular has been my work on Matthew effects in reading development (Stanovich, 1986b). The term Matthew effects derives from the Gospel According to Matthew: "For unto every one that hath shall be given, and he shall have abundance: but from him that hath not shall be taken away even that which he hath" (XXV: 29). It is used to describe rich-get-richer and poor-get-poorer effects that are embedded in the educational process. Herb Walberg (Walberg & Tsai, 1983) had focused attention on the process by which early educational achievement spawns faster rates of subsequent achievement, and in a 1986 paper I specifically explored the idea of Matthew effects in the domain of reading achievement. I outlined a model of how individual differences in early reading acquisition were magnified by the differential cognitive, motivational, and educational experiences of children who vary in early reading development.

In that particular paper, I detailed several developmental mechanisms that are of continuing theoretical and empirical interest. Put simply, the story went something like this: Children who begin school with little phonological awareness have trouble acquiring alphabetic coding skill and thus have difficulty recognizing words. Reading for meaning is greatly hindered when children are having too much trouble with word recognition. When word recognition processes demand too much cognitive capacity, fewer cognitive resources are left to allocate to higher-level processes of text integration and comprehension. Trying to read without the cognitive resources to allocate to understanding the meaning of the text is not a rewarding experience. Such unrewarding early reading experiences lead to less involvement in reading-related activities. Lack of exposure and practice on the part of the less-skilled reader further delays the development of automaticity and speed at the word recognition level. Thus, reading for meaning is hindered, unrewarding reading experiences multiply, practice is avoided or merely tolerated without real cognitive involvement, and the negative spiral of cumulative disadvantage continues. Troublesome emotional side effects begin to be associated with school experiences and these become a further hindrance to school achievement.

Conversely, children who quickly develop efficient decoding processes find reading enjoyable because they can concentrate on the meaning of the text. They read more in school and, of equal importance, reading becomes a self-chosen activity for them. The additional exposure and practice that they get further develops their reading abilities. I speculated that reading develops syntactic knowledge, facilitates vocabulary growth, and broadens the general knowledge base. This facilitates the reading of more difficult and interesting texts. Thus, the increased reading experiences of these children have important positive feedback effects that are denied the slowly progressing reader.

My description of the different developmental trajectories due to differences in the ease of early reading acquisition struck a responsive chord of recognition with many practitioners who thought that the theoretical description captured some things that they had observed. Critiques by researchers were also largely supportive. Subsequent work in which I have tried to generate empirical support for the role of print exposure in cognitive development has been equally well received. My research group has tried to develop alternative methods of assessing differences in amount of print exposure in children and adults (Allen, Cipielewski, & Stanovich, 1992; Cunningham & Stanovich, 1991; Stanovich & West, 1989). Using some new methods, as well as some instruments designed by other investigators, we have documented an important role for print exposure in cognitive development (Stanovich, 1993a; Stanovich & Cunningham, 1992, 1993). Amount of print exposure is a potent predictor of vocabulary growth, knowledge acquisition, and a host of other verbal skills. Exposure to print does seem to be implicated in some educational Matthew effects.

More optimistically, however, we have found that exposure to print seems to be efficacious regardless of the level of the child's cognitive and reading abilities. Using some fairly sophisticated statistical analyses, we found that print exposure was a significant predictor of verbal growth even after the children had been equated on their general cognitive abilities. Print exposure was a strong predictor of cognitive growth in even the least advantaged children in our research samples. Thus, the child with limited reading skills and low general ability will build vocabulary and cognitive structures through immersion in literacy activities just as his/her high-achieving counterpart. An encouraging message for teachers of low-achieving children is implicit here, and this research program of mine has been almost universally well received. Not so, however, with some other research that I have done.

RESEARCH I HAVE DONE THAT NOT EVERYONE LIKES

One of the first research problems in reading that I investigated was the role of context in word recognition. At the time I began these investigations with my colleague Richard West (in the early 1970s), several popular theories posited that the ability to use contextual information to predict upcoming words was an important factor in explaining individual differences in reading ability. Fluent readers were said to have attained their skill because of a heavy reliance on context in identifying words. Reading difficulties were thought to arise because some readers could not, or would not, use context to predict upcoming words. To our surprise at the time (West and I had started these investigations thinking that the context view was correct), our initial investigations of this problem revealed just the opposite: It was the less-skilled readers who were more dependent upon context for word recognition (West & Stanovich, 1978; Stanovich, West, & Feeman, 1981). The reason for this finding eventually became apparent: the word recognition processes of the skilled reader were so rapid and automatic that they did not need to rely on contextual information. Over ten years later, this finding is one of the most consistent and well-replicated in all of reading research. It has been found with all types of readers, in all types of texts, and in a variety of different paradigms (e.g., Bruck, 1988; Leu, DeGroff, & Simons, 1986; Nicholson, 1991; Nicholson, Lillas, &

Rzoska, 1988). Reviews of the dozens of different studies that converge on this conclusion are contained in Perfetti (1985), Rayner and Pollatsek (1989), and Stanovich (1980, 1984, 1986b, 1991b).

Perhaps understandably, at the time our initial findings were published they were not warmly received by researchers invested in the context-use theory which the results falsified. Today, however, the implications of these results have been incorporated into all major scientific models of the reading process (e.g., Just & Carpenter, 1987; Rayner & Pollatsek, 1989). Scientifically, the results are now uncontroversial. However, they are still not welcomed by some reading educators who would perpetuate the mistaken view that an emphasis on contextual prediction is the way to good reading.

It should be noted here that the findings I have referred to concern the use of context as an aid to *word recognition* rather than as a mechanism in the comprehension process. Although good readers employ contextual information more fluently in the comprehension process, they are not more reliant on contextual information for word recognition. A tendency to conflate these two levels of processing in discussions of context effects has caused enormous confusion among both researchers and practitioners. Additional confusion has been caused by the use of imprecise labels such as "word calling." Despite the frequency with which this term occurs in reading publications, it is rare to find an author who spells out exactly what they mean by the term "word caller." However, the implicit assumptions behind its use appear to be as follows: (1) Word calling occurs when the words in the text are efficiently decoded into their spoken forms without comprehension of the passage taking place. (2) This is a bad thing, because (3) it means that the child does not understand the true purpose of reading, which is extracting meaning from the text. (4) Children engaging in word calling do so because they have learned inappropriate reading strategies. (5) The strategic difficulty is one of over-reliance on phonic strategies.

The idea of a "word-caller" embodying the assumptions outlined above has gained popularity despite the lack of evidence that it applies to an appreciable number of poor readers. There is no research evidence indicating that decoding a known word into a phonological form often takes place without meaning extraction. To the contrary, a substantial body of evidence indicates that even for young children, word decoding automatically leads to meaning activation (Ehri, 1977; Stanovich, 1986b) *when the meaning of the word is adequately established in memory.* The latter requirement is crucial. Reports of "word calling" rarely indicate whether the words that are "called" are even in the child's listening vocabulary. If the child would not understand the meaning of the word or passage when spoken, then overuse of decoding strategies can hardly be blamed if the child does not understand the written words. In short, a minimal requirement for establishing "word calling" is the demonstration that the written material being pronounced is within the listening comprehension abilities of the child.

Secondly, it is necessary to show that the "word calling" is not a simple consequence of poor decoding. Although reasonably efficient decoding would appear to be an integral part of any meaningful definition of "word calling," decoding skills are rarely carefully assessed before a child is labeled a "word caller." It is quite possible for accurate decoding to be so slow and capacity-demanding that it strains available cognitive resources and causes comprehension breakdowns. Such accurate but capacity-demanding decoding with little comprehension should not be considered "word calling" as defined above. To the contrary, it is a qualitatively different type of phenomenon. Comprehension fails not because of over-reliance on decoding, but because decoding skill is not developed *enough*.

Another line of my research that has not been universally applauded concerns the role of phonological skills in early reading acquisition. Early insights from the work of Chall, Roswell, and Blumenthal (1964), Bruce (1963), and Liberman et al. (1974) came to fruition in the early 1980s when numerous investigators began to document the importance of phonological awareness skills in early reading acquisition. Our own work (e.g., Stanovich, Cunningham, & Cramer, 1984; Stanovich, Cunningham, & Feeman, 1984a) was part of the "second generation" of research on these processes.

Reading researchers have for years sought the cognitive predictors of individual differences in early reading acquisition. The list of candidate processes and behaviors is long (short-term memory, intelligence, processes of contextual prediction, etc.). In the last ten years, researchers have come to a strong consensus about the cognitive processes that best predict reading progress in the earliest stages. These cognitive processes have been called phonological awareness and they are measured by some of the tasks briefly summarized in Table 20.1. The term phonological awareness refers to the ability to deal explicitly and segmentally with sound units smaller than the syllable. Researchers argue intensely about the meaning of the term phonological awareness and about the nature of the tasks used to measure it. However, in the present context, it is only critical to establish that it is indicated by performance on the generic type of task that we see in this table. These tasks vary in difficulty. Some can be successfully completed before others. But all are highly

TABLE 20.1. Examples of Phonological Awareness Tasks

Phoneme deletion: What word would be left if the /k/ sound were taken away from "cat"?

Word to word matching: Do "pen" and "pipe" begin with the same sound?

Blending: Tell me what word we would have if you put these sounds together, /s/, /a/, /t/

Sound isolation: What is the first sound in "rose"?

Phoneme segmentation: What sounds do you hear in the word "hot"?

Phoneme counting: How many sounds do you hear in the word "bake"?

Deleted phoneme: What sound do you hear in "meat" that is missing in "eat"?

Odd word out: What word starts with a different sound: "bag," "nine," "beach," "bike"?

Sound to word matching: Is there a /k/ in "bike"?

correlated with each other. Most importantly, they are the best predictors of the ease of early reading acquisition—better than anything else that we know of, including IQ.

The latter is a somewhat startling finding if you think about it. Consider that I can spend an hour and a half giving a child any of a number of individually administered intelligence tests; then I can take about seven minutes and administer 15 items of the type illustrated in the table. And, when I am done, the seven minute phonological awareness test will predict ease of initial reading acquisition better than the two hour intelligence test! This is why both researchers and practitioners have been greatly interested in research on phonological awareness. Additionally, research has shown that phonological awareness appears to play a causal role in reading acquisition—that it is a good predictor not just because it is an incidental correlate of something else, but because phonological awareness is a foundational ability underlying the learning of spelling–sound correspondences. Numerous training studies have demonstrated that preschool and kindergarten children exposed to programs designed to facilitate phonological awareness become better readers (Ball & Blachman, 1991; Bradley & Bryant, 1985; Cunningham, 1990; Lie, 1991; Lundberg, Frost, & Peterson, 1988). Programs incorporating aspects of phonological awareness have recently been described in the pages of *The Reading Teacher* (e.g., Griffith & Olson, 1992; Yopp, 1992).

Like my findings on context use in reading—but unlike my research on Matthew effects and print exposure—my research on phonological awareness was less than welcome in some quarters of the reading education community. What accounts for these differential responses to research emanating from the same investigator? It is certainly possible that when I did the work on print exposure I had a "good day" and that when I did the work on phonological awareness and context effects I was having a "bad day." However, those who have followed the dreadful "reading wars" in North American education will be aware that there is a more parsimonious explanation: research topics that I investigated that were closer to the heart of the Great Debate over reading education were more controversial.

THE GREAT DEBATE—AGAIN

Simply put, the work on phonological awareness and context effects contradicted the philosophical tenets of the more "hard line" whole language advocates. Although almost all teachers recognize from their own experience that encouraging "contextual guessing" in those children experiencing early reading difficulty does not help, heavy reliance on context to facilitate word recognition is still emphasized by some whole language proponents. Similarly, phonological awareness training violates a fundamental tenet because it isolates components of the reading process.

What really is the heart of this controversy? I hesitate here, because so much contention and vitriol has surrounded the "phonics versus whole language" debate that I almost balk at the thought of contributing to it further! Nevertheless, ever the optimist, in what follows I offer a five-step strategy for attenuating the dispute. My strategy has the following logic:

1. First look for points of agreement between opposing positions.
2. When doing so, invoke a "spirit of charity" whereby all sides are encouraged to stretch their principles to the maximum to accommodate components of the other position.
3. Step back and take a look at what might be a larger degree of agreement than anyone supposed.
4. Next, isolate the crucial differences. Try to make these few in number but clearly defined so that they are amenable to scientific test.
5. However, before arguing about the outcomes of the tests, both sides should take a look at the set of defining differences and ask themselves whether they are worth the cost of war.

It is really not difficult to demonstrate that there is more agreement among reading educators than is sometimes apparent to those obsessively focused on the so-called reading wars. For example, Chall (1989) has repeatedly pointed out that many of the recommendations and practices that are commonly associated with whole language have appeared repeatedly in her writings. She reminds us that "teaching only phonics—and in isolation—was not a recommendation of the Great Debate in 1967 or 1983" (p. 525). Chall is at pains to remind her readers that, in common with many whole language advocates, she "also recommended that library books, rather than workbooks, be used by children not working with the teacher and that writing be incorporated into the teaching of reading" (p. 525). Chall (1989) has no compunctions about admitting that "some teachers may inadvertently overdo the teaching of phonics, leaving little time for the reading of stories and other connected texts," but she notes that "the history of reading instruction teaches us that literature, writing, and thinking are not exclusive properties of any one approach to beginning reading" (p. 531). Clearly there is plenty of scope for the "principle of charity" to operate here. Corresponding to Chall's statement that "some teachers may inadvertently overdo the teaching of phonics" we simply need the companion admission that "some children in whole language classrooms do not pick up the alphabetic principle through simple immersion in print and writing activities, and such children need explicit instruction in alphabetic coding"—a concession having the considerable advantage of being consistent with voluminous research evidence (Adams, 1990; Vellutino, 1991). It seems inconceivable that we will continue wasting energy on the "reading wars" simply because we cannot get both sides to say, simultaneously, "some teachers overdo phonics" and "some children need explicit instruction in alphabetic coding."

Adams (1991) is likewise boggled at what, seemingly, is the cause of all our strife. She points to the defining features of the whole language philosophy that Bergeron (1990) gleaned from an extensive review of the literature:

> Construction of meaning, wherein an emphasis is placed on comprehending what is read; functional language, or language that has purpose and relevance to the learner; the use of literature in a variety of forms; the writing process, through which learners write, revise, and edit their written works; cooperative student work; and an emphasis on affective aspects of the students' learning experience, such as motivation, enthusiasm, and interest. (p. 319)

Adams (1991) asks rhetorically "Is this what the field has been feuding about?" (p. 41). Probably not. Instead, she argues that "the whole language movement carries or is carried by certain other issues that do merit serious concern. . . . These issues are: (1) teacher empowerment, (2) child-centered instruction, (3) integration of reading and writing, (4) a disavowal of the value of teaching or learning phonics, and (5) subscription to the view that children are naturally predisposed toward written language acquisition" (p. 41). Educators working from a variety of different perspectives might well endorse points #1 to #3. Clearly the key points of difference are issues #4 and #5. However, Adams (1991) makes the seemingly startling—but actually very wise—suggestion that the

> positions of the whole language movement on teaching and learning about spellings and sounds are historical artifacts. Although they are central to its rhetoric and focal to its detractors, they may well be peripheral to the social and pedagogical concerns that drive the movement. . . . Yet their continuing centrality to the rhetoric of the movement may be owed no less to their historical precedence than to the fact that . . . they were tightly connected to the other issues of teacher empowerment, child-centered education, and the reading–writing connection. I believe, moreover, that it is these latter issues that inspire the deepest commitment and passion of the movement. . . . To treat it today as an issue of phonics versus no phonics is not only to misrepresent it, but to place all of its valuable components at genuine risk. (pp.42, 51)

Adams is pointing toward some dangers that lie in wait for whole language advocates but also toward a possible rapprochement within the reading education community. The danger is this: In holding to an irrationally extreme view on the role of phonics in reading education—for failing to acknowledge that some children do not discover the alphabetic principle on their own and need systematic direct instruction in the alphabet principle, phonological analysis, and alphabetic coding—whole language proponents threaten all of their legitimate accomplishments. Eventually—perhaps not for a great while, but eventually—the weight of empirical evidence will fall on their heads. That direct instruction in alphabetic coding facilitates early reading acquisition is one of the most well established conclusions in all of behavioral science (Adams, 1990; Anderson et al., 1985; Chall, 1983b, 1989; Perfetti, 1985; Stanovich,

1986b). Conversely, the idea that learning to read is just like learning to speak is accepted by no responsible linguist, psychologist, or cognitive scientist in the research community (see Liberman & Liberman, 1990). To stand, Canute-like, against this evidence is to put at risk all of the many hard-won victories of the whole language movement:

> The whole language movement should be a movement that is a core component of a long overdue and highly constructive educational revolution. It should be about restoring the confidence and authority of teachers. It should be an affirmation that education can only be as effective as it is sensitive to the strengths, interests, and needs of its students. . . . It should be about displacing such outmoded instructional regimens with highly integrated, meaningful, thoughtful, and self-engendering engagement with information and ideas. If, in fact, these are goals that drive the whole language movement then they must be supported whole-heartedly by all concerned. These goals are of paramount importance to our nation's educational health and progress. At the same time, however, they are strictly independent from issues of the nature of the knowledge and processes involved in reading and learning to read. Only by disentangling these two sets of issues, can we give either the attention and commitment that it so urgently deserves. (Adams, 1991, p. 52)

"Only by disentangling these issues" is the key phrase here. The whole language movement is currently burdened with, shall we say, entangling alliances—in particular, an alliance with an extreme view on the role of direct instruction of decoding skills that is seriously out of step with current evidence. I would give essentially the same medical advice that Adams is pointing to: only amputation will save the patient. And, make no mistake, we do risk losing the patient. Several months ago, in the same Distinguished Educator Series in which the current essay appears, Goodman (1992) excoriated the Bush administration for its hostility to universal public education and pointed to a "group of individuals who want to limit education to a small elite group of technicians needed to run our industry. . . . The Bush initiative would further the development of a two-tiered work force by limiting educational expense for those not needed as technicians" (p. 198). I share all of Goodman's concerns, and I am in sympathy with his indictment of the Bush administration and the many special interest groups with a vested interest in privatized education (The Edison Project of the Whittle Corporation comes to mind). The "savage inequalities" (Kozol, 1991) in American education are indeed a national disgrace and deserve a revolutionary political response. But future historians will find it difficult to explain how the political goal of restructuring educational resources got tied up with the issue of whether teachers should say "s makes the /s/ sound."

But, paradoxically, the latter point does relate—in an unexpected way—to some broader political issues such as the integrity of the public education system. Parents with children who have trouble in early reading acquisition and who have not been given explicit instruction in alphabetic coding will add fuel to the movement toward privatized education in North America. "Parents

Question Results of State-Run School System" (Enchin, 1992) is an increasingly frequent newspaper headline in Canadian provinces (e.g., Ontario) where phonics instruction is neglected or de-emphasized. The January 11, 1993, cover of *Maclean's*, Canada's weekly newsmagazine, was titled "What's Wrong at School?" and featured numerous reports of parents seeking private education for children struggling in reading due to a lack of emphasis on alphabetic coding in school curricula. Featured stories in the magazine had titles such as "Angry Parents Press for Change," and photographs were highlighted with labels such as "Accusing the Schools of Taking Part in a Costly, Failed Experiment." It is reported that Canada's private school enrollment jumped 15% in the single year of 1992. In short, parents who notice that their second and third graders cannot decode simple words will become the unwitting pawns of the corporate advocates of privatized education whose motives Goodman rightly questions.

I have faith, though, that in the end, teachers will save us from some of the more nefarious goals of the Bush administration (now thankfully gone) and its like-minded allies. Teachers, like scientists, are committed pragmatists. Increasingly we are seeing examples of practitioners and teacher-educators finding the "middle way"—some in the pages of this very journal (Spiegel, 1992; Stahl, 1992; Trachtenberg, 1990).

Mosenthal (1989) has characterized whole language as a "romantic" approach to literacy, and its affinities with Rousseauan ideas are commented upon by both advocates and detractors. But we are all aware that a shockingly high number of romantically inspired marriages end in divorce. Often, a little reality testing in the early stages of a romance can prevent a doomed marriage. Better yet, some early reality testing and adjustment can sometimes *prolong* a romance. Appropriately chosen direct instruction in the spelling–sound code is the reality that will enable our romance with whole language to be a long-lasting one.

THE CONNECTING THREAD: SCIENCE

Although I have dichotomized my research projects in this essay, I really do not think of them this way. The projects, to me, are all similar in a mundane way: they are interesting problems about the reading process that were amenable to scientific test. And the latter point is really the common thread. I believe in letting scientific evidence answer questions about the nature of the reading process. Nothing has retarded the cumulative growth of knowledge in the psychology of reading more than the failure to deal with problems in a scientific manner. Education has suffered because its dominant model for adjudicating disputes is political (with corresponding factions and interest groups) rather than scientific. Education's well-known susceptibility to the "authority syndrome" stems from its tacit endorsement of a personalistic view of knowledge acquisition: the belief that knowledge resides within particular individuals who then dispense it to others. Such a conception is completely antithetical to that of science. Knowledge in science is depersonalized and publicly verifiable (see Stanovich, 1992a) and thus depersonalized in the sense that it is not the unique possession of particular individuals or groups (Popper, 1972).

An adherence to a subjective, personalized view of knowledge is what continually leads to educational fads which could easily be avoided by grounding teachers and other practitioners in the importance of scientific thinking in solving educational problems. This training should include an explicit discussion of some of the common misconceptions that people hold about science, for example, that the idea of objective, depersonalized knowledge in the social sciences "dehumanizes" people. Such facile slogans compromise both research and practice in many educational domains. What science actually accomplishes with its conception of publicly verifiable knowledge is the *democratization* of knowledge, an outcome that frees practitioners and researchers from slavish dependence on authority; and it is subjective, personalized views of knowledge that degrade the human intellect by creating conditions in which it is inevitably subjugated to an elite whose "personal" knowledge is not accessible to all (Bronowski, 1956, 1977; Medawar, 1982, 1984, 1990; Popper, 1971).

The scientific criteria for evaluating knowledge claims are not complicated and could easily be included in teacher-training programs, but they usually are not (thus a major opportunity to free teachers from reliance on authority is lost right at the beginning). These criteria include the publication of findings in refereed journals (scientific publications that employ a process of peer review), the duplication of the results by other investigators, and a consensus within a particular research community on whether or not there is a critical mass of studies that point toward a particular conclusion. These mechanisms—such things as the publication of findings in peer reviewed journals and the criterion of replication of results—are some of the best "consumer protections" that we can give teachers.

Teachers should also be introduced to the values of science. Although the technological products of science are "value free" in that they can be used for good or ill, it is not true that the *process* of science is value free (Bronowski, 1956, 1977). For example, objectivity is a value that is fundamental to science and simply means that we let nature "speak for itself" without imposing our wishes on it. The fact that this goal is unattainable for any single human being should not dissuade us from holding objectivity as a value (this would be confusing what *is* the case with what *ought* to be). The sorry state of fields that have abandoned objectivity is perhaps the strongest argument for holding to it as a value. To use a convenient and well-known example, the inability of parapsychologists to screen out subjective wishes and desires from their observations has filled their field with charlatans and scandal, made progress impossible, and alienated a scientific world that was once quite supportive of the field (Alcock, 1990; Hines, 1988).

My view on these matters is considered old fashioned in many educational circles. There is much loose talk in education now about paradigms, incommensurability, frameworks, and such. The whole melange is sometimes termed constructivism and it is commonly employed to support various relativistic doctrines such as the view that there is no objective truth, that all investigators construct their evidence from what they already know is true, that we all live in different realities, that correspondence to reality is not a valid scientific criterion, etc.—or, more technically, that "equally rational, competent, and informed observers are, in some sense, free (of external realist and internal innate constraints) to constitute for themselves different realities" (Shweder, 1991, p. 156).

These ideas have unfortunately come into education half-baked and twice distorted. Legitimate philosophy of science was picked up and reworked by scholars in a variety of humanities disciplines who were not philosophers by training and who used the work for their own—often political—agendas. Educational theorists have taken these worked-over ideas and recooked them once again so that they are now almost unrecognizable from the original. For example, constructivist theorists in education cite Thomas Kuhn constantly. They are greatly enamored with Kuhn's (1970) incommensurability thesis in philosophy of science: the idea that competing frameworks "cannot be compared and evaluated on rational grounds" (Bechtel, 1988, p. 55). These theorists seem unaware of the fact that Kuhn's concept of incommensurability has been seriously disputed by numerous historians and philosophers of science (Gutting, 1980; Lakatos & Musgrave, 1970; Laudan, 1984; Leplin, 1984; Siegel, 1980; Suppe, 1984)—and that Kuhn has largely abandoned the idea (see the 1970 Postscript to *The Structure of Scientific Revolutions* and the commentary on the Postscript by Musgrave, 1980; see also Siegel, 1980). Numerous philosophers of science—the very scholars who did the original work that the educational theorists are parodying—have objected to the distortion of their work by social scientists and educators. For example, Ian Hacking (1983), a leading contributor to these debates in philosophy of science, has written of how

> slightly off-key inferences were drawn from work of the first rank. . . . Kuhn was taken aback by the way in which his work (and that of others) produced a crisis of rationality. He subsequently wrote that he never intended to deny the customary virtues of scientific theories. Theories should be accurate, that is, by and large fit existing experimental data. They should be both internally consistent and consistent with other accepted theories. They should be broad in scope and rich in consequences. They should be simple in structure, organizing facts in an intelligible way. (pp. 2, 13)

Larry Laudan, another key figure in the debate within philosophy of science, echoes Hacking's comments:

> Many who are not philosophers of science (from cultural philosophers like Rorty and Winch to sociologists like Barnes and Collins) appear to believe that contem-

porary philosophy of science provides potent arguments on behalf of a radical relativism about knowledge in general and scientific knowledge in particular. . . .
My belief, by contrast, is that strong forms of epistemic relativism derive scant
support from a clearheaded understanding of the contemporary state of the art in
philosophy of science. I am not alone in that conviction; most of my fellow philosophers of science would doubtless wholeheartedly concur. But that consensus
within the discipline apparently cuts little ice with those outside it. . . . Many scientists (especially social scientists), literati, and philosophers outside of philosophy of science proper have come to believe that the epistemic analysis of science
since the 1960s provides potent ammunition for a general assault on the idea that
science represents a reliable or superior form of knowing. . . . My larger target is
those contemporaries who—in repeated acts of wish fulfillment—have appropri-
ated conclusions from the philosophy of science and put them to work in aid of a
variety of social cum political causes for which those conclusions are ill adapted.
(1990, pp. viii–ix)

The worst example of this distortion is how the concept of incommensurability has been used. The dehumanizing implications of this concept
seem to have entirely escaped educational theorists in the literacy area. The
seeming delight in the view that we are all "locked into our paradigms" is
puzzling. The very thing that incommensurability seeks to deny—the cumulative nature of human knowledge—provides the key rationale that commands
a member of the intellectual community to show respect for the ideas of others. Although the social and *moral* motivation for attempting to view the
world from inside another person's framework is to gain a more humanized
understanding of another individual, the *intellectual* motivation must be that
by doing so I may gain a better (i.e., more accurate) view of the world. If we,
as educators, deny the *last* possibility, we will undercut the motivation to shift
frameworks for even the *first*—the humanistic—purpose. It is one thing to
deny the possibility of attaining certain knowledge. Most scientists admit this
impossibility. It is another thing entirely to argue that we lose nothing by giving up even the *attempt* at attaining objective knowledge. Such a stratagem
undermines the rationale for the scientific quest for knowledge and in this
quest lies the only hope of escaping our continuing dilemma.

CHAPTER 21

Twenty-Five Years of Research on the Reading Process

The Grand Synthesis and What It Means for our Field

One of the purposes of my address is to celebrate the remarkable progress that has been made in the last 25 years toward understanding the basic psychological processes that underlie the act of reading. The convergence of basic research on the reading process over this period is so strong that it is a synthesis of the type other sciences choose to give a name—I have chosen to call ours the Grand Synthesis. This synthesis is actually easy to describe. One only has to take the names of the Oscar Causey Award recipients and add to that list the names of the research award winners from our sister organizations—IRA and SSSR—and you basically have the history of the Grand Synthesis.

Consider a sampling of work from these scholars that, taken together, provides an outline of the Grand Synthesis. Due to the precision eye-movement computer paradigms developed by George McConkie and Keith Rayner, we now have very refined information about how the eyes fixate on words in text and how visual information is extracted. Importantly, they found that fluent readers fixate on virtually every content word in text and that visual information is rather exhaustively sampled from the visual array. Even fluent readers do not engage in a wholesale skipping of words and they actually do extract most of the visual information available.

These findings from the eye movement studies are consistent with the importance of the word recognition process that Causey recipients Linnea Ehri and Phil Gough taught us many years ago. That it is important that this process be rapid and automatic was vividly illustrated in the automaticity model of LaBerge and Samuels—the latter our 1985 Causey winner. That efficient decoding processes provided the underpinning for rapid automatic word recognition was demonstrated by Causey recipients Joanna Williams, Phil Gough, and Isabel Beck—and I should add, by Causey winner John Guthrie in some papers in the early 1970s that are some of his least cited work, but which used the reading level match design even before its more recent popularization. That the underpinning of these decoding skills was phonological processing and phonological awareness was demonstrated by Isabelle and Al Liberman, Don Shankweiler, and others at the Haskins laboratories (with again converging evidence from Oscar Causey recipients Beck, Williams, and Gough). Another Causey recipient, Linnea Ehri, prevented us from slipping into an overly simplified model of these effects by showing us, in some of the most elegantly designed studies in the psychology of reading, that experience with orthography shapes and sculpts phonological awareness.

At the same time, we were finding out how these processes of word recognition fit within the more global process of reading comprehension. Causey recipient Ron Carver taught us the importance of quantifying models of comprehension. Oscar Causey winner Ken Goodman conducted the well-known 1965 study that focused so many of us in the early 1970s on the study of the effects of context on reading (for example, my colleague Richard West and I). This led to several important insights. First, that it is important to distinguish the word recognition level of processing from comprehension when talking about textual context effects because the individual difference relationships are quite different at the two levels of analysis. For example, there is considerable evidence that better readers are better able to use contextual information to facilitate their comprehension processes. However, research in recent years has shown that hypotheses about context use as an individual difference variable were inappropriately generalized to the *word recognition* level. That is, the hypothesis that the superior word recognition skills of the better reader were due to their superior context-use skills—a hypothesis that once had great popularity in the reading literature—is now known to be false. A large amount of research has consistently indicated that the word recognition of better readers is *not* characterized by more reliance on contextual information. It is the *poorer* reader who is more reliant on contextual information at the word recognition level. The reason for this finding eventually became apparent—it is related to other parts of the Grand Synthesis that I have just mentioned: specifically, the word recognition processes of the skilled reader are so rapid and automatic that facilitation from less reliable contextual information is not needed.

The capacity freed by automatic word recognition processes is available for various comprehension strategies—strategies elucidated by two other Causey recipients: David Pearson and Dick Anderson, along with Mike Pressley and many others. Other work by Dick Anderson on out-of-school free-reading and vocabulary growth helped to direct attention toward so-called Matthew effects that I have written about—rich-get-richer and poor-get-poorer effects that are embedded in the educational process. These effects have been incorporated into the synthesis as well.

[material omitted; see Part III and Chapter 20]

I could go on and further sketch details of the conclusions about reading processes reached in this remarkable period of scientific progress, but of course many extensive research summaries already exist (Adams & Bruck, 1993, 1995; Blachman, 1997b; Ehri, 1995, 1997; Frost, 1998; Liberman & Liberman, 1990; Lyon, 1995; Olson, 1994; Perfetti, 1985, 1994, 1995; Rayner & Pollatsek, 1989; Share, 1995; Share & Stanovich, 1995; Siegel, 1993; Snowling, 1995, 1996; Stanovich, 1980, 1986b; Stanovich & Stanovich, 1995). One of the best historical sketches of the period has been written by Linnea Ehri (1996, 1998) in the form of her research autobiography.

FINDING COMMONALITY IN OUR BASIC RESEARCH BASE

Instead, I want to argue that we have utterly failed to use our remarkable basic research database to unify and integrate our field. I have in mind here the fractious nature of our field—the so-called reading wars (for an overview, see Gough, 1995; Kamil, 1995; McKenna, Stahl, & Reinking, 1994; Perfetti, 1991, 1995; Stanovich, 1990a, 1994c), the camps, the acrimonious, unscholarly debates about reading carried out through the media—and in some cases through our journals and conferences. And now, of course, we have the opportunity to hurl invective into cyberspace! For example, one author in an IRA publication accuses researchers of a certain school of clinging to "hocus pocus rhetoric" (Otto, 1993, p. 413). Another accuses those who challenge his conclusions of "insincerity" (Shannon, cited in McKenna et al., 1994, p. 219). A third calls his opponents "amoral elitists" (Goodman, 1992, p. 198)— again, in an IRA publication. And finally, in an IRA publication, certain research is opposed by terming it "asinine," "meaningless," and "nonsensical" (Taylor, 1994). National news publications (*The Atlantic Monthly, Time, Education Week*, and their ilk) now recount these debates and convey their lack of civility to the general public.

How can we knit ourselves back together again? I would argue that we can begin by acknowledging and taking pride in our common research base on the reading process—that is, we can *respect* our differences about practice, and still acknowledge our common research accomplishments. The practice debates won't go away—as I will recount shortly, the basic research evidence does not necessarily *dictate* conclusions about practice. *But* in accepting the common research base on the process of reading, we will have gotten ourselves into the habit of existing in a common community whose conclusions are determined by evidence. It will be the first step in knitting our field back together again. Other fields gain confidence, unity, and common purpose from their common research base. They still dispute areas of application, of course—but they establish their professionalism and unify their discourse by accepting a common point of contact in their scientific accomplishments.

Instead, we have a situation where disputants think that in order to win a particular debate about practice, they must falsify and distort the evidence about the basic process of reading. I see email exchanges every day in which the basic facts about the reading process I have just outlined are distorted and misrepresented. A submission to the California legislature circulated on NRC email and a letter to the IRA publication *Reading Today* in the same *week* implied that the defining feature of adult word recognition was the use of context—a palpably false conclusion that contradicts a broad range of research that I have alluded to previously. The proper conclusion is, as stated earlier, that although better readers are better able to use contextual information to facilitate their comprehension processes, the word recognition of better readers is *not* characterized by more reliance on contextual information (Stanovich, 1986b, 1991b; West, Stanovich, & Cunningham, 1995).

The attempt to distort the truth about the basic research base drains our field of all pretense of professionalism. If we cannot let evidence decide the basic facts about the reading process, how are we to fight off the public bodies and state legislatures that want to dictate our practice? Are we to tell them that we police our own professional practice? This simply has no credibility when our literature, spokespersons, media representatives, and dissemination mechanisms willfully deny a basic research consensus developed over thirty years, comprising hundreds of different studies by dozens of different investigators. The public rightly uses our treatment of the basic research evidence as an indicator of our attitude toward evidence on issues more directly concerning practice. By this criterion we lack credibility.

And this is all totally unnecessary. As mentioned previously, the link between basic facts about reading and educational practice is not tight but loose. As David Pearson said in a lucid NRC email message (December 5, 1995):

> In a perfect world, we might expect a high degree of isomorphism between a cognitive or perceptual process on the one hand and instructional practices on the other. But we must, I think, be prepared for great discontinuities between basic processes and instructional practices. Put differently, theories of instruction are, by their nature, much more complex . . . than theories of the processes the instruction aims at ameliorating.

And again, there is nothing unusual about this. There is no direct application from basic science to practice in any other field, but instead the idealized laws of basic science must be combined with so-called bridge laws covering the specific environmental conditions of interest. So, for example, the idealized laws of physics that work in a vacuum or in frictionless environments must be supplemented with information about air resistance and the special conditions in which the idealized laws will be applied. As Pearson points out, developing bridging laws of special conditions is immensely complex in our case (because the bridging laws must themselves be scientifically validated).

THE LINK FROM RESEARCH TO PRACTICE

Many basic research findings about the reading process only very loosely prescribe practice. Others *are* more tightly linked to practice. Let me give you some examples of each. As a first example: To say that efficient word recognition is a prerequisite to good reading comprehension *doesn't* say *how* that efficient word recognition is best developed. Likewise, to say that phonological awareness is important in reading acquisition *doesn't* tell us *how* that phonological awareness is best developed. In these two cases, we know that word recognition is important, and that phonological awareness is important, but there is plenty of room for disagreement about the bridging principles—about how we should play out these basic facts about the reading process in practice. Basic process researchers are wrong to imply *too* strong and automatic a connection between basic process research and practice.

However, there are *other* cases where the basic research finding is more closely linked with practice. Consider some of the findings that I mentioned earlier—that research using sophisticated eye movement tracking instrumentation has indicated that fluent readers do not generally skip content words in text and that they fairly exhaustively process the information in the visual array, and, further, that they recognize words less by contextual priming and more by powerful and automatic context-free word recognition processes. Now these basic findings *do* put a huge burden of proof on claims that people can be taught to flit through the text—Evelyn Wood–style—and still comprehend. The basic findings do make it less likely that an emphasis on contextual guessing for word recognition is efficacious.

Another example comes from the area of reading disability. Consider that recent developments in basic research have demonstrated that certain ways of classifying children having reading difficulties seem empirically unjustified. For example, one idea that has a long history in the learning disabilities field is that less-skilled readers who display a discrepancy with a measure of so-called aptitude (typically defined as performance on an intelligence test) are different from less-skilled readers who do not display such a discrepancy. It was thought that the reading-related cognitive characteristics of these groups were different and that they needed different types of treatment. In contrast, recent research has indicated that the reading-related cognitive profiles of these two groups of readers at the word recognition level is remarkably similar (Fletcher, Shaywitz, Shankweiler, Katz, Liberman, Stuebing, Francis, Fowler, & Shaywitz, 1994; Stanovich & Siegel, 1994). Although, again, this finding does not automatically dictate practice, it certainly is the case that the burden of proof in this area has shifted. It is now clearly on those who wish to advocate differential treatment for these groups of children, because they have lost—on empirical grounds—the right to their foundational assumption at the basic process level: that the cognitive processes underlying the reading problems of these groups of children are fundamentally different.

KNITTING OUR FIELD TOGETHER THROUGH A RETURN TO SCIENTIFIC VALUES

Thus, we have here examples of the continuum of the link between basic process research and practice. But regardless of where on this continuum we are for a particular problem, there is a unifying function of the basic empirical research of our discipline—it links us together in a social community dedicated to allowing empirical evidence to resolve our disputes. And this is the second function that our basic research base can serve for our field: knitting us together in the same community where scientific scholarly discourse is our currency.

Nothing has impeded the cumulative growth of knowledge in our field more than the failure to deal with problems in a scientific manner. Education in general suffers because its dominant model for adjudicating disputes is political (with corresponding factions, "leaders," and interest groups) rather than scientific. It is much commented upon that we are "marked by the authority syndrome that is antagonistic to the critical tradition of science" (Kavale & Forness, 1985, p. 89). An adherence to a subjective, personalized view of knowledge is what continually leads education down the well-traveled road of fads and politicized disputes. In contrast, what science accomplishes with its conception of publicly verifiable knowledge (Stanovich, 1998a) is the *democratization* of knowledge, an outcome that frees practitioners from reliance on authority.

The liberating aspect of empirical science is that it generates knowledge that is in the public domain. No one need rely on my personal reading of the research literature—it is publicly available for teachers to consult and to decide for themselves whether the state of the literature is as I portray it. In fact, with the exception of a few select areas such as the eye movement research mentioned previously, much of the research I have described could easily be replicated by teachers themselves. With apologies to my research colleagues, what we do is not rocket science. With knowledge of a few uncomplicated principles—control, manipulation, randomization and so forth—anyone can enter the open, public discourse about these empirical findings.

But even more than the methods of science, the *values* of science might help us in adjudicating our professional controversies. For example, objectivity is a value that is fundamental to science and simply means that we let nature "speak for itself" without imposing our wishes on it. The fact that this goal is unattainable for any single human being should not dissuade us from holding objectivity as a value (this would be confusing what *is* the case with what *ought* to be). As anthropologist and ethnographer Clifford Geertz (1973) has noted, "I have never been impressed by the argument that, as complete objectivity is impossible in these matters (as, of course, it is), one might as well let one's sentiments run loose. As Robert Solow has remarked, that is like saying that as a perfectly aseptic environment is impossible, one might as well conduct surgery in a sewer" (p. 30).

The sorry state of fields that have abandoned objectivity is perhaps the strongest argument for holding to it as a value. The solipsism that results— and its concomitant knowledge adjudication by power conflict is simply too damaging—a damage that is discernible in the fragmentation of the reading research community.

There is much loose talk in education now about paradigms, incommensurability, frameworks, and such. This whole melange is commonly employed to support various relativistic doctrines such as the view that there is no objective truth, that all investigators are locked in a framework that their work will never contradict, that we all live in different realities, that correspondence to reality is not a valid criterion, etc.

These ideas have unfortunately come into education half-baked and twice distorted. Legitimate philosophy of science was picked up and reworked by scholars in a variety of humanities disciplines. The distortions introduced have been the subject of extensive critique (Bereiter, 1994; Dasenbrock, 1995; Gross & Levitt, 1994; Gross, Levitt, & Lewis, 1997; Haack, 1997; Hacking, 1983; Lakomski, 1992; Laudan, 1990; Lehman, 1991; Loving, 1997; Schrag, 1992; Searle, 1993, 1995; Siegel, 1988, 1997; Sokal, 1996). Oblivious to the critiques, educational theorists have taken the distortions and recooked them once again so that they are now almost unrecognizable from the original.

It is time to be honest about this. In education, much more common than legitimate, scholarly work on constructivist theory is the tendency for these ideas to be wielded like clubs by people who have never read Willard Quine, Hilary Putnam, or Donald Davidson in the original. For those of us who have been around awhile this is all so depressing. Education always seems to get left with the dregs of half-baked ideas from other disciplines. In learning disabilities, it is half-baked and incorrect neurology. In literacy theory, it is half-baked philosophy.

I have written before (Stanovich, 1994c) about one of the worst examples of these distortions: how Thomas Kuhn's concept of incommensurability has been misused. The idea here is that there is no common truth that all observers converge upon, but instead that observers are, in some sense, free to constitute for themselves different realities because the natural world and such evidence as we have about that world do little or nothing to constrain our beliefs—that reality itself is relative to a scheme; what counts as real in one system may not in another (Davidson, 1984; Laudan, 1990; Shweder, 1991).

The dehumanizing implications of this concept seem to have entirely escaped educational theorists in the literacy area. The seeming delight in the view that we are all "locked into our paradigms" is puzzling. The very thing that incommensurability seeks to deny—the cumulative nature of human knowledge—provides the key rationale that commands a member of the intellectual community to show respect for the ideas of others. It is one thing to deny the possibility of attaining certain knowledge. Most scientists admit this impossibility. It is another thing entirely to argue that we lose nothing by giving up even the *attempt* at attaining objective knowledge. Such a stratagem undermines the rationale for the scientific quest for knowledge and in this quest lies the only hope of escaping our continuing dilemma.

On this issue, I want to give you a concrete example—not directly from the reading literature—but from an allied applied field: the study of autism. Recently, considerable media and professional attention has been directed at a method for unlocking communicative capacity in autistic individuals called "facilitated communication." Autistic individuals who had previously been nonverbal have been alleged to type highly literate messages on a keyboard if their hands and arms are supported over the typewriter by a sympathetic "facilitator." These startlingly verbal performances on the part of autistic children who had previously shown very limited linguistic behavior have not surprisingly spawned incredible hopes among frustrated parents of autistic children.

Unfortunately, claims for the efficacy of facilitated communication were disseminated to hopeful parents by many media outlets before any controlled studies had been conducted. And unfortunately, a number of studies have appeared in journals in speech science, linguistics, and psychology and each one has unequivocally demonstrated the same thing: that the autistic child's performance is dependent upon tactile cuing from the facilitator. In the experiments, it was shown that when both child and facilitator were looking at the same drawing, the child typed the correct name of the drawing. When the viewing was occluded so that the child and the facilitator were shown different drawings, the child typed the name of the facilitator's drawing, not the one that the child herself was looking at (Hudson, Melita, & Arnold, 1993; Jacobson, Mulick, & Schwartz, 1995; Wheeler, Jacobson, Paglieri, & Schwartz, 1993).

But we should also be clear that there also exists in the literature detailed and intense case studies of the experiences of the *facilitators* of the children. These individuals invariably deny that they are cuing the children and give heartfelt, detailed reports of their empathic connections with the children.

The hopes of hundreds of parents rest on how the educational and scientific community adjudicates these conflicting forms of evidence. Here, we have a clear example of some of the points mentioned previously: that this conflict *will* be adjudicated and *how* it is adjudicated will have concrete, practical consequences for many people. The example leads to another important realization: that incommensurability is not a humane doctrine in cases like this. It is simply not helpful to say that the experimental studies of this phenomenon and the ethnographic studies have constituted different worlds. In this case, it appears to me extremely more helpful to argue that these modes of inquiry are telling us different things about the *same* world. The ethnographic studies may be leading us to some new and profound knowledge about the social connections between these children and their facilitators; whereas the experimental studies are telling us that the claim that the technique unlocks heretofore hidden linguistic skills appears to be false. There is no unbridgeable incommensurability between the modes of inquiry. The example cautions us not to unnecessarily erect barriers among modes of inquiry within the reading research field by utilizing concepts such as incommensurability.

We have much to lose from a divisive zero-sum game that separates the efforts of researchers working from different traditions. I simply do not think that the field has weighed the costs of conceptual relativism because—in a smokescreen of confusing philosophy and rhetoric—a basic claim of conceptual relativism has been obscured and thus we have lost sight of its cost. The claim is, startlingly, that we cannot really talk to each other—that insurmountable barriers exist between conceptual universes that are so fundamental that conversation is literally impossible (Davidson, 1984). Such a view is precisely what will sustain the current divisive and acrimonious situation in the reading community.

POLITICS AND THE GREAT DEBATE: ENDING THE CARICATURES

My next recommendation is less philosophical and more political. It is that too many things have become conjoined in our arguments about best practice. Because of rhetorical ploys, too many things have become linked in our literature that are neither logically nor empirically connected—for example, the silly connection that some people want to make between research methods, positions in the Great Debate on reading instruction, and views on social justice. Qualitative and ethnographic methods are supposedly connected with whole language and liberal views on social justice—and the use of statistics and rigorous experimental design with phonics and with conservative views on social justice. This is some of the most unadulterated nonsense in the history of intellectual discourse.

Again, it shows the dismal state we have gotten ourselves into regarding empirical evidence—that no amount of falsifying instances seems to stop this distortion. This is not to mention that such a view is historical nonsense. It of course totally ignores the fact that the push for quantitative social statistics in the nineteenth century was led by *radical* social reformers. European socialism of the early century was built on this foundation. In Victorian England poverty was exposed by the florid prose of Dickens *and* the exhaustive statistical studies of Charles Booth in his monumental *Life and Labour of the People of London*. Social justice was then (and still is) built on a foundation of both humanism and quantitative science.

Why this tendency to caricature opponents? I am repeatedly amazed at the people who think they can predict my opinion on things that are in principle orthogonal. Take, for example, several educational issues that were burning up the listservs in late 1997. Three examples: 1. The NICHD–funded Houston study of early reading acquisition has received intense scrutiny and has become a lightening rod for contentious argument. 2. California's low state ranking on some standardized tests has been used to excoriate whole language. 3. State legislators are attacked for pushing legislation that would dictate teacher practice. My work is referred to in these debates as if people could predict what I felt about these issues from empirical research on the reading process that I have published. But they can't.

One: I think it is extremely unfortunate that attention has focused on the Houston study in the way it has and I find this attention disproportionate to the contribution of that study. Two: I think it is wrong to use the California state ranking to excoriate whole language practice. Three: I do not advocate state legislatures mandating the teaching of phonics.

But let me contextualize these issues. First, the Houston study. Both sides—NICHD officials and whole language advocates—seem to have lost sight of the crucial scientific principles of convergence and consensus (Stanovich, 1998a). The Houston study is not going to *decide* the issue for us. It is going to shift the consensus a little in one direction or the other. The current scientific consensus is that direct instruction in alphabetic coding facilitates early reading acquisition, especially among disadvantaged children. The Houston study, when finally integrated and interpreted—with the hundreds of other relevant studies (the hundreds of studies synthesized in the review papers cited previously)—will either strengthen the moderate–strong consensus in the direction of strong, or weaken it a bit in the direction of moderate. There has been decades of work preceding the Houston study with which it must be integrated. However, critics of this study are acting as if we are at some neutral balance point and that this study is going to tip things definitively in one direction or another. This is a mischaracterization of the literature—and of science. The flailing and uninformed critiques of this study by whole language advocates have badly missed the mark and are embarrassing in what they reveal about the critics' grounding in the logic and evolution of scientific knowledge.

The case of using the low California ranking to excoriate whole language is an even simpler example of flawed reasoning. Any undergraduate who could not think of about ten alternative hypotheses for California's drop would flunk his or her introductory methodology course. We should not just grab at any evidence to advance our case, particularly when the evidence is tenuous. The California finding is salient—and because salience and rhetoric are often used to win battles in our field, it is tempting to pick up this tenuous evidence as a club. But I advise against it.

And finally the state legislatures. This is also a no-brainer—because I have consistently been an advocate of teacher professionalism, academic freedom, and autonomy. But, and it is a big "but," we would be remiss if we did not ask ourselves *why* this is happening. And no—it is not because a secret society of right-wing millionaires directs an international conspiracy whose primary aim is to destroy progressive education. There is a *reason* why we suffer legislative intrusion and the reason reflects a real problem with the field that we must recognize. We do not want to be policed by outsiders—by legislators and state officials. We want to police ourselves by collegial professional interchange and by internal professional standards and sanctions. One important aspect of policing ourselves—of developing our own professional practices and standards—is *being responsive to empirical evidence*. And we have not lived up to standards of professionalism in this respect. Precisely five years ago today I wrote:

> In holding to an irrationally extreme view on the role of phonics in reading education—for failing to acknowledge that some children do not discover the alphabetic principle on their own and need systematic direct instruction in the alphabet principle, phonological analysis, and alphabetic coding—whole language proponents threaten all of their legitimate accomplishments. Eventually—perhaps not for a great while, but eventually—the weight of empirical evidence will fall on their heads. That direct instruction in alphabetic coding facilitates early reading acquisition is one of the most well established conclusions in all of behavioral science (Adams, 1990; Anderson et al., 1985; Chall, 1983b, 1989; Perfetti, 1985; Stanovich, 1986b). Conversely, the idea that learning to read is just like learning to speak is accepted by no responsible linguist, psychologist, or cognitive scientist in the research community (see Liberman & Liberman, 1990). To stand, Canute-like, against this evidence is to put at risk all of the many hard-won victories of the whole language movement. (Stanovich, 1994c, pp. 285–286)

THE SHARED EPISTEMOLOGY OF READING RESEARCHERS AND READING EDUCATORS

This was written five years ago. What the many recent legislative actions across North America reflect is that that evidence has indeed begun to fall on our heads. We still have prominent reading educators, publications, and inservice providers traveling the country promulgating views of the reading process that directly contradict what the research says.

As the Grand Synthesis that I have outlined earlier becomes more broadly known among the public—as the slow process of diffusion of science to the public occurs—the inability of the field to respond to evidence and to police itself will lead to outcries by the public, will spawn more articles in *The Atlantic Monthly*, *Education Week*, and *The New York Times*, which in turn will spawn grandstanding politicians to propose regulating our practice. In contrast to this grim future, the field could choose another course—a course that would assure our professional autonomy. That course is to present a united front to the public—united around our basic research findings—a front that would not stifle debate, that would still contain spirited debate about the practical implications of the basic facts about the reading process—but that would establish not only our knowledge but our shared entry into the community of science where issues are ultimately decided by empirical means.

I also argued five years ago that a consensus was sitting right there waiting for us to grab it. I pointed out that many of the recommendations and practices that are commonly associated with whole language have appeared repeatedly in the writings of, for instance, Marilyn Adams and Jeanne Chall. [*material omitted here; see Chapter 20*] However, I would like this time to state our potential for consensus and unity through the words of a teacher of 18 years classroom experience. This teacher (Paula—who happens to be my wife and love of over 30 years) gave me her metaphor for consensus while we stood outside the Queen's Park legislature in Toronto waiting for the speakers to begin at a rally of over 50,000 in support of the teachers of Ontario who were engaged in the largest teacher strike in the history of North America in November of 1997. Getting bored waiting for the speakers and always anxious to steal any material I can when I have an hour long talk coming up in the next few weeks, I urged her to let me transcribe her thoughts. She said the following:

> Sometimes when I put my special education hat on, I see this controversy as simply another issue of accessibility. Installing ramps at building entrances doesn't keep me (a temporarily able-bodied person) out of the building, but it does allow others in, those, for example, who happen to use assitive devices for mobility. Providing a sign-language interpreter for a public meeting doesn't keep me from listening to the speakers, but it does allow our deaf citizens to participate in the democratic process. Teaching decoding and phonemic awareness doesn't hinder those lucky children who would become readers almost effortlessly, but it does allow those children who need the explicit instruction to become readers too. It allows them access to the world of literacy. If you think about it, opening up the world in this way also has benefits for the rest of us. In the first example, those of us who may be pushing a child in a pram or push chair can use the ramps that were originally installed for users of wheelchairs. In the second example, as I'm listening to the speaker at that public meeting, I can perhaps benefit from the interpreter's use of body language and other nonverbal expression to enrich my understanding of the speaker's intentions. Surely, there is such an enrichment for the able reader who is exposed to the wonderful songs, word play, and word games that we use for teaching decoding and phonemic awareness? (P. Stanovich, November 6, 1997)

In this comment, we have a fine example illustrating that teachers, like scientists, are committed pragmatists. Teachers and scientists are kindred spirits at the epistemological level. They both single-mindedly pursue "what works"—ignoring philosophical strictures along the way. Currently, those of us who hope for medical cures for our health problems will be reassured to know that biochemists in their laboratories are blissfully unaware of philosophical arguments against the idea that one criterion of a good theory is that it should correspond to physical reality. Teachers are likewise shockingly unpostmodern. They think there is a real world out there—a world in flux obviously—but still one that is trackable by triangulating observations and observers. They believe in a world that is predictable and controllable by manipulations which they instantiate in their professional practice—just as scientists do. Their "what works" epistemology makes me confident that they will find a "middle way" between the rhetorical blasts and political posturings of our field. I hope our authentic research base can help them.

BIBLIOGRAPHY

Publications in Reading
by Keith E. Stanovich

EDITED BOOK

Stanovich, K. E. (Ed.). (1988). *Children's reading and the development of phonological awareness*. Detroit: Wayne State University Press.

JOURNAL ARTICLES AND CHAPTERS

Chiappe, P., Stringer, R., Siegel, L. S., & Stanovich, K. E. (in press). Why the timing deficit does not explain reading disability in adults. *Reading and Writing: An Interdisciplinary Journal*.

Stringer, R., & Stanovich, K. E. (2000). The connection between reaction time and variation in reading ability: Unravelling covariance relationships with cognitive ability and phonological sensitivity. *Scientific Studies of Reading, 4,* 41–53.

Gottardo, A., Chiappe, P., Siegel, L. S., & Stanovich, K. E. (1999). Patterns of word and nonword processing in skilled and less-skilled readers. *Reading and Writing: An Interdisciplinary Journal, 11,* 465–487.

Stanovich, K. E. (1999). The sociopsychometrics of learning disabilities. *Journal of Learning Disabilities, 32,* 350–361.

Stanovich, K. E. (1999). Foreword. In R. J. Sternberg & L. Spear-Swerling (Eds.), *Perspectives on learning disabilities: Biological, cognitive, and contextual* (pp. vii–xiii). New York: Westview Press.

Stanovich, K. E. (1999). The search for theoretically meaningful subtypes of reading disability. *Thalamus, 17*(1), 2–20.

Metsala, J. L., Stanovich, K. E., & Brown, G.D.A. (1998). Regularity effects and the phonological deficit model of reading disabilities: A meta-analytic review. *Journal of Educational Psychology, 90,* 279–293.

Stanovich, K. E. (1998). Twenty-five years of research on the reading process: The

Grand Synthesis and what it means for our field. In T. Shanahan & F. Rodriguez-Brown (Eds.), *Forty-seventh yearbook of the National Reading Conference* (pp. 44–58). Chicago: National Reading Conference.

Siddiqui, S., West, R. F., & Stanovich, K. E. (1998). The influence of print exposure on syllogistic reasoning and knowledge of mental-state verbs. *Scientific Studies of Reading, 2,* 81–96.

Cunningham, A. E., & Stanovich, K. E. (1998). What reading does for the mind. *American Educator, 22*(1–2), 8–15.

Stanovich, K. E., Cunningham, A. E., & West, R. F. (1998). Literacy experiences and the shaping of cognition. In S. Paris & H. Wellman (Eds.), *Global prospects for education: Development, culture, and schooling* (pp. 253–288). Washington, DC: American Psychological Association.

Cunningham, A. E., & Stanovich, K. E. (1998). The impact of print exposure on word recognition. In J. Metsala & L. Ehri (Eds.), *Word recognition in beginning literacy* (pp. 235–262). Mahwah, NJ: Erlbaum.

Stanovich, K. E. (1998). Refining the phonological core deficit model. *Child Psychology and Psychiatry Review, 3,* 17–21.

Stanovich, K. E., & Siegel, L. S. (1998). The role of IQ in the diagnosis of reading disorders: The quest for a subtype based on aptitude–achievement discrepancy. In J. Rispens, T. van Yperen, & W. Yule (Eds.), *Perspectives on the classification of specific developmental disorders* (pp. 105–136). Dordrecht, The Netherlands: Kluwer Academic.

Stanovich, K. E., & Stanovich, P. J. (1998). Ending the Reading Wars. *Orbit: OISE/UT's Magazine for Schools, 28*(4), 49–55.

Cunningham, A. E., & Stanovich, K. E. (1997). Early reading acquisition and its relation to reading experience and ability ten years later. *Developmental Psychology, 33,* 934–945.

Stanovich, K. E., Siegel, L. S., & Gottardo, A. (1997). Converging evidence for phonological and surface subtypes of reading disability. *Journal of Educational Psychology, 89,* 114–127.

Gottardo, A., Stanovich, K. E., & Siegel, L. S. (1997). The assessment of adults with reading disabilities: What can we learn from experimental tasks? *Journal of Research in Reading, 20,* 42–54.

Stanovich, K. E., Siegel, L. S., Gottardo, A., Chiappe, P., & Sidhu, R. (1997). Subtypes of developmental dyslexia: Differences in phonological and orthographic coding. In B. Blachman (Ed.), *Foundations of reading acquisition and dyslexia: Implications for early intervention* (pp. 115–141). Mahwah, NJ: Erlbaum.

Stanovich, K. E., & Stanovich, P. J. (1997). Further thoughts on aptitude–achievement discrepancy. *Educational Psychology in Practice, 13,* 3–8.

Stanovich, K. E., Siegel, L. S., & Gottardo, A. (1997). Progress in the search for dyslexia subtypes. In C. Hulme & M. Snowling (Eds.), *Dyslexia: Biology, cognition, and intervention* (pp. 108–130). London: Whurr.

Stanovich, K. E., & Stanovich, P. J. (1997). Prevention and remediation of reading disabilities: A classic glass half empty and half full. *Journal of Academic Language Therapy, 1,* 48–51.

Stanovich, K. E. (1996). Toward a more inclusive definition of dyslexia. *Dyslexia, 2,* 154–166.

Gottardo, A., Stanovich, K. E., & Siegel, L. S. (1996). The relationships between phonological sensitivity, syntactic processing, and verbal working memory in the reading performance of third-grade children. *Journal of Experimental Child Psychology, 63,* 563–582.

Echols, L. D., West, R. F., Stanovich, K. E., & Zehr, K. S. (1996). Using children's literacy activities to predict growth in verbal cognitive skills: A longitudinal investigation. *Journal of Educational Psychology, 88,* 296–304.

Stanovich, K. E., & Stanovich, P. J. (1996). Rethinking the concept of learning disabilities: The demise of aptitude–achievement discrepancy. In D. Olson & N. Torrance (Eds.), *Handbook of education and human development: New models of learning, teaching, and schooling* (pp. 117–147). Cambridge, MA: Blackwell.

Stanovich, K. E. (1996). Toward a scientifically responsible philosophy of reading instruction. In J. Shimron (Ed.), *Literacy and education: Essays in Memory of Dina Feitelson* (pp. 185–208). Cresskill, NJ: Hampton Press.

Stanovich, K. E., West, R. F., Cunningham, A. E., Cipielewski, J., & Siddiqui, S. (1996). The role of inadequate print exposure as a determinant of reading comprehension problems. In C. Cornoldi & J. Oakhill (Eds.), *Reading comprehension disabilities* (pp. 15–32). Hillsdale, NJ: Erlbaum.

Wagner, R. K., & Stanovich, K. E. (1996). Expertise in reading. In A. Ericsson (Ed.), *The road to excellence: The acquisition of expert performance in the arts and sciences, sports and games* (pp. 189–225). Mahwah, NJ: Erlbaum.

West, R. F., Stanovich, K. E., & Cunningham, A. E. (1995). Compensatory processes in reading. In R. Dixon & L. Backman (Eds.), *Compensating for psychological deficits and declines: Managing losses and promoting gain* (pp. 275–296). Hillsdale, NJ: Erlbaum.

Stanovich, K. E., West, R. F., & Harrison, M. (1995). Knowledge growth and maintenance across the life span: The role of print exposure. *Developmental Psychology, 31,* 811–826.

Hoien, T., Lundberg, I., Stanovich, K. E., & Bjaalid, I. (1995). Components of phonological awareness. *Reading and Writing: An Interdisciplinary Journal, 7,* 171–188.

Stanovich, K. E., & Stanovich, P. J. (1995). How research might inform the debate about early reading acquisition. *Journal of Research in Reading, 18,* 87–105.

Share, D. L., & Stanovich, K. E. (1995). Cognitive processes in early reading development: Accommodating individual differences into a model of acquisition. *Issues in Education: Contributions from Educational Psychology, 1,* 1–57.

Share, D. L., & Stanovich, K. E. (1995). Accommodating individual differences in critiques: Replies to our commentators. *Issues in Education: Contributions from Educational Psychology, 1,* 105–121.

Stanovich, K. E. (1995). Review of *Reading Development and Dyslexia*, by C. Hulme and M. Snowling. *Journal of Child Psychology and Psychiatry, 36,* 1499–1500.

Stanovich, K. E. (1994). Are discrepancy-based definitions of dyslexia empirically defensible? In K. van den Bos, L. Siegel, D. Bakker, & D. Share (Eds.), *Current directions in dyslexia research* (pp. 15–30). Lisse, The Netherlands: Swets & Zeitlinger.

Stanovich, K. E. (1994). Does dyslexia exist? *Journal of Child Psychology and Psychiatry, 35,* 579–595.

Stanovich, K. E., & Siegel, L. S. (1994). The phenotypic performance profile of reading-disabled children: A regression-based test of the phonological-core variable-difference model. *Journal of Educational Psychology, 86,* 24–53.

Stanovich, K. E. (1994). Constructivism in reading education. *Journal of Special Education, 28,* 259–274.

Cunningham, A. E., Stanovich, K. E., & West, R. F. (1994). Literacy environment and the development of children's cognitive skills. In H. Assink (Ed.), *Literacy acquisition and social context* (pp. 70–90). New York: Harvester Wheatsheaf.

Gottardo, A., & Stanovich, K. E. (1994). Everything you always wanted to know about orthography (Review of *Orthography, Phonology, Morphology, and Meaning,* by Frost and Katz). *Contemporary Psychology, 39,* 277–279.

Stanovich, K. E. (1993). Distinguished Educator Series: Romance and reality. *The Reading Teacher, 47*(4), 280–291; *48*(1), 10–12.

Stanovich, K. E. (1993). Dysrationalia: A new specific learning disability. *Journal of Learning Disabilities, 26,* 501–515.

Stanovich, K. E. (1993). It's practical to be rational. *Journal of Learning Disabilities, 26,* 524–532; *27*(5), 267–269.

Stanovich, K. E. (1993). Does reading make you smarter? Literacy and the development of verbal intelligence. In H. Reese (Ed.), *Advances in child development and behavior* (Vol. 24, pp. 133–180). San Diego: Academic Press.

Stanovich, K. E. (1993). A model for studies of reading disability. *Developmental Review, 13,* 225–245.

Stanovich, K. E., & Cunningham, A. E. (1993). Where does knowledge come from? Specific associations between print exposure and information acquisition. *Journal of Educational Psychology, 85,* 211–229.

Cunningham, A. E., & Stanovich, K. E. (1993). Children's literacy environments and early word recognition skills. *Reading and Writing: An Interdisciplinary Journal, 5,* 193–204.

Stanovich, K. E. (1993). Buy reading, get cognitive psychology free (Review of *The Psychology of Reading: An Introduction* (2nd ed.), by Crowder and Wagner). *Contemporary Psychology, 38,* 622–623.

Stanovich, K. E. (1993). Introduction. In D. Willows, R. Kruk, & E. Corcos (Eds.), *Visual processes in reading and reading disabilities* (pp. xxi–xxiii). Hillsdale, NJ: Erlbaum.

Stanovich, K. E. (1993). Problems in the differential diagnosis of reading disabilities. In R. M. Joshi & C. K. Leong (Eds.), *Reading disabilities: Diagnosis and component processes* (pp. 3–31). Dordrecht, The Netherlands: Kluwer Academic.

Stanovich, K. E. (1993). The construct validity of discrepancy definitions of reading disability. In G. R. Lyon, D. Gray, J. Kavanagh, & N. Krasnegor (Eds.), *Better understanding of learning disabilities: New views from research and their implications for education and public policies* (pp. 273–307). Baltimore: Brookes.

West, R. F., Stanovich, K. E., & Mitchell, H. R. (1993). Reading in the real world and its correlates. *Reading Research Quarterly, 28,* 34–50; *29,* 290–291.

Stanovich, K. E. (1993). The language code: Issues in word recognition. In S. Yussen & M. C. Smith (Eds.), *Reading across the life span* (pp. 111–135). New York: Springer-Verlag.

Stanovich, K. E. (1993). Reading development: All subprocesses are not created equal (Review of *Understanding and Teaching Reading: An Interactive Model,* by Emerald Dechant). *American Journal of Psychology, 106,* 456–466.

Stanovich, K. E. (1993). Two conceptually rich longitudinal studies: Commentary on Ellis. In H. Grimm & H. Skowronek (Eds.), *Language acquisition problems and reading disorders: Aspects of diagnosis and interaction* (pp. 283–293). Berlin: Walter de Gruyter.

Stanovich, K. E. (1993). Organizing the literature on interventions for reading and writing disabilities. In H. Grimm & H. Skowronek (Eds.), *Language acquisition problems and reading disorders: Aspects of diagnosis and interaction* (pp. 353–360). Berlin: Walter de Gruyter.

Cipielewski, J., & Stanovich, K. E. (1992). Predicting growth in reading ability from children's exposure to print. *Journal of Experimental Child Psychology, 54,* 74–89.

Allen, L., Cipielewski, J., & Stanovich, K. E. (1992). Multiple indicators of children's reading habits and attitudes: Construct validity and cognitive correlates. *Journal of Educational Psychology, 84,* 489–503.

Stanovich, K. E., & Cunningham, A. E. (1992). Studying the consequences of literacy within a literate society: The cognitive correlates of print exposure. *Memory and Cognition, 20,* 51–68.

Stanovich, K. E. (1992). The psychology of reading: Evolutionary and revolutionary developments. *Annual Review of Applied Linguistics, 12,* 3–30.

Stanovich, K. E. (1992). Speculations on the causes and consequences of individual differences in early reading acquisition. In P. Gough, L. Ehri, & R. Treiman (Eds.), *Reading acquisition* (pp. 307–342). Hillsdale, NJ.: Erlbaum.

Stanovich, K. E. (1992). Developmental reading disorder. In S. Hooper, G. Hynd, & R. Mattison (Eds.), *Developmental disorders: Diagnostic criteria and clinical assessment* (pp 173–208). Hillsdale, NJ: Erlbaum.

Stanovich, K. E. (1992). Are we overselling literacy? In C. Temple & P. Collins (Eds.), *Stories and readers: New perspectives on literature in the elementary classroom* (pp. 209–231). Norwood, MA: Christopher-Gordon.

Solman, R. T., & Stanovich, K. E. (1992). Information processing models. In N. Singh & I. Beale (Eds.), *Current perspectives in learning disabilities* (pp. 352–371). New York: Springer.

Stanovich, K. E. (1992). Differences in reading acquisition: Causes and consequences. *Reading Forum New Zealand, 3,* 3–21.

Stanovich, K. E. (1991). Discrepancy definitions of reading disability: Has intelligence led us astray? *Reading Research Quarterly, 26,* 7–29, 175–176, 279–280.

West, R. F., & Stanovich, K. E. (1991). The incidental acquisition of information from reading. *Psychological Science, 2,* 325–330.

Nathan, R. G., & Stanovich, K. E. (1991). The causes and consequences of differences in reading fluency. *Theory into Practice, 15,* 176–184.

Cunningham, A. E., & Stanovich, K. E. (1991). Tracking the unique effects of print exposure in children: Associations with vocabulary, general knowledge, and spelling. *Journal of Educational Psychology, 83,* 264–274.

Stanovich, K. E. (1991). Cognitive science meets beginning reading. *Psychological Science, 2,* 70–81.

Stanovich, K. E., West, R. F., & Cunningham, A. E. (1991). Beyond phonological processes: Print exposure and orthographic processing. In S. Brady & D. Shankweiler (Eds.), *Phonological processes in literacy* (pp. 219–235). Hillsdale, NJ: Erlbaum.

Stanovich, K. E. (1991). The theoretical and practical consequences of discrepancy definitions of dyslexia. In M. Snowling & M. Thomson (Eds.), *Dyslexia: Integrating theory and practice* (pp. 125–143). London: Whurr.

Stanovich, K. E., & Cunningham, A. E. (1991). Reading as constrained reasoning. In S. Sternberg & P. Frensch (Eds.), *Complex problem solving: Principles and mechanisms* (pp. 3–60). Hillsdale, NJ: Erlbaum.

Stanovich, K. E. (1991). Reading disability: Assessment issues. In H. L. Swanson (Ed.),

Handbook on the assessment of learning disabilities (pp. 147–175). Austin, TX: Pro-Ed.

Stanovich, K. E. (1991). Comprehension in context (Review of *Becoming a Skilled Reader*, by Oakhill and Garnham). *Contemporary Psychology, 36,* 145–146.

Stanovich, K. E. (1991). Word recognition: Changing perspectives. In R. Barr, M. L. Kamil, P. Mosenthal, & P. D. Pearson (Eds.), *Handbook of reading research* (Vol. 2, pp. 418–452). New York: Longman.

Stanovich, K. E. (1991). Conceptual and empirical problems with discrepancy definitions of reading disability. *Learning Disability Quarterly, 14,* 269–280.

Stanovich, K. E. (1991). Changing models of reading and reading acquisition. In L. Rieben & C. Perfetti (Eds.), *Learning to read: Basic research and its implications* (pp. 19–31). Hillsdale, NJ: Erlbaum.

Stanovich, K. E. (1991). Comprehensible comprehension research (Review of *Comprehension Processes in Reading*, by Balota, Flores d'Arcais, and Rayner). *Contemporary Psychology, 36,* 864–865.

Cunningham, A. E., & Stanovich, K. E. (1990). Assessing print exposure and orthographic processing skill in children: A quick measure of reading experience. *Journal of Educational Psychology, 82,* 733–740.

Stanovich, K. E. (1990). A call for an end to the Paradigm Wars in reading research. *Journal of Reading Behavior, 22,* 221–231.

Cunningham, A. E., & Stanovich, K. E. (1990). Early spelling acquisition: Writing beats the computer. *Journal of Educational Psychology, 82,* 159–162.

Stanovich, K. E. (1990). Concepts in developmental theories of reading skill: Cognitive resources, automaticity, and modularity. *Developmental Review, 10,* 72–100.

Cunningham, A. E., Stanovich, K. E., & Wilson, M. R. (1990). Cognitive variation in adult college students differing in reading ability. In T. Carr & B. Levy (Eds.), *Reading and its development: Component skills approaches* (pp. 129–159). San Diego, CA: Academic Press.

Stanovich, K. E. (1989). Review of *The Psychology of Reading*, by Rayner and Pollatsek. *Journal of Reading Behavior, 21,* 425–429.

Stanovich, K. E., & West, R. F. (1989). Exposure to print and orthographic processing. *Reading Research Quarterly, 24,* 402–433.

Stanovich, K. E. (1989). An improving classic in reading research (Review of *Research in Literacy: Merging Perspectives*, by Readence and Scott). *Contemporary Psychology, 34,* 925–926.

Stanovich, K. E. (1989). Has the learning disabilities field lost its intelligence? *Journal of Learning Disabilities, 22,* 487–492.

Stanovich, K. E. (1989). Various varying views on variation. *Journal of Learning Disabilities, 22,* 366–369.

Stanovich, K. E. (1989). L'evolution des modéles de la lecture et de l'apprentissage de la lecture [Changing models of reading and reading acquisition]. In L. Rieben & C. Perfetti (Eds.), *L'apprenti lecteur: Recherches empiriques et implications pédagogiques* (pp. 43–59). Neuchâtel and Paris: Delachaux/Niestle.

Stanovich, K. E. (1989). Learning disabilities in broader context. *Journal of Learning Disabilities, 22,* 287–297.

Stanovich, K. E. (1988). Explaining the differences between the dyslexic and the garden-variety poor reader: The phonological-core variable-difference model. *Journal of Learning Disabilities, 21,* 590–612. (Reprinted in J. Torgesen (Ed.), *Cogni-*

tive and behavioral characteristics of children with learning disabilities. Austin, TX: Pro-Ed, 1990.)

Stanovich, K. E. (1988). The right and wrong places to look for the cognitive locus of reading disability. *Annals of Dyslexia, 38*, 154–177.

Stanovich, K. E., Nathan, R. G., Zolman, J. E. (1988). The developmental lag hypothesis in reading: Longitudinal and matched reading-level comparisons. *Child Development, 59*, 71–86.

Stanovich, K. E. (1988). Science and learning disabilities. *Journal of Learning Disabilities, 21*, 210–214.

West, R. F., & Stanovich, K. E. (1988). The neutral condition in sentence context experiments: Empirical studies. *Bulletin of the Psychonomic Society, 26*, 87–90.

West, R. F., & Stanovich, K. E. (1988). How much of sentence priming is word priming? *Bulletin of the Psychonomic Society, 26*, 1–4.

Stanovich, K. E. (1987). Perspectives on segmental analysis and alphabetic literacy. *European Bulletin of Cognitive Psychology, 7*, 514–519.

Stanovich, K. E. (1987). Introduction to invitational issue on children's reading and the development of phonological awareness. *Merrill-Palmer Quarterly, 33*, iii–vi.

Stanovich, K. E. (1987). The impact of automaticity theory. *Journal of Learning Disabilities, 20*, 167–168.

Stanovich, K. E. (1986). Matthew effects in reading: Some consequences of individual differences in the acquisition of literacy. *Reading Research Quarterly, 21*, 360–407.

Stanovich, K. E., Nathan, R., & Vala-Rossi, M. (1986). Developmental changes in the cognitive correlates of reading ability and the developmental lag hypothesis. *Reading Research Quarterly, 21*, 267–283.

Stanovich, K. E. (1986). Cognitive processes and the reading problems of learning disabled children: Evaluating the assumption of specificity. In J. Torgesen & B. Wong (Eds.), *Psychological and educational perspectives on learning disabilities* (pp. 87–131). New York: Academic Press.

Stanovich, K. E. (1986). New beginnings, old problems. In S. Ceci (Ed.), *Handbook of cognitive, social, and neuropsychological aspects of learning disabilities* (Vol. 1). Hillsdale, NJ: Erlbaum.

West, R. F., & Stanovich, K. E. (1986). Robust effects of syntactic structure on visual word processing. *Memory and Cognition, 14*, 104–112.

Stanovich, K. E., Nathan, R., West, R. F., & Vala-Rossi, M. (1985). Children's word recognition in context: Spreading activation, expectancy, and modularity. *Child Development, 56*, 1418–1428.

Stanovich, K. E. (1985). Explaining the variance in reading ability in terms of psychological processes: What have we learned? *Annals of Dyslexia, 35*, 67–96.

Stanovich, K. E., Cunningham, A., & Cramer, B. (1984). Assessing phonological awareness in kindergarten children: Issues of task comparability. *Journal of Experimental Child Psychology, 38*, 175–190.

Stanovich, K. E., Cunningham, A., & Feeman, D. (1984). Intelligence, cognitive skills, and early reading progress. *Reading Research Quarterly, 19*, 278–303.

Stanovich, K. E., Cunningham, A., & Feeman, D. (1984). Relation between early reading acquisition and word decoding with and without context: A longitudinal study of first-grade children. *Journal of Educational Psychology, 76*, 668–677.

Stanovich, K. E. (1984). The interactive–compensatory model of reading: A confluence of developmental, experimental, and educational psychology. *Remedial and Special Education, 5,* 11–19.

Stanovich, K. E., & West, R. F. (1983). On priming by a sentence context. *Journal of Experimental Psychology: General, 112,* 1–36.

Stanovich, K. E., & West, R. F. (1983). The generalizability of context effects on word recognition: A reconsideration of the roles of parafoveal priming and sentence context. *Memory and Cognition, 11,* 49–58.

Stanovich, K. E. (1983). Psychological, neurological, and educational research in dyslexia (Review of *Dyslexia Research and Its Application to Education,* by Pavlidis and Miles). *Contemporary Psychology, 28,* 25–26.

West, R. F., Stanovich, K. E., Feeman, D., & Cunningham, A. (1983). The effect of sentence context on word recognition in second- and sixth-grade children. *Reading Research Quarterly, 19,* 6–15.

Stanovich, K. E., Feeman, D., & Cunningham, A. (1983). The development of the relation between letter naming speed and reading ability. *Bulletin of the Psychonomic Society, 21,* 199–202.

West, R. F., & Stanovich, K. E. (1982). Source of inhibition in experiments on the effect of sentence context on word recognition. *Journal of Experimental Psychology: Learning, Memory, and Cognition, 8,* 385–399.

Irwin, D. E., Bock, J. K., & Stanovich, K. E. (1982). Effects of information structure cues on visual word processing. *Journal of Verbal Learning and Verbal Behavior, 21,* 307–325.

Purcell, D. G., & Stanovich, K. E. (1982). Boundary conditions for a word superiority effect. *Quarterly Journal of Experimental Psychology, 34A,* 117–134.

Stanovich, K. E. (1982). Individual differences in the cognitive processes of reading, 1: Word decoding. *Journal of Learning Disabilities, 15,* 485–493. (Reprinted in the *Annual Review of Learning Disabilities.*)

Stanovich, K. E. (1982). Individual differences in the cognitive processes of reading, 2: Text-level processes. *Journal of Learning Disabilities, 15,* 549–554. (Reprinted in the *Annual Review of Learning Disabilities.*)

Stanovich, K. E. (1982). Word recognition skill and reading ability. In M. Singer (Ed.), *Competent reader, disabled reader: Research and application* (pp. 81–102). Hillsdale, NJ: Erlbaum.

Singer, M. H., & Stanovich, K. E. (1982). Reading disability: Introduction. In M. Singer (Ed.), *Competent reader, disabled reader: Research and application* (pp. 33–37). Hillsdale, NJ: Erlbaum.

Stanovich, K. E. (1981). Relationships between word decoding speed, general name-retrieval ability, and reading progress in first-grade children. *Journal of Educational Psychology, 73,* 809–815.

Stanovich, K. E., West, R. F., & Feeman, D. (1981). A longitudinal study of sentence context effects in second-grade children. *Journal of Experimental Child Psychology, 32,* 185–199.

Stanovich, K. E., & West, R. F. (1981). The effect of sentence context on ongoing word recognition: Tests of a two-process theory. *Journal of Experimental Psychology: Human Perception and Performance, 7,* 658–672.

Stanovich, K. E. (1981). Attentional and automatic context effects in reading. In A. Lesgold & C. Perfetti (Eds.), *Interactive processes in reading* (pp. 241–267). Hillsdale, NJ: Erlbaum.

Stanovich, K. E., Cunningham, A., & West, R. F. (1981). A longitudinal study of the development of automatic recognition skills in first graders. *Journal of Reading Behavior, 13,* 57–74.

Wilkinson, A. C., Guminski, M., Stanovich, K. E., & West, R. F. (1981). Variable interaction between visual recognition and memory in oral reading. *Journal of Experimental Psychology: Human Learning and Memory, 7,* 111–119.

Schwartz, R. M., & Stanovich, K. E. (1981). Flexibility in the use of graphic and contextual information by good and poor readers. *Journal of Reading Behavior, 13,* 263–269.

Stanovich, K. E. (1980). Toward an interactive–compensatory model of individual differences in the development of reading fluency. *Reading Research Quarterly, 16,* 32–71.

Bauer, D., & Stanovich, K. E. (1980). Lexical access and the spelling-to-sound regularity effect. *Memory and Cognition, 8,* 424–432.

Stanovich, K. E., & West, R. F. (1979). The effect of orthographic structure on the word search performance of good and poor readers. *Journal of Experimental Child Psychology, 28,* 258–267.

Stanovich, K. E., & West, R. F. (1979). Mechanisms of sentence context effects: Automatic activation and conscious attention. *Memory and Cognition, 7,* 77–85.

Stanovich, K. E., Purcell, D. G., & West, R. F. (1979). The development of word recognition mechanisms: Inference and unitization. *Bulletin of the Psychonomic Society, 13,* 71–74.

West, R. F., & Stanovich, K. E. (1979). The development of automatic word recognition skills. *Journal of Reading Behavior, 11,* 211–219.

Stanovich, K. E., & Bauer, D. W. (1978). Experiments on the spelling-to-sound regularity effect in word recognition. *Memory and Cognition, 6,* 410–415.

West, R. F., & Stanovich, K. E. (1978). Automatic contextual facilitation in readers of three ages. *Child Development, 49,* 717–727.

Stanovich, K. E., West, R. F., & Pollak, D. (1978). The effect of orthographic structure on word recognition in a visual search task. *Journal of Experimental Child Psychology, 26,* 137–146.

Purcell, D. G., Stanovich, K. E., & Spector, A. (1978). Visual angle and the word superiority effect. *Memory and Cognition, 6,* 3–8.

Related Publications
by Keith E. Stanovich
in Other Areas

BOOK

Stanovich, K. E. (1999). *Who is rational? Studies of individual differences in reasoning.* Mahwah, NJ: Erlbaum.

TEXTBOOK

Stanovich, K. E. (1998). *How to think straight about psychology* 5th ed.. New York: Longman.

JOURNAL ARTICLES AND CHAPTERS

Stanovich, K. E., & West, R. F. (in press). Individual differences in reasoning: Implications for the rationality debate? *Behavioral and Brain Sciences.*

Stanovich, K. E., & West, R. F. (1999). Discrepancies between normative and descriptive models of decision making and the understanding/acceptance principle. *Cognitive Psychology, 38,* 349–385.

Sá, W., West, R. F., & Stanovich, K. E. (1999). The domain specificity and generality of belief bias: Searching for a generalizable critical thinking skill. *Journal of Educational Psychology, 91,* 497–510.

Stanovich, K. E. & West, R. F. (1999). Individual differences in reasoning and the heuristics and biases debate. In P. Ackerman, P. Kyllonen, & R. Roberts (Eds.), *Learning and individual differences: Processes, trait, and content determinants* (pp. 389–407). Washington, DC: American Psychological Association.

Stanovich, K. E., & West, R. F. (1998). Individual differences in framing and conjunction effects. *Thinking and Reasoning, 4,* 289–317.

Stanovich, K. E., & West, R. F. (1998). Cognitive ability and variation in selection task performance. *Thinking and Reasoning, 4,* 193–230.

Stanovich, K. E., & West, R. F. (1998). Individual differences in rational thought. *Journal of Experimental Psychology: General, 127,* 161–188.

Stanovich, K. E., & West, R. F. (1998). Who uses base rates and P(D/~H)? An analysis of individual differences. *Memory and Cognition, 28,* 161–179.

Stanovich, K. E. (1998). Cognitive neuroscience and educational psychology: What season is it? *Educational Psychology Review, 10,* 419–426.

Stanovich, K. E., & West, R. F. (1997). Reasoning independently of prior belief and individual differences in actively open-minded thinking. *Journal of Educational Psychology, 89,* 342–357.

West, R. F., & Stanovich, K. E. (1997). The domain specificity and generality of overconfidence: Individual differences in performance estimation bias. *Psychonomic Bulletin and Review, 4,* 387–392.

Stanovich, P. J., & Stanovich, K. E. (1997). Research into practice in special education. *Journal of Learning Disabilities, 30,* 477–481.

Klein, P., Olson, D. R., & Stanovich, K. E. (1997). Structuring reflection: Teaching argument concepts and strategies enhances critical thinking. *Canadian Journal of School Psychology, 13,* 38–47.

Stanovich, K. E. (1996). Decentered thought and consequentialist decision making (Commentary on "Nonconsequentialist Decisions," by J. Baron). *Behavioral and Brain Sciences, 19,* 323–324.

Stanovich, K. E. (1995). Work on working memory (Review of *Working Memory and Language,* by Gathercole and Baddeley). *Contemporary Psychology, 40,* 857.

Stanovich, K. E. (1994). Reconceptualizing intelligence: Dysrationalia as an intuition pump. *Educational Researcher, 23*(4), 11–22; *23*(7), p. 33.

Stanovich, K. E. (1993). The developmental history of an illusion (Commentary on "How We Know Our Minds: The Illusion of First-Person Knowledge of Intentionality," by A. Gopnik). *Behavioral and Brain Sciences, 16,* 80–81.

Stanovich, K. E. (1993). Introduction to invitational issue on the development of rationality and critical thinking. *Merrill-Palmer Quarterly, 39,* iii–viii.

Stanovich, K. E. (1991). Damn! There goes that ghost again! (Commentary on "Is Human Information Processing Conscious?," by M. Velmans). *Behavioral and Brain Sciences, 15,* 696–698.

Stanovich, K. E. (1990). And then a miracle happens (Commentary on "The Emperor's New Mind: Concerning Computers, Minds, and the Laws of Physics," by R. Penrose). *Behavioral and Brain Sciences, 13,* 684–685.

Stanovich, K. E. (1989). Implicit philosophies of mind: The dualism scale and its relationships with religiosity and belief in extrasensory perception. *Journal of Psychology, 123,* 5–23.

Stanovich, K. E. (1988). Cautions regarding Bonferroni corrections. *Reading Research Quarterly, 23,* 380–381.

Stanovich, K. E., & Purcell, D. G. (1986). Priming without awareness: What was all the fuss about? (Commentary on "Semantic Activation without Conscious Identification," by Holender). *Behavioral and Brain Sciences, 9,* 47–48.

Stanovich, K. E. (1986). Cognitive determinants of reading in mentally retarded individuals. In N. Ellis & N. Bray (Eds.), *International review of research in mental retardation* (Vol. 13). New York: Academic Press.

Stanovich, K. E. (1985). The differences are real—Where do we go from here? *Behavioral and Brain Sciences, 8,* 242–243.

Stanovich, K. E. (1985). A dialogue at last (Review of *Learning and Cognition in the Mentally Retarded,* by Brooks, Sperber, and McCauley). *Contemporary Psychology, 30,* 860–861.

Purcell, D. G., Stewart, A., & Stanovich, K. E. (1983). Another look at semantic priming without awareness. *Perception and Psychophysics, 34,* 65–71.

Stanovich, K. E., & Purcell, D. G. (1981). Comments on "Input Capability and Speed of Processing in Mental Retardation." *Journal of Abnormal Psychology, 90,* 168–171; *90,* 261–262.

Stanovich, K. E. (1981). Age and sex differences in interference proneness. In L. Nadelman (Ed.), *Research manual in child development* (pp. 157–169). New York: Harper & Row.

Stanovich, K. E. (1981). Age and sex differences in two reaction-time tasks. In L. Nadelman (Ed.), *Research manual in child development.* New York: Harper & Row.

Stanovich, K. E. (1979). Studies of letter identification using qualitative error analysis: Effects of speed stress, tachistoscopic presentation, and word context. *Journal of Experimental Psychology: Human Perception and Performance, 5,* 713–733.

Stanovich, K. E., & Stanovich, P. J. (1979). Speaking for themselves: A bibliography of writings by mentally handicapped individuals. *Mental Retardation, 17,* 83–86.

Stanovich, K. E., & West, R. F. (1978). A developmental study of the category effect in visual search. *Child Development, 49,* 1223–1226.

Pachella, R. G., Smith, J., & Stanovich, K. E. (1978). Qualitative error analysis and speeded identification. In F. Restle & N. Castellan (Eds.), *Cognitive theory* (Vol. 3, pp. 169–198). Hillsdale, NJ: Erlbaum.

Stanovich, K. E. (1978). Information processing in mentally retarded individuals. In N. R. Ellis (Ed.), *International review of research in mental retardation* (Vol. 9, pp. 29–60). New York: Academic Press.

Stanovich, K. E. (1978). Technology and mentally handicapped individuals: Speculations on the future. In A. Fink (Ed.), *International perspectives on future special education* (pp. 236–241). Reston, VA: CEC.

Stanovich, K. E. (1977). Note on the interpretation of interactions in comparative research. *American Journal of Mental Deficiency, 81,* 394–396.

Hagen, J., & Stanovich, K. E. (1977). Memory: Strategies of acquisition. In R. Kail & J. Hagen (Eds.), *Perspectives on the development of memory and cognition* (pp. n89–111). Hillsdale, NJ: Erlbaum.

Stanovich, K. E., & Pachella, R. G. (1977). Encoding, stimulus-response compatibility, and stages of processing. *Journal of Experimental Psychology: Human Perception and Performance, 3,* 411–421.

Stanovich, K. E., Pachella, R. G., & Smith, J. (1977). An analysis of confusion errors in naming letters under speed stress. *Perception and Psychophysics, 21,* 545–552.

Stanovich, K. E., & Pachella, R. G. (1976). The effect of stimulus probability on the speed and accuracy of naming alphanumeric stimuli. *Bulletin of the Psychonomic Society, 8,* 281–284.

References

Aaron, P. G. (1987). Developmental dyslexia: Is it different from other forms of reading disability? *Annals of Dyslexia, 37,* 109–125.

Aaron, P. G. (1989a). *Dyslexia and hyperlexia.* Dordrecht, The Netherlands: Kluwer Academic.

Aaron, P. G. (1989b). Qualitative and quantitative differences among dyslexic, normal, and nondyslexic poor readers. *Reading and Writing: An Interdisciplinary Journal, 1,* 291–308.

Aborn, M., Rubenstein, H., & Sterling, T. D. (1959). Sources of contextual constraint upon words in sentences. *Journal of Experimental Psychology, 57,* 171–180.

Ackerman, B. A., & Alstott, A. (1999). *The stakeholder society.* New Haven, CT: Yale University Press.

Ackerman, P. T., Dykman, R. A., & Gardner, M. Y. (1990). ADD students with and without dyslexia differ in sensitivity to rthyme and alliteration. *Journal of Learning Disabilities, 23,* 279–283.

Adams, M. J. (1990). *Beginning to read: Thinking and learning about print.* Cambridge, MA: MIT Press.

Adams, M. J. (1991). Why not phonics and whole language? In W. Ellis (Ed.), *All language and the creation of literacy* (pp. 40–52). Baltimore: Orton Dyslexia Society.

Adams, M. J. (1998). The three-cueing system. In J. Osborn & F. Lehr (Eds.), *Literacy for all: Issues in teaching and learning* (pp. 73–99). New York: Guilford Press.

Adams, M. J. (1999). Afterword: The science and politics of beginning reading practices. In J. Oakhill & R. Beard (Eds.), *Reading development and the teaching of reading* (pp. 213–227). Oxford, England: Blackwell.

Adams, M. J., & Bruck, M. (1993). Word recognition: The interface of educational policies and scientific research. *Reading and Writing: An Interdisciplinary Journal, 5,* 113–139.

Adams, M. J., & Bruck, M. (1995, Summer). Resolving the "Great Debate." *American Educator, 19,* 7–20.

Adams, M. J., Foorman, B. R., Lundberg, I., & Beeler, T. (1998). *Phonemic awareness in young children: A classroom curriculum.* Baltimore: Brookes.

Adelman, K. A., & Adelman, H. S. (1987). Rodin, Patton, Edison, Wilson, Einstein: Were they really learning disabled? *Journal of Learning Disabilities, 20,* 270–279.

Adlard, A., & Hazan, V. (1998). Speech perception in children with specific reading difficulties (dyslexia). *Quarterly Journal of Experimental Psychology, 51A,* 153–177.

Akinnaso, F. N. (1981). The consequences of literacy in pragmatic and theoretical perspectives. *Anthropology and Education Quarterly, 12,* 163–200.

Akinnaso, F. N. (1982). On the difference between spoken and written language. *Language and Speech, 25,* 97–125.

Alcock, J. E. (1990). *Science and supernature: An appraisal of parapsychology.* Buffalo, NY: Prometheus Books.

Alegria, J., Pignot, E., & Morais, J. (1982). Phonetic analysis of speech and memory codes in beginning readers. *Memory and Cognition, 10,* 451–456.

Alexander, P. A. (1992). Domain knowledge: Evolving themes and emerging concerns. *Educational Psychologist, 27,* 33–51.

Alford, J. A. (1980, May). *Predicting predictability: Identification of sources of contextual constraint on words in text.* Paper presented at the meeting of the Midwestern Psychological Association, St. Louis.

Algozzine, B., & Ysseldyke, J. (1983). Learning disabilities as a subset of school failure: The over-sophistication of a concept. *Exceptional Children, 50,* 242–246.

Allen, L., Cipielewski, J., & Stanovich, K. E. (1992). Multiple indicators of children's reading habits and attitudes: Construct validity and cognitive correlates. *Journal of Educational Psychology, 84,* 489–503.

Allerup, P., & Elbro, C. (1998). Comparing differences in accuracy across conditions or individuals: An argument for the use of log odds. *Quarterly Journal of Experimental Psychology, 51A,* 409–424.

Allington, R. L. (1977). If they don't read much, how they ever gonna get good? *Journal of Reading, 21,* 57–61.

Allington, R. L. (1978a). Effects of contextual constraints upon rate and accuracy. *Perceptual and Motor Skills, 46,* 1318.

Allington, R. L. (1978b). Sensitivity to orthographic structure as a function of grade and reading ability. *Journal of Reading Behavior, 10,* 437–439.

Allington, R. L. (1980). Poor readers don't get to read much in reading groups. *Language Arts, 57,* 872–876.

Allington, R. L. (1982). The persistence of teacher beliefs in facets of the visual perceptual deficit hypothesis. *Elementary School Journal, 82,* 351–359.

Allington, R. L. (1983). The reading instruction provided readers of differing reading abilities. *Elementary School Journal, 83,* 548–559.

Allington, R. L. (1984). Content coverage and contextual reading in reading groups. *Journal of Reading Behavior, 16,* 85–96.

Allington, R. L., & Fleming, J. T. (1978). The misreading of high-frequency words. *Journal of Special Education, 12,* 417–421.

Allington, R. L., & Strange, M. (1977). Effects of grapheme substitutions in connected text upon reading behaviors. *Visible Language, 11,* 285–297.

Allington, R. L., & Strange, M. (1978). Word prediction of good and poor readers. In P. D. Pearson (Ed.), *Reading: Disciplined inquiry in process and practice* (pp. 25–39). Clemson, SC: National Reading Conference.

Allport, D. A. (1980). Attention and performance. In G. Claxton (Ed.), *Cognitive psychology: New directions* (pp. 112–153). London: Routledge & Kegan Paul.

Allport, D. A. (1987). Selection for action: Some behavioral and neurophysiological considerations of attention and action. In H. Heuer & A. F. Sanders (Eds.), *Perspectives on perception and action* (pp. 395–419). London: Routledge & Kegan Paul.

Aman, M., & Singh, N. (1983). Specific reading disorders: Concepts of etiology reconsidered. In K. Gadow & I. Bialer (Eds.), *Advances in learning and behavioral disabilities* (Vol. 2, pp. 1–47). Greenwich, CT: JAI Press.

Ames, L. (1968). A low intelligence quotient often not recognized as the chief cause of many learning difficulties. *Journal of Learning Disabilities, 1,* 45–48.

Anastasi, A. (1988). *Psychological testing* (6th ed.). New York: Macmillan.

Anbar, A. (1986). Reading acquisition of preschool children without systematic instruction. *Early Childhood Research Quarterly, 1,* 69–83.

Anderson, M., Kaufman, A., & Kaufman, N. (1976). Use of the WISC-R with a learning disabled population: Some diagnostic implications. *Psychology in the Schools, 13,* 381–386.

Anderson, R. C. (1984). Some reflections on the acquisition of knowledge. *Educational Researcher, 13*(9), 5–10.

Anderson, R. C. (1996). Research foundations to support wide reading. In V. Greaney (Ed.), *Promoting reading in developing countries* (pp. 55–77). Newark, DE: IRA.

Anderson, R. C., & Freebody, P. (1979). *Vocabulary knowledge* (Tech. Rep. No. 136). Urbana-Champaign: University of Illinois, Center for the Study of Reading.

Anderson, R. C., & Freebody, P. (1983). Reading comprehension and the assessment and acquisition of word knowledge. In B. Huston (Ed.), *Advances in reading/ language research* (Vol. 2, pp. 231–256). Greenwich, CT: JAI Press.

Anderson, R. C., Hiebert, E. H., Scott, J. A., & Wilkinson, I. (1985). *Becoming a nation of readers.* Washington, DC: National Institute of Education.

Anderson, R. C., Mason, J., & Shirey, L. (1984). The reading group: An experimental investigation of a labyrinth. *Reading Research Quarterly, 20,* 6–38.

Anderson, R. C., & Pearson, P. D. (1984). A schema-theoretic view of basic processes in reading comprehension. In P. D. Pearson (Ed.), *Handbook of reading research* (pp. 255–291). New York: Longman.

Anderson, R. C., Wilson, P. T., & Fielding, L. G. (1988). Growth in reading and how children spend their time outside of school. *Reading Research Quarterly, 23,* 285–303.

Andolina, C. (1980). Syntactic maturity and vocabulary richness of learning disabled children at four age levels. *Journal of Learning Disabilities, 13,* 372–377.

Andrews, S. (1982). Phonological recoding: Is the regularity effect consistent? *Memory and Cognition, 10,* 565–575.

Applebee, A. N. (1971). Research in reading retardation: Two critical problems. *Journal of Child Psychology and Psychiatry, 12,* 91–113.

Applebee, A. N., Langer, J. A., & Mullis, I. V. S. (1988). *Who reads best?* Princeton, NJ: Educational Testing Service.

Aram, D., Morris, R., & Hall, N. (1992). The validity of discrepancy criteria for identifying children with developmental language disorders. *Journal of Learning Disabilities, 25,* 549–554.

Armstrong, D. M., & Malcolm, N. (1984). *Consciousness and causality.* Oxford, England: Blackwell.

Arter, J., & Jenkins, J. (1979). Differential diagnosis–prescriptive teaching: A critical appraisal. *Review of Educational Research, 49,* 517–555.

Ashton, C. (1996). In defence of discrepancy definitions of specific learning difficulties. *Educational Psychology in Practice, 12,* 131–140.

Auerbach, E. (1992). Literacy and ideology. *Annual Review of Applied Linguistics, 12,* 71–85.

August, D., Flavell, J., & Clift, R. (1984). Comparison of comprehension monitoring of skilled and less skilled readers. *Reading Research Quarterly, 20,* 39–53.

Austin Peay State University. (1990). *Area Concentration Achievement Test in Psychology.* Clarksville, TN: Austin Peay State University, Project for Area Concentration Achievement Tests.

Ayres, L. (1998). *The phonological zoo: Program guide.* Dubuque, IA: Kendall/Hunt.

Bachman, J., & O'Malley, P. (1977). Self-esteem in young men: A longitudinal analysis of the impact of educational and occupational attainment. *Journal of Personality and Social Psychology, 35,* 365–380.

Backman, J. (1983). The role of psycholinguistic skills in reading acquisition: A look at early readers. *Reading Research Quarterly, 18,* 466–479.

Backman, J., Bruck, M., Hebert, M., & Seidenberg, M. (1984). Acquisition and use of spelling–sound correspondences in reading. *Journal of Experimental Child Psychology, 38,* 114–133.

Backman, J., Mamen, M., & Ferguson, H. (1984). Reading level design: Conceptual and methodological issues in reading research. *Psychological Bulletin, 96,* 560–568.

Baddeley, A. D., Ellis, N. C., Miles, T. R., & Lewis, V. J. (1982). Developmental and acquired dyslexia: A comparison. *Cognition, 11,* 185–199.

Baddeley, A. D., Logie, R. H., & Ellis, N. C. (1988). Characteristics of developmental dyslexia. *Cognition, 30,* 198–227.

Baddeley, A. D., Logie, R. H., Nimmo-Smith, I., & Brereton, N. (1985). Components of fluent reading. *Journal of Memory and Language, 24,* 119–131.

Badian, N. A. (1999). Reading disability defined as a discrepancy from listening comprehension: A longitudinal study of stability, gender differences, and prevalence. *Journal of Learning Disabilities, 32,* 138–148.

Baines, L. (1996). From page to screen: When a novel is interpreted for film, what gets lost in translation? *Journal of Adolescent and Adult Literacy, 39,* 612–622.

Baker, L. (1982). An evaluation of the role of metacognitive deficits in learning disabilities. *Topics in Learning and Learning Disabilities, 2,* 27–35.

Baker, L. A., Decker, S. N., & DeFries, J. C. (1984). Cognitive abilities in reading-disabled children: A longitudinal study. *Journal of Child Psychology and Psychiatry, 25,* 11–117.

Ball, E. (1993). Phonological awareness: What's important and to whom? *Reading and Writing: An Interdisciplinary Journal, 5,* 141–159.

Ball, E. W., & Blachman, B. A. (1991). Does phoneme segmentation training in kindergarten make a difference in early word recognition and developmental spelling? *Reading Research Quarterly, 26,* 49–66.

Ball, F., Wood, C., & Smith, E. E. (1975). When are semantic targets detected faster than visual or acoustic ones? *Perception and Psychophysics, 17,* 1–8.

Balota, D., Pollatsek, A., & Rayner, K. (1985). The interaction of contextual constraints and parafoveal visual information in reading. *Cognitive Psychology, 17,* 364–390.

Baltes, P. B. (1987). Theoretical propositions of life-span developmental psychology: On the dynamics between growth and decline. *Developmental Psychology, 23,* 611–626.

Barber, P. J., & Millar, D. G. (1982). Subjective judgments of spelling–sound correspondences: Effects of word regularity and word frequency. *Memory and Cognition, 10*, 457–464.

Barker, K., Torgesen, J. K., & Wagner, R. K. (1992). The role of orthographic processing skills on five different reading tasks. *Reading Research Quarterly, 27*, 334–345.

Baron, J. (1978). Intelligence and general strategies. In G. Underwood (Ed.), *Strategies in information processing* (pp. 403–450). London: Academic Press.

Baron, J. (1979). Orthographic and word-specific mechanisms in children's reading of words. *Child Development, 50*, 60–72.

Baron, J. (1985). *Rationality and intelligence.* Cambridge, England: Cambridge University Press.

Baron, J. (1988). *Thinking and deciding.* Cambridge, England: Cambridge University Press.

Baron, J. (1994). *Thinking and deciding* (2nd ed.). Cambridge, England: Cambridge University Press.

Baron, J., & Strawson, C. (1976). Use of orthographic and word-specific knowledge in reading words aloud. *Journal of Experimental Psychology: Human Perception and Performance, 2*, 386–393.

Baron, J., & Treiman, R. (1980). Use of orthography in reading and learning to read. In J. F. Kavanagh & R. L. Venezky (Eds.), *Orthography, reading, and dyslexia.* Baltimore: University Park Press.

Barr, R. (1974–1975). The effect of instruction on pupil reading strategies. *Reading Research Quarterly, 10*, 555–582.

Barr, R., Kamil, M. L., Mosenthal, P., & Pearson, P. D. (1991). *Handbook of reading research* (Vol. 2). New York: Longman.

Barron, R. W. (1978a). Access to the meanings of printed words: Some implications for reading and learning to read. In F. Murray (Ed.), *The recognition of words: IRA series on the development of the reading process* (pp. 34–56). Newark, DE: International Reading Association.

Barron, R. W. (1978b). Reading skill and phonological coding in lexical access. In M. Gruneberg, R. Sykes, & P. Morris (Eds.), *Practical aspects of memory* (pp. 468–475). London: Academic Press.

Barron, R. W. (1979). Visual-orthographic and phonological strategies in reading and spelling. In U. Frith (Ed.), *Cognitive processes in spelling* (pp. 195–213). London: Academic Press.

Barron, R. W. (1980). Development of visual word recognition: A review. In T. G. Waller & G. E. MacKinnon (Eds.), *Reading research: Advances in theory and practice* (Vol. 2, pp. 119–151). New York: Academic Press.

Barron, R. W. (1981). Reading skill and spelling strategies. In A. Lesgold & C. Perfetti (Eds.), *Interactive processes in reading* (pp. 299–327). Hillsdale, NJ: Erlbaum.

Barron, R. W. (1986). Word recognition in early reading: A review of the direct and indirect access hypotheses. *Cognition, 24*(1–2), 93–119.

Barron, R. W., & Baron, J. (1977). How children get meaning from printed words. *Child Development, 48*, 587–594.

Barzun, J. (1959). *The house of intellect.* New York: Harper & Row.

Bast, J., & Reitsma, P. (1998). Analyzing the development of individual differences in terms of Matthew effects in reading: Results from a Dutch longitudinal study. *Developmental Psychology, 34*, 1373–1399.

Batey, O., & Sonnenschein, S. (1981). Reading deficits in learning disabled children. *Journal of Applied Developmental Psychology, 2,* 237–246.

Bauer, D., & Stanovich, K. E. (1980). Lexical access and the spelling-to-sound regularity effect. *Memory and Cognition, 8,* 424–432.

Bauer, R. (1977). Memory processes in children with learning disabilities: Evidence for deficient rehearsal. *Journal of Experimental Child Psychology, 24,* 415–430.

Bauer, R. (1979). Memory, acquisition, and category clustering in learning-disabled children. *Journal of Experimental Child Psychology, 27,* 365–383.

Bauer, R. (1982). Information processing as a way of understanding and diagnosing learning disabilities. *Topics in Learning and Learning Disabilities, 2,* 33–45.

Beauvois, M. F., & Derouesne, J. (1979). Phonological alexia: Three dissociations. *Journal of Neurology, Neurosurgery, and Psychiatry, 42,* 1115–1124.

Bechtel, W. (1988). *Philosophy of science.* Hillsdale, NJ: Erlbaum.

Beck, I. L. (1996, April). *Discovering reading research: Why I didn't go to law school.* Paper presented at the Reading Hall of Fame, International Reading Association, New Orleans.

Beck, I. L. (1998). Understanding beginning reading: A journey through teaching and research. In J. Osborn & F. Lehr (Eds.), *Literacy for all: Issues in teaching and learning* (pp. 11–31). New York: Guilford Press.

Beck, I. L., Perfetti, C. A., & McKeown, M. G. (1982). Effects of long-term vocabulary instruction on lexical access and reading comprehension. *Journal of Educational Psychology, 74,* 506–521.

Becker, C. A. (1982). The development of semantic context effects: Two processes or two strategies? *Reading Research Quarterly, 17,* 482–502.

Becker, C. A. (1985). What do we really know about semantic context effects during reading? In D. Besner, T. Waller, & G. MacKinnon (Eds.), *Reading research: Advances in theory and practice* (Vol. 5, pp. 125–166). New York: Academic Press.

Becker, C. A., & Killion, T. H. (1977). Interaction of visual and cognitive effects in word recognition. *Journal of Experimental Psychology: Human Perception and Performance, 3,* 389–401.

Beech, J., & Harding, L. (1984). Phonemic processing and the poor reader from a developmental lag viewpoint. *Reading Research Quarterly, 19,* 357–366.

Beech, J. R., & Awaida, M. (1992). Lexical and nonlexical routes: A comparison between normally achieving and poor readers. *Journal of Learning Disabilities, 25,* 196–206.

Bell, L. C., & Perfetti, C. A. (1994). Reading skill: Some adult comparisons. *Journal of Educational Psychology, 86,* 244–255.

Ben-Dror, I., Pollatsek, A., & Scarpati, S. (1991). Word identification in isolation and in context by college dyslexic students. *Brain and Language, 40,* 471–490.

Benson, N., Lovett, M. W., & Kroeber, C. L. (1997). Training and transfer-of-learning effects in disabled and normal readers: Evidence of specific deficits. *Journal of Experimental Child Psychology, 64,* 343–366.

Bentin, S. (1992). Phonological awareness, reading, and reading acquisition. In R. Frost & L. Katz (Eds.), *Orthography, phonology, morphology, and meaning* (pp. 193–210). Amsterdam, The Netherlands: North-Holland.

Bereiter, C. (1994). Implications of postmodernism for science; or, Science as progressive discourse. *Educational Psychologist, 29,* 3–12.

Berent, I., & Perfetti, C. A. (1995). A rose is a REEZ: The two-cycles model of phonology assembly in reading English. *Psychological Review, 102,* 146–184.

Berger, K. W. (1977). *The most common 100,000 words used in conversations*. Kent, OH: Herald Publishing House.

Berger, N. (1978). Why can't John read? Perhaps he's not a good listener. *Journal of Learning Disabilities, 11*, 633–638.

Bergeron, B. (1990). What does the term "whole language" mean? Constructing a definition from the literature. *Journal of Reading Behavior, 22*, 301–329.

Berliner, D. C., & Biddle, B. (1995). *The manufactured crisis: Myths, fraud, and the attack on America's public schools*. Reading, MA: Addison-Wesley.

Berndt, R., D'Autrechy, C. L., & Reggia, J. (1994). Functional pronunciation units in English words. *Journal of Experimental Psychology: Learning, Memory, and Cognition, 20*, 977–991.

Berndt, R., Reggia, J., & Mitchum, C. (1987). Empirically derived probabilities for grapheme-to-phoneme correspondences in English. *Behavior Research Methods, Instruments, and Computers, 19*, 1–9.

Berninger, V. (Ed.). (1994). *Varieties of orthographic knowledge* (Vol. 1). Dordrecht, The Netherlands: Kluwer Academic.

Berninger, V. (Ed.), (1995). *Varieties of orthographic knowledge* (Vol. 2). Dordrecht, The Netherlands: Kluwer Academic.

Besner, D., Twilley, L., McCann, R., & Seergobin, K. (1990). On the association between connectionism and data: Are a few words necessary? *Psychological Review, 97*, 432–446.

Biber, D. (1986). Spoken and written textual dimensions in English: Resolving the contradictory findings. *Language, 62*, 384–414.

Bickley, A. C., Ellington, B. J., & Bickley, R. T. (1970). The cloze procedure: A conspectus. *Journal of Reading Behavior, 2*, 232–249.

Biemiller, A. (1970). The development of the use of graphic and contextual information as children learn to read. *Reading Research Quarterly, 6*, 75–96.

Biemiller, A. (1977–1978). Relationships between oral reading rates for letters, words, and simple text in the development of reading achievement. *Reading Research Quarterly, 13*, 223–253.

Biemiller, A. (1979). Changes in the use of graphic and contextual information as functions of passage difficulty and reading achievement level. *Journal of Reading Behavior, 11*, 307–319.

Birnbaum, R. (1990). IQ and the definition of LD. *Journal of Learning Disabilities, 23*, 330.

Bisanz, G. L., Das, J. P., & Mancini, G. (1984). Children's memory for phonemically confusable and nonconfusable letters. *Child Development, 55*, 1845–1854.

Bishop, D., & Adams, C. (1990). A prospective study of the relationship between specific language impairment, phonological disorders, and reading retardation. *Journal of Child Psychology and Psychiatry, 31*, 1027–1050.

Bishop, D., & Butterworth, G. (1980). Verbal-performance discrepancies: Relationship to both risk and specific reading retardation. *Cortex, 16*, 375–389.

Bissex, G. L. (1980). *Gnys at wrk*. Cambridge, MA: Harvard University Press.

Bjorklund, D. (1987). How age changes in knowledge base contribute to the development of children's memory: An interpretive review. *Developmental Review, 7*, 93–130.

Bjorklund, D., & Bernholtz, J. (1986). The role of knowledge base in the memory performance of good and poor readers. *Journal of Experimental Child Psychology, 41*, 367–393.

Bjorklund, D., & Harnishfeger, K. (1987). Developmental differences in the mental effort requirements for the use of an organizational strategy in free recall. *Journal of Experimental Child Psychology, 44*, 109–125.

Bjorklund, D., & Weiss, S. (1985). Influence of socioeconomic status on children's classification and free recall. *Journal of Educational Psychology, 77*, 119–128.

Blachman, B. A. (1984). Relationship of rapid naming ability and language analysis skills to kindergarten and first-grade reading achievement. *Journal of Educational Psychology, 76*, 610–622.

Blachman, B. A. (1989). Phonological awareness and word recognition: Assessment and intervention. In A. G. Kamhi & H. W. Catts (Eds.), *Reading disabilities* (pp. 133–158). Austin, TX: PRO-ED.

Blachman, B. A. (1997a). Early intervention and phonological awareness: A cautionary tale. In B. A. Blachman (Ed.), *Foundations of reading acquisition and dyslexia: Implications for early intervention* (pp. 409–430). Mahweh, NJ: Erlbaum.

Blachman, B. A. (Ed.). (1997b). *Foundations of reading acquisition and dyslexia: Implications for early intervention.* Mahweh, NJ: Erlbaum.

Blachman, B. A., Ball, E. W., Black, R. S., & Tangel, D. M. (1994). Kindergarten teachers develop phoneme awareness in low-income, inner-city classrooms. *Reading and Writing: An Interdisciplinary Journal, 6*, 1–18.

Blachman, B. A., Tangel, D. M., Ball, E., Black, R., & McGraw, C. (1999). Developing phonological awareness and word recognition skills: A two-year intervention with low-income, inner-city children. *Reading and Writing: An Interdisciplinary Journal, 11*, 239–273.

Blackmore, S. (1999). *The meme machine.* New York: Oxford University Press.

Blanchard, J. (1980). Preliminary investigation of transfer between single-word decoding ability and contextual reading comprehension by poor readers in grade six. *Perceptual and Motor Skills, 51*, 1271–1281.

Blanchard, J., & McNinch, G. (1980). Commentary: Testing the decoding sufficiency hypothesis. A response to Fleisher, Jenkins, and Pany. *Reading Research Quarterly, 15*, 559–564.

Bloom, A., Wagner, M., Reskin, L., & Bergman, A. (1980). A comparison of intellectually delayed and primary reading disabled children on measures of intelligence and achievement. *Journal of Clinical Psychology, 36*, 788–790.

Bobrow, D. G., & Norman, D. A. (1975). Some principles of memory schemata. In D. G. Bobrow & A. Collins (Eds.), *Remembering and understanding* (pp. 131–149). New York: Academic Press.

Boden, M. A. (1988). *Computer models of mind.* Cambridge, England: Cambridge University Press.

Bodor, E. (1973). Developmental dyslexia: A diagnostic approach based on three atypical reading–spelling patterns. *Developmental Medicine and Child Neurology, 15*, 375–389.

Booth, J. R., & Hall, W. S. (1994). Role of the cognitive internal state lexicon in reading comprehension. *Journal of Educational Psychology, 86*, 413–422.

Booth, J. R., Perfetti, C. A., & MacWhinney, B. (1999). Quick, automatic, and general activation of orthographic and phonological representations in young readers. *Developmental Psychology, 35*, 3–19.

Bos, C., & Filip, D. (1982). Comprehension monitoring skills in learning disabled and average students. *Topics in Learning and Learning Disabilities, 2*, 79–85.

Bowers, P., Steffy, R., & Tate, E. (1988). Comparison of the effects of IQ control methods on memory and naming speed predictors of reading disability. *Reading Research Quarterly, 23,* 304–319.

Bowers, P. G., & Swanson, L. B. (1991). Naming speed deficits in reading disability: Multiple measures of a singular process. *Journal of Experimental Child Psychology, 51,* 195–219.

Bowers, P. G., & Wolf, M. (1993). Theoretical links among naming speed, precise timing mechanisms, and orthographic skill in dyslexia. *Reading and Writing: An Interdisciplinary Journal, 5,* 69–85.

Bowey, J. A. (1982). Memory limitations in the oral reading comprehension of fourth-grade children. *Journal of Experimental Child Psychology, 34,* 200–216.

Bowey, J. A. (1986). Syntactic awareness in relation to reading skill and ongoing reading comprehension monitoring. *Journal of Experimental Child Psychology, 41,* 282–299.

Bowey, J. A. (1999). The limitations of orthographic rime analogies in beginners' word reading: A reply to Goswami (1999). *Journal of Experimental Child Psychology, 72,* 220–231.

Bowey, J. A., Cain, M. T., & Ryan, S. M. (1992). A reading-level design study of phonological skills underlying fourth-grade children's word reading difficulties. *Child Development, 63,* 999–1011.

Bradburn, N. M., Rips, L. J., & Shevell, S. K. (1987). Answering autobiographical questions: The impact of memory and inference on surveys. *Science, 236,* 157–161.

Bradley, L., & Bryant, P. E. (1978). Difficulties in auditory organization as a possible cause of reading backwardness. *Nature, 271,* 746–747.

Bradley, L., & Bryant, P. E. (1983). Categorizing sounds and learning to read: A causal connection. *Nature, 301,* 419–421.

Bradley, L., & Bryant, P. E. (1985). *Rhyme and reason in reading and spelling.* Ann Arbor: University of Michigan Press.

Brady, S. A. (1997). Ability to encode phonological representations: An underlying difficulty of poor readers. In B. A. Blachman (Ed.), *Foundations of reading acquisition and dyslexia: Implications for early intervention* (pp. 21–47). Mahweh, NJ: Erlbaum.

Brady, S. A., & Shankweiler, D. (Eds.) (1991). *Phonological processes in literacy.* Hillsdale, NJ: Erlbaum.

Brady, S. A., Shankweiler, D., & Mann, V. (1983). Speech perception and memory coding in relation to reading ability. *Journal of Experimental Child Psychology, 35,* 345–367.

Brainerd, C. J., & Kingma, J. (1985). On the independence of short-term memory and working memory in cognitive development. *Cognitive Psychology, 17,* 210–247.

Brainerd, C. J., Kingma, J., & Howe, M. (1986). Long-term memory development and learning disability: Storage and retrieval loci of disabled/nondisabled differences. In S. Ceci (Ed.), *Handbook of cognitive, social, and neuropsychological aspects of learning disabilities* (Vol. 1, pp. 161–184). Hillsdale, NJ: Erlbaum.

Brainerd, C. J., & Reyna, V. F. (1988). Generic resources, reconstructive processing, and children's mental arithmetic. *Developmental Psychology, 24,* 324–334.

Brainerd, C. J., & Reyna, V. F. (1989). Output-interference theory of dual-task deficits in memory development. *Journal of Experimental Child Psychology, 47,* 1–18.

Bransford, J., Stein, B., & Vye, N. (1982). Helping students learn how to learn from written texts. In M. Singer (Ed.), *Competent reader, disabled reader: Research and application* (pp. 141–150). Hillsdale, NJ: Erlbaum.

Bransford, J. D., & Franks, J. J. (1971). The abstraction of linguistic ideas. *Cognitive Psychology, 2,* 331–350.

Bransford, J. D., & Johnson, M. K. (1973). Consideration of some problems in comprehension. In W. G. Chase (Ed.), *Visual information processing* (pp. 383–438). New York: Academic Press.

Braten, I., Lie, R., Andreassen, R., & Olaussen, B. S. (1999). Leisure time reading and orthographic processes in word recognition among Norwegian third- and fourth-grade students. *Reading and Writing: An Interdisciplinary Journal, 11,* 65–88.

Briggs, P., Austin, S., & Underwood, G. (1984). The effects of sentence context in good and poor readers: A test of Stanovich's interactive–compensatory model. *Reading Research Quarterly, 20,* 54–61.

Briggs, P., & Underwood, G. (1982). Phonological coding in good and poor readers. *Journal of Experimental Child Psychology, 34,* 93–112.

Bristow, P. S. (1985). Are poor readers passive readers? Some evidence, possible explanation, and potential solutions. *Reading Teacher, 39,* 318–325.

Britton, B. K. (1980). Use of cognitive capacity in reading: Effects of processing information from text for immediate recall and retention. *Journal of Reading Behavior, 12,* 129–137.

Britton, B. K., Glynn, S., Meyer, B., & Penland, M. (1982). Effects of text structure on use of cognitive capacity during reading. *Journal of Educational Psychology, 74,* 51–61.

Britton, B. K., Holdredge, T. S., Curry, C., & Westbrook, R. D. (1979). Use of cognitive capacity in reading identical texts with different amounts of discourse level meaning. *Journal of Experimental Psychology: Human Learning and Memory, 5,* 262–270.

Britton, B. K., & Tesser, A. (1982). Effects of prior knowledge on use of cognitive capacity in three complex cognitive tasks. *Journal of Verbal Learning and Verbal Behavior, 21,* 421–436.

Britton, B. K., Westbrook, R. D., & Holdredge, T. S. (1978). Reading and cognitive capacity usage: Effects of text difficulty. *Journal of Experimental Psychology: Human Learning and Memory, 4,* 582–591.

Bronfenbrenner, U., McClelland, P., Wethington, E., Moen, P., & Ceci, S. J. (1996). *The state of Americans.* New York: Free Press.

Bronowski, J. (1956). *Science and human values.* New York: Harper & Row.

Bronowski, J. (1973). *The ascent of man.* Boston: Little, Brown.

Bronowski, J. (1977). *A sense of the future.* Cambridge, MA: MIT Press.

Brown, A. (1972). A rehearsal deficit in retardates' continuous short-term memory: Keeping track of variables that have few or many states. *Psychonomic Science, 29,* 373–376.

Brown, A. (1981). Metacognition: The development of selective attention strategies for learning from texts. In M. Kamil (Ed.), *30th yearbook of the National Reading Conference* (pp. 21–43). Clemson, NC: National Reading Conference.

Brown, G. D. A. (1987). Resolving inconsistency: A computational model of word naming. *Journal of Memory and Language, 26,* 1–23.

Brown, G. D. A., Loosemore, R., & Watson, F. (1993). Normal and dyslexic spelling: A connectionist approach. Unpublished manuscript.

Brown, G. D. A. (1984). A frequency count of 190,000 words in the London–Lund Corpus of English Conversation. *Behavior Research Methods, Instruments, and Computers, 16,* 502–532.

Brown, G. D. A. (1997). Connectionism, phonology, reading, and regularity in developmental dyslexia. *Brain and Language, 59,* 207–235.

Brown, G. D. A., & Deavers, R. P. (1999). Units of analysis in nonword reading: Evidence from children and adults. *Journal of Experimental Child Psychology, 73,* 208–242.

Brown, G. D. A., & Watson, F. L. (1991). Reading development in dyslexia: A connectionist approach. In M. Snowling & M. Thomson (Eds.), *Dyslexia: Integrating theory and practice* (pp. 165–182). London: Whurr.

Brown, I. S., & Felton, R. H. (1990). Effects of instruction on beginning reading skills in children at risk for reading disability. *Reading and Writing: An Interdisciplinary Journal, 2,* 223–241.

Bruce, D. (1964). The analysis of word sounds by young children. *British Journal of Educational Psychology, 34,* 158–170.

Bruck, M. (1988). The word recognition and spelling of dyslexic children. *Reading Research Quarterly, 23,* 51–69.

Bruck, M. (1990). Word-recognition skills of adults with childhood diagnoses of dyslexia. *Developmental Psychology, 26,* 439–454.

Bruck, M. (1992). Persistence of dyslexics' phonological awareness deficits. *Developmental Psychology, 28,* 874–886.

Bruck, M., & Treiman, R. (1990). Phonological awareness and spelling in normal children and dyslexics: The case of initial consonant clusters. *Journal of Experimental Child Psychology, 50,* 156–178.

Bruck, M., & Waters, G. (1988). An analysis of the spelling errors of children who differ in their reading and spelling skills. *Applied Psycholinguistics, 9,* 77–92.

Bruck, M., & Waters, G. (1990). An analysis of the component reading and spelling skills of good readers–good spellers, good readers–poor spellers, and poor readers–poor spellers. In T. Carr & B. A. Levy (Eds.), *Reading and its development: Component skills approaches* (pp. 161–206). New York: Academic Press.

Bryan, T. (1974). Learning disabilities: A new stereotype. *Journal of Learning Disabilities, 7,* 46–51.

Bryant, P. E., & Bradley, L. (1985). *Children's reading problems.* Oxford, England: Blackwell.

Bryant, P. E., Bradley, L., Maclean, M., & Crossland, D. (1989). Nursery rhymes, phonological skills, and reading. *Journal of Child Language, 16,* 407–428.

Bryant, P. E., & Goswami, U. (1986). Strengths and weaknesses of the reading level design: A comment on Backman, Mamen, and Ferguson. *Psychological Bulletin, 100,* 101–103.

Bryant, P. E., & Impey, L. (1986). The similarities between normal readers and developmental and acquired dyslexics. *Cognition, 24,* 121–137.

Burns, M. S., Griffin, P., & Snow, C. E. (Eds.). (1999). *Starting out right: A guide to promoting children's reading success.* Washington, DC: National Academy Press.

Burt, C. D. B., & Kemp, S. (1991). Retrospective duration estimation of public events. *Memory and Cognition, 19,* 252–262.

Butkowsky, S., & Willows, D. (1980). Cognitive-motivational characteristics of children varying in reading ability: Evidence for learned helplessness in poor readers. *Journal of Educational Psychology, 72,* 408–422.

Butler, B., & Hains, S. (1979). Individual differences in word recognition latency. *Memory and Cognition, 7,* 68–76.

Byrne, B. (1981). Deficient syntactic control in poor readers: Is a weak phonetic memory code responsible? *Applied Psycholinguistics, 2,* 201–212.

Byrne, B. (1984). On teaching articulatory phonetics via an orthography. *Memory and Cognition, 12,* 181–189.

Byrne, B. (1986, March). *Learning to read the first few items: Evidence of a nonanalytic acquisition procedure in adults and children.* Paper presented at the Conference on the Process of Reading Acquisition, Center for Cognitive Science, University of Texas, Austin.

Byrne, B. (1992). Studies in the acquisition procedure for reading: Rationale, hypotheses, and data. In P. B. Gough, L. C. Ehri, & R. Treiman (Eds.), *Reading acquisition* (pp. 1–34). Hillsdale, NJ: Erlbaum.

Byrne, B. (1998). *The foundation of literacy: The child's acquisition of the alphabetic principle.* Hove, England: Psychology Press.

Byrne, B., & Fielding-Barnsley, R. (1991). Evaluation of a program to teach phonemic awareness to young children. *Journal of Educational Psychology, 83,* 451–455.

Byrne, B., & Fielding-Barnsley, R. (1993). Evaluation of a program to teach phonemic awareness to young children: A 1-year follow-up. *Journal of Educational Psychology, 85,* 104–111.

Byrne, B., & Liberman, A. M. (1999). Meaninglessness, productivity, and reading: Some observations about the relation between the alphabet and speech. In J. Oakhill & R. Beard (Eds.), *Reading development and the teaching of reading* (pp. 157–173). Oxford, England: Blackwell.

Byrne, B., & Shea, P. (1979). Semantic and phonetic memory codes in beginning readers. *Memory and Cognition, 7,* 333–338.

Cahan, S., & Cohen, N. (1989). Age versus schooling effects on intelligence development. *Child Development, 60,* 1239–1249.

Calfee, R. (1982). Literacy and illiteracy: Teaching the nonreader to survive in the modern world. *Annals of Dyslexia, 32,* 71–91.

Calfee, R. (1983). Review of *Dyslexia: Theory and research. Applied Psycholinguistics, 4,* 69–79.

Calfee, R., Chapman, R., & Venezky, R. (1972). How a child needs to think to learn to read. In L. Gregg (Ed.), *Cognition in learning and memory* (pp. 139–182). New York: Wiley.

Calfee, R., Lindamood, P., & Lindamood, C. (1973). Acoustic–phonetic skills and reading—Kindergarten through twelfth grade. *Journal of Educational Psychology, 64,* 293–298.

California Reading Initiative. (1999). *Read all about it! Readings to inform the profession.* Sacramento: California State Board of Education.

Campbell, J., Voelkl, K., & Donahue, P. (1997). *NAEP 1996 trends in academic progress.* Washington, DC : National Center for Education Statistics.

Campione, J., & Brown, A. (1978). Toward a theory of intelligence: Contributions from research with retarded children. *Intelligence, 2,* 279–304.

Cardon, L. R., Smith, S., Fulker, D., Kimberling, W., Pennington, B., & DeFries, J. (1994). Quantitative trait locus for reading disability on chromosome 6. *Science, 266,* 276–279.

Carlisle, J. F. (1989). The use of the sentence verification technique in diagnostic assessment of listening and reading comprehension. *Learning Disabilities Research,* *5,* 33–44.

Carp, F. M., & Carp, A. (1981). The validity, reliability, and generalizability of diary data. *Experimental Aging Research, 7,* 281–296.

Carr, T. H. (1981). Building theories of reading ability: On the relation between individual differences in cognitive skills and reading comprehension. *Cognition, 9,* 73–114.

Carr, T. H. (1992). Automaticity and cognitive anatomy: Is word recognition "automatic"? *American Journal of Psychology, 105,* 201–237.

Carr, T. H., Brown, T. L., & Vavrus, L. G. (1985). Using component skills analysis to integrate findings on reading development. In T. H. Carr (Ed.), *The development of reading skills* (pp. 95–108). San Francisco: Josey-Bass.

Carr, T. H., & Levy, B. A, (Eds.). (1990). *Reading and its development: Component skills approaches.* San Diego, CA: Academic Press.

Carr, T. H., & Pollatsek, A. (1985). Recognizing printed words: A look at current models. In D. Besner, T. G. Waller, & G. E. MacKinnon (Eds.), *Reading research: Advances in theory and practice* (Vol. 5, pp. 1–82). Orlando, FL: Academic Press.

Carroll, J. B. (1972). Defining language comprehension: Some speculations. In J. B. T. Carroll & R. Freedle (Eds.), *Language, comprehension, and the acquisition of knowledge* (pp. 1–29). Washington, DC: Winston & Sons.

Carroll, J. B. (1977). Developmental parameters of reading comprehension. In J. T. Guthrie (Ed.), *Cognition, curriculum, and comprehension* (pp. 1–15). Newark, DE: IRA.

Carroll, J. B., Davies, P., & Richman, B. (1971). *Word frequency book.* Boston: Houghton Mifflin.

Carver, R. P. (1981). *Reading comprehension and reading theory.* Springfield, IL: Thomas.

Carver, R. P. (1990). Intelligence and reading ability in grades 2–12. *Intelligence, 14,* 449–455.

Castles, A., & Coltheart, M. (1993). Varieties of developmental dyslexia. *Cognition, 47,* 149–180.

Castles, A., & Coltheart, M. (1996). Cognitive correlates of developmental surface dyslexia: A single case study. *Cognitive Neuropsychology, 13,* 25–50.

Castles, A., Datta, H., Gayan, J., & Olson, R. K. (1999). Varieties of developmental reading disorder: Genetic and environmental influences. *Journal of Experimental Child Psychology, 72,* 73–94.

Catts, H. W. (1986). Speech production/phonological deficits in reading-disordered children. *Journal of Learning Disabilities, 19,* 504–508.

Catts, H. W. (1991). Early identification of reading disabilities. *Topics in Language Disorders, 12*(1), 1–16.

Catts, H. W., Fey, M. E., Zhang, X., & Tomblin, J. B. (1999). Language basis of reading and reading disabilities: Evidence from a longitudinal investigation. *Scientific Studies of Reading, 3,* 331–361.

Catts, H. W., & Kamhi, A. G. (1999). *Language and reading disabilities.* Boston: Allyn & Bacon.

Catts, H. W., & Vartianen, T. (1993). *Sounds abound: Listening, rhyming, and reading.* East Moline, IL: LinguiSystems.

Ceci, S. J. (1986). *Handbook of cognitive, social, and neuropsychological aspects of learning disabilities* (Vol. 1). Hillsdale, NJ: Erlbaum.

Ceci, S. J. (1990). *On intelligence . . . more or less: A bio-ecological treatise on intellectual development.* Englewood Cliffs, NJ: Prentice-Hall.

Ceci, S. J. (1991). How much does schooling influence general intelligence and its cognitive components? A reassessment of the evidence. *Developmental Psychology, 27,* 703–722.

Ceci, S. J. (1993). Contextual trends in intellectual development. *Developmental Review, 13,* 403–435.

Ceci, S. J., & Liker, J. K. (1986). A day at the races: A study of IQ, expertise, and cognitive complexity. *Journal of Experimental Psychology: General, 115,* 255–266.

Ceponiene, R., Service, E., Kurjenluoma, S., Cheour, M., & Naatanen, R. (1999). Children's performance on pseudoword repetition depends on auditory trace quality: Evidence from event-related potentials. *Developmental Psychology, 35,* 709–720.

Chafe, W., & Danielewicz, J. (1987). Properties of spoken and written language. In R. Horowitz & S. J. Samuels (Eds.), *Comprehending oral and written language* (pp. 83–113). San Diego, CA: Academic Press.

Chall, J. S. (1967). *Learning to read: The great debate.* New York: McGraw-Hill.

Chall, J. S. (1983a). *Learning to read: The Great Debate* (2nd ed.). New York: McGraw-Hill.

Chall, J. S. (1983b). *Stages of reading development.* New York: McGraw-Hill.

Chall, J. S. (1989). Learning to read: The Great Debate 20 years later. *Phi Delta Kappan, 70*(7), 521–538.

Chall, J. S., Jacobs, V. A., & Baldwin, L. E. (1990). *The reading crisis: Why poor children fall behind.* Cambridge, MA: Harvard University Press.

Chall, J. S., Roswell, F., & Blumenthal, S. (1963). Auditory blending ability: A factor in success in beginning reading. *Reading Teacher, 17,* 113–118.

Chapman, L. J., Chapman, J. P., Curran, T., & Miller, M. (1994). Do children and the elderly show heightened semantic priming? How to answer the question. *Developmental Review, 14,* 159–185.

Chard, D. J., & Osborn, J. (1999). Phonics and word recognition in early reading programs: Guidelines for accessibility. *Learning Disabilities Research and Practice, 14,* 107–117.

Chateau, D., & Jared, D. (2000). Exposure to print and word recognition processes. *Memory and Cognition, 28,* 143–153.

Chen, C., & Stevenson, H. W. (1989). Homework: A cross-cultural examination. *Child Development, 60,* 551–561.

Chen, R. S., & Vellutino, F. R. (1997). Prediction of reading ability: A cross-validation study of the simple view of reading. *Journal of Literacy Research, 29,* 1–24.

Chi, M., Glaser, R., & Rees, E. (1982). Expertise in problem solving. In R. Sternberg (Ed.), *Advances in the psychology of human intelligence* (Vol. 1, pp. 7–75). Hillsdale, NJ: Erlbaum.

Chi, M. T. H. (1985). Changing conception of sources of memory development. *Human Development, 28,* 50–56.

Chi, M. T. H., Hutchinson, J. E., & Robin, A. F. (1989). How inferences about novel domain-related concepts can be constrained by structured knowledge. *Merrill-Palmer Quarterly, 35,* 27–62.

Chiappe, P., Stringer, R., Siegel, L. S., & Stanovich, K. E. (in press). Why the timing deficit does not explain reading disability in adults. *Reading and Writing: An Interdisciplinary Journal.*

Chomsky, C. (1972). Stages in language development and reading exposure. *Harvard Educational Review, 42,* 1–33.

Churchland, P. M. (1979). *Scientific realism and the plasticity of mind.* Cambridge, England: Cambridge University Press.

Churchland, P. M. (1988). *Matter and consciousness* (2nd ed.). Cambridge, MA: MIT Press.

Churchland, P. M., & Churchland, P. S. (1998). *On the contrary: Critical essays, 1987–1997.* Cambridge, MA: MIT Press.

Churchland, P. S. (1983). Consciousness: The transmutation of a concept. *Pacific Philosophical Quarterly, 64,* 80–95.

Churchland, P. S. (1986). *Neurophilosophy: Toward a unified science of the mind/brain.* Cambridge, MA: MIT Press.

Chwilla, D. J., Hagoort, P., & Brown, C. M. (1998). The mechanism underlying backward priming in a lexical decision task: Spreading activation versus semantic matching. *Quarterly Journal of Experimental Psychology, 51A,* 531–560.

Cipielewski, J., & Stanovich, K. E. (1992). Predicting growth in reading ability from children's exposure to print. *Journal of Experimental Child Psychology, 54,* 74–89.

Claxton, G. (1980). Cognitive psychology: A suitable case for what sort of treatment? In G. Claxton (Ed.), *Cognitive psychology: New directions* (pp. 1–25). London: Routledge & Kegan Paul.

Cohen, A. S. (1974–1975). Oral reading errors of first-grade children taught by a code emphasis approach. *Reading Research Quarterly, 10,* 615–650.

Cohen, J., & Cohen, P. (1975). *Applied multiple regression/correlation analysis for the behavioral sciences.* Hillsdale, NJ: Erlbaum.

Cohen, J., & Cohen, P. (1983). *Applied multiple regression/correlation analysis for the behavioral sciences* (2nd ed.). Hillsdale, NJ: Erlbaum.

Cohen, R. L. (1982). Individual differences in short-term memory. In N. Ellis (Ed.), *International review of research in mental retardation* (Vol. 11, pp. 43–77). New York: Academic Press.

Cohen, R. L., & Netley, C. (1981). Short-term memory deficits in reading disabled children, in the absence of opportunity for rehearsal strategies. *Intelligence, 5,* 69–76.

Cohen, R. L., Netley, C., & Clark, M. A. (1984). On the generality of the short-term memory/reading ability relationship. *Journal of Learning Disabilities, 17,* 218–221.

Cohen, S. (1976). The fuzziness and the flab: Some solutions to research problems in learning disabilities. *Journal of Special Education, 10,* 129–136.

Cohen, S., Glass, D. C., & Singer, J. E. (1973). Apartment noise, auditory discrimination, and reading ability in children. *Journal of Experimental Social Psychology, 9,* 407–422.

Cole, K. N., Dale, P. S., & Mills, P. E. (1990). Defining language delay in young children by cognitive referencing: Are we saying more than we know? *Applied Psycholinguistics, 11,* 291–302.

Coleman, J. S., Hoffer, T., & Kilgore, S. (1982). *High school achievement.* New York: Basic Books.

Coles, G. S. (1978). The learning-disabilities test battery: Empirical and social issues. *Harvard Educational Review, 48,* 313–340.

Coles, G. S. (1987). *The learning mystique.* New York: Pantheon Books.

Collins, A. M., & Loftus, E. F. (1975). A spreading-activation theory of semantic processing. *Psychological Review, 82,* 407–428.

Coltheart, M. (1978). Lexical access in simple reading tasks. In G. Underwood (Ed.), *Strategies of information processing* (pp. 151–216). London: Academic Press.

Coltheart, M., Besner, D., Jonasson, J. T., & Davelaar, E. (1979). Phonolgical encoding in the lexical decision task. *Quarterly Journal of Experimental Psychology, 31,* 489–508.

Coltheart, M., Curtis, B., Atkins, P., & Haller, M. (1993). Models of reading aloud: Dual-route and parallel-distributed-processing approaches. *Psychological Review, 100,* 589–608.

Coltheart, M., & Jackson, N. E. (1998). Defining dyslexia. *Child Psychology and Psychiatry Review, 3,* 12–16.

Coltheart, M., Masterson, J., Byng, S., Prior, M., & Riddich, J. (1983). Surface dyslexia. *Quarterly Journal of Experimental Psychology, 35A,* 469–485.

Coltheart, M., Patterson, K., & Marshall, J. C. (1980). *Deep dyslexia.* London: Routledge & Kegan Paul.

Coltheart, M., & Rastle, K. (1994). Serial processing in reading aloud: Evidence for dual-route models of reading. *Journal of Experimental Psychology: Human Perception and Performance, 20,* 1197–1211.

Comstock, G., & Paik, H. (1991). *Television and the American child.* San Diego, CA: Academic Press.

Conners, F. A., & Olson, R. K. (1990). Reading comprehension in dyslexic and normal readers: A component-skills analysis. In D. A. Balota, G. B. Flores d'Arcais, & K. Rayner (Eds.), *Comprehension processes in reading* (pp. 557–579). Hillsdale, NJ: Erlbaum.

Consortium on Reading Excellence. (1999). *Reading research anthology: The why? of reading instruction.* Novato, CA: Arena Press.

Cooksey, R. W., & Freebody, P. (1987). Aspects of a computer-managed test of children's reading vocabulary: Reliability, validity, and characterization of knowledge. *Reading Psychology, 8,* 103–118.

Coomber, J. E. (1972, September). *A psycholinguistic analysis of oral reading errors made by good, average, and poor readers* (Tech. Rep. No. 232). Madison: University of Wisconsin, Wisconsin Research and Development Center.

Cornelissen, P. L., Hansen, P. C., Bradley, L., & Stein, J. F. (1996). Analysis of perceptual confusions between nine sets of constant-vowel sounds in normal and dyslexic adults. *Cognition, 59,* 275–306.

Corson, D. (1985). *The lexical bar.* Oxford, England: Pergamon.

Corson, D. (1995). *Using English words.* Boston: Kluwer Academic.

Cossu, G., & Marshall, J. C. (1986). Theoretical implications of the hyperlexia syndrome: Two new Italian cases. *Cortex, 22,* 579–589.

Cossu, G., Shankweiler, D., Liberman, I. Y., Katz, L., & Tola, G. (1988). Awareness of phonological segments and reading ability in Italian children. *Applied Psycholinguistics, 9,* 1–16.

Crijnen, A., Feehan, M., & Kellman, S. (1998). The course and malleability of reading achievement in elementary school: The application of growth curve modeling in the evaluation of a mastery learning intervention. *Learning and Individual Differences, 10,* 137–157.

Critchley, M. (1970). *The dyslexic child.* London: William Heinemann Medical Books.

Cromer, W. (1970). The difference model: A new explanation for some reading difficulties. *Journal of Educational Psychology, 61,* 471–483.

Cronbach, L. J. (1984). *Essentials of psychological testing* (4th ed.). New York: Harper & Row.

Crowder, R. G. (1984). Is it just reading? *Developmental Review, 4,* 48–61.

CTB/McGraw-Hill. (1981). *Listening test.* Monterey, CA: Author.

Cunningham, A. E. (1990). Explicit versus implicit instruction in phonemic awareness. *Journal of Experimental Child Psychology, 50,* 429–444.

Cunningham, A. E., & Stanovich, K. E. (1990). Assessing print exposure and orthographic processing skill in children: A quick measure of reading experience. *Journal of Educational Psychology, 82,* 733–740.

Cunningham, A. E., & Stanovich, K. E. (1991). Tracking the unique effects of print exposure in children: Associations with vocabulary, general knowledge, and spelling. *Journal of Educational Psychology, 83,* 264–274.

Cunningham, A. E., & Stanovich, K. E. (1993). Children's literacy environments and early word recognition skills. *Reading and Writing: An Interdisciplinary Journal, 5,* 193–204.

Cunningham, A. E., & Stanovich, K. E. (1997). Early reading acquisition and its relation to reading experience and ability ten years later. *Developmental Psychology, 33,* 934–945.

Cunningham, A. E., Stanovich, K. E., & Wilson, M. R. (1990). Cognitive variation in adult college students differing in reading ability. In T. Carr & B. A. Levy (Eds.), *Reading and its development: Component skills approaches* (pp. 129–159). San Diego, CA: Academic Press.

Cunningham, J. W., & Cunningham, P. M. (1991). Review of Handbook of Reading Research (Vol. 2). *Journal of Reading Behavior, 23,* 365–370.

Cunningham, P. M., Moore, S. A., Cunningham, J. W., & Moore, D. W. (1995). *Phonics they use: Words for reading and writing.* New York: HarperCollins.

Curtis, M. (1980). Development of components of reading skill. *Journal of Educational Psychology, 72,* 656–669.

Damasio, A. R. (1994). *Descartes' error.* New York: Putnam.

Daneman, M., & Carpenter, P. A. (1980). Individual differences in working memory and reading. *Journal of Verbal Learning and Verbal Behavior, 19,* 450–466.

Daneman, M., & Tardif, T. (1987). Working memory and reading skill re-examined. In M. Coltheart (Ed.), *Attention and performance* (Vol. 12, pp. 491–508). London: Erlbaum.

Danks, J. H. (1978). Models of language comprehension. *Polish Psychological Bulletin, 9,* 183–192.

Darlington, R. (1990). *Regression and linear models.* New York: McGraw-Hill.

Das, J. P., Mensink, D., & Mishra, R. K. (1990). Cognitive processes separating good and poor readers when IQ is covaried. *Learning and Individual Differences, 2,* 423–436.

Dasenbrock, R. W. (1995). Truth and methods. *College English, 57,* 546–561.

Davidson, D. (1984). On the very idea of a conceptual scheme. In D. Davidson (Ed.), *Inquiries into truth and interpretation* (pp. 183–198). Oxford, England: Oxford University Press.

Davidson, J. E. (1990). Intelligence recreated. *Educational Psychologist, 25,* 337–354.

Dawes, R. M. (1988). *Rational choice in an uncertain world*. San Diego, CA: Harcourt Brace Jovanovich.

Dawkins, R. (1976/1989). *The selfish gene* (2nd ed.). New York: Oxford University Press.

Dawkins, R. (1998). *Unweaving the rainbow*. Boston: Houghton Mifflin.

de Groot, I., & Bus, A. (1995). *Boekenpret voor baby's*. Leiden: Boekenpret.

de Sousa, R. (1987). *The rationality of emotion*. Cambridge, MA: MIT Press.

Deegan, D. H. (1995). The necessity of debate: A comment on commentaries. *Reading Teacher, 48(8),* 688–695.

Denckla, M. B., & Rudel, R. G. (1976). Rapid "automatized" naming (R. A. N.): Dyslexia differentiated from other learning disabilities. *Neuropsychologia, 14,* 471–479.

Dennett, D. (1969). *Content and consciousness*. London: Routledge & Kegan Paul.

Dennett, D. (1978). *Brainstorms*. Cambridge, MA: MIT Press.

Dennett, D. (1987). *The intentional stance*. Cambridge, MA: MIT Press.

Dennett, D. (1988). When philosophers encounter artificial intelligence. *Daedalus, 117,* 284–295.

Dennett, D. (1991). *Consciousness explained*. Boston: Little, Brown.

Dennett, D. (1998). *Brainchildren: Essays on designing minds*. Cambridge, MA: MIT Press.

Denny, J. P. (1991). Rational thought in oral culture and literate decontextualization. In D. R. Olson & N. Torrance (Eds.), *Literacy and orality* (pp. 66–89). Cambridge, England: Cambridge University Press.

Desoto, J., & Desoto, C. (1983). Relationship of reading achievement to verbal processing abilities. *Journal of Educational Psychology, 75,* 116–127.

Detterman, D. (1982). Does "g" exist? *Intelligence, 6,* 99–108.

Devitt, M. (1991). *Realism and truth* (2nd ed.). Cambridge, MA: Blackwell.

Diener, C., & Dweck, C. (1978). An analysis of learned helplessness: Continuous changes in performance, strategy, and achievement cognitions following failure. *Journal of Personality and Social Psychology, 36,* 451–462.

DiVesta, F. J., Hayward, K. G., & Orlando, V. P. (1979). Developmental trends in monitoring text for comprehension. *Child Development, 50,* 97–105.

Doehring, D. G. (1976). Acquisition of rapid reading responses. *Monographs of the Society for Research in Child Development, 41*(2, Serial No. 165).

Doehring, D. G. (1978). The tangled web of behavioral research on developmental dyslexia. In A. L. Benton & D. Pearl (Eds.), *Dyslexia* (pp. 123–135). New York: Oxford University Press.

Doehring, D. G., Trites, R. L., Patel, P. G., & Fiedorowicz, C. A. M. (1981). *Reading disabilities: The interaction of reading, language, and neuropsychological deficits*. New York: Academic Press.

Donaldson, M. (1978). *Children's minds*. London: Fontana/Collins.

Donaldson, M. (1984). Speech and writing and modes of learning. In H. Goelman, A. Oberg, & F. Smith (Eds.), *Awakening to literacy* (pp. 174–184). London: Heinemann.

Donaldson, M. (1993). *Human minds: An exploration*. New York: Viking Penguin.

Donaldson, M., & Reid, J. (1982). Language skills and reading: A developmental perspective. In A. Hendry (Ed.), *Teaching reading: The key issues* (pp. 25–41). London: Heinemann.

Doris, J. (1986). Learning disabilities. In S. J. Ceci (Ed.), *Handbook of cognitive, social, and neuropsychological aspects of learning disabilities* (Vol. 1, pp. 3–53). Hillsdale, NJ: Erlbaum.

Downing, J. (1980). Learning to read with understanding. In C. M. McCullough (Ed.), *Persistent problems in reading education* (pp. 163–178). Newark, DE: International Reading Association.

Duane, D. D. (1983). Neurobiological correlates of reading disorders. *Journal of Educational Research, 77,* 5–15.

Duane, D. D., & Gray, D. B. (Eds.). (1991). *The reading brain: The biological basis of dyslexia.* Parkton, MD: York Press.

Duffy, G. G., Roehler, L. R., & Mason, J. (1984). *Comprehension instruction.* New York: Longman.

Dunn, L. M., & Dunn, L. M. (1981). *Peabody Picture Vocabulary Test—Revised.* Circle Pines, MN: American Guidance Service.

Dunn, L. M., & Markwardt, F. (1970). *Peabody Individual Achievement Test: Manual.* Circle Pines, MN: American Guidance Service.

Dunn, L. M., & Markwardt, F. (1979). *Peabody Individual Achievement Test.* Circle Pines, MN: American Guidance Service.

Durgunoglu, A. Y. (1988). Repetition, semantic priming, and stimulus quality: Implications for the interactive–compensatory model. *Journal of Experimental Psychology: Learning, Memory, and Cognition, 14,* 590–603.

Durkin, D. (1982). *A study of poor black children who are successful readers* (Reading Education Report No. 33). Urbana-Champaign: University of Illinois, Center for the Study of Reading.

Durrell, D. D. (1969). Listening comprehension versus reading comprehension. *Journal of Reading, 12,* 455–460.

Durrell, D. D., & Hayes, M. (1969). *Durrell listening-reading series.* New York: Psychological Corporation.

Dyer, F. N. (1973). The Stroop phenomenon and its use in the study of perceptual, cognitive, and response processes. *Memory and Cognition, 1,* 106–120.

Echols, L. D., West, R. F., Stanovich, K. E., & Zehr, K. S. (1996). Using children's literacy activities to predict growth in verbal cognitive skills: A longitudinal investigation. *Journal of Educational Psychology, 88,* 296–304.

Edwards, J., & Lahey, M. (1998). Nonword repetitions of children with specific language impairment: Exploration of some explanations for their inaccuracies. *Applied Psycholinguistics, 19,* 279–309.

Ehri, L. C. (1977). Do adjectives and functors interfere as much as nouns in naming pictures? *Child Development, 48,* 697–701.

Ehri, L. C. (1979). Linguistic insight: Threshold of reading acquisition. In T. Waller & G. MacKinnon (Eds.), *Reading research: Advances in research and theory* (Vol. 1, pp. 63–114). New York: Academic Press.

Ehri, L. C. (1980). The development of orthographic images. In U. Frith (Ed.), *Cognitive processes in spelling* (pp. 311–338). London: Academic Press.

Ehri, L. C. (1984). How orthography alters spoken language competencies in children learning to read and spell. In J. Downing & R. Valtin (Eds.), *Language awareness and learning to read* (pp. 119–147). New York: Springer-Verlag.

Ehri, L. C. (1985). Effects of printed language acquisition on speech. In D. Olson, N. Torrance, & A. Hildyard (Eds.), *Literacy, language, and learning* (pp. 333–367). Cambridge, England: Cambridge University Press.

Ehri, L. C. (1987). Learning to read and spell words. *Journal of Reading Behavior, 19*, 5–31.

Ehri, L. C. (1989). The development of spelling knowledge and its role in reading acquisition and reading disability. *Journal of Learning Disabilities, 22*, 356–365.

Ehri, L. C. (1992). Reconceptualizing the development of sight word reading and its relationship to recoding. In P. B. Gough, L. C. Ehri, & R. Treiman (Eds.), *Reading acquisition* (pp. 107–143). Hillsdale, NJ: Erlbaum.

Ehri, L. C. (1995). Phases of development in learning to read words by sight. *Journal of Research in Reading, 18*, 116–125.

Ehri, L. C. (1996). Researching how children learn to read: Controversies in science are not like controversies in practice. In G. Brannigan (Ed.), *The enlightened educator: Research adventures in the schools* (pp. 178–204). New York: McGraw-Hill.

Ehri, L. C. (1997). Sight word learning in normal readers and dyslexia. In B. Blachman (Ed.), *Foundations of reading acquisition and dyslexia: Implications for early intervention* (pp. 163–189). Mahweh, NJ: Erlbaum.

Ehri, L. C. (1998). Research on learning to read and spell: A personal–historical perspective. *Scientific Studies of Reading, 2*, 97–114.

Ehri, L. C., & Saltmarsh, J. (1995). Beginning readers outperform older disabled readers in learning to read words by sight. *Reading and Writing: An Interdisciplinary Journal, 7*, 295–326.

Ehri, L. C., & Soffer, A. G. (1999). Graphophonemic awareness: Development in elementary students. *Scientific Studies of Reading, 3*, 1–30.

Ehri, L. C., & Wilce, L. S. (1979). Does word training increase or decrease interference in a Stroop task? *Journal of Experimental Child Psychology, 27*, 352–364.

Ehri, L. C., & Wilce, L. S. (1985). Movement into reading: Is the first stage of printed word learning visual or phonetic? *Reading Research Quarterly, 20*, 163–179.

Ehri, L. C., & Wilce, L. S. (1987). Cipher versus cue reading: An experiment in decoding acquisition. *Journal of Educational Psychology, 79*, 3–13.

Ehri, L. C., Wilce, L. S., & Taylor, B. B. (1987). Children's categorization of short vowels in words and the influence of spellings. *Merrill-Palmer Quarterly, 33*, 393–421.

Ehrlich, S. (1981). Children's word recognition in prose context. *Visible Language, 15*, 219–244.

Ehrlich, S., & Rayner, K. (1981). Contextual effects on word perception and eye movements during reading. *Journal of Verbal Learning and Verbal Behavior, 20*, 641–655.

Eisenberg, L. (1978). Definitions of dyslexia: Their consequences for research and policy. In A. L. Benton & D. Pearl (Eds.), *Dyslexia* (pp. 29–42). New York: Oxford University Press.

Eisenberg, L. (1979). Reading disorders: Strategies for recognition and management. *Bulletin of the Orton Society, 29*, 39–55.

Eisenstadt, M., & Kareev, Y. (1975). Aspects of human problem solving: The use of internal representations. In D. A. Norman & D. E. Rumelhart (Eds.), *Explorations in cognition* (pp. 308–346). San Francisco: Freeman.

Elbro, C. (1996). Early linguistic abilities and reading development: A review and a hypothesis. *Reading and Writing: An Interdisciplinary Journal, 8*, 453–485.

Elbro, C., Borstrom, I., & Peterson, D. K. (1998). Predicting dyslexia from kindergarten: The importance of distinctness of phonological representations of lexical items. *Reading Research Quarterly, 33*, 36–60.

Elbro, C., Nielson, I., & Petersen, D. (1994). Dyslexia in adults: Evidence for deficits in non-word reading and in the phonological representation of lexical items. *Annals of Dyslexia, 44,* 205–226.

Ellis, A. W. (1979). Developmental and acquired dyslexia: Some observations on Jorm. *Cognition, 7,* 413–420.

Ellis, A. W. (1984). *Reading, writing, and dyslexia: A cognitive analysis.* Hillsdale, NJ: Erlbaum.

Ellis, A. W. (1985). The cognitive neuropsychology of developmental (and acquired) dyslexia: A critical survey. *Cognitive Neuropsychology, 2,* 169–205.

Ellis, A. W., McDougall, S., & Monk, A. F. (1996). Are dyslexics different? 2. Individual differences among dyslexics, reading age controls, poor readers, and precocious readers. *Dyslexia, 2,* 59–68.

Ellis, N., & Large, B. (1987). The development of reading: As you seek so shall you find. *British Journal of Psychology, 78,* 1–28.

Enchin, H. (1992, December 29). Parents question results of state-run school system. *Toronto Globe and Mail,* p. 1.

Ennis, P. H. (1965). *Adult book reading in the United States* (National Opinion Research Center Report No. 105). Chicago: University of Chicago Press.

Erickson, F. (1984). School literacy, reasoning, and civility: An anthropologist's perspective. *Review of Educational Research, 54,* 525–546.

Estes, T. H. (1971). A scale to measure attitudes toward reading. *Journal of Reading, 15,* 135–138.

Evans, M. A., & Carr, T. H. (1985). Cognitive abilities, conditions of learning, and the early development of reading skill. *Reading Research Quarterly, 20,* 327–350.

Farmer, M., & Klein, R. (1995). The evidence for a temporal processing deficit linked to dyslexia: A review. *Psychonomic Bulletin and Review, 2,* 460–493.

Feitelson, D., & Goldstein, Z. (1986). Patterns of book ownership and reading to young children in Israeli school-oriented and nonschool-oriented families. *Reading Teacher, 39,* 924–930.

Feldman, C. F. (1991). Oral metalanguage. In D. R. Olson & N. Torrance (Eds.), *Literacy and orality* (pp. 47–65). Cambridge, England: Cambridge University Press.

Felton, R. H. (1993). Effects of instruction on the decoding skills of children with phonological-processing problems. *Journal of Learning Disabilities, 26,* 583–589.

Felton, R. H., & Wood, F. B. (1992). A reading level match study of nonword reading skills in poor readers with varying IQ. *Journal of Learning Disabilities, 25,* 318–326.

Ferreira, F., & Morrison, F. J. (1994). Children's metalinguistic knowledge of syntactic constituents: Effects of age and schooling. *Developmental Psychology, 30,* 663–678.

Fielding, L., Wilson, P., & Anderson, R. (1986). A new focus on free reading: The role of trade books in reading instruction. In T. Raphael & R. Reynolds (Eds.), *The contexts of school-based literacy* (pp. 1496). New York: Longman.

Fincher-Kiefer, R., Post, T. A., Greene, T. R., & Voss, J. F. (1988). On the role of prior knowledge and task demands in the processing of text. *Journal of Memory and Language, 27,* 416–428.

Firth, I. (1972). *Components of reading disability.* Unpublished doctoral dissertation, University of New South Wales.

Fischer, F. W., Shankweiler, D., & Liberman, I. Y. (1985). Spelling proficiency and sensitivity to word structure. *Journal of Memory and Language, 24,* 423–441.

Fischhoff, B. (1977). Perceived informativeness of facts. *Journal of Experimental Psychology: Human Perception and Performance, 3,* 349–358.

Fischler, I. (1977). Associative facilitation without expectancy in a lexical decision task. *Journal of Experimental Psychology: Human Perception and Performance, 3,* 18–26.

Fischler, I., & Bloom, P. A. (1979). Automatic and attentional processes in the effects of sentence contexts on word recognition. *Journal of Verbal Learning and Verbal Behavior, 18,* 1–20.

Fischler, I., & Goodman, G. O. (1978). Latency of associative activation in memory. *Journal of Experimental Psychology: Human Perception and Performance, 4,* 455–470.

Fisk, A. D., Derrick, W. L., & Schneider, W. (1986–1987). A methodological assessment and evaluation of dual-task paradigms. *Current Psychological Research and Reviews, 5,* 315–327.

Fleisher, L. S., Jenkins, J. R., & Pany, D. (1979). Effects on poor readers' comprehension of training in rapid decoding. *Reading Research Quarterly, 15,* 30–48.

Fletcher, J. M. (1981). Linguistic factors in reading acquisition. In F. Pirozzolo & M. Wittrock (Eds.), *Neuropsychology and cognitive processes in reading* (pp. 261–294). New York: Academic Press.

Fletcher, J. M. (1992). The validity of distinguishing children with language and learning disabilities according to discrepancies with IQ: Introduction to the Special Series. *Journal of Learning Disabilities, 25,* 546–548.

Fletcher, J. M., Espy, K., Francis, D., Davidson, K., Rourke, B., & Shaywitz, S. (1989). Comparisons of cutoff and regression-based definitions of reading disabilities. *Journal of Learning Disabilities, 22,* 334–338.

Fletcher, J. M., Francis, D. J., Rourke, B. P., Shaywitz, B. A., & Shaywitz, S. E. (1992). The validity of discrepancy-based definitions of reading disabilities. *Journal of Learning Disabilities, 25,* 555–561.

Fletcher, J. M., Francis, D. J., Shaywitz, S. E., Lyon, G. R., Foorman, B. R., Stuebing, K., & Shaywitz, B. A. (1998). Intelligent testing and the discrepancy model for children with learning disabilities. *Learning Disabilities Research and Practice, 13,* 186–203.

Fletcher, J. M., Satz, P., & Scholes, R. (1981). Developmental changes in the linguistic performance correlates of reading achievement. *Brain and Language, 13,* 78–90.

Fletcher, J. M., Shaywitz, S. E., Shankweiler, D., Katz, L., Liberman, I., Stuebing, K., Francis, D. J., Fowler, A., & Shaywitz, B. A. (1994). Cognitive profiles of reading disability: Comparisons of discrepancy and low achievement definitions. *Journal of Educational Psychology, 86,* 6–23.

Flynn, J. R. (1987). Massive IQ gains in 14 nations: What IQ tests really measure. *Psychological Bulletin, 101,* 171–191.

Fodor, J. A. (1983). *Modularity of mind.* Cambridge, MA: MIT Press.

Fodor, J. A. (1985). Precis of Modularity of Mind. *Behavioral and Brain Sciences, 8,* 1–42.

Foorman, B. R., Francis, D. J., & Fletcher, J. M. (1995, March). *Growth of phonological processing skills in reading: The lag versus deficit model revisited.* Paper presented at the meeting of the Society for Research in Child Development, Indianapolis, IN.

Foorman, B. R., Francis, D. J., Fletcher, J. M., & Lynn, A. (1996). Relation of phonological and orthographic processing to early reading: Comparing two approaches to regression-based, reading-level-match design. *Journal of Educational Psychology, 88,* 639–652.

Foorman, B. R., Francis, D. J., Fletcher, J. M., Schatschneider, C., & Mehta, P. (1998). The role of instruction in learning to read: Preventing reading failure in at-risk children. *Journal of Educational Psychology, 90,* 37–55.

Foorman, B. R., Francis, D. J., Novy, D. M., & Liberman, D. (1991). How letter-sound instruction mediates progress in first-grade reading and spelling. *Journal of Educational Psychology, 83,* 456–469.

Forell, E. R. (1985). The case for conservative reader placement. *Reading Teacher, 35,* 857–862.

Forrest, D., & Barron, R. W. (1977, March). *Meta-cognitive aspects of reading skill.* Paper presented at the meeting of the Society for Research in Child Development.

Forster, K. I. (1976). Accessing the mental lexicon. In R. Wales & E. Walker (Eds.), *New approaches to language mechanisms.* Amsterdam, The Netherlands: North-Holland.

Forster, K. I. (1979). Levels of processing and the structure of the language processor. In W. E. Cooper & E. Walker (Eds.), *Sentence processing: Psycholinguistic studies presented to Merrill Garrett* (pp. 27–85). Hillsdale, NJ: Erlbaum.

Forster, K. I., & Chambers, S. (1973). Lexical access and naming time. *Journal of Verbal Learning and Verbal Behavior, 12,* 627–635.

Foster, R., & Gavelek, J. (1983). Development of intentional forgetting in normal and reading-delayed children. *Journal of Educational Psychology, 75,* 431–440.

Fowler, A. (1991). How early phonological development might set the stage for phoneme awareness. In S. A. Brady & D. P. Shankweiler (Eds.), *Phonological processes in literacy* (pp. 97–117). Hillsdale, NJ: Erlbaum.

Fowler, A. E. (1988). Grammaticality judgments and reading skill in grade 2. *Annals of Dyslexia, 38,* 73–94.

Fowler, J., & Peterson, P. (1981). Increasing reading persistence and altering attributional style of learned helpless children. *Journal of Educational Psychology, 73,* 251–260.

Fox, B., & Routh, D. K. (1975). Analyzing spoken language into words, syllables, and phonemes: A developmental study. *Journal of Psycholinguistic Research, 4,* 331–342.

Fox, B., & Routh, D. K. (1976). Phonemic analysis and synthesis as word-attack skills. *Journal of Educational Psychology, 68,* 70–74.

Fox, B., & Routh, D. K. (1980). Phonemic analysis and severe reading disability. *Journal of Psycholinguistic Research, 9,* 115–119.

Fox, B., & Routh, D. K. (1983). Reading disability, phonemic analysis, and dysphonic spelling: A follow-up study. *Journal of Clinical Child Psychology, 12,* 28–32.

Fox, B., & Routh, D. K. (1984). Phonemic analysis and synthesis as word attack skills: Revisited. *Journal of Educational Psychology, 76,* 1059–1064.

Francis, D. J., Shaywitz, S. E., Stuebing, K., Shaywitz, B. A., & Fletcher, J. M. (1996). Developmental lag versus deficit models of reading disability: A longitudinal, individual growth curve analysis. *Journal of Educational Psychology, 88,* 3–17.

Francis, W. N., & Kucera, H. (1982). *Frequency analysis of English usage: Lexicon and grammar.* Boston: Houghton Mifflin.

Frank, R. H. (1999). *Luxury fever.* New York: Free Press.

Frank, R. H., & Cook, P. J. (1995). *The winner-take-all society.* New York: Free Press.

Frankenberger, W., & Fronzaglio, K. (1991). A review of states' criteria and procedures for identifying children with learning disabilities. *Journal of Learning Disabilities, 24,* 495–500.

Frankenberger, W., & Harper, J. (1987). States' criteria and procedures for identifying learning disabled children: A comparison of 1981/82 and 1985/86 guidelines. *Journal of Learning Disabilities, 20,* 118–121.

Frazier, J. A., & Morrison, F. J. (1998). The influence of extended-year schooling on growth of achievement and perceived competence in early elementary school. *Child Development, 69,* 495–517.

Frederiksen, J. R. (1978). Assessment of perceptual, decoding, and lexical skills and their relation to reading proficiency. In A. Lesgold, J. Pellegrino, S. Fokkema, & R. Glaser (Eds.), *Cognitive psychology and instruction* (pp. 153–169). New York: Plenum Press.

Frederiksen, J. R. (1980). Component skills in reading: Measurement of individual differences through chronometric analysis. In R. Snow, P. Federico, & W. Montague (Eds.), *Aptitude, learning, and instruction* (Vol. 1, pp. 105–138). Hillsdale, NJ: Erlbaum.

Fredman, G., & Stevenson, J. (1988). Reading processes in specific reading retarded and reading backward 13-year-olds. *British Journal of Developmental Psychology, 6,* 97–108.

Freebody, P., & Byrne, B. (1988). Word-reading strategies in elementary school children: Relations to comprehension, reading time, and phonemic awareness. *Reading Research Quarterly, 23,* 441–453.

Frith, U. (1980). Unexpected spelling problems. In U. Frith (Ed.), *Cognitive processes in spelling* (pp. 495–515). London: Academic Press.

Frith, U. (1985). Beneath the surface of developmental dyslexia. In K. Patterson, J. Marshall, & M. Coltheart (Eds.), *Surface dyslexia* (pp. 301–330). London: Erlbaum.

Frith, U., & Snowling, M. (1983). Reading for meaning and reading for sound in autistic and dyslexic children. *British Journal of Developmental Psychology, 1,* 329–342.

Frost, R. (1998). Toward a strong phonological theory of visual word recognition: True issues and false trails. *Psychological Bulletin, 123,* 71–99.

Frost, R. & Katz, L. (Eds.). (1992). *Orthography, phonology, morphology, and meaning.* Amsterdam, The Netherlands: North-Holland.

Fuller, B., Edwards, J., & Gorman, K. (1987). Does rising literacy spark economic growth? Commercial expansion in Mexico. In D. A. Wagner (Ed.), *The future of literacy in a changing world* (pp. 319–340). Oxford, England: Pergamon Press.

Furnham, A. (1986). Response bias, social desirability, and dissimulation. *Personality and Individual Differences, 7,* 385–400.

Gajar, A. (1979). Educable mentally retarded, learning disabled, emotionally disturbed: Similarities and differences. *Exceptional Children, 45,* 470–472.

Galaburda, A. (1991). Anatomy of dyslexia: Argument against phrenology. In D. Duane & D. Gray (Eds.), *The reading brain: The biological basis of dyslexia* (pp. 119–131). Parkton, MD: York Press.

Galaburda, A. (1994). Developmental dyslexia and animal studies: At the interface between cognition and neurology. *Cognition, 50,* 133–149.

Gambrell, L. B., Wilson, R. M., & Gantt, W. N. (1981). Classroom observations of task-attending behaviors of good and poor readers. *Journal of Educational Research, 74,* 400–404.

Garner, R., & Reis, R. (1981). Monitoring and resolving comprehension obstacles: An investigation of spontaneous text lookbacks among upper-grade good and poor comprehenders. *Reading Research Quarterly, 16,* 569–582.

Gaskins, I. W., Ehri, L. C., Cress, C., O'Hara, C., & Donnelly, K. (1997). Procedures for word learning: Making discoveries about words. *Reading Teacher, 50,* 312–327.

Gates, A., & McKillop, A. (1962). *Gates–McKillop Reading Diagnostic Tests.* New York: Teachers College Press.

Gathercole, S. E., & Baddeley, A. D. (1987). The processes underlying segmental analysis. *European Bulletin of Cognitive Psychology, 7,* 462–464.

Gathercole, S. E., & Baddeley, A. D. (1989). Evaluation of the role of phonological STM in the development of vocabulary in children: A longitudinal study. *Journal of Memory and Language, 28,* 200–213.

Gathercole, S. E., & Baddeley, A. D. (1993). *Working memory and language.* Hove, England: Erlbaum.

Gee, J. P. (1988). The legacies of literacy: From Plato to Freire through Harvey Graff. *Harvard Educational Review, 58,* 195–212.

Geertz, C. (1973). *The interpretation of cultures.* New York: Basic Books.

Gellner, E. (1985). *Relativism and the social sciences.* Cambridge, England: Cambridge University Press.

Geyer, J. J. (1970). Models of perceptual processes in reading. In H. Singer & R. B. Ruddell (Eds.), *Theoretical models and processes of reading* (pp. 47–97). Newark, DE: International Reading Association.

Ghiselli, E. E., Campbell, J. P., & Zedeck, S. (1981). *Measurement theory for the behavioral sciences.* San Francisco: Freeman.

Gibson, E. J., & Levin, H. (1975). *The psychology of reading.* Cambridge, MA: MIT Press.

Gillet, J. W., & Temple, C. (1986). *Understanding reading problems: Assessment and instruction* (2nd ed.). Boston: Little, Brown.

Gilovich, T. (1991). *How we know what isn't so: The fallibility of human reason in everyday life.* New York: Free Press.

Gitlin, T. (1995). *The twilight of common dreams: Why America is wracked by culture wars.* New York: Metropolitan Books.

Glaser, R. (1984). Education and thinking: The role of knowledge. *American Psychologist, 39,* 93–104.

Glushko, R. J. (1979). The organization and activation of orthographic knowledge in reading aloud. *Journal of Experimental Psychology: Human Perception and Performance, 5,* 674–691.

Glushko, R. J. (1981). Principles for pronouncing print: The psychology of phonography. In A. Lesgold & C. Perfetti (Eds.), *Interactive processes in reading* (pp. 61–84). Hillsdale, NJ: Erlbaum.

Godfrey, J. J., Syrdal-Lasky, A. K., Millay, K. K., & Knox, C. M. (1981). Performance of dyslexic children on speech perception tests. *Journal of Experimental Child Psychology, 32,* 401–424.

Goldberg, R. A., Schwartz, S., & Stewart, M. (1977). Individual differences in cognitive processes. *Journal of Educational Psychology, 69,* 9–14.

Goldman, R., Fristoe, M., & Woodcock, R. (1974). *GFW Sound–Symbol Tests.* Circle Pines, MN: American Guidance Service.

Goldsmith, J. S., & Nicolich, M. J. (1977). Word boundaries revisited: A first grade study. In P. D. Pearson & J. Hansen (Eds.), *Reading: Theory, research, and practice* (pp. 112–126). Clemson, SC: National Reading Conference.

Goldstein, D. (1976). Cognitive-linguistic functioning and learning to read in preschoolers. *Journal of Educational Psychology, 68,* 680–688.

Golick, M. (1977). *Language disorders in children: A linguistic investigation.* Unpublished doctoral dissertation, McGill University, Montreal, Canada.

Golinkoff, R. M. (1975–1976). A comparison of reading comprehension processes in good and poor comprehenders. *Reading Research Quarterly, 11,* 623–659.

Golinkoff, R. M. (1978). Phonemic awareness skills and reading achievement. In F. Murray & J. Pikulski (Eds.), *The acquisition of reading* (pp. 23–41). Baltimore: University Park Press.

Golinkoff, R. M., & Rosinski, R. R. (1976). Decoding, semantic processing, and reading comprehension skill. *Child Development, 47,* 252–258.

Gombert, J. E. (1992). *Metalinguistic development.* Hemel Hempstead, England: Harvester Wheatsheaf.

Goodman, G. S., Haith, M. M., Guttentag, R. E., & Rao, S. (1985). Automatic processing of word meaning: Intralingual and interlingual interference. *Child Development, 56,* 103–118.

Goodman, K. S. (1965). A linguistic study of cues and miscues in reading. *Elementary English, 42,* 639–643.

Goodman, K. S. (1968). The psycholinguistic nature of the reading process. In K. S. Goodman (Ed.), *The psycholinguistic nature of the reading process* (pp. 13–26). Detroit, MI: Wayne State University Press.

Goodman, K. S. (1973). The 13th easy way to make learning to read difficult: A reaction to Gleitman and Rozin. *Reading Research Quarterly, 8,* 484–493.

Goodman, K. S. (1976). Reading: A psycholinguistic guessing game. In H. Singer & R. B. Ruddell (Eds.), *Theoretical models and processes of reading* (pp. 497–508). Newark, DE: International Reading Association.

Goodman, K. S. (1986). *What's whole in whole language?* Portsmouth, NH: Heinemann.

Goodman, K. S. (1992). I didn't found whole language. *Reading Teacher, 46,* 188–199.

Goodman, K. S. (1993). *Phonics phacts.* Toronto: Scholastic Canada.

Goodman, K. S. (1996). *On reading.* Portsmouth, NH: Heinemann.

Goodman, K. S., & Gollasch, F. V. (1980). Word omissions: Deliberate and nondeliberate. *Reading Research Quarterly, 16,* 6–31.

Goody, J. (1977). *The domestication of the savage mind.* New York: Cambridge University Press.

Goody, J. (1980). Thought and writing. In E. Gellner (Ed.), *Soviet and Western anthropology* (pp. 119–133). London: Duckworth.

Goody, J. (1987). *The interface between the written and the oral.* Cambridge, England: Cambridge University Press.

Goody, J., & Watt, I. (1968). The consequences of literacy. In J. Goody (Ed.), *Literacy in traditional societies* (pp. 27–68). London: Cambridge University Press.

Goswami, U. (1993). Toward an interactive analogy model of reading development: Decoding vowel graphemes in beginning reading. *Journal of Experimental Child Psychology, 56,* 443–475.

Goswami, U. (1996). *Rhyme and analogy teacher's guide.* Oxford, England: Oxford University Press.

Goswami, U. (1998). The role of analogies in the development of word recognition. In J. L. Metsala & L. C. Ehri (Eds.), *Word recognition in beginning literacy* (pp. 41–63). Mahwah, NJ: Erlbaum.

Goswami, U. (1999). Orthographic analogies and phonological priming: A comment on Bowey, Vaughan, and Hansen (1998). *Journal of Experimental Child Psychology, 72*, 210–219.

Goswami, U., & Bryant, P. (1989). The interpretation of studies using the reading level design. *Journal of Reading Behavior, 21*, 413–424.

Goswami, U., & Bryant, P. (1990). *Phonological skills and learning to read.* Hove, England: Erlbaum.

Goswami, U., Schneider, W., & Scheurich, B. (1999). Picture naming deficits in developmental dyslexia in German. *Developmental Science, 2*, 53–58.

Gottardo, A., Chiappe, P., Siegel, L. S., & Stanovich, K. E. (1999). Patterns of word and nonword processing in skilled and less-skilled readers. *Reading and Writing: An Interdisciplinary Journal, 11*, 465–487.

Gottardo, A., Siegel, L. S., & Stanovich, K. E. (1997). The assessment of adults with reading disabilities: What can we learn from experimental tasks? *Journal of Research in Reading, 20*, 42–54.

Gottesman, R., Croen, L., & Rotkin, L. (1982). Urban second grade children: A profile of good and poor readers. *Journal of Learning Disabilities, 15*, 268–272.

Gottfredson, L. S. (1997). Why g matters: The complexity of everyday life. *Intelligence, 24*, 79–132.

Gough, P. B. (1972). One second of reading. In J. Kavanagh & I. Mattingly (Eds.), *Language by ear and eye* (pp. 331–358). Cambridge, MA: MIT Press.

Gough, P. B. (1983). Context, form, and interaction. In K. Rayner (Ed.), *Eye movements in reading* (pp. 203–211). New York: Academic Press.

Gough, P. B. (1984). Word recognition. In P. D. Pearson (Ed.), *Handbook of reading research* (pp. 225–253). New York: Longman.

Gough, P. B. (1993). The beginning of decoding. *Reading and Writing: An Interdisciplinary Journal, 5*, 181–192.

Gough, P. B. (1995). The new literacy: Caveat emptor. *Journal of Research in Reading, 18*, 79–86.

Gough, P. B., & Cosky, M. J. (1977). In N. J. Castellan, D. B. Pisoni, & G. R. Potts (Eds.), *Cognitive theory* (Vol. 2, pp. 271–286). Hillsdale, NJ: Erlbaum.

Gough, P. B., Ehri, L. C., & Treiman, R. (Eds.). (1992). *Reading acquisition.* Hillsdale, NJ: Erlbaum.

Gough, P. B., & Hillinger, M. L. (1980). Learning to read: An unnatural act. *Bulletin of the Orton Society, 30*, 171–176.

Gough, P. B., Hoover, W. A., & Peterson, C. L. (1996). Some observations on a simple view of reading. In C. Cornoldi & J. Oakhill (Eds.), *Reading comprehension difficulties* (pp. 1–13). Mahweh, NJ: Erlbaum.

Gough, P. B., & Juel, C. (1991). The first stages of word recognition. In L. Rieben & C. Perfetti (Eds.), *Learning to read: Basic research and its implications* (pp. 47–56). Hillsdale, NJ: Erlbaum.

Gough, P. B., Juel, C., & Griffith, P. (1992). Reading, spelling, and the orthographic cipher. In P. B. Gough, L. C. Ehri, & R. Treiman (Eds.), *Reading acquisition* (pp. 35–48). Hillsdale, NJ: Erlbaum.

Gough, P. B., & Tunmer, W. E. (1986). Decoding, reading, and reading disability. *Remedial and Special Education, 7*, 6–10.

Graesser, A. C., Hoffman, N. L., & Clark, L. F. (1980). Structural components of reading time. *Journal of Verbal Learning and Verbal Behavior, 19*, 135–151.

Graff, H. J. (1979). *The literacy myth.* New York: Academic Press.

Graff, H. J. (1986). The legacies of literacy: Continuities and contradictions in Western society and culture. In S. de Castell, A. Luke, & K. Egan (Eds.), *Literacy, society, and schooling* (pp. 61–86). England: Cambridge University Press.

Graff, H. J. (1987). *The labyrinths of literacy.* London: Falmer.

Gray, D. B., & Kavanagh, J. K. (1985). *Biobehavioral measures of dyslexia.* Parkton, MD: York Press.

Greaney, V. (1980). Factors related to amount and time of leisure time reading. *Reading Research Quarterly, 15,* 337–357.

Greaney, V., & Hegarty, M. (1987). Correlates of leisure-time reading. *Journal of Research in Reading, 10,* 3–20.

Greenberg, D., Ehri, L. C., & Perin, D. (1997). Are word-reading processes the same or different in adult literacy students and fifth-graders matched for reading level? *Journal of Educational Psychology, 89,* 262–275.

Greenfield, P. (1972). Oral or written language: The consequences for cognitive development in Africa, the United States, and England. *Language and Speech, 15,* 169–178.

Griffith, P. L., & Olson, M. W. (1992). Phonemic awareness helps beginning readers break the code. *Reading Teacher, 45,* 516–523.

Grigorenko, E. L. (1999). Heredity versus environment as the basis of cognitive ability. In R. J. Sternberg (Ed.), *The nature of cognition* (pp. 665–696). Cambridge, MA: MIT Press.

Gross, J., & Gottlieb, J. (1982). The mildly handicapped: A service distinction for the future? In T. Miller & E. Davis (Eds.), *The mildly handicapped student* (pp. 497–511). New York: Grune & Stratton.

Gross, P. R., & Levitt, N. (1994). *Higher superstition: The academic left and its quarrel with science.* Baltimore: Johns Hopkins University Press.

Gross, P. R., Levitt, N., & Lewis, M. (1997). *The flight from science and reason.* New York: New York Academy of Science.

Grundin, H. (1994). Who's romancing reality? A response to Keith Stanovich. *Reading Teacher, 48,* 8–10.

Guthrie, J. T. (1973). Reading comprehension and syntactic responses in good and poor readers. *Journal of Educational Psychology, 65,* 294–299.

Guthrie, J. T. (1981). Reading in New Zealand: Achievement and volume. *Reading Research Quarterly, 17,* 6–27.

Guthrie, J. T., & Greaney, V. (1991). Literacy acts. In R. Barr, M. L. Kamil, P. Mosenthal, & P. D. Pearson (Eds.), *Handbook of reading research* (Vol. 2, pp. 68–96). New York: Longman.

Guthrie, J. T., & Seifert, M. (1983). Profiles of reading activity in a community. *Journal of Reading, 26,* 498–508.

Guthrie, J. T., Schafer, W. D., & Hutchinson, S. R. (1991). Relations of document literacy and prose literacy to occupational and societal characteristics of young black and white adults. *Reading Research Quarterly, 26,* 30–48.

Guthrie, J. T., Wigfield, A., Metsala, J. L., & Cox, K. E. (1999). Motivational and cognitive predictors of text comprehension and reading amount. *Scientific Studies of Reading, 3,* 231–256.

Guttentag, R. E. (1984a). Semantic memory organization in second graders and adults. *Journal of General Psychology, 110,* 81–86.

Guttentag, R. E. (1984b). The mental effort requirement of cumulative rehearsal: A developmental study. *Journal of Experimental Child Psychology, 37,* 92–106.

Guttentag, R. E., & Haith, M. M. (1978). Automatic processing as a function of age and reading ability. *Child Development, 49*, 707–716.

Guttentag, R. E., & Haith, M. M. (1979). A developmental study of automatic word processing in a picture classification task. *Child Development, 50*, 894–896.

Guttentag, R. E., & Haith, M. M. (1980). A longitudinal study of word processing by first-grade children. *Journal of Educational Psychology, 72*, 701–705.

Gutting, G. (1980). *Paradigms and revolutions.* Notre Dame, IN: University of Notre Dame Press.

Haack, S. (1997). Science, scientism, and anti-science in the age of preposterism. *Skeptical Inquirer, 21*(6), 37–42.

Haack, S. (1998). *Manifesto of a passionate moderate.* Chicago: University of Chicago Press.

Hacking, I. (1983). *Representing and intervening.* Cambridge, England: Cambridge University Press.

Hacking, I. (1999). *The social construction of what?* Cambridge, MA: Harvard University Press.

Hagen, J., Barclay, C., & Newman, R. (1982). Metacognition, self-knowledge, and learning disabilities: Some thoughts on knowing and doing. *Topics in Learning and Learning Disabilities, 2*, 19–26.

Halford, G. S., Maybery, M. T., & Bain, J. D. (1986). Capacity limitations in children's reasoning: A dual-task approach. *Child Development, 57*, 616–627.

Hall, J., & Humphreys, M. (1982). Research on specific learning disabilities: Deficits and remediation. *Topics in Learning and Learning Disabilities, 2*, 68–78.

Hall, J., Wilson, K., Humphreys, M., Tinzmann, M., & Bowyer, P. (1983). Phonemic similarity effect in good versus poor readers. *Memory and Cognition, 11*, 520–527.

Hall, S. L., & Moats, L. C. (1999). *Straight talk about reading: How parents can make a difference during the early years.* Chicago: Contemporary Books.

Hall, V. C., Chiarello, K., & Edmondson, B. (1996). Deciding where knowledge comes from depends on where you look. *Journal of Educational Psychology, 88*, 305–313.

Hall, W. S., Nagy, W. E., & Linn R. (1984). *Spoken words: Effects of situation and social group on oral word usage and frequency.* Hillsdale, NJ: Erlbaum.

Hallahan, D., & Bryan, T. (1981). Learning disabilities. In J. Kauffman & D. Hallahan (Eds.), *Handbook of special education* (pp. 141–164). Englewood Cliffs, NJ: Prentice-Hall.

Hallahan, D., & Kauffman, J. (1977). Labels, categories, behaviors: ED, LD, and EMR reconsidered. *Journal of Special Education, 11*, 139–149.

Hammill, D., Leigh, J., McNutt, G., & Larsen, S. (1981). A new definition of learning disabilities. *Learning Disability Quarterly, 4*, 336–342.

Hansen, J., & Bowey, J. A. (1994). Phonological analysis skills, verbal working memory, and reading ability in second-grade children. *Child Development, 65*, 938–950.

Harding, L. M. (1984). Reading errors and style in children with a specific reading disability. *Journal of Research in Reading, 7*, 103–112.

Harm, M. W., Altmann, L., & Seidenberg, M. S. (1994). Using connectionist networks to examine the role of prior constraints in human language. In *Proceedings of the sixteenth annual conference of the Cognitive Science Society* (pp. 392–396). Hillsdale, NJ: Erlbaum.

Harm, M. W., & Seidenberg, M. S. (1999). Phonology, reading acquisition, and dyslexia: Insights from connectionist models. *Psychological Review, 106*, 491–528.

Harris, A. J., & Sipay, E. R. (1985). *How to increase reading ability* (8th ed.). White Plains, NY: Longman.

Hatcher, P. J., & Hulme, C. (1999). Phonemes, rhymes, and intelligence as predictors of children's responsiveness to remedial reading instruction: Evidence from a longitudinal intervention study. *Journal of Experimental Child Psychology, 72*, 130–153.

Hatcher, P. J., Hulme, C., & Ellis, A. W. (1994). Ameliorating early reading failure by integrating the teaching of reading and phonological skills: The phonological linkage hypothesis. *Child Development, 65*, 41–57.

Havelock, E. A. (1963). *Preface to Plato.* Cambridge, MA: Harvard University Press.

Havelock, E. A. (1980). The coming of literate communication to Western culture. *Journal of Communication, 30*, 90–98.

Haviland, S. E., & Clark, H. H. (1974). What's new? Acquiring new information as a process in comprehension. *Journal of Verbal Learning and Verbal Behavior, 13*, 512–521.

Hayduk, S., Bruck, M., & Cavanagh, P. (1992, September). *Do adult dyslexics show low level visual processing deficits?* Paper presented at the meeting of the Rodin Remediation Society, New York Academy of Sciences, New York.

Hayduk, S., Bruck, M., & Cavanagh, P. (1996). Low-level visual processing skills of adults and children with dyslexia. *Cognitive Neuropsychology, 13*, 975–1015.

Hayes, D. P. (1988). Speaking and writing: Distinct patterns of word choice. *Journal of Memory and Language, 27*, 572–585.

Hayes, D. P., & Ahrens, M. (1988). Vocabulary simplification for children: A special case of "motherese"? *Journal of Child Language, 15*, 395–410.

Hayes, D. P., & Grether, J. (1983). The school year and vacations: When do students learn? *Cornell Journal of Social Relations, 17*(1), 56–71.

Helfgott, J. (1976). Phonemic segmentation and blending skills of kindergarten children: Implication for beginning reading acquisition. *Contemporary Educational Psychology, 1*, 157–169.

Henderson, L. (1982). *Orthography and word recognition in reading.* London: Academic Press.

Henderson, L. (1985). Issues in the modeling of pronunciation assembly in normal reading. In K. Patterson, J. Marshall, & M. Coltheart (Eds.), *Surface dyslexia* (pp. 459–508). London: Erlbaum.

Herdman, C., & Dobbs, A. (1989). Attentional demands of visual word recognition. *Journal of Experimental Psychology: Human Perception and Performance, 15*, 124–132.

Herman, P. A. (1985). The effect of repeated readings on reading rate, speech pauses, and word recognition accuracy. *Reading Research Quarterly, 20*, 553–565.

Herrnstein, R. J., & Murray, C. (1994). *The bell curve.* New York: Free Press.

Hessler, G. L. (1987). Educational issues surrounding severe discrepancy. *Learning Disabilities Research, 3*, 43–49.

Hiebert, E. H. (1983). An examination of ability grouping for reading instruction. *Reading Research Quarterly, 18*, 231–255.

Hines, T. (1988). *Pseudoscience and the paranormal.* Buffalo, NY: Prometheus Books.

Hinshelwood, J. (1895). Word-blindness and visual memory. *Lancet, 2*, 1564–1570.

Hinshelwood, J. (1917). *Congenital word-blindness.* London: Lewis.

Hinton, G., & Shallice, T. (1991). Lesioning an attractor network: Investigations of acquired dyslexia. *Psychological Review, 98,* 74–95.

Hirsch, E. D. (1987). *Cultural literacy.* Boston: Houghton Mifflin.

Hirsch, E. D. (1996). *The schools we need: And why we don't have them.* New York: Doubleday.

Hirsch, E. D. (1997, Winter–Spring). An address to the California State Board of Education. *Common Knowledge,* pp. 4–8.

Hirst, W., & Kalmar, D. (1987). Characterizing attentional resources. *Journal of Experimental Psychology: General, 116,* 68–81.

Hochberg, J. (1970). Components of literacy: Speculation and exploratory research. In H. Levin & J. Williams (Eds.), *Basic studies in reading* (pp. 74–89). New York: Basic Books.

Hoffman, J., & Rutherford, W. (1984). Effective reading programs: A critical review of outlier studies. *Reading Research Quarterly, 20,* 79–92.

Hofstadter, D. R. (1985). *Metamagical themas.* New York: Basic Books.

Hogaboam, T. W., & Perfetti, C. A. (1978). Reading skill and the role of verbal experience in decoding. *Journal of Educational Psychology, 70,* 717–729.

Hohnen, B., & Stevenson, J. (1999). The structure of genetic influences on general cognitive, language, phonological, and reading abilities. *Developmental Psychology, 35,* 590–603.

Hoien, T., Lundberg, I., Stanovich, K. E., & Bjaalid, I. (1995). Components of phonological awareness. *Reading and Writing: An Interdisciplinary Journal, 7,* 171–188.

Holligan, C., & Johnston, R. S. (1988). The use of phonological information by good and poor readers in memory and reading tasks. *Memory and Cognition, 16,* 522–532.

Hollis, M., & Lukes, S. (Eds.). (1982). *Rationality and relativism.* Cambridge, MA: MIT Press.

Hood, J., & Dubert, L. A. (1983). Decoding as a component of reading comprehension among secondary students. *Journal of Reading Behavior, 15,* 51–61.

Hooker, C. A. (1975). Systematic philosophy and meta-philosophy of science. *Synthese, 32,* 177–231.

Hooper, S., & Hynd, G. (1985). Differential diagnosis of subtypes of developmental dyslexia with the Kaufman Assessment Battery for Children. *Journal of Clinical Child Psychology, 14,* 145–152.

Hooper, S., Hynd, G., & Mattison, R. (Eds.), *Developmental disorders: Diagnostic criteria and clinical assessment.* Hillsdale, NJ: Erlbaum.

Hoover, H. D. (1984, Winter). The most appropriate scores for measuring educational development in the elementary schools: GE's. *Educational Measurement: Issues and Practices, 3*(4), 8–14.

Hoover, W. A., & Gough, P. B. (1990). The simple view of reading. *Reading and Writing: An Interdisciplinary Journal, 2,* 127–160.

Horn, C. C., & Manis, F. R. (1987). Development of automatic and speeded reading of printed words. *Journal of Experimental Child Psychology, 44,* 92–108.

Horn, J. L., & Hofer, S. (1992). Major abilities and development in the adult period. In R. J. Sternberg & C. A. Berg (Eds.), *Intellectual development* (pp. 44–99). Cambridge, England: Cambridge University Press.

Horn, W. F., & O'Donnell, J. (1984). Early identification of learning disabilities: A comparison of two methods. *Journal of Educational Psychology, 76,* 1106–1118.

Horowitz, R, & Samuels, S. J. (1985). Reading and listening to expository text. *Journal of Reading Behavior, 17,* 185–198.

Howe, M. L., & Rabinowitz, F. M. (1989). On the uninterpretability of dual-task performance. *Journal of Experimental Child Psychology, 47,* 32–38.

Hoyer, W. (1987). Acquisition of knowledge and the decentralization of g in adult intellectual development. In C. Schooler & K. W. Schaie (Eds.), *Cognitive functioning and social structure over the life course* (pp. 120–141). Norwood, NJ: Ablex.

Hudson, A., Melita, B., & Arnold, N. (1993). A case study assessing the validity of facilitated communication. *Journal of Autism and Developmental Disorders, 23,* 165–173.

Hudson, L. (1989, November 3–9). Recalling a scapegoat: Review of "The Burt Affair" by Robert B. Joynson. *Times Literary Supplement,* p. 1201.

Huey, E. B. (1908/1968). *The psychology and pedagogy of reading.* Cambridge, MA: MIT Press.

Hull, D. L. (1988). *Science as a process: An evolutionary account of the social and conceptual development of science.* Chicago: University of Chicago Press.

Hulme, C. (1988). The implausibility of low-level visual deficits as a cause of children's reading difficulties. *Cognitive Neuropsychology, 5,* 369–374.

Hulme, C., & Snowling, M. (1992). Deficits in output phonology: An explanation of reading failure. *Cognitive Neuropsychology, 9,* 47–72.

Hulme, C., Snowling, M., & Quinlan, P. (1991). Connectionism and learning to read: Steps towards a psychologically plausible model. *Reading and Writing: An Interdisciplinary Journal, 3,* 159–168.

Hulme, C., Thomson, N., Muir, C., & Lawrence, A. (1984). Speech rate and the development of short-term memory span. *Journal of Experimental Child Psychology, 38,* 241–253.

Humphreys, G. W. (1985). Attention, automaticity, and autonomy in visual word processing. In D. Besner, T. Waller, & G. MacKinnon (Eds.), *Reading research: Advances in theory and practice* (Vol. 5, pp. 253–309). New York: Academic Press.

Humphreys, G. W., & Evett, L. J. (1985). Are there independent lexical and nonlexical routes in word processing? An evaluation of the dual-route theory of reading. *Behavioral and Brain Sciences, 8,* 689–740.

Humphreys, L. G. (1979). The construct of general intelligence. *Intelligence, 3,* 105–120.

Hunt, E. (1995). *Will we be smart enough? A cognitive analysis of the coming workforce.* New York: Russell Sage Foundation.

Hunt, E. (1999). Intelligence and human resources: Past, present, and future. In P. Ackerman, P. Kyllonen, & R. Richards (Eds.), *Learning and individual differences: Process, trait, and content determinants* (pp. 3–28). Washington, DC: American Psychological Association.

Hurford, D. P., Schauf, J. D., Bunce, L., Blaich, T., & Moore, K. (1994). Early identification of children at risk for reading disabilities. *Journal of Learning Disabilities, 27,* 371–382.

Huston, A., Watkins, B. A., & Kunkel, D. (1989). Public policy and children's television. *American Psychologist, 44,* 424–433.

Huttenlocher, J., Levine, S., & Vevea, J. (1998). Environmental input and cognitive growth: A study using time-period comparisons. *Child Development, 69,* 1012–1029.

Hynd, G. W., Marshall, R., & Gonzalez, J. (1991). Learning disabilities and presumed central nervous system dysfunction. *Learning Disability Quarterly, 14*, 283–296.

Hynd, G. W., & Hynd, C. R. Dyslexia: Neuroanatomical/neurolinguistic perspectives. *Reading Research Quarterly, 19*, 482–498.

Hynd, G. W., Clinton, A., & Hiemenz, J. R. (1999). The neuropsychological basis of learning disabilities. In R. J. Sternberg & L. Spear-Swerling (Eds.), *Perspectives on learning disabilities* (pp. 60–79). New York: Westview/HarperCollins.

Ijzendoorm, M., & Bus, A. G. (1994). Meta-analytic confirmation of the nonword reading deficit in developmental dyslexia. *Reading Research Quarterly, 29*, 266–275.

Iversen, S., & Tunmer, W. E. (1993). Phonological processing skills and the Reading Recovery Program. *Journal of Educational Psychology, 85*, 112–126.

Iyengar, S., & Kinder, D. R. (1987). *News that matters: Television and American opinion.* Chicago: University of Chicago Press.

Jackson, M. (1980). Further evidence for a relationship between memory access and reading ability. *Journal of Verbal Learning and Verbal Behavior, 19*, 683–694.

Jackson, M. D., & McClelland, J. L. (1975). Sensory and cognitive determinants of reading speed. *Journal of Verbal Learning and Verbal Behavior, 14*, 565–574.

Jackson, M. D., & McClelland, J. L. (1979). Processing determinants of reading speed. *Journal of Experimental Psychology: General, 108*, 151–181.

Jackson, N. E., & Biemiller, A. J. (1985). Letter, word, and text reading times of precocious and average readers. *Child Development, 56*, 196–206.

Jackson, N. E., & Butterfield, E. C. (1989). Reading-level-match designs: Myths and realities. *Journal of Reading Behavior, 21*, 387–412.

Jackson, N. E., Ju, D., & Lu, W. (1994). Chinese readers of English: Orthographic and phonological processing, word identification, and exposure to print. In V. Berninger (Ed.), *Varieties of orthographic knowledge: Theoretical and developmental issues* (Vol. 1, pp. 73–109). Dordrecht, The Netherlands: Kluwer Academic.

Jacobson, J. W., Mulick, J. A., & Schwartz, A. A. (1995). A history of facilitated communication: Science, pseudoscience, and antiscience. *American Psychologist, 50*, 750–765.

Jakimik, J., Cole, R. A., & Rudnicky, A. I. (1985). Sound and spelling in spoken word recognition. *Journal of Memory and Language, 24*, 165–178.

Jared, D., Levy, B. A., & Rayner, K. (1999). The role of phonology in the activation of word meanings during reading: Evidence from proofreading and eye movements. *Journal of Experimental Psychology: General, 128*, 219–264.

Jastak, J. F., & Jastak, S. R. (1978). *The Wide Range Achievement Test—Revised.* Wilmington, DE: Jastak Associates.

Jastak, J. F., Bijou, S. W., & Jastak, S. R. (1965). *Wide Range Achievement Test. Wilmington, DE: Guidance Associates.*

Jastak, S. R., & Wilkinson, G. S. (1984). *The Wide Range Achievement Test—Revised. Wilmington, DE: Jastak Associates.*

Jencks, C. (1972). *Inequality.* New York: Basic Books.

Jenkins, J., & Dixon, R. (1983). Vocabulary learning. *Contemporary Educational Psychology, 8*, 237–260.

Jenkins, J., Stein, M., & Wysocki, K. (1984). Learning vocabulary through reading. *American Educational Research Journal, 21*, 767–787.

Jensen, A. R. (1980). *Bias in mental testing.* New York: Free Press.

Jensen, A. R. (1998). *The g factor: The science of mental ability.* Westport, CT: Praeger.

Jensen, A. R., & Rohwer, W. D. (1966). The Stroop Color-Word Test: A review. *Acta Psychologica, 25,* 36–93.

Jimerson, S., Egeland, B., & Teo, A. (1999). A longitudinal study of achievement trajectories: Factors associated with change. *Journal of Educational Psychology, 91,* 116–126.

Johnson, D. J. (1988). Review of research on specific reading, writing, and mathematics disorders. In J. F. Kavanagh, & T. J. Truss (Eds.), *Learning disabilities: Proceedings of the national conference* (pp. 79–163). Parkston, MD: York Press.

Johnston, P. H., & Winograd, P. N. (1985). Passive failure in reading. *Journal of Reading Behavior, 17,* 279–301.

Johnston, R. S., Rugg, M., & Scott, T. (1987). Phonological similarity effects, memory span, and developmental reading disorders: The nature of the relationship. *British Journal of Psychology, 78,* 205–211.

Jonides, J., Naveh-Benjamin, M., & Palmer, J. (1985). Assessing automaticity. *Acta Psychologica, 60,* 157–171.

Jorgenson, G. (1977). Relationship of classroom behavior to the accuracy of the match between material difficulty and student ability. *Journal of Educational Psychology, 69,* 24–32.

Jorm, A. (1979). The cognitive and neurological bases of developmental dyslexia: A theoretical framework and review. *Cognition, 7,* 19–33.

Jorm, A. (1983). Specific reading retardation and working memory: A review. *British Journal of Psychology, 74,* 311–342.

Jorm, A., & Share, D. (1983). Phonological recoding and reading acquisition. *Applied Psycholinguistics, 4,* 103–147.

Jorm, A., Share, D., Maclean, R., & Matthews, R. (1984). Phonological recoding skills and learning to read: A longitudinal study. *Applied Psycholinguistics, 5,* 201–207.

Jorm, A., Share, D., Maclean, R., & Matthews, R. (1986). Cognitive factors at school entry predictive of specific reading retardation and general reading backwardness: A research note. *Journal of Child Psychology and Psychiatry, 27,* 45–54.

Joyce, B. R. (1999). Reading about reading: Notes from a consumer to the scholars of literacy. *Reading Teacher, 52*(7), 662–671.

Juel, C. (1980). Comparison of word identification strategies with varying context, word type, and reader skill. *Reading Research Quarterly, 15,* 358–376.

Juel, C. (1983). The development and use of mediated word identification. *Reading Research Quarterly, 18,* 306–327.

Juel, C. (1988). Learning to read and write: A longitudinal study of 54 children from first through fourth grades. *Journal of Educational Psychology, 80,* 437–447.

Juel, C., Griffith, P. L., & Gough, P. B. (1986). Acquisition of literacy: A longitudinal study of children in first and second grade. *Journal of Educational Psychology, 78,* 243–255.

Juola, J. F., Schadler, M., Chabot, R., & McCaughey, M. (1978). The development of visual information processing skills related to reading. *Journal of Experimental Child Psychology, 25,* 459–476.

Jusczyk, P. (1977). Rhymes and reasons: Some aspects of the child's appreciation of poetic form. *Developmental Psychology, 13,* 599–607.

Just, M. A., & Carpenter, P. A. (1980). A theory of reading: From eye fixations to comprehension. *Psychological Review, 4,* 329–354.

Just, M. A., & Carpenter, P. A. (1987). *The psychology of reading and language comprehension*. Boston: Allyn & Bacon.

Kaestle, C. F. (1991). *Literacy in the United States*. New Haven, CT: Yale University Press.

Kahneman, D., & Chajczyk, D. (1983). Tests of the automaticity of reading: Dilution of Stroop effects by color-irrelevant stimuli. *Journal of Experimental Psychology: Human Perception and Performance, 9*, 497–509.

Kahneman, D., Slovic, P., & Tversky, A. (1982). *Judgment under uncertainty: Heuristics and biases*. Cambridge, England: Cambridge University Press.

Kahneman, D., & Treisman, A. (1984). Changing views of attention and automaticity. In R. Parasuraman & R. Davies (Eds.), *Varieties of attention* (pp. 29–61). New York: Academic Press.

Kamhi, A. G. (1992). Response to historical perspective: A developmental language perspective. *Journal of Learning Disabilities, 25*, 48–52.

Kamhi, A. G., & Catts, H. W. (1989). *Reading disabilities: A developmental language perspective*. Boston: College-Hill Press.

Kamil, M. L. (1995). Some alternatives to paradigm wars in literacy research. *Journal of Reading Behavior, 27*, 243–261.

Kavale, K. A. (1987). Theoretical issues surrounding severe discrepancy. *Learning Disabilities Research, 3*, 12–20.

Kavale, K. A., & Forness, S. R. (1985). *The science of learning disabilities*. San Diego, CA: College-Hill Press.

Kavale, K. A., & Mattson, P. (1983). "One jumped off the balance beam": Meta-analysis of perceptual-motor training. *Journal of Learning Disabilities, 16*, 165–173.

Kavale, K. A., & Nye, C. (1981). Identification criteria for learning disabilities: A survey of the research literature. *Learning Disability Quarterly, 4*, 363–388.

Kavanagh, J. F., & Truss, T. J. (Eds.). (1988). *Learning disabilities: Proceedings of the national conference*. Parkston, MD: York Press.

Kay, J., & Bishop, D. (1987). Anatomical differences between nose, palm, and foot; or, The body in question: Further dissection of the processes of sub-lexical spelling–sound translation. In M. Coltheart (Ed.), *Attention and performance* (Vol. 12, pp. 449–469). London: Erlbaum.

Kee, D. W., & Davies, L. (1988). Mental effort and elaboration: A developmental analysis. *Contemporary Educational Psychology, 13*, 221–228.

Keil, F. C. (1984). Mechanisms of cognitive development and the structure of knowledge. In R. Sternberg (Ed.), *Mechanisms of cognitive development* (pp. 81–99). New York: Freeman.

Kelman, M., & Lester, G. (1997). *Jumping the queue: An inquiry into the legal treatment of students with learning disabilities*. Cambridge, MA: Harvard University Press.

Keppel, G., & Zedeck, S. (1989). *Data analysis for research designs*. New York: Freeman.

Kerlinger, F. N., & Pedhazur, E. J. (1973). *Multiple regression in behavioral research*. New York: Holt, Rinehart & Winston.

Kibby, M. W. (1979). Passage readability affects the oral reading strategies of disabled readers. *Reading Teacher, 32*, 390–396.

Kihlstrom, J. (1987). The cognitive unconscious. *Science, 237*, 1445–1452.

Kimmel, S., & MacGinitie, W. H. (1984). Identifying children who use a perseverative text processing strategy. *Reading Research Quarterly, 19*, 162–172.

Kimura, Y., & Bryant, P. (1983). Reading and writing in English and Japanese: A cross-cultural study of young children. *British Journal of Developmental Psychology, 1,* 143–154.

Kintsch, W. (1988). The role of knowledge in discourse comprehension: A construction–integration model. *Psychological Review, 95,* 163–182.

Kirk, S., & Elkins, J. (1975). Characteristics of children enrolled in the child service demonstration centers. *Journal of Learning Disabilities, 8,* 630–637.

Kirk, S., McCarthy, J., & Kirk, W. (1968). *Illinois Test of Psycholinguistic Ability.* Urbana, IL: University of Chicago Press.

Kirsch, I., & Jungeblut, A. (1986). *Literacy: Profiles of America's young adults.* Princeton, NJ: Educational Testing Service.

Kitcher, P. (1993). *The advancement of science.* New York: Oxford University Press.

Klein, H. A. (1976). The role of material level on the development of word identification. *Journal of Psychology, 94,* 225–232.

Klein, H. A., Klein, G. A., & Bertino, M. (1974). Utilization of context for word identification decisions in children. *Journal of Experimental Child Psychology, 17,* 79–86.

Klinge, V., Rennick, P., Lennox, K., & Hart, Z. (1977). A matched-subject comparison of underachievers with normals on intellectual, behavioral, and emotional variables. *Journal of Abnormal Child Psychology, 5,* 61–68.

Kochnower, J., Richardson, E., & DiBenedetto, B. (1983). A comparison of the phonic decoding ability of normal and learning disabled children. *Journal of Learning Disabilities, 16,* 348–351.

Kolers, P. A. (1972). Experiments in reading. *Scientific American, 227,* 84–91.

Kolers, P. A. (1975). Pattern-analyzing disability in poor readers. *Developmental Psychology, 11,* 282–290.

Korten, D. C. (1999). *The post-corporate world: Life after capitalism.* San Francisco: Berrett-Koehler.

Kotsonis, M., & Patterson, C. (1980). Comprehension-monitoring skills in learning-disabled children. *Developmental Psychology, 16,* 541–542.

Kozol, J. (1991). *Savage inequalities.* New York: Crown.

Krashen, S. (1989). We acquire vocabulary and spelling by reading: Additional evidence for the input hypothesis. *Modern Language Journal, 73,* 440–464.

Kraut, A. G., & Smothergill, D. W. (1980). New method for studying semantic encoding in children. *Developmental Psychology, 16,* 149–150.

Kreuz, R. J. (1987). The subjective familiarity of English homophones. *Memory and Cognition, 15,* 154–168.

Krueger, L. E. (1979). Features versus redundancy: Comments on Massaro, Venezky, and Taylor's "Orthographic regularity, positional frequency, and visual processing of letter strings." *Journal of Experimental Psychology: General, 108,* 125–130.

Krueger, L. E., Keen, R. H., & Rublevich, B. (1974). Letter search through words and nonwords by adults and fourth-grade children. *Journal of Experimental Psychology, 102,* 845–849.

Kruk, R. (1991). *Functional consequences of a transient visual processing deficit in reading disabled children.* Unpublished doctoral dissertation. Ontario Institute for Studies in Education, Toronto.

Kucera, H., & Francis, W. N. (1967). *Computational analysis of present-day American English.* Providence, RI: Brown University Press.

Kuhn, T. S. (1970). *The structure of scientific revolutions* (2nd ed.). Chicago: University of Chicago Press.

Kuttner, R. (1998). *Everything for sale: The virtues and limits of markets.* Chicago: University of Chicago Press.

La Heij, W. L. (1988). Components of Stroop-like interference in picture naming. *Memory and Cognition, 16,* 400–410.

LaBerge, D., & Samuels, S. (1974). Toward a theory of automatic information processing in reading. *Cognitive Psychology, 6,* 293–323.

Labuda, M., & DeFries, J. C. (1989). Differential prognosis of reading-disabled children as a function of gender, socioeconomic status, IQ, and severity: A longitudinal study. *Reading and Writing: An Interdisciplinary Journal, 1,* 25–36.

Lachman, R., Lachman, J., & Butterfield, E. (1979). *Cognitive psychology and information processing: An introduction.* Hillsdale, NJ: Erlbaum.

Lakatos, I., & Musgrave, A. (1970). *Criticism and the growth of knowledge.* Cambridge, England: Cambridge University Press.

Lakomski, G. (1992). Unity over diversity: Coherence and realism in educational research. *Curriculum Inquiry, 22,* 191–203.

Landauer, T. K. (1998). Learning and representing verbal meaning: The latent semantic analysis theory. *Current Directions in Psychological Science, 7,* 161–164.

Landauer, T. K., & Dumais, S. (1996). How come you know so much? In D. Herrmann, C. Hertzog, C. McEvoy, P. Hertel, & M. Johnson (Eds.), *Basic and applied memory: Memory in context* (pp. 105–126). Mahwah, NJ: Erlbaum.

Landauer, T. K., & Dumais, S. (1997). A solution to Plato's problem: The latent semantic analysis theory of acquisition, induction, and representation of knowledge. *Psychological Review, 104,* 211–240.

Lane, D. M. (1977). Attention allocation and the relationship between primary and secondary task difficulty: A reply to Kantowitz and Knight. *Acta Psychologica, 41,* 493–495.

Larkin, J., McDermott, J., Simon, D., & Simon, H. (1980). Expert and novice performance in solving physics problems. *Science, 208,* 1335–1342.

Larochelle, S., McClelland, J. L., & Rodriguez, E. (1980). Context and the allocation of resources in word recognition. *Journal of Experimental Psychology: Human Perception and Performance, 6,* 686–694.

Larsen, P., Hoien, T., Lundberg, I., & Odegaard, H. (1990). MRI evaluation of the size and symmetry of the planum temporale in adolescents with developmental dyslexia. *Brain and Language, 39,* 289–301.

Laudan, L. (1990). *Science and relativism.* Chicago: University of Chicago Press.

Lee, S. (1996). Free voluntary reading and writing competence in Taiwanese high school students. *Perceptual and Motor Skills, 83,* 687–690.

Lefton, L. A., Spragins, A. B., & Byrnes, J. (1973). English orthography: Relation to reading experience. *Bulletin of the Psychonomic Society, 2,* 281–282.

Lehman, D. (1991). *Signs of the times: Deconstruction and the fall of Paul de Man.* New York: Poseidon Press.

Leinhardt, G., Seewald, A., & Zigmond, N. (1982). Sex and race differences in learning disabilities classrooms. *Journal of Educational Psychology, 74,* 835–843.

Leplin, J. (1984). *Scientific realism.* Berkeley and Los Angeles: University of California Press.

Lerner, R., & Busch-Rossnagel, N. (1981). *Individuals as producers of their development: A life-span perspective.* New York: Academic Press.

Lesgold, A., & Perfetti, C. (1978). Interactive processes in reading comprehension. *Discourse Processes, 1,* 323–336.

Lesgold, A., & Resnick, L. (1982). How reading difficulties develop: Perspectives from a longitudinal study. In J. Das, R. Mulcahey, & A. Wall (Eds.), *Theory and research in learning disabilities* (pp. 155–187). New York: Plenum Press.

Lesgold, A., Resnick, L., & Hammond, K. (1985). Learning to read: A longitudinal study of word skill development in two curricula. In G. MacKinnon & T. Waller (Eds.), *Reading research: Advances in theory and practice* (Vol. 4, pp. 107–138). London: Academic Press.

Leu, D. (1982). Oral reading error analysis: A critical review of research and application. *Reading Research Quarterly, 17,* 420–437.

Leu, D. J., DeGroff, L., & Simons, H. D. (1986). Predictable texts and interactive-compensatory hypotheses: Evaluating individual differences in reading ability, context use, and comprehension. *Journal of Educational Psychology, 78,* 347–352.

Levin, H., & Kaplan, E. L. (1970). Grammatical structure and reading. In H. Levin & J. Williams (Eds.), *Basic studies in reading* (pp. 119–133). New York: Basic Books.

Levin, J. (1973). Inducing comprehension in poor readers: A test of a recent model. *Journal of Educational Psychology, 65,* 19–24.

Levine, K. (1982). Functional literacy: Fond illusions and false economies. *Harvard Educational Review, 52,* 249–266.

Levinthal, C., & Hornung, M. (1992). The role of orthographic processing skills on five different reading tasks. *Reading and Writing: An Interdisciplinary Journal, 4,* 231–243.

Levy, B. A. (1978). Speech analysis during sentence processing: Reading and listening. *Visible Language, 12,* 81–101.

Levy, B. A. (1981). Interactive processes during reading. In A. Lesgold & C. Perfetti (Eds.), *Interactive processes in reading* (pp. 1–35). Hillsdale, NJ: Erlbaum.

Levy, B. A., Bourassa, D. C., & Horn, C. (1999). Fast and slow namers: Benefits of segmentation and whole word training. *Journal of Experimental Child Psychology, 73,* 115–138.

Lewellen, M. J., Goldinger, S., Pisoni, D. B., & Greene, B. (1993). Lexical familiarity and processing efficiency: Individual differences in naming, lexical decision, and semantic categorization. *Journal of Experimental Psychology: General, 122,* 316–330.

Lewis, R., & Teale, W. H. (1980). Another look at secondary school students' attitudes toward reading. *Journal of Reading Behavior, 12,* 187–201.

Lewkowicz, N. (1980). Phonemic awareness training: What to teach and how to teach it. *Journal of Educational Psychology, 72,* 686–700.

Liberman, A. M. (1999). The reading researcher and the reading teacher need the right theory of speech. *Scientific Studies of Reading, 3,* 95–111.

Liberman, I. Y. (1973). Segmentation of the spoken word and reading acquisition. *Bulletin of the Orton Society, 23,* 65–77.

Liberman, I. Y. (1982). A language-oriented view of reading and its disabilities. In H. Mykelbust (Ed.), *Progress in learning disabilities* (Vol. 5, pp. 81–101). New York: Grune & Stratton.

Liberman, I. Y., & Liberman, A. M. (1990). Whole language versus code emphasis:

Underlying assumptions and their implications for reading instruction. *Annals of Dyslexia, 40,* 51–77.

Liberman, I. Y., & Liberman, A. M. (1992). Whole language versus code emphasis: Underlying assumptions and their implications for reading instruction. In P. B. Gough, L. C. Ehri, & R. Treiman (Eds.), *Reading acquisition* (pp. 343–366). Hillsdale, NJ: Erlbaum.

Liberman, I. Y., Rubin, H., Duques, S., & Carlisle, J. (1985). Linguistic abilities and spelling proficiency in Kindergarteners and adult poor spellers. In D. Gray & J. Kavanagh (Eds.), *Biobehavioral measures of dyslexia* (pp. 163–175). Parkton, MD: York Press.

Liberman, I. Y., & Shankweiler, D. (1979). Speech, the alphabet, and teaching to read. In L. Resnick & P. Weaver (Eds.), *Theory and practice of early reading* (Vol. 2, pp. 109–132). Hillsdale, NJ: Erlbaum.

Liberman, I. Y., & Shankweiler, D. (1985). Phonology and the problems of learning to read and write. *Remedial and Special Education, 6,* 8–17.

Liberman, I. Y., Shankweiler, D., Fischer, F. W., & Carter, B. (1974). Explicit syllable and phoneme segmentation in the young child. *Journal of Experimental Child Psychology, 18,* 201–212.

Liberman, I. Y., Shankweiler, D., Liberman, A. M., Fowler, C., & Fischer, W. F. (1977). Phonetic segmentation and recoding in the beginning reader. In A. Reber & D. Scarborough (Eds.), *Toward a psychology of reading* (pp. 207–225). Hillsdale, NJ: Erlbaum.

Licht, B., & Dweck, C. (1984). Determinants of academic achievement: The interaction of children's achievement orientations with skill area. *Developmental Psychology, 20,* 628–636.

Lie, A. (1991). Effects of a training program for stimulating skills in word analysis in first-grade children. *Reading Research Quarterly, 26,* 234–250.

Lieberman, P., Meskill, R. H., Chatillon, M., & Schupack, H. (1985). Phonetic speech perception deficits in dyslexia. *Journal of Speech and Hearing Research, 28,* 480–486.

Lindgren, S. D., De Renzi, E., & Richman, L. C. (1985). Cross-national comparisons of developmental dyslexia in Italy and the United States. *Child Development, 56,* 1404–1417.

Lipps Birch, L. (1976). Age trends in children's time-sharing performance. *Journal of Experimental Child Psychology, 22,* 331–345.

Lipps Birch, L. (1978). Baseline differences, attention, and age differences in time-sharing performance. *Journal of Experimental Child Psychology, 25,* 505–513.

Lipson, M. Y., & Wixson, K. L. (1986). Reading disability research: An interactionist perspective. *Review of Educational Research, 56,* 111–136.

Logan, G. D. (1985). Skill and automaticity: Relations, implications, and future directions. *Canadian Journal of Psychology, 39,* 367–386.

Logan, G. D. (1988). Toward an instance theory of automatization. *Psychological Review, 95,* 492–527.

Logan, G. D., Zbrodoff, N. J., & Fostey, A. R. (1983). Costs and benefits of strategy construction in a speeded discrimination task. *Memory and Cognition, 11,* 485–493.

Lohman, D. (1999). Minding our p's and q's: On finding relationships between learning and intelligence. In P. Ackerman, P. Kyllonen, & R. Richards (Eds.), *Learning* and individual differences: Process, trait, and content determinants (pp. 55–72). Washington, DC: American Psychological Association.

Lomax, R. (1983). Applying structural modeling to some component processes of reading comprehension development. *Journal of Experimental Education, 52,* 33–40.

Lonigan, C. J., Burgess, S. R., Anthony, J. L., & Barker, T. A. (1998). Development of phonological sensitivity in 2- to 5-year-old children. *Journal of Educational Psychology, 90,* 294–311.

Lott, D., & Smith, F. (1970). Knowledge of intraword redundancy by beginning readers. *Psychonomic Science, 19,* 343–344.

Lovegrove, W. (1992). The visual deficit hypothesis. In N. Singh & I. Beale (Eds.), *Learning disabilities: Nature, theory, and treatment* (pp. 246–269). New York: Springer-Verlag.

Lovegrove, W., & Slaghuis, W. (1989). How reliable are visual differences found in dyslexics? *Irish Journal of Psychology, 10,* 542–550.

Lovegrove, W., Martin, F., & Slaghuis, W. (1986). A theoretical and experimental case for a visual deficit in specific reading disability. *Cognitive Neuropsychology, 3,* 225–267.

Lovett, M. W. (1979). The selective encoding of sentential information in normal reading development. *Child Development, 50,* 897–900.

Lovett, M. W. (1984). A developmental perspective on reading dysfunction: Accuracy and rate criteria in the subtyping of dyslexic children. *Brain and Language, 22,* 67–91.

Lovett, M. W. (1986). Sentential structure and the perceptual spans of two samples of disabled readers. *Journal of Psycholinguistic Research, 15,* 153–175.

Lovett, M. W., Borden, S., DeLuca, T., Lacerenza, L., Benson, N., & Brackstone, D. (1994). Treating the core deficits of developmental dyslexia. *Developmental Psychology, 30,* 805–822.

Lovett, M. W., Ransby, M., & Barron, R. (1988). Treatment, subtype, and word type effects in dyslexic children's response to remediation. *Brain and Language, 34,* 328–349.

Lovett, M. W., Warren-Chaplin, P., Ransby, M., & Borden, S. (1990). Training the word recognition skills of reading disabled children: Treatment and transfer effects. *Journal of Educational Psychology, 82,* 769–780.

Loving, C. C. (1997). From the summit of truth to its slippery slopes: Science education's journey through positivist-postmodern territory. *American Educational Research Journal, 34,* 421–452.

Lundberg, I. (1985). Longitudinal studies of reading and reading difficulties in Sweden. In G. MacKinnon & T. Waller (Eds.), *Reading research: Advances in theory and practice* (Vol. 4, pp. 65–105). London: Academic Press.

Lundberg, I., Frost, J., & Peterson, O. (1988). Effects of an extensive program for stimulating phonological awareness in preschool children. *Reading Research Quarterly, 23,* 263–284.

Lundberg, I., & Hoien, T. (1989). Phonemic deficits: A core symptom of developmental dyslexia? *Irish Journal of Psychology, 10,* 579–592.

Lundberg, I., Oloffson, A., & Wall, S. (1980). Reading and spelling skills in the first school years predicted from phonemic awarness in kindergarten. *Scandinavian Journal of Psychology, 21,* 159–173.

Luria, A. R. (1976). *Cognitive development: Its cultural and social foundations.* Cambridge, MA: Harvard University Press.

Lynch, A. (1996). *Thought contagion.* New York: Basic Books.

Lyon, G. R. (1985). Educational validation studies of learning disability subtypes. In B. P. Rourke (Ed.), *Neuropsychology of learning disabilities* (pp. 228–253). New York: Guilford Press.

Lyon, G. R. (1987). Learning disabilities research: False starts and broken promises. In S. Vaughn & C. S. Bos (Eds.), *Research in learning disabilities* (pp. 69–85). Boston: College-Hill Press.

Lyon, G. R. (1995). Toward a definition of dyslexia. *Annals of Dyslexia, 45,* 3–27.

Lyons, W. (1986). *The disappearance of introspection.* Cambridge, MA: MIT Press.

Maclean, M., Bryant, P., & Bradley, L. (1987). Rhymes, nursery rhymes, and reading in early childhood. *Merrill-Palmer Quarterly, 33,* 255–281.

Mamen, M., Ferguson, H., & Backman, J. E. (1986). No difference represents a significant finding. *Psychological Bulletin, 100,* 107–109.

Mander, J., & Goldsmith, E. (Eds.). (1996). *The case against the global economy.* San Francisco: Sierra Club Books.

Manis, F. R. (1985). Acquisition of word identification skills in normal and disabled readers. *Journal of Educational Psychology, 77,* 78–90.

Manis, F. R., Custodio, R., & Szeszulski, P. A. (1993). Development of phonological and orthographic skill: A 2-year longitudinal study of dyslexic children. *Journal of Experimental Child Psychology, 56,* 64–86.

Manis, F. R., Keating, D. P., & Morrison, F. J. (1980). Developmental differences in the allocation of processing capacity. *Journal of Experimental Child Psychology, 29,* 156–169.

Manis, F. R., Seidenberg, M. S., & Doi, L. M. (1999). See Dick RAN: Rapid naming and the longitudinal prediction of reading subskills in first and second graders. *Scientific Studies of Reading, 3,* 129–157.

Manis, F. R., Seidenberg, M. S., Doi, L. M., McBride-Chang, C., & Peterson, A. (1996). On the bases of two subtypes of developmental dyslexia. *Cognition, 58,* 157–195.

Manis, F. R., Szeszulski, P. A., Holt, L. K., & Graves, K. (1990). Variation in component word recognition and spelling skills among dyslexic children and normal readers. In T. H. Carr & B. A. Levy (Eds.), *Reading and its development: Component skills approaches* (pp. 207–259). San Diego, CA: Academic Press.

Manis, F. R., Szeszulski, P., Howell, M., & Horn, C. (1986). A comparison of analogy- and rule-based decoding strategies in normal and dyslexic children. *Journal of Reading Behavior, 18,* 203–218.

Mann, V. (1984). Reading skill and language skill. *Developmental Review, 4,* 1–15.

Mann, V. (1986). Why some children encounter reading problems. In J. Torgesen & B. Wong (Eds.), *Psychological and educational perspectives on learning disabilities* (pp. 133–159). New York: Academic Press.

Mann, V. A. (1993). Phoneme awareness and future reading ability. *Journal of Learning Disabilities, 26,* 259–269.

Mann, V. A., Shankweiler, D., & Smith, S. (1984). The association between comprehension of spoken sentences and early reading ability: The role of phonetic representation. *Journal of Child Language, 11,* 627–643.

Mann, V. A., Tobin, P., & Wilson, R. (1987). Measuring phonological awareness through the invented spellings of kindergartners. *Merrill-Palmer Quarterly, 33,* 365–391.

Manning, M. (1988). *The standard periodical directory* (11th ed.). New York: Oxbridge Communications.

Marcel, T. (1974). The effective visual field and the use of context in fast and slow readers of two ages. *British Journal of Psychology, 65,* 479–492.

Maria, K., & MacGinitie, W. H. (1982). Reading comprehension disabilities: Knowledge structures and non-accommodating text processing strategies. *Annals of Dyslexia, 32,* 33–59.

Marsh, G., & Mineo, R. (1977). Training preschool children to recognize phonemes in words. *Journal of Educational Psychology, 69,* 748–753.

Marshall, J. C., & Newcombe, F. (1973). Patterns of paralexia: A psycholinguistic approach. *Journal of Psycholinguistic Research, 2,* 175–199.

Marslen-Wilson, W. D. (1975). Sentence perception as an interactive parallel process. *Science, 189,* 226–227.

Martin, F., & Lovegrove, W. (1988). Uniform and field flicker in control and specifically disabled readers. *Perception, 17,* 203–214.

Maruyama, G., Rubin, R., & Kingsbury, G. (1981). Self-esteem and educational achievement: Independent constructs with a common cause? *Journal of Personality and Social Psychology, 40,* 962–975.

Mason, M. (1975). Reading ability and letter search time: Effects of orthographic structure defined by single-letter positional frequency. *Journal of Experimental Psychology: General, 104,* 146–166.

Mason, M. (1978). From print to sound in mature readers as a function of reader ability and two forms of orthographic regularity. *Memory and Cognition, 6,* 568–581.

Mason, M. (1980). Reading ability and the encoding of item and location information. *Journal of Experimental Psychology: Human Perception and Performance, 6,* 89–98.

Masonheimer, P. E., Drum, P. A., & Ehri, L. C. (1984). Does environmental print identification lead children into word reading? *Journal of Reading Behavior, 16,* 257–271.

Massaro, D. W. (1975). Primary and secondary recognition in reading. In D. W. Massaro (Ed.), *Understanding language: An information processing analysis of speech perception, reading, and psycholinguistics* (pp. 241–289). New York: Academic Press.

Massaro, D. W. (1978). A stage model of reading and listening. *Visible Language, 12,* 3–26.

Massaro, D. W., Jones, R. D., Lipscomb, C., & Scholz, R. (1978). Role of prior knowledge on naming and lexical decisions with good and poor stimulus information. *Journal of Experimental Psychology: Human Learning and Memory, 4,* 498–512.

Massaro, D. W., Venezky, R. L., & Taylor, G. A. (1979). Orthographic regularity, positional frequency, and visual processing of letter strings. *Journal of Experimental Psychology: General, 108,* 107–124.

Masson, M. E. J. (1995). A distributed memory model of semantic priming. *Journal of Experimental Psychology: Learning, Memory, and Cognition, 21,* 3–23.

Masson, M. E. J., & Sala, L. S. (1978). Interactive processes in sentence comprehension and reading. *Cognitive Psychology, 10,* 244–270.

McBride-Chang, C. (1995). Phonological processing, speech perception, and reading disability: An integrative review. *Educational Psychologist, 30,* 109–121.

McBride-Chang, C., & Chang, L. (1995). Memory, print exposure, and metacognition: Components of reading in Chinese children. *International Journal of Psychology, 30,* 607–616.

McBride-Chang, C., Manis, F. R., Seidenberg, M. S., Custodio, R., & Doi, L. (1993). Print exposure as a predictor of word reading and reading comprehension in disabled and nondisabled readers. *Journal of Educational Psychology, 85,* 230–238.

McBride-Chang, C., Wagner, R. K., & Chang, L. (1997). Growth modeling of phonological awareness. *Journal of Educational Psychology, 89,* 621–630.

McCall, R. B. (1981). Nature–nurture and the two realms of development: A proposed integration with respect to mental development. *Child Development, 52,* 1–12.

McClelland, J. L., & Rumelhart, D. E. (1981). An interactive activation model of context effects in letter perception: Part 1. An account of basic findings. *Psychological Review, 88,* 375–407.

McClure, J., Kalk, M., & Keenan, V. (1980). Use of grammatical morphemes by beginning readers. *Journal of Learning Disabilities, 13,* 262–267.

McConkie, G. W., & Rayner, K. (1976). Identifying the span of the effective stimulus in reading: Literature review and theories of reading. In H. Singer & R. Ruddell (Eds.), *Theoretical models and processes of reading* (2nd ed., pp. 137–162). Newark, DE: International Reading Association.

McConkie, G. W., & Zola, D. (1981). Language constraints and the functional stimulus in reading. In A. M. Lesgold & C. A. Perfetti (Eds.), *Interactive processes in reading* (pp. 155–175). Hillsdale, NJ: Erlbaum.

McConkie, G. W., & Zola, D. (1985, April). *Computer aided reading: An environment for developmental research.* Paper presented at the annual meeting of the Society for Research in Child Development, Toronto, ON.

McCormick, C., & Samuels, S. J. (1979). Word recognition by second graders: The unit of perception and interrelationships among accuracy, latency, and comprehension. *Journal of Reading Behavior, 11,* 107–118.

McCusker, L. X., Hillinger, M. L., & Bias, R. G. (1981). Phonological recoding and reading. *Psychological Bulletin, 89,* 217–245.

McDougall, S., Hulme, C., Ellis, A., & Monk, A. (1994). Learning to read: The role of short-term memory and phonological skills. *Journal of Experimental Child Psychology, 58,* 112–133.

McGill-Franzen, A. (1987). Failure to learn to read: Formulating a policy problem. *Reading Research Quarterly, 22,* 475–490.

McGuinness, D. (1997). *Why our children can't read: And what we can do about it.* New York: Free Press.

McKenna, M., Stahl, S., & Reinking, D. (1994). A critical commentary on research, politics, and whole language. *Journal of Reading Behavior, 26,* 1–22.

McKenna, M. C., & Kear, D. J. (1990). Measuring attitude toward reading: A new tool for teachers. *Reading Teacher, 43,* 626–639.

McKenna, M. C., & Robinson, R. D. (1999). The impact of the *Journal of Reading Behavior* on reading scholarship. *Journal of Literacy Research, 31,* 93–104.

McKeown, M., Beck, I., Omanson, R., & Perfetti, C. (1983). The effects of long-term vocabulary instruction on reading comprehension. *Journal of Reading Behavior, 15,* 3–18.

McKinney, J. D. (1987). Research on the identification of learning-disabled children:

Perspectives on changes in educational policy. In S. Vaughn & C. Bos (Eds.), *Research in learning disabilities* (pp. 215–233). Boston: College-Hill.

McLeod, P. (1978). Does probe RT measure central processing demand? *Quarterly Journal of Experimental Psychology, 30,* 83–89.

McLeod, P., McLaughlin, C., & Nimmo-Smith, I. (1985). Information encapsulation and automaticity: Evidence from the visual control of finely timed actions. In M. Posner & O. Marin (Eds.), *Attention and performance* (Vol. 11, pp. 391–406). Hillsdale, NJ: Erlbaum.

McLeskey, J. (1989). The influence of level of discrepancy on the identification of students with learning disabilities. *Journal of Learning Disabilities, 22,* 435–438.

McLeskey, J., & Rieth, H. (1982). Controlling IQ differences between reading disabled and normal children: An empirical example. *Journal of Learning Disabilities, 15,* 481–483.

McPike, E. (1998, Spring–Summer). The unique power of reading and how to unleash it. *American Educator, 22*(1–2), pp. 4–5.

Meara, P., & Buxton, B. (1987). An alternative to multiple choice vocabulary tests. *Language Testing, 4,* 142–151.

Medawar, P. B. (1979). *Advice to a young scientist.* New York: Harper & Row.

Medawar, P. B. (1982). *Pluto's republic.* Oxford, England: Oxford University Press.

Medawar, P. B. (1984). *The limits of science.* New York: Harper & Row.

Medawar, P. B. (1990). *The threat and the glory.* New York: HarperCollins.

Menyuk, P., & Flood, J. (1981). Linguistic competence, reading, writing problems, and remediation. *Bulletin of the Orton Society, 31,* 13–28.

Mercy, J., & Steelman, L. (1982). Familial influence on the intellectual attainment of children. *American Sociological Review, 47,* 532–542.

Merrill, E., Sperber, R., & McCauley, C. (1981). Differences in semantic encoding as a function of reading comprehension skill. *Memory and Cognition, 9,* 618–624.

Merton, R. (1968). The Matthew effect in science. *Science, 159,* 56–63.

Metcalf, S. D. (1998, March). Attention deficits. *Lingua Franca, 8*(2), 60–64.

Metsala, J. L. (1997a). An examination of word frequency and neighborhood density in the development of spoken word recognition. *Memory and Cognition, 25,* 47–56.

Metsala, J. L. (1997b). Spoken word recognition in reading disabled children. *Journal of Educational Psychology, 89,* 159–169.

Metsala, J. L. (1999). Young children's phonological awareness and nonword repetition as a function of vocabulary development. *Journal of Educational Psychology, 91,* 3–19.

Metsala, J. L., & Brown, G. D. A. (1998). Normal and dyslexic reading development: The role of formal models. In C. Hulme & R. M. Joshi (Eds.), *Reading and spelling: Development and disorder* (pp. 235–261). Hove, England: Erlbaum.

Metsala, J. L., & Ehri, L. C. (Eds.). (1999). *Word recognition in beginning literacy.* Mahwah, NJ: Erlbaum.

Metsala, J. L., & Stanovich, K. E. (1995, April). *An examination of young children's phonological processing as a function of lexical development.* Paper presented at the annual meeting of the American Educational Research Association, San Francisco.

Metsala, J. L., Stanovich, K. E., & Brown, G. D. A. (1998). Regularity effects and the phonological deficit model of reading disabilities: A meta-analytic review. *Journal of Educational Psychology, 90,* 279–293.

Metsala, J. L., & Walley, A. C. (1998). Spoken vocabulary growth and the segmental restructuring of lexical representations: Precursors to phonemic awareness and early reading ability. In J. L. Metsala & J. L. Ehri (Eds.), *Word recognition in beginning literacy* (pp. 89–119). Mahwah, NJ: Erlbaum.

Meyer, B., Brandt, D., & Bluth, G. (1980). Use of top-level structure in text: Key for reading comprehension of ninth-grade students. *Reading Research Quarterly, 16,* 72–103.

Meyer, D. E., & Schvaneveldt, R. W. (1971). Facilitation in recognizing pairs of words: Evidence of a dependence between retrieval operations. *Journal of Experimental Psychology, 90,* 227–234.

Meyer, D. E., Schvaneveldt, R. W., & Ruddy, M. G. (1974). Functions of graphemic and phonemic codes in visual word recognition. *Memory and Cognition, 2,* 309–321.

Meyer, D. E., Schvaneveldt, R. W., & Ruddy, M. G. (1975). Loci of contextual effects on word recognition. In P. M. A. Rabbitt & S. Dornic (Eds.), *Attention and performance* (Vol. 5, pp. 98–118). New York: Academic Press.

Mezynski, K. (1983). Issues concerning the acquisition of knowledge: Effects of vocabulary training on reading comprehension. *Review of Educational Research, 53,* 253–279.

Miller, G. A., & Gildea, P. M. (1987). How children learn words. *Scientific American, 257*(3), 94–99.

Miller, G. R., & Coleman, E. B. (1967). A set of thirty-six prose passages calibrated for complexity. *Journal of Verbal Learning and Verbal Behavior, 6,* 851–854.

Miller, T., & Davis, E. (1982). *The mildly handicapped student.* New York: Grune & Stratton.

Minsky, M. L. (1987). *The society of mind.* New York: Simon & Schuster.

Mishler, E. (1990). Validation in inquiry-guided research: The role of exemplars in narrative studies. *Harvard Educational Review, 60,* 415–442.

Mitchell, D. (1982). *The process of reading: A cognitive analysis of fluent reading and learning to read.* New York: Wiley.

Mitchell, D. C., & Green, D. W. (1978). The effects of context and content on immediate processing in reading. *Quarterly Journal of Experimental Psychology, 30,* 609–636.

Mody, M., Studdert-Kennedy, M., & Brady, S. (1997). Speech deficits in poor readers: Auditory processing or phonological coding? *Journal of Experimental Child Psychology, 62,* 199–231.

Monaghan, E. J. (1980). A history of the syndrome of dyslexia with implications for its treatment. In C. McCullough (Ed.), *Inchworm, inchworm: Persistent problems in reading education* (pp. 87–101). Newark, DE: IRA.

Morais, J., Bertelson, P., Cary, L., & Alegria, J. (1986). Literacy training and speech segmentation. *Cognition, 24,* 45–64.

Morais, J., Cary, L., Alegria, J., & Bertelson, P. (1979). Does awareness of speech as a sequence of phones arise spontaneously? *Cognition, 7,* 323–331.

Morris, J. (1984). Children like Frank, deprived of literacy unless. . . . In D. Dennis (Ed.), *Reading: Meeting children's special needs* (pp. 16–28). London: Heinemann.

Morris, R. D., Stuebing, K., Fletcher, J. M., Shaywitz, S. E., Lyon, G. R., Shankweiler, D., Katz, L., Francis, D. J., & Shaywitz, B. A. (1998). Subtypes of reading disability: Variability around a phonological core. *Journal of Educational Psychology, 90,* 347–373.

Morrison, F. J. (1984). Word decoding and rule-learning in normal and disabled readers. *Remedial and Special Education, 5*, 20–27.

Morrison, F. J. (1987a). The nature of reading disability: Toward an integrative framework. In S. Ceci (Ed.), *Handbook of cognitive, social, and neuropsychological aspects of learning disabilities* (pp. 33–62). Hillsdale, NJ: Erlbaum.

Morrison, F. J. (1987b, November). The "5–7" shift revisited: A natural experiment. Paper presented at the annual meeting of the Psychonomic Society, Seattle, WA.

Morrison, F. J. (1991). Learning (and not learning) to read: A developmental framework. In L. Rieben & C. Perfetti (Eds.), *Learning to read: Basic research and its implications* (pp. 163–174). Hillsdale, NJ: Erlbaum.

Morrison, F. J., Giordani, B., & Nagy, J. (1977). Reading disability: An information processing analysis. *Science, 196*, 77–79.

Morrison, F. J., Griffith, E., & Alberts, D. (1997). Nature–nurture in the classroom: Entrance age, school readiness, and learning in children. *Developmental Psychology, 33*, 254–262.

Morrison, F. J., & Manis, F. R. (1982). Cognitive processes and reading disability: A critique and proposal. In C. Brainerd & M. Pressley (Eds.), *Verbal processes in children* (pp. 59–93). New York: Springer-Verlag.

Morrison, F. J., Smith, L., & Dow-Ehrensberger, M. (1995). Education and cognitive development: A natural experiment. *Developmental Psychology, 31*, 789–799.

Morrow, L. M., Tracey, D. H., Woo, D. G., & Pressley, M. (1999). Characteristics of exemplary first-grade literacy instruction. *Reading Teacher, 52*, 462–476.

Morton, J. (1969). The interaction of information in word recognition. *Psychological Review, 76*, 165–178.

Morton, J. A. (1970). A functional model for memory. In D. A. Norman (Ed.), *Models of human memory* (pp. 203–254). New York: Academic Press.

Mosenthal, P., Walmsley, S., & Allington, R. (1978). Word recognition reconsidered: Toward a multi-context model. *Visible Language, 12*, 448–468.

Mosenthal, P. B. (1989). The whole language approach: Teachers between a rock and a hard place. *Reading Teacher, 42*(8), 628–629.

Musgrave, A. (1980). Kuhn's second thoughts. In G. Gutting (Ed.), *Paradigms and revolutions* (pp. 39–53). Notre Dame, IN: University of Notre Dame Press.

Musgrove, F. (1982). *Education and anthropology*. New York: Wiley.

Muter, V., Hulme, C., Snowling, M., & Taylor, S. (1998). Segmentation, not rhyming, predicts early progress in learning to read. *Journal of Experimental Child Psychology, 71*, 3–27.

Nagel, T. (1997). *The last word*. New York: Oxford University Press.

Nagy, W. E., & Anderson, R. C. (1984). How many words are there in printed school English? *Reading Research Quarterly, 19*, 304–330.

Nagy, W. E., & Herman, P. A. (1987). Breadth and depth of vocabulary knowledge: Implications for acquisition and instruction. In M. McKeown & M. Curtis (Eds.), *The nature of vocabulary acquisition* (pp. 19–35). Hillsdale, NJ: Erlbaum.

Nagy, W. E., Herman, P. A., & Anderson, R. C. (1985). Learning words from context. *Reading Research Quarterly, 20*, 233–253.

Nation, K. (1999). Reading skills in hyperlexia: A developmental perspective. *Psychological Bulletin, 125*, 338–355.

Nation, K., & Hulme, C. (1997). Phonemic segmentation, not onset-rime segmentation, predicts early reading and spelling skills. *Reading Research Quarterly, 32*(2), 154–167.

Nation, K., & Snowling, M. J. (1998). Individual differences in contextual facilitation: Evidence from dyslexia and poor reading comprehension. *Child Development, 69*, 996–1011.

Navon, D. (1984). Resources—A theoretical soup stone? *Psychological Review, 91*, 216–234.

Navon, D. (1985). Attention division or attention sharing? In M. Posner & O. Marin (Eds.), *Attention and performance* (Vol. 11, pp. 133–146). Hillsdale, NJ: Erlbaum.

Navon, D. (1989). The importance of being visible: On the role of attention in a mind viewed as an anarchic intelligence system: 1. Basic tenets. *European Journal of Cognitive Psychology, 1*, 191–213.

Navon, D., & Gopher, D. (1980). Task difficulty, resources, and dual-task performance. In R. Nickerson (Ed.), *Attention and performance* (Vol. 8, pp. 297–315). Hillsdale, NJ: Erlbaum.

Neely, J. H. (1976). Semantic priming and retrieval from lexical memory: Evidence for facilitatory and inhibitory processes. *Memory and Cognition, 4*, 648–654.

Neely, J. H. (1977). Semantic priming and retrieval from lexical memory: Roles of inhibitionless spreading activation and limited-capacity attention. *Journal of Experimental Psychology: General, 106*, 226–254.

Neisser, U. (1967). *Cognitive psychology.* New York: Appleton-Century-Crofts.

Nell, V. (1988). The psychology of reading for pleasure: Needs and gratification. *Reading Research Quarterly, 23*, 6–50.

Neuman, S. B. (1999). Books make a difference: A study of access to literacy. *Reading Research Quarterly, 34*, 286–311.

Neumann, O. (1987). Beyond capacity: A functional view of attention. In H. Heuer & A. F. Sanders (Eds.), *Perspectives on perception and action* (pp. 361–394). London: Routledge & Kegan Paul.

Neville, M. H., & Pugh, A. K. (1976–1977). Context in reading and listening: Variations in approach to cloze tasks. *Reading Research Quarterly, 12*, 13–31.

Newcomer, P., & Magee, P. (1977). The performance of learning (reading) disabled children on a test of spoken language. *Reading Teacher, 30*, 896–900.

Newman, D. S., & Hagen, J. W. (1981). Memory strategies in children with learning disabilities. *Journal of Applied Developmental Psychology, 1*, 297–312.

Nicholson, T. (1986). Reading is not a guessing game—The Great Debate revisited. *Reading Psychology, 7*, 197–210.

Nicholson, T. (1991a). *Overcoming the Matthew effect: Solving reading problems across the curriculum.* Wellington: New Zealand Council for Educational Research.

Nicholson, T. (1991b). Do children read words better in context or in lists? A classic study revisited. *Journal of Educational Psychology, 83*, 444–450.

Nicholson, T., Lillas, C., & Rzoska, M. (1988). Have we been misled by miscues? *Reading Teacher, 42*(1), 6–10.

Nicolson, R. I. (1996). Developmental dyslexia: Past, present, and future. *Dyslexia, 2*, 190–207.

Nisbett, R., & Ross, L. (1980). *Human inference: Strategies and shortcomings of social judgment.* Englewood Cliffs, NJ: Prentice-Hall.

Nisbett, R., & Wilson, T. (1977). Telling more than we know: Verbal reports on mental processes. *Psychological Review, 84*, 231–259.

Norman, C., & Zigmond, N. (1980). Characteristics of children labeled and served as learning disabled in school systems affiliated with child service demonstration centers. *Journal of Learning Disabilities, 13,* 16–21.

Norman, D. A. (1976). *Memory and attention.* New York: Wiley.

Norris, D. (1990). Connectionism: A case for modularity. In D. Balota, G. Flores d'Arcais, & K. Rayner (Eds.), *Comprehension processes in reading* (pp. 331–343). Hillsdale, NJ: Erlbaum.

Nystrand, M. (1987). The role of context in written communication. In R. Horowitz & S. J. Samuels (Eds.), *Comprehending oral and written language* (pp. 197–214). San Diego, CA: Academic Press.

Oakan, R., Wiener, M., & Cromer, W. (1971). Identification, organization, and reading comprehension for good and poor readers. *Journal of Educational Psychology, 62,* 71–78.

Oakhill, J., & Garnham, A. (1988). *Becoming a skilled reader.* Oxford, England: Blackwell.

Oatley, K. (1992). *Best laid schemes: The psychology of emotions.* Cambridge, England: Cambridge University Press.

Ogden, W. C., Martin, D. W., & Paap, K. R. (1980). Processing demands of encoding: What does secondary task performance reflect? *Journal of Experimental Psychology: Human Perception and Performance, 6,* 355–367.

Oka, E., & Paris, S. (1986). Patterns of motivation and reading skills in underachieving children. In S. Ceci (Ed.), *Handbook of cognitive, social, and neuropsychological aspects of learning disabilities* (Vol. 2, pp. 115–145). Hillsdale, NJ: Erlbaum.

Olofsson, A., & Lundberg, I. (1985). Evaluation of long-term effects of phonemic awareness training in kindergarten. *Scandinavian Journal of Psychology, 26,* 21–34.

Olson, D. R. (1977). From utterance to text: The bias of language in speech and writing. *Harvard Educational Review, 47,* 257–281.

Olson, D. R. (1986a). Intelligence and literacy: The relationships between intelligence and the technologies of representation and communication. In R. J. Sternberg & R. K. Wagner (Eds.), *Practical intelligence* (pp. 338–360). Cambridge, England: Cambridge University Press.

Olson, D. R. (1986b). The cognitive consequences of literacy. *Canadian Psychology, 27,* 109–121.

Olson, D. R. (1988). Mind and media: The epistemic functions of literacy. *Journal of Communication, 38,* 27–36.

Olson, D. R. (1994). *The world on paper.* Cambridge, England: Cambridge University Press.

Olson, D. R., & Torrance, N. (Eds.). (1991). *Literacy and orality.* Cambridge, England: Cambridge University Press.

Olson, D. R., Torrance, N., & Hildyard, A. (Eds.). (1985). *Literacy, language, and learning.* New York: Cambridge University Press.

Olson, R. K. (1991, September). *Genetic etiologies of reading disability.* Paper presented at the NATO Advanced Study Institute on Differential Diagnosis and Treatments of Reading and Writing Disorders, Chateau de Bonas, France.

Olson, R. K. (1994). Language deficits in "specific" reading disability. In M. Gernsbacher (Ed.), *Handbook of psycholinguistics* (pp. 895–916). San Diego, CA: Academic Press.

Olson, R. K. (1999). Genes, environment, and reading disabilities. In R. J. Sternberg &

L. Spear-Swerling (Eds.), *Perspectives on learning disabilities* (pp. 3–21). New York: Westview/HarperCollins.

Olson, R. K., Datta, H., Gayan, J., Hulslander, J., Ring, J., Wise, B. W., DeFries, J., Pennington, B., & Wadsworth, S. (1999, April). *Does IQ matter for the reading profile, etiology, and remediation of reading disability?* Paper presented at the annual meeting of the Society for the Scientific Study of Reading, Montreal, Canada.

Olson, R. K., Davidson, B., Kliegl, R., & Davies, S. (1984). Development of phonetic memory in disabled and normal readers. *Journal of Experimental Child Psychology, 37,* 187–206.

Olson, R. K., Foltz, G., & Wise, B. (1986). Reading instruction and remediation with the aid of computer speech. *Behavior Research Methods, Instruments, and Computers, 18,* 93–99.

Olson, R. K., Forsberg, H., & Wise, B. (1994). Genes, environment, and the development of orthographic skills. In V. Berninger (Eds.), *Varieties of orthographic knowledge: Theoretical and developmental issues* (Vol. 1, pp. 27–71). Dordrecht, The Netherlands: Kluwer Academic.

Olson, R. K., Kliegl, R., & Davidson, B. (1983). Dyslexic and normal readers' eye movements. *Journal of Experimental Psychology: Human Perception and Performance, 9,* 816–825.

Olson, R. K., Kliegl, R., Davidson, B., & Foltz, G. (1985). Individual and developmental differences in reading disability. In G. E. MacKinnon & T. Waller (Eds.), *Reading research: Advances in theory and practice* (Vol. 4, pp. 1–64). London: Academic Press.

Olson, R. K., Rack, J., Conners, F., DeFries, J., & Fulker, D. (1991). Genetic etiology of individual differences in reading disability. In L. Feagans, E. Short, & L. Meltzer (Eds.), *Subtypes of learning disabilities* (pp. 113–135). Hillsdale, NJ: Erlbaum.

Olson, R. K., Wise, B., Conners, F., & Rack, J. (1990). Organization, heritability, and remediation of component word recognition and language skills in disabled readers. In T. Carr & B. A. Levy (Eds.), *Reading and its development: Component skills approaches* (pp. 261–322). New York: Academic Press.

Olson, R. K., Wise, B., Conners, F., Rack, J., & Fulker, D. (1989). Specific deficits in component reading and language skills: Genetic and environmental influences. *Journal of Learning Disabilities, 22,* 339–348.

Olson, R. K., Wise, B., Johnson, M., & Ring, J. (1997). The etiology and remediation of phonologically based word recognition and spelling disabilities: Are phonological deficits the "hole" story? In B. Blachman (Ed.), *Foundations of reading acquisition: Implications for early intervention* (pp. 305–326). Mahweh, NJ: Erlbaum.

Ong, W. J. (1967). *The presence of the word.* Minneapolis: University of Minnesota Press.

Ong, W. J. (1982). *Orality and literacy.* London: Methuen.

Orwell, G. (1937/1989). *The road to Wigan Pier.* London: Penguin Books.

Orwell, G. (1952). *Homage to Catalonia.* New York: Harcourt, Brace & World, Inc.

Orwell, S., & Angus, I. (Eds.). (1968). *The collected essays, journalism and letters of George Orwell* (Vols. 1–4). New York: Harcourt Brace Jovanovich.

Otto, W. (1993). What I should have said. *Journal of Reading, 36*(5), 412–415.

Paap, K. R., Newsome, S. L., McDonald, J. E., & Schvaneveldt, R. W. (1982). An activation-verification model for letter and word recognition: The word superiority effect. *Psychological Review, 89,* 573–594.

Paap, K. R., & Ogden, W. C. (1981). Letter encoding is an obligatory but capacity-demanding operation. *Journal of Experimental Psychology: Human Perception and Performance, 7,* 518–527.

Pace, A. J., & Golinkoff, R. M. (1976). Relationship between word difficulty and access of single-word meaning by skilled and less skilled readers. *Journal of Educational Psychology, 68,* 760–767.

Page, M. (in press). Connectionist modeling in psychology: A localist manifesto. *Behavioral and Brain Sciences.*

Palmer, J., MacLeod, C. M., Hunt, E., & Davidson, J. E. (1985). Information processing correlates of reading. *Journal of Memory and Language, 24,* 59–88.

Paraskevopoulos, J., & Kirk, S. (1969). *The development and psychometric characteristics of the Revised Illinois Test of Psycholinguistic Abilities.* Urbana: University of Illinois Press.

Paris, S., & Myers, M. (1981). Comprehension monitoring, memory, and study strategies of good and poor readers. *Journal of Reading Behavior, 13,* 5–22.

Paris, S. G. (1987). Introduction to current issues in reading comprehension. *Educational Psychologist, 22,* 209–212.

Paris, S. G., Lipson, M. Y., & Wixson, K. K. (1983). Becoming a strategic reader. *Contemporary Educational Psychology, 8,* 293–316.

Parkin, A. G. (1982). Phonological recoding in lexical decision: Effects of spelling-to-sound regularity depend on how regularity is defined. *Memory and Cognition, 10,* 43–53.

Parkin, A. G., & Underwood, G. (1983). Orthographic vs. phonological irregularity in lexical decision. *Memory and Cognition, 11,* 351–355.

Pashler, H. E. (1998). *The psychology of attention.* Cambridge, MA: MIT Press.

Patberg, J. P., & Yonas, A. (1978). The effects of the reader's skill and the difficulty of the text on the perceptual span in reading. *Journal of Experimental Psychology: Human Perception and Performance, 4,* 545–552.

Patterson, K., & Coltheart, V. (1987). Phonological processes in reading: A tutorial review. In M. Coltheart (Ed.), *Attention and performance* (Vol. 12, pp. 421–447). London: Erlbaum.

Patterson, K., Marshall, J., & Coltheart, M. (1985). *Surface dyslexia.* London: Erlbaum.

Patterson, K. E., & Morton, J. (1985). From orthography to phonology: An attempt at an old interpretation. In K. Patterson, J. Marshall, & M. Coltheart (Eds.), *Surface dyslexia* (pp. 335–359). London: Erlbaum.

Paulhus, D. L. (1984). Two-component models of socially desirable responding. *Journal of Personality and Social Psychology, 46,* 598–609.

Pearson, P., & Camperell, K. (1981). Comprehension of text structures. In J. T. Guthrie (Ed.), *Comprehension and teaching* (pp. 27–55). Newark, DE: International Reading Association.

Pearson, P. D. (Ed.). (1984). *Handbook of reading research.* New York: Longman.

Pearson, P. D. (1999). A historically based review of preventing reading difficulties in young children. *Reading Research Quarterly, 34,* 231–246.

Pearson, P. D., & Kamil, M. L. (1977–1978). What hath Carver raud? A reaction to Carver's "Toward a theory of reading comprehension and rauding." *Reading Research Quarterly, 13,* 92–115.

Pellegrino, J. W., & Glaser, R. (1979). Cognitive correlates and components in the analysis of individual differences. In R. J. Sternberg & D. K. Detterman (Eds.), *Human intelligence: Perspectives on its theory and measurement* (pp. 61–88). Norwood, NJ: Ablex.

Pennington, B. F. (1986). Issues in the diagnosis and phenotype analysis of dyslexia: Implications for family studies. In S. D. Smith (Ed.), *Genetics and learning disabilities* (pp. 69–96). San Diego, CA: College-Hill Press.

Pennington, B. F. (1991). Genetic and neurological influences on reading disability: An overview. *Reading and Writing: An Interdisciplinary Journal, 3,* 191–201.

Pennington, B. F., Gilger, J., Olson, R. K., & DeFries, J. C. (1992). The external validity of age- versus IQ-discrepancy definitions of reading disability: Lessons from a twin study. *Journal of Learning Disabilities, 25,* 562–573.

Pennington, B. F., McCabe, L. L., Smith, S., Lefly, D., Bookman, M., Kimberling, W., & Lubs, H. (1986). Spelling errors in adults with a form of familial dyslexia. *Child Development, 57,* 1001–1013.

Pennington, B. F., Van Orden, G. K., Kirson, D., & Haith, M. (1991). What is the causal relation between verbal STM problems and dyslexia? In S. A. Brady & D. P. Shankweiler (Eds.), *Phonological processes in literacy* (pp. 173–186). Hillsdale, NJ: Erlbaum.

Pennington, B. F., Van Orden, G. C., Smith, S. D., Green, P. A., & Haith, M. M. (1990). Phonological processing skills and deficits in adult dyslexics. *Child Development, 61,* 1753–1778.

Perfetti, C. A. (1984). Reading acquisition and beyond: Decoding includes cognition. *American Journal of Education, 92,* 40–60.

Perfetti, C. A. (1985). *Reading ability.* New York: Oxford University Press.

Perfetti, C. A. (1986). Continuities in reading acquisition, reading skill, and reading disability. *Remedial and Special Education, 7,* 11–21.

Perfetti, C. A. (1991). The psychology, pedagogy, and politics of reading. *Psychological Science, 2,* 70–76.

Perfetti, C. A. (1992). The representation problem in reading acquisition. In P. B. Gough, L. C. Ehri, & R. Treiman (Eds.), *Reading acquisition* (pp. 145–174). Hillsdale, NJ: Erlbaum.

Perfetti, C. A. (1994). Psycholinguistics and reading ability. In M. Gernsbacher (Ed.), *Handbook of psycholinguistics* (pp. 849–894). San Diego, CA: Academic Press.

Perfetti, C. A. (1995). Cognitive research can inform reading education. *Journal of Research in Reading, 18*(2), 106–115.

Perfetti, C. A., Beck, I., Bell, L., & Hughes, C. (1987). Phonemic knowledge and learning to read are reciprocal: A longitudinal study of first grade children. *Merrill-Palmer Quarterly, 33,* 283–319.

Perfetti, C. A., Beck, I., & Hughes, C. (1981, March). *Phonemic knowledge and learning to read.* Paper presented at the annual meeting of the Society for Research in Child Development, Boston.

Perfetti, C. A., & Curtis, M. E. (1986). Reading. In R. F. Dillon & R. J. Sternberg (Eds.), *Cognition and instruction* (pp. 13–57). New York: Academic Press.

Perfetti, C. A., Finger, E., & Hogaboam, T. W. (1978). Sources of vocalization latency differences between skilled and less skilled young readers. *Journal of Educational Psychology, 70,* 730–739.

Perfetti, C. A., Goldman, S. R., & Hogaboam, T. W. (1979). Reading skill and the identification of words in discourse context. *Memory and Cognition, 7,* 273–282.

Perfetti, C. A., & Hogaboam, T. W. (1975). The relationship between single word decoding and reading comprehension. *Journal of Educational Psychology, 67,* 461–469.

Perfetti, C. A., & Lesgold, A. M. (1977). Discourse comprehension and sources of individual differences. In M. Just & P. Carpenter (Eds.), *Cognitive processes in comprehension* (pp. 141–183). Hillsdale, NJ: Erlbaum.

Perfetti, C. A., & Lesgold, A. M. (1979). Coding and comprehension in skilled reading and implications for reading instruction. In L. B. Resnick & P. A. Weaver (Eds.), *Theory and practice of early reading* (Vol. 1, pp. 57–85). Hillsdale, NJ: Erlbaum.

Perfetti, C. A., & McCutchen, D. (1982). Speech processes in reading. In N. Lass (Eds.), *Speech and language: Advances in basic research and practice* (Vol. 7, pp. 237–269). New York: Academic Press.

Perfetti, C. A., & McCutchen, D. (1987). Schooled language competence: Linguistic abilities in reading and writing. In S. Rosenberg (Ed.), *Advances in applied psycholinguistics* (Vol. 2, pp. 105–141). Cambridge, England: Cambridge University Press.

Perfetti, C. A., & Roth, S. (1981). Some of the interactive processes in reading and their role in reading skill. In A. M. Lesgold & C. A. Perfetti (Eds.), *Interactive processes in reading* (pp. 269–297). Hillsdale, NJ: Erlbaum.

Perin, D. (1983). Phonemic segmentation and spelling. *British Journal of Psychology, 74,* 129–144.

Peterson, S. W., Fox, P. T., Posner, M. I., & Raichle, M. E. (1988). Positron emission tomographic studies of the cortical anatomy of single-word processing. *Nature, 331,* 585–589.

Piaget, J. (1926). *The language and thought of the child.* London: Routledge & Kegan Paul.

Pinker, S. (1997). *How the mind works.* New York: Norton.

Plaut, D. C., McClelland, J. L., Seidenberg, M. S., & Patterson, K. (1996). Understanding normal and impaired word reading: Computational principles in quasi-regular domains. *Psychological Review, 103,* 56–115.

Plaut, D. C., & Shallice, T. (1994). *Connectionist modelling in cognitive neuropsychology: A case study.* Hove, England: Erlbaum.

Plomin, R. (1991). A behavioral genetic approach to learning disabilities and their subtypes. In L. Feagans, E. Short, & L. Meltzer (Eds.), *Subtypes of learning disabilities* (pp. 83–109). Hillsdale, NJ: Erlbaum.

Plomin, R., & Bergeman, C. S. (1991). The nature of nurture: Genetic influences on "environmental" measures. *Behavioral and Brain Sciences, 14,* 373–427.

Plomin, R., Corley, R., DeFries, J. C., & Fulker, D. W. (1990). Individual differences in television viewing in early childhood: Nature as well as nurture. *Psychological Science, 1,* 371–377.

Plomin, R., DeFries, J., & Loehlin, J. (1977). Genotype–environment interaction and correlation in the analysis of human behavior. *Psychological Bulletin, 84,* 309–322.

Plomin, R., DeFries, J. C., & McClearn, G. E. (1990). *Behavioral genetics: A primer* (2nd ed.). New York: Freeman.

Popper, K. R. (1963). *Conjectures and refutations: The growth of scientific knowledge.* New York: Harper & Row.

Popper, K. R. (1971). *The open society and its enemies* (Vols. 1 & 2). Princeton, NJ: Princeton University Press.

Popper, K. R. (1972). *Objective knowledge.* Oxford, England: Oxford University Press.

Posnansky, C. J., & Rayner, K. (1977). Visual–feature and response components in a picture-word interference task with beginning and skilled readers. *Journal of Experimental Child Psychology, 24,* 440–460.

Posner, M. I. (1992). Attention as a cognitive and neural system. *Current Directions in Psychological Science, 1,* 11–14.

Posner, M. I., & Boies, S. J. (1971). Components of attention. *Psychological Review, 78,* 391–408.

Posner, M. I., & Carr, T. H. (1992). Lexical access and the brain: Anatomical constraints on cognitive models of word recognition. *American Journal of Psychology, 105,* 1–26.

Posner, M. I., Peterson, S. W., Fox, P. T., & Raichle, M. E. (1988). Localization of cognitive operations in the human brain. *Science, 240,* 1627–1631.

Posner, M. I., & Rogers, M. G. K. (1978). Chronometric analysis of abstraction and recognition. In W. K. Estes (Ed.), *Handbook of learning and cognitive processes* (Vol. 5, pp. 143–188). Hillsdale, NJ: Erlbaum.

Posner, M. I., & Snyder, C. R. R. (1975a). Attention and cognitive control. In R. L. Solso (Ed.), *Information processing and cognition: The Loyola Symposium* (pp. 55–84). Hillsdale, NJ: Erlbaum.

Posner, M. I., & Snyder, C. R. R. (1975b). Facilitation and inhibition in the processing of signals. In P. M. A. Rabbitt & S. Dornic (Eds.), *Attention and performance*(Vol. 5, pp. 669–682). New York: Academic Press.

Postman, N. (1985). *Amusing ourselves to death.* New York: Viking Penguin.

Pratt, A. C., & Brady, S. (1988). Relation of phonological awareness to reading disability in children and adults. *Journal of Educational Psychology, 80,* 319–323.

Pressley, M. (1998). *Reading instruction that works: The case for balanced teaching.* New York: Guilford Press.

Pressley, M., & Levin, J. R. (1987). Elaborative learning strategies for the inefficient learner. In S. J. Ceci (Ed.), *Handbook of cognitive, social, and neuropsychological aspects of learning disabilities* (Vol. 2, pp. 175–212). Hillsdale, NJ: Erlbaum.

Pring, L., & Snowling, M. (1986). Developmental changes in word recognition: An information-processing account. *Quarterly Journal of Experimental Psychology, 38A,* 395–418.

Prior, M., & McCorriston, M. (1985). Surface dyslexia: A regression effect? *Brain and Language, 25,* 52–71.

Pugh, K., Shaywitz, B. A., Shaywitz, S. E., Shankweiler, D. P., Katz, L., Fletcher, J. M., Skudlarski, P., Fulbright, R., Constable, R., Bronen, R., Lacadie, C., & Gore, J. (1997). Predicting reading performance from neuroimaging profiles: The cerebral basis of phonological effects in printed word identification. *Journal of Experimental Psychology: Human Perception and Performance, 23,* 299–318.

Pulvermuller, F. (1999). Words in the brain's language. *Behavioral and Brain Sciences, 22,* 253–336.

Purcell, D. G., Stanovich, K. E., & Spector, A. (1978). Visual angle and the word superiority effect. *Memory and Cognition, 6,* 3–8.

Purcell-Gates, V. (1988). Lexical and syntactic knowledge of written narrative held by well-read-to kindergartners and second graders. *Research in the Teaching of English, 22,* 128–157.

Pylyshyn, Z. W. (1981). The imagery debate: Analogue media versus tacit knowledge. *Psychological Review, 88,* 16–45.

Pylyshyn, Z. W. (1999). Is vision continuous with cognition? The case for cognitive impenetrability of visual perception. *Behavioral and Brain Sciences, 22,* 341–423.

Rabbitt, P. (1988). Human intelligence. *Quarterly Journal of Experimental Psychology, 40A,* 167–185.

Rack, J. (1985). Orthographic and phonetic coding in developmental dyslexia. *British Journal of Psychology, 76,* 325–340.

Rack, J. P., Snowling, M. J., & Olson, R. K. (1992). The nonword reading deficit in developmental dyslexia: A review. *Reading Research Quarterly, 27,* 28–53.

Rapala, M. M., & Brady, S. (1990). Reading ability and short-term memory: The role of phonological processing. *Reading and Writing: An Interdisciplinary Journal, 2,* 1–25.

Ravitch, D., & Finn, C. E. (1987). *What do our 17–year-olds know?* New York: Harper & Row.

Rayner, K. (1978). Eye movements in reading and information processing. *Psychological Bulletin, 85,* 618–660.

Rayner, K. (1985a). Do faulty eye movements cause dyslexia? *Developmental Neuropsychology, 1,* 3–15.

Rayner, K. (1985b). The role of eye movements in learning to read and reading disability. *Remedial and Special Education, 6,* 53–60.

Rayner, K. (1998). Eye movements in reading and information processing: 20 Years of research. *Psychological Bulletin, 124,* 372–422.

Rayner, K., & Bertera, J. H. (1979). Reading without a fovea. *Science, 206,* 468–469.

Rayner, K., Inhoff, A. W., Morrison, R. E., Slowiaczek, M. L., & Bertera, J. H. (1981). Masking of foveal and parafoveal vision during eye fixations in reading. *Journal of Experimental Psychology: Human Perception and Performance, 7,* 167–179.

Rayner, K., & Pollatsek, A. (1989). *The psychology of reading.* Englewood Cliffs, NJ: Prentice-Hall.

Read, C., & Ruyter, L. (1985). Reading and spelling skills in adults of low literacy. *Remedial and Special Education, 6,* 43–52.

Reading Coherence Initiative. (1999). *Understanding reading: What research says about how children learn to read.* Austin, TX: Southwest Educational Development Laboratory.

Redeker, G. (1984). On differences between spoken and written language. *Discourse Processes, 7,* 43–55.

Reed, J. C. (1970). The deficits of retarded readers—Fact or artifact? *Reading Teacher, 23,* 347–357.

Reed, M. A. (1989). Speech perception and the discrimination of brief auditory cues in reading disabled children. *Journal of Experimental Child Psychology, 48,* 270–292.

Reitsma, P. (1983). Printed word learning in beginning readers. *Journal of Experimental Child Psychology, 36,* 321–339.

Reitsma, P. (1984). Sound priming in beginning readers. *Child Development, 55,* 406–423.

Resnick, D. P., & Resnick, L. B. (1977). The nature of literacy: An historical exploration. *Harvard Educational Review, 47,* 370–385.

Reynolds, C. R. (1985). Measuring the aptitude–achievement discrepancy in learning disability diagnosis. *Remedial and Special Education, 6,* 37–55.

Rice, G. E. (1986). The everyday activities of adults: Implications for prose recall: 1. *Educational Gerontology, 12,* 173–186.

Rice, M., Howes, M., & Connell, P. (1998, July). *The Prison Reading Survey: A report to HM Prison Service Planning Group.* No. Cambridge, England: Author.

Richardson, E., DiBenedetto, B., & Adler, A. (1982). Use of the decoding skills test to study differences between good and poor readers. In K. Gadow & I. Bialer (Eds.), *Advances in learning and behavioral disabilities* (Vol. 1, pp. 25–74). Greenwich, CT: JAI Press.

Richek, M. (1977–1978). Readiness skills that predict initial word learning using two different methods of instruction. *Reading Research Quarterly, 13,* 200–222.

Rode, S. S. (1974). Development of phrase and clause boundary reading in children. *Reading Research Quarterly, 10,* 124–142.

Rodgers, B. (1983). The identification and prevalence of specific reading retardation. *British Journal of Educational Psychology, 53,* 369–373.

Rodrigo, V., McQuillan, J., & Krashen, S. (1996). Free voluntary reading and vocabulary knowledge in native speakers of Spanish. *Perceptual and Motor Skills, 83,* 648–650.

Rollman, G. B., & Nachmias, J. (1972). Simultaneous detection and recognition of chromatic flashes. *Perception and Psychophysics, 12,* 309–314.

Rorty, R. (1979). *Philosophy and the mirror of nature.* Princeton, NJ: Princeton University Press.

Rosinski, R. (1977). Picture–word interference is semantically based. *Child Development, 48,* 643–647.

Rosinski, R. R., & Wheeler, K. E. (1972). Children's use of orthographic structure in word discrimination. *Psychonomic Science, 26,* 97–98.

Rosinski, R. R., Golinkoff, R. M., & Kukish, K. S. (1975). Automatic semantic processing in a picture–word interference. *Child Development, 46,* 247–253.

Rosson, M. B. (1985). The interaction of pronunciation rules and lexical representations in reading aloud. *Memory and Cognition, 13,* 90–99.

Royer, J. M., Kulhavy, R., Lee, S., & Peterson, S. (1986). The relationship between reading and listening comprehension. *Educational and Psychological Research, 6,* 299–314.

Royer, J. M., Sinatra, G. M., & Schumer, H. (1990). Patterns of individual differences in the development of listening and reading comprehension. *Contemporary Educational Psychology, 15,* 183–196.

Rozin, P., & Gleitman, L. (1977). The structure and acquisition of reading: 2. The reading process and the acquisition of the alphabetic principle. In A. Reber & D. Scarborough (Eds.), *Toward a psychology of reading*)pp. 55–141). Hillsdale, NJ: Erlbaum.

Rubenstein, H., & Aborn, M. (1958). Learning, prediction, and readability. *Journal of Applied Psychology, 42,* 28–32.

Rubenstein, H., Lewis, S. S., & Rubenstein, M. (1971). Evidence for phonemic recoding in visual word recognition. *Journal of Verbal Learning and Verbal Behavior, 10,* 645–657.

Ruddell, R. B. (1965). The effect of similarity of oral and written patterns of language structure on reading comprehension. *Elementary English, 43,* 403–410.

Rumelhart, D. E. (1977). Toward an interactive model of reading. In S. Dornic (Ed.), *Attention and performance* (Vol. 6, pp. 573–603). Hillsdale, NJ: Erlbaum.

Rumelhart, D. E., & McClelland, J. L. (1982). An interactive activation model of context effects in letter perception: Part 2. The contextual enhancement effect and some tests and extensions of the model. *Psychological Review, 89,* 60–94.

Rumelhart, D. E., & McClelland, J. L. (1986). *Parallel distributed processing: Explorations in the microstructure of cognition* (Vol. 1). Cambridge, MA: MIT Press.

Ruse, M. (1999). *Mystery of mysteries: Is evolution a social construction?* Cambridge, MA: Harvard University Press.

Rutter, M. (1978). Prevalence and types of dyslexia. In A. Benton & D. Pearl (Eds.), *Dyslexia: An appraisal of current knowledge* (pp. 5–28). New York: Oxford University Press.

Rutter, M. (1983). School effects on pupil progress: Research findings and policy implications. *Child Development, 54,* 1–29.

Rutter, M., & Madge, N. (1976). *Cycles of disadvantage.* London: Heinemann.

Rutter, M., & Yule, W. (1975). The concept of specific reading retardation. *Journal of Child Psychology and Psychiatry, 16,* 181–197.

Rutter, M., Yule, B., Quintin, D., Rowlands, O., Yule, W., & Berger, M. (1974). Attainment and adjustment in two geographical areas: 3. Some factors accounting for area differences. *British Journal of Psychiatry, 125,* 520–533.

Ryle, G. (1949). *The concept of mind.* New York: Barnes & Noble.

Sá, W., West, R. F., & Stanovich, K. E. (1999). The domain specificity and generality of belief bias: Searching for a generalizable critical thinking skill. *Journal of Educational Psychology, 91,* 497–510.

Salter, D. J., & Stanovich, K. E. (1996, August). *Exposure to print in kindergarten and acquisition of literacy skills.* Paper presented at the annual meeting of the American Psychological Association, Toronto, Canada.

Salthouse, T. A. (1988). Resource-reduction interpretations of cognitive aging. *Developmental Review, 8,* 238–272.

Samuels, S. J. (1977). Introduction to theoretical models of reading. In W. Otto, C. Peters, & N. Peters (Eds.), *Reading problems: A multidisciplinary perspective* (pp. 7–41). Reading, MA: Addison-Wesley.

Samuels, S. J., Begy, G., & Chen, C. C. (1975–1976). Comparison of word recognition speed and strategies of less skilled and more highly skilled readers. *Reading Research Quarterly, 11,* 72–86.

Samuels, S. J., Dahl, P., & Archwamety, T. (1974). Effect of hypothesis/test training on reading skill. *Journal of Educational Psychology, 66,* 835–844.

Samuelsson, S., Gustafson, S., & Ronnberg, J. (1998). Visual and auditory priming in Swedish poor readers: A double dissociation. *Dyslexia, 4,* 16–29.

Sanford, A. J., Garrod, S., & Boyle, J. M. (1977). An independence of mechanism in the origins of reading and classification-related semantic distance effects. *Memory and Cognition, 5,* 214–220.

Santa, C. M., & Hoien, T. (1999). An assessment of Early Steps: A program for early intervention. *Reading Research Quarterly, 34,* 54–79.

Sattler, J. (1982). *Assessment of children's intelligence and special abilities* (2nd ed.). Boston: Allyn & Bacon.

Satz, P., & Friel, J. (1974). Some predictive antecedents of specific reading disability: A preliminary two-year follow-up. *Journal of Learning Disabilities, 7,* 437–444.

Satz, P., Morris, R., & Fletcher, J. M. (1985). Hypotheses, subtypes, and individual differences in dyslexia: Some reflections. In D. B. Gray & J. F. Kavanagh (Eds.), *Biobehavioral measures of dyslexia* (pp. 25–40). Parkton, MD: New York Press.

Satz, P., Taylor, H., Friel, J., & Fletcher, J. (1978). Some developmental and predictive precursors of reading disabilities: A six-year follow-up. In A. Benton & D. Pearl (Eds.), *Dyslexia: An appraisal of current knowledge* (pp. 325–347). New York: Oxford University Press.

Scanlon, D. M., & Vellutino, F. R. (1997). A comparison of the instructional backgrounds and cognitive profiles of poor, average, and good readers who were initially identified as at risk for reading failure. *Scientific Studies of Reading, 1*, 191–215.

Scarborough, H. S. (1984). Continuity between childhood dyslexia and adult reading. *British Journal of Psychology, 75*, 329–348.

Scarborough, H. S. (1990). Very early language deficits in dyslexic children. *Child Development, 61*, 1728–1743.

Scarborough, H. S., Ehri, L. C., Olson, R. K., & Fowler, A. E. (1998). The fate of phonemic awareness beyond the elementary schoopl years. *Scientific Studies of Reading, 2*, 115–142.

Scarr, S., & McCartney, K. (1983). How people make their own environments. *Child Development, 54*, 424–435.

Schadler, M., & Thissen, D. M. (1981). The development of automatic word recognition and reading skill. *Memory and Cognition, 9*, 132–141.

Schank, R. (1978). Predictive understanding. In R. Campbell & P. Smith (Eds.), *Recent advances in the psychology of language: Formal and experimental approaches* (pp. 91–101). New York: Plenum Press.

Schatschneider, C., Francis, D. J., Foorman, B. R., Fletcher, J. M., & Mehta, P. (1999). The dimensionality of phonological awareness: An application of item response theory. *Journal of Educational Psychology, 91*, 439–449.

Schatz, E. K., & Baldwin, R. S. (1986). Context clues are unreliable predictors of word meanings. *Reading Research Quarterly, 21*, 439–453.

Scheerer-Neumann, G. (1978). A functional analysis of reading disability: The utilization of intraword redundancy by good and poor readers. In A. Lesgold, J. Pellegrino, S. Fokkema, & R. Glaser (Eds.), *Cognitive psychology and instruction* (pp. 171–179). New York: Plenum Press.

Scheffler, I. (1985). *Of human potential.* New York: Routledge & Kegan Paul.

Schick, F. (1997). *Making choices: A recasting of decision theory.* Cambridge, England: Cambridge University Press.

Schmookler, A. B. (1993). *The illusion of choice: How the market economy shapes our destiny.* Albany: State University of New York Press.

Schneider, W. (1987). Connectionism: Is it a paradigm shift for psychology? *Behavior Research Methods, Instruments, and Computers, 19*, 73–83.

Schrag, F. (1992). In defense of positivist research paradigms. *Educational Researcher, 21*(5), 5–8.

Schuberth, R. E., & Eimas, P. D. (1977). Effects of context on the classification of words and nonwords. *Journal of Experimental Psychology: Human Perception and Performance, 3*, 27–36.

Schvaneveldt, R., Ackerman, B., & Semlear, T. (1977). The effect of semantic context on children's word recognition. *Child Development, 48*, 612–616.

Schwantes, F. M. (1981). Effect of story context on children's ongoing word recognition. *Journal of Reading Behavior, 13*, 305–311.

Schwantes, F. M. (1982). Text readability level and developmental differences in context effects. *Journal of Reading Behavior, 14*, 5–12.

Schwantes, F. M. (1985). Expectancy, integration, and interactional processes: Age differences in the nature of words affected by sentence context. *Journal of Experimental Child Psychology, 39,* 212–229.

Schwantes, F. M. (1991). Children's use of semantic and syntactic information for word recognition and determination of sentence meaningfulness. *Journal of Reading Behavior, 23,* 335–350.

Schwantes, F. M., Boesl, S., & Ritz, E. (1980). Children's use of context in word recognition: A psycholinguistic guessing game. *Child Development, 51,* 730–736.

Schwartz, R. M. (1977). Strategic processes in beginning reading. *Journal of Reading Behavior, 9,* 17–26.

Schwartz, R. M. (1980). Resource allocation and context utilization in the reading process. *Journal of Educational Psychology, 72,* 841–849.

Schwartz, R. M., & Stanovich, K. E. (1981). Flexibility in the use of graphic and contextual information by good and poor readers. *Journal of Reading Behavior, 13,* 263–269.

Schwartzman, A., Gold, D., Andres, D., Arbuckle, T., & Chaikelson, J. (1987). Stability of intelligence: A 40-year follow-up. *Canadian Journal of Psychology, 41,* 244–256.

Scribner, S. (1986). Thinking in action: Some characteristics of practical thought. In R. J. Sternberg & R. K. Wagner (Eds.), *Practical intelligence* (pp. 13–30). Cambridge, England: Cambridge University Press.

Scribner, S., & Cole, M. (1978). Literacy without schooling: Testing for intellectual effects. *Harvard Educational Review, 48,* 448–461.

Scribner, S., & Cole, M. (1981). *The psychology of literacy.* Cambridge, MA: Harvard University Press.

Searle, J. R. (1993). Rationality and realism: What is at stake? *Daedalus, 122*(4), 55–83.

Searle, J. R. (1995). Postmodernism and the Western rationalist tradition. In J. Arthur & A. Shapiro (Eds.), *Campus wars: Multiculturalism and the politics of difference* (pp. 28–48). Boulder, CO: Westview Press.

Seidenberg, M. S. (1985a). Lexicon as module. *Behavioral and Brain Sciences, 8,* 31–32.

Seidenberg, M. S. (1985b). The time course of information activation and utilization in visual word recognition. In D. Besner, T. Waller, & G. MacKinnon (Eds.), *Reading research: Advances in theory and practice* (Vol. 5, pp. 199–252). New York: Academic Press.

Seidenberg, M. S. (1985c). The time course of phonological code activation in two writing systems. *Cognition, 19,* 1–30.

Seidenberg, M. S. (1992). Dyslexia in a computational model of word recognition in reading. In P. B. Gough, L. C. Ehri, & R. Treiman (Eds.), *Reading acquisition* (pp. 243–273). Hillsdale, NJ: Erlbaum.

Seidenberg, M. S. (1999, April). *How can theoretical models of learning to read incorporate more realistic learning environments?* Paper presented annual meeting of the at the Society for the Scientific Study of Reading, Montreal, Canada.

Seidenberg, M. S., Bruck, M., Fornarolo, G., & Backman, J. (1985). Word recognition processes of poor and disabled readers: Do they necessarily differ? *Applied Psycholinguists, 6,* 161–180.

Seidenberg, M. S., Bruck, M., & Fornarolo, G., & Backman, J. (1986). Who is dyslexic? Reply to Wolf. *Applied Psycholinguistics, 7,* 77–84.

Seidenberg, M. S., & McClelland, J. L. (1989a). A distributed, developmental model of word recognition and naming. *Psychological Review, 96*, 523–568.

Seidenberg, M. S., & McClelland, J. L. (1989b). Visual word recognituion and pronunciation: A computational model of acquisition, skilled performance, and dyslexia. In A. M. Galaburda (Eds.), *From reading to neurons* (pp. 256–305). Cambridge, MA: MIT Press.

Seidenberg, M. S., & Tanenhaus, M. K. (1979). Orthographic effects on rhyme monitoring. *Journal of Experimental Psychology: Human Learning and Memory, 5,* 546–554.

Seidenberg, M. S., Waters, G. S., Barnes, M. A., & Tanenhaus, M. K. (1984). When does irregular spelling or pronunciation influence word recognition? *Journal of Verbal Learning and Verbal Behavior, 23,* 383–404.

Seidenberg, M. S., Waters, G. S., Sanders, M., & Langer, P. (1984). Pre- and post-lexical loci of contextual effects on word recognition. *Memory and Cognition, 12,* 315–328.

Sejnowski, T. J., & Rosenberg, C. R. (1986). *NETtalk: A parallel network that learns to read aloud* (Tech. Rep. No. JHU/EECS-86/01). BaltimoreJohns Hopkins University, Department of Electrical Engineering and Computer Science.

Semel, E., & Wiig, E. (1975). Comprehension of syntactic structures and critical verbal elements by children with learning disabilities. *Journal of Learning Disabilities, 8,* 53–58.

Senechal, M., LeFevre, J., Hudson, E., & Lawson, E. P. (1996). Knowledge of storybooks as a predictor of young children's vocabulary. *Journal of Educational Psychology, 88,* 520–536.

Senechal, M., LeFevre, J., Thomas, E. M., & Daley, K. E. (1998). Differential effects of home literacy experiences on the development of oral and written language. *Reading Research Quarterly, 33,* 96–116.

Senf, G. F. (1986). LD research in sociological and scientific perspective. In J. K. Torgesen & B. Y. L. Wong (Eds.), *Psychological and educational perspectives on learning disabilities* (pp. 27–53). Orlando, FL: Academic Press, Inc.

Sennett, R. (1998). *The corrosion of character.* New York: Norton.

Seymour, P. H. K. (1976). Contemporary models of the cognitive process, 2: Retrieval and comparison operations in permanent memory. In V. Hamilton & M. D. Vernon (Eds.), *The development of cognitive processes* (pp. 43–108). New York: Academic Press.

Seymour, P. H. K., & Elder, L. (1986). Beginning reading without phonology. *Cognitive Neuropsychology, 3,* 1–36.

Seymour, P. H. K., & Porpodas, C. D. (1980). Lexical and non-lexical processing in developmental dyslexia. In U. Frith (Ed.), *Cognitive processes in spelling* (pp. 443–473). London: Academic Press.

Shalit, R. (1997, August 25). Defining disability down. *New Republic,* pp, 16–22.

Shankweiler, D. (1989). How problems of comprehension are related to difficulties in decoding. In D. Shankweiler & I. Y. Liberman (Eds.), *Phonology and reading disability* (pp. 35–68). Ann Arbor: University of Michigan Press.

Shankweiler, D. (1999). Words to meaning. *Scientific Studies of Reading, 3,* 113–127.

Shankweiler, D., Crain, S., Brady, S., & Macaruso, P. (1992). Identifying the causes of reading disability. In P. B. Gough, L. C. Ehri, & R. Treiman (Eds.), *Reading acquisition* (pp. 275–305). Hillsdale, NJ: Erlbaum.

Shankweiler, D., & Liberman, I. Y. (1972). Misreading: A search for causes. In J.

Kavanagh & I. Mattingly (Eds.), *Language by ear and eye* (pp. 106–133). Cambridge, MA: MIT Press.

Shankweiler, D., Liberman, I. Y., Mark, L. S., Fowler, D. A., & Fischer, F. W. (1979). The speech code and learning to read. *Journal of Experimental Psychology: Human Learning and Memory, 5,* 531–545.

Shankweiler, D., Lundquist, E., Katz, L., Stuebing, K., Fletcher, J., Brady, S., Fowler, A., Dreyer, L., Marchione, K., Shaywitz, S., & Shaywitz, B. (1999). Comprehension and decoding: Patterns of association in children with reading difficulties. *Scientific Studies of Reading, 3,* 69–94.

Share, D. L. (1995). Phonological recoding and self-teaching: Sine qua non of reading acquisition. *Cognition, 55,* 151–218.

Share, D. L. (1996). Word recognition and spelling processes in specific reading disabled and garden-variety poor readers. *Dyslexia, 2,* 167–174.

Share, D. L. (1999). Phonological recoding and orthographic learning: A direct test of the self-teaching hypothesis. *Journal of Experimental Child Psychology, 72,* 95–129.

Share, D. L., Jorm, A. F., Maclean, R., & Matthews, R. (1984). Sources of individual differences in reading acquisition. *Journal of Educational Psychology, 76,* 1309–1324.

Share, D. L., McGee, R., McKenzie, D., Williams, S., & Silva, P. A. (1987). Further evidence relating to the distinction between specific reading retardation and general reading backwardness. *British Journal of Developmental Psychology, 5,* 35–44.

Share, D. L., McGee, R., & Silva, P. (1989). IQ and reading progress: A test of the capacity notion of IQ. *Journal of the American Academy of Child and Adolescent Psychiatry, 28,* 97–100.

Share, D. L., & Silva, P. A. (1987). Language deficits and specific reading retardation: Cause or effect? *British Journal of Disorders of Communication, 22,* 219–226.

Share, D. L., & Stanovich, K. E. (1995). Cognitive processes in early reading development: Accommodating individual differences into a model of acquisition. *Issues in Education: Contributions from Educational Psychology, 1,* 1–57.

Sharon, A. T. (1973–1974). What do adults read? *Reading Research Quarterly, 9,* 148–169.

Shaywitz, B. A., Fletcher, J. M., Holahan, J. M., & Shaywitz, S. E. (1992). Discrepancy compared to low achievement definitions of reading disability: Results from the Connecticut Longitudinal Study. *Journal of Learning Disabilities, 25,* 639–648.

Shaywitz, B. A., Holford, T., Holahan, J., Fletcher, J. M., Stuebing, K., Francis, D. J., & Shaywitz, S. E. (1995). A Matthew effect for IQ but not for reading: Results from a longitudinal study. *Reading Research Quarterly, 30,* 894–906.

Shaywitz, B. A., Shaywitz, S. E., Pugh, K., Fulbright, R., Constable, R., Mencl, W., Shankweiler, D. P., Liberman, A. M., Skudlarski, P., Fletcher, J. M., Katz, L., Marchione, K., Lacadie, C., Gatenby, C., & Gore, J. (1998). Functional disruption in the organization of the brain for reading and dyslexia. *Proceedings of the National Academy of Sciences USA, 95,* 2636–2641.

Shaywitz, S. E. (1996). Dyslexia. *Scientific American, 275*(5), 98–104.

Shaywitz, S. E., Shaywitz, B. A., Fletcher, J. M., & Escobar, M. D. (1990). Prevalence of reading disability in boys and girls. *Journal of the American Medical Association, 264,* 998–1002.

Shepard, L. (1980). An evaluation of the regression discrepancy method for identifying children with learning disabilities. *Journal of Special Education, 14,* 79–91.

Shepard, L., Smith, M., & Vojir, C. (1983). Characteristics of pupils identified as learning disabled. *American Educational Research Journal, 20,* 309–332.

Shiffrin, R. M., & Schneider, W. (1977). Controlled and automatic human information processing: 2. Perceptual learning, automatic attending, and a general theory. *Psychological Review, 84,* 127–190.

Shulman, H. G. (1970). Encoding and retention of semantic and phonemic information in short-term memory. *Journal of Verbal Learning and Verbal Behavior, 9,* 499–508.

Shulman, H. G., & Davison, T. C. B. (1977). Control properties of semantic coding in a lexical decision task. *Journal of Verbal Learning and Verbal Behavior, 16,* 91–98.

Shweder, R. A. (1991). *Thinking through cultures.* Cambridge, MA: Harvard University Press.

Siddiqui, S., West, R. F., & Stanovich, K. E. (1998). The influence of print exposure on syllogistic reasoning and knowledge of mental-state verbs. *Scientific Studies of Reading, 2,* 81–96.

Sidhu, R., Stringer, R., Chiappe, P., & Stanovich, K. E. (1999, April). *What does Rapid Automatized Naming (RAN) Measure?: A covariance structure analysis of RAN's relationship to phonological awareness, temporal processing, and word recognition.* Paper presented at the annual meeting of the Society for the Scientific Study of Reading, Montreal, Canada.

Siegel, H. (1980). Objectivity, rationality, incommensurability, and more. *British Journal for the Philosophy of Science, 31,* 359–384.

Siegel, H. (1987). *Relativism refuted: A critique of contemporary epistemological relativism.* Dordrecht, The Netherlands: D. Reidel.

Siegel, H. (1988). *Educating reason: Rationality, critical thinking, and education.* New York: Routledge.

Siegel, H. (1997). *Rationality redeemed? Further dialogues on an educational ideal.* New York: Routledge.

Siegel, L. S. (1985). Psycholinguistic aspects of reading disabilities. In L. Siegel & F. Morrison (Eds.), *Cognitive development in atypical children* (pp. 45–65). New York: Springer-Verlag.

Siegel, L. S. (1988). Evidence that IQ scores are irrelevant to the definition and analysis of reading disability. *Canadian Journal of Psychology, 42,* 201–215.

Siegel, L. S. (1989). IQ is irrelevant to the definition of learning disabilities. *Journal of Learning Disabilities, 22,* 469–479.

Siegel, L. S. (1992). An evaluation of the discrepancy definition of dyslexia. *Journal of Learning Disabilities, 25,* 618–629.

Siegel, L. S. (1993a). Alice in IQ land: or, Why IQ is still irrelevent to learning disabilities. In R. M. Joshi & C. K. Leong (Eds.), *Reading disabilities: Diagnosis and components processes* (pp. 71–84). Dordrecht, The Netherlands: Kluwer Academic.

Siegel, L. S. (1993b). The development of reading. In H. Reese (Ed.), *Advances in child development and behavior* (pp. 63–97). San Diego, CA: Academic Press.

Siegel, L. S., & Faux, D. (1989). Acquisition of certain grapheme–phoneme correspondences in normally achieving and disabled readers. *Reading and Writing: An Interdisciplinary Journal, 1,* 37–52.

Siegel, L. S., & Heaven, R. K. (1986). Categorization of learning disabilities. In S. J. Ceci (Ed.), *Handbook of cognitive, social, and neuropsychological aspects of learning disabilities* (Vol. 1, pp. 95–121). Hillsdale, NJ: Erlbaum.

Siegel, L. S., & Linder, B. (1984). Short-term memory processes in children with reading and arithmetic learning disabilities. *Developmental Psychology, 20,* 200–207.

Siegel, L. S., & Ryan, E. B. (1984). Reading disability as a language disorder. Remedial and Special Education, 5, 28–33.

Siegel, L. S., & Ryan, E. B. (1988). Development of grammatical-sensitivity, phonological, and short-term memory skills in normally achieving and learning disabled children. Developmental Psychology, 24, 28–37.

Siegel, L. S., & Ryan, E. B. (1989). Subtypes of developmental dyslexia: The influence of definitional variables. Reading and Writing: An Interdisciplinary Journal, 1, 257–287.

Siler, E. R. (1974). The effects of syntactic and semantic constraints on the oral reading performance of second and fourth graders. *Reading Research Quarterly, 9,* 603–621.

Silva, P. A., McGee, R., & Williams, S. (1985). Some characteristics of 9-year-old boys with general reading backwardness or specific reading retardation. *Journal of Child Psychology and Psychiatry, 26,* 407–421.

Simons, H. D., & Leu, D. J. (1987). The use of contextual and graphic information in word recognition by second-, fourth-, and sixth-grade readers. *Journal of Reading Behavior, 19,* 33–47.

Simpson, G., & Foster, M. (1985, April). *Lexical ambiguity and children's word recognition.* Paper presented at the annual meeting of the Society for Research in Child Development, Toronto, Canada

Simpson, G. B., & Foster, M. R. (1986). Lexical ambiguity and children's word recognition. *Developmental Psychology, 22,* 147–154.

Simpson, G., & Lorsbach, T. (1983). The development of automatic and conscious components of contextual facilitation. *Child Development, 54,* 760–772.

Simpson, G. B., Lorsbach, T., & Whitehouse, D. (1983). Encoding and contextual components of word recognition in good and poor readers. *Journal of Experimental Child Psychology, 35,* 161–171.

Sincoff, J. B., & Sternberg, R. J. (1987). Two faces of verbal ability. *Intelligence, 11,* 263–276.

Singer, M., & Crouse, J. (1981). The relationship of context-use skills to reading: A case for an alternative experimental logic. *Child Development, 52,* 1326–1329.

Singer, M. H. (1982). *Competent reader, disabled reader.* Hillsdale, NJ: Erlbaum.

Slemrod, J., & Bakija, J. (1996). *Taxing ourselves: A citizen's guide to the great debate over tax reform.* Cambridge, MA: The MIT Press.

Sloboda, J. (1980). Visual imagery and individual differences in spelling. In U. Frith (Ed.), *Cognitive processes in spelling* (pp. 231–248). London: Academic Press.

Smiley, S., Oakley, D., Worthen, D., Campione, J., & Brown, A. (1977). Recall of thematically relevant material by adolescent good and poor readers as a function of written versus oral presentation. *Journal of Educational Psychology, 69,* 381–387.

Smith, E. B., Goodman, K. S., & Meredith, R. (1976). *Language and thinking in school.* New York: Holt, Rinehart & Winston.

Smith, E. E., & Spoehr, K. T. (1974). The perception of printed English: A theoretical perspective. In B. H. Kantowitz (Ed.), *Human information processing: Tutorials in performance and cognition* (pp. 231–275). Hillsdale, NJ: Erlbaum.

Smith, F. (1971). *Understanding reading.* New York: Holt, Rinehart & Winston.

Smith, F. (1973). *Psycholinguistics and reading.* New York: Holt, Rinehart & Winston.

Smith, F. (1975). The role of prediction in reading. *Elementary English, 52*, 305–311.

Smith, F. (1978). *Understanding reading* (2nd ed.). New York: Holt, Rinehart & Winston.

Smith, F. (1979). *Reading without nonsense.* New York: Teachers College Press.

Smith, F. (1982). *Understanding reading* (3rd ed.). New York: Holt, Rinehart & Winston.

Smith, F. (1983). *Essays into literacy.* Portsmouth, NH: Heinemann.

Smith, F. (1989). Overselling literacy. *Phi Delta Kappan, 70*(5), 353–359.

Smith, F., & Holmes, D. L. (1971). The independence of letter, word, and meaning identification in reading. *Reading Research Quarterly, 6*, 394–415.

Smith, M. C. (1996). Differences in adults' reading practices and literacy proficiencies. *Reading Research Quarterly, 31*, 196–219.

Smith, M. D., Coleman, J. M., Dokecki, P. R., & Davis, E. E. (1977). Intellectual characteristics of school labeled learning disabled children. *Exceptional Children, 43*, 352–357.

Smith, P., & Jones, O. R. (1986). *The philosophy of mind.* Cambridge, England: Cambridge University Press.

Snodgrass, J. G., & Corwin, J. (1988). Pragmatics of measuring recognition memory: Applications to dementia and amnesia. *Journal of Experimental Psychology: General, 117*, 34–50.

Snow, C. E., Barnes, W., Chandler, J., Goodman, I., & Hemphill, L. (1991). *Unfulfilled expectations: Home and school influences on literacy.* Cambridge, MA: Harvard University Press.

Snow, C. E., Burns, M. S., & Griffin, P. (Eds.). (1998). *Preventing reading difficulties in young children.* Washington, DC: National Academy Press.

Snowling, M. (1980). The development of grapheme–phoneme correspondence in normal and dyslexic readers. *Journal of Experimental Child Psychology, 29*, 294–305.

Snowling, M. (1981). Phonemic deficits in developmental dyslexia. *Psychological Research, 43*, 219–234.

Snowling, M. (1983). The comparison of acquired and developmental disorders of reading: A discussion. *Cognition, 14*, 105–118.

Snowling, M. (1985). The assessment of reading and spelling skills. In M. Snowling (Ed.), *Children's written language difficulties* (pp. 80–95). Windsor, England: NFER-Nelson.

Snowling, M. (1987). *Dyslexia.* Oxford, England: Blackwell.

Snowling, M. (1991). Developmental reading disorders. *Journal of Child Psychology and Psychiatry, 32*, 49–77.

Snowling, M. (1995). Phonological processing and developmental dyslexia. *Journal of Research in Reading, 18*, 132–138.

Snowling, M. (1996). Contemporary approaches to the teaching of reading. *Journal of Child Psychology and Psychiatry, 37*, 139–148.

Snowling, M., Bryant, P., & Hulme, C. (1996). Theoretical and methodological pitfalls in making comparisons between developmental and acquired dyslexia: Some comments on Castles and Coltheart (1993). *Reading and Writing: An Interdisciplinary Journal, 8*, 443–451.

Snowling, M., & Hulme, C. (1989). A longitudinal case study of developmental phonological dyslexia. *Cognitive Neuropsychology, 6*, 379–401.

Snowling, M., Stackhouse, J., & Rack, J. (1986). Phonological dyslexia and dysgraphia: A developmental analysis. *Cognitive Neuropsychology, 3,* 309–339.

Sokal, A. (1996, May–June). A physicist experiments with cultural studies. *Lingua Franca,* pp. 62–64.

Sokal, A., & Bricmont, J. (1998). *Fashionable nonsense: Postmodern intellectuals' abuse of science.* New York: Picador.

Solman, R. T., & May, J. G. (1990). Spatial localization discrepancies: A visual deficiency in poor readers. *American Journal of Psychology, 103,* 243–263.

Spache, G. D. (1981). *Diagnostic reading scales.* Monterey, CA: CTB/McGraw-Hill.

Spear-Swerling, L., & Sternberg, R. J. (1996). *Off Track: When poor readers become "learning disabled."* Boulder, CO: Westview Press.

Speel, H. C. (1995, June). *Memetics: On a conceptual framework for cultural evolution.* Paper presented at the symposium "Einstein Meets Magritte," Free University of Brussels.

Sperber, D. (1985). Apparently irrational beliefs. In D. Sperber, *On anthropological knowledge* (pp. 35–63). Cambridge, England: Cambridge University Press.

Sperber, R. D., McCauley, C., Ragain, R. D., & Weil, C. M. (1979). Semantic priming effects on picture and word processing. *Memory and Cognition, 7,* 339–345.

Sperling, G. (1967). Successive approximations to a model for short-term memory. *Acta Psychologica, 27,* 285–292.

Spiegel, D. L. (1992). Blending whole language and systematic direct instruction. *Reading Teacher, 46*(1), 38–44.

Spiro, R. J., Bruce, B. C., & Brewer, W. F. (Eds.). (1980). *Theoretical issues in reading comprehension.* Hillsdale, NJ: Erlbaum.

Spring, C., & Capps, C. (1974). Encoding speed, rehearsal, and probed recall of dyslexic boys. *Journal of Educational Psychology, 66,* 780–786.

Spring, C., & Farmer, R. (1975). Perceptual span of poor readers. *Journal of Reading Behavior, 7,* 297–305.

Spring, C., & French, L. (1990). Identifying children with specific reading disabilities from listening and reading discrepancy scores. *Journal of Learning Disabilities, 23,* 53–58.

Springer, S., & Deutsch, G. (1985). *Left brain, right brain* (Rev. ed.). New York: Freeman.

Stage, S. A., & Wagner, R. K. (1992). Development of young children's phonological and orthographic knowledge as revealed by their spelling. *Developmental Psychology, 28,* 287–296.

Stahl, S. A. (1983). Differential word knowledge and reading comprehension. *Journal of Reading Behavior, 15,* 33–50.

Stahl, S. A. (1992). Saying the "p" word. *Reading Teacher, 45,* 618–625.

Stahl, S. A. (1998). Understanding shifts in reading and its instruction. *Peabody Journal of Education, 73,* 31–67.

Stahl, S. A., Duffy-Hester, A. M., & Stahl, K. A. D. (1998). Everything you wanted to know about phonics (but were afraid to ask). *Reading Research Quarterly, 33,* 338–355.

Stahl, S. A., & Murray, B. (1998). Issues involved in defining phonological awareness and its relation to early reading. In J. L. Metsala & L. C. Ehri (Eds.), *Word recognition in beginning literacy* (pp. 65–87). Mahwah, NJ: Erlbaum.

Stahl, S. A., Osborn, J., & Lehr, F. (1990). *A summary of "Beginning to Read" by Marilyn Jager Adams.* Urbana-Champaign, IL: Center for the Study of Reading.

Stainthorp, R. (1997). A children's Author Recognition Test: A useful tool in reading research. *Journal of Research in Reading, 20,* 148–158.

Staller, J., & Sekuler, R. (1975). Children read normal and reversed letters: A simple test of reading skill. *Quarterly Journal of Experimental Psychology, 27,* 539–550.

Stanley, G., Smith, G., & Howell, E. (1983). Eye-movements and sequential tracking in dyslexic and control children. *British Journal of Psychology, 74,* 181–187.

Stanley, G., Smith, G., & Powys, A. (1982). Selecting intelligence tests for studies of dyslexic children. *Psychological Reports, 50,* 787–792.

Stanovich, K. E. (1978). Information processing in mentally retarded individuals. In N. R. Ellis (Ed.), *International review of research in mental retardation* (Vol. 9, pp. 29–60)). New York: Academic Press.

Stanovich, K. E. (1979). Studies of letter identification using qualitative error analysis: Effects of speed stress, tachistoscopic presentation, and word context. *Journal of Experimental Psychology: Human Perception and Performance, 5,* 713–733.

Stanovich, K. E. (1980). Toward an interactive–compensatory model of individual differences in the development of reading fluency. *Reading Research Quarterly, 16,* 32–71.

Stanovich, K. E. (1981a). Attentional and automatic context effects in reading. In A. Lesgold & C. Perfetti (Eds.), *Interactive processes in reading* (pp. 241–267). Hillsdale, NJ: Erlbaum.

Stanovich, K. E. (1981b). Relationships between word decoding speed, general name-retrieval ability, and reading progress in first-grade children. *Journal of Educational Psychology, 73,* 809–815.

Stanovich, K. E. (1982a). Individual differences in the cognitive processes of reading: 1. Word decoding. *Journal of Learning Disabilities, 15,* 485–493.

Stanovich, K. E. (1982b). Individual differences in the cognitive processes of reading: 2. Text-level processes. *Journal of Learning Disabilities, 15,* 549–554.

Stanovich, K. E. (1982c). Word recognition skill and reading ability. In M. Singer (Ed.), *Competent reader, disabled reader: Research and application* (pp. 81–102). Hillsdale, NJ: Erlbaum.

Stanovich, K. E. (1984). The interactive–compensatory model of reading: A confluence of developmental, experimental, and educational psychology. *Remedial and Special Education, 5,* 11–19.

Stanovich, K. E. (1986a). Cognitive processes and the reading problems of learning disabled children: Evaluating the assumption of specificity. In J. Torgesen & B. Wong (Eds.), *Psychological and educational perspectives on learning disabilities* (pp. 87–131). New York: Academic Press.

Stanovich, K. E. (1986b). Matthew effects in reading: Some consequences of individual differences in the acquisition of literacy. *Reading Research Quarterly, 21,* 360–407.

Stanovich, K. E. (1987). Perspectives on segmental analysis and alphabetic literacy. *Cahiers Psychologie Cognitive, 7,* 514–519.

Stanovich, K. E. (1988a). Explaining the differences between the dyslexic and the garden-variety poor reader: The phonological-core variable-difference model. *Journal of Learning Disabilities, 21,* 590–612.

Stanovich, K. E. (1988b). The right and wrong places to look for the cognitive locus of reading disability. *Annals of Dyslexia, 38,* 154–177.

Stanovich, K. E. (1989a). Has the learning disabilities field lost its intelligence? *Journal of Learning Disabilities, 22,* 487–492.

Stanovich, K. E. (1989b). Learning disabilities in broader context. *Journal of Learning Disabilities, 22*, 287–297.

Stanovich, K. E. (1990a). A call for an end to the Paradigm Wars in reading research. *Journal of Reading Behavior, 22*, 221–231.

Stanovich, K. E. (1990b). Concepts in developmental theories of reading skill: Cognitive resources, automaticity, and modularity. *Developmental Review, 10*, 72–100.

Stanovich, K. E. (1991a). Discrepancy definitions of reading disability: Has intelligence led us astray? *Reading Research Quarterly, 26*, 7–29.

Stanovich, K. E. (1991b). Word recognition: Changing perspectives. In R. Barr, M. L. Kamil, P. Mosenthal, & P. D. Pearson (Eds.), *Handbook of reading research* (Vol. 2, pp. 418–452). New York: Longman.

Stanovich, K. E. (1992a). *How to think straight about psychology* (3rd ed.). New York: HarperCollins.

Stanovich, K. E. (1992b). Speculations on the causes and consequences of individual differences in early reading acquisition. In P. Gough, L. Ehri, & R. Treiman (Eds.), *Reading acquisition* (pp. 307–342). Hillsdale, NJ: Erlbaum.

Stanovich, K. E. (1993a). Does reading make you smarter? Literacy and the development of verbal intelligence. In H. Reese (Ed.), *Advances in child development and behavior* (Vol. 24, pp. 133–180). San Diego, CA: Academic Press.

Stanovich, K. E. (1993b). Dysrationalia: A new specific learning disability. *Journal of Learning Disabilities, 26*, 501–515.

Stanovich, K. E. (1993c). The language code: Issues in word recognition. In S. Yussen & M. C. Smith (Eds.), *Reading across the life span* (pp. 111–135). New York: Springer-Verlag.

Stanovich, K. E. (1994a). Does dyslexia exist? *Journal of Child Psychology and Psychiatry, 35*, 579–595.

Stanovich, K. E. (1994b). Reconceptualizing intelligence: Dysrationalia as an intuition pump. *Educational Researcher, 23*(4), 11–22.

Stanovich, K. E. (1994c). Romance and reality. *Reading Teacher, 47*(4), 280–291.

Stanovich, K. E. (1996a). *How to think straight about psychology* (4th ed.). New York: HarperCollins.

Stanovich, K. E. (1996b). Toward a more inclusive definition of dyslexia. *Dyslexia, 2*, 154–166.

Stanovich, K. E. (1998a). *How to think straight about psychology* (5th ed.). New York: Longman.

Stanovich, K. E. (1998b). Cognitive neuroscience and educational psychology: What season is it? *Educational Psychology Review, 10*, 419–426.

Stanovich, K. E. (1999a). The sociopsychometrics of learning disabilities. *Journal of Learning Disabilities, 32*, 350–361.

Stanovich, K. E. (1999b). *Who is rational? Studies of individual differences in reasoning.* Mahweh, NJ: Erlbaum.

Stanovich, K. E., & Bauer, D. W. (1978). Experiments on the spelling-to-sound regularity effect in word recognition. *Memory and Cognition, 6*, 410–415.

Stanovich, K. E., & Cunningham, A. E. (1991). Reading as constrained reasoning. In S. Sternberg & P. Frensch (Eds.), *Complex problem solving: Principles and mechanisms* (pp. 3–60). Hillsdale, NJ: Erlbaum.

Stanovich, K. E., & Cunningham, A. E. (1992). Studying the consequences of literacy within a literate society: The cognitive correlates of print exposure. *Memory and Cognition, 20*, 51–68.

Stanovich, K. E., & Cunningham, A. E. (1993). Where does knowledge come from? Specific associations between print exposure and information acquisition. *Journal of Educational Psychology, 85*, 211–229.

Stanovich, K. E., Cunningham, A. E., & Cramer, B. (1984). Assessing phonological awareness in kindergarten children: Issues of task comparability. *Journal of Experimental Child Psychology, 38*, 175–190.

Stanovich, K. E., Cunningham, A. E., & Feeman, D. J. (1984a). Intelligence, cognitive skills, and early reading progress. *Reading Research Quarterly, 19*, 278–303.

Stanovich, K. E., Cunningham, A. E., & Feeman, D. J. (1984b). Relation between early reading acquisition and word decoding with and without context: A longitudinal study of first-grade children. *Journal of Educational Psychology, 76*, 668–677.

Stanovich, K. E., Cunningham, A. E., & West, R. F. (1981). A longitudinal study of the development of automatic recognition skills in first graders. *Journal of Reading Behavior, 13*, 57–74.

Stanovich, K. E., Cunningham, A. E., & West, R. F. (1998). Literacy experiences and the shaping of cognition. In S. Paris & H. Wellman (Eds.), *Global prospects for education: Development, culture, and schooling* (pp. 253–288). Washington, DC: American Psychological Association.

Stanovich, K. E., Feeman, D. J., & Cunningham, A. E. (1983). The development of the relation between letter-naming speed and reading ability. *Bulletin of the Psychonomic Society, 21*, 199–202.

Stanovich, K. E., Nathan, R. G., & Vala-Rossi, M. (1986). Developmental changes in the cognitive correlates of reading ability and the developmental lag hypothesis. *Reading Research Quarterly, 21*, 267–283.

Stanovich, K. E., Nathan, R. G., West, R. F., & Vala-Rossi, M. (1985). Children's word recognition in context: Spreading activation, expectancy, and modularity. *Child Development, 56*, 1418–1429.

Stanovich, K. E., Nathan, R. G., Zolman, J. E. (1988). The developmental lag hypothesis in reading: Longitudinal and matched reading-level comparisons. *Child Development, 59*, 71–86.

Stanovich, K. E., & Pachella, R. G. (1977). Encoding, stimulus-response compatibility, and stages of processing. *Journal of Experimental Psychology: Human Perception and Performance, 3*, 411–421.

Stanovich, K. E., Purcell, D. G., & West, R. F. (1979). The development of word recognition mechanisms: Inference and unitization. *Bulletin of the Psychonomic Society, 13*, 71–74.

Stanovich, K. E., & Siegel, L. S. (1994). The phenotypic performance profile of reading-disabled children: A regression-based test of the phonological-core variable-difference model. *Journal of Educational Psychology, 86*, 24–53.

Stanovich, K. E., Siegel, L. S., & Gottardo, A. (1997). Converging evidence for phonological and surface subtypes of reading disability. *Journal of Educational Psychology, 89*, 114–127.

Stanovich, K. E., & Stanovich, P. J. (1995). How research might inform the debate about early reading acquisition. *Journal of Research in Reading, 18*, 87–105.

Stanovich, K. E., & Stanovich, P. J. (1997). Further thoughts on aptitude–achievement discrepancy. *Educational Psychology in Practice, 13*, 3–8.

Stanovich, K. E., & West, R. F. (1979a). The effect of orthographic structure on the word search performance of good and poor readers. *Journal of Experimental Child Psychology, 28*, 258–267.

Stanovich, K. E., & West, R. F. (1979b). Mechanisms of sentence context effects in reading: Automatic activation and conscious attention. *Memory and Cognition, 7,* 77–85.

Stanovich, K. E., & West, R. F. (1981). The effect of sentence context on ongoing word recognition: Tests of a two-process theory. *Journal of Experimental Psychology: Human Perception and Performance, 7,* 658–672.

Stanovich, K. E., & West, R. F. (1983a). On priming by a sentence context. *Journal of Experimental Psychology: General, 112,* 1–36.

Stanovich, K. E., & West, R. F. (1983b). The generalizability of context effects on word recognition: A reconsideration of the roles of parafoveal priming and sentence context. *Memory and Cognition, 11,* 49–58.

Stanovich, K. E., & West, R. F. (1989). Exposure to print and orthographic processing. *Reading Research Quarterly, 24,* 402–433.

Stanovich, K. E., & West, R. F. (1997). Reasoning independently of prior belief and individual differences in actively open-minded thinking. *Journal of Educational Psychology, 89,* 342–357.

Stanovich, K. E., & West, R. F. (1998). Individual differences in rational thought. *Journal of Experimental Psychology: General, 127,* 161–188.

Stanovich, K. E., West, R. F., & Cunningham, A. E. (1991). Beyond phonological processes: Print exposure and orthographic processing. In S. Brady & D. Shankweiler (Eds.), *Phonological processes in literacy* (pp. 219–235). Hillsdale, NJ: Erlbaum.

Stanovich, K. E., West, R. F., Cunningham, A. E., Cipielewski, J., & Siddiqui, S. (1996). The role of inadequate print exposure as a determinant of reading comprehension problems. In C. Cornoldi & J. Oakhill (Eds.), *Reading comprehension disabilities* (pp. 15–32). Hillsdale, NJ: Erlbaum.

Stanovich, K. E., West, R. F., & Feeman, D. J. (1981). A longitudinal study of sentence context effects in second-grade children: Tests of an interactive–compensatory model. *Journal of Experimental Child Psychology, 32,* 185–199.

Stanovich, K. E., West, R. F., & Harrison, M. (1995). Knowledge growth and maintenance across the life span: The role of print exposure. *Developmental Psychology, 31,* 811–826.

Stanovich, K. E., West, R. F., & Pollak, D. (1978). The effect of orthographic structure on word recognition in a visual search task. *Journal of Experimental Child Psychology, 26,* 137–146.

Stedman, L. (1996). As assessment of literacy trends, past and present. *Research in the Teaching of English, 30,* 283–302.

Stein, C. L., Cairns, H. S., & Zurif, E. B. (1984). Sentence comprehension limitations related to syntactic deficits in reading-disabled children. *Applied Psycholinguistics, 5,* 305–322.

Stein, M., Johnson, B., & Gutlohn, L. (1999). Analyzing beginning reading programs: The relationship between decoding instruction and text. *Remedial and Special Education, 20,* 275–287.

Steinheiser, F., & Guthrie, J. T. (1978). Reading ability and efficiency of graphemic–phonemic encoding. *Journal of General Psychology, 99,* 281–291.

Steinmetz, H., & Galaburda, A. M. (1991). Planum temporale asymmetry: In-vivo morphometry affords a new perspective for neuro-behavioral research. *Reading and Writing: An Interdisciplinary Journal, 3,* 331–343.

Sternberg, R. J. (1980). Sketch of a componential subtheory of human intelligence. *Behavioral and Brain Sciences, 3,* 573–584.

Sternberg, R. J. (1982). Introduction: Some common themes in contemporary approaches to the training of intelligent performances. In D. K. Detterman & R. J. Sternberg (Eds.), *How and how much can intelligence be increased?* (pp. 141–146). Norwood, NJ: Ablex.

Sternberg, R. J. (1985a). *Beyond IQ: A triarchic theory of human intelligence.* Cambridge, England: Cambridge University Press.

Sternberg, R. J. (1985b). Controlled versus automatic processing. *Behavioral and Brain Sciences, 8*, 32–33.

Sternberg, R. J. (1987). Most vocabulary is learned from context. In M. G. McKeown & M. E. Curtis (Eds.), *The nature of vocabulary acquisition* (pp. 89–105). Hillsdale, NJ: Erlbaum.

Sternberg, R. J. (1988). *The triarchic mind.* New York: Viking.

Sternberg, R. J. (1990). *Metaphors of mind: Conceptions of the nature of intelligence.* Cambridge, England: Cambridge University Press.

Sternberg, R. J., & Detterman, D. K. (Eds.). (1986). *What is intelligence?* Norwood, NJ: Ablex.

Sternberg, R. J., & Powell, J. (1983). Comprehending verbal comprehension. *American Psychologist, 38*, 878–893.

Sternberg, R. J., Powell, J., & Kaye, D. (1982). The nature of verbal comprehension. *Poetics, 11*, 155–187.

Sternberg, R. J., & Spear-Swerling, L. (Eds.). (1999). *Perspectives on learning disabilities.* New York: Westview/HarperCollins.

Sternberg, R. J., & Wagner, R. K. (1986). *Practical intelligence.* Cambridge, England: Cambridge University Press.

Sternberg, S. (1969). The discovery of processing stages: Extensions of Donder's method. In W. G. Koster (Ed.), *Attention and performance* (Vol.2). Amsterdam, The Netherlands: North-Holland.

Stevenson, H. W., & Lee, S. (1990). Contexts of achievement. *Monographs of the Society for Research in Child Development (Serial No. 221), 55*, 1–123.

Stevenson, H. W., Parker, T., Wilkinson, A., Hegion, A., & Fish, E. (1976). Longitudinal study of individual differences in cognitive development and scholastic achievement. *Journal of Educational Psychology, 68*, 377–400.

Stevenson, H. W., Stigler, J. W., Lee, S. Y., Lucker, G. W., Kitamura, S., & Hsu, C. C. (1985). Cognitive performance and academic achievement of Japanese, Chinese, and American children. *Child Development, 56*, 718–734.

Stevenson, J. (1991). Which aspects of processing text mediate genetic effects? *Reading and Writing: An Interdisciplinary Journal, 3*, 249–269.

Stevenson, J. (1992). Identifying sex differences in reading disability: Lessons from a twin study. *Reading and Writing: An Interdisciplinary Journal, 4*, 307–326.

Stevenson, J., Graham, P., Fredman, G., & McLoughlin, V. (1987). A twin study of genetic influences on reading and spelling ability and disability. *Journal of Child Psychology and Psychiatry, 28*, 229–247.

Stich, S. (1983). *From folk psychology to cognitive science.* Cambridge, MA: MIT Press.

Sticht, T. (1979). Applications of the audread model to reading evaluation and instruction. In L. B. Resnick & P. Weaver (Eds.), *Theory and practice of early reading* (pp. 209–226). Hillsdale, NJ: Erlbaum.

Sticht, T. G., Hofstetter, C. R., & Hofstetter, C. H. (1996). Assessing adult literacy by telephone. *Journal of Literacy Research, 28*, 525–559.

Sticht, T. G., & James, J. H. (1984). Listening and reading. In P. D. Pearson (Ed.), *Handbook of reading research* (pp. 293–317). New York: Longman.

Stock, B. (1983). *The implications of literacy.* Princeton, NJ: Princeton University Press.

Stolz, J. A., & Besner, D. (1999). On the myth of automatic semantic activation in reading. *Current Directions in Psychological Science, 8,* 61–65.

Stolz, J. A., & Neely, J. H. (1995). When target degradation does and does not enhance semantic context effects in word recognition. *Journal of Experimental Psychology: Learning, Memory, and Cognition, 21,* 596–611.

Strange, M. (1979). The effect of orthographic anomalies upon reading behavior. *Journal of Reading Behavior, 11,* 153–161.

Street, B. V. (1984). *Literacy in theory and practice.* Cambridge, England: Cambridge University Press.

Street, B. V. (1988). Literacy practices and literacy myths. In R. Saljo (Ed.), *The written word: Studies in literate thought and action* (pp. 59–72). Berlin: Springer-Verlag.

Stringer, R. (1997). *Adult reading disability and temporal processing deficits.* Unpublished doctoral dissertation, Ontario Institute for Studies in Education, University of Toronto, Canada

Stringer, R., & Stanovich, K. E. (2000). The connection between reaction time and variation in reading ability: Unravelling covariance relationships with cognitive ability and phonological sensitivity. *Scientific Studies of Reading, 4,* 41–53.

Stuckey, J. E. (1991). *The violence of literacy.* Portsmouth, NH: Boynton/Cook.

Studdert-Kennedy, M., & Mody, M. (1995). Auditory temporal perception deficits in the reading-impaired: A critical review of the evidence. *Psychonomic Bulletin and Review, 2,* 506–514.

Suppe, F. (1984). Beyond Skinner and Kuhn. *New Ideas in Psychology, 2,* 89–104.

Suskind, R. (1998). *A hope in the unseen.* New York: Broadway Books.

Swan, D., & Goswami, U. (1997a). Phonological awareness deficits in developmental dyslexia and the phonological representations hypothesis. *Journal of Experimental Child Psychology, 66,* 18–41.

Swan, D., & Goswami, U. (1997b). Picture naming deficits in developmental dyslexia: The phonological representations hypothesis. *Brain and Language, 56,* 334–353.

Swanson, H. L. (1988). Toward a metatheory of learning disabilities. *Journal of Learning Disabilities, 21,* 196–209.

Swinney, D. A., Onifer, W., Prather, P., & Hirshkowitz, M. (1979). Semantic facilitation across sensory modalities in the processing of individual words and sentences. *Memory and Cognition, 7,* 159–165.

Szeszulski, P., & Manis, F. R. (1987). A comparison of word recognition processes in dyslexic and normal readers at two reading-age levels. *Journal of Experimental Child Psychology, 44,* 364–376.

Tabachnick, B., & Fidell, L. (1983). *Using multivariate statistics.* New York: Harper & Row.

Tallal, P. (1980). Auditory temporal perception, phonics, and reading disabilities in children. *Brain and Language, 9,* 182–198.

Tallal, P., Sainburg, R. L., & Jernigan, T. (1991). The neuropathology of developmental dysphasia: Behavioral, morphological, and physiological evidence for a pervasive temporal processing disorder. *Reading and Writing: An Interdisciplinary Journal, 3,* 363–377.

Tan, L. H., & Perfetti, C. A. (1998). Phonological codes as early sources of constraint in Chinese word identification: A review of current discoveries and theoretical accounts. *Reading and Writing: An Interdisciplinary Journal, 10,* 165–200.

Tanenhaus, M. K., Dell, G. S., & Carlson, G. (1987). Context effects in lexical processing: A connectionist approach to modularity. In J. Garfield (Ed.), *Modularity in knowledge representation and natural language understanding* (pp. 83–109). Cambridge, MA: MIT Press.

Tanenhaus, M. K., & Lucas, M. M. (1987). Context effects in lexical processing. *Cognition, 25,* 213–234.

Tannen, D. (1982). The myth of orality and literacy. In W. Frawley (Ed.), *Linguistics and literacy* (pp. 37–50). New York: Plenum Press.

Tarver, S. G. (1982). Characteristics of learning disabilities. In T. Miller & E. Davis (Eds.), *The mildly handicapped student* (pp. 17–36). New York: Grune & Stratton.

Tarver, S. G., Hallahan, D. P., Kauffman, J. M., & Ball, D. W. (1976). Verbal rehearsal and selective attention in children with learning disabilities: A developmental lag. *Journal of Experimental Child Psychology, 22,* 275–285.

Taylor, B. M., Frye, B. J., & Maruyama, G. M. (1990). Time spent reading and reading growth. *American Educational Research Journal, 27,* 351–362.

Taylor, D. (1989). Toward a unified theory of literacy learning and instructional practices. *Phi Delta Kappan, 71*(3), 184–193.

Taylor, D. (1994). The trivial pursuit of reading psychology in the "real world": A response to West, Stanovich, and Mitchell. *Reading Research Quarterly, 29,* 276–288.

Taylor, H. G., Lean, D., & Schwartz, S. (1989). Pseudoword repetition ability in learning-disabled children. *Applied Psycholinguistics, 10,* 203–219.

Taylor, H. G., Satz, P., & Friel, J. (1979). Developmental dyslexia in relation to other childhood reading disorders: Significance and clinical utility. *Reading Research Quarterly, 15,* 84–101.

Taylor, H. G., & Schatschneider, C. (1992). Academic achievement following childhood brain disease: Implications for the concept of learning disabilities. *Journal of Learning Disabilities, 25,* 630–638.

Temple, C. M., & Marshall, J. C. (1983). A case study of developmental phonological dyslexia. *British Journal of Psychology, 74,* 517–533.

Theios, J. (1973). Reaction time measurements in the study of memory processes: Theory and data. In G. Bower (Ed.), *The psychology of learning and motivation: Advances in research and theory* (Vol. 7, pp. 43–85). New York: Academic Press.

Thompson, G. B., & Nicholson, T. (Eds.). (1999). *Learning to read: Beyond phonics and whole language.* New York: Teachers College Press/IRA.

Thompson, L. A., Detterman, D. K., & Plomin, R. (1991). Associations between cognitive abilities and scholastic achievement: Genetic overlap but environmental differences. *Psychological Science, 2,* 158–165.

Thomson, M. (1982). Assessing the intelligence of dyslexic children. *Bulletin of the British Psychological Society, 35,* 94–96.

Thorndike, R. L. (1963). *The concepts of over- and under-achievement.* New York: Teachers College Press

Thorndike, R. L. (1973–1974). Reading as reasoning. *Reading Research Quarterly, 9,* 135–147.

Tindal, G., & Marston, D. (1986). Approaches to assessment. In J. K. Torgeson & B. Y. L. Wong (Eds.), *Psychological and educational perspectives on learning disabilities* (pp. 55–84). Orlando, FL: Academic Press.

Tinker, M. (1958). Recent studies of eye movements in reading. *Psychological Bulletin, 55*, 215–231.

Tizard, J. (1975). Race and IQ: The limits of probability. *New Behaviour, 1*, 6–9.

Torgesen, J. K. (1977a). Memorization processes in reading-disabled children. *Journal of Educational Psychology, 69*, 571–578.

Torgesen, J. K. (1977b). The role of nonspecific factors in the task performance of learning disabled children: A theoretical assessment. *Journal of Learning Disabilities, 10*, 27–34.

Torgesen, J. K. (1978–1979). Performance of reading disabled children on serial memory tasks. *Reading Research Quarterly, 14*, 57–87.

Torgesen, J. K. (1982). The use of rationally defined subgroups in research on learning disabilities. In J. Das, R. Mulcahey, & A. Wall (Eds.), *Theory and research in learning disabilities* (pp. 111–131). New York: Plenum Press.

Torgesen, J. K. (1985). Memory processes in reading disabled children. *Journal of Learning Disabilities, 18*, 350–357.

Torgesen, J. K. (1986). Controlling for IQ. *Journal of Learning Disabilities, 19*, 452.

Torgesen, J. K. (Ed.). (1990). *Cognitive and behavioral characteristics of children with learning disabilities.* Austin, TX: Pro-Ed.

Torgesen, J. K., & Bryant, B. (1994). *Test of Phonological Awareness.* Austin, TX: PRO-ED.

Torgesen, J. K., & Burgess, S. R. (1998). Consistency of reading-related phonological processes throughout early childhood: Evidence from longitudinal-correlational and instructional studies. In J. L. Metsala & L. C. Ehri (Eds.), *Word recognition in beginning literacy* (pp. 161–187). Mahwah, NJ: Erlbaum.

Torgesen, J. K., & Dice, C. (1980). Characteristics of research in learning disabilities. *Journal of Learning Disabilities, 13*, 531–535.

Torgesen, J. K., & Goldman, T. (1977). Verbal rehearsal and short-term memory in reading-disabled children. *Child Development, 48*, 56–60.

Torgesen, J. K., & Houck, D. (1980). Processing deficiencies of learning-disabled children who perform poorly on the digit span test. *Journal of Educational Psychology, 72*, 141–160.

Torgesen, J. K., & Licht, B. (1983). The learning disabled child as an inactive learner: Retrospect and prospects. In J. McKinney & L. Feagans (Eds.), *Topics in learning disabilities* (Vol. 1, pp. 100–130). Norwood, NJ: Ablex.

Torgesen, J. K., Morgan, S., & Davis, C. (1992). Effects of two types of phonological awareness training on word learning in kindergarten children. *Journal of Educational Psychology, 84*, 364–370.

Torgesen, J. K., & Murphey, H. A. (1979). Verbal versus nonverbal and complex versus. simple responses in the paired-associate learning of poor readers. *Journal of General Psychology, 101*, 219–226.

Torgesen, J. K., & Wagner, R. K. (1998). Alternative diagnostic approaches for specific developmental reading disabilities. *Learning Disabilities: Research and Practice, 13*(4), 220–232.

Torgesen, J. K., Wagner, R. K., & Rashotte, C. A. (1997). Prevention and remediation of severe reading disabilities: Keeping the end in mind. *Scientific Studies of Reading, 1*, 217–234.

Torgesen, J. K., & Wong, B. (1986). *Psychological and educational perspectives on learning disabilities*. New York: Academic Press.

Torneus, M. (1984). Phonological awareness and reading: A chicken and egg problem? *Journal of Educational Psychology, 70*, 1346–1358.

Trachtenburg, P. (1990). Using children's literature to enhance phonics instruction. *Reading Teacher, 43*, 648–654.

Tranel, D., & Damasio, A. (1985). Knowledge without awareness: An autonomic index of facial recognition by prosopagnosics. *Science, 228*, 1453–1454.

Treiman, R. (1984). Individual differences among children in reading and spelling styles. *Journal of Experimental Child Psychology, 37*, 463–477.

Treiman, R. (1998). Why spelling? The benefits of incorporating spelling into beginning reading instruction. In J. L. Metsala & L. C. Ehri (Eds.), *Word recognition in beginning literacy* (pp. 289–313). Mahwah, NJ: Erlbaum.

Treiman, R., & Baron, J. (1981). Segmental analysis ability: Development and relation to reading ability. In T. Waller & G. MacKinnon (Eds.), *Reading research: Advances in theory and practice* (Vol. 3, pp. 159–198). New York: Academic Press.

Treiman, R., & Baron, J. (1983). Phonemic-analysis training helps children benefit from spelling–sound rules. *Memory and Cognition, 11*, 382–389.

Treiman, R., & Baron, J. (1984). Individual differences in spelling: The Phoenician-Chinese distinction. *Topics in Learning and Learning Disabilities, 3*, 33–40.

Treiman, R., Goswami, V., & Bruck, M. (1990). Not all words are alike: Implications for reading development and theory. *Memory and Cognition, 18*, 559–567.

Treiman, R., & Hirsh-Pasek, K. (1985). Are there qualitative differences in reading behavior between dyslexics and normal readers? *Memory and Cognition, 13*, 357–364.

Treiman, R., Mullennix, J., Bijeljac-Babic, R., & Richmond-Welty, E. D. (1995). The special role of rimes in the description, use, and acquisition of English orthography. *Journal of Experimental Psychology: General, 124*, 107–136.

Trites, R. L., & Fiedorowicz, C. (1976). Follow-up study of children with specific (or primary) reading disability. In R. Knights & D. Bakker (Eds.), *The neuropsychology of learning disorders* (pp. 41–50). Baltimore: University Park Press.

Tulving, E., & Gold, D. (1963). Stimulus information and contextual information as determinants of tachistoscopic recognition of words. *Journal of Experimental Psychology, 66*, 319–327.

Tunmer, W. E., & Chapman, J. W. (1998). Language prediction skill, phonological recoding, and beginning reading. In C. Hulme & R. M. Joshi (Eds.), *Reading and spelling: Development and disorder* (pp. 33–67). Hove, England: Erlbaum.

Tunmer, W., Herriman, M., & Nesdale, A. (1988). Metalinguistic abilities and beginning reading. *Reading Research Quarterly, 23*, 134–158.

Tunmer, W. E., & Hoover, W. (1992). Cognitive and linguistic factors in learning to read. In P. B. Gough, L. C. Ehri, & R. Treiman (Eds.), *Reading acquisition* (pp. 175–214). Hillsdale, NJ: Erlbaum.

Tunmer, W. E., & Nesdale, A. R. (1985). Phonemic segmentation skill and beginning reading. *Journal of Educational Psychology, 77*, 417–427.

Tversky, A., & Kahneman, D. (1981). The framing of decisions and the psychology of choice. *Science, 211*, 453–458.

Tversky, B., Havousha, S., & Poller, A. (1979). Noun-modifier order in a semantic verification task. *Bulletin of the Psychonomic Society, 13*, 31–34.

Tweedy, J. R., Lapinski, R. H., & Schvaneveldt, R. W. (1977). Semantic-context effects on word recognition: Influence of varying the proportion of items presented in an appropriate context. *Memory and Cognition, 5,* 84–89.

Underwood, G. (1977). Contextual facilitation from attended and unattended messages. *Journal of Verbal Learning and Verbal Behavior, 16,* 99–106.

Underwood, G. (1985). Information processing in skilled readers. In G. MacKinnon & T. Waller (Eds.), *Reading research: Advances in theory and practice* (Vol. 4, pp. 139–181). London: Academic Press.

Uttal, D. H., Lummis, M., & Stevenson, H. W. (1988). Low and high mathematics achievement in Japanese, Chinese, and American elementary-school children. *Developmental Psychology, 24,* 335–342.

Valtin, R. (1978–1979). Deficit in reading or deficit in research? *Reading Research Quarterly, 14,* 201–221.

Van den Bos, K. P. (1989). Relationship between cognitive development, decoding skill, and reading comprehension in learning disabled Dutch children. In P. Aaron & M. Joshi (Eds.), *Reading and writing disorders in different orthographic systems* (pp. 75–86). Dordrecht, The Netherlands: Kluwer Academic.

van der Wissel, A. (1987). IQ profiles of learning disabled and mildly mentally retarded children: A psychometric selection effect. *British Journal of Developmental Psychology, 5,* 45–51.

van der Wissel, A., & Zegers, F. E. (1985). Reading retardation revisited. *British Journal of Developmental Psychology, 3,* 3–9.

Van Orden, G. C., Pennington, B. F., & Stone, G. O. (1990). Word identification in reading and the promise of subsymbolic psycholinguistics. *Psychological Review, 97,* 488–522.

Varnhagen, C. K., Morrison, F. J., & Everall, R. (1994). Age and schooling effects in story recall and story production. *Developmental Psychology, 30,* 969–979.

Vaughn, S., & Bos, C. S. (1987). *Research in learning disabilities: Issues and future directions.* Boston: College-Hill Press.

Vellutino, F. R. (1977). Alternative conceptualizations of dyslexia: Evidence in support of a verbal-deficit hypothesis. *Harvard Educational Review, 47,* 334–354.

Vellutino, F. R. (1978). Toward an understanding of dyslexia: Psychological factors in specific reading disability. In A. L. Benton & D. Pearl (Eds.), *Dyslexia* (pp. 59–111). New York: Oxford University Press.

Vellutino, F. R. (1979). *Dyslexia: Theory and research.* Cambridge, MA: MIT Press.

Vellutino, F. R. (1991). Introduction to three studies on reading acquisition: Convergent findings on theoretical foundations of code-oriented versus whole-language approaches to reading instruction. *Journal of Educational Psychology, 83,* 437–443.

Vellutino, F. R., & Scanlon, D. M. (1987). Phonological coding, phonological awareness, and reading ability: Evidence from a longitudinal and experimental study. *Merrill-Palmer Quarterly, 33,* 321–363.

Vellutino, F. R., & Scanlon, D. M. (1989). Some prerequisites for interpreting results from reading level matched designs. *Journal of Reading Behavior, 21,* 361–385.

Vellutino, F. R., Scanlon, D. M., Sipay, E., Small, S., Pratt, A., Chen, R., & Denckla, M. (1996). Cognitive profiles of difficult to remediate and readily remediated poor readers: Early intervention as a vehicle for distinguishing between cognitive and experiential as basic causes of specific reading disability. *Journal of Educational Psychology, 88,* 601–638.

Venezky, R. L. (1970). *The structure of English orthography.* The Hague, The Netherlands: Mouton.

Venezky, R. L. (1976). *Theoretical and experimental base for teaching reading.* The Hague, The Netherlands: Mouton.

Venezky, R. L. (1977). Research on reading processes: A historical perspective. *American Psychologist, 32,* 339–345.

Venezky, R. L. (1999). *American English orthography.* New York: Guilford Press.

Venezky, R. L., & Massaro, D. W. (1987). Orthographic structure and spelling-sound regularity in reading English words. In A. Allport, D. MacKay, W. Prinz, & E. Scheerer (Eds.), *Language perception and production* (pp. 159–179). London: Academic Press.

Vernon, P. A. (Ed.). (1987). Speed of information-processing and intelligence. Norwood, NJ: Ablex.

Vogel, S. (1974). Syntactic abilities in normal and dyslexic children. *Journal of Learning Disabilities, 7,* 103–109.

Vogler, G., Baker, L. A., Decker, S. N., DeFries, J. C., & Huizinga, D. (1989). Cluster analytic classification of reading disability subtypes. *Reading and Writing: An Interdisciplinary Journal, 1,* 163–177.

Wachs, T., & Mariotto, M. (1978). Criteria for the assessment of organism–environment correlation in human developmental studies. *Human Development, 21,* 268–288.

Wagner, D. A. (1987). Literacy futures: Five common problems from industrializing and developing countries. In D. A. Wagner (Ed.), *The future of literacy in a changing world* (pp. 3–16). Oxford, England: Pergamon Press.

Wagner, R. K. (1988). Causal relations between the development of phonological processing abilities and the acquisition of reading skills: A meta-analysis. *Merrill-Palmer Quarterly, 34,* 261–279.

Wagner, R. K., & Torgesen, J. K. (1987). The nature of phonological processing and its causal role in the acquisition of reading skills. *Psychological Bulletin, 101,* 192–212.

Wagner, R. K., Torgesen, J. K., Laughon, P., Simmons, K., & Rashotte, C. A. (1993). Development of young readers' phonological processing abilities. *Journal of Educational Psychology, 85,* 83–103.

Wagner, R. K., Torgesen, J. K., & Rashotte, C. A. (1994). The development of reading-related phonological processing abilities: New evidence of bi-directional causality from a latent variable longitudinal study. *Developmental Psychology, 30,* 73–87.

Wagner, R. K., Torgesen, J. K., Rashotte, C. A., Hecht, S. A., Barker, T. A., Burgess, S. R., Donahue, J., & Garon, T. (1997). Changing causal relations between phonological processing abilities and word-level reading as children develop from beginning to skilled readers: A 5-year longitudinal study. *Developmental Psychology, 33,* 468–479.

Walberg, H. J., Strykowski, B. F., Rovai, E., & Hung, S. S. (1984). Exceptional performance. *Review of Educational Research, 54,* 87–112.

Walberg, H. J., & Tsai, S. (1983). Matthew effects in education. *American Educational Research Journal, 20,* 359–373.

Walberg, H. J., & Tsai, S. (1984). Reading achievement and diminishing returns to time. *Journal of Educational Psychology, 76,* 442–451.

Walczyk, J. J., & Taylor, R. W. (1996). How do the efficiencies of reading subcomponents relate to looking back in text? *Journal of Educational Psychology,* 88(3), 537–545.

Walley, A. C. (1993). The role of vocabulary development in children's spoken word recognition and segmentation ability. *Developmental Review, 13,* 286–350.

Warren, R. E. (1974). Association, directionality and stimulus encoding. *Journal of Experimental Psychology, 102,* 151–158.

Waters, G. S., Bruck, M., & Seidenberg, M. (1985). Do children use similar processes to read and spell words? *Journal of Experimental Child Psychology, 39,* 511–530.

Waters, G. S., & Seidenberg, M. (1985). Spelling-sound effects in reading: Time-course and decision criteria. *Memory and Cognition, 13,* 557–572.

Waters, G. S., Seidenberg, M., & Bruck, M. (1984). Children's and adults' use of spelling-sound information in three reading tasks. *Memory and Cognition, 12,* 293–305.

Watson, F., & Brown, G. (1992). Single-word reading in college dyslexics. *Applied Cognitive Psychology, 6,* 263–272.

Weaver, C. (1989). The basalization of America: A cause for concern. In C. Weaver & P. Groff (Eds.), *Two reactions to the Report Card on Basal Readers* (pp. 4–7, 14–22, 33–37). Bloomington, IN: ERIC Clearinghouse on Reading and Communication Skills.

Weber, R. M. (1970a). A linguistic analysis of first-grade reading errors. *Reading Research Quarterly, 5,* 427–451.

Weber, R. M. (1970b). First graders' use of grammatical context in reading. In H. Levin & J. Williams (Eds.), *Basic studies on reading.* New York: Basic Books.

Wechsler, D. (1974). *Manual for the Wechsler Intelligence Scale for Children—Revised.* San Antonio, TX: Psychological Corp.

Weinstein, P., & Rabinovitch, M. S. (1971). Sentence structure and retention in good and poor readers. *Journal of Educational Psychology, 62,* 25–30.

Wells, G (1986). *The meaning makers.* Portsmouth, NH: Heinemann.

Werker, J. F., & Tees, R. C. (1987). Speech perception in severely disabled and average reading children. *Canadian Journal of Psychology, 41,* 48–61.

West, R. F., & Stanovich, K. E. (1978). Automatic contextual facilitation in readers of three ages. *Child Development, 49,* 717–727.

West, R. F., & Stanovich, K. E. (1979). The development of automatic word recognition skills. *Journal of Reading Behavior, 11,* 211–219.

West, R. F., & Stanovich, K. E. (1982). Source of inhibition in experiments on the effect of sentence context on word recognition. *Journal of Experimental Psychology: Learning, Memory, and Cognition, 8,* 385–399.

West, R. F., & Stanovich, K. E. (1986). Robust effects of syntactic structure on visual word processing. *Memory and Cognition, 14,* 104–112.

West, R. F., & Stanovich, K. E. (1988a). The neutral condition in sentence context experiments: Empirical studies. *Bulletin of the Psychonomic Society, 26,* 87–90.

West, R. F., & Stanovich, K. E. (1988b). How much of sentence priming is word priming? *Bulletin of the Psychonomic Society, 26,* 1–4.

West, R. F., & Stanovich, K. E. (1991). The incidental acquisition of information from reading. *Psychological Science, 2,* 325–330.

West, R. F., Stanovich, K. E., & Cunningham, A. E. (1995). Compensatory processes in reading. In R. Dixon & L. Backman (Eds.), *Compensating for psychological deficits and declines: Managing losses and promoting gain* (pp. 275–296). Hillsdale, NJ: Erlbaum.

West, R. F., Stanovich, K. E., Feeman, D. J., & Cunningham, A. E. (1983). The effect of sentence context on word recognition in second- and sixth-grade children. *Reading Research Quarterly, 19,* 6–15.

West, R. F., Stanovich, K. E., & Mitchell, H. R. (1993). Reading in the real world and its correlates. *Reading Research Quarterly, 28,* 34–50.

Whaley, J., & Kibby, M. (1981). The relative importance of reliance on intraword characteristics and interword constraints for beginning reading achievement. *Journal of Educational Research, 74,* 315–320.

Wheeler, D. L., Jacobson, J. W., Paglieri, R. A., & Schwartz, A. A. (1993). An experimental assessment of facilitated communication. *Mental Retardation, 31,* 49–60.

White, T. G., Slater, W. H., & Graves, M. F. (1989). Yes/no method of vocabulary assessment: Valid for whom and useful for what? In S. McCormick & J. Zutell (Eds.), *Cognitive and social perspectives for literacy research and instruction, 38th yearbook of the National Reading Conference* (pp. 391–397). Chicago: National Reading Conference.

Whitehurst, G. J., & Lonigan, C. J. (1998). Child development and emergent literacy. *Child Development, 69*(3), 848–872.

Whitehurst, G. J., Zevenbergen, A., Crone, D. A., Schultz, M., Velting, O., & Fischel, J. E. (1999). Outcomes of an emergent literacy intervention from Head Start through second grade. *Journal of Educational Psychology, 91,* 261–272.

Wildman, D. M., & Kling, M. (1978–1979). Semantic, syntactic, and spatial anticipation in reading. *Reading Research Quarterly, 14,* 128–164.

Wilkes, K. V. (1984). Is consciousness important? *British Journal of Philosophy of Science, 35,* 223–243.

Wilkinson, A. C., Guminski, M., Stanovich, K. E., & West, R. F. (1981). Optional interaction between visual recognition and memory in oral reading. *Journal of Experimental Psychology: Human Learning and Memory, 7,* 111–119.

Williams, J. P. (1980). Teaching decoding with an emphasis on phoneme analysis and phoneme blending. *Journal of Educational Psychology, 72,* 1–15.

Williams, J. P. (1984). Phonemic analysis and how it relates to reading. *Journal of Learning Disabilities, 7,* 240–245.

Williams, J. P. (1986). The role of phonemic analysis in reading. In J. Torgesen & B. Wong (Eds.), *Psychological and educational perspectives on learning disabilities* (pp. 399–416). New York: Academic Press.

Willows, D. M. (1991). Visual processes in learning disabilities. In B. Wong (Ed.), *Learning about learning disabilities* (pp. 163–193). San Diego, CA: Academic Press.

Willows, D. M., & Ryan, E. B. (1986). The development of a grammatical sensitivity and its relation to early reading achievement. *Reading Research Quarterly, 21,* 253–266.

Wilson, E. O. (1998). *Consilience: The unity of knowledge.* New York: Knopf.

Wilson, L. R., & Cone, T. (1984). The regression equation method of determining academic discrepancy. *Journal of School Psychology, 22,* 95–110.

Wirtz, W. (1977). *On further examination.* New York: College Entrance Examination Board.

Wise, B. W., Ring, J., & Olson, R. K. (1999). Training phonological awareness with and without explicit attention to articulation. *Journal of Experimental Child Psychology, 72,* 271–304.

Wisher, R. A. (1976). The effects of syntactic expectations during reading. *Journal of Educational Psychology, 68,* 597–602.

Wixson, K. K., & Peters, C. W. (1987). Comprehension assessment: Implementing an interactive view of reading. *Educational Psychologist, 22,* 333–356.

Wixson, K. L. (1979). Miscue analysis: A critical review. *Journal of Reading Behavior, 11,* 163–175.

Wolf, M. (1984). Naming, reading, and the dyslexias: A longitudinal overview. *Annals of Dyslexia, 34,* 87–115.

Wolf, M. (1991a). Naming speed and reading: The contribution of the cognitive neurosciences. *Reading Research Quarterly, 26,* 123–141.

Wolf, M. (1991b). The word-retrieval deficit hypothesis and developmental dyslexia. *Learning and Individual Differences, 3,* 205–223.

Wolf, M. (1997). A provisional, integrative account of phonological and naming-speed deficits in dyslexia: Implications for diagnosis and intervention. In B. Blachman (Ed.), *Foundations of reading acquisition and dyslexia: Implications for early intervention* (pp. 67–94). Mahweh, NJ: Erlbaum.

Wolf, M., & Bowers, P. G. (1999). The double-deficit hypothesis for the developmental dyslexias. *Journal of Educational Psychology, 91,* 415–438.

Wolf, M., & Goodglass, H. (1986). Dyslexia, dysnomia, and lexical retrieval: A longitudinal investigation. *Brain and Language, 28,* 154–168.

Wolford, G., & Fowler, C. (1984). Differential use of partial information by good and poor readers. *Developmental Review, 6,* 16–35.

Wong, B. (1984). Metacognition and learning disabilities. In T. Waller, D. Forrest, & G. MacKinnon (Eds.), *Metacognition, cognition, and human performance* (pp. 137–180). New York: Academic Press.

Wong, B., Wong, R., & Foth, D. (1977). Recall and clustering of verbal materials among normal and poor readers. *Bulletin of the Psychonomic Society, 10,* 375–378.

Woodcock, R. W. (1987). *Woodcock Reading Mastery Tests—Revised: Examiner's manual.* Circle Pines, MN: American Guidance Service.

Yaden, D. (1984). Reading research in metalinguistic awareness: Findings, problems, and classroom applications. *Visible Language, 18,* 5–47.

Yates, J. (1978). Priming dominant and unusual senses of ambiguous words. *Memory and Cognition, 6,* 636–643.

Yopp, H. K. (1988). The validity and reliability of phonemic awareness tests. *Reading Research Quarterly, 23,* 159–177.

Yopp, H. K. (1992). Developing phonemic awareness in young children. *Reading Teacher, 45,* 696–703.

Ysseldyke, J., & Algozzine, B. (1979). Perspectives on assessment of learning disabled students. *Learning Disability Quarterly, 2,* 3–13.

Yule, W. (1973). Differential prognosis of reading backwardness and specific reading retardation. *British Journal of Educational Psychology, 43,* 244–248.

Yule, W. (1984). The operationalizing of "underachievement"—Doubts dispelled. *British Journal of Clinical Psychology, 23,* 233–234.

Yussen, S. R. (1990). Rethinking child development. *Contemporary Psychology, 35,* 677–678.

Zbrodoff, N. J., & Logan, G. D. (1986). On the autonomy of mental processes: A case study of arithmetic. *Journal of Experimental Psychology: General, 115,* 118–130.

Ziegler, J. C., Stone, G. O., & Jacobs, A. M. (1997). What is the pronunciation for -ough and the spelling for /u/? A database for computing feedforward and feedback consistency in English. *Behavior Research Methods, Instruments, and Computers, 29*, 600–618.

Zifcak, M. (1981). Phonological awareness and reading acquisition. *Contemporary Educational Psychology, 6*, 117–126.

Zigler, E. (1969). Developmental versus difference theories of mental retardation and the problem of motivation. *American Journal of Mental Deficiency, 73*, 536–556.

Zill, N., & Winglee, M. (1990). *Who reads literature?* Cabin John, MD: Seven Locks Press.

Zimmerman, J., Broder, P. K., Shaughnessy, J. J., & Underwood, B. J. (1977). A recognition test of vocabulary using signal-detection measures, and some correlates of word and nonword recognition. *Intelligence, 1*, 5–31.

Zola, D. (1984). Redundancy and word perception during reading. *Perception and Psychophysics, 36*, 277–284.

Author Index

Subject Index